MANAGEMENT INFORMATION SYSTEM

MANAGEMENT INFORMATION SYSTEM

By
VERSHA MEHTA
A.S. SUDAN
SUDHIR DAWRA

ANMOL PUBLICATIONS PVT. LTD.
NEW DELHI - 110 002 (INDIA)

ANMOL PUBLICATIONS PVT. LTD.
4374/4B, Ansari Road, Daryaganj
New Delhi - 110 002
Phones: 23261597, 23278000
Visit us at: www.anmolpublications.com

Management Information System

First Published, 2003

ISBN 81-261-1630-7

PRINTED IN INDIA

Published by J.L. Kumar for Anmol Publications Pvt. Ltd., New Delhi and Printed at Mehr Offset Press, Delhi.

Contents

SECTION 4
MIS in Functional Areas

SECTION 5
How to Build Management Information System
Or
Requirements of Information Systems

Preface

Information is the backbone of any organization. Information is prepared on the basis of Raw data. Raw data is processed and converted to useful information which is effectively used by management for the smooth running of the organization.

Management information system is that part of management information which provides information for taking the decisions in the organization. It includes Decision Support System, Management Reporting System, Transaction Processing System, Office Automation System, Transaction Processing System and Security areas.

Information system department works under the leadership of Chief Information Officer who co-ordinates and formulates the different policies and procedures for the Information Department.

Fundamentals of hardware and software which are to be used for the better procurement of information in the organization is also appended in this text.

Nowadays information plays a vital role in any organization. It support in taking decisions, generating Reports and providing details about the transactions.

Various parameters of security like Network security, maintaining firewalls, and DBA's are appointed for minimizing the data redundancy and for security of information.

In India, some big organizations have already implemented MIS and have their own department for maintaining the information. Some of them are LIC, Hindustan Lever, Proctor & Gamble, L&T and Nirma.

The subject matter of the book has been taken from various books, journals and case studies. An humble attempt is made to do the justice with the topics dealt herein. We are deeply beholden to all those great scholars whose works are cited and substantially borrowed in the present venture.

While preparing the text of this book, we received active cooperation, moral support and miscellaneous assistance from various quarters. Our colleagues, friends and well-wishers deserve all appreciation for motivating us to undertake this project. We owe a deep sense of gratitude to all of them. Mr. J.L. Kumar, Managing Director, Anmol Publications Pvt. Ltd., remains a constant source of inspiration. We are thankful to him. Any suggestions for the improvement of the book are welcome and subsequently added in the revised edition.

—Authors

Section 1

Management Information System (Introduction and Structure)

1

Introduction to Management Information System

Information processing is a major societal activity. A significant art of an individual's working and personal time is spent recording, searching for, and absorbing information. As much as 80 percent of a typical executive's time is spent in the processing and communication of information. More than 50 percent of the United States works force is employed in jobs that primarily involve some form of information processing. A large proportion of these employees are "knowledge workers"; their duties involve the production and use of information outputs—documents, reports, analyses, plans, etc.

Computers have become an essential part of organisational information processing because of the power of the technology and the volume of data to be processed. The application of computers to information processing began in 1954 when one of the first computer was programmed to process payroll. Today, computerised processing of the transaction data is a routine activity of large organisations. Moreover, the capability to automate information processing has permitted an expansion in the scope of formalised organisational information use. The current challenge in information processing is to use the capabilities of computers to support knowledge work, including managerial activities and decision-making. The wide variety of computer resources to perform transaction processing, to provide processing for a formal information and reporting system, and to accomplish managerial-decision support are broadly classified as the organisation's *management information system* or MIS.

The design and implementation of management information systems in an organisation necessitates the identification of information requirements. The requirements for routine transaction processing tend to be stable and relatively easy to identify; information requirement for management and decision-making activities are more changeable and more difficult to define. The content of this text is useful both for those who design, implement, and manage information systems and for those who specify information requirements and use the systems. The text can help systems analysts to understand the structure of a management information system and the type of requirements to be included; it can aid information systems executives in planning and management; it can help users to understand how their information requirements fit into the system and how to analyse and formulate those requirements. It can also aid users who develop their own systems.

How Long Can An Organisation Operate Without Computer Information Processing?

When asked how long different business functions would be able to operate without the information processing capabilities of computers, 36 companies responded with the following results for all operational applications: On average, the companies estimated that only 28 percent of the operational activities would be functioning within 5.5 days without computer data processing. Finance companies in the sample estimated that only 13 percent of operations would be functioning after 5.5 days without computing. (Figure 1.1).

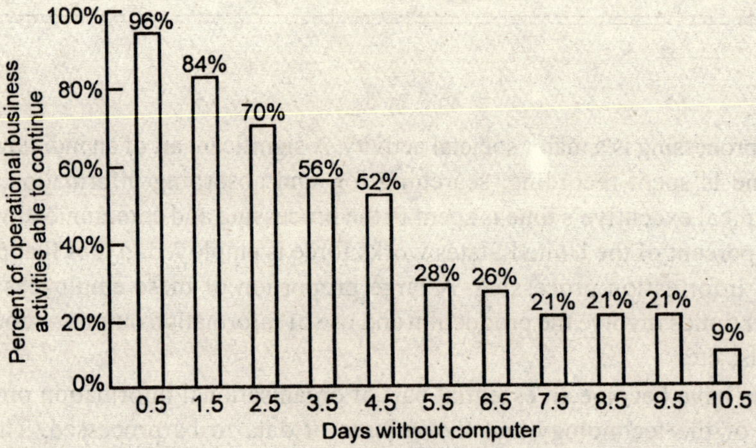

Figure 1.1. Decline in operational business activities following a complete computer data processing failure.

Definition of a Management Information System

There is no consensus on the definition of the term "management information system." Some writers prefer alternative terminology such as "information processing system," "information and decision system," "organisational information system," or simply "information system" to refer to the computer-based information processing system which supports the operations, management, and decision-making functions of an organisation. This text uses "MIS" because it is descriptive and generally understood; it also frequently uses "information system" instead of "MIS" to refer to an organisational information system.

A definition of a management information system, as the term is generally understood, is *an integrated, user-machine system for providing information to support operations, management, and decision-making functions in an organisation. The system utilizes computer hardware and software; manual procedures; models for analysis, planning, control and decision-making; and a database*. The fact that it is an integrated system does not mean that it is a single, monolithic structure; rather, it means that the parts fits into an overall design. The elements of the definition are highlighted below.

What's in a Name?

A 1983 survey of 334 large organisations identified the following name used for the information systems function:

Name	**Percent**
Management information systems	**33**
Information services	**17**
Information systems	**14**
Data processing	**12**
Information resources management	**3**
Other	**21**
	100

"Information System Planning to Meet Business Objectives: A Survey of Practice," Cresap, McCormick and Paget, New York.

Definition of a Management Information System

A management information system is

- An integrated user-machine system
- For providing information
- To support the operations, management, analysis, and decision-making functions
- In an organisation

The system utilizes

- Computer hardware and software
- Manual procedures
- Models for analysis, planning, control, and decision-making, and
- A database

The management information system has been described as a pyramid structure (Figure 1.2) in which the bottom layer consists of information for transaction processing, status inquiries, etc.; the next level consists of information resources in support of day-to-day operations and control; the third level consists of information system resources to aid in tactical planning and decision-making for management control; and the top level consists of information resources to support strategic planning and policy-making by higher levels of management. Each level of information processing may make use of data provided for lower levels; but new data may also be introduced. For example, some of the information to support management and decision-making is provided by the data obtained for transaction processing, while some may be new data about activities external to the organisation.

In order to further clarify the definition, the following sections elaborate on certain key concepts: the user-machine systems, the concept of an integrated system, the need for a database, and the role of planning and decision models. In addition, there is a discussion of the relationship of MIS to other information system structural concepts: Information Resources Management (IRM), Decision Support System (DSS), Transactional Processing System (TPS) and Management Reporting System (MRS).

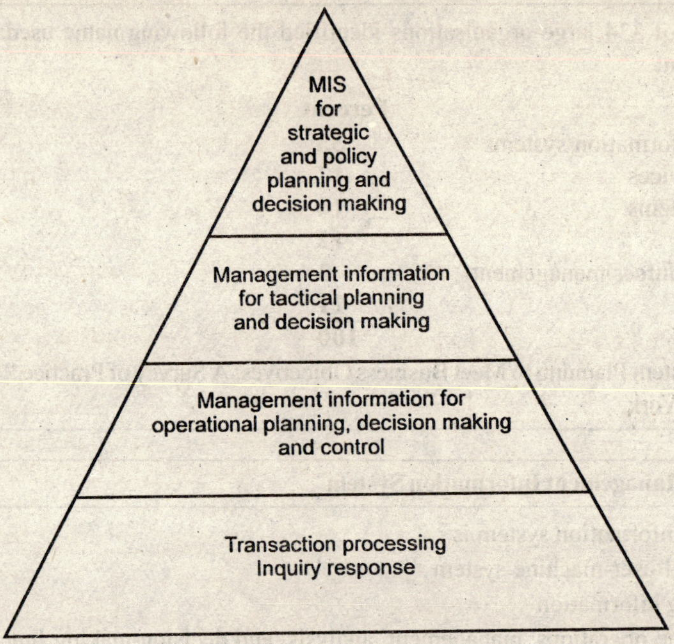

Figure 1.2. Management information system.

Computer-Based User-Machine System

Conceptually, a management information system can exist without computers, but it is the power of the computer which makes MIS feasible. The question is not whether computers should be used in management information systems, but the extent to which information use should be computerised. The concept of a user-machine system implies that some tasks are best performed by humans, while others are best done by machine. The user of an MIS is any person responsible for entering input data, instructing the system, or utilizing the information output of the system. For many problems, the user and the computer form a combined system with results obtained through a set of interactions between the computer and the user.

User-machine interactions is facilitated by operations in which the user's input-output devices (usually a visual display terminal) is connected to the computer. The computer can be personal computer serving only one user or a large computer that serves a number of users through terminals connected by communication lines. The user input-output device permits input of data and immediate output of results. For instance, a person using the computer interactively in financial planning poses "what if" questions by entering input at the terminal keyboard; the results are displayed on the screen in a few seconds.

The computer-based user-machine characteristics of an MIS affect the knowledge requirements of both system developer and system user. "Computer-based" mean that the designer of a management information system must have a knowledge of computers and of their use in information processing. The "user-machine" concept means that system designer should also understand the capabilities of humans as system components (as information processors) and the behaviour of humans as users of information.

Information system applications should not require users to be computer experts. However, users need to be able to specify their information requirements; some understanding of computers, the nature of information, and its use in various management functions aids users in this task.

Integrated System of All the Systems

Management information systems typically provide the basis for integration of organisational information processing. Individual applications within information systems are developed for and by diverse sets of users. If there are no integrating processes and mechanisms, the individual applications may be inconsistent and incompatible. Data items may be specified differently and may not be compatible across application that use the same data. There may be redundant development of separate applications when actually a single application could serve more than one need. A user wanting to perform analysis using data from two different applications may find the task very difficult and sometimes impossible.

The first step in integration of diverse information system applications is an overall information system plan. Even though application systems are implemented one at a time, their design can be guided by the overall plan, which determines how they fit in with other functions. In essence, the information system is designed as a planned federation of small systems.

Information system integration is also achieved through standards, guidelines, and procedures set by the MIS functions. The enforcement of such standards and procedures permits diverse applications to share data, meet audit and control requirements, and be shared by multiple users. For instance, an application may be developed to run on a particular small computer. Standards for integration may dictate that the equipment selected be compatible with existing computers and that the application be designed for communication with centralized database.

The trend in information system design is toward separate application processing from the data used to support it. The separate database is the mechanism by which data items are integrated across many applications and made consistently available to a variety of users. The need for a database in MIS is discussed below.

Importance of Database

The terms "information" and "data" are frequently used interchangeably; however, information is generally defined as data that is meaningful or useful to the recipient. Data items are therefore the raw material for producing information.

The underlying concept of a database is that data needs to be managed in order to be available for processing and have appropriate quality. This data management includes both software and organisation. The software to create and manage a database is a *database management system.*

When all access to and use of the database is controlled through a database management system, all applications utilizing a particular data item access the same data item which is stored in only one place. A single updating of the data item updates it for all uses. Integration through a database management system requires a central authority for the database. The data can be stored in one central computer or dispersed among several computers; the overriding requirement is that there can be an organisational function to exercise control.

Utilisation of Models

It is usually insufficient for human recipients to receive only raw data or even summarized data. Data usually needs to be processed and presented in such a way that the result is directed toward the decision to be made. To do this, processing of data items is based on a decision model. For example, an investment decision relative to new capital expenditures might be processed in terms of a capital expenditure decision model.

Decision models can be used to support different stages in the decision-making process. "Intelligence" models can be used to search for problems and/or opportunities. Models can be used to identify and analyse possible solutions. Choice models such as optimisation models may be used to find the most desirable solution.

Using Information in Finding Problems

"Communities across the U.S. are starting to use information as well as fire hoses to combat arson. Boston, New Haven, Knoxville, Phoenix, San Francisco, and Seattle all run programmes that collate fire department records with tax, building ownership, and other data... And growing number of insurance companies... are using similar surveys to reduce arson fraud by policy-holders."

"The new arson information tracking programme are already paying off... Last year the Federal Bureau of investigation reported a 12% drop in arson in the U.S. Although experts say it is too early to link the national drop in arson directly to information management systems, the results from cities that have installed such systems are encouraging. For example, in Phoenix, which installed an arson information programme in 1978, arson cases dropped last year to 497, or 35% of all fires, from 739, 49% of the total, in 1978."

For an arson information system to be effective, cities have found they must strike up a cooperative relationship with insurance companies, which already collect many of the same data. The new arson prevention system encourages the exchange of information instead of duplicating efforts.

Excerpts from "Data Programs Helps Stamp Out Arson."

In other words, multiple approaches are needed to meet a variety of decision situations. The following are some examples of problems and the type of model that might be included in an MIS to aid in analysis in support of decision-making:

Problem	Example of Model
Amount of inventory Safety Stock	Inventory model which computes safety stock under a variety of assumptions
Personnel selection	Personnel search and ranking-of-alternatives model
New product pricing	New product introduction model
Expenditure control	Budgetary control model

In a comprehensive information system, the decision maker has available a set of general models that can be applied to many analysis and decision situations plus a set of very specific models for unique decisions. Similar models are available for planning and control. The set of models is the model base for the MIS.

Models are generally most effective when the manager can use interactive dialog to build a plan or to iterate through several decision choices under different conditions.

MIS as an Evolving Concept

MIS is known as evolving concept due to its functionality. When the concept of MIS was first introduced, many proponents envisioned a single, highly integrated system that would bring together processing for all organisational functions. Others questioned whether it was possible to design adequate computer-based information systems to support management planning and decision making functions, especially strategic planning.[1] They questioned the value of applying advanced information technology to an ill-defined judgement process.

Over time, the concept of a single, highly integrated system was demonstrated to be too complex to implement. The MIS concept is now that of a federation of subsystems, developed and implemented as needed but confirming to the overall plan, standard, and procedures for the MIS. Thus, rather than a single, global MIS, an organisation may have many related information systems which serve managerial needs in various ways.

MIS as a concept continues to evolve. It is related to, but no equivalent with, data processing and other information systems-related concepts. Two such concepts that can be considered extensions of the MIS concept are decision support systems (DSS) and information resources management (IRM). An emerging trend consistent with the evolution of the MIS concept is end-user computing.

MIS/Data Processing

A data processing system processes transactions and produces reports. It represents the automation of fundamental, routine processing to support operations. Prior to computers, data processing was performed manually or with simple machines. A management information system is more comprehensive; it encompass processing in support of a wider range of organisational functions and management processes. However, every MIS will also include transactions processing as one of its functions.

What does it takes to make a data processing system into a management information system? Can a rather mundane data processing system be an MIS if a simple database, retrieval capabilities, and one or two decision models are added? This is not a useful question. MIS is a concept and an orientation toward which an information system design moves rather than an absolute state. Therefore, the significant issue is the extent to which an information system adopt the MIS orientation and supports the management functions of an organisation. The answer is usually a matter of degree rather than a simple yes or no.

One important aspect of the difference between MIS and routine data processing is the capability to provide analysis, planning, and decision making support. An MIS orientation means users have access to decision model and methods for querying the database on an ad hoc basis; the database is also, of course, an essential part of routine transaction processing and reporting. Furthermore, an MIS orientation means information resources are utilised so as to improve decision-making and achieve improved organisational effectiveness. Information resources are also used as a means of achieving a competitive advantage.

MIS and Decision Support Systems

A decision support system (DSS) is an information system application that assists decision making. DSS tend to be used in planning, analysing alternatives and trial and error search for solutions. They are generally operated through terminal-based interactive dialogs with users. They incorporate a variety of decision models. DSS represent a significant class of MIS applications which will be discussed in details.

Using Information Analysis to Win at Football

"We can describe everything to the computer, says Chuck Clausen, defensive line coach for the Philadelphia Eagles. We can identify formations, draw picture, define pass patterns, who caught the ball, yardage, what every receiver was doing, and how the blocking was.

"Because of the number of players on the field and the diversity of possible plays, football is particularly suitable to computer analysis. Neal Dahlen, a scout for the San Francisco 49, says he can analyze and evaluate nearly 40 variables in any individual play on the team's computer. Based on information gleaned from computer printouts, 49ers coach Bill Walsh often scripts the first 20 plays of a game before he even arrives at the stadium.

As an example of the value of this analysis, a weakness was uncovered by a computer analysis of the lineup patterns of the Kansas City Chiefs. When the ball was between the 20-yard line and the goal line, the Chiefs lined up in the same formation 70 percent of the time. The San Diego Chargers' 372F Shoot Pump play was developed to exploit the weakness.

"Currently an NFL rule bars computer terminals from the sidelines or the press boxes. The hometown advantage would be too great for teams that have complex computer systems on their own turf, says Pete Adimante, an NFL spokesman. Nevertheless, football insiders expect the rule will be made more liberal within the next few years.

Excerpts from "The Computer Scores Big on the Gridiron," *Business Week.*

MIS and Information Resource Management

Information resource management (IRM) is an approach to management based on the concept that information is an organisational resource. Given that view, the task of the information system executive is to manage the resource. The resource is defined very broadly. The scope of IRM includes data communications, word processing, and personal computers as well as traditional data processing. The IRM concept tends to emphasise the organisational effectiveness of the information system resource rather than the technical sophistication or efficiency of the hardware and software. The MIS concept, as defined in this text, includes the resource view of information. The IRM concept is applicable to management of the MIS function.

End-User Computing

A recent major development affecting the structure and design of MIS is end-user computing. Users are provided with terminals or personal computers and powerful software for accessing data, developing models, and performing information processing directly. This development, made possible by the increasing power and decreasing cost of the technology, is a significant force for change in the way information resources are organised, provided, and used. In many organisations, the MIS function is undergoing a transition from centralized control of information systems resources toward provision of support to users who control their own development and operation of information systems. System support for end user computing and issues of MIS management in the end user environment are discussed in detail in the text.

Handling Increased Demand for Information

"The Essex Group, a unit of United Technologies Corp., is taking a pragmatic approach to office automation...Much of the company's $900 million in annual sales depends on two highly cyclical industries: housing and automobiles. Timely information on housing starts, auto order backlogs, and production schedules was increasingly crucial in fine-tuning Essex's costly inventories.

"Employee requests for data soared 45% in 1982, to 429 inquiries. But the backlog of the central data processing department was so large that it was taking a year or more to full many of these requests for information." Had Essex not acted to provide better response to information needs, disgruntled managers might have started installing their own personal computers. The result would have been loss of access and control over organisational information maintained on the micros.

"Managers who have completed training through Essex's newly-formed information centre no longer have to wait for the data processing department. They can use one of 550 terminals linked to Essex's mainframe computer or one of the company's 40 personal computers to gain access to and analyse copies of data files themselves. Since the centre opened, in early 1982, about 400 Essex employees—from senior executives to engineer and secretaries—have completed one or more computer courses."

Excerpted and adapted from "Taking the Anxiety out of Office Automation."

Significance of MIS in other Academic Disciplines

Many of the ideas which are part of management information systems are found in other academic disciplines. Four major academic areas are especially significant to the MIS concept: managerial accounting, operation research, management and organisation theory, and computer science.

Accounting (Financial|Managerial)

It is useful to think of the field of accounting as having two major areas: financial and managerial accounting. Financial accounting is concerned with the measurement of income for specific periods of time such as a month or a year (the income statement) and the reporting of financial status at the end of the period (the balance sheet). Financial accounting reports are oriented toward investors. As a result, financial accounting has limited usefulness for managerial decision-making. Managerial accounting, on the other hand, is concerned with determining relevant costs and performing other analysis useful for managerial control and managerial decisions. It tends to be the focus for the preparation of budgets and performance analysis based on budget. Historically the accounting department was always responsible for data processing because the first applications were related to accounting functions.

The MIS concepts includes mush of the content of managerial accounting; however, the support systems which provide users with access to data and models are beyond the scope of traditional managerial accounting. Current organisational practice is usually to retain cost and budget analysis within the managerial accounting function and to have the MIS function provide data and model support.

Operations Research Techniques

Operations research is the application of the scientific method and quantitative analysis techniques to management problems. Some of its key concepts are:

1. Emphasis on systematic approaches to problem solving
2. Use of mathematical models and mathematical and statistical procedure in analysis
3. Goal of seeking optimal decisions or optimal policy.

Operations research is important relative to management information system because it has developed procedures for the analysis and computer-based solutions of many types of decision problems. The systematic approach to problem solving, use of models, and computer-based solution algorithms are generally incorporated in the decision support system component of MIS.

How MIS Helps in Organisational Behaviour

Since the MIS is a support system for organisational functions, it draws upon concepts of organisation, organisation behaviour, management, and decision-making. The fields of management (or organisation behaviour) and organisation theory provide several important concepts which are key to understanding the function of an MIS in an organisation. Some of these concepts are:

1. Behavioural theory of organisational and individual decision-making
2. Individual motivation
3. Group processes and group decision-making
4. Leadership techniques
5. Organisational change processes
6. Organisational structure and design

Importance of Computer Science in MIS

Computer science is important to management information systems because it covers topics such as algorithms, computation, software, and data structures. However, the academic field of management information systems is not an extension of computer science; rather it is an extension of management and organisational theory. The fundamental processes of management information systems are more related to organisational processes and organisational effectiveness than computational algorithms. The emphasis in MIS is on the application of the technical capabilities computer science has made possible.

Subsystem of an MIS

MIS is a collaboration of subsystems. MIS has been introduced as a broad concept referring to a federation of subsystems. Two approaches to defining the subsystems of an MIS are according to the organisational functions which they support and according to managerial activities for which they are used.

Organisational Function Subsystems

Because organisational functions are somewhat separable in terms of activities and are defined managerially as separate responsibilities—one for each major organisational function. There may be common support system used by more than one subsystem, but each functional system is unique in its procedures, programmes, models, etc. Typical major subsystems for a business organisation engaged in manufacturing are:

Major Functional Subsystem	Some Typical Uses
Marketing	Sales forecasting, sales planning, customer and sales analysis
Manufacturing	Production planning and scheduling, cost control analysis
Logistics	Planning and control of purchasing, inventories, distribution
Personnel	Planning personnel requirements, analysing performance, salary administration
Finance and accounting	Financial analysis, cost analysis, capital requirements planning, income measurement
Information processing	Information system planning, cost-effectiveness analysis
Top management	Strategic planning, resource allocation

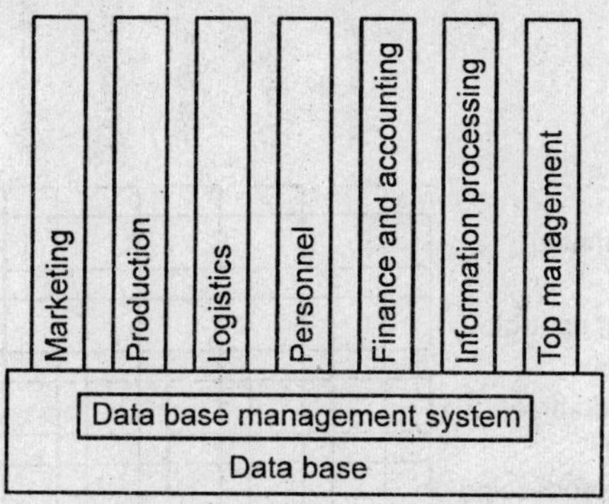

Figure 1.3. *Functional subsystems in an MIS used by a manufacturing concern.*

The database is the primary means of integration of the various subsystems. A data item that is stored or updated by one subsystem is then available to the other subsystem. For instance, the sales and inventory information used by the marketing subsystem; the same data is used by the manufacturing subsystem for production planning and scheduling.

Activities Subsystems

Another approach to understanding the structure of an information system is in terms of the subsystems which perform various activities. Some of the activities subsystems will be useful for more than one organisational functional subsystem; other will be useful for only one function. Example of major activities subsystems are:

Activity subsystem	Some typical uses
Transaction processing	Processing of orders, shipments, and receipts
Operational control	Scheduling of activities and performance reports
Management control	Formulation of budgets and resource allocation
Strategic planning	Formulation of objectives and strategic plans

Note that these activities subsystem correspond to the levels of the pyramid structure that defines MIS. The relationship of activities subsystems to functional subsystems is illustrated in Figure given below:

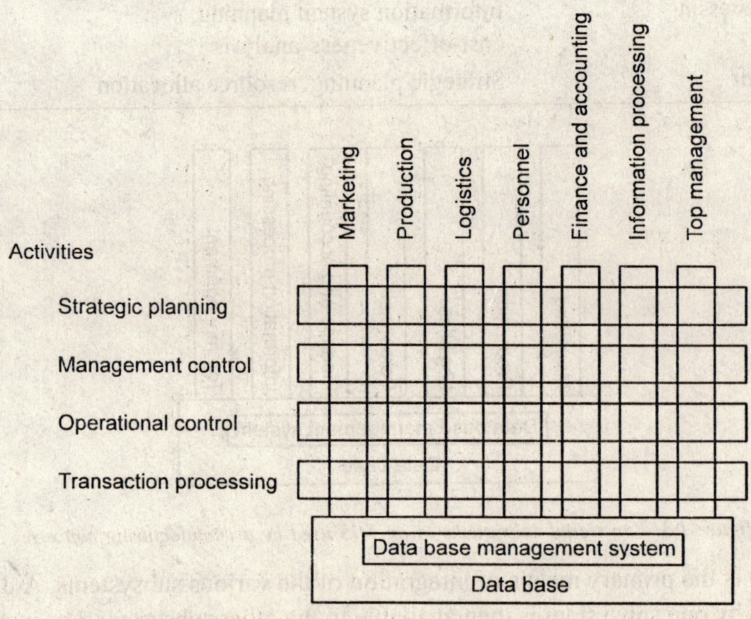

Figure 1.4. Relation of activities to functional subsystems.

MIS at the User End

The major users of a computer-based information system are the following:

User	Uses
Clerical personnel	Handle transactions, process input data and answer inquiries.
First-level Managers	Obtain operations data. Assistance with planning, scheduling, identifying out-of-control situations, and making decisions.
Staff specialists	Information for analysis. Assistance with analysis, planning, and reporting.
Management	Regular reports. Ad hoc retrieval requests. Ad hoc analyses. Ad hoc reports. Assistance in identifying problems and opportunities. Assistance in decision-making analysis.

Clerical personal are responsible for input and data control rather than being primary users of the output of the system. The job of the clerical person may be altered significantly when transaction processing is changed from manual to computer-based, especially if the system is online. For instance, an order clerk who takes orders over the phone previously worked with paper order forms and used an inventory book to check whether requested items were in stock. Now the clerk sits at a terminal; when an order is received, the clerk can instantly check inventory and complete the order, making substitutions if necessary while the customer is still on the telephone. In addition, the address and credit status of the customer can be verified immediately.

Since most of the information required by first-level managers is operational in nature, it can be supplied through the database and transaction processing systems. These also provide access to status information. Thus the supervisor can easily take action on items needing attention; without the report they would be difficult to identify.

The staff specialist assisting management in particular functional areas makes substantial use of the capabilities of MIS. The database is searched for problems. The data analysed to find possible solutions. Planning models are utilised to arrive at a first approximation of plans for management to examine. The model base provides the means for intelligence and design as staff specialists formulate data for managerial use. They may also examine and analyse data from external sources and incorporate them into models.

Since, currently, many decision models are somewhat difficult to use and require some knowledge of data processing, higher-level managers may not take the time to do analyses themselves. There is a trend toward the creation of specialist staff positions to handle such processing for managers.

Higher levels of management are affected by MIS through improved response to inquiries, continuous monitoring of important variables (rather than periodic reporting), and improved capability to identify problems or opportunities. Management control is enhanced by planning models and analytical models. For the highest level of management, strategic planning is aided by strategic planning models and analysis methods which support their use.

Information as a Strategic Weapon / Significance of Information

Sear sends reminders to customers that it is time to renew their service contracts. "It also sends letters offering special package deals to customers who have bought several appliances but have not purchased maintenance contracts for any of them. By keeping track of the appliances purchases made by each customer, as well as the service plans and maintenance calls for those appliances. Sears has been able to create a powerful marketing tool that is helping to boost service revenue and win customer goodwill."

"Owens-Corning Fiberglass Corp... is turning information developed by in-house research and development into what could prove a lucrative new marketing tool. The Toledo company generated substantial data on the energy efficiency of a wide variety of house designs when it was conducting research to develop new insulation materials severals years ago. Now, to boost sales of its home insulation products, Owens-Corning has developed a computer programme that uses these data to come up with energy-efficiency ratings for new designs. Owens has begun to offer builders free evaluations of their designs if they agree to buy all of their insulation from the manufacturer and meet a minimum standard of energy efficiency."

"Fidelity Brokerage Services Inc. spent $8 million for a proprietary system that has vaulted it into the No. 2 slot in the discount brokerage business—a move that was made against much larger rivals. Its system allows a broker using a terminal on his desk to execute stock trades more quickly and less expensively than most competitors who buy their services from outside computing companies."

"Xerox Corp. decided to put a good deal of value on faster information, and it is reaping significant rewards. By year end, Xerox expects it will have cut manufacturing costs in its copier division by 18% from those of three year ago. To accomplish that, it had to revamp 10 key manufacturing operations and change a number of business practices, including those in materials handling and inventory control. Xerox now exchanges quality-control information with its suppliers via computer terminals to eliminate the expensive inspection of incoming parts. In turn, the copier maker gives suppliers it master manufacturing schedule so they can ship parts at precisely the time that Xerox needs on its production line, thus keeping inventories lean."

Excerpted from "Business in Turning Data into a Potent Strategic Weapon."

MIS Professionals

An organisation typically has a separate MIS function which is responsible for acquiring and operating system hardware, acquiring or developing software, and managing the overall MIS resource. MIS professionals with a diverse area of skills are required to staff the MIS function. There is also a need for MIS professionals whose primary role is to adequately service the needs of a diverse user community.

The field of computing did not, in the beginning, emphasise formal education as a preparation. The field is now so broad and complex that come amount of formal education is generally necessary for a career in information systems. Two obvious alternatives are computer science and management information systems.

Although very useful, computer science alone is generally not sufficient for the management information systems specialist. Understanding basic organisational functions (marketing, finance, manufacturing, accounting, management, etc.) is as important as knowledge of computers. Understanding decision making and human behaviour in interaction with computer systems is as important as knowledge of programming. Understanding the dynamics of organisational change is as important as technical skills.

An example of academic preparation suitable for MIS is the curriculum recommendation of the Association for Computing Machinery (ACM) for those who wish to specialise in computer-based organisational information system.[2] The curriculum is a post-bachelor's degree program to provide educational preparation for a career in information systems. Figure 1-5 shows the basic structure of the proposed curriculum. A similar, but scaled-down, curriculum has been proposed for undergraduates.[3] A somewhat comparable curriculum has been proposed by a committee of IFIP (The International Federation for Information Processing). A curriculum with a slightly different orientation has been developed by DPMA (the Data Processing Management Association).[4]

The ACM curriculum is especially interesting in the context of MIS because it specifies academic preparation for two types of information systems professionals: the information analyst who works with users to define information requirements and the system designer who specifies hardware and software requirements. The information analyst is concerned with organisational information needs, whereas the system designer has more technical computer training. The role of the information analyst includes facilitation of organisational change; an information analyst includes the basic organisational functions and may even report to the functional area for which information services are being provided.

Users of This Text

The text is designed to serve the purpose of two sets of readers. The first group includes people who are or will be managers of an organisational function that is supported by MIS or their staff support specialists. Such persons need to know how MIS can provide them with information that will help them function more effectively. They also need to understand principles of information systems in order to effectively develop and use end user systems. The second group are computer professional who need to broaden their knowledge of information systems and learn to comprehend user needs for information. This group needs an orientation to MIS as a concept and philosophy to aid them in designing more effective information systems.

The book emphasizes the role of the user in the design, development, and operation of information systems. The design methods and designs principles presented in the text are applicable both to the MIS professional as a designer and to the end user who specifies requirements and/ or develops applications.

Goal of the Text

This text is different from most other books on computers and information systems. A person who studies or works in information systems in organisations may be able to describe the different components of a system but still not understand how and why the parts fit together. The text emphasizes not only alternatives in information system development, design, and use; it also specifies conditions and decision criteria for selecting among alternatives. The book thus contains descriptive material for conceptual understanding, but emphasizes developing an ability to discriminate and select among alternatives.

The last point is often related to contingency theory. The idea is that the selection of a method, format, design, procedure, etc., is *contingent* on the characteristics of the problem or situation. A contingency theory specifies the characteristics, the alternatives, and the rules or criteria for selection. The text presents contingency theories for a number of important decisions in MIS design, implementation, and operation.

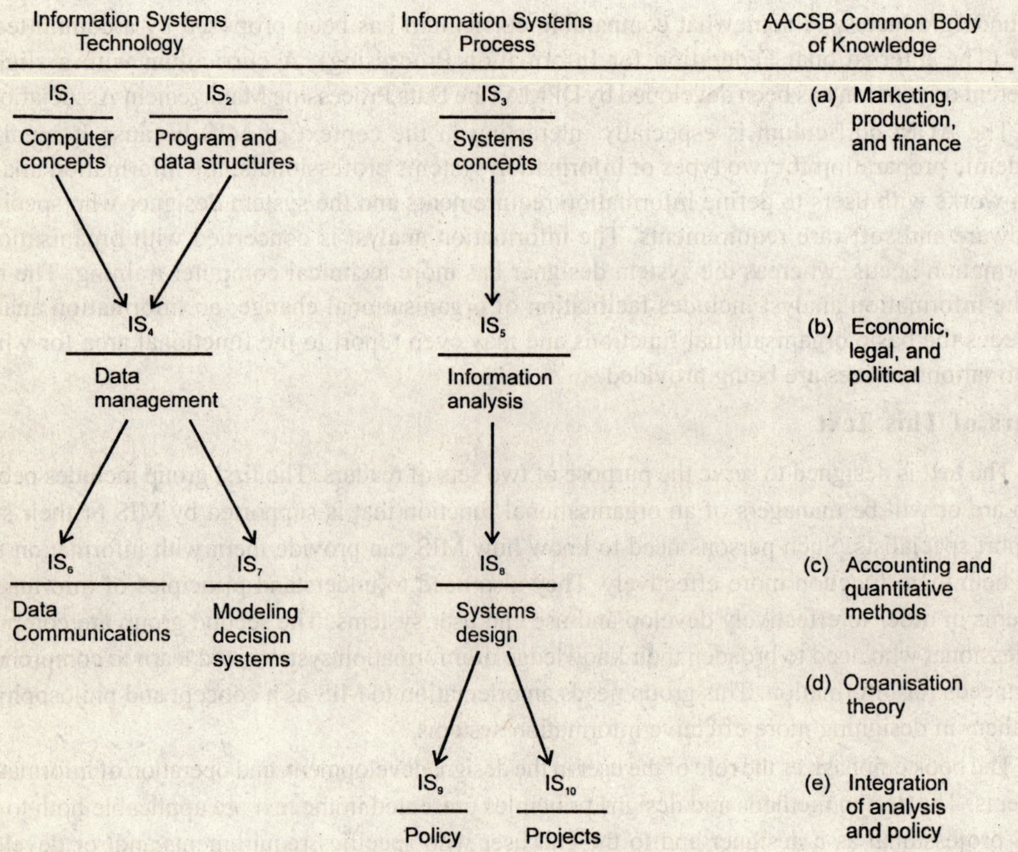

***Figure 1.5.** Curriculum for professional program in information systems. (Figure 1 from J.F. Nunamaker, J.D.Couger, and G.B. Davis, "Information Systems Curriculum Recommendations for the 80s: Undegraduate and Graduate Programs.)*

Organisation of the Text

In the remainder of this section, the structure of an MIS will be explained. In coming chapters, the technical environment surrounding MIS will be described. This includes an overview of hardware, software, and communication facilities; storage and retrieval of data; and transaction processing, office automation, and information processing control functions.

A complete understanding of computer-based organisational information systems requires an understanding of information use and information value, and how they relate to the organisation and humans as information processors. Last section of the text covers these conceptual foundations. It is a key section of the text. To illustrate the coverage, the concepts covered are listed below with comments on their relevance to an MIS.

Concepts	Comments
The decision-making process	MIS design should reflect not only rational approaches for optimisation in making decisions but also the behavioural theory of organisational decision-making.
Concepts of information	Information is that which adds to a representation. It has attributes of age and quality. It also has value in that it changes decisions.
Humans as information processors	The capabilities of humans as information processors impose limitations on information systems and suggest principles for their design.
System concepts	Because a management information system is system, and also part of an organisational systems, the concepts of systems are useful in designing approaches to information system development.
Concepts of planning and control	Information processing is a significant part of the important organisational activities of planning and control.
Organisational structure and management concepts	An information system exists within an organisation and is designed to support management functions; information is an important determinant of organisational form.

An underlying assumption is that information systems add value to an organisation. Information is viewed as a resource much like land, labour, and capital. It is not a free good. It must be obtained, processed, stored, retrieved, manipulated and analysed, distributed, etc. An organisation with a well-designed information system will generally have a competitive advantage over organisations with poorer systems.

Summary/Conclusion

Information is a vital ingredient for the operations and management of any organisation. The scope of a formal information system in an organisation is limited by the data that can be obtained, the cost of obtaining, processing, and storing the data; the cost of retrieval and distribution; the value of the information to the user; and the capability of humans to accept and act on the information. A computer-based management information system is designed to both reduce the costs and increase the capabilities of organisational information processing.

A definition of a management information system is an integrated, user-machine system for providing information to support the operations, management, and decision-making functions in an organisation. The system utilizes computer hardware and software; manual procedure; models for analysis, planning, control, and decision-making; and a database. Online operations facilitate user-machines dialog and interactive analysis, planning and decision-making. MIS is an evolving concept. Rather than a single large system, an MIS is a federation of loosely integrated subsystem. Functional subsystems of an MIS may be developed separately, guided by a master development plan, and integrated through the database. Rather than being distinct from data processing, MIS is an orientation which guides the development and operation of data processing systems. Three concepts which are incorporated into the MIS orientation are decision support systems, information resources management, and end user computing.

The concepts of MIS may be viewed as a substantial extension of the concepts of managerial accounting, operation research, and organisational theories related to management and decision-making. The content of computer science is relevant, but management information systems as an academic discipline is more of an extension of organisational behaviour and management than computer science.

Subsystems of MIS can be described in terms of organisational functional (such as marketing and production) or activities (such as planning and transaction processing). Each functional subsystem can be viewed as containing activity subsystems related to that function.

Different classes of users of MIS will use it differently. Clerical users primarily provide input and data control. First-line supervisor use it for operational control and detailed exception reporting. Management uses it for special reports and analyses, often employing a staff specialist to manipulate decision models and perform analyses. Because of the complexity of the process of MIS development and need for judgement, there is a need for comprehensive academic training for MIS professionals.

The text is directed at both users and developers of an MIS. It has a unique emphasis on conceptual foundations and contingency theory. The study of the text should aid in developing an understanding of what MIS is, why it is that way, and how it is developed and managed.

Notes

1. John Dearden, "MIS is a Mirage," *Harvard Business Review,* January–February 1972.
2. Jay F. Nunamaker, J. Daniel Couger, and Gordon B. Davis, "Information Systems Curriculum Recommendations for the 80s: Undergraduate and Graduate Programs—A Report of the ACM Curriculum Committee on Information Systems."
3. Nunamaker, Couger, and Davis, "Information Systems Curriculum."
4. The IFIP Curriculum has not yet been published; "DPMA Model Curriculum for Undergraduate Computer Information System Education," prepared by the Data Processing Management Association Education Foundation Committee on Curriculum Development.

2

Skeleton of a Management Information System

Operating Elements of an Information System
- Physical Components
- Processing Functions
- Outputs for Users

How MIS Helps in Decision Making
- Procedural Programmable Decisions
- Nonprocedural, Nonprogrammable Decisions

Management Information System Structure Based on Management Activity
- Hierarchy of Management Activity
- Role of Information Systems for Operational Control
- Role of Information Systems for Management Control
- Importance of Information Systems for Strategic Planning

Management Information System Works on Organisational Function
- Sales and Marketing Subsystems of MIS
- Production Subsystem of MIS
- Logistics Subsystem of MIS
- Personnel Subsystem of MIS
- Finance and Accounting Subsystem of MIS
- Information Processing Subsystem
- Top Management Subsystem

Synthesis of Management Information System Structure
- Conceptual Structure of Management Information System
- Physical Structure of Management Information System

Some Critical Issues about Management Information System Structure
- Advantage of Formal System over Informal Information System
- Extent of Integration
- Extent of User-Machine Interaction

Summary/Conclusion

What does a management information system look like? What is its conceptual structure? What is its physical structure? This chapter addresses these questions. There is no standard, agreed-upon framework for describing management information systems. However, the central tendency is reflected in this chapter.

This chapter emphasizes the scope of MIS as a broad concept and thus reflects an "ideal" toward which an organisation may move as it designs or redesigns its information systems. The organisation's management information system is not a distinct entity, separate from its other information systems. Rather it represents a broad framework within which individual information systems (or subsystems) fit. In the text, "management information system" and "information system" are used interchangeably to refer to this broad framework.

Like most complex systems, a management information system can be described in a number of different ways. For example, imagine describing an automobile to someone without prior experience with a car. It might be explained in terms of its physical characteristics of shape, colour, seating capacity, number of doors, etc. It could also be described in terms of the component systems such as chassis, engine, or transmission, and how these components are related to achieve a working automobile. One might also classify cars in terms of major use, such as a station wagon, sedan, and sports car. Each of these classifications would provide insight to the person seeking to understand automobiles.

Multiple approaches are used in this chapter to explain the structure of an organisational information system or management informational system. The information system is described in terms of four separate but related classifications:

- Operating elements
- Decision support
- Management activity
- Organisational function

After describing management information systems from these four perspectives, the chapter presents a synthesis of the last three categories into a single model of a management information system.

Operating Elements of an Information System

If one requested to be shown the information systems of an organisation, he or she would probably be shown its physical components. An enquiry as to what these physical components do might be answered in terms of processing functions or perhaps in terms of system outputs for users.

Physical Components (Hardware, Software, Database, Procedures and Operational Personnel)

The physical components required for an organisational information system are hardware, software, database, procedures, and operations personnel. These elements shown below:

Physical components	Description
Hardware	Hardware refers to physical computers equipment and associated devices. Hardware must provide for five major functions: 1. Input or entry 2. Output 3. Secondary storage for data and programs 4. Central processor (computation, control, and primary storage) 5. Communications
Software	Software is a broad term given to the instructions that direct the operation of the hardware. The software can be classified into two major types: system software and application software.
Database	The database contains all data utilised by application software. An individual set of stored data is often referred to as a file. The physical existence of stored data is evidenced by the physical storage media (computer tapes, disk packs, diskettes , etc.) used for secondary storage.
Procedures	Formal operating procedures are physical components because they exist in a physical form such as a manual or instruction booklet. Three major types of procedures are required: 1. User instructions (for users of the application to record data, employ a terminal to enter or retrieve data, or use the result) 2. Instructions for preparation of input by data preparation personnel 3. Operating instructions for computer operations personnel
Operations personnel	Computer operators, systems analysts, programmers, data preparation personnel, information systems management, data administrators, etc.

Processing Functions (Process Transactions, Maintain Master Files, Produce Reports, Process Inquiries, Process Interactive Support Applications)

A description of an information system in terms of physical components does not explain what the system does, just as a description of a hardware configuration does not explain why it is configured in that way. Another way to describe an information system is in terms of processing functions (Figure 2.1). The major processing are on the next page in table:

Outputs for End Users

The user of a management information system provides inputs and receives outputs. The user's assessment of the information system is therefore dependent somewhat on the ease of input but is primarily based on the usefulness of the output the user sees. The outputs thus form one description of an information system and can be classified as being of five major types:

1. Transaction documents or screens
2. Preplanned reports
3. Preplanned inquiry responses
4. Ad hoc reports and inquiry responses
5. User-machine dialog results

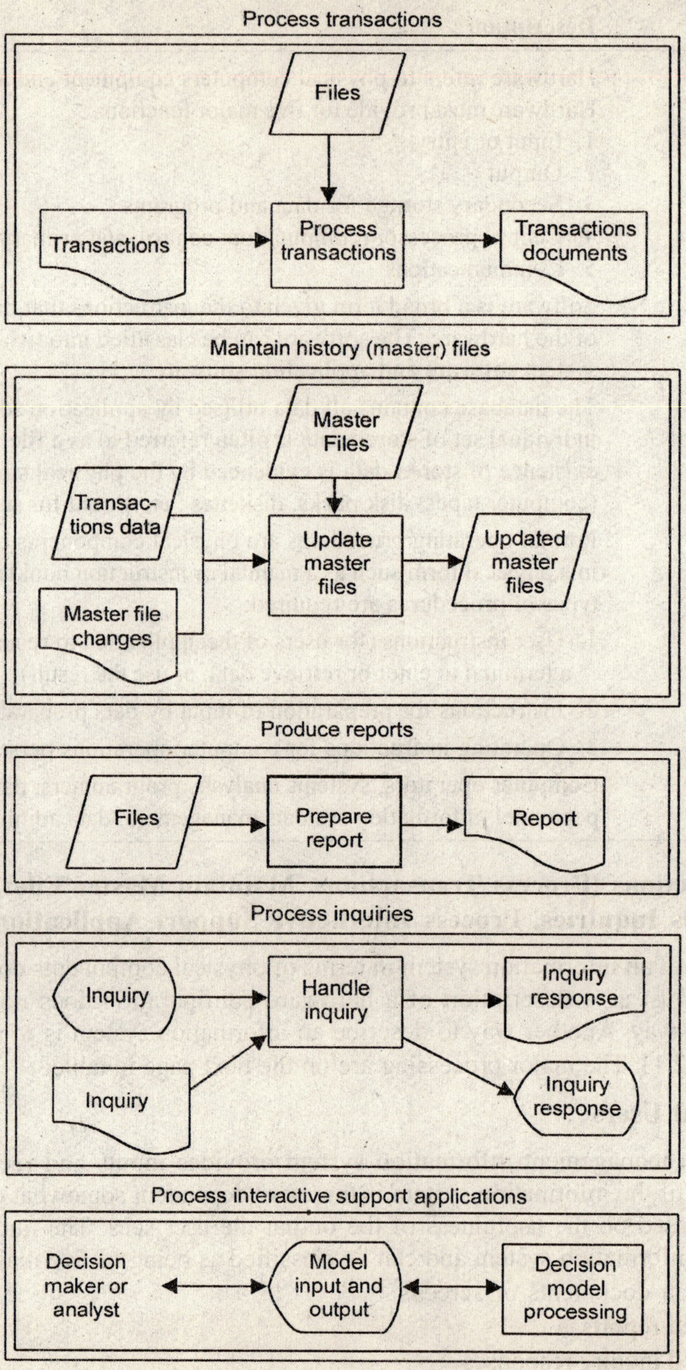

Figure 2.1. Processing functions.

Processing function	Comments
Process transactions	A transaction is an activity such as making a purchase or a sale or manufacturing product. It may be internal to the organisation or may involve the organisation and an external entity. Performance of a transaction requires records to (1) direct a transaction to take place, (2) report, confirm, or explain its performance, or (3) communicate the transaction to those needing a record for background information or reference.
Maintain master files	Many processing activities require creation and files maintenance of master files, which store relatively permanent or historical data about organisational entities. For example, processing to prepare an employee's paycheck requires data items for the employee's rate of pay, deductions, etc. When transactions are processed, master file data items are updated to reflect the most current information.
Produce reports	Reports are significant products of an information system. Scheduled reports are produced on a regular basis. An information system should also be able to produce special reports quickly based on ad hoc (unscheduled) requests.
Process inquiries	Other outputs of the information systems are responses to inquiries using the database. These may be regular inquiries with a preset format or ad hoc inquiries. The essential function of inquiry processing is to make any record or any item in the database easily accessible to authorised personnel.
Process interactive support application	The information system contains applications designed to support systems for planning, analysis, and decision-making. The computer performs processing based on a planning model, decision model, etc.; the mode of operation is interactive with the user responding to questions and requests for data and receiving immediate results in order to alter inputs until a solution or satisfactory result is achieved.

Examples of transaction documents are items such as sales invoices, payroll checks, customer billings, and purchase orders. Transaction documents refer directly to the operations of the organisations, while the other types of outputs support management and control of those operations.

Reports, inquiry responses, and dialog results provide four types of information:

1. **Monitoring information.** The information confirms that actions have been taken and reports status in financial or other terms. The information also provides the recipient with background for understanding other reports and analyses. Monitoring information may provide a basis for problem finding and diagnosis and may lead to action, but no action is specified by the information itself.
2. **Problem finding information.**[1] The information is presented in a format that promotes identification of problems. Examples are comparisons between enterprise data and standards (internal standards, industry averages, or competitor data) and projections of current performance to the end of a reporting period.

3. **Action information.** The information is presented with action specified or implied.
4. **Decision support.** The report, inquiry, result, or dialog is oriented to performing analysis and making a decision.

Transaction document type	Explanation about these translations with examples
Informational	Reports or confirms that action will be or has been taken. Examples are a sales order confirmation verifying receipt of an order from a customer and a report describing receipt of goods previously ordered. Their purpose is to provide feedback to persons connected in some way with the action or later reference.
Action	Requests or instructions for action. A purchase order initiates a purchase, a check instruct the bank to pay, a production order instructs production actions.
Investigational	Reports exceptions, errors, or other conditions that may require investigation. Used for control and future reference.

Preplanned reports have a regular content and format and are usually run on a regularly scheduled basis. Examples are sales analysis, inventory status, and budget variance reports. Prepared at a given time, they reflect one of three conditions with respect to the time period they cover:

1. They describe status or condition at a point in time (such as inventory status as a January 31, 1985);
2. They summarise what has occurred during a period such as a week, month, or year (e.g., sales during month of March 1985);
3. They present result to date and project to the end of the period (such as a year).

Preplanned inquiries are generally associated with limited output, usually with respect to a small number of items, and result in such output as inventory on hand of part 37518, pay rate of employee 518238142, or balance due from customer XYZ Industries. Inquiries are typically handled online, which means the inquiry is entered and response received immediately via terminal. Since the inquiry has been preplanned, the input format of the inquiry is generally quite simple, and therefore the terminal may be operated directly by the user requesting the information.

Ad hoc reports and inquiry responses occur at irregular intervals and require data or analysis whose format has not been preplanned. If the data items needed are not available, a data collection procedure must be planned and implemented. If the data is already stored in the information system, the ad hoc request may be handled in two ways:

1. The user may be provided with a means for preparing and processing the request. The inquiry may, for example, be formulated by use of an inquiry language using either an online terminal or special coding forms for subsequent transcription to machine-readable form.
2. An information service (often called an information centre) may be available to process ad hoc requests. Specialists staffing the information service aid user to analyse requests and specify the retrieval and processing necessary to provide the requested data or analysis.

User-machine dialog differs from reports or inquiries. It is essentially a way in which a user can interact with a model to arrive at an analysis or a solution. User-machine interaction employs a terminal such as a visual display terminal or a stand-alone personal computer plus computer processing of a model such as an analysis, planning, or decision model. Examples are site planning models, capital investment analysis models, and portfolio management models.

How MIS Helps in Decision-Making

Decisions vary with respect to the structure that can be provided for making them. A highly structured decision can be preplanned or prespecified, whereas a highly unstructured decision cannot. A structured decision can be said to be programmable, in the sense that unambiguous decision rules can be specified in advance. The term does not necessarily mean that the decision is automated, although many programmable decisions are automated. An unstructured decision is said to be nonprogrammable. The structured, programmable decision tends to be routine and frequently repeated; the unstructured decision tends to occur with less frequency and tends to be nonroutine. Decision-making will be explained in more.

Information system support will differ for the two types of decisions. Some decisions will fit easily into this classification, but many decisions are more or less structured and have some elements that are programmable and some that are not.

Procedural, Programmable Decisions

When a decision can be programmed, an organisation can prepare a decision rule or decision procedure. This can be expressed as a set of steps to follow, a flowchart, a decision table, or a formula. The decision procedure will also specify the information to be acquired before the decision rules are applied. Since structured, programmable decisions can be already specified, many of these decisions can be handled by lower-level personnel with little specialised knowledge. In fact, many highly structured decisions may be completely automated, although human review is generally considered desirable. Examples of highly structured decisions are inventory reorder formulas and rules for granting credit.

The information system requirements for structured decisions are clear and unambiguous procedures for entering the required input data, validation procedures to ensure correct and complete input, processing of the input using the decision logic, and output of the programmed decision in a form that is useful for action.

In many cases, it is not possible to define a decision procedure or decision rule to handle all possible situations. In these cases, the decision rules are written to apply to the most common situations, and the uncommon or unusual situations that do not apply are referred to a human maker, usually one with some specialised knowledge.

Nonprocedural, Nonprogrammable Decisions

The unstructured decision has no preestablished decision procedure, either because the decision is too infrequent to justify the organisational cost of preparing a decision procedure (even though it may be partly programmable) or because the decision process is not understood well enough or is too changeable to allow a stable preestablished decision procedure. The support requirements for unstructured decision-making are access to data and a variety of analysis and decision procedures that can be applied to the solution of the problem. The data requirements are not completely known in advance, so data retrieval must allow for ad hoc retrieval requests. Interactive decision support systems with generalised inquiry and analysis capabilities are appropriate information system support for unstructured decision-making.

Management Information System Structure Based on Management Activity

Management information systems support management activity. This means that the structure of an information system can be classified in terms of a hierarchy of management planning and control activities.

Hierarchy of Management Activity

The following categories of management planning and control were defined by Anthony:[2]

Level	Comments
Strategic planning	Definition of goals, policies, and general guidelines charting course for organisation. Determination of organisational objectives.
Management control and planning	Acquisition of resources. Acquisition tactics, plant location, new products. Establishment and monitoring of budgets.
Operational planning and control	Effective and efficient use of existing facilities and resources to carry out activities within budget constraints.

The three levels of management activity can be differentiated on the basis of the planning horizon for each level. Strategic planning deals with long-range considerations. The decisions to be made are concerned with the choice of business direction, market strategy, product mix, etc. Management control and tactical planning has a medium-term planning horizon. It includes acquisition and organisation of resources, structuring of work, and acquisition and training of personnel. It is reflected in the capital expenditure budget, the three-year staffing plan, etc. Operational planning and control is related to short-term decisions for current operations. Pricing, production levels, inventory levels, etc., are a result of operational planning and control activities.

A particular manager may have responsibility for a mix of management activities, but proportions shift with management level. For instance, a shop floor supervisor will spend most of his or her time on operational planning and control. An executive vice president will devote, by comparison, more time to strategic planning.

The activities and information processing for the three levels are interrelated. For example, inventory control at the operational level depends on accurate processing of transactions; at the level of management of control, decisions made about safety stock and reorder frequency are dependent on correct summarisation of results of operations; at the strategic level, results in operations and management control are related to strategic objectives, competitor behaviour, and so forth to arrive at inventory strategy. There is a marked contrast between characteristics required of information for strategic planning and for operational control, with management control and tactical planning being somewhat in the middle. Table 2-1 shows the difference for seven information characteristics. Given these differences, information system support for strategic planning should be quite different from information system support for operational control.

Table 2.1
Information Requirements by Level of Management Activity

Characteristics of Information	Operational control	Management control	Strategic planning
Source	Largely internal		External
Scope	Well-defined, narrow		Very wide
Level of aggregation	Detailed		Aggregate
Time horizon	Historical		Future
Currency	Highly current		Quite old
Required accuracy	High		Low
Frequency of use	Very frequent		Infrequent

Source: G.A. Gorry and M. S. Scott Morton, "Framework for Management Information Systems."

Decisions vary as to the degree of structure within each level of management activity, although the majority of decisions at the operational control level are relatively structured and the majority of decisions at the strategic planning level are relatively unstructured. Table 2.2 shows examples of structured and unstructured decisions at each management level. The table also shows that information systems to support structured versus unstructured decisions are characteristically different. Structured decision systems provide decision rules and exception reports but are relatively inflexible as to content and format. Decision support systems (DSS), on the other hand, are characterised by flexible access to the database, a variety of flexible outputs formats, and a collection of decision models. Such components are required to "support" the manager in the decision-making *process*, rather than attempting to provide solutions or make decisions for the user.

Table 2.2
Types of Decision by Management Activity

		Operational control	Management control	Strategic planning
	Structured ↑			
Structured decision systems		Inventory reorder decisions Production scheduling Selection of vendor	Pricing of bids Selection of credit line institutions Allocation of advertising	Acquisition of a company Addition of new product line Entry into new market
Decision support system		Hiring of new supervisor	Internal organisation of a department	New organisation of company
	↓ **Unstructured**			

The following three sections summarise the characteristics of information system support for the three levels of the hierarchy of management planning and control.

Role of Information System for Operational Control

Operational control is the process of ensuring that operational are carried out effectively and efficiently. Operational control makes use of preestablished procedures and decision rules. A large percentage of the decisions are programmable. The procedures to follow are generally quite stable. The operating decisions and resulting actions usually cover short time periods (a day to a week). Individual transactions are often important, so that the operational system must be able to respond to both individual transactions and summaries of transactions.

Processing support for operational control consists of:

1. Transaction processing
2. Report processing
3. Inquiry processing

These three types of processing contain various decision-making routines which implement prespecified decision rules or provide output describing the decision that will be taken unless the user responsible overrides it. Some examples will illustrate the type of decision procedure that can be designed into operational control system.

- An inventory withdrawal transaction produces a transaction document. The transaction processing programme can also examine the balance on hand, etc., and decide (using preestablished criteria) if a replenishment order should be placed. If so, the order quantity is calculated by use of an order quantity algorithm, and an action document is produced which specifies the need for an order plus the order quantity. The human recipient (e.g., inventory analyst) may accept the order as it is or may choose to override the programmed decision by canceling it or adjusting the order quantity.
- An inquiry to a personnel file describe the requirements for a position. The computer search of the employee file uses preprogrammed rules to select and rank candidates.
- A telephone order clerk taking an order enters the data online using a visual display terminal. In the case of a stockout, programmed decision rules are applied to identify substitute items which the order taker can suggest to the customer.
- A programmed decision rule in a report processing procedure may cause issuance of special reports to provide information in a problem area. An example might be a report showing orders still outstanding after 30 days, produced as a result of an unusually high (the limit prespecified) 30-day balance.

The database for operational control and operational decision making contains primarily internal data generated from transactions. The data items are generally quite current. Care must be taken to interpret data being recorded from operations, since the sequence of processing is often significant; for example, additions to inventory are processed before withdrawals in order to avoid the appearance of being out of stock when new stock has been received.

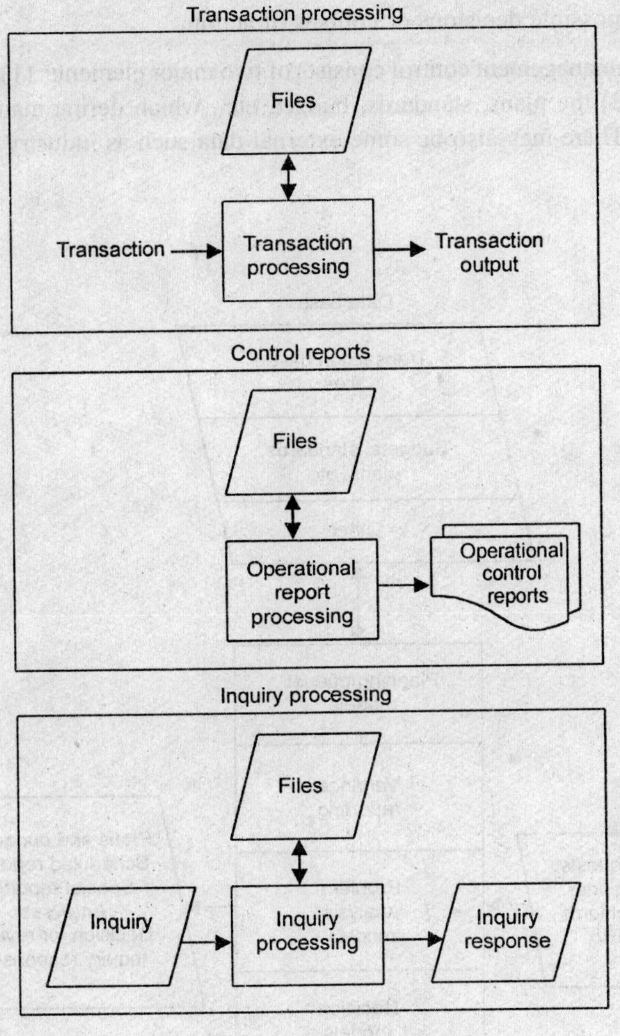

Figure 2.2. *Processing to support operational control.*

Role of Information System for Management Control

Management control information is required by managers of departments, profit centres, etc., to measure performance, decide on control actions, formulate new decision rules to be applied by operational personnel, and allocate resources. Summary information is needed; it must be processed so that trends may be observed, reasons for performance variances may be understood, and solutions may be suggested. The control process requires the following types of information:

- Planned performance (standard, expected, budgeted, etc.)
- Variances from planned performance
- Reasons for variances
- Analysis of possible decisions or courses of action.

The database for management control consists of two major elements: (1) the database provided by operations, and (2) the plans, standards, budget, etc., which define management expectations about performance. There may also be some external data such as industry comparisons and cost indices (Figure 2-3).

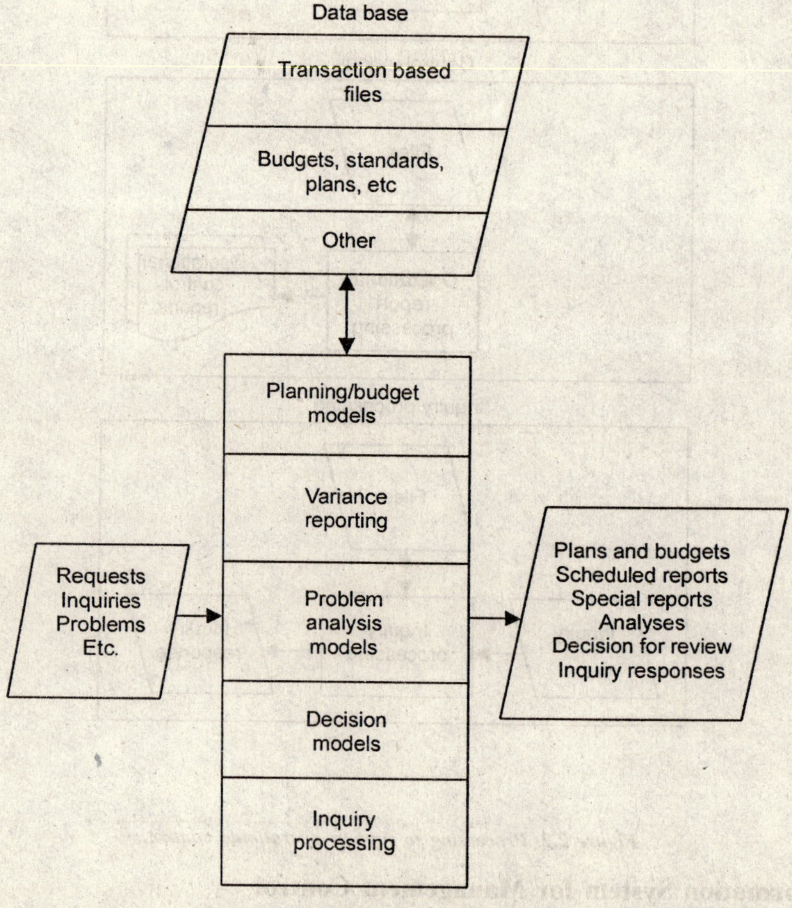

Figure 2.3. Management control and processing support.

The processing requirements to support management control activities are the following:

1. Planning and budget models to assist managers in finding problems in direction and preparing and revising plans and budgets. This includes projections of effects of current actions.
2. Variance reporting programmes to process scheduled reports showing performance and variances from planned performance or other standards such as competitor performance.
3. Problem database models to analyze data to provide input for decision-making.
4. Decision models to analyse a problem situation and provide possible solutions for management evaluation.
5. Inquiry models to assist in responding to inquiries.

The outputs from the management control information system are plans and budgets, scheduled reports, special reports, analyses of problem situation, decision for review, and inquiry responses.

Importance of Information Systems for Strategic Planning

The purpose of strategic planning is to develop strategies by which an organisation will be able to achieve its objectives. The time horizon for strategic planning tends to be fairly long, so that fundamental shifts in the organisation may be made. For example:

- A department store chain may decide to diversify into the mail order business.
- A department store chain with stores in the central city may decide to change to a discount type of operation in the subrubs.
- A company manufacturing industrial products may decide to diversify into consumer lines.

Strategic planning activities do not have to occur on a periodic, regular cycle as do management control activities. They can be somewhat irregular, although some strategic planning may be scheduled into the yearly planning and budgeting cycle. Data requirements for strategic planning are generally for processed, summarised data from a variety of sources. There is need for considerable external data. Some examples of types of data that are useful in strategic planning illustrate the nature of the data requirements:

1. Outlook for the economy in the company's current and prospective areas of activity
2. Current and prospective political environment
3. Current capabilities and performance of the organisation by market, country, etc. (based on current policies)
4. Prospect for the industry in each country
5. Capabilities of competitors and their market shares.

This database contains some "hard" facts, but much is based on judgment. Much of the data cannot be collected on a regular basis, and much of it cannot be specified completely in advance. For this reason, some have argued that it is impossible (or certainly impractical) to have a management information system for strategic planning activities. They point out the difficulty to efficiently coding, storing, and retrieving the multitude of rumors, facts, hunches, etc., that enter into an assessment of prospects for an industry, a market, or an economy.

An alternative to this view is that information system support cannot be as complete for strategic planning as it is for management control and operational control, but the system is one source of information that can provide substantial aid to the process of strategic planning. For example:

- The evaluation of current capabilities is based on internal data generated by operational processing requirements, but it may need to be summarised in a special way for planning use.
- The initial projections of future capability can be developed by analysis of past data. This first approximation is adjusted by management on the basis of judgement and experience.
- Fundamental market data on the industry and competitors can probably be kept in the organisation's database.
- Databanks of public information regarding the industry and competitors may be purchased in machine-readable form for use with planning and decision models.

Management Information System Works on Organisational Function

The structure of an information system can also be described in terms of the organisational functions which use information. There is no standard classification of functions, but a typical set of functions in a manufacturing organisation includes production, sales and marketing, finance and accounting, logistics, personnel, and information systems. Top management can also be considered as a separate function. Each of these functions has unique information needs and each requires information system support designed for it. An organisation may not actually be organised along functional lines, but in general the logical information subsystem will follow functional lines.

As explained already, a management information system is essentially a federation of information systems that are designed to support the functional subsystems of the organisation. Each functional subsystem requires applications to perform all information processing related to the function, although this may involve calling upon a database, a model base, and some computer programmes which are common to all functional subsystems. Within each functional subsystem, there will be applications for transaction processing, operational control, managerial control, and strategic planning (Figure 2.4).

Subsystems of MIS

MIS has several subsystems. Each subsystem has its own importance. Some of the subsystems are given below:

Sales and Marketing Subsystems of MIS: The sales and marketing function generally includes all activities related to the promotion and sales of products or services. The transactions are sales orders, promotion orders, etc. The operational control activities include the hiring and training of the sales force, the day-to-day scheduling of sales and promotion efforts, and periodic analyses of sales volumes by region, product, customer, etc. Managerial control concerns comparisons of overall performance against a marketing plan. Information for managerial control may include data on customers, competitor, competitor products, and sales force requirements. Strategic planning for the marketing function involves consideration of new markets and new marketing strategies. The information requirement for strategic planning include customer analyses, competitor analyses, consumer survey information, income projection, demographic projections, and technology projections.

Production Subsystem of MIS: The responsibilities of the production or manufacturing functions include product engineering, planning of production facilities, scheduling and operation of production facilities, employment and training of production personnel, and quality control and inspection. Typical transactions to be processed are production orders (based on an explosion of the sales orders and inventory requirements into components parts), assembly orders, finished parts tickets, scrap tickets, and time-keeping tickets. Operational control requires detailed reports comparing actual performance to the production schedule and highlighting areas where bottlenecks occur. Management control requires summary reports which compare overall planned or standard performance to actual performance for such classifications as cost per unit and labour used. Strategic planning for manufacturing includes alternative manufacturing approaches and alternative approaches to automation.

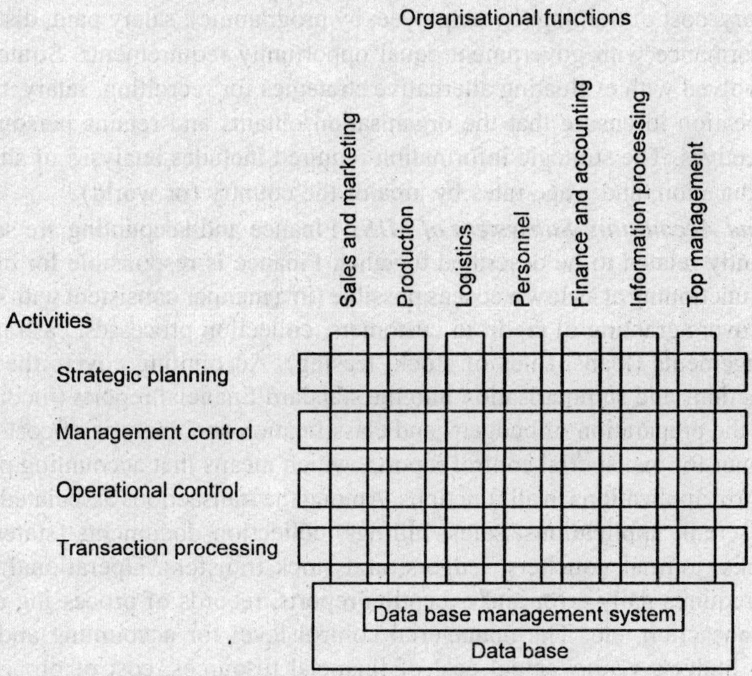

Figure 2.4. The matrix of functional and management activities.

Logistics Subsystem of MIS: The logistics function encompasses such activities as purchasing, receiving, inventory control, and distribution. The transactions to be processed include purchase requisitions, purchase orders, manufacturing orders, receiving reports, tickets for inventory, shipping orders, and bill of lading. The operational control function uses information contained in reports such as past-due purchases, past-due shipments to customers, out-of-stock items, overstocked items, inventory turnover reports, vendor performance summaries, and shipper performance analyses. Managerial control information for logistics consists of overall comparisons between planned and actual inventory levels, costs for purchased items, stockouts, inventory turnover, etc. Strategic planning involves the analysis of new distribution strategies, new policies with regard to vendors, and "make *versus* buy" strategies. Information on new technology, distribution alternatives, etc., is required.

Personnel Subsystem of MIS: The personnel subsystem includes hiring, training, record keeping, payment, and termination of personnel. The transactions result in documents describing employment requisitions, job descriptions, training specifications, personnel data (background, skills, experience), pay rate changes, hours worked, paychecks, benefits, and termination notices. Operational control for personnel requires decision procedures for action such as hiring, training, termination, changing pay rates, and issuing benefits. Management control of the personnel function is supported by reports and analysis showing the variances resulting from differences between planned and actual performance for such classifications as number of employees hired, cost of recruiting, composition of skills inventory, cost of training (by employee, by programme), salary paid, distribution of wage rates, and conformance with government equal opportunity requirements. Strategic planning for personnel is involved with evaluating alternative strategies for recruiting, salary, training, benefits, and building location to ensure that the organisation obtains and retains personnel necessary to achieve its objectives. The strategic information required includes analyses of shifting patterns of employment, education, and wage rates by area of the country (or world).

Finance and Accounting Subsystem of MIS: Finance and accounting are separate functions but are sufficiently related to be described together. Finance is responsible for ensuring adequate organisational functioning at as low a cost as possible (in a manner consistent with other objectives). This function covers granting of credit to customers, collection processes, cash management, and financing arrangements (loans, sales of stock, leasing). Accounting covers the classification of financial transactions and summarisation into the standard financial reports (income statement and balance sheet), the preparation of budgets, and classification and analysis of cost data. Budget and cost data are input for managerial control reports, which means that accounting provides input for managerial control applications in all functions. Among the transactions associated with finance and accounting are credit applications, sales, billings, collection documents (statements), payment vouchers, checks, journal vouchers, ledgers, and stock transfers. Operational control over the function itself requires daily error and exception reports, records of processing delays, reports of unprocessed transaction, etc. The managerial control level for accounting and finance utilizes information on budgets *versus* actual cost of financial resources, cost of processing accounting data, and error rates. The strategic planning level for accounting and finance involves a long-run strategy to ensure adequate financing, a long-range tax accounting policy to minimize the impact of taxes, and planning of systems for cost accounting and budgeting.

Information Processing Subsystem of MIS: The information processing functions is responsible for ensuring that the other functions are provided the necessary information processing services and resources. Typical transactions for information processing are requests for processing, requests for corrections or changes in data and programs, reports of hardware and programme performance, and project proposals. Operational control of information processing operations requires information on the daily schedule of jobs, error rates, and equipment failures; for new project development it requires daily or weekly schedules of programmer progress and test time. Managerial control over information processing require data on planned *versus* actual utilization, equipment costs, overall programmer performance, and progress compared to schedule for projects to develop and implement new applications. Strategic planning for information systems involves the organisation of the function (such as centralized or decentralized), the overall information system plan, selection of strategic uses of information, and the general structure of the hardware and software environment. For example, a major strategic decision might be to implement microcomputer workstations for all analysts, planner, and managers.

Office automation may be defined as a separate subsystem or included within information processing. Office automation includes a wide range of support facilities for knowledge work and clerical activities. Examples are word processing, electronic mail, electronic filing, and data and voice communications.

***Top Management Subsystem*:** The top management function (chief executive officer plus staff) operates separately from the functional areas, but also includes the functional vice presidents acting in a top management capacity such as in management committees. The transactions processed by top management are primarily inquiries for information and support of decisions. The transaction documents, therefore, tends to be letters and memoranda. Responding to the inquiries and making decisions requires either access to the database and decision models of the organisation or transmittal of the requests to other parts of the organisation. The information for operational control in the top management function includes meeting schedules, correspondence control files, and contact files. Managerial control by top management uses information which summarises the management control being exercised by other functions to evaluate whether the functions are performing as planned. This requires access to the plans and actual performance of all the functions. Strategic planning activities relate to matters such as direction of the company (which business it should be in) and plans for ensuring necessary resources. The strategy determined by top management sets the framework for strategic planning within function and also coordinates planning to remove major inconsistencies. Strategic planning at the top management levels requires a wide variety of summarised external and internal data. Information system support for strategic planning may include ad hoc retrieval of data, ad hoc analyses, and decision support systems.

External Information Dominates EIS

In the design of an executive information system (EIS) for the chief officers of a large regional banking system, the requirements were dominated by external information not produced by the transaction system of data processing. Examples of external information requirements were:

- Competitor information
- Regulatory information
- Regional economic indicators
- Customer preferences for services
- Quality of services being provided.

Synthesis of a Management Information System Structure

The MIS structure has been described in terms of support for decision-making, management activity, and organisational functions. These three approaches will now be synthesized into a management information system structure. This is essentially a conceptual framework which allows one to describe an existing or planned information system. There is also a physical structure which defines the way an MIS is implemented.

Conceptual Structure of Management Information System: The conceptual structure of a management information system is defines as a federation of functional subsystems, each of which is divided into four major information processing components: transaction processing, operational control information system support, managerial control information system support, and strategic planning information system support. Each of the functional subsystems of the information system has some unique data files which are used only by that subsystem. There are also files which need to be accessed by more than one application and need to be available for general retrieval. These files are organised into a general database managed by a database management system.

A further amplification of the structure is the introduction of common software. In addition to application programmes written especially for each subsystem, there are common applications which serve multiple functions. Each subsystem has linkages to these common applications. There are also many analytical and decision models that can be used by many applications. These form the model base for the information system.

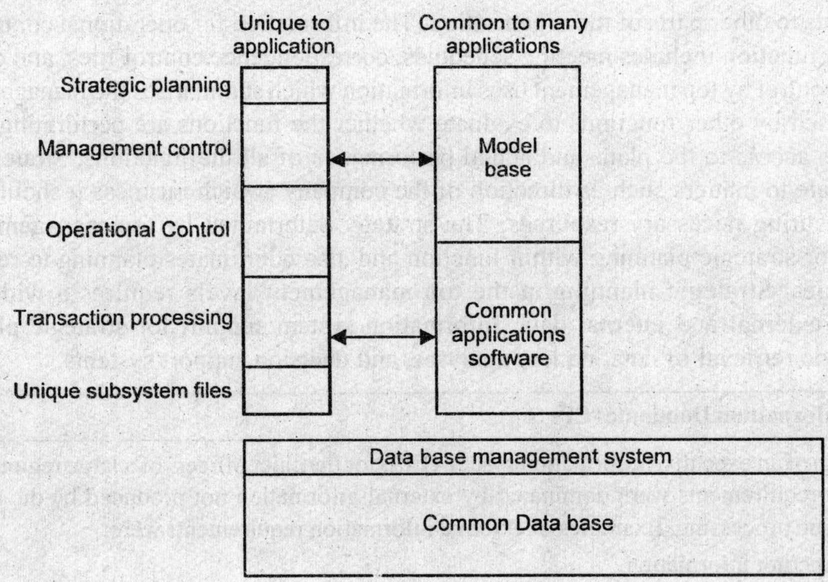

Figure 2.5. The Information subsystem for a function (such as marketing or production).

The subsystem has unique programmes and unique files for its basic activities. It shares the use of common application software, a model base, a database management system. The database management system controls all files in the common database, and may also be used for storage and retrieval of the files unique to a function. The combination of all subsystems forms the management system for the organisation.

Within the three management activity classifications of a functional subsystem of the information system, application can be classified as to thze type of management information support provided. These can be monitoring information, action information, and decision support.

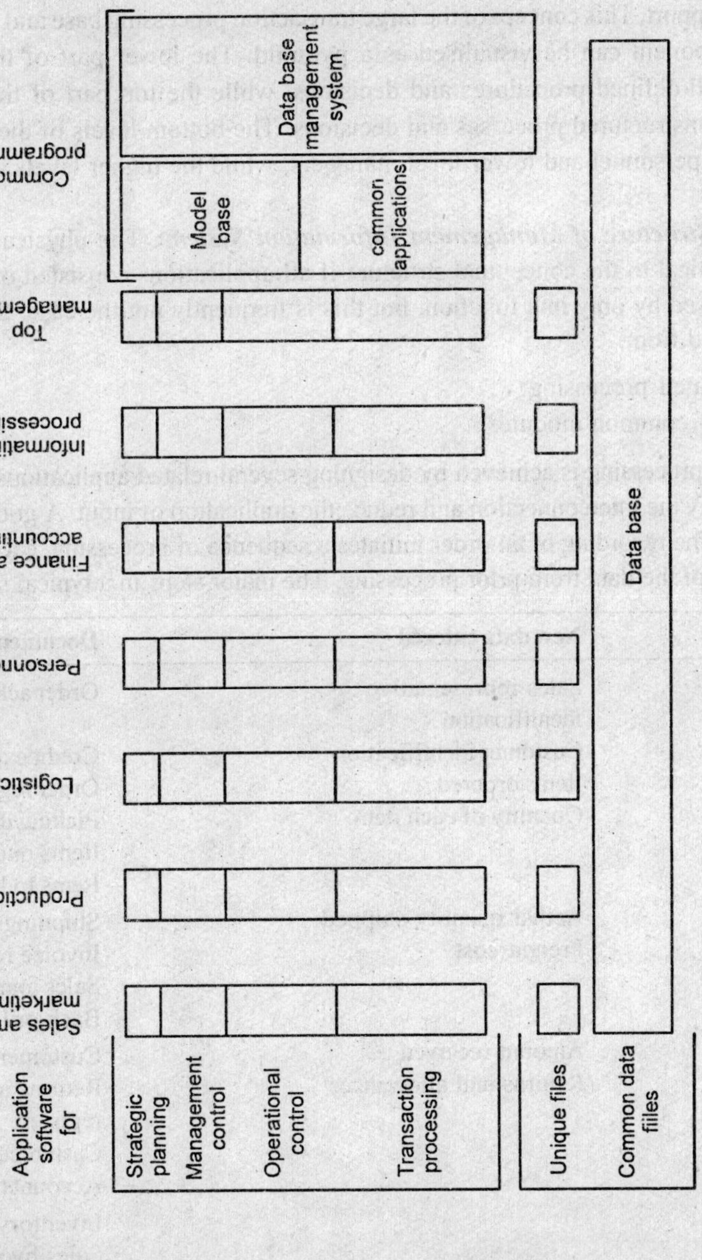

Figure 2.6. The organisational MIS.

The amount of information processing resources required varies by level of management activity. Transaction processing is substantially more significant in terms of processing time, data volume, etc., than strategic planning. Transaction processing systems provide the base for all other internal information support. This concept of the large transaction processing base and a fairly small strategic planning component can be visualised as a pyramid. The lower part of the pyramid describes structured, well-defined procedures and decisions, while the top part of the pyramid represents more ad hoc, unstructured processes and decisions. The bottom levels of the pyramid are of more use to clerical personnel and lower-level managers, while the higher levels apply primarily to top management.

***Physical Structure of Management Information System*:** The physical structure of an MIS would be identical to the conceptual structure if all applications consisted of completely separate programmes used by only one function, but this is frequently not the case. Substantial economies can be achieved from:

1. Integrated processing
2. Use of common modules.

Integrated processing is achieved by designing several related applications as a single system in order to simplify the interconnection and reduce the duplication of input. A good example is an order entry system. The recording of an order initiates a sequence of processing, each step using new data but also much of the data from prior processing. The major steps in a typical sequence are:

Step	New data entered	Documents produced
Order entry	Sales representative identification Customer identification Items ordered Quantity of each item	Order acknowledgement Credit exception notice Order register Picking document Items out of stock Items to be ordered
Shipping	Actual quantity shipped	Shipping document
Invoicing	Freight cost	Invoice register Sales journal Back-order register
Collection	Amount received Returns and allowances	Customer statements Returns and allowances register Cash receipts journal Accounts receivable aging
Analysis		Inventory status Sales by representative, district, customer, or other category

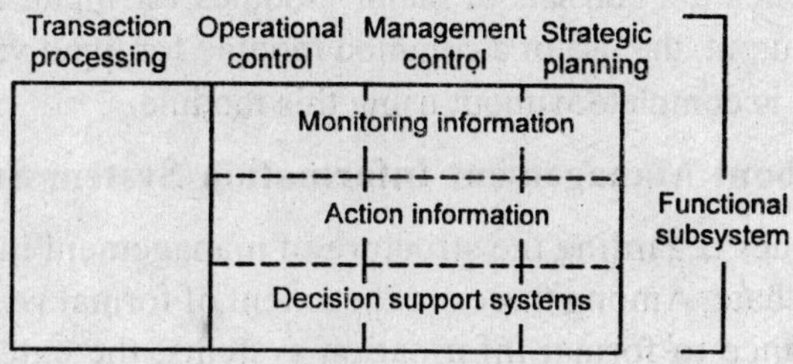

Figure 2.7. *Type of management information support within a functional subsystem.*

Note that a large number of documents and reports are prepared from the initial entry of the order plus later entry of actual quantity shipped, freight, amounts received on account, and returns and allowances. The assumption is made that the customer name, address, and credit status, plus price of each item, are contained in customer files and billing files. The documents and reports from order entry are not associated with a single function but with the sales and marketing, logistics, and accounting and finance functions. In other words, an integrated order entry system crosses functional boundaries.

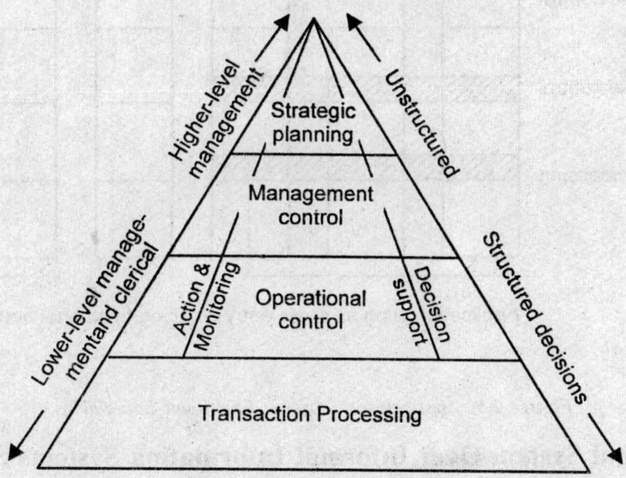

Figure 2-8. *The management information system as a pyramid.*

Modularity is the design of an information system as a number of smallest of processing instructions called modules. Some modules are used only once in a single application; others are used in a large number of applications. The use of modules even in cases where each has a single purpose is desirable because it improves control over system development and modification. The modules can be written and tested separately, allowing more efficient maintenance by identification of the boundaries of the module being changed. The use of modules is thus an application of system principles.

The physical structure of an information system is affected by the use of common modules for many processing operations. For example, a common input data validation routine may be used for all applications. If an application consists of major modules for input, input validation and error control, processing, and output, the use of a common module for input validation and error control means that no application is complete without using this module.

Some Critical Issue About Management Information System Structure

There are several issues regarding the structure of management information systems about which there is ongoing debate. Among these are the extent of formal *versus* informal information systems, manager resistance to formal information systems, the extent of integration of files and processing, the extent of user-machine interaction, and generalised *versus* individualised systems.

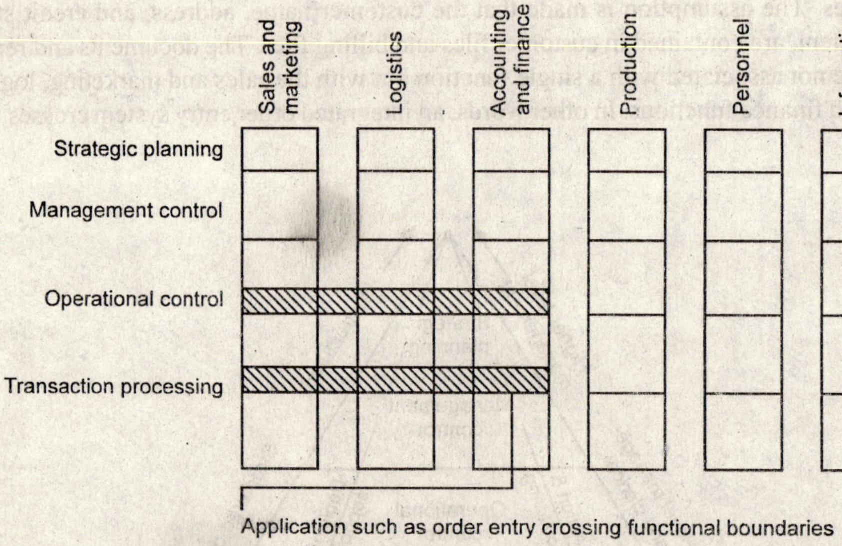

Figure 2.9. Applications crossing functional boundaries.

Advantage of Formal System Over Informal Information Systems

The management information system as described in this chapter encompasses only part of the total information processing that takes place in an organisation. The complete information processing system of an organisation consists of both the public systems and private systems. "Public" is used in the sense of being known to relevant persons in the organisation and available to all who have authority to access the information. Private systems are kept by individuals. These may supplement or duplicate the public systems, and they may be unsanctioned and discouraged or sanctioned and encouraged. There are within the public and private systems both formal and informal information systems. The formal information system is manifested by documents and other records, usually indicating compliance with prespecified rules and procedures. The informal information system may process information that is vital to organisational functioning but without formal records of that process.

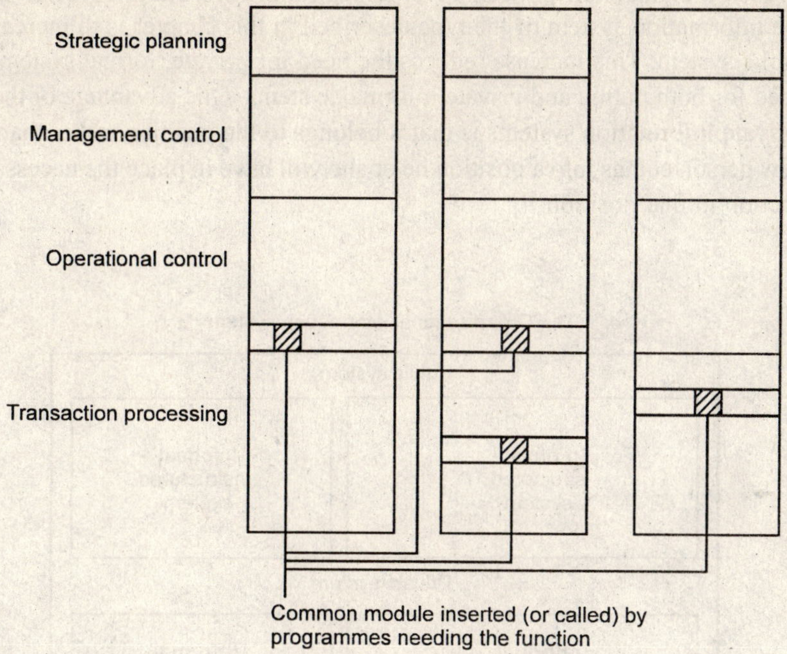

Figure 2.10. *Use of common modules in physical structure of MIS.*

It is organisationally public and access is dependent only upon having appropriate organisational authority to enter or retrieve data or to receive reports or inquiry responses. There is also an informal public system that serves all persons in the organisation who connect with it. The informal system has few predetermined rules. Examples of the public informal information systems are electronic mail, telephone calls, conversations at gathering points such as the water cooler, notes on the bulletin board, articles and other publications distributed in the office (perhaps annotated), and presentations by external information sources such as sales representatives.

In addition to these formal and informal public systems, many private information systems tend to exist in organisations. Some of these are quite formal, at least for the individual owner and any support staff who help maintain it. For example, an industrial sales manager might maintain a separate file of performance data on sales representatives which she uses to augment the information received from the formal sales information system. The manager's secretary might collect and maintain the data (for instance, from the sales representatives' daily customer call reports), but the information is available only for the sales manager's use, possibly without the sales representatives' knowledge. This is a formal private system. It is based not upon the function or the job title but upon the person who occupies the position. Many individuals also have their own private informal information systems. Primarily through personal contact they maintain a flow of information which may be critical to decision-making but is available to them as individuals rather than as occupiers of a formal position.

The public information system of an organisation tends to be larger than the private system, but the latter includes a significant portion of organisational information flows. The effect of a comprehensive information system of the type described in this chapter is to increase the scope of the formal, public system. This increase reduces the need for private, formal systems and probably reduces the need for both public and private informal systems. One advantage of the formal public system over private information systems is that it belongs to the position rather than the person, so that when a new person comes into a position he or she will have in place the necessary information support to function in that position.

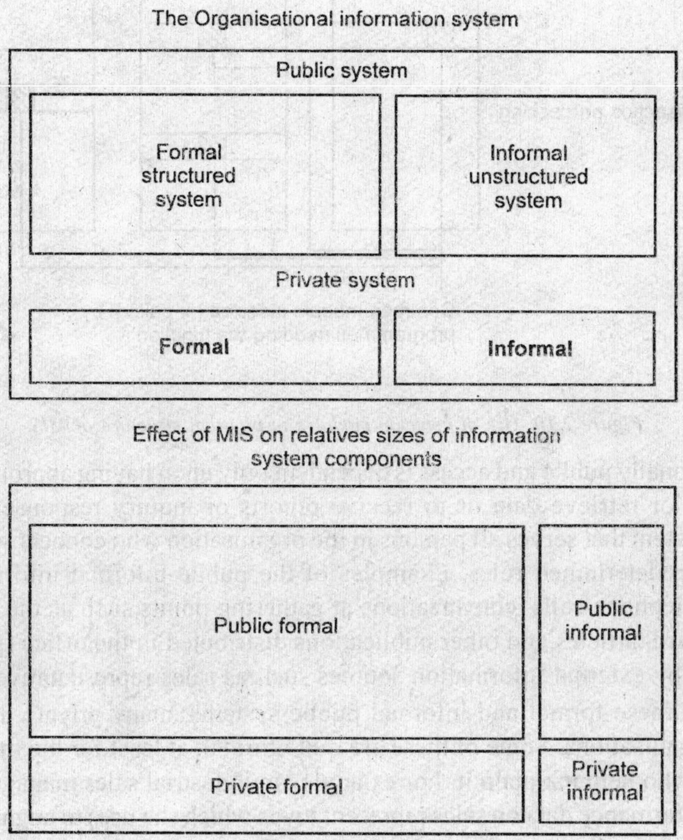

Figure 2.11. *Public or private and formal* versus *informal information systems.*

Increasing the scope of the public formal system also has associated costs. There are the costs of eliciting requirements, designing the system, programming, testing, and writing procedures for operating and using the system. Because of the high cost of developing systems, the tendency has been to only automate systems that can be justified as public systems so that the costs are shared over many users. However, the trend to end user computing, as described already, means users have access to terminals or personal computers and powerful application development languages which facilitate having them develop their own systems. Many applications developed by users on personal computers are highly individualized, and are thus formal, private systems.

There is ongoing debate as to how much organisational information processing can effectively be made part of the formal system and how much should remain in the informal systems. It can be argued that many important decisions are based on information received through informal channels that cannot be formalized, especially at top management levels. A well-known study by Mintzberg[3] shows that as much as 80 percent of a chief executive's time is spent in verbal communication. A study of information systems managers by Ives and Olson[4] showed a similar pattern. This is especially noteworthy because these managers cannot be said to be unfamiliar with the capabilities of the formal, public information system.

Advocates of increasing the scope of the formal public system claim that if it can reduce the time spent by managers in informal communication, their productivity will increase and thus benefit the organisation. Skeptics of this view claim that the only information systems that will affect managerial productivity are enhancements to informal systems such as electronic mail and to formal private systems such as user-developed decision support systems. This debate will be considered again in later chapter.

Extent of Integration

Some advocates of "total systems" have argued for complete integration of all formal information processing. The experience to date suggests that such a tightly integrated system is impractical. There are too many factors to consider all at once, and maintenance is difficult. For this reason, information systems tends to have a modular design with integration only where required (as in the order entry system example). Inconsistencies among subsystems are reduced by the use of standards and the common database.

Data integration is accomplished by the use of a common database. A common database does not necessarily eliminate the need for separate files. Some files are significant only to one application and therefore may be designed for and maintained by that application.

Data requirements for different levels of management activity also suggest the need for more than one database rather than complete integration. For example, the data collected from external sources and stored for strategic planning is so different from internal data for operation control that some different database may be desirable.

Extent of User-Machine Interaction

The information system structure does not specify online user-machine interaction; it indicates only support for various operational and management activities. Online processing of transactions is often desirable because the transaction is completed immediately. Inquiries are generally more effective if immediate response is available. The use of analysis, planning, and decision models is frequently enhanced if the analyst, planner, or decision-maker can interact directly with the computer programme, asking "what if" question during problem analysis. With the decreasing costs of both computer and communications technology, the trend is to online interactive processing for both transaction processing and decision support systems.

The computer system that supports online transaction processing may not be able to support interactive models. However, having an information system does not imply that a single computer system must be used. An organisation may use its in-house computer for transaction processing but provide alternatives for interactive models such as providing a small in-house interactive system, renting time on an outside computer through timesharing, or providing personal computers. These approaches encourage managers and staff specialists to develop their own support models, rather than depending on the staff of the information processing function to provide them.

Summary/Conclusion

This chapter has defined a conceptual structure for a management information system. An actual organisational informational system will differ from his model become certain elements are not cost-justified or because the implementation is performed in an evolutionary manner rather than all at once.

The information system may be described in term of its operating elements. Its physical components are hardware, software, database, procedures, and personnel. Its processing requirements are to process transactions, maintain master files, produce reports, process inquiries, and process interactive support applications. The outputs for users are transaction documents, preplanned reports, preplanned inquiry responses, ad hoc reports and inquiry responses, and user-machine dialog responses. These provide management and other decision-makers with monitoring information, action information, and decision support. Information can be provided for both structured, programmable decisions and unstructured, nonprogrammable decisions.

Management information system structure is affected by management activity and organisational function. Information requirements vary with the level of management activity supported: strategic planning, managerial control, or operational control. They also vary depending on the degree of structure of the decision supported. Each organisational function supported by the information system has its own unique information processing requirements as well as some which are common to several functions.

The conceptual structure of an information system consists of a federation of information subsystems for different functions. Each subsystem provides support for transaction processing, operational control, management control, and strategic planning. Some typical subsystem might be marketing, production, logistics, personnel, finance and accounting, information systems, and top management. The conceptual structure includes some unique files for each subsystem plus a common database. There is unique software for each subsystem, and there is common software used by or available to all subsystems—a database management system, common software routines, and a model base of analysis, planning, and decision models.

Some issues of MIS structure around which there is an ongoing debate are the extent of the formal information system *versus* information systems, the extent of integration of processing and data, and the extent of user-machine interaction.

Notes

1. Based on C. H. P. Brookes, "A Framework for DSS Development," Information Systems Forum Research Report.
2. R. N. Anthony, *Planning and Control Systems: A Framework for Analysis.*
3. Henry Mintzberg, *The Nature of Managerial Work,* Harper & Row.
4. B. Ives and M. H. Olson, "Manager or Technician? The Nature of the Information System Manager's Job.

Section 2

Management and Management Information System

3

Role and Importance of Management

Introduction

Management as defined by Mary Follett is "the art of getting things done through people". A manager is defined as a person who achieves the organisation's goals by motivating others to perform–not by performing himself. Whether management is an art or a science is a very subjective question. But it can be said without doubt that modern management in the environment of technology is becoming more of a science than an art. We define management for the purpose of Management Information Systems as the process of planning, organising, staffing, coordinating and controlling the efforts of the members of the organisation to achieve common stated goals of the organisation.

In the process of management, a manager uses human skills, material resources and scientific methods to perform all the activities leading to the achievement of goals. The management process involves a continuous resolution of conflicts of one kind or the other which effects the achievement of goals. In the management of any activity, a manager comes across human conflict, conflict of goals, conflict between alternative resources, conflict of time, conflict of approach or method and the conflict of choice. The manager uses a variety of tools, techniques and skills while executing the management process of planning, organising, staffing, coordinating and controlling. An effective way of handling this process is to treat the organisation as a system. The result-oriented management approaches the problem of management through the systems view of the organisation.

The key concepts of the systems theory used in the management are as follows:

1. A system is a comprehensive assembly of parts becoming an organisation to achieve the stated goals.
2. A system is called OPEN if it has an interaction with the environment, and CLOSED if it does not have an interaction with the environment.
3. A system is defined, described and understood by the boundaries within which it performs.
4. The systems are subject to entropy, i.e., the tendency to "run down". Closed systems suffer from entropy as they are cut off from the environment, which open systems interact with the environment and draw upon the support of resources to maintain a given condition.
5. Systems try to remain in an equilibrium or a steady state by taking recourse to corrective action. This is possible when the system has its own feedback, i.e., an informational input about the state of the system.

The advantage of viewing the management as a system is that it enables us to see the critical variables, constraints and their interaction with one another. It forces the manager to look at the situation in such a way that due regard is given to the consequences arising out of interaction with the related elements or subjects. The process of management explained earlier consists of steps which are relationally linked and locked with each other.

In the context of the MIS, the systems approach to management is the most efficient one. The understanding of the basic principles of management theory evolved by the scholars Henry Fayol, Chester Barnard and Alvin Brown is very much essential. The application of management principles in an environment, recognising the specific situation, is the accepted practice of management. Deviating from the principles to honour the situation and at the same time not diluting the management principle is the managerial skill. The manager must have a knowledge of management theory and principles as well as the skill to use them in a particular environment.

Approaches to Management

Frederick W Taylor*, is recognised as the father of scientific management. His principles can be summarised as follows:

1. Replace the rules of thumb with scientific rules.
2. Obtain a harmony in group action.
3. Achieve cooperation of human beings, rather than chaotic individualism.
4. Work for a maximum output.
5. Develop all workers to the fullest possible potential for their own highest possible prosperity.

Carl George Barth, Henry L Gantt, Frank and Lillian Gilberth are the disciples of Taylor, who promoted the thought of the scientific management.

The French industrialist Henri Fayol** promoted the theory of operational management. Fayol is of the view that all the activities of an industrial or a business undertaking can be broken into operational functions such as technical, commercial, financial, security, accounting, and so on. He evolved the principles of operational management. These are as given in Table 3-1.

Fayol regarded the elements of management as planning, organising, commanding, coordinating and controlling. He believed that the operational management would succeed through the elements of management. During the same period when Taylor, Fayol and others were concentrating on the scientific management, another group of scholars was concentrating on industrial psychology and social theory as the basis for the scientific management.

Robert Owen, Rountree, Lyndall Urwick are credited to evolve the management with a focus on the personnel management. Max Weber, Vilfredo Pareto, Mayo Elton are the scholars who thought that productivity can be improved through the social factors as morale and satisfactory relation between the members of work group, and an effective management is possible only if human behaviour and group behaviour is managed through the interpersonal skills, viz., motivating, counselling, leading and communicating.

---

* F W Taylor, *The Priciples of Scientific Management.*

** Henri Fayol, *General and Industrial Management*, translated by Constance Storrs, London.

Hawthorne's studies brought out the theory that man is a "Social Animal" operating in the socio-technical system and, therefore, the emphasis in effective management is on behavioural sciences. Chester Barnard advocated the theory of systems as an approach to the management. Barnard said that due to the physical and biological limitations of individuals, they cooperate in the work environment. The cooperation increases with effective and efficient incentives. He further said that the cooperation is more effective if the members of the group communicate with one another, are willing to contribute to group action, and have a conscious common purpose. He further said that a group of people in the system work as an organisation. An effective management is possible if the organisation is looked upon as a system of functions, a system of incentives, a system of authority and a direction and a system of logical decision making. The emergence of the modern management thought is credited to the social scientists, the behavioural scientists, the systems scientists and the practicing managers.

Table 3.1 Principles of Operational Management

Principle	Comments
Division of work	Efficient handling of work.
Authority and responsibility	Pinpoints accountability.
Discipline	Adherence to rules, regulations, norms and priorities.
Unity of command	Single source direction to avoid confusion.
Unity of direction	Efforts should be directed towards one objective.
Subordination of individual to corporate interest	Ignore the individual interests for overall betterment of the organisation.
Remuneration	Should be fair for maximum satisfaction.
Centralisation	Authority should be centralised just enough for control. Overcentralisation is unproductive.
Scalar chains	Chain of authority vested into the people should not be short-circuited.
Order	Orderly arrangement of men, material and other resources is necessary.
Equity	Subordinates should be dealt with kindliness and justice to elicit loyalty and devotion.
Stability of tenure	It is necessary to ensure that the turnover of people is controlled for stability.
Initiative	The initiative of subordinates should be encouraged, sacrificing personal vanity of the superior.

Role and Functions of the Manager

An individual who gets the things done is a Manager. It is necessary to distinguish between the tasks and the functions. While managing, a manager may perform the activities such as accounting, selling, manufacturing, purchasing, etc. These activities are called as tasks and not as functions.

The activities that are performed through the managerial functions are Planning, Organising , Staffing, Directing, Coordinating and Controlling.

Planning is a process of determining the goals and objectives and evolving strategies, policies, programmes and procedures for the achievement of these goals. The essence of the process is decision making as there are a number of alternatives in each of these factors.

Organisation involves evolving the structure of the people working in the organisation and their roles. It specifies an authority structure and assigns activities to the people backed by the delegation of authority. Building a meaningful effective structure of authority and the relationship is known as organising.

Staffing involves manning the positions in the organisation structure. It requires defining the manpower needs per position or centre of activity. It requires appropriate selection of the person or persons ensuring that they together will achieve the goals and objectives of the organisation.

Directing is a complex task of implementing the process of management. In the process, the manager is required to guide, clarify and solve the problems of the people and their activities. It is necessary to motivate the people to work for the goal with an interest and a confidence.

Coordinating is the function which brings a harmony and smoothness in the various group activities and individual efforts directed towards the accomplishment of goals. It is a process of synchronising individual actions and the efforts which may differ because of the differences in the personal goals and the common goals, the differences in the interpretation of methods and directions. It is, therefore, necessary to undertake centrally a process of coordinating and reconciling the differences in the approach, timing, efforts and interests towards a common goal. This task is to be carried out by the authority placed at a higher level in the organisation structure.

Controlling is a process of measurement of an output, comparing it with the goals, the objectives and the target, and taking corrective actions, if the output is falling short of the stated norms. Controlling ensures an achievement of the plan. The essence of the control lies in good planning. It helps to evaluate the performance, highlights abnormal deviations, guides a manager to take specific corrective actions. This may call for a change of plan, a reallocation of resources, a modification of methods, procedures and even the organisation structure. The control is central to the managerial function.

The manager's main function, therefore, is planning and control of the business functions and operations. While performing these functions, he resorts to the scientific approach to the management.

Managers and the Environment (Economic, Social, Technological and Political)

All managers, whether they are managing a business, a school, a hospital, Government Department, or any enterprise, work in an environment in which the organisation operates. There are a number of forces which are generated in the environment, which have an impact on the managerial performance. These forces may be from within or from outside the organisation. They affect, directly or indirectly, the process of the management and a manager is required to meet these forces effectively. While to some extent the internal environment is controllable, the external environment is beyond his control. Since it is proven that the external environment also has an impact on the business manager's performance, it is necessary to know and understand the environment. For the purpose of discussion, the external environment is classified into five classes as the economic, the technological, the social, the political and the ethical environment.

Economic Environment

The economic environment comprises capital, labour, price changes, productivity, fiscal and monetary policy and customers.

Capital. It is required to run the organisation. The enterprise needs a long–term and a short-term capital. The capital required can be either from the internal sources or borrowed from the financial institutions. When a capital is borrowed, it is borrowed at an interest. The organisation is forced to borrow for various reasons and the interest charged by the lending financial institutions forms the cost of the capital. Hence management of the capital is an important aspect of the business.

Labour. The next important cost of a business is the cost of labour. The cost of labour is determined every two to three years by a union agreement. The settlement of an agreement is based on the cost of living index, the industry wage standards, the availability of labour, etc. These aspects are external to the organisation and a manager has no control on them.

Price Changes. Price changes occur in the economy for various reasons. The changes occur because of decrease in the demand and supply, the changes in the consumer behaviour, in the consumption pattern and the money supply, and so on. The price changes affect the cost of raw material and labour and on these changes a manager has no control.

Productivity. Productivity is a result of the capital, labour and technology. Many a times and organisation's business is taken over by better technology. The costs are affected by the technology changes affecting the productivity. The manager has to respond quickly to the technological changes to save the business.

Fiscal and Monetary Policy. The Government announces fiscal policies and controls them. The organisation's profit position is affected by these policies. These policies affect the credit terms, the prices of the inputs and the money supply affecting the cash position of the organisation. A manager has a very little leverage to deal with these policy changes.

Customers. The customers rule the business, especially when the business operates in a buyer's market. In a competitive world, it is very difficult to predict the customer behaviour. The changes in the demands occur with growth and technology. The customer does not show consistent preference to the product. The change in the business orientation to suit the changes in the consumer demand is a difficult task for the manager. It is not always possible to predict these changes well in advance in order to take any managerial action to meet the changed situation.

Technological Environment

The technology has a major impact on the business. It affects the business prospects, cuts down the profit and forces the management to change the course of the business operations. It requires changes in the product design and promotes new concepts. It generates new business opportunities. Any change in technology changes the work culture, the methods and the systems. It affects the speed of the operations and gives a boost to the productivity of the production systems. Examples of technological changes are seen in aviation, electronics, energy, communication, consumer goods industry, optics, medicines and manufacturing.

Social Environment

The social environment is built around the attitudes, the desires, the expectations, the degree of intelligence and education, the beliefs and customs, the religion, the caste and creed of the people.

The social environment is built in centuries and hence it is deeply rooted in the society. The social environment has an important impact on the business and the organisational productivity.

Social factors create an attitude towards the work, generate the product choices, and manipulate the consumer behaviour. It is well known that it took a lot of time to convince the farmers in India about the use of fertilisers. It is recognised that rural marketing is different from the urban marketing. In spite of the technological advances, frozen foods are not finding consumer preferences. Introduction of computers in the service industry is still a difficult proposition. A number of such examples can be cited to prove that the social environment effects business and makes the manager's task very difficult and challenging.

Political Environment

The political factor is the most important factor which affects the business in Indian environment. The unstable political environment brings stagnancy in the business development. The changes in ruling party bring economic policy changes, affecting the business. The sectoral preferences, such as an agricultural *versus* an industrial, an educational *versus* a basic research, an investment in the service sector *versus* a core sector come about with change in the ruling political party and its policies. Such changes have a long-term impact on business performance. The manager has to deal with such changes effectively.

Ethical Environment (System of a Moral Behaviour)

Some business problems arise due to failing on the ethical grounds. The government has enacted many laws and regulations to bring about harmonious operations in business. However, some aspects of the business operations are left as ethics, called the business ethics. The business ethics emerge from the professional conduct, the business norms and codes on confidentiality, the payment and documentation, the adherence to generally accepted standards of accounting and auditing. Business ethics is a set of norms which are universally accepted as a business behaviour.

All these factors discussed so far, are beyond the control of the manager. At best he can predict, assess, evaluate and take such actions which will help him to control the situation.

Management as a Control System

Planning, organising, staffing, coordinating, directing and controlling are the various steps in a management process. All the steps prior to a control are necessary but are not necessarily self-assuring the results unless it is followed by a strong control mechanism. The management experts have viewed these steps as 'Management Control System'. They postulate the hypothesis that unless a control is exercised on the process, the goals will not be achieved. They advocate a system of effective control to ensure achievement of the business objectives.

A definition of control is the process through which managers assure that actual activities conform to the planned activities, leading to the achievement of the stated common goals. The control process measures a progress towards those goals, and enables the manager to detect the deviations from the original plan in time to take corrective actions before it is too late. Robert J Mockler defines and points out the essential elements of the control process. The basic steps of the control process are given in Fig 3.1.

The management is a systematic effort to set the performances standards in line with the performances objectives, to design the information feedback systems, to compare the actual performance with these predetermined standards, to identify the deviations from the standards, to measure its significance and to take corrective actions in case of significant deviations. This systematic effort is undertaken through the management control system.

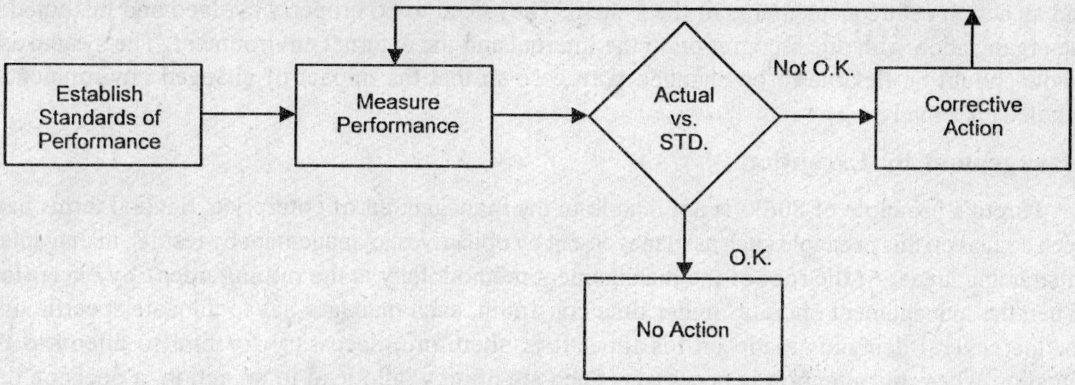

Figure 3.1.

The control system is essential to meet the environmental changes discussed earlier, to meet the complexity of today's business, to correct the mistakes made by the people, and to effectively monitor the delegation process. A reliable and effective control systems has the following features.

Early Warning Mechanism. This is a mechanism of predicting the possibility of achieving the goals and the standards before it is too late and allowing the manager to take corrective actions.

Performance Standard. The performance standard must be measurable and acceptable to all the organisation. The system should have meaningful standards relating to the work areas, responsibility, managerial functions and so on. For example, the top management would have standards relating to the business performance, such as production, sales, inventory, quality, etc. The operational management would have standards relating to the shift production, rejections, down time, utilisation of resources, sale in a typical market segment and so on. The chain of standards, when achieved, will ensure an achievement of the goals of the organisation.

Strategic Controls. In every business there are strategic areas of control known as the critical success factors. The system should recognise them and have controls instituted on them.

Feedback. The control system would be effective, if it continuously monitors the performance and sends the information to the control centre for action. It should not only highlight the progress but also the deviations.

Accurate and Timely. The feedback should be accurate in terms of results and should be communicated on time for corrective action.

Realistic. The system should be realistic so that the cost of control is far less than the benefits. The standards are realistic and are believed as achievable. Sufficient incentive and rewards are to be provided to motivate the people.

The Information Flow. The system should have the information flow aligned with the organisation structure and the decision makers should ensure that the right people get the right information for action and decision making.

Exception Principle. The system should selectively approve some significant deviations from the performance standards on the principle of management by exception.

A standard is meaningful when it is achievable and provides a challenge to the achiever. A management control system has a set of objectives, standards to measure, a feedback mechanism and an action centre as elements of the system. They need to be properly evolved and instituted in the organisation with due recognition to the internal and the external environment. The system as a whole should be flexible to be changed with ease so that the impact of changed environment is handled effectively.

Management by Exception

Pareto's principle of 80:20 is applicable to the management of enterprise. Several terms have been coined on this principle such as management by objectives, management by results, management of strategic areas. At the root of the management methodology is the **management by exception.** When the management operates under time constraint, each manager has to allocate specific time for the several demands made on his time. It is, therefore, necessary for him to attend to the situation where his attention is necessary. Such attention would lead to an action, a decision or a wait-and-see approach.

If all the situations are considered in a routine manner, it consumes time and tends to be neglected over a period of time. An efficient manager tries for selective attention to manage within the available time resource. The principle evolved, therefore, is of the management by exception. The exception is decided on the impact a situation would make on the performance, the process and the standards set in the management control system.

The exception is defined as a significant deviation from the performance, or the process and the standard. The deviation could be abnormal on a positive or on a negative side of the standard. The deviation could be predictive or could be arising out of random causes in the business operations. It is, therefore, necessary to assess whether the deviation is sporadic or consistently coming in, calling for managerial attention. The manager is interested in knowing the significant deviation by the yardsticks of consistency and not out of random causes. The significant deviations are exceptional in nature and require to be attended to immediately. A manager is further interested in knowing the reasons behind the exceptional nature of the situation. It is possible to trace the reasons of deviation, and it is possible to take a corrective action.

The significant deviation can occur on account of wrong performance standards and wrong management process. Many a times the standards are set very low and they need to be looked into to avoid the misuse of resources. If the standards are set too high, then the people fail to achieve them on account of demotivating factor of the high standards.

A wrong management process refers to a variety of decisions a manager has taken in the planning, organising, staffing, directing and controlling a given management task. These decisions relate to the choice and the allocation of resources, the methods of using resources, the application of the tools and the techniques, the use of manpower by way of staffing and the manner in which the efforts are coordinated in the organisation. For an efficient and an effective management, without loss of time, it is, therefore, necessary to report the significant deviations to the right persons in the organisation. In this regard a manager himself has to provide the conditions of exceptions in the control system so that they are highlighted and informed. The management by exception commands grip on the management process. The managerial effort gets directed towards the goal with the purpose of achievement.

MIS: A Support to the Management

The management process is executed through a variety of decisions taken at each step of planning, organising, staffing, directing, coordinating and control. The MIS aids decision making. If the management is able to spell out the decisions required to be taken, the MIS can be designed suitably. The decisions required to be taken in these steps are tabulated in Table 3.2.

Table 3.2 Decisions in Management

Steps in management	Decision
Planning	A selection from various alternatives–strategies, resources, methods, etc.
Organisation	A selection of a combination out of several combinations of the goals, people, resources, method, and authority.
Staffing	Providing a proper manpower complement.
Directing	Choosing a method from the various methods of directing the efforts in the organisation.
Coordinating	Choice of the tools and the techniques for coordinating the efforts for optimum results.
Controlling	A selection of the exceptional conditions and the decision guidelines.

The objectives of the MIS is to provide information for a decision support in the process of management. It should help in such a way that the business goals are achieved in the most efficient manner. Since the decision making is not restricted to a particular level, the MIS is expected to support all the levels of the management in conducting the business operations. Unless the MIS becomes a management aid, it is not useful to the organisation.

4

Management Process

Effectiveness of Management

Negandhi Estafen provides a good model for the analysis of management effectiveness, which generates an enterprise effectiveness in achieving the goals and objectives. The model puts a lot of emphasis on the management philosophy and the environment factors on which the effectiveness is dependent. The environment factors provide the opportunities to survive and grow with certain constraints, while the management philosophy sets the guidelines for deciding the management practices to run the enterprise.

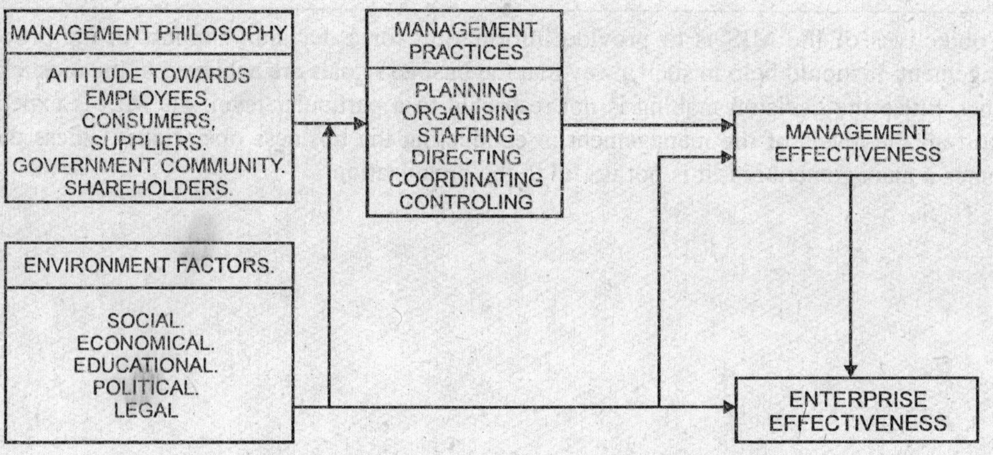

Figure 4.1. Negandhi Estafen Model for Analysis of Management Effectiveness.

While the environment factors are difficult to control, it is left for the management to change its philosophy towards the various players in the business, viz., the employees, the consumers, the suppliers, the government, the community and the shareholders. Basically, it is a change in attitude towards these players. For example, how to look at the employees? If the attitude is to treat them as business partners, you will empower them and create a sense of belonging to the organisation. Such an attitude will have an impact on the management practices, where the employee will play a decisive critical role. It will affect the organisation structure by reducing its size and the reporting levels.

If the attitude towards the consumer is changed to fulfil the expectations giving rise to a higher satisfaction, then the management practices in the product design, manufacturing and marketing will undergo a significant change. The product life cycle will then be short, and more features and functions will be added to the product fulfilling not only the functional needs but also the service needs of the consumer.

The management practices, therefore, emerge out of the management philosophy and the environment, in which it operates. The Management effectiveness, would largely depend on both these factors. The MIS design would, therefore, be different depending upon the management practices followed by several organisations in the same industry. Such design improves the management effectiveness leading to an improvement in the enterprise effectiveness.

Aim, Objectives and Targets

The process of management begins with setting of goals, objectives and targets. The goals and long-term aims to be achieved by the organisation; objective are relatively short-term milestones to be accomplished, while the targets generally refer to physical achievements in the organisation's business. The goals, objectives and targets are so set that they are consistent which each other and help to achieve each other. These are to be achieved within a stipulated time and failing to achieve the same, means loss of business profit and image. The difference between these entities can be best understood by examples in the three type of organisations given in Table 4.1.

Table 4.1

	Business organisation	Hospital	State transport organisation
AIM	Be a leader in the household consumer goods industry, with modern amenities.	Be a hospital providing total service to the patients.	Connect all villages of population 5000 and above by S.T. service.
OBJECTIVES	Provide complete product range in the area of cleaning, preserving and entertainment.	Establish 300 bed hospital in three years.	Manage state transport at the rate of Rs 5 per kilometre travelled.
TARGETS	20 per cent growth per annum in turnover.	Achieve Rs 800 per bed per day earnings.	Achieve 90 per cent average seat occupancy everyday.

The setting of goals, objectives and targets is a top management function. It has its implications on the business operations and profits. These are set considering the environment and changes expected in it. It considers social technological, political, educational and economical changes expected to occur in about five to six years. The organisation is expected to consider and cater for these changes and, translate them into business operations. The setting of goals, objectives and targets helps to pull the resources of the organisation in one direction and solve. It helps to build the strategies, frame the policies and set the rules of conducting the business. It provides an efficient measure to monitor the managerial process. The people in the organisation can have common understanding of the purpose of the managerial process. The people in the organisation can have common understanding of the purpose of the business operations.

In an organisation, as time progresses, business goals, departmental goals, functional goals and personal goals emerge, which create conflicting environment in the organisation. The goals, objectives and targets form a network. Achievement of targets helps in accomplishing objectives, and accomplishment of objectives leads to the attainment of goals. Careful determination of these entities is, therefore, essential for a successful management process. The goals, objectives and targets become reference points for strategic planning, resource planning, and operations planning.

It further helps the management to identify key areas of business and key areas of management attention. It helps appropriate and consistent business review. The performance appraisal of the manager becomes impersonal and unbiased as it is done with reference to achievement of goals, objectives and targets. McGregor saw appraisal against the goals and objectives as a better means of performance evaluation and more meaningful because it emphasised on results and not only personality. Its advantage is that it stimulates the development of people and provides motivation. According to Peter Drucker, "goals and objective are necessary in every area where performance and results directly and vitally affect the survival, growth and prosperity of business".

Planning

Planning is basic to all managerial functions. It is a process of selecting one course of action, from different alternatives, for achieving the stated goals, objectives and targets. It is a decision making process determining in advance what to do, how to do, when to do and who is to do. Planning creates a frame of activity and events which are to happen or a runway for achieving corporate goals, objectives and targets. Planning process demands resource allocation through decision making. The organisation may have a plan; but question is how effective the plan is.

The efficiency of a plan is measured by the amount it contributes towards achievement of goals. The plan is efficient if it achieves the goals with less investment or with less resources. Therefore, efficient planning involves selecting a plan among several alternative plans. An efficient plan enables the management to handle uncertainty and risk in the business. It helps to handle the change occurring in the environment and affecting the plan itself.

Procedure of Planning

Planning is a process and hence it has methodology. The first step in planning is forecasting the environment, in which the plan it to be made and operated. Forecasting provides information on population, growth, price trends, market changes, new opportunities, changes in technology and the external factors affecting the business. Forecasting provides the base on which the plan will be developed and implemented.

The second step in planning is determining alternative course of action. The management's ability lies in creating a number of alternatives. The effective way of creating a number of alternatives is to build a model of the situation and use it as a tool for the generation of alternatives. These models are known as system models, operational research model and mathematical models. Consequent to the development of alternative courses of actions, the necessity is to analyse the feasibility of each. As, a model can give infinite alternatives, only some of them can be feasible in the given conditions and constraints. The constraints may be man-made or environmental; but they affect the feasibility of the action. Evaluating the feasibility of each alternative brings the infinite number of alternatives to a limited number.

The third step in the planning process is to evaluate the best among all the feasible alternatives. The analysis and evaluation is done with reference to the objectives such as, minimisation of cost, maximisation of profit, yield, and productivity, etc. The right choice of an objective is a crucial factor in the selection process. The planning begins with the setting of goals and objectives and ends up in selecting the most rational course of action.

As mentioned earlier, the organisation has a network of goals, objectives and targets. It is necessary to develop the network of plans corresponding to this network. The process leads to the development of corporate plans, functional plans, departmental plans and so on. For example, the organisation may have business plans, investment plans, marketing plans, and advertising plans. Normally, the corporate plans are for a longer period and the derived plans are for shorter periods. Since the plan has a commitment to time, it is necessary to build a flexible plan capable of undergoing a suitable change to alter the goals and objectives within the same time. The flexibility, as far as possible, should be built in, so that the cost of changes is not very high and the implementation is still possible without loss of time. The implementation of plans is made through developing the strategies, policies, systems, rules, procedures, programmes and the budgets. The strategy shows the direction, focus, emphasis and development of resources. Many a times good plans fail because of strategic failure. The purpose of the strategy is not to outline a precise method of implementation; but to provide a boost or thrust to the plans of implementation. An appropriate strategy helps to cut down the use of resources and accelerates the process of achieving the goals.

The policy is a statement of management which stands on the top of all plans or courses of action. A rational plan or a decision can be rejected on the premise of policy. The policies are evolved in the wider frame of strategies and are generally not questionable; but these can be changed. For example, the organisation can have a policy of recruiting personnel only with the qualification of MBA or it may have a policy of changing the prices once a year and not too frequently. The policy, therefore, is a general guideline and is to be followed by all.

The system is a vehicle for the implementation of a plan. The system provides pathways, gates and structures for communication and control. The strategies and policies are important for successful implementation of the plans. Depending upon the plans, systems will be built as closed or open systems. The rules, procedures and programmes help to implement the operational plans. They provide a common basis and an understanding of conducting business operations. A strict adherence to the rules and the procedures builds discipline in the organisation. A smooth implementation of the plan calls for the rules, procedures and programmes to be observed properly. When the organisation becomes bigger, the adherence to rules, procedures and systems brings a higher degree of formalisation in the process of implementation.

The effectiveness of the plan depends on how it is implemented. A successful implementation requires appropriate timing of launching the basic plan and its derivatives. Lack of knowledge creates the problems of going away in a totally different direction. The plan must be evolved by people who are going to implement it. Their participation brings their involvement and commitment to the plan. For effective planning, participation should be encouraged.

An effective planning should begin at the top and flow down the line. The effectiveness is brought in by taking a series of decisions, committing resources, giving directions, and executing controls to achieve the goals and objectives. The process of planning, therefore, is to develop the alternatives, evaluate them by meaningful analysis of costs and benefits, and make a rational selection based on some choice about goals. If the situation is that of uncertainty, then the evaluation is done through risk analysis and preference theory using utility as a criteria.

Organising (Managerial Process)

Organising is an important step in the managerial process and relates to the people in an enterprise. It deals with a quantitative and a qualitative aspect of manpower in terms of placement, the roles they play and the relations amongst them, with the aim that they work together effectively towards accomplishing the goals, objectives and the targets of the organisation. In essence, it deals with organising the manpower resources for a given plan of execution.

The organisation could be formal or informal. The organisation is formal when the roles, the relations of the people and the objectives they should achieve are well defined. In an informal organisation, it is left to the people to understand and evolve suitable roles and relationships to achieve the objectives.

While creating the organisation, attention is given to an appropriate splitting of the enterprise activities, by way of function, and grouping them in such a way that they form a division, a department, a section or a formal group. The people heading these entities should have enough authority to decide, and should exercise a discretion in using the authority. The people should be put in such a structure of roles and relationships that it is designed to work effectively and the members of the structure are able to contribute substantially towards the achievement of goals. The structure would be productive, if it is manned properly. The process of meaning involves selecting people in right number.and placing them at appropriate levels.

Peter Drucker recommends three ways to determine the structure:

- activity analysis,
- decision analysis, and
- relations analysis.

Organising is a process by which the manager can bring a smoothness of operations, by way of conflict resolution, assigning work responsibility, and creating appropriate work environment of teamwork while deciding on the process of organising. There are certain important factors to which attention should be paid and which are discussed as follows.

Organisation Levels and the Span of Control

This factors deals with grouping the people in hierarchical form, determining the levels in the organisation. The levels get determined by the span of control, i.e., in the organisation how many subordinates a superior can manage. This number can vary anywhere between four to eight in higher levels of management and eight to fifteen in lower levels of management. The span of control is determined on the basis of the task to be performed, decisions to be taken, and the strengths and weakness of the people and the degree of the delegation of the responsibilities that a superior is willing to attain. The span of control can be increased and the number the levels can be brought down by training the subordinates, precise planning, use of objective standards, effective communications and formalising the administration by way of rules, programme and policies.

Departmentation

Departmentation is a process of breaking an enterprise into smaller groups and levels. There are a number of ways to break the enterprise. A widely accepted practice is by functions of the enterprise, viz., Marketing, Production, Finance, Personnel, Materials, etc. The second method is based on geographic area distribution. This method is resorted to when the distances are long, the activities are many and the decision making is decentralised. Many organisations have divisions, branches and territories through which the business operations are conducted.

The third method to departmentalise is by way of the product or the services the organisation is providing. The departmentation of the organisation brings operational convenience, creates appropriate responsibility centres, facilitates a formal and an informal communication, permits an evaluation of activities by a smaller group, and provides control and decision points for the top management. Each method of a departmentalising has advantages and disadvantages and, therefore, it is to be chosen based on the needs of the management.

Relationship of Line and Staff Functions

The function of a department can be as a line or a staff. The functions which have a direct responsibility of achieving the targets for production or sales are line functions. The staff functions are those which do not participate directly in the activity but aid line functions to achieve the targets. Production Planning, Marketing, Purchasing, etc. are staff functions. The distinction is more clear and precise at higher levels. The staff function is advisory but owns the responsibility for the results and is accountable for non-performance.

The relationship between the line and the staff functions, is always strained. The performance of the line function depends upon how the staff function has planned the activities. Deficient planning leads to an unutilisation of line capacity and non attainment of targets. A line function does not have resources, leverages and powers to overcome the problems arising out of the staff functions.

Delegation of Authority

The function may either be a line function or a staff function; but still it requires decision making. As one person cannot plan, execute and control all the tasks in the functions, owing to the limitations of time and capacity, it is necessary that the decision making is not centralised at one point.

Handing over limited authority of decision making to the subordinates is called delegation. The concept of delegation is based on the premise that an individual can take decisions if supported by information, knowledge and guidance, and is motivated enough to perform. The concept of delegation accepts the responsibility of non-performance of the delegated person or the mistakes made by him. Hence, most routine types of decisions are delegated with the support of rules, conditions and the method of decision making.

The failures in delegation occur not because of the lack of understanding of the principle of delegation, but because of the inability to implement it into practice. A lot depends upon the ability of the manager to delegate and upon the capabilities of the subordinates to use the authority. The manager is not able to delegate, if he does not have a positive attitude towards delegation, if he is not receptive to the subordinates' ideas and is not willing to accept the risk of failure or mistakes of his subordinates. A failure to use the delegated authority emanates from a lack of communication, guidance, training and motivation.

Towards Effective Organising

Organising is an activity of building a structure of roles and relations of the people to secure coordination of individual efforts to achieve common stated goals, objectives and targets. The failure in organising occurs due to the failure to plan properly, to delegate the authority and due to the confusion of roles, relations and authority. The failure also occurs on account of imbalance in the line and staff functions and their relations. Organising becomes effective, if it is designed for the unity of goals and objectives with precise planning and optimum span of control. It becomes further effective, if it works on the principle of command, delegation and parity of authority and responsibility. It becomes productive if it is flexible enough to change and is headed by a manager with leadership qualities.

Staffing in the Organisation

The function of staffing deals with manning the enterprise as per the organisation structure so that they together implement the process of the management. Staffing involves not only selection of a persons but also their appraisal and development so that they perform their designated roles. The selection of a person is a difficult task. However, the chances of selecting a wrong person are very less if a proper method is used. Since people cannot be easily replaced because of socio-political and legal reasons, their selection, in terms of quality and quantity, is of paramount importance.

Staffing of enterprise should be for today's needs, as well as that of the future. The requirement of the future is difficult to predict in precise terms and this requirement needs to be forecasted for more than five to six years. So the purpose of staffing is not manning for the current plan of business but to create a manpower potential capable of undergoing development, so that the same manpower is able to perform the changed roles in the future.

Hence the selection of a person in terms of age, qualification and potential becomes an important task in human resource development.

The selection of individuals for line functions is not that difficult because the role and the tasks are well defined and do not undergo any significant change over a period of time. The difficulty lies in the selection of management positions. The manager is a multi-faceted personality. A person is said to have good managerial potential, if he has the following qualities apart from the function knowledge:

- The person must have the desire to manage.
- He must have the necessary drive and self-motivation to manage.
- He must be able to identify himself with the corporate goals and be committed to them.
- The person must have the capability of applying knowledge to real life situations in the right perspective, locating the problem areas and generating a number of alternate courses of action. In short, he must be a person with analytical ability.
- The person must be able to perform effectively. This is possible only if he has the ability to communicate effectively. If not properly communicated, his ideas and management plans cannot take off. For good communication skills, the person must have a good command

over the language in written and spoken form. Many times the person may have the skills, but due to the psychological barriers he cannot communicate. These barriers come on account of personality conflicts, power games and dissatisfaction on rewards and promotion.

- The manager must be a person of integrity.
- He should be honest, trustworthy and high achiever. This can be judged by the track record of the person and his work experience and the extra curricular activities he may be performing.

The staffing, therefore, deals with creation of human resources in the enterprise to achieve goals, objectives and targets set by the top management.

Role of Manager in Coordinating and Directing

After organising the resources and staffing the planned activities, the business plan is launched. The process of implementing the plan is dynamic. It calls upon the manager to perform a number of things in a coordinated manner so that the plan remains valid and the development takes place as per the plan.

The process meets with a number of difficulties and the manager is supposed to resolve them. There will be a lag and lead in many activities. There could be shortfalls and overruns. There could be sudden developments which may disturb the plans and the process of implementation. The manager's role, in this situation, is to coordinate all the activities and provide leadership to the group to keep the plan moving. Directing and leading are the methods, whereby the subordinates are lead to understand the purpose of the activity, and by way of guidance, a direction is given to them to march towards the goals. Their difficulties and conflicts are resolved, bottlenecks removed and a clear path is created to progress on plan achievement.

The task of directing and leading becomes more effective if the human side of the enterprise is taken care of by motivating the people. The manager is required to create an environment in which everybody can perform their best. The work environment becomes conducive to good performance if work becomes satisfying and provides an opportunity to expand the scope of work and his influence.

The manager is a leader if he possesses the art of influencing the subordinates in such a way that they willingly perform towards the achievement of the goals, objectives and targets. The process of coordinating and directing takes place through communication. Good communication has been defined by the American Society of Training Directives as an interchange of thought or information to bring about mutual understanding and confidence or good human relations. The coordinating and directing effect is more effective if the manager is able to motivate the subordinates and provide leadership by way of an effective communication.

Importance of Manager in Controlling

The last but the most important step in the process of management is controlling, the successful execution of management plan. Without control, the process becomes unproductive. The purpose of control is to regulate the process in such a way that the management process continuously strives for the achievement of the goals, objectives and targets.

The control is exercised through a system. The system measures the performance of the management in terms of some predefined measures of output. it compares the output with the standard, identifies the deviations from the standard, corrects the management process to ensure that the plan continues to be effective in terms of achieving goals, objectives and targets.

The control system works on the principle of feedback. The feedback on the performance should be quick without any loss of time, so that corrective action can be taken immediately. The process of correction involves changes in the plan, reallocation of resources, application of new systems, procedures and rules. The best control is the one which brings the process back into operation on the main track without outside intervention. The control system must get into action automatically to correct the midstream adverse development.

Time is the essence of control. If the corrective action is taken late on account of delayed feedback, it is ineffective and may result in heavy losses. Most of the managers look for real time control system, a system which provides an instant negative feedback from the standard and an instantaneous corrective action without any time delay.

Since the management control systems are not physical systems, where one can desire real time control mechanism, the managers look for feedforward control. The feedforward control gives an advance warning, an indication that the deviations are likely to occur in the near future calling for a corrective action. The techniques used in the feedforward control are forecasting, trend analysis and judging the performance from the standpoint of input *versus* output.

Auditing is also a tool of control. There are several types of audits possible in a business organisation. Managerial audit deals with how effectively the plans are made and implemented. It is addressed to the managerial performance to judge whether it was up to the mark, and whether there are any lapses, failures or weaknesses. The operational audit deals with an adherence to the rules and the policies of the management. It identifies whether the operations of the organisation are being carried out as per the managerial directives, rules and policies. The financial audit addresses the business and financial transactions to find out whether they are carried out with due regard to the accounting principles, practices and statutes. It also examines whether all the transactions are covered completely and correctly for the year.

With the advancement of information technology and computers, a variety of planning and control tools have been developed. Planning and budget models, financial models, risk analysis models, PERT/CPM, operations research models are some of the examples of the control tools.

MIS: An Efficient Tool for Management Process

The process of management requires a lot of data and information for execution of the plan. This requirement arises on account of the fact that in each step of management, a variety of decisions are taken to correct the course of development. The decisions or actions are prompted due to the feedback given by the control system incorporated in the management system. The control of overall performance is made possible by way of budget summaries and reports. The summary showing sales, costs, profit and return on investment throws light on the direction the organisation is moving to. The exception reports identify the weaknesses in the system of management.

If effective management system is to be assured, it has to rest on business information. The management performance improves if the business risk and uncertainties are handled effectively. If the information provided is adequate, one can deal with these factors squarely. The information support improves the lack of knowledge, enriches experience and improves analytical abilities leading to better business judgement. So, if efficient information support is to be provided, it calls for a system with the goals of generating management information. A good MIS must furnish information to the managers to expand their knowledge base. He must know the adverse trends in business, the shortfalls and failures in the management process.

The MIS should provide the support to act and to act decisively. It should support management in terms of basic business information at the corporate level and meet the specific needs of the managers . It should highlight on the critical success factors and support key areas of management. MIS should have, wherever possible, decision support systems to help the manager in decision making.

Modern management systems rely on MIS. The complexity of business management and competitive nature of business requires handling of business operations with skill and foresight to avert the crisis. Modern business management requires shift from the traditional controls to managerial control. The shift requires the manager to become more efficient in handling the tasks he is entrusted with. The manager becomes more efficient if he is well informed made richer in knowledge, experience and analytical skills and is able to face the uncertainties and the risks of business. This is possible only if he is supported by MIS, in his specific task of management of business.

Modern business has become more technology-oriented wherein the manager is required to be up-to-date on technological advancement, not only in his field of operations but also in the other technologies. The emerging new technologies are posing threats to current business and are opening new opportunities for new business ventures. The manager has to keep himself abreast on the information of how these technologies affect his business prospects. A good MIS designed for such a support is absolutely essential. MIS, therefore, is a tool for effective execution of the management process.

5

Organisation Structure Theory and Practices

Basic Model of Organisation Structure

The word organisation means two things. The first meaning of the word organisation is an institution or a functional group. A business organisation, a hospital, a school, a university are some such institutions. There is another meaning of 'organisation', that is an arrangement of people in an institution keeping in view the concept of division of labour, authority, responsibility and decision making so that the institution, as a stable system, works coherently towards the achievement of goals.

The organisation structure is built by arrangement of organisational subsystems. The organisation structure is built on four basic principles, viz. hierarchy of authority, specialisation, standardisation or formalisation and, centralisation. The structure is built to achieve goals and objectives fitting into the environment. The structure built on any principle shows division of work, managerial and non-managerial manpower allocation as well as flow of decision responsibility and exchange of information.

Hierarchy of Authority in Organisation

The authority rests with individual in the organisation. The degree and strength of authority depends on the level at which a person is holding position. The authority is measured on the basis of command on control of resources, the risk of business, and the decision making power to manage the risks and rewards. When the authority is distributed in a vertical order in terms of levels, the organisation is built on the principles of hierarchy of authority. The effectiveness of the authority is based on the span of control, i.e., the number of persons being managed and controlled by a person. Depending on the organisation, and business, the span may differ from four to seven. The span outside this range has proved to be unproductive and inefficient.

Specialisation

The second principle of building organisation structure is specialisation. Specialisation can be decided in a number of ways, arranging all similar and associated tasks under one head. For example, a business organisation can be structured on the specialisation such as Manufacturing, Marketing, Accounting and Personnel. A hospital can be structured on the basis of specialisation such as General Medicine, Surgery, Heart diseases, Orthopedics and so on. The specialisation principle brings clarity in organisation functions, helps to select right people and group them properly, aids in functional planning and control of the activities of the organisation.

Standardisation (Formalisation)

The purpose of standardisation or formalisation is to make a person in an organisation independent, whereby the interaction between the individuals in the organisation is minimum. The people work on the basis of rules, procedures, systems, guidelines and policies. If the degree of such specialisation is very high a person can supervise more number of people. In other words, it affects the span of control favourably. With specialisation, the delegation of work and its control has become easier. Where standardisation is not possible owing to the nature of business, the risk in business and decision making complexity span of control is reduced as the number of people handle similar range of operations. Requirement of manpower then increases making the organisation top heavy.

Centralisation of Authority and Responsibility

Centralisation refers to the location or position where the decision-making centre is localised. In a highly centralised organisation, the decision making is at the top and in a decentralised organisation, it is delegated down the line in the organisation hierarchy. When business risks are high and difficult to manage, the organisation emerges as centralised.

The organisation is structured on the basis of the above four principles. The blend of these principles is decided on the nature of business, risk of business, size of business, management style and the environment of business. The blending of these principles would undergo a change as the business grows. The organisation is under a continuous process of change to meet the changing needs of business. The organisation will have a different structure in its various business stages namely, inception, growth, maturity and decline. The structure of organisation affects organisational productivity, individual performance, growth of human resource, and the manpower itself. A considerable amount of saving in manpower and overhead expenses is possible, if the organisation is properly structured to the business needs and towards fulfilling the objectives.

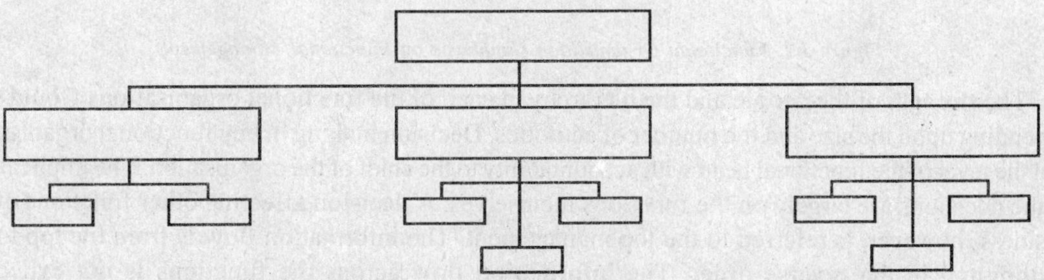

Figure 5.1. *Basic Model of Organisation*

Independent of the blend of these principles, the effectiveness of the structure largely depends on the quality of people—ability, skills, knowledge, attitude and motivation. The basic model of the organisation structure is shown in Figure 5.1. It shows the arrangement of the people in a reverse tree structure.

The basic model will have more levels if the size of the organisation is very large. The number of levels will be determined on the basis of the span of control and the nature of work. The appropriateness of the structure can be decided based on the factors like responsibility and authority, economy in conducting the business, the ability to achieve the goals and objectives, a smooth flow of information exchange and communication. There are four variations of the basic model which are widely used in real life.

Modifications to the Basic Model of Organisation Structure

There are four modifications to the basic model of organisation as under:
1. Functional; 2. Product/Market/Service; 3. Project; and 4. Matrix.

Functional Organisation

The functional organisation is most suitable where the organisation business can be split into clear divisions of activity and all of them are equally important. For example, the business organisation can be functionally organised into four or five functions such as marketing, manufacturing, finance, personnel, and materials.

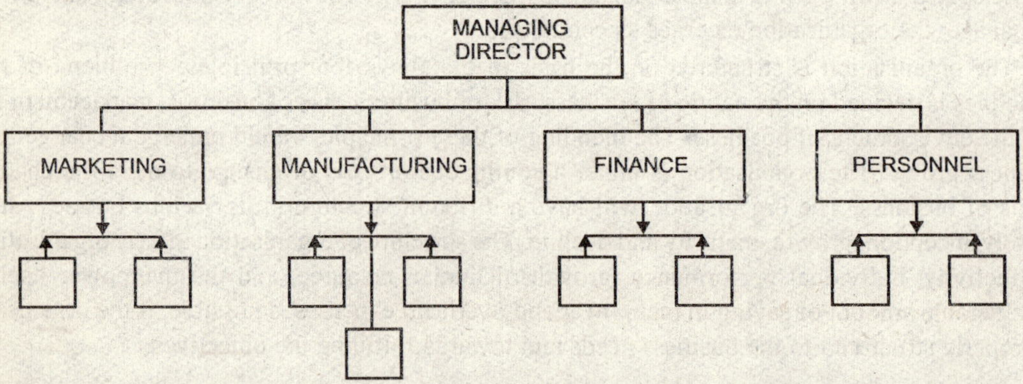

Figure 5.2. Functional Organisation (Emphasis on Functional Management).

The strength of the people and the hierarchy in each of the functional organisations would vary depending upon the size and the number of activities. Decision making in any functional organisation is at the level of the functional head with accountability to the chief of the organisation. The implications of the decisions are largely on the functions themselves. A decision affecting other functions of the business, however, is referred to the top management. The information flow is from the top to the bottom and in the reverse order. The information flow across the functions is not expected. Accumulation of information is at the chief executive's level and is shared by the others.

The functional organisation is most suited where each function is a speciality and calls for an expertise in the field; and where coordination is of a very low order and can be handled easily through the management process. The organisation works efficiently when the business is stable and is expected to grow in a steady manner. When the business becomes competitive and develops threats to its growth, the functional structure undergoes a change. The development of people is on the specialized functions and hence they are not equipped to handle other functions if required. The people in a functional organisation develop a narrow outlook restricted to their own functions and responsibilities. The corporate culture is difficult to imbibe in a functional set-up. Most of the manufacturing, selling organisations in their initial period are structured on the functional lines. The government departments and agencies are organised on the functional principle.

Product/Market/Service Organisation

When the organisation grows large in turnover and strength, and when the decisionmaking relates to, either the product or the market or the service, the organisation structure is built around one of these factors. In this structure, the total responsibility rests with the product/market/service head. He is expected to take all the decisions regarding finance, material, etc. The people in the organisation report to the product head.

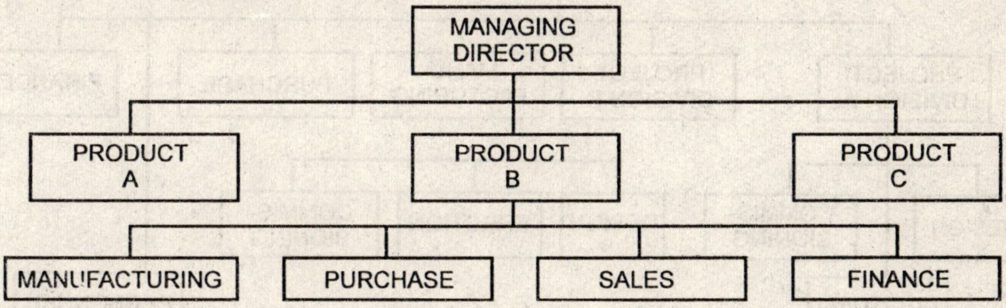

***Figure 5.3.** Product Organisation (Emphasis on Product Management)*

The decision making in this structure is faster and to some extent centralised. The inter-functional conflicts are avoided resulting in speedy business progress. In this structure, people work more for product goals than the corporate goals. The contribution to profit by product can be easily measured as profit is earned by product business unit. In this structure, the manpower requirement is higher and the people develop specialisations in the specific technology and management.

Project Organisation

A project organisation is a special case of product organisation where the common services like finance, purchase, etc. are organised at the functional level. But project resources are allocated to the project manager. Since the business responsibility rests with the project manager, necessary authority is given to him with the requisite resources. This type of organisation structure helps in making quick decisions for project control in terms of cost, resources and time. In a project organisation some of the functions are of corporate responsibility and some of them are the project manager's responsibility.

In a project business, the activity is one at a time and has implications on the subsequent activities in the project. Therefore, any problem or conflict relating to the activity needs to be resolved immediately. This calls for quick decisions. This is possible by organising all the functional resources under one command of the project manager.

Matrix Organisation

In all the three organisation structures discussed so far, the communication protocol is vertical in the hierarchy. The information flow is within the hierarchy. The lateral communication between the functions is not permitted. In a matrix organisation a vertical as well as a lateral communication and information flow is allowed. The matrix organisation integrates functional responsibility with product responsibility. It is a combination of the functional and the product organisation structure. A product manager is responsible for the total performance of the product and he will have the production manager, the marketing manager, the accounts manager as his counterparts in the manufacturing, marketing and accounting functions respectively. These functional managers report to the functional head vertically and the product manager laterally.

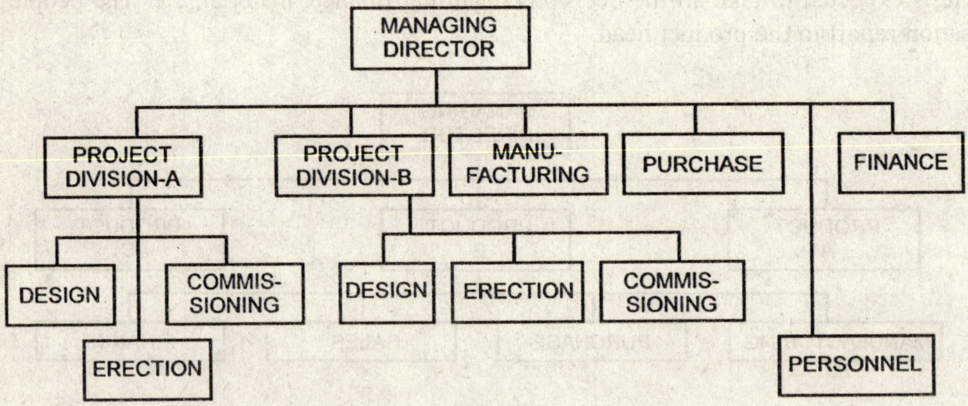

Figure 5.4. *Project Organisation (Emphasis on Project Management).*

The matrix organisation structure is used in big companies having diverse business activities. The business units, known as strategic business units, are organised with a unit head at the top. The structure enjoys the advantages of a functional as well as of a product organisation. It should be noted that the organisation structure is a dynamic model. It is effective for the purpose it is set to fulfil under certain conditions. The moment the business conditions change, the structure should undergo a suitable change. The structural changes do not limit themselves from one type to the other but many other qualitative changes are also desirable.

There has to be a change in the people in terms of strengths, skills and abilities. A functional head in the functional organisation may not be suitable to shoulder the responsibility of the Product Manager in a product organisation structure, because of inherent limitation of narrow specialised experience as a functional head.

With the standardisation and formalisation drive in the organisation, the span of control can be enlarged than before. With the delegation of authority, backed by the rules and policies, the junior level personnel become more knowledgeable, experienced and capable of shouldering higher responsibility. This would affect the levels in hierarchy.

Behaviour of Organisation

Though an organisation is structured according to the goals and objectives to be achieved, the actual performance is at variance for various reasons. There are some factors, beyond the control of the management, which affect the performance of the organisation. However there are some factors, which relate to the organisation (independent of the type of structure). The performance is affected due to organisational behaviour: The behaviour of the organisation is a result of the following factors:

1. Organisational Culture; 2. Organisational Power; 3. Organisational Change; 4. Organisational Learning; and 5. Organisational Motivation.

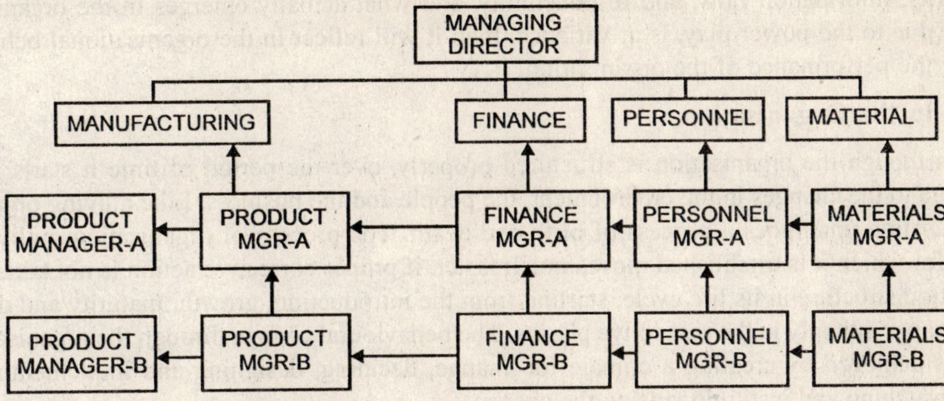

Figure 5.5. *Matrix Organisation (Emphasis on Product/Functional Management).*

Organisational Culture

The culture is a set of attitudes, beliefs , values, norms and understandings, the people have in the organisation. The culture is a collective behavioural result of the people who man the organisation. Depending upon the person, whether he is a manager, an officer or a worker, the cultural pattern emerges and it is known as a managerial culture and a work culture, etc. Long-term performance and managerial actions depend on the managerial culture and the achievement of the targets depends on the work culture.

Let us take an example of quality of product which a particular organisation manufactures and markets. The attitude of the employees towards quality must be positive and it must be seen in the organisation in all the activities. Unless the attitude is positive, it cannot be seen in the product as desired. The employees must believe and show a concern towards quality. They should believe that the quality norms are achievable and they must be committed to it. The commitment towards the achievement of quality will come only if a high value tag is reserved for quality by the employees.

Above all, the organisation must have norms of quality set in all its activities and they must be understood by all the employees.

The culture may be reflected in the philosophy, policy, strategy, goals and managerial style of the organisation. If the organisation culture is generating a behaviour which affects the performance adversely, it can be changed by management actions such as training, education, creating awareness, transferring people, encouraging young recruitments and talent in the organisation.

Organisational Power

The organisational power is the ability of the organisation structure to use human and material resources to achieve the stated goals and objectives of the organisation. The power of the organisation is not distributed uniformly all over the organisation but it may be concentrated in small groups representing a function, a department or a section. It might be localised with the individuals.

Some individuals by virtue of their position, responsibility and seniority, enjoy more power than others. Some individuals by virtue of their nearness to the management and a strong personality, derive power in the organisation structure. If what is meant to be the organisation structure in terms of authority, information flow, and responsibility, and what actually emerges in the organisation structure due to the power play, is at variance, then it will reflect in the organisational behaviour affecting the performance of the organisation.

Change in the Organisation

Even though the organisation is structured properly, over the period of time it starts failing slowly due to the changes in the environment, the people and the business. Like a living organism, an organisation undergoes a process of birth and death. The process of organisation outlives the purpose for which it is established moves much faster, if proper corrective action is not taken. The organisation structure in its life cycle, starting from the introduction, growth, maturity and decline should change suitably in the respective phases. The behavioural change through the organisational change is achieved by creating a climate for change, deciding, designing and implementing the change, watching and institutionalising the change.

Organisational Learning

The organisational behaviour improves with the experience it gathers from all business fronts. With experience, people are in a position to identify the cause and effect relationship. It is possible to predict the errors and probable mistakes in the business operations. The rules, systems and procedures are streamlined over a period of time. With this learning experience, some changes in the organisation structure are inevitable and they should be carried out.

The individuals in the organisation are able to assess the strength and weaknesses within them and are able to take steps to improve. As organisational learning increases the organisation's behaviour shows maturity. With increased learning, the organisation moves towards high degree of formalisation, affecting the structure itself. The organisational learning is faster, if people and management are dynamic and progressive.

Motivation in the Organisational Support and Organisational Behaviour

Organisational behaviour can be monitored and directed if proper motivation is provided to the people. Motivation inspires the people to perform. Monetary rewards, presentation are the known methods of motivation. If a proper leadership is provided it is observed that the people perform beyond expectations. The leadership is an interpersonal influence on the subordinates which persuades or motivates them to perform to achieve the goal.

There are two leadership styles, autocratic and supportive. In an autocratic style, the leader determines everything and dictates decisions. The decisions are enforced by the power of authority. Under such a leadership style people are not trained to shoulder higher responsibilities. The enterprising ones are frustrated under such a leadership style.

The supportive leadership style calls for participation, consultation and respects the opinion of the subordinates. The process evokes initiative amongst the subordinates and gives them a feeling of importance and satisfaction.

Another method of motivation is through job environment. A job is to be designed in such a way that it provides challenge to the skills of an employee. It should be a complete task identifiable with the person and with a potential to create an impact on other people or on the business. The person should feel an autonomy in its operation and should get the direct feedback of the result.

Organisation System

A system is an assembly of elements arranged in a logical order to achieve certain objectives. The organisation is also a system–of people. The individuals in the organisation are selected in terms of number, quality and ability and are placed in hierarchical order to plan and execute the business activities to achieve certain goals and objectives. This is the simplest justification for calling the organisation a system.

The management theorists, however, have seen organisation in different views and perspectives. They have identified more elements in the system besides the people. H. J. Leavitt identified task, technology and structure as additional three elements of the organisation system. He says that the task, technology and people structure are dependent on each other and their significance cannot be ignored as elements of the system.

The arrangement of task in terms of process and work design is dependent on the people. The choice of technology of handling the task is dependent on the people. You may choose the best technology and well designed tasks, but they have to be suited for the people. Over and above, these are to be arranged in proper structure. Further, a fourth element has been added as culture. According to Leavitt an organisation should be viewed as a socio-technical system consisting of people, tasks, technology, culture and structure. The modified Leavatt's model is shown if Fig. 5.6.

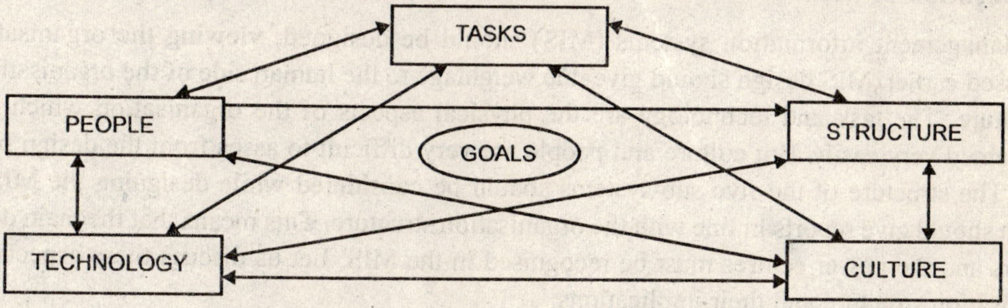

Figure 5.6. Modified Model of the Organisation system.

In view of the nature of the task, the organisation is supposed to carry out, it has to be designed as an open system capable of adjusting itself to the changing environment. The organisation continuously exchanges the information with the environment and is influenced by the changes in it. The organisation, therefore, has to be built in such a fashion that it adjusts with the changes in the environment and that the goals and objectives are achieved.

Hence, the organisation is a socio-technical system whose sub-systems are tasks, people, technology, culture and structure, each having its own input and output satisfying at first its own objectives and eventually the corporate organisation's goals and objectives. If the sub-system's goals and objectives are not congruent with the goals and objectives of the corporate organisation, poor performance, resistance to change and non-attainment of corporate goals will be the consequences.

The systems and their goals are not stable. The goals change in response to the changes in the business focus, the environment and in the people in the organisation. A significant change calls for change in the organisation structure. A goal displacement is said to have occurred when the system goals replace the organisation system goals. When a goal displacement occurs, it affects the organisation's goals significantly. Another reason for goals change is due to the natural process of growth and decline. This phenomenon is best described by a sigmoid or S curve.

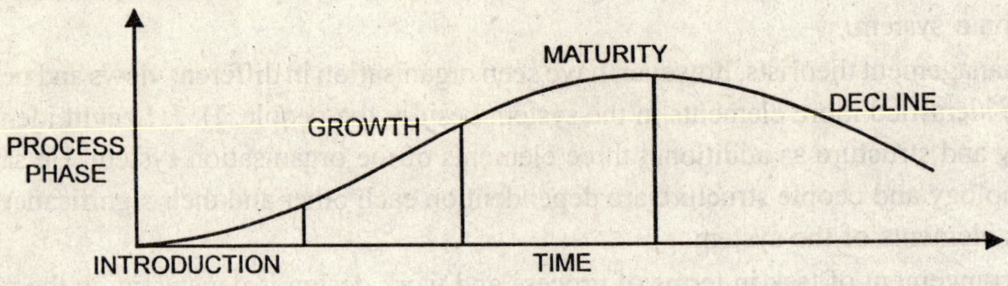

Figure 5.7.

All organisations and their business go through the different phases of growth cycle in stages as, Introduction, Growth, Maturity and Decline. Each phase generates new goals to be served. If the changed or displaced goals are not reflected in the organisation as a system the organisation is bound to suffer from decay.

Organisation of MIS

Management information systems (MIS) should be designed, viewing the organisation as discussed earlier. MIS design should give due weightage to the human side of the organisation and its culture. The task and technology are the physical aspects of the organisation which can be ascertained very easily. But culture and people are very difficult to asses from the design point of view. The structure of the five sub-systems should be considered while designing the MIS. MIS design should give reports in line with the organisation structure. This means that the main decision makers and the power centres must be recognised in the MIS. Let us discuss these aspects of the organisation structure and their implications.

In a tall hierarchy with a high degree of centralisation, the MIS should give control information to the higher management where decision making is concentrated. If the system is structured on the functional basis where the functional head is a key decision maker and all the functions have equally important role to play, then the MIS will have a functional design with the information support to the functional head. Further, in such a set-up, an integrated MIS would be necessary, reporting the corporate status of the business to the top management.

If the organisation works on a standardised system where rules, policies, systems and procedures have been laid down, then these become part of the MIS. The processing routine in the MIS incorporate these features as an integral part. This is safe as it has already been approved by the management of the organisation. Along with the information, if the decision-making responsibilities are also clearly defined and allocated, then the MIS can product information reports by processing the data and summarising the results in line with the decision maker's position in the structure.

If the basic model of the organisation is modified as a product or a project organisation system, then the MIS should focus on the management of product or project where the concerned manager has a composite responsibility or planning and control of the multiple functions. Besides these functions, he has to know the status of the other support functions. The information should be such that it highlights the trouble spots and shows the interconnection with the other functions. It must summarise all information relating to the span of control of product or project manger. The MIS should be able to cater to the view of the product or the project manager and also of the top management.

If the organisation culture provides sufficient incentive for efficiency and results, the MIS should support this culture by providing such information which will aid the promotion of efficiency. If the culture encourages delegation of power and authority, then the MIS should incorporate the decision making rules in the system.

The organisation system is an open system and MIS should be so designed that it highlights the critical business, operational , technological and environmental changes to the concerned level in the organisation, so that the action can be taken to correct the situation. The principle of the feed forward control should be extensively used as a design feature to provide a prior warning to the decision maker.

Since the organisation systems has a dynamic role to play to meet the changing needs of a business, the MIS becomes a common support system for playing the dynamic role. When an organisation is moving through the business phases of introduction, growth, maturity and decline, MIS should provide an information support, relevant to that phase of the business cycle. This means the designer of MIS should foresee such requirements and make the design flexible enough to support such requirements.

The organisational learning helps to tone up the behaviour of the organisation. The MIS should support the learning mechanism by identifying the cause and effect in a given situation. It should keep the records of action and provide help to analyse the best action in a given situation. It should help to build various decision models for use by the managers. The information support should be such that the group of enterprising managers should be able to improve their capabilities to perform better.

The design of the MIS, in isolation from organisational factors, is destined to fail as it just does not fit into the structure. Since organisation systems in the same business differ for various reasons such as the leadership style, the management style, culture and group of people as a body and so on, it is difficult to evolve a standard model of the MIS for a business and/or an industry.

MIS plays a very important role in creating organisation behaviour which in turn sets the goals for achievement. Technology and people decide the organisation structure and style of the management. Figure 5.8 explains the impact and relationship of MIS on the organisation behaviour.

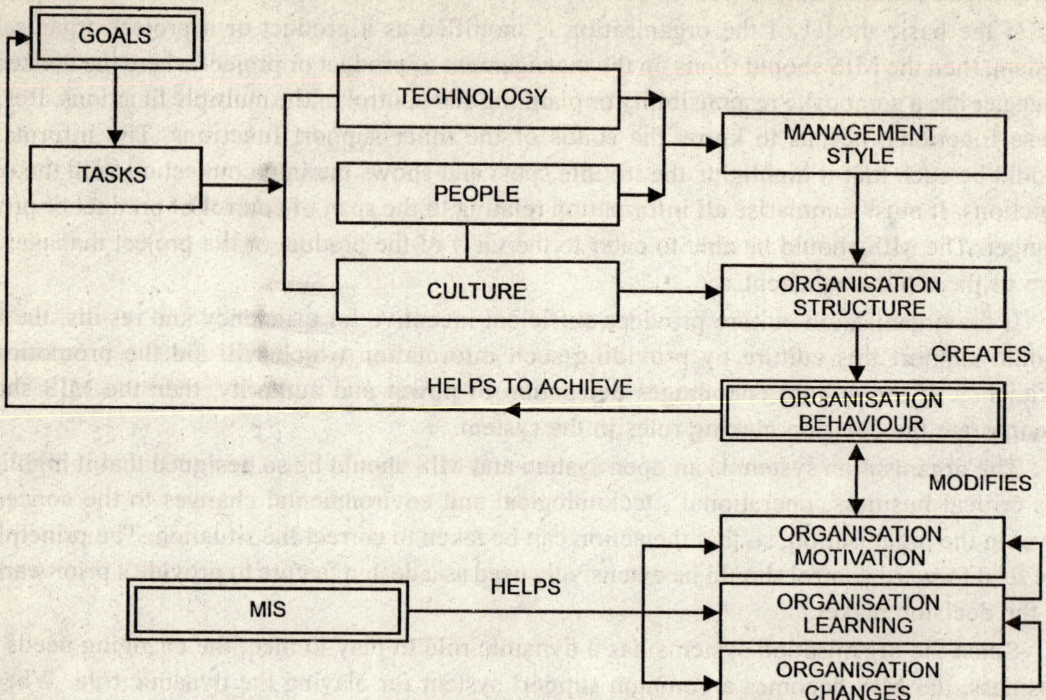

Figure 5.8. Organisational Behaviour and Management Information System.

6

Strategic Management of Business in the 21st Century

Meaning of Corporate Planning

A plan is a predetermined course of action to be taken in the future. It is a document containing the details of how the action will be executed, and it is made against a time scale. The goals and the objectives that a plan is supposed to achieve, are the pre-requisites of a plan. The setting of the goals and the objectives is the primary task of the Management without which planning cannot begin.

Planning means taking a deep look into the future and assessing the likely events in the total business environment and taking a suitable action to meet any eventuality. It further means generating the courses of actions to meet the most likely eventuality. Planning is a dynamic process. As the further becomes the present reality, the course of action decided earlier may require a change. Planning, therefore, calls for a continuous assessment of the predetermined course of action versus the current requirements of the environment. The essence of planning is to see the opportunities and the threats in the future and predetermine the course of action to convert the opportunity into a business gain, and to meet the threat to avoid any business loss.

Planning involves a chain of decisions, one dependent on the other, since it deals with a long term period. A successful implementation of a plan means the execution of these decisions in a right manner one after another.

Planning, in terms of future, can be long-range or short-range. Long-range planning is for a period of five years or more, while short-range planning is for one year at the most. The long-range planning is more concerned about the business as a whole, and deals with subjects like the growth and the rate of growth, the direction of business, establishing some position in the business world by way of a corporate image, a business share and so on. On the other hand, short-range planning is more concerned with the attainment of the business results of the year. It could also be in terms of action by certain business tasks, such as launching of a new product, starting a manufacturing facility, completing the project, achieving intermediate milestones on the way to the attainment of goals. The goals relate to long-term planning and the objectives relate to the short-term planning. There is a hierarchy of objectives which together take the company to the attainment of goals. The plans, therefore, relate to the objectives when they are short-range and to goals when they are the long-range.

Long-range planning deals with resource selection, its acquisition and allocation. It deals with the technology and not with the methods or the procedures. It talks about the strategy of achieving the goals. The right strategy improves the chances of success tremendously. At the same time, a wrong strategy means a failure in achieving the goals.

Corporate business planning deals with the corporate business goals and objectives. The business may be a manufacturing or a service; it may deal with the industry or trade; may operate in a public or a private sector; may be a national or an international business. Corporate business planning is a necessity in all cases. Though the corporate business planning deals with a company, its universe is beyond the company. The corporate business plan considers the world trends in the business, the industry, the technology, the international markets, the national priorities, the competitors, the business plans, the corporate strengths and the weaknesses for preparing a corporate plan. Planning, therefore, is a complex exercise of steering the company through the complexities, the difficulties, the inhibitions and the uncertainties towards the attainment of goals and objectives.

Dimensions of Planning

The corporate business plan has five dimensions. These are time, entity, organisation, elements and characteristics.

Time. The plan may either by long-range or short-range, but the execution of the plan is, year after year. The plan is made on a rolling basis where every year it is extended by one year, keeping the plan period as the next five years. The rolling plan provides an opportunity to correct or revise the plan in the light of any new information the planner may receive.

Entity. The plan entity is the thing on which the plan is focussed. The entity could be the production in terms of quantity or it could be a new product. It could be about the finance, the marketing, the capacity, the manpower or the research and development. The goals, and the objectives would be stated in terms of these entities. A corporate plan may have several entities.

Organisation. The corporate plan would deal with the company as a whole, but it has to be broken down for its subsidiaries, if any, such as the functional groups, the divisions, the product groups and the projects. The breaking of the corporate business plan into smaller organisational units helps to fix the responsibility for execution. The corporate plan, therefore, would be a master plan and it would comprise several subsidiary plans.

Elements. The plan is made out of several elements. The plan begins with the mission and goal which the organisation would like to achieve. It may provide a vision statement for all to understand as also the purpose, focus, and direction the organisation would like to move towards. It would, at the outset, place certain policy statements emerging out of management's business philosophy, culture and style of functioning, followed by policy statements. Next it would declare the strategies in various business functions, which would enable the organisation to achieve the business objectives and targets. It would spell out a programme of execution of plan and achievements. It provides support on rules, procedures and methods of plan implementation, wherever necessary. One important element of the plan is a budget stipulated for achieving certain goals and business targets. The budgets are provided for sales, production, stocks, resources, expenses which are monitored against the time in execution period. The budgets and performance provide meaningful measure about success and failure of the plan designed to achieve certain goals.

Characteristics. There are no definite characteristics of a corporate plan. The choice of characteristics is a matter of convenience helping to communicate to everybody concerned in the organisation and for an easy understanding in execution. The features of a plan could be several and could have several parts. The plan is a confidential written document subject to change, and known to a limited few in the organisation. It is described in the quantitative and qualitative terms. The long-term plan is normally flexible while the short-term one is generally not. The plan is based on the rational assumptions about the future and gives weightage to the past achievements and corporate strength and weaknesses. The typical characteristics of a corporate plan are the goals, the resources, the important milestones, the investment details and a variety of schedules.

Requirements of Strategic Planning

There are some compelling reasons which force all the organisations to resort to strategic business planning. The following reasons make planning an essential management process to keep the business in a good shape and conditions:

1. Forces of Market.
2. Change in the Technology.
3. Diversification of business.
4. Facing Competition.
5. Environment of the Organisation.

Forces of Market

It is very difficult to predict the market forces such as the demand and supply, the trend of the market growth, the consumer behaviour and the choices, the emergence of new products and the new product concepts. The ability of the organisation to predict these forces and plan the strategies is limited for the various reasons. The market forces affect the sales, the growth and the profitability. With the problems arising out of market forces, it is difficult to reorient the organisation quickly to meet the eventualities adversely affecting the business unless the business is managed through a proper business plan.

Change in the Technology

There are a number of illustrative cases throughout the world on the technological break-throughs and changes which have threatened the current business creating new business opportunities. The emergence of the microchip, plastic, laser technology, fibre optics technology, nuclear energy, wireless communication, audio-visual transmission, turbo engines, thermal conductivity and many more, are the examples which have made some products obsolete, threatening the current business, but at the same time, have created new business opportunities. The technological changes have affected not only the business prospects but the managerial and operational styles of the organisations.

In the absence of any corporate plan, such a technological change can bring the organisation into some difficult problems and, in some cases, can pose a threat to its survival. The corporate plan is expected to ensure the recovery of the business investment before such a technological change takes over.

Diversification of Business

The scope of business is wide, touching many fronts. The variety of products, the different market segments, the various methods of manufacturing, the multiple locations, the dependence on the external factors, such as the transport, the communications and the manufacturing resources brings complexity in the management of business. Many factors are uncontrollable and unless there is a plan, prepared with due consideration to the diverse and complex nature of business, handling these factors is not possible. This might lead to the loss of business opportunity.

As the business grows, it reaches a stage where the strategies such as the expansion–vertical or horizontal, integration–forward or backward, diversification–in the same line or in the diverse line of business, are the issues which the management is required to handle. These issues are investment-oriented and have a far-reaching effect on the business growth, direction and profitability.

Facing Competition

Facing competition in the business means fighting on a number of fronts. Competition could be direct or indirect. It may share the market or create a new product which will shift the market affecting your business. Competition could be solely in the management of business, when there is hardly any product distinction or it may come from certain sectors which are being promoted by the government. The companies compete on the merits such as the know how, quality, prompt delivery, after sales service, etc.

Competition is a natural phenomenon in business, and it has to be dealt with in a proper manner to protect business interests. This means that the management has to continuously evolve new strategies to deal with the competition. Evolving strategies and their implementation, calls for forward thinking and planning, without which it is not possible to handle competition.

Competition forces the management to look for new products, new markets, and new technologies to keep the market share intact, the process controlled and the quality improved. Strategies also have to be implemented in a proper sequence as business competition demands an intricate planning, testing and implementation of the strategies. The competition should never be underestimated and has to be met squarely through corporate planning.

Environment of the Organisation

The environment is beyond the control of the management. Depending upon the organisation's business and its purpose, different environments have bearing on the fortunes of business. It could be one of the social, business, economic, industrial, technological environments affecting the business. Many a times, it could be a mix of different environments. The environmental changes are difficult to predict and are generally slow. Therefore, many times the managements, are caught unaware by the environmental changes. To illustrate the environment's impact on business, some examples of recent origin are mentioned as follows.

Widespread education programmes have created new opportunities for knowledge processing and communication. The introduction of television has adversely affected the film industry and its immense popularity has considerably restricted other amusement activities like going for a picnic or to a circus. Personal computers are fast replacing the typewriters on account of changing office environment.

Values and attitudes make the penetration in the market difficult. The difference in the values and attitudes of the rural and urban consumers calls for separate products, with different advertising strategies for them. The attitude of the consumer towards fast food or frozen food decides its spread and popularity. Similarly continuous increase in the cost of transport affects the tourism and hotel industry, but promotes the home entertainment industry. The policies of the Government also affects the business and the industry. The international laws and agreements create new opportunities and threats to the business.

Forecasting the probable environment changes like the change in population, population mix, consumer preferences and their behaviour, government policies, new opportunities and so on and so forth, is a major task under corporate planning. Evolving the strategies to meet these changes is another major task.

Business planning, therefore, is absolutely essential for the survival of the business. Peter Drucker defines long-range planning as the process of making the present managerial (risk taking) decisions systematically and with the best possible knowledge of their futurity, organising systematically the efforts needed to carry out these decisions and measuring the results of these decisions against the expectations through organised systematic feedback. Planning is neither forecasting nor making future decisions today; it is making current decisions in the light of future.

Planning does not eliminate the risk but provides an effective tool to face it. Comprehensive corporate planning is not an aggregate of the functional plans, but it is a systematic approach aiming to manoeuvre the enterprise direction over a period of time through an uncertain environment, to achieve the stated goals and the objectives of the organisation.

HOW TO DEVELOP BUSINESS STRATEGIES

Long-Range Strategic Planning

Like any other business activity, planning also has a process and methodology. It goes without any extra emphasis that the corporate planning is a top management responsibility. It begins with deciding the social responsibility, and proceeds to spell out the business mission and goals, and the strategies to achieve them.

In the very beginning of the planning process, it is necessary to establish and communicate to all concerned, the social and economic responsibilities of the organisation. In order to discharge these responsibilities, it is necessary to decide the purpose of the organisation for which it works. Many organisations call it a mission.

The mission or the aim of an organisation is a broad statement of the organisation's existence which sets the direction of the organisation and decides the scope and the boundaries of the business.

The task after deciding the mission or the aim is to set the goal (s) for the organisation. The goal is more specific and has a time scale of three to five years. It is described in the quantitative terms in the form of a ratio, a norm or a level of certain business aspects such as the largest share, leader in the industry, dominate in certain product, quality, reach and distribution, etc. The goals become a reference for the top management in planning the business activities.

After determining the mission and the goals, the next task is to set various objectives for the organisation. The objectives are described in terms of business results to be achieved in a short duration of a year or two. The objectives are measurable and can be monitored with the help of business tools and technologies. Objectives may be the profitability, the sales, the quality standard, the capacity utilisation etc. When achieved, the objectives will contribute to the accomplishment of the goals and subsequently the mission.

The next step in the planning process is to set targets for more detailed working and references. The objective of the business is to be translated in terms of functional and operational units for easy communication and decision making. The targets may be monthly for the sales, production, inventory and so on. The targets will be the direct descendants of the objective(s).

The success in achieving the goals and objectives is directly dependent on the management's business strategies. Business is like a war where two or more business competitors are set against each other to win and are constantly in search of a strategy to win. The strategy means the manner in which the resources, such as the men, the material, the money and the know-how will be put to use over a period to achieve the goals. The resources of an organisation are deployed based on its goals and its business strategies but also the competition being faced by it. The game is of evolving strategies and counter strategies to win.

The development of the strategy also considers the environmental factors such as the technology, the markets, the life style, the work culture, the attitudes, the policies of the Government and so on. A strategy helps to meet the external forces affecting the business development effectively and further ensures that the goals and the objectives are achieved. The development of the strategy considers the strength of the organisation in deploying the resources and at the same time it compensates for the weaknesses. The strategy formulation, therefore, is an unstructured exercise of a complex nature riddled with the uncertainties (see Figure 6.1). It sets the guidelines for use of the resources in kind and manner during the planning period.

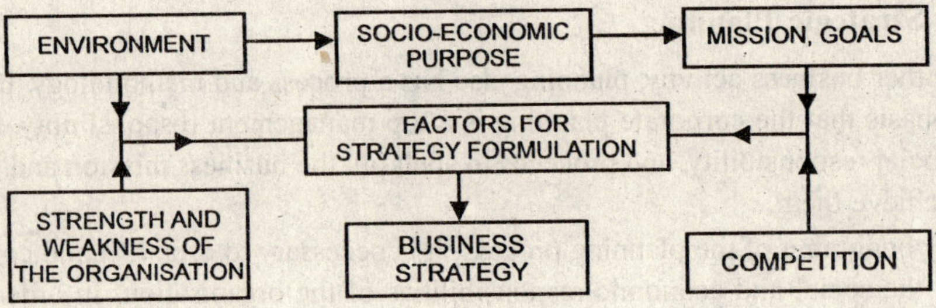

Figure 6.1.

Different Types of Strategies

A strategy means a specific decision(s) usually, but not always, regarding the deployment of the resources to achieve the mission or goals of the organisation. The right strategy beats competition and ensures the attainment of goals, while a wrong strategy fails to achieve the goals. Correction and improvement, in case of a wrong strategy is possible at a very high cost. Such a situation is described as a strategic failure.

If a strategy considers a single point of attack by a specified method, it is a *pure strategy.* If a strategy acts on many fronts by different means, then it is a *mixed strategy.* The business strategy could be a series of pure strategies handling several external forces simultaneously.

Hence, the strategy, may fall in any area of the business and may deal with any aspects of the business. It could be aspects like price, market, product, technology, process, quality, service, finance, management strength and so on. When the management decides to fight the external forces of a single area by choice, it becomes a pure strategy. If it uses or operates in more than one area, then it becomes a mixed strategy.

The success of an organisation, in spite of its strength, depends on the strategic moves or planning the management pursues. The strategy may be pure or mixed. It can be classified into four broad classes: 1. Overall Company Strategy; 2. Growth Strategy; 3. Product Strategy; and 4. Marketing Strategy.

These strategies are applicable to all the types of businesses and industries.

Overall Strategies of the Company

This strategy considers a very long-term business perspective, deals with the overall strength of the entire company and evolves those policies of the business which will dominate the course of the business movement. It is the most productive strategy, if chosen correctly and fatal if chosen wrongfully. The other strategies act under the overall company strategy. To illustrate the overall company strategy, following examples are given:

1. A two wheeler manufacturing company will have a strategy of mass production and an aggressive marketing.
2. A computer manufacturer will have a strategy of adding new products every two or three years.
3. A consumer goods manufacturer will have a strategy of maximum reach to the consumer and exposure by way of a wide distribution network.
4. A company can have a strategy of remaining in the low price range and catering to the masses.
5. Another company can have a strategy of expanding very fast to capture the market.
6. A third company can have a strategy of creating a corporate brand image to build a brand loyalty, e.g., Escorts, Kirloskar, Godrej, Tata, Bajaj, Bhel, MTNL.

The overall company strategy is broad-based having a far reaching effect on the different facets of the business, and forming the basis for generating strategies in the other areas of business.

Strategy of Growth

An organisation may grow in two different ways. Growth may either mean the growth of the existing business turnover, year after year, or it may mean the expansion and diversification of the business.

A two wheeler manufacturing company's growth was very rapid on a single product for more than two decades; then it brought out the new models, then came the range of products, finally the company had manufacturing units at multiple locations. This is an example of the growth of the existing business structure.

There is another organisation which manufactures a variety of products, and it positions them into multiple markets. It has the products from, say, soaps and oils to machinery. Its policy, therefore, is to grow with diversification.

Growth strategy means the selection of a product with a very fast growth potential. It means choice of industries such as electronics, communication, transport, textile, plastic, and so on where the growth potential exists for expansion, diversification and integration. The growth strategy means acquisition of business of the other firms and opening new market segments.

Growth strategies are adopted to establish, consolidate, and maintain a leadership and acquire a competitive edge in the business and industry. It has a direct, positive impact on the profitability.

Strategy of the Product

A growth strategy, where the company chooses a certain product with particular characteristics, becomes a product strategy. A product strategy means choice of a product which can expand as a family of products and provide the basis for adding associated products. It can be positioned into the expanding markets by way of model, type, and price.

The product strategy can be innovated continuously for new markets. Some examples are as follows:

1. A company producing pressure cookers enters the business of making ovens, boilers, washing machines and mixers—the products for home market.
2. A company producing a low priced detergent powder enters the business of washing soap and bath soap.
3. A company producing refrigerators offers a wide range of models with different capacities and features, and further enters into the market of Coolers, Window Air Conditioner, etc.

When a consumer need exists, has a potential of expanding in several dimensions and a product can be conceived satisfying that need, it becomes the product strategy.

Strategy of the Market

The product and the marketing strategies are closely related. The marketing strategies deal with the distribution, services, market research, pricing, advertising, packing and choice of the market itself. A few examples of marketing strategies are as follows.

1. Many companies adopt the strategy of providing after sales service of the highest order. They may offer a free after sales service or establish service organisations to solve customer complaints and problems.
2. A company can offer its products in different packages keeping in mind the consumer budget.
3. A company can arrange for loan facilities to buy its products and keeps the prices low.
4. A computer company manufactures computers and markets them through the market leader under their brand name.

The marketing strategies act as an expediting and activating force for the product and the growth strategy and as the force which accelerates business development. They are generated to create loyalty and preference, for holding market share, for communicating consumer needs and also explaining how the product satisfies it. Marketing strategies are generally centred around one of the factors such as quality, price, service, and availability.

The corporate management formulates the strategies and implements them. The choice of strategy and the method of implementation affects the corporate success. Development of a strategy is a difficult task and it is an exercise in multidisciplinary fields. It can be developed by the business analyst under the directions of the management. The attitude and philosophy of the management will be reflected in the strategy formulation. There are no ready-made formulae or procedures to ensure the selection of a correct strategy, only the results can prove its worth.

The last but not the least point is the business policy evolved by the top management. All the strategies are governed by the business policy. The policies mirror the management's bias, preference, attitude, strength and weakness. Business policy is the frame within which the strategies are sketched.

Business policies provide the necessary guidelines to decide and act across the company and they generally remain effective for a long time. The business policies inform people in the organisation about the intentions of management to conduct the business in a particular direction and in a particular manner. The policies should be clearly stated as they would be used by the people in the organisation without recourse to consultation. This is also true for a strategy formulation.

Short-Range Planning

Short-range planning deals with the targets and the objectives of the organisation. Based on the goals and the objectives, a short-range plans provide the scheme for implementation of the long-range plan. Short-range plans are made for one year in terms of the targets which are to be achieved within the given budgets. The organisation translates long-range plans into the target covering all the critical areas of business, to be achieved by the organisation on a time scale. A manufacturing organisation will make targets for production, sales, capacity, etc. Most of the companies after deciding the targets, work on the budgets.

A budget gives details of the resources required to achieve the targets. The budgets are prepared first in terms of physical units and then converted into the financial units. The companies prepare budgets for sales, production, expenses, capital expenditure, raw materials, advertising and cash, and use them for a decision making and control.

Sensitivity Analysis

The sensitivity analysis helps to test the validity of the solution in variable conditions. The problem situation is handled with certain assumptions and conditions. Based on these considerations, a rational solution is found. Sensitivity analysis requires to know whether the solution will still remain valid if the assumptions changed, constraints were relaxed and new conditions emerged. It helps to assess the impact of change on the solution in economic terms. If various factors are involved, the sensitivity analysis helps to assess the criticality of the factor against the impact it makes on the solution. Some factors will be highly sensitive and some will not be so. Most of the decision making problems are resolved on the principle of optimality, where you are trying to balance the two aspects of the problems, such as, inventory carrying cost *versus* ordering cost, waiting time cost *versus* idle time cost, costs *versus* benefits, opportunity loss *versus* investment cost and so on. The sensitivity analysis helps to test the validity of the optimal solution under changed conditions.

Sensitivity analysis helps to test the solutions on the principle of utility. A solution which is economically rational and is based on a sound business principles may be rejected on the principle of utility. The utility profiles of all the people in the organisation are not the same. The utility profile, alternately known as a preference curve, shows the attitude and preference of the decision maker towards the gains and the losses against a time scale. The profile shows indirectly the risk-taking ability of the decision maker. It uses techniques such as the decision tree analysis, methods of discounting, payoff matrix, simulation, and the modelling.

Modelling (Meaningful Representation)

A model is a meaningful representation of a real situation on a mini scale, where only the significant factors of the situation are highlighted. The purpose of a model is to understand the complex situation based on only the significant factors.

There are several types of models. The model could be a physical model, like a model of a house, a park, a sports complex, etc. The model could be a scale model reducing a large body to a small one. The model could be mathematical model like break even analysis model, linear programming model, queuing model, network model etc. Here a situation is represented in a mathematical form such as equations, matrices graphs and polynomials.

A complex situation is represented using variables, constants and parameters which play a significant role in that situation. The model is based on the relations the variables have. The relation among the variables may be linear or non-linear. The model only considers the relations of high significance. The model, when a situation is complex, tries to simplify the complexity by ignoring minor factors and emphasising only minor important factors.

A model could be static or dynamic. The physical models are static models. Some business models, like the break even analysis model, the statistical regression models and some of the O.R. programming models are static models. The static model does not change over a time period.

All the planning models and all the forecasting models are dynamic models. In a dynamic model, in addition to the variables considered, time is a dimension of the variables. The values of these variables change with the change in time. Such variables are called the stochastic variables.

A model, physical or mathematical, static or dynamic, needs to be tested for its utility or effectiveness. The model can be tested by using the control results already obtained. This would show the difference between the result given by the model and the actual result in a real life situation. If the difference is not significant, then one can say that the model represnents the real situation. Once the model is proved useful, it is used for testing the various solution alternatives. The selection of a solution, from many alternatives solutions, depends on the objective chosen. In a linear programming model, a solution is selected on the principle of maximisation of the profit or minimisation of the cost. In the queuing model a solution is selected, when the cost of the waiting time of a customer is less than the cost of the idle time of facility. The selection of a solution is based on the attainment of certain value of some aspect of the business, such as the turnover, the cost and the profit and so on.

The planning model considers those business variables which affect the business prospects and which show a significant impact on the business results. The long-range strategic models are, generally, dynamic models and the short-range management and operations models are mostly static models.

Business Planning of Supported by MIS

Business environment is prone to changes and this factor makes business planning very complex. Some factors such as the market forces, technological changes, complex diversity of business and competition have a significant impact on any business prospects. MIS is designed to assess and monitor these factors. The MIS design is supposed to provide some insight into these factors enabling the management to evolve some strategy to deal with them. Since these factors are a part of the environment, MIS design is required to keep watch on environment factors and provide information to the management for a strategy formulation.

Strategy formulated is a complex task based on the strength and the weakness of the organisation and the mission and goals it wishes to achieve. Strategy formulation is the responsibility of the top management and the top management relies on the MIS for information .

There are various business strategies such as overall company growth, product, market financing and so on. MIS should provide the relevant information that would help the management in deciding the type of strategies the business needs. Every business may not require all the strategies all the time. The type of strategy is directly related to the current status of business and the goals it wishes to achieve. The MIS is supposed to provide current information on the status of the business vis-a-vis the goals. MIS is supposed to give a status with regard to whether the business is on a growth path or is stagnant or is likely to decline, and the reasons thereof. If the status of the business shows a declining trend, the strategy should by of growth. If business is losing in a particular market segment, then the strategy should be market or a product strategy.

The continuous assessment of business progress in terms of sales, market, quality, profit and its direction becomes the major role of MIS. It should further aid the top management in strategy formulation at each stage of business. The business does not survive on a single strategy but it requires a mix of strategy operating at different levels of the management. For example, when a business is on the growth path, it would require a mix of price, product and market strategies. If a business is showing a decline, it would need a mix of price discount, sales promotion and advertising strategies.

The MIS is supposed to evaluate the strategies in terms of the impact they have on business and provide an optimum mix. The MIS is supposed to provide a strategy-pay off matrix for such an evaluation.

In business planning, MIS should provide support to top management for focusing its attention on decision making and action. In business management, the focus shifts from one aspect to another. In the introductory phase, the focus would be on a product design and manufacturing. When the business matures and requires to sustain or to consolidate, the focus would be on the post sales services and support. The MIS should provide early warning to change the focus of the management from one aspect to the other.

When the strategies are being implemented, it is necessary that the management gets a continuous feedback on its effectiveness in relation to the objective which they are supposed to achieve. MIS is supposed to give a critical feedback on the strategy performance. According to the nature of the feedback, the management may or may not make a change in the strategy mix, the focus and the resource allocation.

MIS has certain other characteristics for the top management. It contains forecasting models to probe into the future—the business model evaluation of the strategy performance by simulating business conditions. It contains functional models such as the model for a new product launching, budgeting, scheduling and the models using PERT/CPM technique for planning.

MIS for the top management relies heavily on databases which are external to the organisation. The management also relies heavily on the internal data which is evolved out of transaction processing. Management uses the standards, the norms, the ratios and the yardsticks while planning and controlling the business activities. They are also used for designing strategies and their mix. The MIS is supposed to provide correct, precise and unbiased standards to the top management for planning.

We can summarise the role of the MIS in the top management function as follows: MIS supports by way of information, to

1. decide the goals and objectives,
2. determine the correct status of the future business and projects,
3. provide the correct focus for the attention and action of the management,
4. evolve, decide and determine the mix of the strategies,
5. evaluate the performance and give a critical feedback on the strategic failures.

Success of a business depends on the quality of support the MIS gives to the management. The quality is assured only through an appropriate design of the MIS integrating the business plan with the MIS plan.

Section 3

Information Technology Concept

7

Computer Hardware

- Pointing Device
- Pen-Based Computing
- Voice Recognition and Response
- Optical Scanning
- Other Input Technologies
- Output Technologies and Trends
- Video Output
- Printed Output
- Storage Trends and Trade-Offs
  - *Computer Storage Fundamentals*
  - *Direct and Sequential Access*
- Semiconductor Memory
- Magnetic Disk Storage
  - *Types of Magnetic Disks*
- Magnetic Tape Storage
- Optical Disk Storage
  - *Business Applications*

Real World Case: AG Communication Systems: The Business Case for Notebook Computers

SECTION I

COMPUTER SYSTEMS: END USER AND ENTERPRISE COMPUTING

All computers are systems of input, processing, output, storage, and control components. In this section, we will discuss the trends, applications, and some basic concepts of the many types of computer systems in use today. In section II, we will cover the changing technologies for input, output, and storage that are provided by the peripheral devices that are part of modern computer systems.

Analyzing SpeedServe and Merrill Lynch

SpeedServe switched from a high-powered server to a mainframe computer system to handle the 1 million transactions and growing processing load it expects at its Web site. Merrill Lynch decided to use an existing mainframe to host a Web site of stock market data because most of the data needed by the site was already stored on the mainframe system. In both cases, the mainframe systems were chosen as Web servers because their processing power, reliability, security, and manageability were considered superior to the use of networked server computers. Though mainframe computers are too expensive and overpowered for many Web site applications, SpeedServe and Merrill Lynch needed mainframe processing capacity, and believe that of operating cost of mainframes will be less than the labour and support costs of using multiple servers to run a Web site.

Trends in Computer Systems

Today's computer systems come in a variety of sizes, shapes, and computing capabilities. Rapid hardware and software developments and changing end user needs continue to drive the emergence of new models of computers, from the smallest hand-held *personal digital assistant* for end users, to the largest multiple-CPU mainframe for the enterprise.

Categories such as ***mainframe, midrange computers,*** and ***microcomputers*** are still used to help us express the relative processing power and number of end users that can be supported by different types of computers. But as Figure 7.2 illustrates, these are not precise classifications, and they do overlap each other. Thus, other names are commonly given to highlight the major uses of particular types of computers. Examples include personal computers, network servers, network computers, and technical workstations.

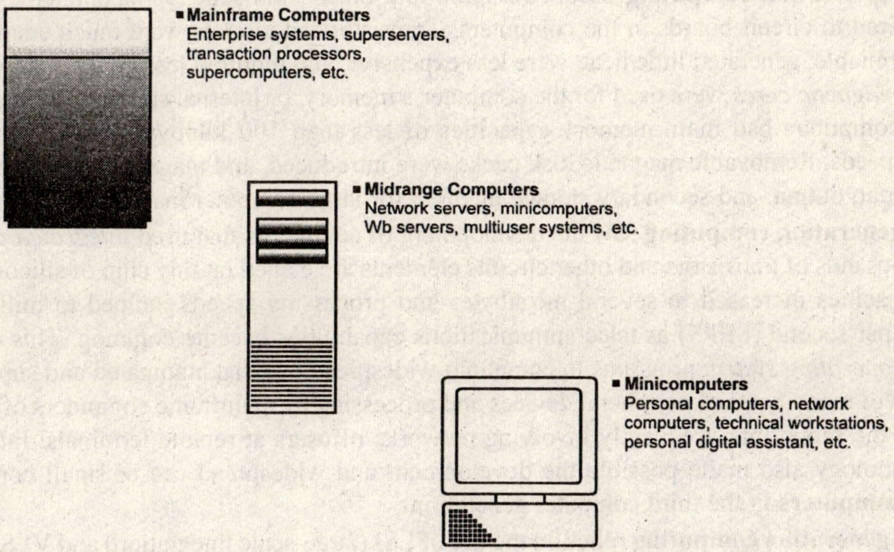

Figure 7.1. Examples of computer system categories.

In addition, experts continue to predict the merging or disappearance of several computer categories. They feel, for example, that many midrange and mainframe systems have been made obsolete by the power and versatility of *clients/server* networks of end user microcomputers and servers. Most recently, some industry experts have predicted that the emergence of network computers for applications on the Internet and corporate intranets will replace many personal computers specially in large organisations and in the home computer market. Only time will tell whether such predictions will equal the expectations of industry forecasters.

Computer Generations

It is important to realize that major changes and trends in computer systems have occurred during the major stages—or **generations**—of computing, and will continue into the future. The first generation of computers developed in the early 1950s, the second generation blossomed during the late 1960s, the third generation took computing into the 1970s, and the fourth generation has been the computer technology of the 1980s and 1990s. A fifth generation of computers that accelerates the trends of the previous generations is expected to evolve as we enter the 21st century. Figure 7.3 highlights trends in the characteristics and capabilities of computers. Notice that computers continue to become smaller, faster, more reliable, less costly to purchase and maintain, and interconnected within computer networks.

First-generation computing involved massive computers using hundreds or thousands of *vacuum tubes* for their processing and memory circuitry. These large computers generated enormous amounts of heat; their vacuum tubes had to be replaced frequently. Thus, they had large electrical power, air conditioning, and maintenance requirements. First-generation computers had main memories of only a few thousand characters and millisecond processing speeds. They used magnetic drums or tape for secondary storage and punched cards or paper tape as input and output media.

Second-generation computing used *transistors* and other solid-state, semiconductor devices that were wired to circuit boards in the computers. Transistorized circuits were much smaller and much more reliable, generated little heat, were less expensive, and required less power than vacuum tubes. Tiny *magnetic cores* were used for the computer's memory, or internal storage. Many second-generation computers had main memory capacities of less than 100 kilobytes and microsecond processing speeds. Removable magnetic disk packs were introduced, and magnetic tape emerged as the major input, output, and secondary storage medium for large computer installations.

Third-generation computing saw the development of computers that used *integrated circuits,* in which thousands of transistors and other circuits elements are etched on tiny chip of silicon. Main memory capacities increased to several megabytes and processing speeds jumped to millions of instructions per second (MIPS) as telecommunications capabilities became common. This made it possible for *operating system* programs to come into widespread use that automated and supervised the activities of many types of peripheral devices and processing by mainframe computers of several programs at the same time, frequently involving networks of users at remote terminals. Integrated circuits technology also made possible the development and widespread use of small computers called **minicomputers** in the third computer generation.

Fourth-generation computing relies on the use of LSI (large-scale integration) and VLSI (very-large scale integration) technologies that cram hundreds of thousands or millions of transmission and other circuit elements on each chip. This enabled the development of **microprocessors**, in which all of the circuits of a CPU are contained on a single chip with processing speeds of millions of instructions per second. Main memory capacities ranging from a few megabytes to several gigabytes can also be achieved by *memory chips* that replaced magnetic core memories. **Microcomputers,** which use microprocessor CPUs and a variety of peripheral devices and easy-to-use software packages to form small personal computer (PC), systems or *client/server* networks of linked PCs and servers, are a hallmark of the fourth generation of computing, which accelerated the **downsizing** of computing systems.

Whether we are moving into a **fifth generation** of computing is a subject of debate since the concept of generations may no longer fit the continual, rapid changes occurring in computer hardware, software, data, and networking technologies. But in any case, we can be sure that progress in computing will continue to accelerate, and that the development of Internet-based technologies and applications will be one of the major forces driving computing into the 21st century.

	First Generation	Second Generation	Third Generation	Fourth Generation	Fifth Generation?
SIZE (Typical computers)	Room Size Mainframe	Closet Size Mainframe	Desk-Size Minicomputer	Desktop and Laptop Microcomputers	Networked Computers of all sizes
NETWORKING	None	Mainframe-Based Networks of Video Terminals	Mainframe and Minicomputer-Based Networks	Local Area and Client/Server Networks	The Internet, Intranets and Extranets
CIRCUITRY	Vacuum Tubes	Transistors	Integrated Semi-conductor Cricuits	Large-Scale Integ-ated (LSI) Semi-Conductor Circuits	Very-Large-Scale Integrated (VLSI) Seminconductor Circuits
DENSITY (Circuits per componont)	One	Hundreds	Thousands	Hundreds of Thousands	Millions
SPEED (Instructions/second)	Hundreds	Thousands	Millions	Tens of Millions	Billions
RELIABILITY (Failure of circuits)	Hours	Days	Weeks	Months	Years
MEMORY (Capacity in characters)	Thousands	Tens of Thousands	Hundreds of Thousands	Millions	Billions
COST (Per million instructions)	$10	$1.00	$.10	$.001	$.0001

Figure 7.2. Major trends in computer system capabilities.

Microcomputer Systems

Cheaper, faster, better remains the iron law of the computer industry. The immense power of the new microprocessor—from Intel and its competitors—means that this year's state-of-the-art personal computer is an astonishingly capable machines [5].

Microcomputers are the most important category of computer systems for end users. Though usually called a *personal computer*, or PC, a microcomputers is much more than a small computer for use by an individual. The computing power of microcomputers now exceeds that of the mainframes of previous computer generations at a fraction of their cost. Thus, they have become powerful networked *professional workstations* for end users in business.

Microcomputers come in a variety of sizes and shapes for a variety of purposes. For example, PCs are available as handheld, notebook, laptop, portable, desktop, and floor-standing models. Or, based on their use, they include home, personal, professional, workstation, and multiuser systems. Most microcomputers are *desktop* designed to fit on an office desk, or *notebooks* for those who want a small, portable PC for their work activities.

Some microcomputers are powerful **workstation computers** (technical workstations) that support applications with heavy mathematical computing and graphics display demands such as computer-aided design (CAD) in engineering, or investment and portfolio analysis in the securities industry. Other microcomputers are used as **network servers.** They are usually more powerful microcomputers that coordinate telecommunications and resource sharing in small local area networks (LANs), and Internet and intranets Web sites. Another important microcomputer category includes handled microcomputer devices known as **personal digital assistants** (PDAs), designed for convenient mobile communications and computing. PDAs use touch-screens, pen-based handwriting recognition, or keyboards to help mobile workers send and receive E-mail and exchange information such as appointments, to-do lists, and sales contacts with their desktop PCs or Web servers.

Dream Machine Checklist

- **The Ultimate Business Box.** If your dream machine is mainly for business, you'll want at least 32MB of RAM for those big software programs, a 56Kbps modem to pull down research and news from the Web, a 5GB hard drive, and a 300 MHz processor. Don't sweat high-end graphics processor, audio, and other frills, but look for a Universal Serial Bus for easy connections to printers and other peripherals.
- **The Graphics Workstation.** If you're crunching 3-D architectural renderings, you'll want 64MB of main memory, 20MB of graphics memory, a fast microprocessor with Level 2 cache of 512KB, and a replaceable hard drive for those large graphics files.
- **The Ultimate Multimedia.** PC enthusiasts want it all. Top-end processor, 32MB RAM, a 5GB hard drive, 56Kbps modem. For browsing multimedia on the Web, look for 16-bit, full-duplex audio boards with Wave Table Synchronous. It gaming is your focus, go for 3-D rendering boards with 4MB of fast Synchronous DRAM.

Source: Adapted from "Dream Machines," in "Technology Buyer's Guide," *Fortune*, Winter 1998.

Figure 7.3. Business PC checklist. Some of the key features to evaluate when purchasing a high-end business PC, graphics workstation, or multimedia PC.

Multimedia Systems

While sound, videos, and animation are still most important for games and educational software, multimedia technology has begun to suffuse business applications as well. The cost of videoconferencing has plummeted while its quality has improved. Film clips and animations—already a staple in PC-based presentations—are turning up in tutorials and training materials. Shared documents annotated with voice, digitized photographs, or 3-D graphics are beginning to make the rounds on the company network. The highly graphical Web, for good or ill, is as commonplace as bad coffee in today's office [7].

Multimedia PCs are designed to present you with information in a variety of media, including text and graphics displays, voice and other digitized audio, photographs, animation, and video clips. Mention multimedia, and many people think of computer videos games, multimedia encyclopedias, educational videos, and multimedia home pages on the World Wide Web. However, multimedia systems are widely used in business for training employees, educating customers, making sales presentations and adding impact to other business presentation.

The basic hardware and software requirements of a multimedia computer system depend on whether you wish to create as well as enjoy multimedia presentations. Owners of low-cost multimedia PCs marketed for home use do not need authoring software or high-powered hardware capabilities in order to enjoy multimedia games and other entertainment and educational multimedia products. These computers come equipped with a CD-ROM drive, stereo speakers, additional memory, a high-performance processor, and other multimedia processing capabilities.

People who want to create their own multimedia productions may have to spend several thousand dollars to put together a high-performance *multimedia authoring system.* This includes a high-resolution colour graphics monitor, sound and video capture boards, a high-performance microprocessor with multimedia capabilities, additional megabytes of memory, and several gigabytes of hard disk capacity. *Sound cards* and video capture boards are circuit boards that contain *digital signal processor* (DSPs) and additional megabytes of memory for digital processing of sound and video. A digital camera, digital video camcorder, optical scanner, and software such as authoring tools and programs for image editing and graphics creation can add several thousand dollars to the start-up costs of a multimedia authoring system.

Network Computers

"As the mainframes were to the 60s, minicomputers were to the 70s and PCs to the 80s, [the] network computer will be to the 90s." So says Ed Zander, president of Sun—Microsystems [18].

Whether there is enough of the 90s left is debatable, but not the reality of **network computers** (NCs) as a serious business computing platform. Through Microsoft and Intel ridiculed the NC concept at first, they have since agreed to support moves toward "thin client" as well as traditional "fat client" full featured PCs. The Wintel duo (Windows OS and Intel microprocessor) proposed a tripped-down, locked-up PC called the NetPC. Microsoft went one step further and proposed an even more stripped-down device than the NC or NetPC called the *Windows terminal*, that would be dependent on network servers for software, processing power, and storage [10].

Network computers are thus a major new microcomputer category designed primarily for use with the Internet and corporate intranets by clerical workers, operational employees, and knowledge workers with specialized or limited computing applications. NCs are low-cost, sealed, networked microcomputers with no or minimal disk storage. Users of NCs depend primarily on Internet and intranet servers for their operating system and Web browser, Java-enabled application software, and data access and storage. Examples include Sun's JavaStations, IBM's Network Station, and the NCD Explora network computers.

One of the main attractions of network computers is their lower cost of purchase, upgrades, maintenance, and support compared to full-featured PCs. Other benefits to business include ease of software distribution and licensing, computing platform standardization, reduced end user support requirements, and improved manageability through centralized management and enterprisewide control of computer network resources [9,10].

Special-purpose NCs that take the form of *set-top boxes* that connect to your home TV set are another category of network computer. These devices enable you to surf the World Wide Web or send and receive E-mail and watch TV programs at the same time in multiple windows. Examples include the Sony WebTV Internet Terminal and Phillips Magnavox WebTV Plus Receiver, which use Microsoft's WebTV network services. Another example is the RCA Network Computer, which is based on Oracle's *information appliances* NC standards, and uses the NetChannel Internet service. The Sony and Phillips models include a TV tuner, 56 Kbps modem, and 1.1 GB hard drive for downloading files. Prices for these devices start around $300, plus optional peripherals such as keyboards and printers [8].

Network Computer

- Operating system, application software, and data storage are provided by the server
- Uses a Web browser and runs Java-enabled software applications called *applets*
- Managed remotely and centrally
- Generally has no hard disk drive

NetPC

- Works like a PC, with its own software
- Has a hard drive, but no floppy drive or CD-ROM
- Box is sealed so user can't change its configuration
- Operating system and application are managed and loaded centrally

Windows terminals

- An inexpensive terminal-like device without disk storage
- Multiuser version of Windows NT as the server operating system
- Microsoft Office-like multiuser software on the server

Source: Adapted from April Jacobs and Lisa Picatrille, "Microsoft Now Says Thin Is In," *Computerworld,* April 14, 1997.

Figure 7.4. Comparing the network computer to the NetPC and the Windows terminal.

Computer Terminals

Computer terminals are undergoing a major conversion to networked computer devices. *Dumb terminals*, which are keyboard/video monitor devices with limited processing capabilities, are being replaced by *intelligent terminals,* which are modified networked PCs, networked computers, or other networked devices. Intelligent terminals can perform data entry and some information processing tasks independently. This includes the widespread use of the **transaction terminals** in banks, retail stores, factories and other work sites. Examples are automated teller machines (ATMs), factory production reorders, and retail point-of-sale (POS) terminals. These intelligent terminals use keypads, touch screens, and other input methods to capture data and interact with end users during a transaction, while relying on servers or other computers in the network for further transaction processing.

Midrange Computer Systems

Midrange computers, including minicomputer and high-end network servers, are multiuser systems that can manage networks of PCs and terminals. Though not as powerful as mainframe computers, they are less costly to buy, operate, and maintain than mainframe systems, and thus meet the computing needs of many organisations.

Midrange computers first became popular as **mini-computers** for scientific research, instrumentation systems, engineering analysis and industrial process monitoring and control. Minicomputers could easily handle such uses because these applications are narrow in scope and do not demand the processing versatility of mainframe systems. Thus, midrange computers serve as industrial process-control and manufacturing plant computers, and they still play a major role in computer-aided manufacturing (CAM). They can also take the form of powerful technical workstations for computer-aided design (CAD) and other computation and graphics-intensive applications. Midrange computers are also used as *front-end computer* to assist mainframe computers in telecommunications processing and network management.

Burgeoning data warehouses and related applications such as data mining and online analytical processing are forcing IT shops into higher and higher levels of server configurations. Similarly, Internet-based applications, such as Web servers and electronic commerce, are forcing IT managers to push the envelope of processing speed and storage capacity and other [business] applications fueling the growth of high-end servers [17].

Midrange computers have become popular as powerful **network servers** to help manage large Internet Web sites, corporate intranets and extranets, and client/server networks. Electronic commerce and other business uses of the Internet are popular high-end server applications, as are integrated enterprisewide manufacturing, distribution, and financial applications. Other applications, like data warehouse management, data mining, and online analytical processing, are contributing to the growth of high-end server and other midrange systems [17].

Mainframe Computer Systems

Six years after dire pronouncements that the mainframe was dead, quite the opposite is true: Mainframe usage is actually on the rise. And it's not just a short-term blip. One factor that's been driving mainframe sales is cost reductions [of 35 percent or more]. Price reductions aren't the only factor fueling mainframe acquisitions. IS organisations are teaching the old dog new tricks by putting mainframes at the centre stage of emerging applications such as data mining and warehousing, decision support, and a variety of Internet-based applications, most notably electronic commerce [16].

Mainframe computers are large, fast, and powerful computer systems. For example, mainframes can process hundreds of million instructions per second (MIPS). Mainframes also have large primary storage capacities. Their main memory capacity can range from hundreds of megabytes to many gigabytes of primary storage. And mainframes have slimmed down drastically in the last few years, dramatically reducing their air-conditioning needs, electrical power consumption, and floor space requirements, and thus their acquisition and operating costs. Most of these improvements are the result of a move from water-cooled mainframes to a new CMOS air-cooled technology for mainframe systems.

Thus, mainframe computers continue to handle the information processing needs of major corporations and government agencies with many employees and customers or with complex computational problems. For example, major international banks, airlines, oil companies and other large corporations process millions of sales transactions and customer inquiries each day with the help of large mainframe systems. Mainframes are still used for computation-intensive applications such as analyzing seismic data from oil field explorations or simulating flight conditions in designing aircraft. Mainframes are also widely used as *superservers* for the large client/server networks and high-volume Internet Web sites of large companies. And as previously mentioned, mainframes are becoming a popular business computing platform for data mining and warehousing, and electronic commerce applications.

IBM	ES/3090 Model 600E (water cooled)	S/390 Ry4 (CMOS air cooled)
Processors	6-way	10-way
Processing power	390 MIPS	400 MIPS
Electrical needs	138.8 KVA	5 KVA
Floor space	974 sq. ft.	52 sq. ft.
Weight	31,590 pounds	2,057 pounds

Source: Adapted from Tim Ouellette, "Goodbye to the Glass House," *Computerworld,* May 26, 1997.

Figure 7.5. Comparing a traditional water-cooled mainframe with a comparable air-cooled CMOS system.

Supercomputer Systems

Supercomputers have now become "scalable servers" at the top end of product lines that start with desktop workstations. Market-driven companies, like Silicon Graphics, Hewlett-Packard, and IBM, have a much broader focus than just building the world's fastest computer, and the software of the desktop computer has a much greater overlap with that of the supercomputer than it used to, because both are built from the same cache-based microprocessor [12].

The term **supercomputer** describes a category of extremely powerful computer systems specifically designed for scientific, engineering, and business applications requiring extremely high speeds for massive numeric computations. The market for supercomputers includes government research agencies, large universities, and major corporations. They use supercomputers for applications such as global weather forecasting, military defense systems, computational cosmology and astronomy, microprocessor research and design, large-scale data mining, and so on.

Supercomputers use *parallel processing* architectures of interconnected microprocessors (which can execute many instructions at the same time in parallel). They can perform arithmetic calculations at speeds of billions of floating-point operations per second (gigaflops). Teraflop (1 trillion floating-point operations per second) supercomputers, which used advanced massively parallel processing (MPP) designs of thousands of interconnected microprocessors, are becoming available. Purchase prices for large supercomputers are in the $5 million to $50 million range.

However, the use of symmetric multiprocessing (SMP) and distributed shared memory (DSM) designs of smaller numbers of interconnected microprocessors has spawned a breed of *minisupercomputers* with prices that start in the hundreds of thousands of dollars. For example,

IBM's RS/6000 SP starts at $150,000 for a one-processing-node SMP computer. However, it can be expanded to a maximum of 512 processing nodes, which drives its price into the tens of millions of dollars. Deep Blue, which beat world chess champions Garry Kasparov in May 1997, was a 32-node version of the RS/6000 SP [11]. Thus, supercomputers continue to advance the state of the art for the entire computer industry.

- Most critical business data may already be stored on the mainframe.
- Mainframe scalability can handle growing Internet traffic.
- Mainframe applications were designed to work with thin clients such as NetPCs and NCs.
- Built-in mainframe security can be combined with new cryptographic coprocessors and upcoming fire wall capabilities.
- Data is safer on the mainframe than on many servers.
- Internet tools are integrated right into the mainframe's OS/390 operating system.
- New mainframes offer huge savings in size, energy, and maintenance.

Source: Adapted from Tim Ouellette, "Mainframes Ripe for Web Serving."

Figure 7.6. Why companies are using mainframes as servers for electronic commerce.

Technical Note: Computer System Concepts and Components

As a business end user, you do not need a detailed technical knowledge of computers. However, you do not need to understand some basic facts and concepts about computer systems. This should help you be an informed and productive user of computer system resources. Therefore, this section presents basic concepts about the components and functions of a computer system. Other topics include the central processing unit, computer memory, and variations in computer processors.

The Computer System Concepts

A computer is more than a high-powered collection of electronic devices performing a variety of information processing chores. A computer is a system, an interrelated combination of components that performs the basic system functions of input, processing, output, storage, and control, thus providing end users with a powerful information processing tool. Understanding the computer as a **computer system** is vital to the effective use and management of computers. You should be able to visualize any computer this way, from a microcomputer like that shown in Figure 7.16, to a large computer system whose components are interconnected by a telecommunications network and spread throughout a building or geographic area.

Figure 7.17 illustrates that a computer is a system of hardware devices organised according to the following system functions:

- **Input**. The input devices of a computer system include keyboard, touch screens, pens, electronic mice, optical scanners, and so on. They convert data into electronic machine-readable form for direct entry or through telecommunications links into a computer system.

- **Processing**. The central processing unit (CPU) is the main processing components of a computer system. (In microcomputers, it is the main microprocessor.) In particular, the electronic circuits of the arithmetic-logic unit, one of the CPU's major components, perform the arithmetic and logic functions required in computer processing.
- **Output**. The output devices of a computer system include video display units, printers, audio response units, and so on. They convert electronic information produced by the computer system into human-intelligible form for presentations to end users.
- **Storage**. The storage functions of a computer system takes place in the storage circuits of the computer's primary storage unit, or *memory*, and in secondary storage devices such as magnetic disk and tape units. These devices store data and program instructions needed for processing.
- **Control**. The control unit of the CPU is the control component of a computer system. Its circuits interpret computer program instructions and transmit directions to the other components of the computer system.

The Central Processing Unit

The **central processing unit** is the most important hardware components of a computer system. It is also known as the CPU, the central processor or instruction processor, and the **main microprocessor** in a microcomputer. Conceptually, the circuitry of a CPU can be subdivided into two major subunits: the arithmetic-logic unit and the control unit. The CPU also includes circuitry for devices such as *registers* and *cache memory* for high-speed, temporary storage of instruction and data elements, and various subsidiary processors such as those for arithmetic operations, input/output, and telecommunications support.

The **control unit** obtain instruction from software segments stored in the primary storage unit and interprets them. Then it transmit electronic signals to the other components of the computer system to perform required operations. The **arithmetic-logic unit** performs required arithmetic and comparison operations. A computer can make logical changes from one set of program instructions to another (e.g., overtime pay *versus* regular pay calculations) based on the results of comparisons made in the ALU during processing.

Primary and Secondary Storage

A computer's **primary storage unit** is commonly called **main memory,** and holds data and program instructions between processing steps and supplies them to the control unit and arithmetic-logic unit during processing. Most of a computer's memory consists of microelectronic semiconductor memory chips known as RAM (random access memory). The contents of these memory chips can be instantly changed to store new data. Other, more permanent memory chips, called ROM (read only memory) may also be used.

Secondary storage devices like magnetic disk and optical disks are used to store data and programs, and thus greatly enlarge the storage capacities of computer systems. Also, since memory circuits typically lose their contents when electric power is turned off, most secondary storage media provide a more permanent type of storage. However, the contents of hard disk drives, floppy disks, CD-ROM disks, and other secondary storage media cannot be processed without first being brought into memory. Thus, secondary storage devices play a supporting role to the primary storage of a computer system.

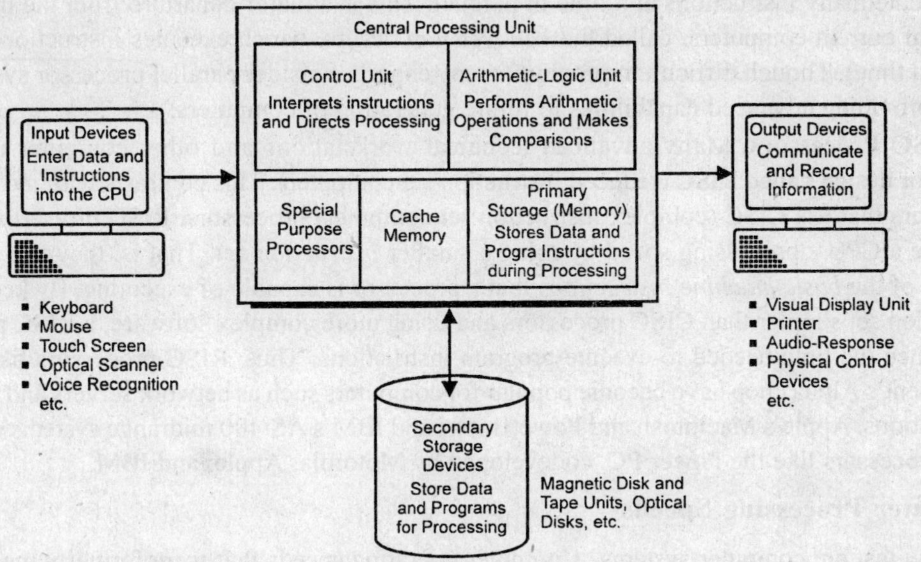

Figure 7.7. The computer system concept. A computer is a system of hardware components and functions.

Multiple Processors

Many current computers, from microcomputers to large mainframes, use multiple processors for their processing functions. Instead of having one CPU with a single control unit and arithmetic-logic unit, the CPUs of these computers contain several types of processing units. Let's briefly look at the major types of such **multiprocessor** designs.

A **support processor** design relies on specialized microprocessor to help the main CPU perform a variety of functions. These microprocessor may be used for input/output, memory management, arithmetic computations, multimedia processing, and telecommunications, thus freeing the main processor to do the primary job of executing program instructions. For example, many microcomputers rely on support microprocessors such as arithmetic co-processors, video display controllers, and magnetic disk controllers to reduce the processing load on their main microprocessors. A large computer may use support microprocessors called *channels* to control the movement of data between the CPU and input/output devices. Advanced microprocessor designs integrate the functions of several support processors on a single main microprocessor.

A **coupled processor** design uses multiple CPUs or main microprocessors to do multiprocessing, that is, executing more than one instruction at the same time. Some configurations provide a *fault-tolerant* capability in which multiple CPUs provide a built-in backup to each other should one of them fail.

A **parallel processor** design uses a group of instruction processors to execute several program instructions at the same time. Sometimes, hundreds or thousands of processors are organised in clusters or networks in *massively parallel processing* (MPP) computers. Other parallel processor designs are based on simple models of the human brain called *neural networks.* All these systems can execute many instructions at a time in parallel. This is a major departure from the traditional design of current computers, called the *Von Neuman design,* which executes instructions serially (one at a time). Though difficult to program, many experts consider parallel processor systems the key to providing advanced capabilities to future generation of computers.

RISC Processors. Many advanced technical workstations and other computer rely on a processor design called RISC (reduced instruction set computer). This contrasts with most current computers that use CISC (complex instruction set computer) processors. RISC processor designs optimize a CPU's processing speed by using a smaller *instruction set.* That is, they use a smaller number of the *basic machine instructions* that a processor is capable of executing. By keeping the instruction set simpler than CISC processors and using more complex software, a RISC processor can reduce the time needed to execute program instructions. Thus, RISC processors like Digital Equipment's Alpha chop have become popular for computers such as network servers and technical workstations. Apple's Macintosh and PowerBooks and IBM's AS/400 midrange systems use RISC microprocessors like the Power PC, codeveloped by Motorola, Apple, and IBM.

Computer Processing Speeds

How fast are computer systems? Computer operating speeds that were formerly measured in milliseconds (thousands of a second) and **microseconds** (millionths of the second) are now in the **nanosecond** (billionth of a second) range, with **picosecond** (trillionth of a second) speed being attained by some computers. Such speeds seem almost incomprehensible. For example, an average person taking one step each nanosecond would circle the earth about 20 times in one second! Many microcomputers and midrange computers, and most mainframe computers, operate in the nanosecond range, and can thus process program instructions at *million instructions per second* (MIPS) speeds. Another measure of processing speed is *megahertz* (MHz), or millions of cycles per second. It is commonly called the *clock speed* of a microprocessor, since it is used to rate microprocessors by the speed of their timing circuits or internal clock.

However, megahertz rating can be misleading indicators of the effective processing speed of microprocessors as measured in MIPS and other measures. That's because processing speed depends on a variety of factors besides a microprocessor's clock speed. Important examples include the size of circuitry paths, or *buses*, that interconnect microprocessor components, the capacity of instruction processing *registers* the use of high-speed *memory caches* and the use of specialized microprocessors such as a math co-processor to do arithmetic calculations faster. For example, Intel's Pentium microprocessor runs at 66 to 200 MHz and is rated at over 100 MIPS, while the PentiumPro microprocessor has a top processing rating of over 200 MIPS at similar megahertz speeds.

***Note:** Registers* are small high-speed storage circuitry elements in a CPU used to temporarily store parts of an instruction or data element during the execution of an instruction. *Cache memory* is a high-speed temporary storage area in a CPU for storing parts of a program or data for faster access by the CPU during processing.

Processor	Pentium	Pentium	Pentium Pro	Pentium II	Pentium II	Pentium II
Clock Speed	200MHz	200MHz-MMX™	200MHz	233 MHz	266MHz	300MHz
Cache Memory (L2)			256KB	512KB	512KB	512KB
Overall Speed	9.8	14.1	11.8	17.5	19.8	21.7
Video	8.4	11.4	7.4	10.4	11.8	12.9
3D Graphics	13	14.2	16.7	22.4	25.5	27.6
Audio	11.2	22.5	16.6	26.9	30.6	34.2
CD-ROM	5.4	5.4	5.4	5.4	5.4	5.4
Imaging	5.7	28.1	17	41.4	46.1	·50.7

Source: Adapted from Jim Cope, "High-End PCs," PC Today, November 1997.

Figure 7.8. A comparison of the Norton Utilities multimedia performance benchmark scores for several models of Intel Pentium microprocessors. Notice how higher megahertz clock speeds and level 2 (L2) external cache capacities increase the multimedia processing speed of the microprocessors tested, so they can accomplish more multimedia operations in the same amount of time.

SECTION II

Computer Peripherals: Input, Output, and Storage Technologies

Introduction

The right peripherals can make all the difference in your computing experience. A top-quality monitor will be easier on your eyes—and may change the way you work. A scanner can edge you closer to that ever-elusive goal—the paperless office. Backup-storage systems can offer bank-vault security against losing your work. CD-ROM drives can be essential for education and entertainment. Memory cards, 3-D graphics, and other devices will help you configure your computer to meet your needs. Some may be the digital equivalent of chrome bumpers and tailfins, but the right choice of peripherals can make a bug difference [7].

A computer is just a high-powered "processing box" without peripherals. **Peripherals** is the generic name given to all input, output, and secondary storage devices that are part of a computer system. Peripherals depend on direct connections or telecommunications links to the central processing unit of a computer system. Thus, all peripherals are **online** devices; that is, they are separate from, but can be electronically connected to and controlled by, a CPU. (This is the opposite of **offline** devices that are separate from and not under the control of the CPU.) The major types of peripherals and media that can be part of a computer system are discussed in this section.

Peripherals Checklist

- **Monitors.** Bigger is better for computer screens. Consider a 17-inch or one of the new 19-inch monitors. That gives you much more room to display spreadsheets, Web pages, line of text, open windows, etc. The stability and clarity of a monitor's image are important, too. Look for a models with a "refresh rate" of at least 75Hz and a resolution of at least 1024 × 768 pixels.
- **Printers.** Your choice is between laser printers or colour inkjet printers. Lasers are better suited for high-volume business use. Moderately priced colour inkjets provide high-quality images and are well-suited for reproducing photographs. Per-page costs are higher than for laser printers.
- **Scanners.** You'll have to decide between a compact, sheet-fed scanner or a flatbed model. Sheet-fed scanners will save desktop space, while bulkier flat-bed model provide higher speed and resolution. Resolution is a key measure of quality; you'll want at least 300 dpi.
- **Hard Disk Drive.** Bigger is better; as with closer space, you can always use the extra capacity. So go 2 gigabytes at the minimum, 8 to 10 gigabytes at the max.
- **CD-ROM Drives.** Once considered a luxury, the CD-ROM drive is becoming a necessity for software installation and multimedia applications. Consider a high-speed variable-speed model (20X or 24X) for faster, smoother presentations.
- **Backup Systems.** Essential. Don't compute without them. Cassette tape backup is OK, but removable mag disk cartridges (like the Iomega Zip and Jazz drives) are more convenient and versatile, and faster too.

Source: Adapted from "Peripherals," in "Technology Buyer's Guide," *Fortune,* Winter 1997.

Figure 7.9. Some advice about peripherals for a business PC.

Input Technology Trends

Figure 7.12 emphasizes that there has been a major trend toward the increased use of input technologies that provide a more **natural user interface** for computer users. You can now enter data and commands directly and easily into a computer system through pointing devices like electronic mice and touch pads, and technologies like optical scanning, handwriting recognition, and voice recognition. These developments have made it unnecessary to always record data on paper *source documents* (such as sales order forms, for example) and then keyboard the data into a computer in an additional data entry step. Further improvements in voice recognition and other technologies should enables an even more natural user interface in the future.

Pointing Devices

Keyboards are still the most widely used devices for entering data and text into computer systems. However, **pointing devices** are a better alternatives for issuing commands, making choices, and responding to prompt displayed on your video screen. This may be with your operating system's **graphical user interface** (GUI), which presents you with icons, menus, windows, buttons, bars, and so on, for your selection. For example, pointing devices such as electronic mice and touchpads allow you to easily choose from menu selections and icon displays using point-and-click or point-and-drag methods.

The **electronic mouse** is the most popular pointing devices used to move the cursor on the screen, as well as to issue commands and make icon and menu selections. By moving the mouse on a desktop or pad, you can move the cursor onto an icon displayed on the screen. Pressing buttons on the mouse activates various activities represented by the icon selected.

The trackball, pointing stick, and touch pad are other pointing devices most often used in place of the mouse. A **trackball** is a stationary device related to the mouse. You turn a roller ball with only its top exposed outside its case to move the cursor on the screen. A **pointing stick** (also called a *trackpoint*) is a small button like device, sometimes likened to the eraserhead of a pencil. It is usually centered one row above the space bar of a keyboard. The cursor moves in the direction of the pressure you place on the stick. The **touchpad** is a small rectangular touch-sensitive surface usually placed below the keyboard. The cursor moves in the directions your finger move on the pad. Trackballs pointing sticks, and touchpads are easier to use than a mouse for portable computer users and are thus built into most notebook computer keyboards.

	First Generation	Second Generation	Third Generation	Fourth Generation	Fifth Generation?
INPUT MEDIA/ METHOD	Punched Cards Paper Tape	Punched Cards	Key to Tape/Disk	Keyboard Data Entry Pointing Device Optical Scanning	Voice Recognition Touch Devices Handwriting Recognition
TREND: Towards Direct Input Devices that Are More Natural and Easy to Use.					

Figure 7.10. *Input technology trends. Note the trend toward input methods that provide a more natural user interface.*

Touch screens are devices that allow you to use a computer by touching the face of its video display scree. Some touch screens emit a grid of infrared beams, sound waves, or a slight electric current that is broken when the screen is touched. The computer senses the point in the grid where the break occurs and responds with an appropriate actions. For example, you can indicate your selection on a menu display by just touching the screen next to that menu item.

Pen-Based Computing

Handwriting-recognition systems convert script into text quickly and are friendly to shaky hands as well as those of block-printing draftsmen. The pen is more powerful than the keyboard in many vertical markets, as evidenced by the popularity of pen-based devices in the utilities, service, and medical trade [7].

Pen-based computing technologies are being used in many hand-held computers and personal digital assistants. These small PCs and PDAs contain fast processors and software that recognizes and digitizes handwriting, handprinting, and hand drawing. They have a pressure-sensitive layer like a graphics pad under their slatelike liquid crystal display (LCD) screen. So instead of writing on a paper form fastened to a clipboard or using a keyboard device, you can use a pen to make selections, send E-mail, and enter handwritten data directly into a computer.

A variety of other penlike devices are available. One example is the digitizer pen and *graphics tablet.* You can use the digitizer pen as a pointing device, or use it to draw or write on the pressure-sensitive surface of the graphics tablet. Your handwriting or drawing is digitized by the computer, accepted as input, displayed on its video screen, and entered into your application.

Voice Recognition and Response

It's been a staple of science fiction for decades—a space traveler speaks to a computer, and the computer automatically records every word. Thanks to [continuous] speech recognition products, speech recognition is moving from science fiction into an office-usable tool [3].

Voice recognition promises to be the easiest method for data entry, word processing, and conversational computing, since speech is the easiest, most natural means of human communication. Voice input has now become technologically and economically feasible for a variety of applications. Early voice recognition products used *discrete speech recognition*, where you had to pause between each spoken word. New *continuous speech recognition* (CSR) software recognizes continuous, conversationally paced speech.

Voice recognition systems analyze and classify speech or vocal tract patterns and convert them into digital codes for entry into a computer system. Typically, voice recognition systems with large vocabularies require training the computer to recognize your voice in order to achieve a high degree of accuracy. Training such systems involves repeating a variety of words and phrases in a training session and using the system extensively. Trained systems regularly achieve a 95 to 99 percent word recognition rate.

Two examples of continuous speech recognition software for word processing are NaturallySpeaking by Dragon Systems and ViaVoice by IBM. Minimum requirements are a 133 MHz Pentium class microprocessor, 32 MB or RAM, an industry standard sound card, and 50 MB of available hard disk capacity. The products have 30,000-words vocabularies expandable to 60,000 words, and sell for less than $200. Training to 95 percent accuracy takes only a few hours. Longer use, faster processors, and more memory make 99 percent accuracy possible [3].

Speaker-independent voice recognition systems, which allow a computer to understand a few words from a voice it has never heard before, are being built into products and used in a growing number of applications. Examples include *voice-messaging computers,* which use voice recognition and voice response software to verbally guide an end user through the steps of a task in many kinds of activities. Typically, they enable computers to respond to verbal and Touch-Tone input over the telephone. Examples of applications include computerized telephone call switching, telemarketing surveys, bank pay-by-phone bill-paying services, stock quotations services, university registration systems, and customer credit and account balance inquiries.

Voice recognition devices in work situations allow operators to perform data entry without using their hands to key in data or instructions and to provide faster and more accurate input. For example, manufacturers use voice recognition systems for the inspection, inventory, and quality control of a variety of products; and airlines and parcel delivery companies use them for voice-directed sorting of baggage and parcels. Voice recognition can also help you operate your computer's operating systems and software packages through voice input of data and commands. In addition, some Internet browsers can be voice-enabled so you can send E-mail and surf the World Wide Web via voice recognition [13].

Optical Scanning

Few people understand how much scanners can a improve a computer system and make your work easier. Their functions is to get documents into your computer with a minimum of time and hassle, transforming just about anything on paper—a letter, a logo, or a photograph—into the

· *digital format that your PC can make sense of Scanners can be a big help in getting loads of paper off your design and into your PC* [7].

Optical scanning devices read text or graphics and convert them into digital input for your computer. Thus, optical scanning enables the direct entry of data from source documents into a computer system. For example, you can use a compact desktop scanner to scan pages of text and graphics into your computer for desktop publishing and Web publishing applications. Or you can scan documents of all kinds into your system and organise them into folders as part of *document management* library system.

There are many types of optical scanners, but they all employ photoelectric devices to scan the characters being read. Reflected light patterns of the data are converted into electronic impulses that are then accepted as input into the computer system. Compact desktop scanners have become very popular due to their low cost and ease of use with personal computer systems. However, larger, more expensive *flatbed scanners* are faster and provide higher resolution colour scanning.

The credit card billing operations of credit card companies, banks, and oil companies use a form of optical scanning called **optical character recognition** (OCR). OCR scanners read the characters and codes on credit card receipts, utility bills, insurance premiums, airlines tickets, and other documents. OCR scanners are also used to automatically sort mail, score tests, and process a wide variety of forms in business and government.

Devices such as handled optical scanning **wands** are frequently used to read OCR coding on merchandise tags and other media. Many business applications involve reading *bar coding*, a code that utilizes bars to represent characters. One common example is the Universal Product Code (UPC) bar coding that you see on packages of food items and many other products. For example, the automated checkout scanners found in supermarkets read UPC bar coding. Supermarket scanners emit laser beams that are reflected off a UPC bar code. The reflected image is converted to electronic impulses that are sent to the in-store computer, where they are matched with pricing information. Pricing information is returned to the terminal, visually displayed, and printed on a receipt for the customer.

Other Input Technologies

Magnetic stripe technology is a familiar form of data entry that helps computers read credit cards. The dark magnetic stripe on the back of such cards is the same iron oxide coating as on magnetic tape. Customer account numbers can be recorded on the mag stripe so it can be read by bank ATMs, credit card authorization terminals, and many other types of magnetic stripe readers.

Smart cards that embed a microprocessor chip and several kilobytes of memory into debit, credit, and other cards are popular in Europe, and becoming available in the United States. One example is Holland, where over 8 million smart debit cards have been issued by Dutch banks. Smart debit cards enable you to store a cash balance on the card and electronically transfer some of it to others to pay for small items and services. The balance on the card can be replenished in ATMs or other terminals.

The smart debit cards used in Holland feature a microprocessor and either 8 or 16 kilobytes of memory, plus the usual 200 byte magnetic stripe. The smart cards are widely used to make payments in parking meters, vending machines, newsstands, pay telephones, and retail stores[6].

Digital cameras represent another fast growing set of input technologies. Digital still cameras and digital video cameras (digital camcorders) enable you to shoot, store and download still photos or full motion video with audio into your PC. Then you can use image-editing software to edit and enhance the digitized images and include them in newsletter, reports, multimedia presentations, and Web pages [4].

The computer systems of the banking industry can magnetically read checks and deposit slips using **magnetic ink character recognition** (MICR) technology. Computers can thus sort and post checks to the proper checking accounts. Such processing is possible because the identification numbers of the bank and the customer's account are preprinted on the bottom of the checks with an iron oxide-based ink. The first bank receiving a check after it has been written must encode the amount of the check in magnetic ink on the check's lower right-hand corner. The MICR systems uses 14 characters (the 10 decimal digits and 4 special symbols) of a standardized design. Equipment known as *reader-sorters* read a check by first magnetizing the magnetic ink characters and on sensing the signal induced by each character as it passes a reading head. In this way, data are electronically captured by the bank's computer system.

Output Technologies and Trends

Computers provide information to you in a variety of forms. As you can see, video displays and printed documents have been, and still are, the most common forms of output from computer systems. But other natural and attractive output technologies such as **voice response** systems and multimedia outputs are increasingly found along with video displays in business applications.

For example, you have probably experienced the voice and audio output generated by speech and audio microprocessors in a variety of consumer products. Voice messaging software enables PCs and servers in voice mail and messaging systems to interact with you through voice responses. And of course, multimedia output is common on the Web sites of the Internet and corporate intranets.

Video Output

Of all the peripherals you can purchase for your system, a [video] monitor is the one addition that can make the biggest difference. Forget about faster processors, bigger hard drives, and the like. The fact is, the monitor is the part of your system you spend the most time interacting with . . . Invest in a quality monitors, and you'll be thankful every time you turn on your computer [7].

Video display are the most common type of computer output. Most desktop computers rely on **video monitors** that use a *cathode ray tube* (CRT) technology similar to the picture tubes used in home TV sets. Usually, the clarity of the video display depends on the type of video monitor you use and the graphics circuits board installed in your computer. These can provide a variety of graphics modes of increasing capability. A high-resolution, flicker-free monitor is especially important if you spend a lot of time viewing multimedia on CDs, or the Web, or complex graphical displays of many software packages.

The biggest use of **liquid crystal displays** (LCDs) is to provide a visual display capability for portable microcomputers and PDAs. LCD display need significantly less electric current and provide a thin, flat display. Advances in technology such as *active matrix* and *dual scan* capabilities have improved the clarity of LCD displays.

Printed Output

Printing information on paper is still the most common form of output after video displays. Thus, most personal computer systems rely on an inkjet or laser printer to produce permanent (hard copy) output in high-quality printed form. Printed output is still a common form of business communications, and is frequently required for legal documentation. Thus, computers can produce printed reports and correspondence, documents such as sales invoices, payroll checks, bank statements, and printed versions of graphics displays.

	First Generation	Second Generation	Third Generation	Fourth Generation	Fifth Generation?
OUTPUT MEDIA/ METHOD	Punched Cards Printed Reports and Documents	Punched Cards Printed Reports and Documents	Printed Reports and Documents Video Displays	Video Displays Audio Responses Printed Reports and Documents	Video Displays Voice Responses Hyperlinked Multi-media Documents
TREND: Towards Direct Output Methods that Communicate Naturally, Quickly, and Clearly.					

Figure 7.11. Output technology trends. Note the trend from paper documents to more natural forms of video, audio, and multimedia output.

Inkjet printers, which spray ink onto a page one line at a time, have become the most popular, low-cost printers for microcomputers systems. They are quiet, produce several pages per minute of high quality output, and can print both black-and-white and high-quality colour graphics. **Laser printers** use an electrostatic process similar to a photocopying machine to produce many pages per minute of high-quality black-and-white output. More expensive colour laser printers and multifunction inkjet and laser models that print, fax, scan, and copy are other popular choices for business offices.

Storage Trends and Trade-Offs

Data and information must be stored until needed using a variety of storage methods. For example, many people and organisations still rely on paper documents stored in filing cabinets as a major form of storage media. However, you and other computer users more likely to depend on the memory circuits and secondary storage devices of computer systems to meet your storage requirements. Progress in very-large-scale integration (VLSI), which packs millions of memory circuit elements on tiny semiconductor memory chips, are responsible for continuing increases in the main-memory capacity of computers. Secondary storage capacities are also expected to escalate into the billions and trillions of characters, due primarily to the use of optical media.

There are many types of storage media and devices. Figure 7.13 illustrates the speed, capacity, and cost relationships of several alternative primary and secondary storage media. Note the cost/ speed/capacity trade-offs as one moves from semiconductor memories to magnetics media, such as magnetic disks and tapes, to optical disks. High-speed storage media cost more per byte and provide lower capacities. Large-capacity storage media cost less per byte but are slower. This is why we have different kinds of storage media.

Note in Figure 7.13 that semiconductor memories are used mainly for primary storage though they are sometimes used as high-speed secondary storage devices. Magnetic disk and tape optical disk devices, on the other hand, are used as secondary storage devices to greatly enlarge the storage capacity of computer systems. Also, since most primary storage circuits use RAM (random access memory) chips, which lose their contents when electrical power is interrupted, secondary storage devices provide a more permanent type of storage media for storage of data and programs.

	First Generation	Second Generation	Third Generation	Fourth Generation	Fifth Generation?
PRIMARY STORAGE	Magnetic Drum	Magnetic Core	Magnetic Core	LSI Semiconductor Memory	VLSI Semiconductor Memory
TREND: Towards Large Capacities Using Smaller Microelectronic Circuits.					
SECONDARY STORAGE	Magnetic Tape Magnetic Drum	Magnetic Tape Magnetic Disk	Magnetic Disk Magnetic Tape	Magnetic Disk Optical Disk	Optical Disk Magnetic Disk
TREND: Towards Massive Capacities Using Magnetic and Optical Media.					

Figure 7.12. Major trends in primary and secondary storage media.

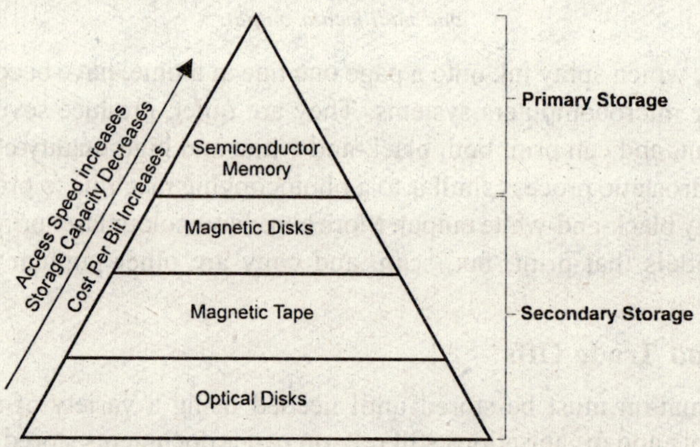

Figure 7.13. Storage media cost, speed, and capacity trade-offs. Note how cost increases with faster access speeds, but decreases with excess capacity.

Computer Storage Fundamentals

Data are processed and stored in a computer system through the presence or absence of electronic or magnetic signals in the computer's circuitry or in the media it uses. This is called a "two-state" or **binary representation** of data, since the computer and the media can exhibit only two possible states or conditions. For example, transistors and other semiconductor circuits are either in a conducting or nonconducting state. Media such as magnetic disks and tapes indicate these two states by having magnetized spots whose magnetic fields have one of two different directions, or polarities. This binary characteristics of computer circuitry and media is what makes the binary number system the basis for representing data in computers. Thus, for electronic circuits, the conducting (ON) state represents the number one, while the nonconducting (OFF) state represents the number zero. For magnetic media, the magnetic field of a magnetized spot in one direction represents a one, while magnetism in the other directions represents a zero.

The smallest element of data is called a **bit,** or binary digit, which can have a value of either zero or one. The capacity of memory chips is usually expressed in terms of bits. A **byte** is a basic grouping of bits that the computer operates as a single unit. Typically, it consists of eight bits and represents one character of data in most computer coding schemes. Thus, the capacity of a computer's memory and secondary storage devices is usually expressed in terms of bytes. Computer codes such as ASCII (American Standard Code and Information Interchange) use various arrangements of bits to form bytes that represent the numbers zero through nine, the letters of the alphabet, and many other characters.

Storage capacities are frequently measured in **kilobytes** (KB), **megabytes** (MB), **gigabytes** (GB), or **terabytes** (TB). Although kilo means 1,000 in the metric system, the computer industry uses K to represent 1,024 (or 2^{10}) storage positions. Therefore, a capacity of 10 megabytes, for example, is really 10,485,760 storage positions, rather than 10 million positions. However, such differences are frequently disregarded in order to simplify description of storage capacity. Thus, a megabyte is roughly 1 million bytes of storage, while a gigabyte is roughly 1 billion bytes and a terabyte represents about 1 trillion bytes.

Character	ASCII Code	Character	ASCII Code
0	00110000	I	01001001
1	00110001	J	01001010
2	00110010	K	01001011
3	00110011	L	01001100
4	00110100	M	01001101
5	00110101	N	01001110
6	00110110	O	01001111
7	00110111	P	01010000
8	00111000	Q	01010001
9	00111001	R	01010010
A	01000001	S	01010011
B	01000010	T	01010100
C	01000011	U	01010101
D	01000100	V	01010110
E	01000101	W	01010111
F	01000110	X	01011000
G	01000111	Y	01011001
H	01001000	Z	01011010

Figure 7.14. *Examples of ASCII computer code.*

Direct and Sequential Access

Primary storage media such as semiconductor memory chips are called **direct access** or random access memories (RAM). Magnetic disk devices are frequently called direct access storage devices (DASDs). On the other hand, media such as magnetic tapes are known as **sequential access** devices.

The term *direct access* describe the same concept. They mean that an element of data or instructions (such as a byte or word) can be directly stored and retrieved by selecting and using any of the locations on the storage media. They also mean that each storage position (1) has a unique address and (2) can be individually accessed in approximately the same length of time without having to search through other storage positions. For example, each memory cell on a microelectronic semiconductor RAM chip can be individually sensed or changed in the same length of time. Also any data record stored on a magnetic or optical disk can be accessed directly in approximately the same time period.

Sequential access storage media such as magnetic tape do not have unique storage addresses that can be directly addressed. Instead, data must be stored and retrieved using a sequential or serial process. Data are recorded one after another in a predetermined sequence (such as in numeric order) on a storage medium. Locating an individual item of data requires searching much of the recorded data on the tape until the desired item is located.

Semiconductor Memory

Memory is the coalman to the CPU's locomotive: For maximum PC performance, it must keep the processor constantly stoked with instructions. Faster CPUs call for larger and faster memories, both in the cache where data and instructions are stored temporarily and in the main memory [7].

The primary storage (main memory) of your computer consists of microelectronic **semiconductor memory** chips. Memory chips with capacities of 4 million bits (4 megabits) and 16 megabits are now common. Plug-in memory circuit boards containing 16 and 32 megabytes or more of memory chips can be added to your PC to increase its memory capacity. Specialized memory can help improve your computer's performance. Examples include external cache memory of 256 or 512 kilobytes to help your microprocessor work faster, or a video graphics accelerator card with 2 megabytes or more of RAM for faster and clearer video performance. Removable credit-card-size and smaller "flash memory" RAM cards can also provide several megabytes of erasable direct access storage for PDAs or handheld PCs.

Some of the major attractions of semiconductor memory are its small size, great speed, and shock and temperature resistance. One major disadvantage of most semiconductor memory is its **volatility**. Uninterrupted electric power must be supplied or the contents of memory will be lost. Therefore, emergency transfer to other devices or standby electrical power (through battery packs or emergency generators) is required if data are to be saved. Another alternative is to permanently "burn in" the contents of semiconductor devices so that they cannot be erased by a loss of power.

Thus, there are two basic types of semiconductor memory: random access memory (RAM) and read only memory (ROM).

- **RAM: random access memory**. These memory chips are the most widely used primary storage medium. Each memory position can be both sensed (read) and changed (written), so it is also called read/write memory. This is volatile memory.
- **ROM: read only memory**. Nonvolatile random access memory chips are used for permanent storage. ROM can be read but not erased or overwritten. Frequently used control instructions in the control unit and programs in primary storage (such as parts of the operating system) can be permanently burned in to the storage cells during manufacture. This is sometimes called firmware. Variations include PROM (programmable read only memory) and EPROM (erasable programmable read only memory) that can be permanently or temporarily programmed after manufacture.

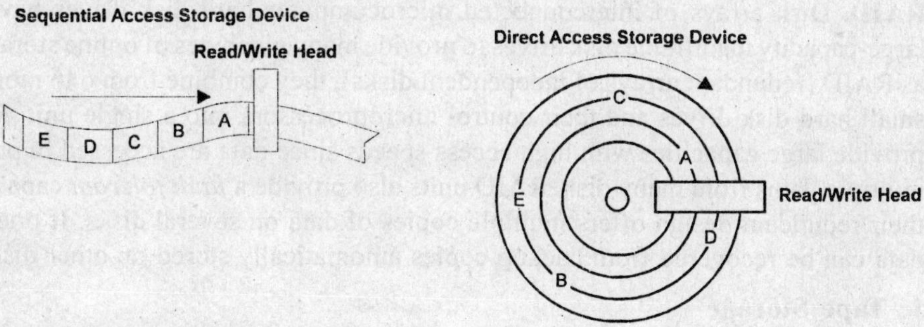

Figure 7.15. *Sequential versus direct access storage. Magnetic tape is a typical sequential access medium. Magnetic disks are typical direct access storage devices.*

Magnetic Disk Storage

Even 2-gigabyte [magnetic disk] drives aren't extravagant, considering that full-motion video files, voice clips, and photo-quality images can consumes colossal amounts of disk space in a blink [7].

Magnetic disks are the most common form of secondary storage for your computer system. That's because they provide fast access and high storage capacities at a reasonable cost. Magnetic disk drives contain metal disks that are coated on both sides with an iron oxide recording material. Several disks are mounted together on a vertical shaft, which typically rotates the disks at speeds of 3,600 to 7,600 revolutions per minute (rpm). Electromagnetic read/write heads are positioned by access arms between the slightly separated disk to read and write data on concentric, circular tracks. Data are recorded on tracks in the form of tiny magnetized spots to form the binary digits of common computer codes. Thousands of bytes can be recorded on each track, and there are several hundred data tracks on each disk surface, thus providing you with billions of storage positions for your software and data.

Types of Magnetic Disks

There are several types of magnetic disk arrangements, including removable disk cartridges as well as fixed disk units. Removable disk devices are popular because they are transportable and can be used to store backup copies of your data offline for convenience and security.

- **Floppy disks**, or magnetic diskettes, consist of polyester film disks covered with an iron oxide compound. A single disk is mounted and rotates freely inside a protective flexible or hard plastic jacket, which has access openings to accommodate the read/write head of a disk drive unit. The 3½-inch floppy disk, with capacities of 1.44 megabytes, is the most widely used version, with a newer LS-120 technology offering 120 megabytes of storage.
- **Hard disk drives** combine magnetic disks, access arms, and read/write heads into a sealed modules. This allows higher speeds, greater data-recording densities, and closer tolerances within a sealed, more stable environment. Fixed or removable disk cartridges versions are available. Capacities of hard drives range from several hundred megabytes to gigabytes of storage.
- **RAID.** Disk arrays of interconnected microcomputer hard disk drives have replaced large-capacity mainframe disk drives to provide many gigabytes of online storage. Known as RAID (redundant arrays of independent disks), they combine from 6 to more than 100 small hard disk drives and their control microprocessors into a single unit. RAID units provide large capacities with high access speeds since data are accessed in parallel over multiple paths from many disk. RAID units also provide a *fault tolerant* capability, since their redundant design offers multiple copies of data on several disks. If one disk fails, data can be recovered from backup copies automatically stored on other disks.

Magnetic Tape Storage

Tape storage is moving beyond backup. Disk subsystems provide the fastest response time for mission-critical data. But the sheer amount of data users need to access these days as part of huge enterprise applications, such as data warehouses, requires affordable [magnetic tape storage] [14].

Magnetic tape is still being used as a secondary storage medium in business applications. The read/write heads of magnetic tape drives record data in the form of magnetized spots on the iron oxide coating of the plastic tape. Magnetic tape devices include tape reels and cartridges in mainframes and midrange systems, and small cassettes or cartridges for PCs. Magnetic tape cartridges have replaced tape reels in many applications, and can hold over 200 megabytes.

One growing business application of magnetic tape involves the use of 36-track magnetic tape cartridges in robotics automated drive assemblies that can hold hundreds of cartridges. These devices serve as slower, but lower cost, storage to supplement magnetic disks to meet massive data warehouse and other business storage requirements. Other major applications for magnetic tape includes long-term *archival* storage and backup storage for PCs and other systems [14].

Optical Disk Storage

CD-ROM technology has become a necessity. Within two years most software companies will stop distribute their elephantine programs on floppies altogether. Many corporations are now rolling their own CDs to distribute product and corporate information that once filled bookshelves [7].

Optical disk are fast-growing storage medium. The version for use with microcomputers is called CD-ROM (compact disk-read only memory). CD-ROM technology uses 12-centimeter (4.7

inch) compact disk (CDs) similar to this used in stereo music systems. Each disk can store more than 600 megabytes. That's the equivalent of over 400 1.44 megabyte floppy disks or more than 300,000 double-spaced pages of text. A laser records data by burning permanent microscopic pits in a spiral track on a master disk from which compact disks can be mass produced. Then CD-ROM disk drives use a laser devices to read the binary codes formed by those pits.

CD-R (compact disk-recordable) is another optical disk technology. It enables computers with CD-R disk drive units to record their own data once on a CD, then be able to read the data indefinitely. The major limitation of CD-ROM and CD-R disks is that recorded data cannot be erased. However, **CD-RW** (CD-rewritable) optical disk systems have now become available which record and erase data by using laser to heat a microscopic point on the disk's surface. In CD-RW versions using a magneto optical technology, a magnetic coil changes the spot's reflective properties from one direction to another, thus recording a binary one or zero. A laser device can then read the binary codes on the disk by sensing the direction of reflected light.

Optical disk capacities and capabilities have increased dramatically with the emergence of an optical disk technology called **DVD** (digital video disk or digital versatile disk), which can hold from 3.0 to 8.5 gigabytes of multimedia data on the each side of a compact disk. The large capacities and high quality images and sound of DVD technology are expected to eventually replace CD-ROM and CD-RW technologies for data storage, and promise to accelerate the use of DVD drives for multimedia products that can be used in both computers and home entertainment systems.

Business Applications

One of the major uses of optical disks in mainframe and midrange systems is in **image processing,** where long-term *archival storage* of historical files of document images must be maintained. Mainframe and midsize computer versions of optical disks use 12-inch plastic disks with capacities of several gigabytes, with up to 20 disks held in *jukebox* drive units. Financial institutions, among others, are using optical scanners to capture digitized document images and store them on WORM (write once, read many) versions of such optical disks as an alternative to microfilm media.

One of the major business uses of CD-ROM disks for personal computers is to provide a publishing medium for fast access to reference materials in a convenient, compact form. This includes catalogs, directories, manuals, periodical abstracts, part listings, and statistical databases of business and economic activity. Interactive multimedia applications in business, education, and entertainment are another major use of CD-ROM disks. The large storage capacities of CD-ROM are a natural choice for computer video games, educational videos, multimedia encyclopedias, and advertising presentations.

Thus, optical disks have become a popular storage medium for image processing and, multimedia business applications, and they appear to be a promising alternative to magnetic disks and tape for very large *mass storage* capabilities for enterprise computing systems. However, rewritable optical technologies are still being perfected. Also, most optical disk devices are significantly slower and more expensive (per byte of storage) than magnetic disk devices. So optical disk systems are not expected to displace magnetic disk technology in the near future for most business applications.

Summary/Conclusion

- **Computer Systems.** Major type and trends in computer systems are summarized in Figures 7.1 and 7.2. A computer is a system of information processing components that perform input, processing, output, storage, and control functions. Its hardware components include input and output devices, a central processing unit (CPU), and primary and secondary storage devices. The major functions and hardware in a computer system are summarized in Figure 7.7.
- **Microcomputer Systems.** Microcomputers are used as personal computers in digital assistants, professional workstations, technical workstations, and network servers. Like most computer systems today, microcomputers are interconnected in a variety of telecommunications networks. This typically includes local area networks, client/server networks, intranets and extranets, the Internet, and other global networks. PCs are also increasingly available with built-in multimedia capabilities that enable them to provide or create video, audio, and other multimedia presentations.
- **Other Computer Systems.** Midrange computers are increasingly used as powerful network servers, and for many multiuser business data processing and scientific applications. Mainframe computers are larger and more powerful than most midsize computers. They are usually faster, have more memory capacity, and can support more input/ouput and secondary storage devices. They are designed to handle the information processing needs of large organisations with many customers and employees, or with complex computational problems supercomputers are a special category of extremely powerful mainframe computer systems designed for massive computational assignments.
- **Peripheral Devices.** Refer to Figures 7.18 and 7.19 for summaries of the functions, characteristics, and capabilities of peripheral devices for input, output, and storage discussed in this chapter.

Peripheral Equipment	Media	Primary Functions	Comments
Video display terminals	None	Keyboard input and video output	Conventional and inexpensive, but limited display capacity and no hard copy
Printers	Paper	Printed output of paper reports and documents	Hard copy, but inconvenient and bulky, many printers are relatively slow
Pointing devices	None	Input by mouse, trackball, pointing stick, touchpad, pen, and touch screen	Input devices are easy to use and inexpensive, but may have limited applications and software
Voice input/ output devices	None	Voice Input and output	Easiest I/O but is slow, has limited vocabulary, and has accuracy problems

Peripheral Equipment	Media	Primary Functions	Comments
Optical scanners	Paper documents	Direct input from written or printed documented	Direct input from paper documents, but some limitations on input format
Magnetic ink character recognition (MICR) readers	MICR paper documents	Direct input of MICR documents	Fast, high-reliability reading, but documents must be preprinted and the character set is limited

Figure 7.16. *A summary of important input/output methods. Note especially the advantages and disadvantages of each method in providing hardware support of the user interface.*

Peripheral Equipment	Media	Primary Functions	Comments
Magnetic disk drive	Hard disk Disk cartridge	Secondary storage (data access) and input/ouput	Large capacity, fast, direct disk access storage device (DASD), low cost/byte
Floppy disk drive	Magnetic diskette	Secondary storage (direct access) and input/output	Small, inexpensive, and convenient, but slower and smaller capacity than hard drives
Magnetic tape drive	Magnetic tape reel and cartridge	Secondary storage (sequential access), input/output, and disk backup	Inexpensive, large capacity, with a fast transfer rate, but only sequential access
Optical disk drive	Optical disk: CD-ROM WORM, CD-R, CD-RW, and DVD	Secondary storage (direct access) and archival storage	Large capacity, high quality storage of data, text, images audio, and video. Primarily a read-only medium

Figure 7.17. *A summary of important computer storage methods. Note the advantages and disadvantages of each method.*

8

Computer Software

Section I

Application Software: End User Applications

- Introduction to Software
- Real World Case: General Motors, Wayne Memorial Hospital, and Others:
- Using Speech Recognition Software
  - *Analyzing General Motors and Others*
  - *Software Trends*
- Application Software for End Users
- Software Suites and Integrated Packages
- Web Browsers and More
- Electronic Mail
- Word Processing and Desktop Publishing
- Electronic Spreadsheets
- Database Management
- Presentation Graphics and Multimedia
  - *Multimedia Technologies*
- Personal Information Managers
- Groupware
- **Real World Case**: Vanguard Cellular, GE Capital, and Others: Application Software for the PalmPilot

Section II

System Software: Computer System Management

- System Software Overview
- Operating Systems
  - *Operating System Functions*

- *Popular Operating Systems*
- Network Management Programs
- Database Management Systems
- Other System Management Programs
- Programming Languages
  - *Machine Languages*
  - *Assembler Languages*
  - *High-Level Languages*
  - *Fourth-Generation Languages*
  - *Object-Oriented Languages*
  - *HTML and Java*
- Programming Packages
  - *Language Translator Programs*
  - *Programming Tools*

Real World Case: Home Depot, Service Merchandise Co., and Time New Media: The Business Benefits of Java

---

SECTION I

Application Software: End User Applications

Introduction to Software

This chapter presents an overview of the major types of software you depend on as you work with computers and access computer networks. It discusses their characteristics and purposes and gives examples of their uses. Before we begin, let's look at an example of one of the newest software technologies in action.

Analyzing General Motors and Others

Read the Real World Case on General Motors, Wayne Memorial Hospital, and others on the next page. We can learn a lot about the benefits and limitations of software used in business from this example.

Continuous speech recognition software such as Naturally Speaking by Dragon Systems and ViaVoice by IBM has finally made it possible to do word processing and other chores by speaking at a natural pace into a microphone attached to your PC. Accuracy is not perfect, and PC hardware requirements are substantial, but these software products are a breakthrough in ease of use for many PC users.

Larry McNally of General Motors is experiencing productivity gains of over 100 percent in word processing with Naturally Speaking. Dr. Gary Flashner of Wayne Memorial Hospitals reports big productivity gains with the macro instructions he has built into ViaVoice. A few word from him are translated into longer, more detailed word processing output by the software. Frank Ricci of Fred Ricci Tool Co. and Dorsey Ruley of Ameritech are PC users with physical challenges who are expecting big production gains when they move from their discrete speech recognition packages to the new continuous speech software. Productivity gains should spread among more PC users as CSR products are built into or bundled with other types of software, including software suites, E-mail packages, and Web browsers.

Let's begin our analysis of software by looking at an overview of the major types and functions of **application software** and **system software** available to computer users, shown in Figure 8.1. This figure summarizes the major categories of system and application software we will discuss in this chapter. Of course, this is a conceptual illustration. The types of software you will encounter depend primarily on the types of computers and networks you use, and on what specific tasks you want to accomplish.

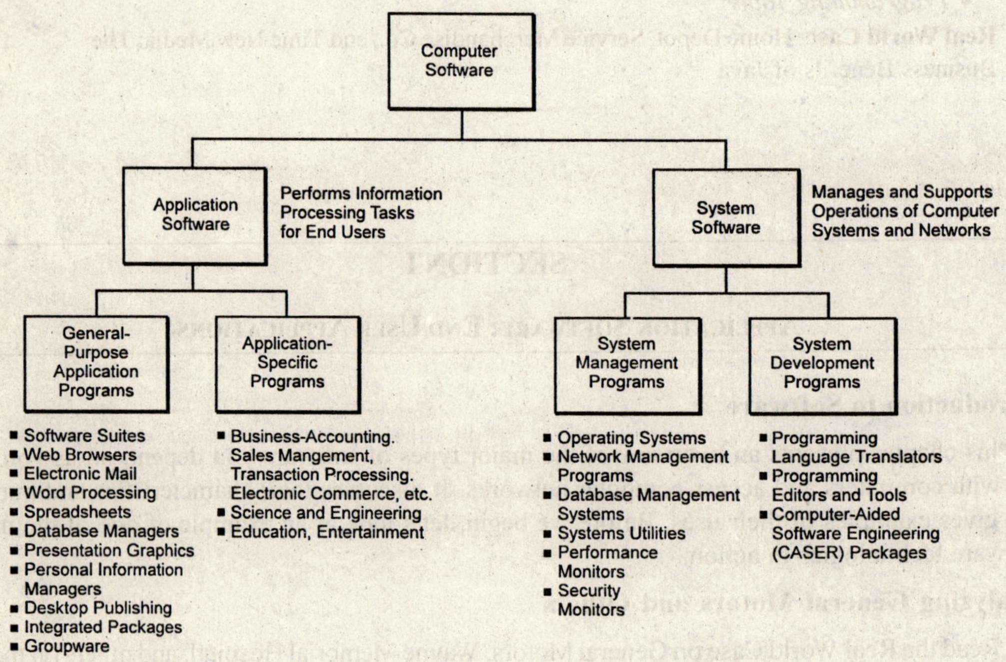

Figure 8.1. An overview of computer software. Note the major types and examples of application and system software.

Software Trends

Figure 8.2 emphasizes several major software trends. First, there has been a major trend away from custom-designed programs developed by the professional programmers of an organisation. Instead, the trend is toward the use of off-the-shelf software packages acquired by end users from software vendors. This trend dramatically increased with the development of relatively inexpensive and easy-to-use application software packages and multipurpose *software suites* for microcomputers.

The trend has accelerated recently, as software packages are designed with networking capabilities and collaboration features that optimize their usefulness for end users and workgroups on the Internet and corporate intranets and extranets.

	FIRST GENERATION	SECOND GENERATION	THIRD GENERATION	FOURTH GENERATION	FIFTH GENERATION?
TREND: Towards Easy-to-Use Multipurpose Network-Enabled Application Packages for Productivity and Collaboration					
Software Trends	User-Written Programs Machine Languages	Packaged Programs Symbolic Languages	Operating System High-Level Languages	Database Management Systems Fourth-Generation Languages Microcomputer Packages	Natural and Object-Oriented Languages Multipurpose Graphic-Interface Network-Enabled Expert-Assisted Packages
TREND: Toward Visual or Conversational Programming languages and Tools					

Figure 8.2. *Trends in computer software. The trend in software is toward multipurpose, network-enabled, expert-assisted packages with natural language and graphical user interfaces.*

Second, their has been a steady trend away from (1) technical, machines-specific programming languages using binary-based or symbolic codes, or (2) *procedural languages,* which use brief statements and mathematical expressions to specify the sequence of instructions a computer must perform. Instead, the trend is toward the use of a visual graphics interface for object-oriented programming, or toward nonprocedural *natural languages* for programming that are closer to human conversation. This trend accelerated with the creation of easy-to-use, nonprocedural *fourth-generation languages* (4GLs). It continues to grow as developments in object technology, graphics, and artificial intelligence produce natural language and graphical user interfaces that make both programming tools and software packages easier to use.

In addition, artificial intelligence features are now being built into a new generation of *expert-assisted* software packages. For example, many software suites provide intelligent help features called *wizards* that help you perform common software functions like graphing parts of a spreadsheet or generating reports from a database. Other software packages use capabilities called *intelligent agents* to perform activities based on instructions from a user. For example, some electronic mail packages can use an intelligent capability to organize, send, and screen E-mail messages for you.

These major trends seem to be converging to produce a fifth generation of powerful, multipurpose, expert-assisted, and network-enabled software packages with natural language and graphical interfaces to support the productivity and collaboration of both end users and IS professional.

Application Software for End Users

Figures 8.1 showed that application software includes a variety of programs that can be subdivided into general-purpose and application-specific categories. Thousands of **application-specific** software packages are available to support specific applications of end users in business and other fields. For example, application-specific packages in business support managerial, professional, and business uses such as transaction processing, decision support, accounting, sales management, investment analysis, and electronic commerce. Application-specific software for science and engineering plays a major role in the research and development programs of industry and the design of efficient production processes for high-quality products. Other software packages help end users with personal finance and home management, or provide a wide variety of entertainment and educational products.

General-purpose application programs are programs that perform common information processing jobs for end users. For example, word processing programs, spreadsheet programs, database management programs, and graphics programs are popular with microcomputer users for home, education, business, scientific, and many other purposes. Because they significantly increase then productivity of end users, they are sometimes known as *productivity packages.* Other examples include Web browsers, electronic mail, and *groupware,* which help support communications and collaboration among workgroups and teams. We will briefly explain some of the most popular types of such packages in this section, and discuss several of them in more detail in later chapters.

Software Suites and Integrated Packages

Let's begin our discussion of popular general-purpose application software by looking at **software suites.** That's because the most widely used productivity packages come bundled together as software suites such as Microsoft Office, Lotus SmartSuite, and Corel WordPerfect Office. Examining their components gives us an overview of the important software tools that you can use to increase your productivity, collaborate with your colleagues, and access intranets, extranets, and the Internet.

Figure 8.3 compares the components programs that make up the top three software suites. Notice that each suite integrates software packages for Web browsing, word processing, spreadsheets, presentation graphics, database management, personal information management, and more. These packages can be purchased as separate stand-alone products. However, a software suite costs a lot less than the total cost of buying its individual packages separately.

Another advantage of software suites us that all programs use a similar **graphical user interface (GUI)** of icons, tool and status bars, menus, and so on, which gives them the same look and feel, and makes them easier to learn and use. Software suites also share common tools, such as spell checkers and help wizards to increase their efficiency. Another big advantage of suits is that their programs are designed to work together seemlessly, and import each other's files easily, no matter which program you are using at the time. These capabilities make them more efficient and easier to use than using a variety of individual package versions.

Of course, putting so many programs and features together in one super-size package does have some disadvantages. Industry critics argue that many software suite features are never used by most end users. The suites take up a lot of disk space, from over 100 megabytes to over 150 megabytes, depending on which version or functions you install. So such software is sometimes derisively called *bloatware* by its critics. The cost of suites can vary from as low as $100 for a competitive upgrade to over $700 for a full version of some editions of the suites.

These drawbacks are one reason for the continued use of **integrated packages** like Microsoft Works, Lotus Works, Claris Works, and so on. Integrated packages combine some of the functions of several programs—word processing, spreadsheets, presentation graphics, database management, and so on—into one software package.

Because Works programs leave out many features and functions that are in individual packages and software suites, they cannot do as much as those packages do. However, they use a lot less disk space (less than 10 megabytes), and cost less than hundred dollars. So integrated packages have proven that they offer enough functions and features for many computer users, while providing some of the advantages of software suites in a smaller package.

Programs	Microsoft Office	Lotus Smartsuite	Corel WordPerfect Office
Web Browser	Internet Explorer	N/A	Netscape Navigator
Word Processor	Word	WordPro	WordPerfect
Spreadsheet	Excel	1-2-3	Quattro Pro
Presentation Graphics	PowerPoint	Freelance	Presentations
Database Manager	Access*	Approach	Paradox
Personal Information Manager	Outlook	Organiser	Corel Central
Others	Commander*	———	CorelDraw**

* Access not included in the Standard editions. Microsoft Publisher, Bookshelf, etc., available depending on the suite edition.

** CorelFlow, TimeLine, Dashboard, etc., available in all versions.

Figure 8.3. The program components of the top three software suites.

Web Browsers and More

The most important software components for many computer uses today is the once simple and limited, but now powerful and feature-rich, **Web browser**. A browser like Netscape Navigator or Microsoft Explorer is the key software interface you use to point and click your way through the hyperlinked resources of the World Wide Web and the rest of the Internet, as well as corporate intranets and extranets. One limited to surfing the Web, browser are becoming the universal software platform on which end users launch into information searches, E-mail, multimedia file transfer, discussion groups, and many other Internet, intranet, and extranets applications.

Industry experts are predicting that the Web browser will be the model for how most people will use networked computers into the next century. So now, whether you want to watch a video, make a phone call, download some software, hold a video conference, check your E-mail, or work on a spreadsheet of your team's business plan, you can use your browser to launch and host such applications. That's why browsers are being called the *universal client*, that is, the software component installed on the workstations of all the clients (users) in client/server networks throughout an enterprise.

The web browser has also become only one components of a new suite of communications and collaborations. Figure 8.4 is a summary of the software components in Netscape Communicator, a suite of software tools that includes the Navigator/Web browser, Messenger for E-mail, Conference for audio and data conferencing, Calendar for scheduling and calendaring, Netcaster for receiving Web broadcasts, Composer for Web page creation and publishing, and Collabra groupware for creating and managing discussion groups and their databases on intranets and extranets.

Electronic Mail

The first thing many people do at work all over the world is check their E-mail. **Electronic** mail has changed the way people work and communicate. Millions of ends users now depend on E-mail software to communicate with each other by sending and receiving electronic messages via the Internet or their organisation's intranets or extranets. E-mail is stored on network servers until you are ready. Whenever you want to you can read your E-mail by displaying it on your workstations. So, with only a few minutes of effort (and a few microseconds or minutes of transmission time), a message to one or many individuals can be composed, sent, and received.

Navigator	Messenger	Collabra	Conference	Calendar	Composer	Netcaster
Web browser	E-mail	Discussion forums and databases	Audio and conferencing, chat, and Internet telephone	Group scheduling and calendaring	Web page editor	Net broadcaster via push channels

Figure 8.4. Components of the Netscape communicator suite of communications and collaboration software.

As we mentioned earlier, E-mail software is now a component of top software suites and some Web browsers. E-mail package like Eudora and Pine are typically provided to Internet users by Internet service providers and educational institutions. Full-featured E-mail software like Microsoft Exchange E-mail or Netscape Messenger can route messages to multiple end users based on predefined mailing lists and provide password security, automatic message forwarding, and remote user access. They also allow you to store messages in folders with provisions for adding attachments to message files. E-mail packages may also enable you to edit and send graphics and multimedia as well as text, and provide bulletin board and computer conferencing capabilities. Finally, your E-mail software may automatically filter and sort incoming messages (even news items from online services) and route them to appropriate user mailboxes and folders.

Word Processing and Desktop Publishing

Software for **word processing** has transformed the process of writing. Word processing packages computerize the creation, editing, revision, and printing of *documents* (such as letter, memos, and reports) by electronically processing your *text data* (word, phrase, sentences, and paragraphs). Top words processing packages like Microsoft Word, Lotus WordPro, and Corel WordPerfect can provide a wide variety of attractively printed documents with their desktop publishing capabilities. These packages can also convert all documents to HTML formats for publication as Web pages on corporate intranets or the World Wide Web.

Word processing packages also provide advanced features. For example, a spelling checker capability can identify and correct spelling errors, and a thesaurus feature helps you to find a better choice of words to express ideas. Or you can identify and correct grammar and punctuation errors, as well as suggest possible improvements in your writing style, with grammar and style checker functions. Another text productivity tool is an idea processor or outline function. It helps you organise and outline your thoughts before you prepare a document or develop a presentation. Besides converting documents to HTML format, you can also use the top packages to design and create Web pages from scratch for an Internet Web site.

End user and organisations can use **desktop publishing** (DTP) software to produce their own printed material that look professionally published. That is, they can design and print their own newsletters, brochures, manuals, and books with several type styles, graphic, photos, and colour on each page. Word processing packages and desktop publishing packages like Adobe PageMaker and QuarkXPress are used to do desktop publishing. Typically, text material and graphics can be generated by word processing and graphics packages and imported as text and graphics files. Optical scanners may be used to input text and graphics from printed material. You can also use files of **clip art**, which are predrawn graphic illustrations provided by the software package or available from other sources.

The heart of desktop publishing is a page design process called *page makeup* or *page composition.* Your video screen becomes an electronic pasteup board with rulers, column guides, and other page design aids. Text material and illustrations are then merged into the page format you design. The software will automatically move excess text to another column or page and help size and place illustrations and headings. Most DTP packages provide WYSIWYG (What You See Is What You Get) displays so you can see exactly what the finished document will look like before it is printed.

Electronic Spreadsheets

Electronic spreadsheet packages like Lotus 1-2-3, Microsoft Excel, and Corel QuattroPro are used for business analysis, planning, and modeling. They help you develop an *electronic spreadsheet*, which is a worksheet of rows and columns that can be stored on your PC or an network server, or converted to HTML format and stored as a Web page or *websheet* on the World Wide Web. Developing a spreadsheet involves designing its format and developing the relationships (formulas) that will be used in the worksheet. In response to your input, the computer performs necessary calculations based on the relationships (formulas) you defined in the spreadsheet, and displays results immediately, whether at your workstation or Web site. Most packages also help you develop graphics display of spreadsheet results.

For example, you could develop a spreadsheet to record and analyse past and present advertising performance for a business. You could also develop hyperlinks to a similar websheet at your marketing team's intranet Web site. Now you have a decision support tool to help you answer *what-if questions* you may have about advertising. For example, "What would happen to market share if advertising expense increased by 10 percent?" To answer this question, you would simply change the advertising expense formula on the advertising performance worksheet you developed. The computer would recalculate the affected figures, producing new market share figures and graphics. You would then have a better insight on the effect of advertising decisions on market share. Then you could share this insight with a note on the worksheet at your team's intranet Web site.

Database Management

Microcomputer versions of database management programs have become so popular that they are now viewed as general-purpose application software packages like word processing and spreadsheet packages. Database management packages such as Microsoft Access, Lotus Approach, or Corel Paradox allow you to set up and manage databases on your PC, network server, or the World Wide Web. Most database managers can perform four primary tasks, which we will discuss further.

- **Database development.** Define and organise the content, relationships, and structure of the data needed to build a database, including any hyperlinks to data on Web pages.
- **Database interrogation.** Access the data in a database to display information in a variety of formats. End users can selectively retrieve and display information and produce forms, reports, and other documents, including Web pages.
- **Database maintenance.** Add, delete, update, and correct the data in database, including hyperlinked data on Web pages.
- **Application development.** Develop prototypes of Web pages, queries, forms, reports, and labels for a proposed business application. Or use a built-in 4GL or application generator to program the application.

Presentation Graphics and Multimedia

Which type of display would you rather see: columns or rows of numbers, or a graphics display of the same information? **Presentation graphics** packages help you convert numeric data into graphics displays such as line charts, bar graphs, pie charts, and many other types of graphics. Most of the top packages also helps you prepare **multimedia presentations** of graphics, photos, animation, and video clips, including publishing to the World Wide Web. Not only are graphics and multimedia displays easier to comprehend and communicate than numeric data but multiple-colour and multiple-media displays also can more easily emphasizes key points, strategic differences, and important trends in the data. Presentations graphics has proved to be much more effective than tabular presentations of numeric data for reporting and communicating in advertising media, management reports, or other business presentations.

Presentation graphics software packages like Microsoft PowerPoint, Lotus Freelance, or Corel Presentations gives you many easy-to-use capabilities that encourage the use of graphics presentations. For example, most packages help you design and manage computer-generated and -orchestrated *slide shows* containing many integrated graphics and multimedia displays. Or you can select from a variety of predesigned *templates* of business presentations, prepare and edit the outline and notes for a presentation, and manage the use of multimedia files of graphics, photos, sounds, and video clips. And of course, the top packages helps you tailor your graphics and multimedia presentation for transfer in HTML format to Web sites on corporate intranets or the World Wide Web.

Multimedia Technologies

Hypertext and hypermedia are foundation technologies for multimedia presentations. By definition hypertext contains only text and a limited amount of graphics. Hypermedia are electronic documents that contain multiple forms of media, including text, graphics, video, and so on. Key terms and topics in hypertext or hypermedia documents are indexed by software links so that they can be quickly searched by the reader. For example, if you click your mouse button on an underlined term on a hypermedia document displayed on your on your computer video screen, the computer instantly brings up a display of a passage of text and graphics related to that term. Once you finish viewing that pop-up display, you can return to what you were reading originally, or jump to another part of the document.

Hypertext and hypermedia are developed using specialized programming languages like Java and the Hypertext Markup Language (HTML), which create Hyperlinks to other parts of the documents, or to the documents and media. Hypertext and hypermedia documents can thus be programmed to let a reader navigate through a multimedia database by following a chain of hyperlinks through various documents. The Web sites on the World Wide Web of the Internet are a popular example of this technology. Thus, the use of hypertext and hypermedia provides an environment for online interactive presentations of multimedia.

- **Authoring language.** A high-level computer programming facility with English language commands specifically designed to implement multimedia applications.
- **Computer Edit System.** A video editing system controlled by a computer and interfaced to several playback and record machines. This type of system is capable of making precise frame-accurate edits.
- **Digital Video Interactive.** This technology compresses video images and can produce animated scenes at over 60 frames per second. Current compression ratios exceed 400 to 1.
- **Interactive Video.** Gives a user control over co-ordinated video program and computer program through the user's actions, choices, and decisions, which affect how the program unfolds.
- **Musical Instrument Digital Interface.** A serial data transmission protocol for transporting musical information between compatible electronic musical devices.
- **Sound Board.** An add-in card with software that captures and plays back sound or music.
- **Storyboard:**
  1. A visualization of the order of a production, using representative frames from each shot or sequence to show a visual skeleton of the production.
  2. Documentation for video production that contains the audio script and a complete description of the visual content often in the form of pictures or sketches.
- **Video Capture Card.** An add-in card that digitizes analog video from a VCR, video camera, or still-image camera. Video can be digitized as a single frame or multiple frames per second to produce full-motion video.

Figure 8.5. Technologies for multimedia productions and presentations.

Multimedia technologies allow end users to digitally capture, edit, and combine video with text, picture, and sound into multimedia business and educational presentations. For example, an interactive video session for training airline flight attendants can be produced on CD-ROM disks. It can combine animated graphics displays of different airplane configurations, presentations graphics of airline statistics, lists of major topics and facts, video clips of flight attendants working on various airplanes, and various announcements and sounds helpful in managing emergencies. Figure 8.5 summarizes many of the technologies that are used to create multimedia presentations.

Personal Information Managers

The **personal information manager (PIM)** is a popular software package for end user productivity and collaboration. PIMs such as Lotus Organiser, Sidekick by Starfish Software, and Microsoft Outlook help end users store, organise, and retrieve information about customers, clients, and prospects, or schedule and manage appointments, meetings, and tasks. The PIM package will organise data you enter and retrieve information in a variety of forms, depending on the style and structure of the PIM and the information you want. For example, information can be retrieved as an electronic calendar or list of appointments, meetings, or other things to do; the timetable for a project; or a display of key facts and financial data about customers, clients, or sales prospects.

Personal information managers are sold as independent programs or are included in software suites, and vary widely in their style, structure, and features. For example, Lotus Organisers uses a notebook with tabs format, while Microsoft Outlook organises data about people as a continuous A-to-Z list. Most PIMs emphasize the maintenance of *contact lists,* that is, customers, clients, or prospects. Scheduling appointments and meetings and task management are other top PIM applications. PIMs are now changing to include the ability to access the World Wide Web as Sidekick does, or provide E-mail capability, as in Microsoft Outlook. Also, some PIMs use Internet and E-mail features to support team collaborations by sharing information such as contact lists, task lists, and schedules with other networked PIM users.

Groupware

Groupware is *collaboration software,* that is, software that helps workgroups and teams work together to accomplish group assignments. Groupware is fast-growing category of general-purpose application software that combines a variety of software features and functions to facilitate collaboration. For example, groupware products like Lotus Notes, Novell GroupWise, Microsoft Exchange, and Netscape Communicator and Collabra support collaboration through electronic mail, discussion groups and databases, scheduling, task management, data, audio and video conferencing, and so on.

Groupware products are changing in several ways to meet the demand for better tools for collaboration. Groupware is now designed to use the Internet and corporate intranet and extranets to make collaboration possible on a global scale by *virtual teams* located anywhere in the world. For example, team members might use the Internet for global E-mail, project discussion forums, and joint Web page development. Or they might use corporate intranets to publish projects news and progress reports, and work jointly on documents stored on Web servers. Collaborative capabilities are also being added to other software to give them groupware features. For example, in the Microsoft Office software suite, Microsoft Word keeps track of who made revisions to each document. Excel tracks all changes made to a spreadsheet, and Outlook lets you keep track of tasks you delegate to other team members.

SECTION II

SYSTEM SOFTWARE: COMPUTER SYSTEM MANAGEMENT

System Software Overview

System software consists of programs that manage and support a computer system and its information processing activities. These programs serve as a *vital software interface* between computer system hardware and the application programs of end users. See Figure 8.6. Note that we can group such programs into two major categories:

- **System management programs.** Programs that manage the hardware, software, network, and data resources of the computer system during its execution of the various information processing jobs of users. Examples of important system management programs are operating systems, network management programs, database management systems, and system utilities.
- **System development programs.** Programs that help users develop information system programs and procedures and prepare user programs for computer processing. Major development programs are programming language translators and editors, other programming tools, and CASE (computer-aided software engineering) packages.

Operating Systems

The most important system software package for any computer is its operating system. An operating system is an integrated system of programs that manages the operations of the CPU, controls the input/output and storage resources and activities of the computer system, and provides various support services as the computer executes the application programs of users.

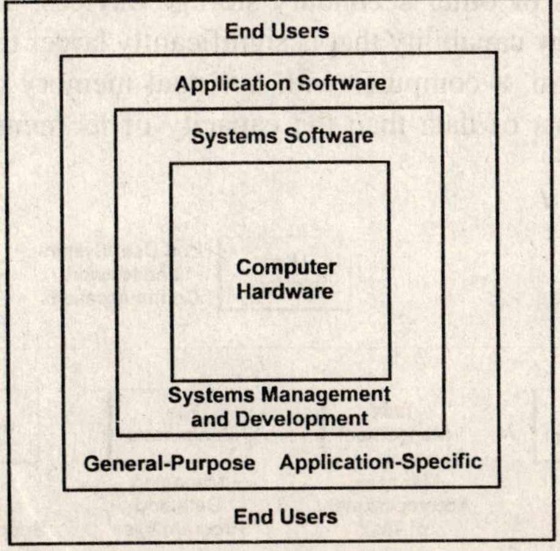

Figure 8.6. The system and application software interface between end users and computer hardware.

The primary purpose of an operating system is to maximize the productivity of a computer system by operating it in the most efficient manner. An operating system minimizes the amount of human intervention required during processing. It helps your application programs perform common operations such as accessing a network, entering data, saving and retrieving files, and printing or displaying output. If you have any hands-on experience on a computer, you know that the operating system must be loaded and activated before you can accomplish other tasks. This emphasizes the fact that operating systems are the most indispensable component of the software interface between users and the hardware of their computer systems.

Operating System Functions

An operating system performs five basic functions in the operations of a computer system: providing a user interface, resource management, task management, file management, and utilities and support services.

The User Interface. The **user interface** is the part of the operating system that allows you to communicate with it so you can load programs, access files, and accomplish other tasks. Three main types of user interfaces are the *command-driven, menu-driven,* and *graphical user interfaces.* The trend in user interfaces for operating systems and other software is moving away from the entry of brief end user commands, or even the selection of choices from menus of options. Instead, the trend is toward an easy-to-use **graphical user interface** (GUI) that uses icons, bars, buttons, boxes, and other images. GUIs rely on pointing devices like the electronic mouse or trackball to make selections that help you get things done.

Resource Management. An operating system uses a variety of resource management programs to manage the hardware and networking resources of a computer system, including its CPU, memory, secondary storage devices, telecommunications processors, and input/output peripherals. For example, memory management programs keep track of where data and programs are stored. They may also subdivide memory into a number of sections and swap parts of programs and data between memory and magnetic desks or other secondary storage devices. This can provide a computer system with a **virtual memory** capability that is significantly larger than the real memory capacity of its primary storage unit. So, a computer with a virtual memory capability can process larger programs and greater amounts of data than the capacity of its memory circuits would normally allow.

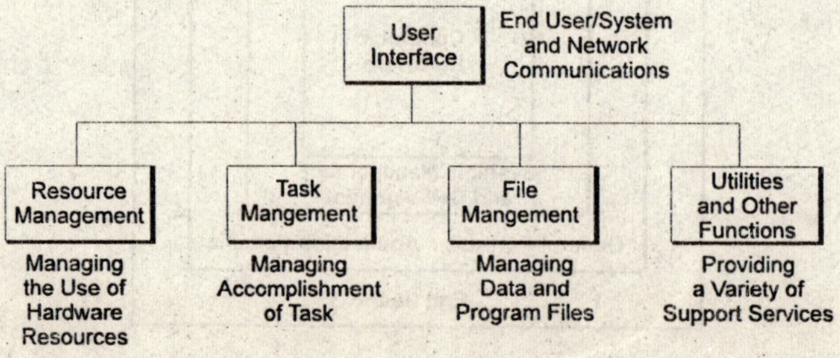

***Figure 8.7.** The basic functions of an operating system include a user interface, resources management, task management, file management, and utilities and other functions.*

File Management. An operating system contains file management programs that control the creation, deletion, and access of files of data and programs. File management also involves keeping track of the physical location of files on magnetic disks and other secondary storage devices. So operating systems maintain directories of information about the location and characteristics of files stored on a computer system's secondary storage devices.

Task Management. The task management programs of an operating system manage the accomplishment of the computing tasks of end users. They give each task a slice of a CPU's time and interrupt the CPU operations to substitute other tasks. Tasks management may involve a **multitasking** capability where several computing tasks can occur at the same time. Multitasking may take the form of *multiprogramming,* where the CPU can process the tasks of several programs at the same time, or *timesharing,* where the computing tasks of several users can be processed at the same time . The efficiency of multitasking operations depends on the processing power of a CPU and the virtual memory and multitasking capabilities of the operating system it uses.

New microcomputer operating systems and most midrange and mainframe operating systems provide a multitasking capability. With multitasking, end users can do two or more operations (e.g., keyboarding and printing) or applications (e.g., word processing and financial analysis) concurrently, that is, at the same time. Multitasking on microcomputers has also been made possible by the development of more powerful microprocessors (like the Intel Pentium II) and their ability to directly address much larger memory capacities (up to 4 gigabytes). This allows an operating system to subdivide primary storage into several large partitions, each of which can be used by a different application program.

In effect, a single computer can act as if it were several computers, or *virtual machines*, since each application program is running independently at the same time. The number of programs that can be run concurrently depends on the amount of memory that is available and the amount of processing each job demands. That's because a microprocessor (or CPU) can become overloaded with too many jobs and provide unacceptably slow response times. However, if memory and processing capacities are adequate, multitasking allows end users to easily switch from one application to another, share data files among applications, and process some applications in a *background* mode. Typically, background tasks include large printing jobs, extensive mathematical computation, or unattended telecommunications sessions.

Popular Operating Systems

MS-DOS (Microsoft Disk Operating System), along with the Windows operating environment, has been the most widely used microcomputer operating system. It is a single-user, single-tasking operating system, but was given a graphical user interface and limited multitasking capabilities by combining it with Microsoft Windows. Microsoft began replacing its DOS/Windows combination in 1995 with the **Windows 95** operating system. Windows 95 is an advanced operating system featuring a graphical user interface, true multitasking, networking multimedia, and many other capabilities. Microsoft plans to ship a Windows 98 version during 1998.

Microsoft introduced another operating system, **Windows NT** (New Technology), in 1995. Windows NT is a powerful, multitasking, multiuser operating system that is being installed on network serves to manage local area networks and on desktop PCs with high-performance computing requirements. New Server and Workstation versions were introduced in 1997. Some industry experts are predicting that Windows NT Workstation will supplant Windows 95 and 98 in a few years.

OS/2 (Operating System/2) is a microcomputer operating system from IBM. Its latest version, **OS/2 Warp 4**, was introduced in 1996 and provides a graphical user interface, voice recognition, multitasking, virtual memory, telecommunications, and may other capabilities. A version for network servers, OS/2 Warp Server, is also available. Originally developed by AT&T, UNIX now is also offered by other vendors, including Solaris by Sun Microsystems and AIX by IBM. UNIX is a multitasking, multiuser, network-managing operating system whose portability allows it to run on mainframes, midrange computers, and microcomputers. UNIX is a popular choice for network servers in many client/server computing networks. The **Macintosh Systems** is an operating system from Apple for Macintosh microcomputers. Now in versions 8.0, the system has a popular graphical user interface as well as multitasking and virtual memory capabilities.

Operating System	MS-DOS	OS/2 Warp 4	Windows 98	Macintosh System 8.0	Windows NT	UNIX
Developer	Microsoft	IBM	Microsoft	Apple	Microsoft	AT&T, Sun, IBM, etc.
Primary Market	PCs	PCs Servers	PCs	Macintoshes	Servers PCs	Workstations Servers Midrange Mainframes
Primary Micro-processors	Intel	Intel Power PC	Intel	Motorola Power PC	Intel Alpha	Many
GUI		X	X	X	X	X
Single User	X	X	X	X	X	
Multitasking		X	X	X	X	X
Virtual Memory		X	X	X	X	X
Networking		X	X	X	X	X
Multiuser		X			X	X
Network Management		X			X	X

Figure 8.8. A comparison of popular operating systems.

Network Management Programs

Today's information systems rely heavily on the Internet, intranets, extranets, local area networks, and other telecommunications networks to interconnect end user workstations, network servers, and other computer systems. This requires a variety of system software for **network management,** including **network operating systems,** network performance monitors, telecommunications monitors, and so on. These programs are used by network servers and other computers in a network to manage network performance. Network management programs perform such functions as automatically checking client PCs and video terminals for input/output activity, assigning priorities to data communications requests from clients and terminals, and detecting and correcting transmission errors and other network problems. In addition, some network management programs functions as *middleware* to help diverse networks communicate with each other.

Examples of network management programs include Novell NetWare, the most widely used network operating system for complex interconnected local area networks. Microsoft's Windows NT Server and IBM's OS/2 Warp Server are two other popular network operating systems. IBM's telecommunications monitor CICS (Customer Identification Operating System) is an example of a widely used *telecommunications monitor* for mainframe-based wide area networks. IBM's NetView and Hewlett-Packard's OpenView are examples of network management programs for managing several mainframe-based or midrange-based computer networks.

Database Management Systems

In Section I, we discussed microcomputer database management programs like Microsoft Access, Lotus Approach, or Corel Paradox. In mainframe and midrange computer systems, a **database management system** (DBMS) is considered an important system software package that controls the development, use, and maintenance of the databases of computer-using organisations. A DBMS program helps organisations use their integrated collections of data records and files known as databases. It allows different user application programs to easily access the same database. For example, a DBMS makes it easy for a employee database to be accessed by payroll, employee benefits, and other human resources programs. A DBMS also simplifies the process of retrieving information from databases in the form of displays and reports. Instead of having to write computer programs to extract information, end users can ask simple questions in a *query language.* Thus, many DBMS packages provide *fourth-generation language* (4GLs) and other application development features. Examples of popular mainframe and midrange packages are DB2 by IBM and Oracle 8 by Oracle Corporation.

Other System Management Programs

Several other types of system management software are marked as separate programs or are included as part of an operating system. Utility programs, or **utilities**, are an important example. Programs like Norton Utilities perform miscellaneous housekeeping and file conversion functions. Examples include data backup, data recovery, virus protection, data compression, and file defragmentation. Most operating systems also provide many utilities that perform a variety of helpful chores for computer users.

Other examples of system support programs include performance monitors and security monitors. **Performance monitors** are programs that monitors and adjust the performance and usage of one or more computer systems to keep them running efficiently. **Security monitors** are packages that monitors and control the use of computer systems and provide warning messages and record evidence of unauthorized use of computer resources. A recent trend is to merge both types of programs into operating systems like Microsoft's Windows NT Server, or into system management software like Computer Associates' CA-Unicenter, that can manage both mainframe systems and servers in a data centre.

Programming Language

To understand computer software, you need a basic knowledge of the role that programming languages play in the development of computer programs. A **programming language** allows a programmer to develop the sets of instructions that constitute a computer program. Many different programming languages have been developed, each with its own unique vocabulary, grammar, and uses.

Machine Languages

Machine languages (or *first-generation language*) are the most basic level of programming languages. In the early stages of computer development, all program instructions had to be written using binary codes unique to each computer. This type of programming involves the difficult task of writing instructions in the form of strings of binary digits (ones and zeros) or other number systems. Programmers must have a detailed knowledge of the internal operations of the specific type of CPU they are using. They must write long series of detailed instructions to accomplish even simple processing tasks. Programming in machine language requires specifying the storage locations for every instruction and item of data used. Instructions must be included for every switch and indicator used by the programs. These requirements make machine language programming a difficult and error-prone task. A machine language program to add two numbers together in the CPU of a specific computer and store the result.

Assembler Languages

Assembler languages (or *second-generation languages*) are the next level of programming languages. They were developed to reduce the difficulties in writing machine language programs. The use of assembler language requires language translator programs called *assemblers* that allow a computer to convert the instructions of such languages into machines instructions. Assembler languages are frequently called symbolic languages because symbols are used to represent operation codes and storage locations. Convenient alphabetic abbreviations called mnemonics (memory aids) and other symbols represent operation codes, storage locations, and data elements. For example, the computation X = Y + Z in an assembler language might take the form shown in Figure 8.9.

• **Machine Languages:** Use binary coded instructions 1010 11001 1011 11010 1100 11011	• **High-Level Languages:** Use brief statements or arithmetic notations BASIC; X = Y + Z COBOL: COMPUTE X = Y + Z
• **Assembler Languages:** Use symbolic coded instructions LOD Y ADD Z STR X	• **Fourth-Generation Languages:** Use natural and nonprocedural statements SUM THE FOLLOWING NUMBERS

Figure 8.9. *Examples of four levels of programming languages. These programming language instructions might be used to compute the sum of two numbers as expressed by the formula X = Y + Z.*

Advantages and Disadvantages. An assembler language use alphabetic abbreviations that are easier to remember in place of the actual numeric addresses of the data. This greatly simplifies programming, since the programmer does not need to know the exact storage locations of data and instructions. However, assembler language is still machine oriented, because assembler language instructions correspond closely to the machine language instructions of the particular computer model being used. Also, note that each assembler instruction corresponds to a single machine instruction, and that the same number of instructions are required in both illustrations.

Assembler languages are still widely used as a method of programming a computer in a machine-oriented language. Most computer manufacturers provide an assembler language that reflects the unique machine language instruction set of a particular line of computers. This feature is particularly desirable to system programmers, who program system software (as opposed to application programmers, who program application software), since it provides them with greater control and flexibility in designing a program for a particular computer. They can then produce more efficient software, that is, programs that require a minimum of instructions, storage, and CPU time to perform a specific processing assignment.

High-level Languages

High-level languages (or *third-generation languages)* use instructions, which are called *statements*, that use brief statements or arithmetic expressions. Individual high-level language statements are actually *macroinstructions*; that is, each individual statement generates several machine instructions when translated into machine language by high-level language translator programs called *compilers* or *interpreters.* High-level language statements resemble the phrases or mathematical expressions required to express the problem or procedure being programmed. The *syntax* (vocabulary, punctuation, and grammatical rules) and the *semantics* (meanings) of such statements do not reflect the internal code of any particular computer. For example, the computation X = Y + Z would be programmed in the high-level languages of BASIC and COBOL.

Ada: Named after Augusta Ada Byron, considered the world's first computer programmer. Developed for the U.S. Department of Defense as a standard "high-order language" to replace COBOL and FORTRAN.

BASIC: (Beginner's All-Purpose Symbolic Instruction Code). A simple procedure-oriented language designed for end user programming.

C: A mid-level structured language developed as part of the UNIX operating system. It resembles a machine-independent assembler language.

COBOL: (Common Business Oriented Language). An Englishlike language widely used for programming business applications.

FORTRAN: (FORmula TRANslation). A high-level language designed for scientific and engineering applications.

Pascal: Named after Blaise Pascal Developed specifically to incorporate structure programming concepts.

Figure 8.10. Highlights of several important high-level languages.

Advantages and Disadvantages: A high level language is obviously easier to learn and understand than an assembler language. Also, high-level languages have less-rigid rules, forms, and syntaxes, so the potential for error is reduced. However, high-level language programs are usually less efficient than assembler language programs and require a greater amount of computer time for translation into machine instructions. Since most high-level languages are machine independent, programs written in a high-level language do not have to be reprogrammed when a new computer is installed, and computer programmers do not have to learn a new language for each computer they program.

Fourth Generation Languages

The term **fourth-generation language** describes a variety of programming languages that are more nonprocedural and conversational than prior languages. These languages are called fourth-generation languages (4GLs) to differentiate them from machine languages (first generation), assembler languages (second generation), and high-level languages (third generation).

Most fourth-generation languages are **nonprocedural languages** that encourage users and programmers to specify the results they want, while the computer determines the sequence of instructions that will accomplish those results. Users and programmers no longer have to spend a lot of time developing the sequence of instructions the computer must follow to achieve a result. Thus, fourth-generation languages have helped simplify the programming process. **Natural languages** are 4GLs that are very close to English or other human languages. Research and development activity in artificial intelligence (AI) is developing programing languages that are easy to use as ordinary conversation in one's native tongue. For example, INTELLECT, a natural language 4GL, would use a statement like, "What are the average exam scores in MIS 200?" to program a simple average exam score task.

Advantages and Disadvantages. There are major differences in the ease of use and technical sophistication of 4GL products. For instance, INTELLECT and English Wizard are examples of natural query languages that impose no rigid grammatical rules, while a query language like SQL requires concise structured statements. However, the ease of use of 4GLs is gained at the expense of some loss in flexibility. It is frequently difficult for an end user to override some of the prespecified formats or procedures of 4GLs. Also, the machine language code generated by a program developed by a 4GL is frequently much less efficient (in terms of processing speed and amount of storage capacity needed) than a program written in a language like COBOL. Major failures have occurred in some large transaction processing applications programmed in a 4GL. These applications were unable to provide reasonable response times when faced with a large amount of realtime transaction processing and end user inquiries. However, 4GLs have shown great success in business applications that do not have a high volume of transaction processing.

Object-Oriented Languages

Object-oriented programming (OOP) languages have been around since Xerox developed Smalltalk in the 1960s. However, object-oriented languages like Visual Basic, C++, and Java have become major tools of software development. Briefly, while most other programming languages separate data elements from the procedures or actions that will be performed upon them, OOP languages tie them together into **objects**. Thus, an object consists of data and the actions that can be performed on the data. For example, an object could be set of data about a bank customer's savings account, and the operations (such as interest calculations) that might be performed upon the data. Or an object could be data in graphic form such as a video display window, plus the display actions that might be used upon it.

In procedural languages, a program consists of procedures to perform actions on each data elements. However, in object-oriented systems, objects tell other objects to perform actions on themselves. For example, to open a window on a computer video display, a beginning menu object could send a window object a message to open and a window will appear on the screen. That's because the window object contains the program code for opening itself.

Object-oriented languages are easier to use and more efficient for programming the graphics-oriented user interface required by many applications. Also, once objects are programmed, they are reusable. Therefore, reusability of objects is a major benefits of object-oriented programming. For example, programmers can construct a user interface for a new program by assembling standard objects such as windows, bars, boxes, buttons, and icons. Therefore, most object-oriented programming packages provide a GUI that supports a "point and click," "drag and drop" visual assembly of objects known as *visual programming.*

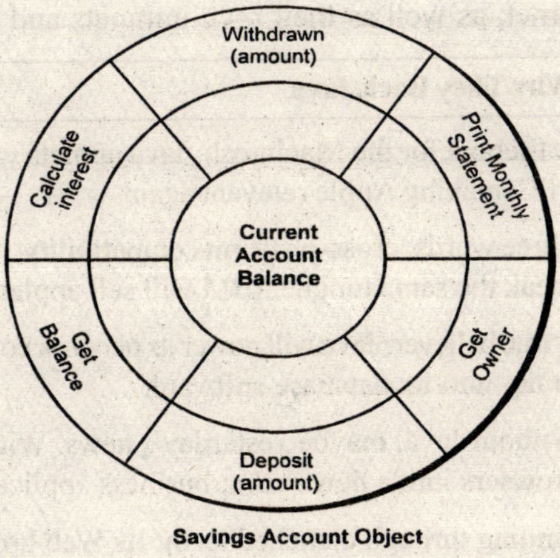

Figure 8.11. *An example of a bank savings account objects. This object consists of data about a customer's account balance and the basic operations that can be performed on those data.*

HTML and Java

HTML and Java are two relatively new programming languages that have become vital tools for building multimedia Web pages, Web sites, and Web-based applications.

HTML (Hypertext Markup Language) is a page description language that creates hypertext or hypermedia documents. HTML inserts control codes within a document at points you can specify that create links (*hyperlinks*) to other parts of the document or to other document anywhere on the World Wide Web. HTML embeds control codes in the ASCII text of a documents that designate titles, headings, graphics, and multimedia components, as well as hyperlinks within the document.

As we mentioned earlier, several of the programs in the top software suites will automatically convert documents into HTML formats. These include Web browsers, word processing and spreadsheet programs, database managers, and presentation graphics packages. These and other specialized *HTML editor* programs provide a range of features to help you design and create multimedia Web pages without formal HTML programming.

Java is an object-oriented programming language created by Sun Microsystems that is revolutionizing the programming of applications for the World Wide Web and corporate intranets and extranets. Java is related to the C++ and Objective C programming languages, but is much simpler and secure, and is computing platform independent. Java is also specifically designed for realtime, interactive, Web-based network applications. So Java applications consisting of small application programs, called **applets**, can be executed by any computer and any operating system anywhere in a network.

The ease of creating Java applets and distributing them from network servers to client PCs and network computers is a major reason for Java's popularity. Applets can be small special-purpose application programs or small modules of larger application programs. Applets can reside at Web sites on a network server until needed by client systems, and are easy to distribute over the Internet or intranets and extranets. Applets are platform independent too—they can run on Windows, OS/2, UNIX, and Macintosh systems without modification. So Java is becoming the programming language alternative to Microsoft's Active X language for many organisations intent on capitalizing on the business potential of the Internet, as well as their own intranets and extranets [10].

Company	Why They Back Java
Apple Computer	A lifeboat for the Macintosh: Java applets will run as well on a Mac as on a PC, making Apple relevant again.
IBM	Three words: cross-platform compatibility. All its computers will finally speak the same tongue. IBM will sell applets too.
Oracle Systems	A true believer: Java will power its network computer, allowing mere mortals to tap into its database software.
Netscape Communications	Without Java, maybe yesterday's news. With Java, Netscape moves past browsers into a new realm: business applications.
Microsoft	Smiling through clenched teeth: Its Web browser must keep up with Netscape's—and that means using Java.

Source: Adapted from Brent Schlender, "Sun's Java: The Threat to Microsoft is Real.

Figure 8.12. *Why the major computer industry players are backing Sun's Java.*

Programming Packages

A variety of software packages are available to help programmers develop computer programs. For example, *programming language translators* are programs that translate other programs into machine language instructions codes that computers can execute. Other software packages, such as programming language editors, are called *programming tools* because they help programmers write programs by providing a variety of program creation and editing capabilities.

Language Translator Programs

Computer programs consist of sets of instructions written in programming languages that must be translated by a **language translator** into the computer's own machine language before they can be processed, or executed, by the CPU. Programming language translator programs (or *language processors*) are known by a variety of names. An **assembler** translates the symbolic instruction codes of programs written in an assembler language into machine language instructions, while **a compiler** translates high-level language statements.

An **interpreter** is a special type of compiler that translates and executes each statement in a program one at a time, instead of first producing a complete machine language program, like compilers and assemblers do. Java is an example of an interpreted language. Thus, the program instructions in Java applets are interpreted and executed *on-the-fly* as the applet is being executed by a client PC.

Programming Tools

Many language translator programs are enhanced by a *graphical programming interface* and a variety of built-in capabilities of add-on packages. Language translators have always provided some editing and diagnostic capabilities to identify programming errors or bugs. However, many language translator programs now include powerful graphics-oriented *programming editors* and *debuggers*. These programs help programmers identify and minimize errors while they are programming. Such programming tools provide a computer-aided programming *environment* or *workbench*. Their goal is to decrease the drudgery of programming while increasing the efficiency and productivity of programmers. Other programming tools include diagramming packages, code generators, libraries of reusable objects and program code, and prototyping tools. Many of these same tools are part of the toolkit provided by *computer-aided software engineering* (CASE) packages.

Summary/Conclusion

- **Software.** Computers software consist of two major types of programs: (1) application software that directs the performance of a particular use, or application, of computers to meet the information processing needs of users, and (2) system software that controls and supports the operations of a computer system as it performs various information processing tasks. Refer to Figure 8.1 for an overview of the major types of software.
- **Application Software.** Application software includes a variety of programs that can be segregated into specific categories. General purpose application programs perform common information processing jobs for end users. Examples are word processing, electronic spreadsheet, database management, telecommunications, and presentation graphics programs. Application-specific programs accomplish information processing tasks that support specific business functions or processes, scientific or engineering applications, and other computer applications in society.
- **System Software.** System software can be subdivided into system management programs and system development programs. System management programs manage the hardware, software, network, and data resources of a computer system during its execution of information processing jobs. Examples of system management programs are operating systems, network management programs, database management systems, system utilities, performance monitors, and security monitors. Network management programs support and manage telecommunications activities and network performance telecommunications networks. Database management systems control the development, integration, and maintenance of databases. Utilities are programs that perform routine computing functions, such as backing up data or copying files, as part of an operating system or as a separate package. System development programs help IS specialists and end users develop computer

programs and information system procedures. Major development programs are language translators, programming editors and other programming tools, and CASE tools.

- **Operating Systems**. An operating system is an integrated system of programs that provides the operation of the CPU, controls the input/output storage functions of the computer system, and provides various support services. An operating system performs five basic functions: (1) a user interface for communication with users and operators, (2) resource management for managing the hardware resources of a computer system, (3) file management for managing files and data and programs, (4) task management for managing the tasks a computer must accomplish, and (5) utilities and other functions that provide miscellaneous support services.
- **Programming Languages**. Programming languages are a major category of system software. They require the use of a variety of programming packages to help programmers develop computer programs, and language translator programs to convert programming language instructions into machine language instruction codes. The five major levels of programming languages are machine languages, assembler languages, high-level languages, fourth-generation languages, and object-oriented languages. Object-oriented languages like Java and special-purpose languages like HTML are being widely used for Web-based business applications.

9

Telecommunications

Section I

Telecommunications and the Internetworked Enterprise

SECTION II

TECHNICAL TELECOMMUNICATIONS ALTERNATIVES

- Telecommunications Alternatives
- Telecommunications Media
  - *Twisted-Pair Wire*
  - *Coaxial Cable*
  - *Fibre Optics*
  - *Terrestrial Microwave*
  - *Communications Satellites*
  - *Cellular Phone Systems*
  - *Wireless LANs*
- Telecommunications Processors
  - *Modems*
  - *Multiplexers*
  - *Internetwork Processors*
- Telecommunication Software
  - *Common Software Functions*
- Telecommunications Network Topologies
  - *Star, Ring, and Bus Networks*
- Network Architectures and Protocols
  - *The OSI Model*
  - *The Internet's TCP/IP*
- Bandwidth Alternatives
- Switching Alternatives
- Access Alternatives

Real World Case: Citibank and AT&T: Improving Global Network Performance

SECTION I

TELECOMMUNICATIONS AND THE INTERNETWORKED ENTERPRISE

Networking the Enterprise

Business are becoming **internetworked enterprises.** As we said already, the Internet and Internet-like networks inside the enterprise (intranets), between an enterprise and its trading partners (extranets), and other types of networks have become the primary information technology infrastructure of many organisations. Such telecommunications networks enables managers, end users, team, and workgroups to electronically exchange data and information anywhere in the world with other end users, customers, suppliers, and business partners. Companies and workgroups can thus collaborate more creatively, manage their business operations and resources more effectively, and compete successfully in today's fast-changing global economy. Most business organisations today could not survive without a variety of interconnected computer networks to service their information processing and communications needs. As manager, entrepreneur, or business professional, you will thus be expected to make or participate in decisions regarding a great variety of telecommunications and network options. That's why you need to study the applications, technology, and managerial implications of telecommunications.

Deckers switched from leasing private high-speed telecommunications lines to a virtual private network (VPN), which provides secure communications links across the Internet. The VPN is saving Deckers $10,000 a month in telecommunications cost, and is crucial to the company's plan for international expansion. Employee project teams in Holland and California use the VPN and Lotus Notes groupware to collaborate on product development for Deckers. The VPN is providing to be quite secure, but slower than Deckers' previous telecommunications service. However, MIS Director Steve Miley expects VPN service to improve as Internet technologies steadily improve.

Deckers plans to add their offices in Hong Kong, Mexico, and Macao to the VPN, as well as using it for videoconferencing applications. This should result in substantial savings in international communications and travel costs.

Business Applications of Telecommunications

Telecommunications is the sending of information in any form (e.g., voice, data, text, and images) from one place to another using electronic or light-emitting media. *Data communications* is a more specific term describes the transmitting and receiving of data over communication links between one or more computer systems and a variety of input/output terminals. The term *teleprocessing, telemetics,* and *telephony* may also be used since they reflect the integration of computer-based information processing with telecommunications and telephone technologies. However, all forms of telecommunications now rely heavily on computers and computerized devices. For this reason, the broader term *telecommunications* can be used as a synonym for data communications activities. Therefore, in this text, we will use these terms interchangeably.

Figure 9.1 illustrates some of the many possible business applications of telecommunications. It groups telecommunications applications into the major categories of enterprise collaboration systems, electronic commerce system, and internal business systems. Figure 9.1 also emphasizes that these applications rely on the telecommunications capabilities of the Internet, intranets, extranets, and other types of enterprise and interorganisational networks.

Enterprise collaboration applications use telecommunications networks to support communication, coordination, and collaboration among the members of business teams and workgroups. For example, employees and external consultants on a project team may use the Internet, intranets, and extranets to support electronic mail, video-conferencing, electronic discussion groups, and multimedia Web pages to communicate and collaborate on business projects. **Electronic commerce** applications support the buying and selling of products, services, and information over the Internet and other computer networks. For example, a business could use the Internet to give customers access to multimedia product catalogs on the World Wide Web, use extranets so large customers can access the company's inventory databases, and use a corporate intranet so employees can easily look up customer records stored on intranets servers.

Internal business applications of telecommunications depend on a variety of computer networks to support a company's business operations. For examples, employee may use an intranet to access benefits information on a human resource department server. Or a company may link wide area and local area networks so managers can make inquiries and generate reports from corporate databases stored on network servers and mainframe systems.

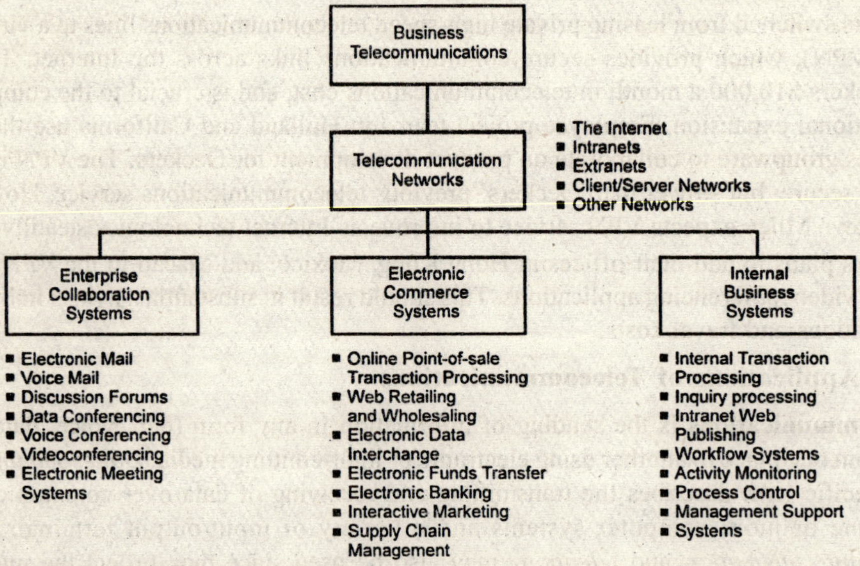

Figure 9.1. *Some of the business applications of telecommunications. Note the many types of applications for enterprise collaboration, electronic commerce, and internal business operation.*

The Business Value of Telecommunications

What *business value* is created by the business applications of telecommunications shown in Figure 9.1. That's what you need to know as a manager, entrepreneur, or business professional. A good way to answer this question is shown in Figure 9.2. Information technology, especially in telecommunications-based business applications, helps a company overcome geographic, time, cost, and structural barriers to business success. Figure 9.2 outlines examples of the business values of these four strategic capabilities of telecommunications and other information technologies. This figures emphasizes how several applications of electronic commerce can help a firm capture and provide information quickly to end users at remote geographic locations are reduced costs, as well as supporting its strategic organisational objectives.

For example, travelling salespeople and those at regional sales office can use the internet, extranet, and other networks to transmit customer orders from their laptop or desktop PCs, thus breaking geographic barriers. Point-of-sale terminals and an online sales transaction processing networks can break time barriers by supporting immediate credit authorization and sales processing. Teleconferencing can be used to cut costs by reducing the need for expensive business trips since it allows customers, suppliers, and employees to participate in meeting and collaborate on joint projects. Finally, electronic data interchange systems are used by the business to establish strategic relationships with their customers and suppliers by making the exchange of electronic business documents fast, convenient, and tailored to the needs of the business partners involved.

Strategic Capabilities	EC Examples	Business Value
Overcome geographic barriers: Capture information about business transactions from remote locations	Use the Internet and extranets to transmit customer orders from traveling salespeople to a corporate data centre for order processing and inventory control	Provides better customer service by reducing delay in filling orders and improves cash flow by speeding up the billing of customers
Overcome time barriers: Provide information to remote locations immediately after it is requested	Credit authorization at the point of sale using online POS networks	Credit inquiries can be made and answered in seconds
Overcome cost barriers: Reduce the cost of more traditional means of communication	Desktop videoconferencing between a company and its business partners using the Internet, intranets, and extranets	Reduce expensive business trips; allows customers, suppliers, and employees to collaborate, thus improving the quality of decisions reached
Overcome structural barriers: Support linkage for competitive advantage	Electronic data interchange (EDI) of transactions data to and from suppliers and customers using extranets or other networks	Fast, convenient service locks in customers and suppliers

Figure 9.2. Examples of the business value of electronic commerce applications of telecommunications.

Trends in Telecommunications

Major trends occurring in the field of telecommunications have a significant impact on management decisions in this area. You should thus be aware of major trends in telecommunications industries, technologies, and applications that significantly increase the decision alternatives confronting the managers of business organisations.

Industry Trends

The competitive arena for telecommunications service has changed dramatically in the United States and several other countries, from a few government-regulated monopolies to many fiercely competitive suppliers of telecommunications services. This telecommunications revolution began in the United States with the breakup of AT&T and the Bell System in 1984, and accelerated with the passage of the Telecommunication Act of 1996, and the tidal wave of Internet users and uses in the 1990s. Now telecommunications networks and services are available from numerous large and small telecommunications companies. Thousands of companies offer business and consumers a choice of everything from local and global telephone services to communications satellite channels, mobile radio, cable TV, cellular phone services, and Internet access.

The explosive growth of the Internet and the World Wide Web has spawned a host of new telecommunications products, services, and providers. Driving and responding to this growth, business firms have dramatically increased their use of the Internet and the Web for electronic commerce and collaboration. Thus, the service and vendor options available to meet a company's telecommunications needs have increased significantly, as have a business manager's decision-making alternatives.

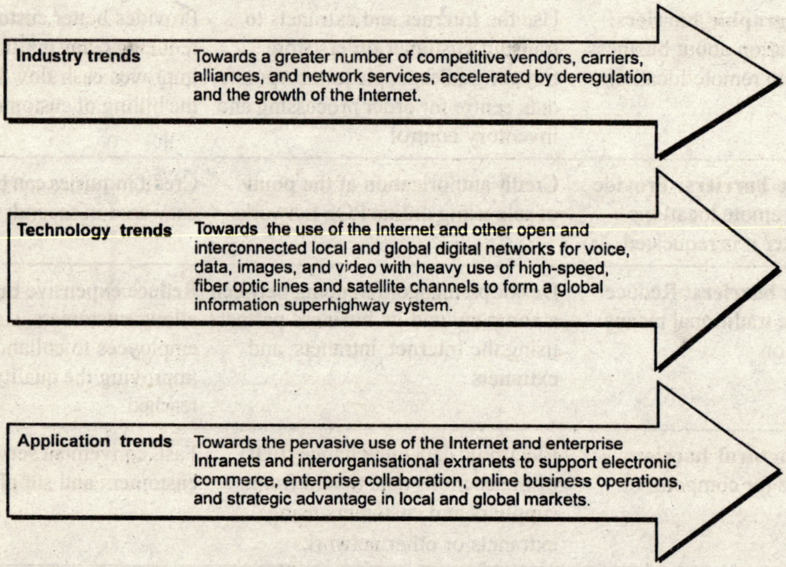

Figure 9.3. Major trends in telecommunications.

The U.S. Telecommunications Deregulation and Reform Act of 1996 has promoted many of the dynamic changes taking place in the telecommunications industry. With a few exceptions, the law overturns virtually all U.S. federal regulations that governed which companies could enter which communications businesses. This encourages the creations of even more telecommunications companies, telecommunications mergers and alliances, and telecommunications services. Key changes in the law include:

- Local telephone companies, including the regional Bell operating companies, can provide long distance telecommunications services.
- Long-distance telephone companies can enter local telephone service markets.
- Local and long-distance telephone companies can expand into the cable TV business.
- Cable TV companies can provide local telephone services.
- Public utilities, such as electric, gas, and water companies, can offer a variety of telecommunications services.
- Telephone companies can offer television programming and other video communications services [2, 22].

Technology Trends

The defining trend of the 1990s, from corporate boardrooms to consumers playrooms, is connecting everyone and everything to everyone and everything else. Interactive television, cellular phones, modems, faxes, personal digital assistants—if they connect, they seem to be in demand. Convinced that this hunger for connectivity will continue, telecommunications and cable companies are investing billions to bring enhanced interactive communications to the American household. All types of businesses are installing local area and wide area networks to connect employees at different locations and to facilitate the exchange of electronic information with vendors and customers.

Many of these enterprise networks [now] share the standards that allow the global Internet to transmit messages and data across international and organisational borders. Companies already linked to the Internet receive the advantages of high-speed telecommunications and continuously evolving technology while learning invaluable lessons about the management of networked organisations [6].

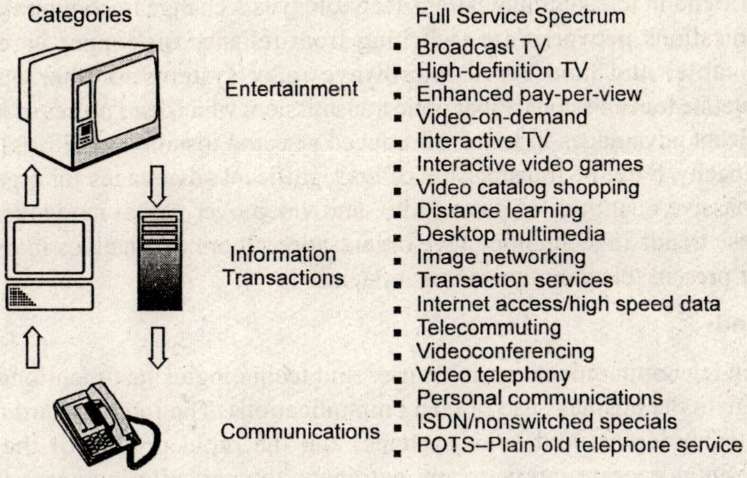

Source: Adapted from Samir Chatterjee, "Requirements for Success in Gigabit Networking." *Communication of the ACM.*

Figure 9.4. *The Spectrum of telecommunications-based services available today.*

Open systems with unrestricted connectivity, using **Internet networking technologies** as their technology platform, are the primary telecommunications technology drivers of the late 1990s. This trend is self-evident in the rapid and continually changing development of thousands of hardware, software, and networking products and services. Their primary goal is to promote easy and secures access by business end users and consumers to the resources of the Internet, especially the World Wide Web, and corporate intranets and extranets. Web browser suites, HTML Web page editors, Internet and intranet servers and network management software, TCP/IP Internet networking products, and network security fire walls are just a few examples. These technologies are being applied in many types of business networks and applications, especially those for electronic commerce and collaborations. This trend has reinforced previous industry and technical moves toward building client/server networks based on an open systems architecture.

Open systems are information systems that use common standards for hardware, software, applications, and networking. Open systems, like the Internet and corporate intranets and extranets, create a computing environment that is open to easy access by end users and their networked computer systems. Open systems provide greater **connectivity**, that is, the ability of networked computers and other devices to easily access and communicate with each other and share information. Any open systems architecture also provides a high degree of network **interoperability.** That is, open systems enable the many different applications of end users to be accomplished using the different varieties of computer systems, software packages, and database provided by a variety of interconnected networks. Frequently, software known as *middleware* may be used to help diverse systems work together. Network architectures like the Open Systems Interconnection (OSI) model of the International Standards Organisation and the Internet's TCP/IP protocol suite promote open, flexible, and efficient standards for the development of open telecommunications networks.

Another major trend in telecommunications technology is a change in communications media. Many telecommunications networks are switching from reliance on copper wire-based media (such as coaxial cable) and land-based microwave relay systems to fiber optic lines and communications satellite transmissions. Fiber optic transmission; which uses pulses of laser-generated light, offers significant advantages in terms of reduced size and installation efforts, vastly greater communication capacity. Satellite transmission offers significant advantages for organisations that need to transmit massive quantities of data, audio, and video over global networks, especially to isolated areas. These trends in technology give organisations more alternatives in overcoming the limitations of their present telecommunications systems.

Application Trends

The changes in telecommunications industries and technologies just mentioned are causing a significant change in the business use of telecommunications. The trend toward more vendors, service, Internet technologies, and open systems, and the rapid growth of the Internet, the World Wide Web and corporate intranets and extranets, dramatically increases the number of feasible telecommunications applications. Thus, telecommunications networks are now playing vital and pervasive roles in electronic commerce, enterprise collaboration , and internal business applications that support the operations, management, and strategic objectives of both large and small companies.

An organisation's telecommunications functions is no longer relegated to office telephone systems, long-distance calling arrangements, and a limited amount of data communications in local area network and with corporate mainframes. Instead, it has become an integral part of local and global computer networks that are used to dramatically out costs, shorten business lead time and response times supports electronic commerce, improve the collaboration of workgroups, develop online operational processes, share resources, lock in customers and suppliers, and develop new products and services. This makes telecommunications a more complex and important decision area for businesses that must increasingly find new ways to compete in both domestic and global markets.

The Internet Revolution

Suddenly it seems that the Internet is everywhere. After two decade of relative obscurity as a government and research network, the internet burst upon the 1990s to penetrate the public consciousness, capturing headlines and attracting millions of users around the world. Analysts estimates that a new computer connects to the Internet about one every 30 minutes, propelling a rate of network expansion that tops 10 percent each month. Every indication points to even faster growth in the future [5].

The explosive growth of the Internet is the revolutionary technology phenomenon of the 1990s. The Internet has become the largest and most important networks of networked today, and is evolving into the information superhighway of tomorrow. The Internet is constantly expanding, as more and more businesses and other organisations and their uses, computers, and networks join its global web. Thousands of business, educational, and research networks now connect millions of computer systems and users in more than 200 countries to each other. The Internet has also become a key platform for a rapidly expanding list of information and entertainment services and business applications, including enterprise collaboration and electronic commerce systems.

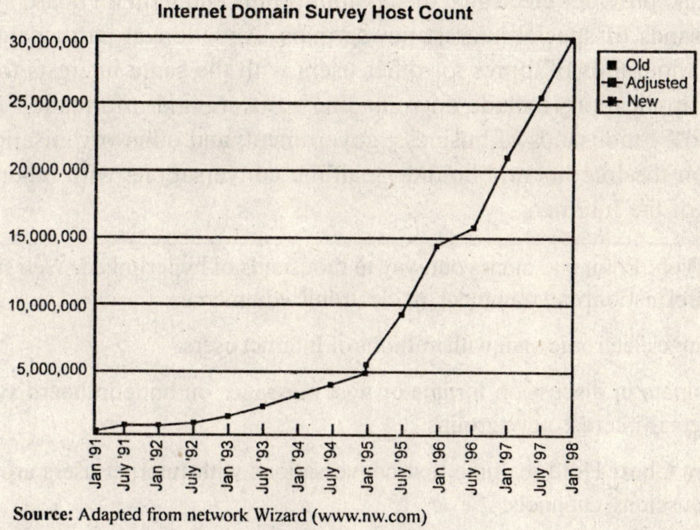

***Figure 9.5.** The rapid growth of the Internet.*

The **Internet** evolved from research and development network (ARPANET) established in 1969 by the U.S. Defence Department to enable corporate, academic, and government researchers to communicate with E-mail and share data and computing resources. The Net doesn't have a central computer system or telecommunications centre. Instead, each messages sent has a unique address code so any Internet server in the network can forward it to its destination. Also, the Internet does not have a headquarters or governing body. The Internet Society in Reston, Virgina, is one of several volunteer groups of individual and corporate members who promote use of the

Internet and development of new communications standards. These common standards are the key to the free flow of messages among the widely different computers and networks in the system.

The Internet is growing rapidly. For example, the Internet is more than doubling in size each year, growing to over 30 million host computers and more than 100 millions users in early 1998. The monthly rate of growth of the Internet was estimated at between 7 to 10 percent. Some industry experts the Internet to eventually interconnect more than 1 billion networks [4, 12].

Internet Applications

The most popular Internet Application are E-mail, browsing the sites on the World Wide Web, and participating in special-interest *newsgroup.* Internet E-mail is faster than many public networks. Messages usually arrive in seconds or a few minutes anywhere in the world, and can take the form of data, text, fax, and video files. Internet browser software like Netscape Navigator and Microsoft Explorer enables millions of users to *surf* the World Wide Web by clicking their way to the multimedia information resources stored on the hyperlinked pages of businesses, government, and other Web sites. Web sites offer information and entertainment, and are the launch sites for electronic commerce transactions between businesses and their suppliers and customers.

The internet also provides electronic discussion forums and bulletin board systems formed and managed by thousands of special-interest newsgroups. Anyone can participate in discussions or post messages on thousands of topics for other users with the same interests to read and respond to. Other popular applications include downloading software and information files and accessing databases provided by thousands of business, government, and other organisations. Logging on to other computers on the Internet and holding realtime conversations with other Internet users are also popular uses of the Internet.

- **World Wide Web:** Point and click your way to thousands of hyperlinked. Web sites and resources for multimedia information, entertainment, or electronic commerce.
- **E-mail:** Exchange electronic mail with millions of Internet users.
- **Usenet:** Participate in discussion forums or post messages on bulletin board systems formed by thousands of special-interest newsgroups.
- **Internet Relay Chat:** Hold realtime text conversations with Internet users around the world on hundreds of discussions channels.
- **File Transfer Protocol (FTP):** Download data files, programs, reports, articles, management, books, pictures, sounds, and other types of files from thousands of sources to your computer system.
- **Telnet:** Log on to and use thousands of Internet computer systems around the world.
- **Other Uses:** Make long-distance phone calls for free, hold desktop videoconferences, listen to radio program, watch television, explore virtual worlds, etc.

Figure 9.6. Popular uses of the Internet.

One of the most important and popular uses of the Internet is gathering information. You can make online searches for information in a variety of ways, using your Web browser and search engines such as AltaVista, Excite, and Infoseek, and directories like Yahoo! Thousands of Web sites, business and government databases, and catalogs from university libraries to the Library of Congress are available, as are electronic versions of numerous consumers, business, and academic publications. You can point and click your way to thousands of Web sites and their databases, downloading everything from the latest satellite weather photos from NASA to world almanac excerpts from the U.S. Central Intelligence Agency.

The Information Superhighway

The trends toward open, high-speed, digital networks with fibre optic and satellite links and the widespread use of the Internet and its technologies have made the concepts of an **information superhighway** technically feasible and captured the interest of both business and government. In this concept, local, regional, nationwide, and global networks will be integrated into a vast network of networks, with more advanced interactive multimedia capabilities than the Internet. The information superhighway system would connect individual, households, businesses, news and entertainment media, government agencies, libraries, universities, and all other institutions, and would support interactive voice, data, video, and multimedia communications.

• **American Online www.aol.com** AOL is the leading commercial online service with more than 11 millions members, including those added through its acquisition of CompuServe. AOL provides E-mail, news, electronic shopping, chat, and original content, as well as access to the Internet for its dial-up users. There are several pricing plans available, including unlimited access for $21.95 per month.
• **AT&T WorldNET www.att.net** AT&T's dial-up Internet access is among the most reliable nationwide Internet service providers (ISP's). At the WorldNet home page, users can find links to all sorts of topics on the Net, including movies, travel, and investing. There are also connections to content providers like AOL, Snap Online, and The Mining Company.
• **Microsoft Network www.msn.com** Microsoft's online service offers plenty of content and services. There's news from MSNBC, gossip from Entertainment Tonight, highbrow, prose from Slate, and lowbrow, humor from Car Talk. You can plan a trip with Expedia, find a movie with Cinemania, or check on your favourite stock with Microsoft Investor. And there's Internet access, too.
• **Netcom www.netcom.com** Netcom is a nationwide ISP that offers high-speed Internet access for both business and individuals. For individual users, Netcom's Homeport offers customized news and information. Netcom will also host a personal Web page and provide a customized news page for each user.

Figure 9.7a. *Some of the leading commercial online services and Internet service providers (ISPs).*

Proponents of the information superhighway say it could provide a national information infrastructure (NII) and economic network with an economic impact equivalent to the transcontinental railway and interstate highway systems combined. Critics question whether the potential benefits of the superhighway as it was proposed would be worth its cost, especially given the rapid growth of the Internet as a worldwide multimedia network. But proponents argue that the information superhighway is needed to create an information infrastructure that would dramatically increase business efficiency and competitiveness by improving economic communications, electronic commerce and collaboration, and information gathering. In any event, the information superhighway concept promises to be a catalyst for the development and improvement of the Internet and other changes in telecommunications network and services in the years to come.

• **AltaVista www.altavista.digital.com** The powerful AltaVista search engine finds information on the Web quickly keywords in 25 different languages. If too much information appears, more sophisticated techniques can be used to refine a search. AltaVista can also check the thousands of newsgroups on the Usenet for postings on various subjects.
• **HotBot www.hotbot.com** *Wired* magazine packs all kinds of searching possibilities into this site. To focus your query, you can limit your search by date, domain, media type, or Internet location. Plus, the *Wired* editors offer picks of their favourite Web-sites in categories like current affairs, culture, and technology. There are also links to popular commerce sites like Virtual Vineyards and Cyberian Outpost.
• **Switchboard www.switchboard.com** Finding people is easier than ever before, thanks to Web site like Switchboard, which compiles the nation's telephone listing under one cyber-roof. You can also find E-mail listings and business address using Switchboard's search technology. And with Switchboard's Sideclick service, you can find related Web sites for any URL you type in.
• **Yahoo! www.yahoo.com** The best-known site for online searches, Yahoo! also offer news, financial information, and free E-mail. Its outline format is perfect for finding information in neat categories from arts and humanities to computers and business. Yahoo! also runs special sites for countries like Germany and France and for cities like Boston and Chicago.

Figure 9.7b. Some of the Top Internet Search Sites.

A Telecommunications Network Model

Before we get any further in our discussion of telecommunications, we should understand the basic components of a telecommunications networks. Generally, a *communications network* is any arrangement where a *sender* transmits a message to a *receiver* over a *channel* consisting of some type of *medium*. Figure 9.8 illustrates a simple conceptual model of a **telecommunications network,** which allows that it consists of five basic categories of components:

- **Terminals**, such as networked personal computers, network computers, or video terminals. Of course, any input/output device that uses telecommunications networks to transmit or receive data is a terminal, including telephones, office equipment, and the transaction terminals.

- **Telecommunications processors**, which support data transmission and reception between terminals and computers. These devices, such as modems, switches, and routers, perform a variety of control and support functions in a telecommunications network. For example, they convert data from digital to analog and back, code and decode data, and control the speed, accuracy, and efficiency of the communications flow between computers and terminals in a telecommunications network.
- **Telecommunications channels** over which data are transmitted and received. Telecommunications channels use combinations of **media**, such as copper wires, coaxial cables, fibre optics cables, microwave systems, and communications satellites, to interconnect the other components of a telecommunications network.
- **Computers** of all sizes and types are interconnected by telecommunications networks so that they can carry out their information processing assignments. For example, a mainframe computer may serve as a *host computer* for a large network, assisted by a midrange computer serving as a *front-end processor*, while a microcomputer may act as a *network server* for a small network of microcomputer workstations.
- **Telecommunication control software** consists of programs that control telecommunications activities and manage the functions of telecommunications networks. Example include network management programs of all kinds, such as *telecommunications monitors* for mainframe host computers, *network operating systems* for microcomputer network servers, and *Web browsers* for microcomputers.

No matter how large and complex real world telecommunications networks may appear to be, these five basic categories of network components must be at work to support an organization's telecommunications activities. This is the conceptual framework you can to help you understand the various types of telecommunications networks in use today.

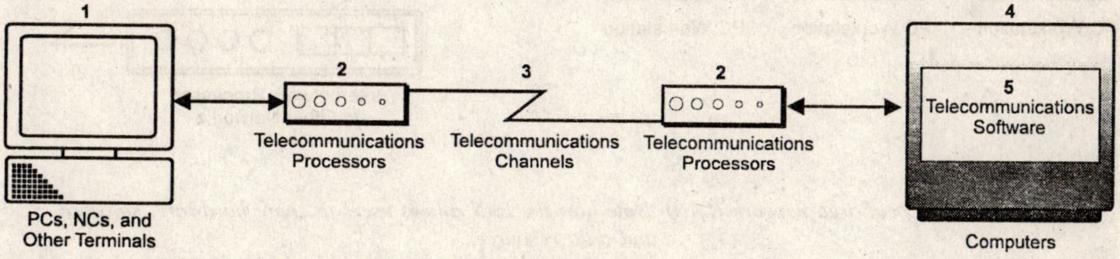

***Figure 9.8.** The five basic components in a telecommunications network: (1) terminals, (2) telecommunications processors, (3) telecommunications channels, (4) computers, and (5) telecommunications software.*

Types of Telecommunications Networks

There are many different types of telecommunications networks. However, from an end user's point of view, there are only a few basic types, such as wide area and local area networks and interconnected networks like the Internet, intranets, and extranets, as well as client/server and interorganisational networks.

Wide Area Networks

Telecommunications networks covering a large geographic area are called **wide area networks (WANs).** Networks that cover a large city or metropolitan area (*metropolitan area networks)* can also be included in this category. Such large networks have become a necessity for carrying out the day-to-day activities of many business and government organisations and their end users. For example, WANs are used by many multinational companies to transmit and receive information among their employees, customers, suppliers, and other organisations across cities, regions, countries, and the world.

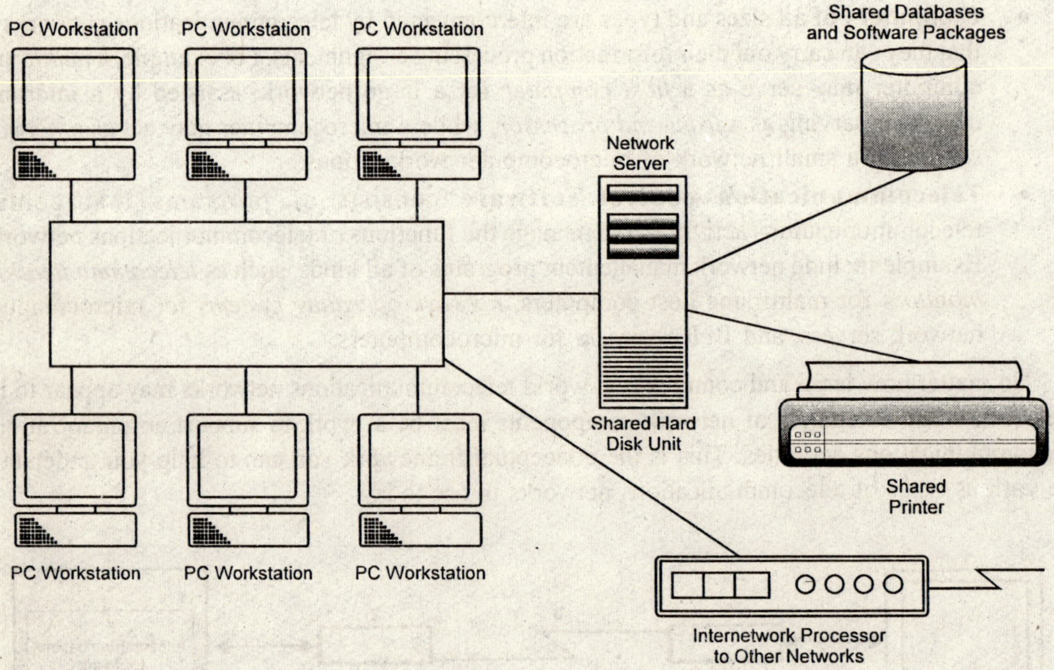

Figure 9.9. A Local area network (LAN). Note how the LAN allows users to share hardware, software, and data resources.

Local Area Networks

Local area networks (LANs) connect computers and other information processing devices within a limited physical area, such as an office, a classroom, a building, manufacturing plant, or other work site. LANs have become commonplace in many organisations for providing telecommunications networks capabilities that link end users in offices, departments, and other workgroups.

LANs use a variety of telecommunications media, such as ordinary telephone writing, coaxial cable, or even wireless radio systems to interconnect microcomputer workstations and computer peripherals. To communicate over the networks, each PC usually has a circuit board called a *network interface card.* Most LANs use a more powerful microcomputer having a large hard disk capacity, called a *file server* or **network server,** that contains a **network operating system** program that controls telecommunications and the use and sharing of network resources. For example, it distributes copies of common data files and software packages to the other microcomputers in the network and controls access to shared laser printers and other network peripherals.

Internetworks

Most local area networks are eventually connected to other LANs in wide area networks. These interconnected networks are generally called **internetworks**, of which the Internet is the largest example. Such networks enables end user to communicate with the workstations of colleagues on other LANs, or to access the computing resources and databases at other company locations or at other organisations. These interconnected telecommunications networks rely on **internetwork processors,** such as switches, routers, hubs, or gateway, to make internetworking connections to other LANs and wide area networks.

Intranets and Extranets

The goal of many internetwork architectures is to create a seamless network of Internet-like networks called *intranets* within each organisations. This networks of intranets is then connected to the Intranet and to networks called *extranets* that provide electronic links to business partners. See Figure 9.10.

Intranets are designed to be open, but secure internal networks whose Web browsing software provides easy point-and-click access by end users to multimedia information on internal Web sites. Intranet Web sites may be established on internal Web servers by a company, its business units, departments, and workgroups. For example, a human resources department may establish an intranet Web sites so employees can easily access up-to-the-minute information on the status of their benefits accounts, as well as latest information on company benefits options.

Extranets are networks that link some of the intranet resources of a company with other organisations and individuals. For example, extranets enable customer, suppliers, subcontractors, consultants, and others to access selected intranet Web sites and other company databases. Organisations can establish private extranets among themselves, or use the Intranet as part of the networks connections between them.

Many organisations use *virtual private networks* (VPNs) to establish secure intranets and extranets. A **virtual private networks** is a secure network that uses the Internet as its main *backbone network,* but relies on the fire walls and other security features of its Internet and intranet connections and those of participating organisations. Thus, for example, VPNs would enables a company to use the Internet to established secure intranets between its distant branch offices and manufacturing plants, and secure extranets between itself and its customer and supplier [6].

Client Server Networks

Client/Server networks have become the predominate information architecture of enterprisewide computing. We introduced client/server networks in already, in our discussion of networked computing systems. Computing power is distributed and interconnected throughout many organisations by networked computer systems that take the form of client/server networks.

In a client/server networks, end user PC or NC workstations are the **clients**. They are interconnected by local area networks and share application processing with network **servers**, which also manage the networks. Local area networks are also interconnected to other LANs and wide area networks of client workstations and servers.

In client/server networks, end users at client workstations can handle a broad range of information processing tasks. They can thus perform some or most of the processing of their business applications. This includes data entry and other user interface activities, inquiry response, transaction processing, updating databases, generating reports, and providing decision support. Networks servers can share application processing, manage workgroup collaboration, and control common hardware, software, and databases. Thus, data can be completely processed locally, where most input and output (and errors and problems) must be handled anyway, while still providing access to the workstations and servers in other networks. This provides computers processing more tailored to the needs of end users and increases information processing efficiency and effectiveness since users and increase information processing efficiency and effectiveness since users share responsibility for their own applications.

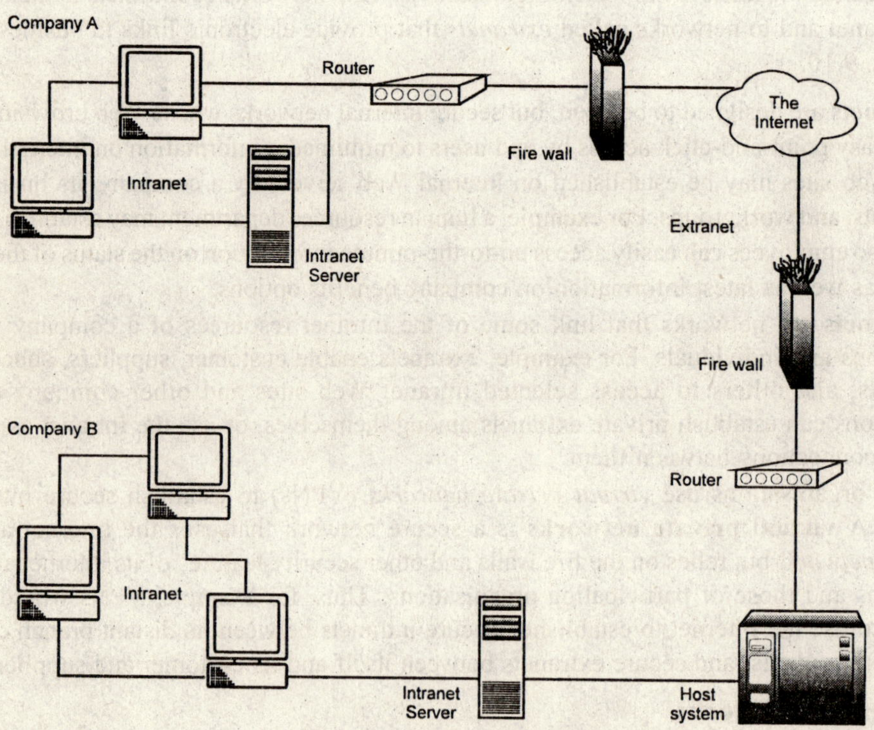

Figure 9.10. *An example of intranets and extranets.*

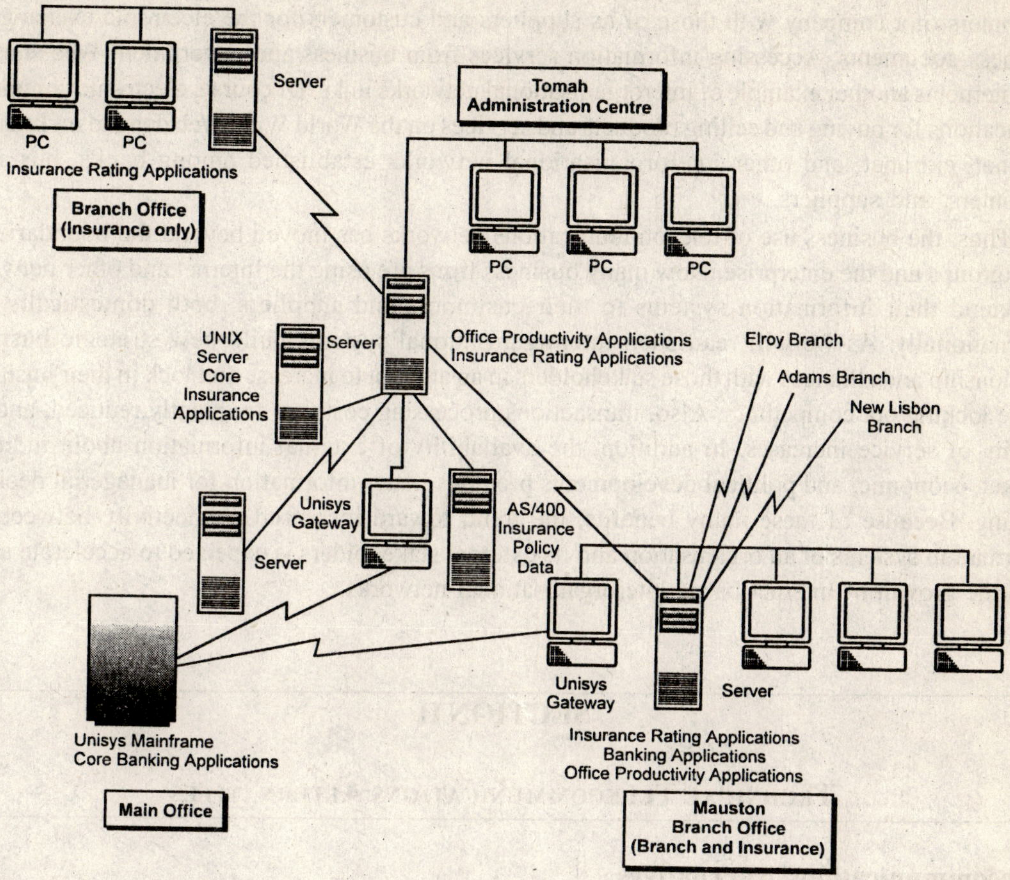

***Figure 9.11.** A client/server network. Note the functions performed by different types of computers acting as clients, servers, and superservers for a Wisconsin banking and insurance company.*

Client/server computing also lets large central-site computers handle those jobs they can do best, such as high-volume transaction processing, communications networks security and control, and maintenance and control of large corporate databases. User clients at local sites can access these superservers to receive corporatewide management information or transmit summary transaction data reflecting local site activities.

Interorganisational Networks

Many of the applications of telecommunications we have just mentioned can be classified as **interorganisational networks.** The Internet, extranets, and other networks may be used to link a company's headquarters and other locations to the networks of its customer, suppliers, and other organisations. For example, you can think of a customer account inquiry system that provides intranets access by employees and extranets access by customers as an example of an interorganisational network. So is the use of electronic data interchange (EDI) systems that link the computers of a company with those of its suppliers and customers for the electronic exchange of business documents. Accessing information services from business and government Web sites on the Internet is another example of interorganisational networks links. Of course, electronic commerce applications for buying and selling products and services on the World Wide Web depend on Internet, intranet, extranet, and other interorganisational networks established among banks, business, customers, and suppliers.

Thus, the business use of telecommunications networks has moved beyond the boundaries of workgroups and the enterprise. Now many business firms are using the Internet and other networks to extend their information systems to their customers and suppliers, both domestically and internationally. As we will read such interorganisational systems build new strategic business relationship and alliances with those stakeholders in an attempt to increase and lock in their business, while locking out competitors. Also, transactions processing costs are frequently reduced, and the quality of service increases. In addition, the availability of external information about industry, market, economic, and political developments provides better information for managerial decision making. Because of these many benefits, the trend toward increased connectivity between the information systems of an organisation and its external stakeholders is expected to accelerate along with the growth of Internet-based interorganisational networks.

SECTION II

Technical Telecommunications Alternatives

Telecommunications Alternatives

Telecommunications is a highly technical, rapidly changing field of information systems technology. Most end users do not need a detailed knowledge of its technical characteristics. However, it is necessary that you understand some of the important characteristics of the basic components of telecommunications networks. This understanding will help you participate effectively in decision-making regarding telecommunications alternatives. It outlines key telecommunications network components and alternatives. Remember, a basic understanding and appreciation, not a detailed knowledge, are sufficient for most business end users.

Telecommunications Media

Telecommunications channels make use of a variety of **telecommunications media.** These include twisted-pair wire, coaxial cables, and fibre optic cables, all of which physically link the devices in a network. Also included are terrestrial microwave, communications satellite, cellular phone systems, and packer and LAN radio, all of which use microwave and other radio waves. In addition, there are infrared systems, which use infrared light to transmit and receive data.

Twisted-Pair Wire

Ordinary telephone wire, consisting of copper wire twisted into pairs (**twisted-pair wire**), is the most widely used media for telecommunications. These lines are used in established communications networks throughout the world for both voice and data transmission. Thus, twisted-pair writing used extensively in home and office telephone systems and many local area networks and wide area networks.

Coaxial Cable

Coaxial cable consists of a sturdy copper or aluminum wire wrapped with spacers to insulate and protect it. The cable's cover and insulation minimize interference and distortion of the signals the cable carries. Groups of coaxial cables may be bundled together in a big cable for ease of installation. These high quality line can be placed underground and laid on the floors of lakes and oceans. They allow high-speed data transmission and are used instead of twisted-pair wire lines in high-service metropolitan areas, for cable TV systems, and for short-distance connection of computers and peripheral devices. Coaxial cables are also used in many offices building and other work sites for local area networks.

Network Component	Examples of Alternatives
Media	Twisted-pair wire, coaxial cable, fibre optics, microwave radio, communications satellite, cellular phone systems, LAN radio, infrared
Processors	Modems, multiplexers, switches, routers, hubs, gateways, front-end processors, private branch exchanges
Software	Network operating systems, telecommunications monitors, Web browser, middleware
Channels	Analog/digital, switched/nonswitched, circuits/message/packets/ cell switching, bandwidth alternatives
Topology/architecture	Point-to-point, multidrop, star/ring/bus, OSI, TCP/IP

Figure 9.12. *Key telecommunications network components and alternatives.*

Fibre Optics

Fibre optics uses cables consisting of one or more hair-thin filaments of glass fibre wrapped in a protective jackets. They can conduct light pulses generated by laser at transmission rates as high as 30 billion bits per second. This is about 60 times greater than coaxial cable and 3,000 times better than twisted-pair wire lines. Fibre optic cables provide substantial size and weight reductions as well as increased speed and greater carrying capacity. A half-inch-diameter fibre optic cable can carry up to 50,000 channels, compared to about 5,500 channels for a standard coaxial cable.

Fibre optic cables are not affected by and do nor generate electromagnetic radiations; therefore, multiple fibres can be placed in the same cable. Fibre optic cables have a minimal need for repeaters for signal retransmissions, unlike electrical wire media. Fibre optics also has a much lower data error rate than other media and is harder to tap than electrical wire and cable. One disadvantage of fibre optics has been the difficulty of splicing the cable to make connections, though this is also a security advantage that limits line tapping. However, improved splicing techniques have made it easier to splice fibre cables. Fibre optic cables have already been installed in many parts of the United States, and they are expected to replace other communications media in many applications in the near future.

Terrestrial Microwave

Terrestrial microwave involves earthbound microwave systems that transmit high-speed radio signals in a line-of-sight path between relay stations spaced approximately 30 miles apart. Microwave antennas are usually placed on top of buildings, towers, hills, and mountain peaks, and they are a familiar sight in many sections of the country. They are still a popular medium for both long-distance and metropolitan area networks.

Communications Satellite

Communication satellites also use microwave radio as their telecommunications medium. There are many communications satellite from several nations and organisations placed into stationary geosynchronous orbits approximately 22,000 miles above the equator. Satellite are powered by solar panels and can transmit microwave signals at a rate of several hundred million bits per second. They serve as relay stations for communications signals transmitted from earth stations. Earth stations use dish antennas to beam microwave signals to the satellite that amplify and retransmit the signal to other earth stations thousands of miles away.

While communications satellite were used initially for voice and vide transmission, they are now also used for high-speed transmission of large volumes of data. Because of time delays caused by the great distance involved, they are not suitable for interactive, realtime processing. Communications satellite systems are operated by several firms, including Comsat, American Mobile Satellite, and Intellsat, an international consortium of more than 100 nations. Many large corporations and other users have developed networks of samll satellite dish antennas known as VSAT (very-small-aperture terminal) to connect their distant work areas. These satellite networks are also called *bypass networks* beacuse firms are bypassing the regular communications networked provided by communications carriers.

Cellular Phone Systems

Cellular phone systems use several radio communications technologies. However, all of them divide a geographic area into small areas, or *cells*, typically from one to several squares miles in area. Each cell has its own low-power transmitter or radio relay antenna device to relay calls from one cell to another. Computers and other communications processors coordinate and control the transmissions of mobile phone users as they move from one area to another.

Cellular phone systems have long used analog communications technologies operating at frequencies in the 800 to 900 MHz cellular band. Newer cellular systems use digital technologies, which provide greater capacity and security, and additional services such as voice mail, paging, messaging, and caller ID. These capabilities are also available with the new PCS (Personal Communication Services) phone systems. PCS operates at 1,900 MHz frequencies using digital technologies that are related to digital cellular. However, PCS phone systems cost substantially less to operate and use than cellular system and have lower power consumption requirements [17].

Digital cellular technologies have become an important communications medium for mobile computing and data communications. Cellular modems enables laptop computer users to digital cellular systems for mobile computing. For example, Federal Express uses digital cellular for data communications using terminals in each of its thousand of delivery vans as part of its competitive edge. The integration of cellulaı and other mobile radio technologies, such as *packet radio*, and the emergence of next few years. These developments will provide a full range of communications and computing capabilities to mobile computer users.

Wireless LANs

Wiring an office or a building for a local area network is often a difficult and costly task. Older buildings frequently do not have conduits for coaxial cables or additional twisted-pair wire, and the conduits in newer buildings may not have enough room to pull additional wiring through. Repairing mistakes and damages to wiring is often difficult and costly, as are major relocations of LAN workstations and other components. One solution to such problems is installing a **wireless LAN**, using one of several wireless technologies. An important example is LAN radio, which may involve a high-frequency radio technology similar to digital cellular, or a low-frequency radio technology called *spread spectrum*. The other wireless LAN technology is called infrared because it uses beams of infrared light to establish network links between LAN components.

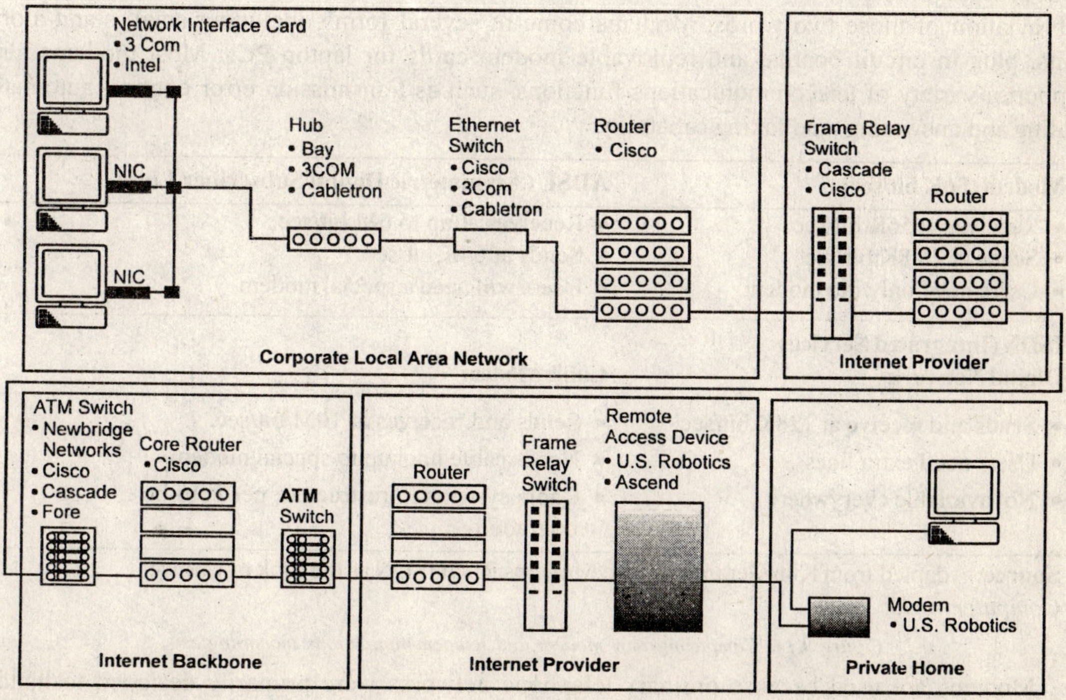

Figure 9.13. The communications processors involved in a typical Internet connection.

Obviously, a wireless LAN eliminates or greatly reduces the need for wires and cables, thus making a LAN easier to set up, relocate, and maintain. However, current wireless technologies have higher initial costs and other limitations. For example, an infrared LAN transmit faster than radio LANs but is limited to line-of-sight arrangements to a maximum of about 80 feet between components. High-frequency radio LANs do not need line-of-sight links, but are limited to 40 to 70 feet between components in enclosed areas. Spread spectrum LANs can penetrate masonry walls and link components from 100 to 200 feet away in enclosed areas, but are more subject to receiving or generating radio interference.

Telecommunications Processors

Telecommunications processors such as modems, multiplexers, switches, and routers perform a variety of support functions between the computers and other devices in a telecommunications network. Let's take a look at some of these processors and their functions.

Modems

Modems are the most common type of communications processor. They convert the digital signals from a computer or transmission terminal at one end of a communications link into analog frequencies that can be transmitted over ordinary telephone lines. A modem at the other end of the communications line converts the transmitted data back into digital form at a receiving terminal. This process is known as *modulation* and *demodulation*, and the word *modem* is a combined abbreviation of those two words. Modems come in several forms, including small stand-alone units, plug-in circuit boards, and removable modem cards for laptop PCs. Most modems also support a variety of telecommunications functions, such as transmission error control, automatic dialing and answering, and faxing capability.

Modem (56K bit/sec)	**ADSL (Asymmetric Digital Subscriber Line)**
• Receives at 56K bit/sec. • Sends at 28.8K bit/sec. • Users need only the modem	• Receives at up to 6M bit/sec. • Sends at 64K bit/sec. • Users will need a special modem
ISDN (Integrated Services Digital Network	**Cable Modem**
• Sends and receive at 128K bit/sec. • Users need extra lines • Not available everywhere	• Sends and receives at 10M bit/sec. • Needs cable hookup to special modem • Cable systems infrastructure needs to be upgraded

Source: Adapted from Kim Gerard, "Juiced Modems Rival ISDN as the Link of Choice," *Computerworld.*

Figure 9.14. *Comparing new modem and telecommunications technologies.*

Modems are used because ordinary telephone networks were primarily designed to handle continuous analog signals (electromagnetic frequencies), such as those generated by the human voice over the telephone. Since data from computers are in digital form (voltage pulses), devices are necessary to convert digital signals into appropriate analog transmission frequencies and vice versa.

However, digital communications networks that use only digital signals and do not need analog/ digital conversion are becoming commonplace. Since most modems also perform a variety of telecommunications support functions, devices called *digital modems* are still used in digital networks. It compares several new modem and telecommunications technologies.

Multiplexers

A **multiplexers** is a communications processor that allows a single communications channel to carry simultaneous data transmissions from many terminals. Thus, a single communications line can be shared by several terminals. Typically, a multiplexer merges the transmissions of several terminals at one end of a communications channel, while a similar unit separates the individual transmission at the receiving end.

This is accomplished in two basic ways. In *frequency division multiplexing* (FDM), a multiplexer effectively divides a high-speed channels into multiple slow-speed channels. In *time division multiplexing* (TDM), the multiplexer divides the time each terminal can use the high-speed line into very short time slots, or time frames. The most advanced and popular type of multiplexer is the *statistical time division multiplexer*, most commonly referred to as a statistical multiplexer. Instead of giving all terminals equal time slots, it dynamically allocates time slots only to active terminals according to priorities assigned by a telecommunications manager.

Modem (56Kbit/sec)	ADSL (Assymmetric Digital Subscriber Line)
• Receives at 56 Kbit/sec • Sends at 28.8 Kbit/sec • Users need only the modem	• Receives at upto 6 Mbit/sec • Sends at 64 bit/sec • Users will need a special modem
ISDN (Integrated Services Digital Network	Cable Modem
• Sends & Receives at a 128 Kbit/sec • Users need extra lines • Not available everywhere	• Sends & Receives at 10 Mbit/sec • Needs Cable hookup to spend modem • Cable System Infrastructure needs to be upgraded

Figure 9.15. Comparing new modem and telecommunications technologies.

Internetwork Processors

As we mentioned in Section I, telecommunications networks are interconnected by special-purpose communications processors called **internetwork processors** such as switches, routers, hubs, and gateways. A *switch* is a communications processor that make connections between telecommunications circuits in a networks so a telecommunications message can reach its intended destination. A *router* is a more intelligent communications processor that interconnects networks based on different rules or *protocols*, so a telecommunications message can be routed to its destination. A *hub* is a port switching communications processor. Workstations, servers, printers, and other network resources are connected to ports, as are switches and routers provided by hub to other networks. Networks that use different communications architectures are interconnected by using a communications processor called a *gateway*. All these devices are essential to providing connectivity and easy access between the multiple LANs and wide area networks that are part of the intranets and client/server networks in many organisations.

Telecommunications Software

Software is a vital component of all telecommunications networks. In already, we discussed telecommunications and network management software, which may reside in PCs, servers, mainframes, and communications processors like multiplexers and routers. For example, mainframe-based wide area networks frequently use *telecommunications monitors* or *teleprocessing* (TP) monitors. CICS (Customer Identification Control System) for IBM mainframes is a typical example. Servers in local area networks rely on network management software called *network operating system*, such as Novell NetWare, IBM's OS/2 Warp Server, or Microsoft Windows NT Server. Corporate intranets use network management software like Netscape's Enterprise Server, which is one of several programs for network management, electronic commerce, and application development in Netscape's SuiteSpot, a suite of software servers for the internet, intranets, and extranets. Many times, telecommunications software known as *middleware* can help diverse networks communicate with each other. A variety of communications software packages are available for microcomputers, especially Internet Web browsers like Netscape Navigator and Microsoft Explorer.

Common Software Functions

Telecommunications software packages provide a variety of communications support services. The number and type of network terminals, computers, communications processors, and communications activities involved determine the capabilities of the program required. However, several major functions are commonly provided by telecommunications packages.

- **Access Control.** This function establishes the connections between terminals and computers in a network. The software works with a communications processor (such as a modem) to connect and disconnect communications link and establish communications parameters such as transmission speed, mode, and direction. Access control may also involve automatic telephone dialing and redialing, logging on and off with appropriate account number and security codes, and automatic answering of telephone calls from another computer. Many communications packages include a script allows you to develop programs to customize access control, such as accessing other computers at night or while you are away.
- **Transmission Control.** This function allows computers and terminals to send and receive commands, messages, data, and programs. Some error checking and correction of data transmissions may also be provided. Data and programs are usually transmitted in the form of files, so this activity is frequently called file transfer.
- **Network Management.** This functions manages communications in a telecommunications network. Software such as LAN network operating system and WAN telecommunications monitors determines transmission priorities; routes (switches) messages, polls, and terminals in the network; and forms waiting lines (queues) of transmission requests. It also logs statistics of network activity and the use of network resources by end user workstations.

- **Error Control.** This function involves detection and correction of transmission errors. Errors are usually caused by distortions in the communications channel, such as line noise and power surges. Communications software and processors control errors in transmission by several methods, including *parity checking*. Parity checking involves determining whether there is an odd or even number of *binary one digits* in a character being transmitted or received. Besides parity bits, additional *control codes* are usually added to the message itself. These specify such information as the destination of the data, their priority, and the beginning and end of the message, plus additional error detecting and correcting information. Most error correction methods involve retransmissions. A signal is sent back to the computer to retransmit the previous message.
- **Security Management.** This function protects a communications network from unauthorized access. Network operating systems or other security programs restrict access to data files and other computing resources in LANs and other types of networks. This restrictions usually involves control procedures that limits access to all or parts of network by various categories of users, as determined by the network manage or administrator of the network. Automatic disconnection and callback procedures may also be used. Data transmission can also be protected by *encryption* techniques. Data are scrambled into a coded form before transmission and decoded upon arrival.

Telecommunications Network Topologies

There are several basic types of network *topologies*, or structures, in telecommunications networks. The two simplest are *point-to-point lines* and *multidrop lines*. When point-to-point lines are used, each terminals is connected by its own line to a computer system. When multidrop lines are used, several terminals share each data communications line to a computer. Obviously, point-to-point line are more expensive than multidrop lines; all of the communications capacity and equipment of a communications line is being used by a single terminal. Therefore, point-to-point line are used only if there will be continuous communications between a computer and a terminal or other computer system. A multidrop line decreases communications costs because each line is shared by many terminals. Communications processors such as multiplexers and concentrators help many terminals share the same line.

Star, Ring, and Bus Networks

Figure 9.16 illustrates three basic topologies used in wide area and local area telecommunications networks. A *star* networks ties end user computers to a central computer. A *ring* network ties local computer processors together in a ring on a more equal basis. A *bus* network in which local processors share the same bus, or communications channel. A variation of the ring network is the mesh network. This uses direct communications line to connect some or all of the computers in the ring to each other. Another variation is the tree network, which joins several bus networks together.

Clients/servers networks may use a combination of star, ring, and bus approaches. Obviously, the star network is more centralized, while ring and bus networks have a more decentralized approach. However, this is not always the case. For example, the central computer in a star configuration may be acting only as a *switch*, or message-switching computer, that handles the data communications between autonomous local computers. Star, ring, and bus networks differ in their performances, reliabilities, and costs. A pure star network is considered less reliable than a ring network, since the other computers in the star are heavily dependent on the central host computer. If it fails, there is no backup processing and communications capability, and the local computer cut off from each other. Therefore, it is essential that the host computer be highly reliable. Having some type of multiprocessor architecture to provide a fault tolerant capability is a common solution.

Ring and bus networks are most common in local area networks. Ring networks are considered more reliable and less costly for the type of communications in such networks. If one computer in the ring goes down, the other computers can continue to process their own work as well as to communicate with each other.

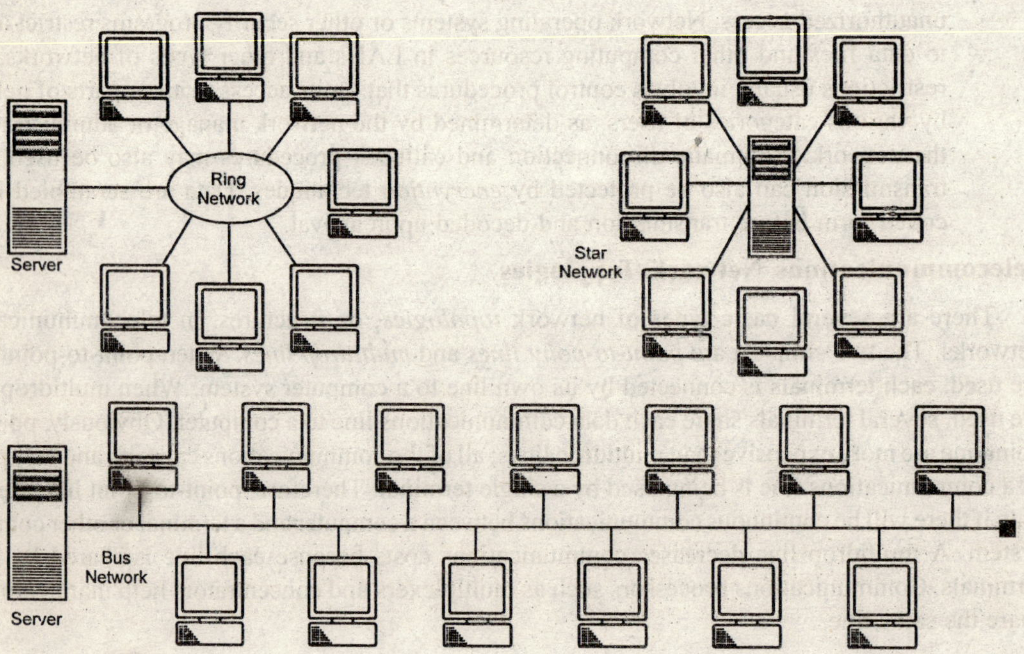

Figure 9.16. The ring, star, and bus network topologies.

Network Architectures and Protocols

Until quite recently, there was a lack of sufficient standards for the interfaces between the hardware, software, and communications channels of data communications networks. For this reason, it is quite common to find a lack of compatibility between the data communications hardware and software of different manufacturers. This situation has hampered the use of data communications, increased its costs, and reduced its efficiency and effectiveness. In response, computer manufacturers and national and international organisations have developed standards called *protocols* and master plan called *network architectures* to support the development of advanced data communications networks.

- **Protocols.** A **protocol** is a standard set of rules and procedures for the control of communications in a network. However, these standards may be limited to just one manufacturer's equipment, or to just one type of data communications. Part of the goal of communications network architectures is to create more standardization and compatibility among communications protocols. One example of a protocol is a standard for the physical characteristics of the cables and connectors between terminals, computer, modems, and communications line. Other examples are the protocols that establish the communications control information needed for *handshaking*, which is the process of exchanging predetermined signals and characters to establish a telecommunications session between terminals and computers. Other protocols deal with control of data transmission reception in a network, switching techniques, internetwork connections, and so on.
- **Network Architectures.** The goal of network architectures is to promote an open. Simple, flexible, and efficient telecommunications environment. This is accomplished by the use of standard protocols, standard communications hardware and software interfaces, and the design of a standard multilevel interface between end users and computer systems.

The OSI Model

The International Standards Organisations (ISO) has developed a seven-layer Open Systems Interconnection (OSI) model to serve as a standard model for network architectures. Dividing data communications functions into seven distinct layers promotes the development of modular network architectures, which assists the development, operations, and maintenance of complex telecommunications networks. Figure 9.17 illustrates the functions of the seven layers of the OSI model architecture.

The Internet's TCP/IP

The Internet uses a system of telecommunications protocols that has become so widely used that it is equivalent to a network architecture. The Internet's protocol suite is called Transmission Control Protocol/Internet Protocol and is known as TCP/IP. As Figure 9.17 shows, TCP/IP consists of five levels of protocols that can be related to the seven layers of the OSI architectures. TCP/IP is used by the Internet and by all intranets and extranets. Many companies and other organisations are also converting their client/server networks to TCP/IP.

Bandwidth Alternatives

The communications speed and capacity of telecommunications networks can be classified by **bandwidth**. This is the frequency range of a telecommunications channel; it determines the channel's maximum transmission rate. The speed and capacity of data transmission rates are typically measured in bits per second (BPS). This is sometimes referred to as the *baud* rate, though baud is more correctly a measure of signal changes in a transmission line.

Low-speed analog channels (*voicehand*) are typically used for transmission rates from 300 to 9,600 BPS, but can now handle up to 1 million BPS (MBPS). They are usually unshielded twisted-pair lines commonly used for voice communications, but are also for data communications by microcomputers, video terminals, and fax machines. Medium-speed channels (*medium-band*) use shielded twisted-pair lines for transmission speeds from 9,600 BPS up to 100 MBPS.

High-speed digital channels (*broadband*) allow transmission rates at specific intervals from 256,000 BPS to several billion BPS. Typically, they use microwave, fibre optics, or satellite transmission. Examples are 1.54 millions BPS for T1 communications channels developed by AT&T and up to 100 MBPS for communications satellite channels.

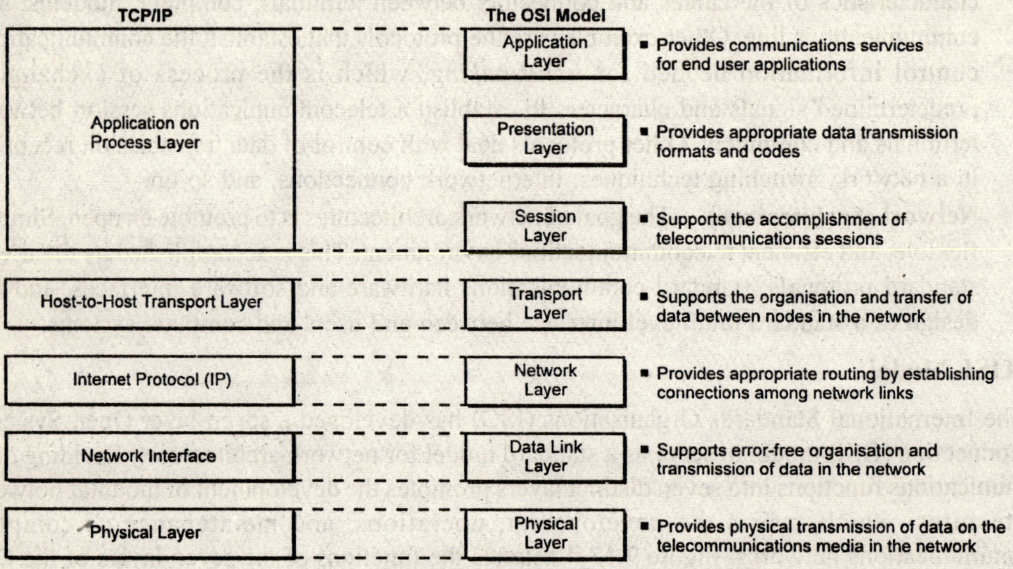

Figure 9.17. *The seven layers of the OSI communications network architecture, and the five layers of the Internet's TCP/IP protocol suite.*

Switching Alternatives

Regular telephone service relies on *circuits switching*, which a switch opens a circuits to establish a link between a sender and receiver; it remains open until the communication session is completed. In messages switching, a message is transmitted a block at a time from one switching device to another.

Packet switching involves subdividing communications messages into fixed of variable groups called packets. For example, in the X.25 protocol, packets are 128 characters long, while they are of variable length in the *frame relay* technology. Packet switching networks are frequently operated by *value-added carriers* who use computers and other communications processors to control the packets switching process and transmit the packets of various users over their networks.

Early packets switching networks were X.25 networks. The X.25 protocols is an international set of standards governing the operations of widely used, but relatively slow, packet switching networks. *Frame relay* is another popular packet switching protocol, and is used by many large companies for their wide area networks. Frame relay is considerably faster than X.25, and is better able to handle the heavy telecommunication traffic of interconnected local area networks within a company's wide area client/server network. ATM (*asynchronous transfer mode*) is an emerging high-capacity *cell switching* technology. An ATM switch breaks voice, video, and other data into fixed cells of 53 bytes (48 bytes of data and 5 bytes of control information), and routes them to their next destination in the network. ATM networks are being developed by many companies needing its fast, high-capacity multimedia capabilities for voice, video, and data communications.

Type of Media	Maximum BPS
Twisted pair—unshielded/shielded	2M–100M
Coaxial cable—baseband/broadband	264M–550M
Satellite/terrestrial microwave	100M
Wireless LAN radio	3.3M
Infrared LAN	4M
Fibre optic cable	30G
Network Technologies	**Typical/Maximum BPS**
Standard Ethernet or token ring	10–16M
High-speed Ethernet	100M–1G
FDDI: fibre distributed data interface	100M
DDN: digital data network	2.4K–2M
PSN: packet switching network	2.4K–64K
Frame relay network	56K/64K–34M
ISDN: integrated services digital network	64K/128K–2M
ATM: asyncronous transfer mode	25/155M–2.4G

KBPS = thousands BPS or kilobits per second GBPS = billions BPS or gigabits per second.
MBPS = millions BPS or megabits per second.

***Figure 9.18.** Examples of the telecommunications transmission speeds by type of media and network technology.*

Access Alternatives

How can terminals and other devices access and share a network to transmit and receive data? As Figure 9.19 indicates, a variety of access methods provides this capacity. In the *polling* approach, a host computer or communications processor polls (contacts) each terminals in sequence to determine which terminals have messages to send. The sequence in which the terminals are polled is based on the communications traffic expected for each terminal. Thus, the transmission of each terminal is based on a roll call of each terminal on the line. Polling can be an effective methods because the speed of mainframe and communications processor computers allow them to poll and control transmission by many terminals sharing the same line, especially if typical communications consists of brief messages and inquiries.

In the *contention* approach, line use is on a first-come, first-served basis, where a terminal can transmit data if the line is not in use but must wait if it is busy. In this method, a computer or other device continually monitors the network and sends a massage only if it senses the network is not in use. If a collision is detected, the computer must stop transmission, wait until the network is clear, and try again. This access methods is used by the Ethernet standard for local area networks.

- **Polling.** A communications processor conducts a roll call of the terminals in a network to determine if they have messages to send.
- **Contention.** Terminals send messages on the network on a first-come, first-served basis.
- **Token passing.** Terminals use an electronic signal code, or *token*, to send messages that are passed onto the appropriate terminal in the network.

***Figure 9.19.** Common telecommunications access methods.*

Another widely used methods in local area networks is token passing. A token is a special signal code sent around the network. If a terminal or other device wants to transmit a message, it must wait for the token to come by, examine it to see if it is in use, and pass it on or use the token to help route its message to its destinations on the network. After transmission is completed, the token is returned to the network by the receiving terminals if it is not needed. This access method is used in all *token ring* local area network, and the high-speed fibre optic-based token ring LAN standard known as Fibre Distribution Data Interface, or FDDI.

Summary/Conclusion

Telecommunication Trends. Many organisations are becoming internetworked enterprises that use the Internet, intranets, and other telecommunications networks to support business operations and collaborations within the enterprises, and with their customers, suppliers, and other business partners. Telecommunications has entered a deregulated and fiercely competitive environment with many vendors, carriers, and services. Telecommunications technology is moving towards open, internetworked digital networks for voice, data, video, and multimedia. A major trend is the pervasive use of the Internet and its technologies to build interconnected enterprise and global networks, like intranets and extranets, that form information superhighways to support enterprise collaboration, electronic commerce, and internal business applications as summarized in Figure 9.1.

Telecommunications Networks. The major generic components of any telecommunications network are (1) terminals, (2) telecommunications processors, (3) communications channels, (4) computers, and (5) telecommunications software. There are several basic types of telecommunications network, including wide area networks (WANs) and local area networks (LANs). Most WANs and LANs are being interconnected to form internetworks such as the Internet, intranets and extranets, and client/server and interorganisational networks.

The Internet Revolution. The explosive growth of the Internet and the use of its enabling technologies are the revolutionary technology phenomena of the 1990s. The Internet has become the key platform for a rapidly expanding list of information and entertainment services and business applications, including enterprise collaboration and electronic commerce systems. Opens systems with unrestricted connectivity using Internet technologies are the primary telecommunications technology drivers of the later 1990s. Their primary goal is to promote easy and secure access by business end users and consumers to the resources of the Internet, enterprise intranets, and interorganisational extranets.

Network Alternatives. Key telecommunications network alternatives and components are summarized in Figure 9.12 for telecommunications media, processors, software, channels, and network architectures. A basic understanding of these major alternatives will help business end users participate effectively in decisions involving telecommunications issues. Telecommunications processors include modems, multiplexers, internetwork processors, and various devices to help interconnect and enhance the capacity and efficiency of telecommunications channels. Telecommunications channels uses such media as twisted-pair wire, coaxial cables, fibre optic cables, terrestrial microwave, communications satellite, cellular phone systems, and wireless LAN technologies. Telecommunications software, such as network operating systems, telecommunications monitors, and Web browsers, controls and supports the communications activity in a telecommunications network.

10

Database Management

SECTION I

DATABASE MANAGEMENT MANAGING DATA RESOURCES

SECTION II

Technical Foundation of Database Management

SECTION I

Database Management: Managing Data Resources

Introduction

Data are a vital organisational resource that need to be managed like other important business assets. Most organisations could not survive or succeed without quality data about their internal operational and external environment.

Organisations are under tremendous pressure to provide better quality decision-making information in forms easy to access and manipulate. Business users are reacting to their own mission-critical needs for better information due to rapidly changing, increasingly volatile and competitive markets, as well as ever-shortening product life cycles [13].

That's why organisations and their managers need to practice data resource management, a managerial activity that applies information systems technologies like database management and other management tools to the task of managing an organisation's data resources to meet the information needs of business users. This chapter will show you the managerial implications of using database management technologies and methods to manage an organisation's data assets to meet the information requirements of a business.

For example, Sears uses consumer demographic data in their data warehouse to improve their new store location decisions. Comparative market data helps Sears compare the performance of their stores and store managers to their competitors. MCI and First American, on the other hand, use warehouse data about the buying habits of their own customers and other companies' customers to significantly improve the success of their joint marketing campaigns. By combining internal and external data about their customers and their chosen markets in data warehouses, these companies can do a better job of analyzing their business performance and designing successful marketing strategies.

Foundation Data Concepts

Before we go any further, let's review some fundamental concepts about how data are organised in information systems. A hierarchy of several levels of data has been devised that differentiates between different groupings, or elements, of data. Thus, data may be logically organised into characters, fields, records, files, and databases, just as writing can be organised in letters, words, sentences, paragraphs, and documents.

Character

The most basic logical data elements is the **character**, which consists of a single alphabetic, numeric, or other symbol. One might argue that the bit or byte is a more elementary data element, but remember that those terms refer to the physical storage elements provided by the computer hardware. From a user's point of view (that is, from a logical as opposed to a physical or hardware view of data), a character is the most basic element of data that can be observed and manipulated.

Field

The next higher level of data is the **field**, or data item. A field consists of a grouping of characters. For example, the grouping of alphabetic characters in a person's name forms a name field, and the grouping of numbers in a sales amount forms a sales amount field.

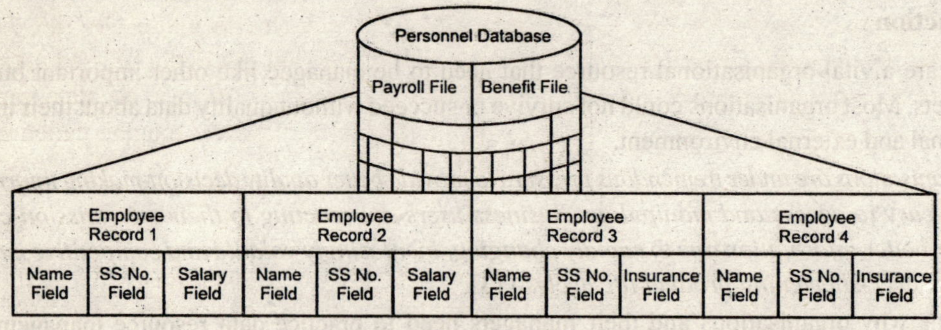

***Figure 10.1** Examples of the logical data elements in information systems. Note especially the examples of how data fields, records, files, and databases are related.*

Specifically, a data field represents an attribute (a characteristic or quality) of some entity (object, person, or event). For example, an employee's salary is an attribute that is a typical data field used to describe an entity who is an employee of a business.

Record

Related fields of data are grouped to form a record. Thus, a record represents a collection of *attributes* that describe an *entity.* An example is the payroll record for a person, which consists of data fields describing attributes such as the person's name, Social Security number, and rate of pay. *Fixed-length* record contain a fixed number of fixed-length data fields. *Variable-length* records contain a variable number of fields and fields lengths.

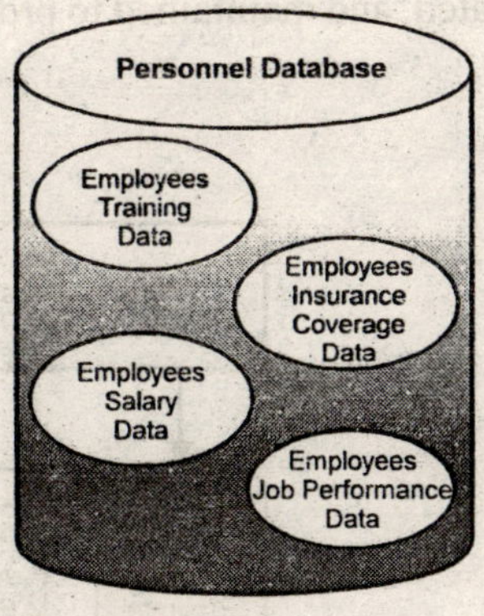

***Figure 10.2** A personal database consolidates data formerly kept in separate files.*

File

A group of related records is a data file, or *table.* Thus, an employee file would contain the records of the employees of a firm. Files are frequently classified by the application for which they are primarily used, such as a *payroll file or an inventory file,* or the type of data they contain, such as a *document file* or *a graphical image file.* Files are also classified by their permanence, for example, a payroll *master file* versus a payroll weekly *transaction file.* A transaction file, therefore, would contain records of all transactions occurring during a period and might be used periodically to update the permanent records contained in a master file. *A history file* is an obsolete transaction or master file retained for backup purposes or for long-term historical storage called *archival storage.*

Database

A database is an integrated collection of logically related records or *objects.* An object consists of data values describing the attributes of an *entity,* plus the operations that can be performed upon the data. We will explain object-oriented databases in Section II.

A database consolidates records previously stored in separate files into a common pool of data records that provides data for many applications. The data stored in a database are independent of the application programs using them and of the type of secondary storage devices on which they are stored. For example, a personnel database consolidates date formerly segregated in separate files such as payroll files, personnel action files, and employee skills files.

The Database Management Approach

The development of databases and database management software is the foundation of modern methods of managing organisational data. The database management approach consolidates data records and objects into databases that can be accessed by many different application programs. In addition, an important software package called a *database management system* (DBMS) serves as a software interface between users and databases. This helps users easily access the records in a database. Thus, database management involves the use of database management software to control how databases are created, interrogated, and maintained to provide information needed by end users and their organisations.

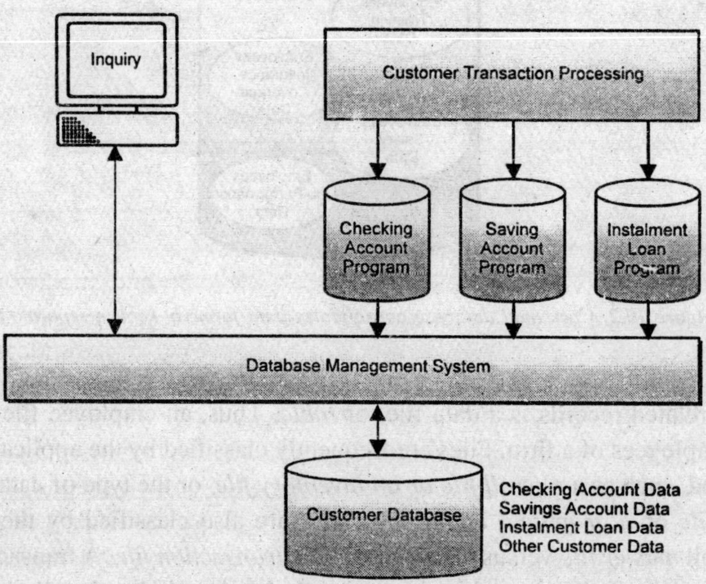

Figure 10.3 *An example of a database management approach in a banking information system. Note how the savings, checking, and instalment loan programs use a database management system to share a customer database. Note also that the DBMS allows a user to make a direct, ad hoc interrogation of the database without using application programs.*

For example, customers records and other common types of data are needed for several different applications in banking, such as check processing, automated teller systems, bank credit cards, savings accounts, and instalment loan accounting. These data can be consolidated into a common *customer database*, rather than being kept in separate files for each of those applications.

Thus, the database management approach involves three basic activities:

- Updating and maintaining common databases to reflect new business transactions and other events requiring changes to an organization's records.
- Providing information needed for each end user's application by using application programs that share the data in common databases. This sharing of data is supported by the common

software interface provided by a database management system package. Thus, end users and programmers do not have to know where or how data are physically stored.

- Providing an inquiry/response and reporting capability through a DBMS package so that end users can easily interrogate databases, generate reports, and receive quick responses to their ad hoc requests for information.

Using Database Management Software

Let's take a closer look at the capabilities provided by database management software. A database management system (DBMS) is a set of computer programs that controls the creation, maintenance, and use of the database of an organisation and its end users. As we said already, database management packages are available for micro, midrange, and mainframe computer systems. The four major uses of a DBMS are illustrated in Figure 10.4. Let's take a look at each of them now.

Database Development

Database management packages like Microsoft Access or Lotus Approach allow end users to easily develop the databases they need. However, large organisations with client/server or mainframe-based systems usually place control of enterprisewide database development in the hands of **database administrators** (DBAs) and other database specialists. This improves the integrity and security of organisational databases. Database developers use the *data definition language* (DDL) in database management system like Oracle 8 or IBM's DB2 to develop and specify the data contents, relationships, and structure of each database, and to modify these database specifications when necessary. Such information is cataloged and stored in a database of data definitions and specifications called a *data dictionary,* which is maintained by the DBA. We will discus database development further in Section II of this chapter.

The Data Dictionary. Data dictionaries are another tool of database administration. A data dictionary is a computer-based catalog or directory containing *metadata,* that is, data about data. A data dictionary includes a software component to manage a database of data definitions, that is, metadata about the structure, data elements, and other characteristics of an organisation's databases. For example, it contains the names and descriptions of all types of data records and their interrelationships, as well as information outlining requirements for end user's access, use of application programs, and database maintenance and security.

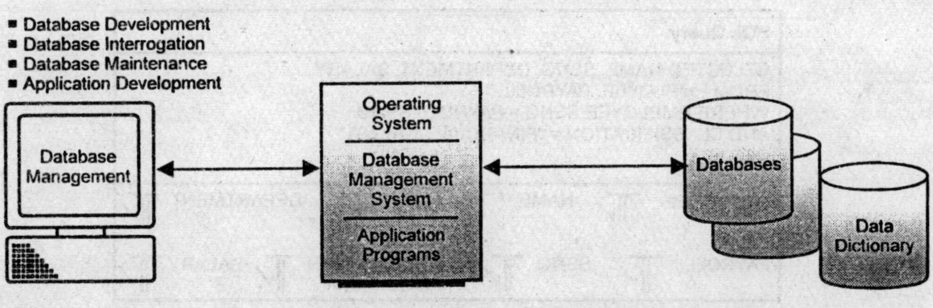

Figure 10.4. The four major uses of a DBMS package are database development, database interrogation, database maintenance, and application development.

Data dictionaries can be queried by the database administrator to report the status of any aspect of a firm's metadata. The administrator can then make changes to the definitions of selected data elements. Some *active* (versus *passive*) data dictionaries automatically enforce standard data element definitions whenever end users and application programs use a DBMS to access an organisation's databases. For example, and active data dictionary would not allow a data entry program to use a nonstandard definition of a customer record, nor would it allow a data entry operator to enter a name a customer that exceeded the defined size of that data element.

Database Interrogation

The database interrogation capability is a major benefit of a database management system. End users can use a DBMS by asking for information from database using a *query language* or a *report generator.* They can receive an immediate response in the form of video displays or printed reports. No difficult programming is required. The query language feature lets you easily obtain immediate responses to ad hoc data requests: you merely key in a few short inquiries. The report generator feature allows you quickly specify a report format for information you want presented as a report.

SQL and QBE. SQL, or Structured Query Language is a query language found in many database management packages. The basic form of an SQL query is:

SELECT. . . FROM . . . WHERE . . .

After SELECT you list the data fields you want retrieved. After FROM you list the files or tables from which the data must be retrieved. After WHERE you specify conditions that limit the search to only those data records in which you are interested. For example, suppose a financial manager wanted to retrieve the names, Social Security numbers, departments, and salaries of all employees who are financial analysts from the employee and payroll files in the company's human resources database. Then she might use the SQL query shown in Figure 10.5 to display such information.

Another query language in some database management packages is QBE, or query by example. QBE's point-and-click capabilities make it easier for end users than SQL. This method displays boxes for each of the data fields in one or more files. You then use your keyboard or mouse to fill in, click on, query, or check boxes to indicate which information you want. For example, a QBE query that would retrieve information similar to the previous SQL query is shown Figure 10.5.

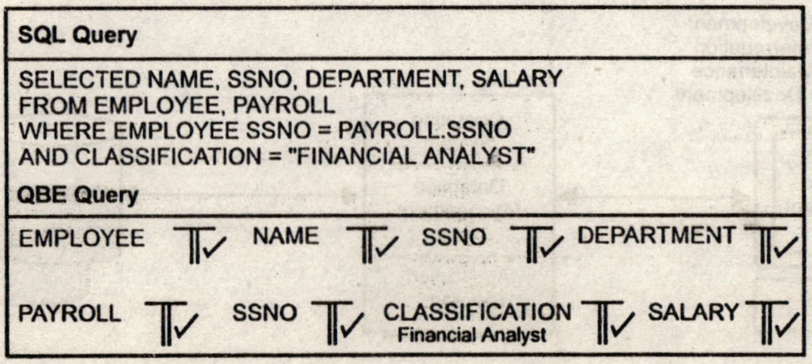

***Figure 10.5.** Using SQL (Structured Query Language) and QBE (query by example) to retrieve information about a company's financial analysts.*

Graphical and Natural Queries. Many end users (and IS professionals) have difficulty correctly phrasing SQL and other database language queries. So most end user database management packages offer GUI (graphical user interface) point-and-click methods, which are easier to use and are translated by the software into SQL commands. Other packages are available that use *natural language* query statements similar to conversational English (or other languages).

Database Maintenance

The database or an organisation need to be updated continually to reflect new business transactions and other events. Other miscellaneous changes must also be made to ensure accuracy of the data in the databases. This **database maintenance** process is accomplished by transaction processing programs and other end user application packages, with the support of the DBMS. End users and information specialists can also employ various utilities provided by a DBMS for database maintenance.

Application Development

DBMS packages play a major role in application **development.** Application developers use the internal 4GL programming language and built-in software development tools provided by many DBMS packages to develop custom application programs. For example, you can use a DBMS to easily develop the data entry screens, forms, reports, or Web pages of a business application. A DBMS also makes the job of application programmers easier, since they do not have to develop detailed data-handling procedures using a conventional programming language every time they write a program. Instead, they can include *data manipulation language* (DML) statements in their programs that call on the DBMS to perform necessary data-handling activities.

A Sample English-to-SQL Translation for
Microsoft's Access Database Manager

English Wizard

WHAT CUSTOMERS DIDN'T HAVE ANY ORDERS LAST MONTH?

SQL

```
SELECT [Customers], [Customers], [Contact Name]
FROM [Customers]
WHERE not Exists {SELECT [Ship Name] FROM [Orders]
  WHERE Month {[Order Date]}=1 and Year {[Orders Date]}=1998 and
  [Customer], [Customer ID]=[Orders]. [Customer ID]}
```

Source: Adapted from Kim Nash, "Wizard turns English into Database Language."

Figure 10.6 Comparing a natural language query with and SQL query.

Types of Databases

Continuing developments in information technology and its business applications have resulted in the evolution of several major types of databases. It illustrates six major conceptual categories of databases that may be found in computer using organisations.

Operational Databases. These databases store detailed data needed to support the operations of the entire organisation. They are also called *subject area data-bases* (SADB), *transaction databases,* and *production databases*. Examples are a customer database, personnel database, inventory database, and other databases containing data generated by business operations.

Analytical Databases. These databases store data information extracted from selected operational and external databases. They consist of summarized data and information most needed by an organisation's managers and other end users. Analytical databases are also called *management databases* or *information databases.* They may also be called *multidimensional databases,* since they frequently use a multidimensional database structure to organise data. These are the databases accessed by the *online analytical processing* (OLAP) systems, decision support systems, and executive information systems.

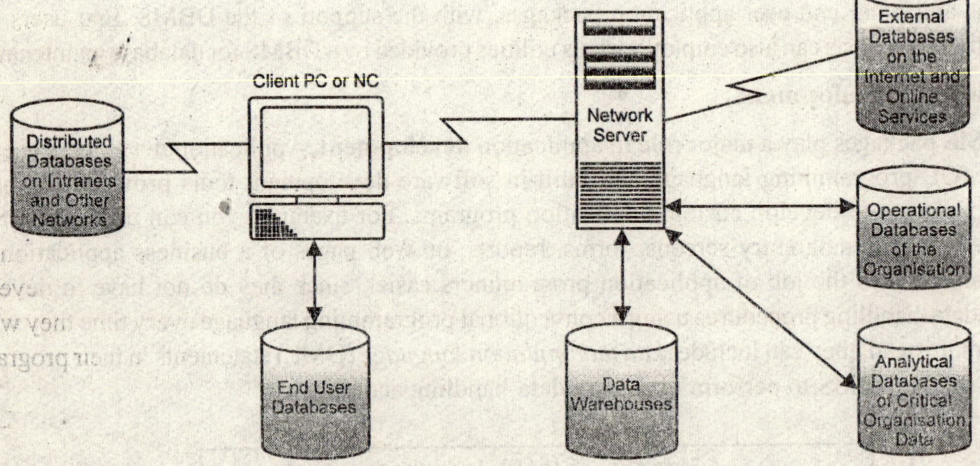

Figure 10.7. Examples of the major types of databases used by organisations and end users.

Data Warehouses. A data warehouse stores data from current and previous years that has been extracted from the various operational databases of an organisation. It is a central source of data that has been screened, edited, standardized, and integrated so it can be used by managers and other end user professionals for a variety of forms of business analysis, market research, and decision support. Data warehouses may by subdivided into *data marts,* which hold specific subsets of data from the warehouse. A major use of data warehouse databases is **data mining.** In data mining, the data in a data warehouse are processed to identify key factors and trends in historical patterns of business activity. This can be used to help managers make decisions about strategic changes in business operations to gain competitive advantages in the marketplace.

Distributed Databases. Many organisations replicate and distribute copies or parts of databases to network servers at a variety of sites. These distributed databases can reside on network servers on the World Wide Web, on corporate intranets or extranets, or on other company networks. Distributed databases may be copies of operational or analytical databases, hypermedia or discussion databases, or any other type of database. Replication and distribution of databases is done to improve database performance and security. Ensuring that all of the data in an organisation's distributed databases are consistently and concurrently updated is a major challenge of distributed database management.

End User Database. These databases consist of a variety of data files developed by end users at their workstations. For example, users may have their own electronic copies of documents they download from the World Wide Web, generate with word processing packages, or receive by electronic mail. Or they may have their own data files generated from using spreadsheet and DBMS packages.

External Databases. Access to a wealth of information from external databases is available for a fee from commercial online services and with or without charge from many sources on the Internet, especially the World Wide Web. Web sites provide an endless variety of hyperlinked pages of multimedia documents in *hypermedia databases* for you to access. Data are available in the form of statistics on economic and demographic activity from *statistical* data banks. Or you can view or download abstracts or complete copies of hundreds of newspapers, magazines, newsletters, research papers, and other published material and other periodicals from *bibliographic* and *full text* databases.

Hypermedia Databases on the Web

The most compelling business driver today is the Internet. Because so much of the information flying across the Internet is [multimedia], companies need databases that can store, retrieve, and manage other data types, particularly documents, video and sound [17].

The rapid growth of the Web sites on the Internet and corporate intranets and extranets has dramatically increased the use of databases of hypertext and hypermedia documents. A Web site stores such information in a **hypermedia database** consisting of a home page and other hyperlinked pages of multimedia or mixed media (text, graphic and photographic images, video clips, audio segments, and so on). That is, from a database management point of view, the set of interconnected multimedia pages at a Web site is a database of interrelated hypermedia pages, rather than interrelated data records [2].

The web site illustrated in Figure 10.8 uses a hypermedia database consisting of HTML (Hypertext Markup Language) pages, GIF (graphics image files) files, and video files. The web server software acts as a database management system to manage the use of the interrelated hypermedia pages of the Web site.

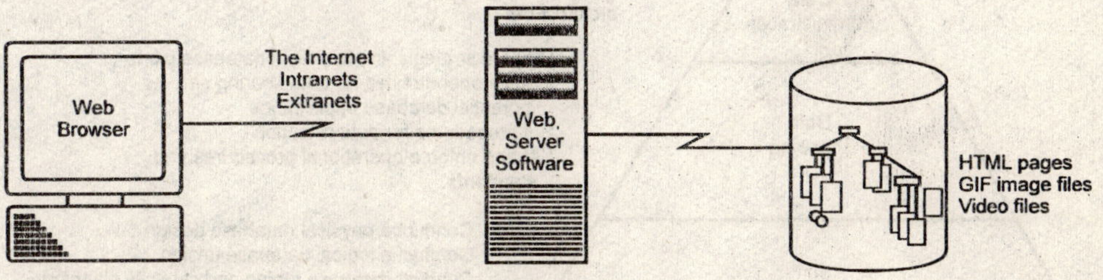

***Figure 10.8.** The components of a Web-based Information system include Web browsers, servers, and hypermedia databases.*

Managerial Considerations for Data Resources Management

Managerial end users should view data as an important resource that they must learn to manage properly to ensure the success and survival of their organisations. But this is easier said than done. Database management is an important application of information systems technology to the management of a firm's data resources. However, other major data management efforts are needed in order to offset some of the problems that can result from the use of a database management approach. Those are (1) database administration, (2) data planning, and (3) data administration.

Database administration is an important data resource management function responsible for the proper use of database management technology. Database administration includes responsibility for developing and maintaining the organisation's data dictionary, designing and monitoring the performance of databases, and enforcing standards for database use and security. Database administrators and analysts work with systems developers and end users to provide their expertise to major systems development projects.

Data Planning is a corporate planning and analysis function that focuses on data resource management. It includes the responsibility for developing and overall data architecture for the firm's data resources that ties in with the firm's strategic mission and plans, and the objectives and processes of its business units. Data planning is done by organisations that have made a formal commitment to long-range planning for the strategic use and management of their data resources.

Data administration is another vital data resource management function. It involves the establishment and enforcement of policies and procedures for managing data as a strategic corporate resource. This means administering the collection, storage, and dissemination of all types of data in such a way that data become a standardized resource available to all end users in the organisation. The focus of data administration is the control of data in support of an organisation's business functions and strategic business objectives. Data administration may also include responsibility for developing policies and setting standards for corporate database design processing, and security arrangements, and for selecting database management and data dictionary software.

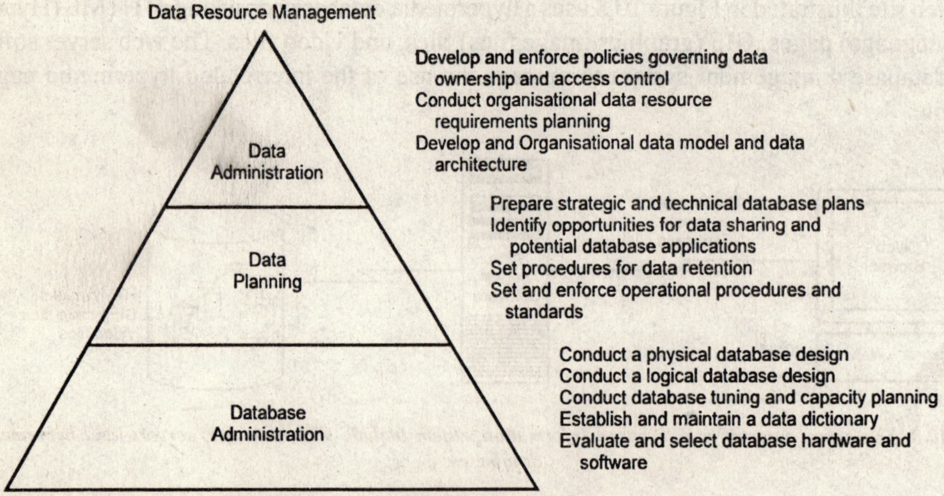

Source: Adapted from Varun Grover and James Teng, "How Effective Is Data Resource Management.

Figure 10.9. ***Data resources management includes database administration, data planning and data administration activities.***

Benefits and Limitations of Database Management

The database management approach provides managerial end users with several important benefits. Database management reduces the duplication of data and integrates data so that they can be accessed by multiple programs and users. Programs are not dependent on the format of the data and the type of secondary storage hardware being used. Users are provided with an inquiry/response and reporting capability that allows them to easily obtain information they need without having to write computer programs. Computer programming is simplified, because programs are not dependent on either the logical format of the data or their physical storage location. Finally, the integrity and security of the data stored in databases can be increased, since access to data and modification of the database are controlled by database management system software, a data dictionary, and a database administrator function.

The limitations of database management arise from its increased technological complexity. Thus, a database management approach can pose problems in data resource management. Developing large databases of complex data types and installing a DBMS can be difficult and expensive. More hardware capability is required, since storage requirements for the organisation's data, overhead control data, and the DBMS programs are greater. Longer processing times may result from high-volume transaction processing applications since an extra layer of software (the DBMS) exists between application programs and the operating system. Finally, if an organisation relies on centralized databases, its vulnerability to errors, fraud, and failures is increased. Yet problems of inconsistency of data can arise if a distributed database approach is used. Therefore, the security and integrity of an organisation's databases are major concerns of an organisation's data resource management effort.

SECTION II

Technical Foundations of Database Management

Just imagine how difficult it would be to get any information from an information system if data were stored in an unorganised way, or if there was no systematic way to retrieve it. Therefore, in all information systems, data resources must be organised and structured in some logical manner so that they can be accessed easily, processed efficiently, retrieved quickly, and managed effectively. Thus, data structures and access methods ranging from simple to complex have been devised to efficiently organise and access data stored by information systems. In this section, we will explore these concepts, as well as more technical concepts of database management.

Database Structures

The relationships among the many individual records stored in databases are based on one of several logical data structures, or models. Database management system packages are designed to use a specific data structure to provide end users with quick, easy access to information stored in databases. Five fundamentals database structures are the hierarchical, network, relational, object-oriented, and multidimensional models. Simplified illustrations of the first three database structures are shown in Figure 10.10.

Hierarchical Structure

Early mainframe DBMS packages used the hierarchical structure, in which the relationships between records form a hierarchy or treelike structure. In the traditional hierarchical model, all records are dependent and arranged on multilevel structures, consisting of one *root* record any number of subordinate levels. Thus, all of the relationships among records are *one-to-many,* since each data element is related to only one element above it. The data element or record at the highest level of the hierarchy (the department data element in this illustration) is called the root element. Any data element can be accessed by moving progressively downward from a root and along the branches of the tree until the desired record (for example, the employee data element) is located.

Network Structure

The network structure can represent more complex logical relationships, and is still used by some mainframe DBMS packages. It allows *many-to-many* relationships among records; that is, the network model can access a data element by following one of several paths, because any data element or record can be related to any number of other data elements. For example, in Figure 10.10, departmental records can be related to more than one employee record, and employee records can be related to more than one project record. Thus, one could locate all employee records for a particular department, or all project records related to a particular employee.

Relational Structure

The relational model has become the most popular of the three database structures. It is used by most microcomputer DBMS packages, as well as by many minicomputer and mainframe systems. In the relational model, all data elements within the database are viewed as being stored in the form of simple **tables**. Figure 10.10 illustrates the relational database model with two tables representing some of the relationships among departmental and employee records. Other tables, or **relations,** for this organisation's database might represent the data element relationships among projects, divisions, product lines, and so on. Database management system packages based on the relational model can link data elements from various tables to provide information to users. For example, a DBMS package could retrieve and display an employee's name and salary from the employee table in Figure 10.10, and the name of the employee's department from the department table, by using their common department number field (Deptno) to link or join the two tables.

Multidimensional Structure

The multidimensional database structure is a variation of the relational model that uses multidimensional structures to organise data and express the relationships between data. You can visualize multidimensional structures as cubes of data and cubes within cubes of data. Each side of the cube is considered a dimension of the data. Figure 10.11 is an example that shows that each dimension can represent a different category, such as product type, region, sales channel, and time.

Hierarchical Structure

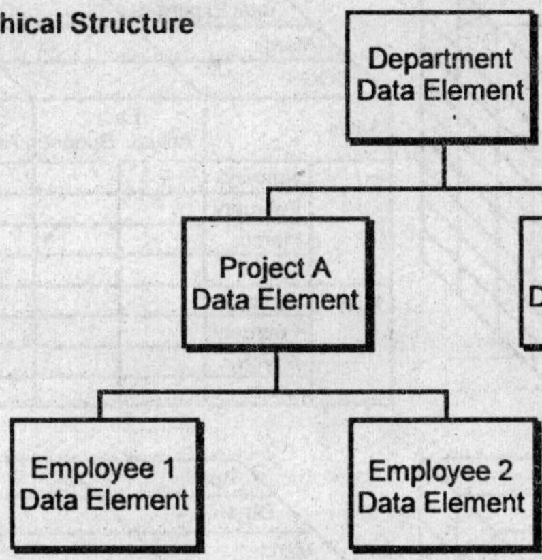

Network Structure

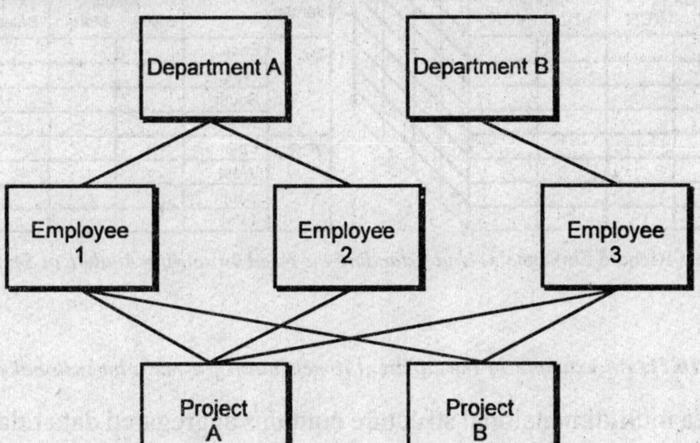

Relational Structure

Department Table

Deptno	Dname	Dloc	Dmgr
Dept A			
Dept B			
Dept C			

Empno	Ename	Etitle	Esalary	Deptno
Emp 1				Dept A
Emp 2				Dept A
Emp 3				Dept B
Emp 4				Dept B
Emp 5				Dept C
Emp 6				Dept D

Figure 10.10. *Examples of three fundamental database structures. They represent three basic ways to develop and express the relationship among the data elements in a database.*

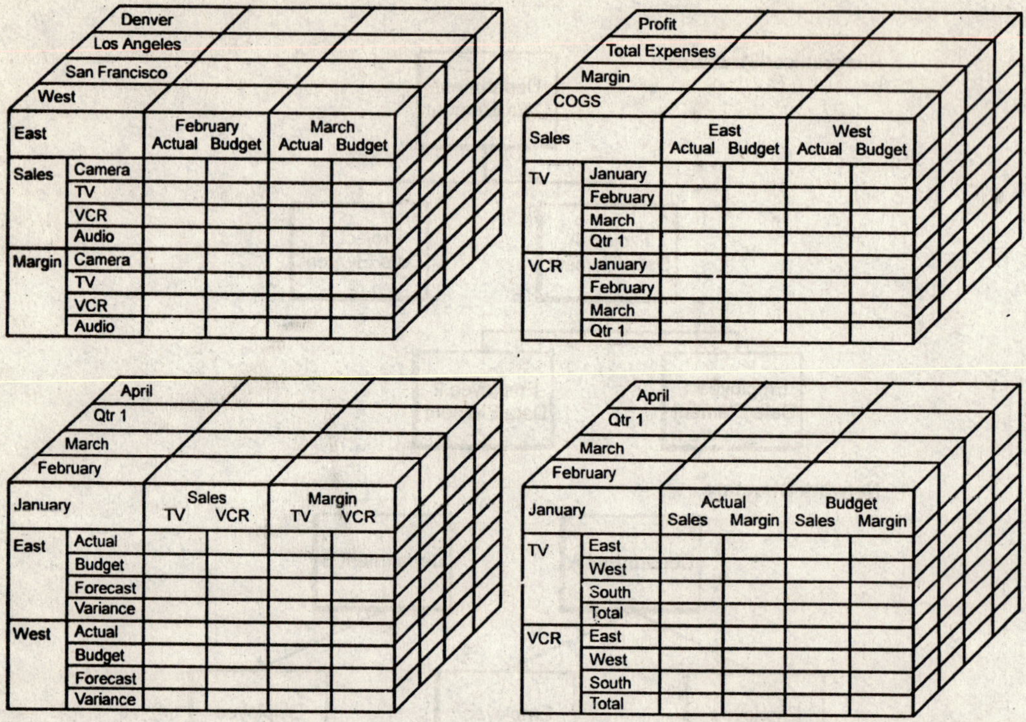

Source: Adapted from Richard Finkelstein, *Understanding the Need for on-line Analytical Servers.*

Figure 10.11. *An example of the different dimensions of a multidimensional database.*

Each cell within a multidimensional structure contains aggregated data related to elements along each of its dimensions. For example, a single cell may contain the total sales for a product in a region for a specific sales channel in a single month. A major benefit of multidimensional databases is that they are a compact and easy-to-understand way to visualize and manipulate data elements that have many interrelationships. So multidimensional database have become the most popular database structure for the analytical databases that support *on-line analytical processing* (OLAP) applications, in which fast answers to complex business queries are expected.

Object-Oriented Structure

The **object-oriented** database model is considered to be one of the key technologies of a new generation of multimedia Web-based applications. We introduced the concept of objects when we discussed object-oriented programming already. It illustrates, an **object** consists of data values describing the attributes of an entity, plus the operations that can be performed upon the data. This *encapsulation* capability allows the object-oriented model to better handle more complex types of data (graphics, pictures, voice, text) than other database structures.

The object-oriented model also supports *inheritance*; that is, new objects can be automatically created by replicating some or all of the characteristics of one or more *parent* objects. Thus, the checking and savings account objects can both inherit the common attributes and operations of the parent bank account object. Such capabilities have made *object-oriented database management systems* (OODBMS) popular in computer-aided design (CAD) and in a growing number of applications. For example, object technology allows designers to develop product designs, store them as objects in an object-oriented database, and replicate and modify them to create new product designs. In addition, multimedia Web-based applications for the Internet and corporate intranets and extranets have become a major application area for object technology, as we will discuss shortly.

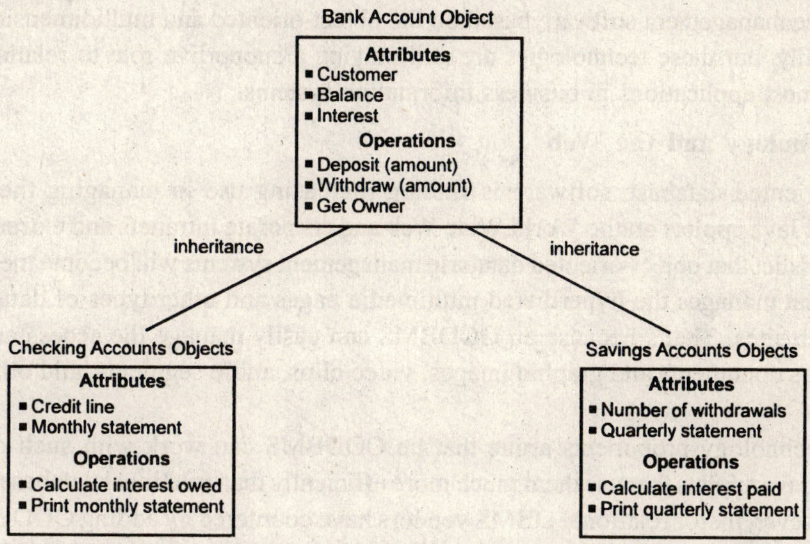

Source: Adapted from Ivar Jacobson, Maria Ericsson, and Ageneta Jacobsen, ***The Object Advantage Business Process Reengineering with Other Technology.***

Figure 10.12. *The checking and savings account objects can inherit common attributes and operations from the bank account object.*

Evaluation of Database Structure

The hierarchical data structure is a natural model for the databases used for many of the structure, routine types of transaction processing characteristics of many business operations. Data for many of these operations can easily be represented by groups of records in a hierarchical relationship. However, there are many cases where information is needed about records that do not have hierarchical relationships. For example, it is obvious that, in some organisations, employees from more than one department can work on more than one project. A network data structure could easily handle this many-to-many relationship. It is thus more flexible than the hierarchical structure in support of database for many types of business operations. However, like the hierarchical structure, because its relationships must be specified in advance, the network model cannot easily handle ad hoc requests for information.

Relational databases, on the other hand, allow an end users to easily receive information in response to ad hoc requests. That's because not all of the relationships between the data elements in a relationally organised database need to be specified when the database is created. Database management software (such as Oracle 8, DB2, Access, and Approach) creates new tables of data relationships using parts of the data from several tables. Thus, relational databases are easier for programmers to work with and easier to maintain than the hierarchical and network models.

The major limitation of the relational model is that database management systems based on it cannot process large amounts of business transactions as quickly and efficiently as those based on the hierarchical and network models, in which all data relationships are prespecified. However, this performance gap is narrowing with the development of advanced relational DBMS software. The use of database management software based on the object-oriented and multidimensional model is growing steadily, but these technologies are still playing a supportive role to relational database software for most applications in business information systems.

Object Technology and the Web

Object-oriented database software is finding increasing use in managing the hypermedia databases and Java applets on the World Wide Web and corporate intranets and extranets. Industry proponents predict that object-oriented database management systems will become the key software component that manages the hyperlinked multimedia pages and other types of data that support corporate Web sites. That's because an OODBMS can easily manage the access and storage of objects such as documents and graphic images, video clips, audio segments, and other subsets of Web pages.

Object technology proponents argue that an OODBMS can work with such *complex data types* and the Java applets that use them much more efficiently than relational database management systems. However, major relational DBMS vendors have countered by adding OODBMS modules to their relational software. Examples include multimedia object extensions to IBM's DB2, Informix's DatsBlades for their Universal Server, and Oracle's object-based "cartridges" for their Universal Server and Oracle 8.

Accessing Databases

Efficient access to data is important. In database maintenance, records or objects have to be continually added, deleted, or updated to reflect business transactions. Data must also be accessed rapidly so information can be produced in response to end user requests.

Key Fields

That's why all data records usually contain one or more identification fields, or *keys*, that identify the record so it can be located. For example, the Social Security number of a person is often used as a *primary* key field that uniquely identifies the data records of individuals in students, employees, and customer files and databases. Other methods also identify and link data records stored in several different database files. For example, hierarchical and network databases may use *pointer fields*. These are fields within a record that indicate (point to) the location of another record that is related to it in the same file, or in another file. Hierarchical and network database management systems use this method to link records so they can retrieve information from several different database file.

Department Table

Deptno	Dname	Dloc	Dmgr
Dept A			
Dept B			
Dept C			

Employee Table

Empno	Ename	Etitle	Esalary	Deptno
Emp 1				Dept A
Emp 2				Dept B
Emp 3				Dept C
Emp 4				Dept D
Emp 5				Dept E
Emp 6				Dept F

Figure 10.13. *Joining the Employee and Department tables in a relational database enables you to selectively access data in both tables at the same time.*

Relational database management packages use primary keys to link records. Each table (file) in a relational database must contain a primary key. This field (or fields) uniquely identifies each record in a file and must also be found in other related files. For example, department number (Deptno) is the primary key in the Department table and is also a field in the Employee table. As we mentioned earlier, a relational database management packages could easily provide you with information from both tables to join the tables and retrieve the information you want.

URLs

The files and databases on the Internet and corporate intranets and extranets use **URLs** (uniform Resources Locators) for data access. The general form of URLs for some of the major services of the Internet is shown in Figure 10.14. Thus, the pages of hyperlinked text and multimedia documents on the World Wide Web and intranet/extranet Web sites are accessed by URLs with the format shown in Figure 10.14. For example, the URL for the home page of the Sun Microsystems Web sites is http://www.sun.com. Thus, a Web site relies on URLs instead of traditional keys and pointer to identify and express the relationships among the interconnected pages of its hypermedia database.

Sequential Access

One of the original and basic ways to access data is **sequential access.** This method uses a *sequential organisation*, in which records are physically stored in a specified order according to a key field in each record. For example, payroll records could be placed in payroll file in a numerical order based on employee Social Security numbers. Sequential access is fast and efficient when dealing with large volumes of data that need to be processed periodically. However, it requires that all new transactions be sorted into the proper sequence for sequential access processing. Also, most of the database or file may have to be searched to locate, store, or modify even small number of data records. Thus, this method is too slow to handle applications requiring immediate updating or responses.

Direct Access

When using **direct access** methods, records do not have to be arranged in nay particular sequence on storage media. However, the computer must keep track of the storage location of each record using a variety of *direct organisation* methods so that data can be retrieved when needed. New transactions data do not have to be sorted, and processing that requires immediate responses or updating is easily handled. There are a number of ways to directly access records in the direct organisation method. Let's take a brief look at three widely used methods tc accomplish such direct access processing.

- Web: http://server.address:port/homepage.html
- Gopher: gopher://server.address:port/directory/filename
- FTP: ftp://server.address/complete.file.name
- TELNET: telnet://server.address:port

***Figure 10.14.** The general form of Uniform Resources Locators for major Internet services.*

One common technique of direct access is **key transformation.** This method performs an arithmetic computations on a key field of record (such as a product number or Social Security number) and uses the number that results from that calculations as an address to store and access that record. Thus, the process is called key transformation because an arithmetic operation is applied to a key field to transform it into the storage location address of a record. Another direct access methods used to store and locate records involves the use of an **index** of record keys and related storage addresses. A new data record is stored at the next available location, and its key and address are placed in an index. The computer uses this index whenever it must access a record.

In the **indexed sequential access method** (ISAM), records are stored in sequential order on a magnetic disk or other direct access storage device based on the key field of each record. In addition, each database contain an index that references one or more key fields of each data record to its storage location address. Thus, an individual record can be directly located by using its key fields to search and locate its address in the database index, just as you can locate key topics in this book by looking them up in its index. As a result, if a few records must be processed quickly, the index is used to directly access the record needed. However, when large numbers of records must be processed periodically, the sequential organisation provided by this method is used. For example, processing the weekly payroll for employees or producing monthly statements for customers could be done using sequential access processing of the records in the database.

Database Development

Developing small, personal databases is relatively easy using microcomputer database management packages. However, developing a large database of complex data types can be a complex task. In many companies, developing and managing large corporates databases are the primary responsibility of the database administrator and database design analysis. They work with end users and systems analysts to model business processes and the data they require. Then they determine (1) what data definitions should be included in the database and (2) what structure or relationships should exist among the data elements.

Data Planning and Database Design

As Figure 10.15 illustrates, database development may start with a top-down **data planning process.** Database administrators and designers work with corporate and end user management to develop an *enterprise model* that defines the basic business processes of the enterprise. Then they define the information needs of end users in a business process, such as the purchasing/receiving process that all businesses have [17].

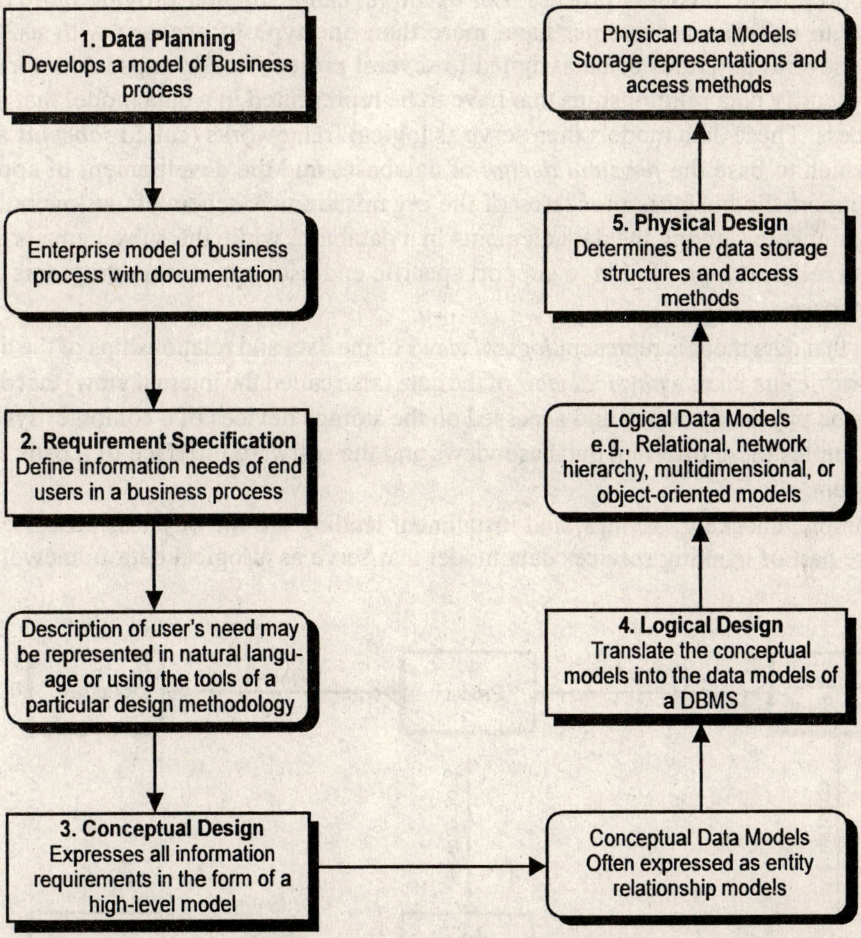

Sources: Adapted from Veda Storey and Robert Goldstein, "Knowledge-based Approaches to Database Design," *MIS Quarterly.*

Figure 10.15. *Database development involves data planning and database design activities. Data models that support business processes are used to develop databases that meet the information needs of users.*

Next, end users must identify the key data elements that are needed to perform their specific business activities. This frequently involves developing *entity relationship diagrams* (ERDs) that model the relationships among the many entities involved in business processes. For example, It illustrates some of the relationships in a purchasing/receiving system. End users and database designers could use ERD models to identify what supplier and product data are necessary in the purchasing/receiving process. Entity relationship diagrams are discussed in more detail in Appendix B at the back of this text.

Such user views are a major part of a **data modeling** process where the relationships between data elements are identified. Each data model the logical relationships among the data elements needed to support a basic business process. For example, can a supplier provide more than one type of product to us? Can a customer have more than one type of account with us? Can an employee have several pay rates or be assigned to several project workgroups? Answering such questions will identify data relationships that have to be represented in a data model that supports a business process. These data models then serve as logical frameworks (called *schemas* and *sub-schemas*) on which to base the *physical design* of databases and the development of application programs to support the business processes of the organisation. A schema is an overall logical view of the relationships among the data elements in a database, while the subschema is a logical view of the data relationships needed to support specific end user application programs that will access that database.

Remember that data models represent *logical views* of the data and relationships of the database. Physical database design takes a *physical view* of the data (also called the internal view) that describes how data are to be physically stored and accessed on the storage devices of a computer system. For example, It illustrates these different database views and the software interface of a bank database processing system.

In this example, checking, savings, and installment lending are the business processes whose data models are part of banking services data model that serve as a logical data framework for all bank services.

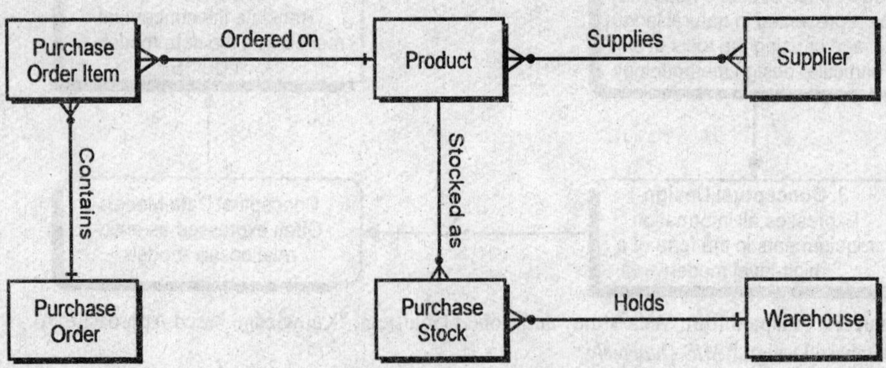

***Figure 10.16.** This entity relationship diagram illustrates some of the relationships among entities in a purchasing/receiving system.*

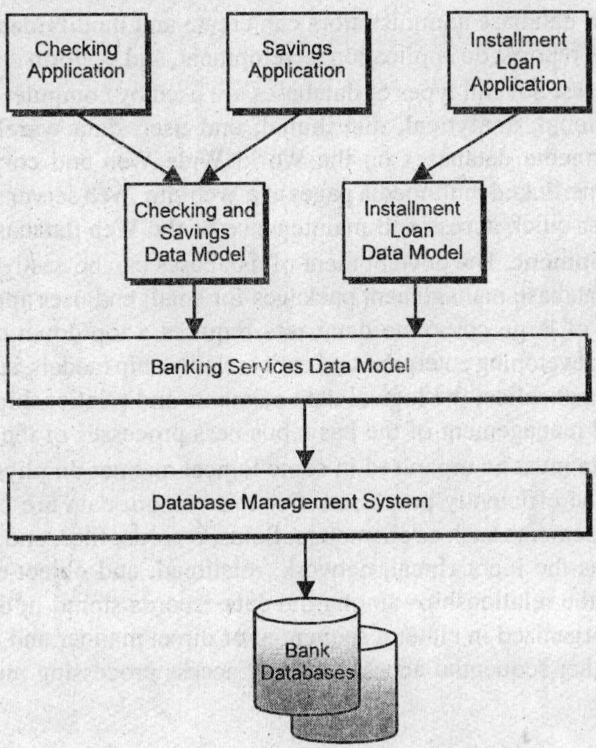

Figure 10.17. Examples of the logical and physical database views and the software interface of a banking services information system.

Summary/Conclusion

- **Data Resources Management.** Data resources management is a managerial activity that applies information systems technology and management tools to the task of managing an organisation's data resources. It includes the database administration function that focuses on developing and maintaining standards and control for an organisation's databases. Data administration, however, focuses on the planning and control of data to support business functions and strategic organisational objectives. This includes a data planning effort that focuses on developing an overall data architecture for a firm's data resources.
- **Database Management.** The database management approach affects the storage and processing of data. The data needed by different applications is consolidated and integrated into several common databases, instead of being stored in many independent data files. Also, the database management approach emphasizes updating and maintaining common databases, having users' application programs share the data in the database, and providing a reporting and an inquiry/response capability so end users can easily receive reports and quick responses to request for information.

- **Database Software.** Database management systems are software packages that simplify the creation, use, and maintenance of databases. They provide software tools so end users, programmers, and database administrators can create and modify databases, interrogate a database, generate reports, do application development, and perform database maintenance.
- **Types of Databases.** Several types of databases are used by computer-using organisations, including operational, analytical, distributed, end user, data warehouse, and external databases. Hypermedia databases on the World Wide Web and corporate intranets and extranets store hyperlinked multimedia pages at a Web site. Web server software can manage such databases for quick access and maintenance of the Web database.
- **Database Development.** The development of databases can be easily accomplished using microcomputer database management packages for small end user applications. However, the development of large corporate databases requires a top-down data planning effort. This may involve developing enterprise and entity relationship models, subject area databases, and data models that reflect the logical data elements and relationships needed to support the operation and management of the basic business processes of the organisation.
- **Data Access.** Data must be organised in some logical manner on physical storage devices so that they can be efficiently processed. For this reason, data are commonly organised into logical data elements such as characters, fields, records, files, and databases. Database structures, such as the hierarchical, network, relational, and object-oriented models, are used to organise the relationships among the data records stored in databases. Databases and files can be organised in either a sequential or direct manner and can be accessed and maintained by either sequential access or direct access processing methods.

Section 4

MIS in Functional Areas

11

Transaction Processing and Management Reporting Systems

- Describe the characteristics of the major subsystems of computer-based information systems.
- Define transaction processing system (TPS) and describe some of the properties that distinguish a TPS from other types of information systems.
- Explain the impact that technology has had on transaction processing.
- Identify and describe several transaction processing subsystems.
- Define management reporting system (MRS) and describe some of the properties that distinguish an MRS for other types of information systems.
- List and describe the major types of reports output by management reporting systems.

In this chapter, we look at two of the earliest types of managerial information systems (MIS): transaction processing systems (TPS), and management reporting systems (MRS). Both of these systems are primarily oriented toward predefined types of data or information.

Most companies must provide regular support to a number of data-oriented, transaction processing operations that involve a massive amount of record keeping. These operations—payroll, order entry, and inventory control, to name just a few—were the first business applications of computers in organisations and are still among the most important. Without their computer-base transaction processing systems, most businesses could not survive in today's fast-paced business environment. In fact, according to a study conducted at the University on Minnesota, banks would have to close after two days without computer based transaction processing systems distribution companies would bog down in four days, and factories would grind to a halt within a week.

In recent years, some computer-based transaction processing systems have produced a new competitive business weapon: the interorganisational system (IOS). In many organisations, electronic data interchange (EDI) and imaging systems impact the manner in which some transactions are processed. Another important trend is the downsizing of transaction processing—moving transaction processing applications from mainframes to minicomputers, microcomputers, and local area networks.

Historically, management reporting systems were the first types of management information systems whose main purpose was to supply information to managers for decision-making purpose. The earliest management reporting systems produced reports that were by-products of transaction processing systems. Some management reporting systems were eventually developed that used their own independent data sources. Today, management reporting systems of both types are still widely used. However, there are not the only sources of data and information used by managers to make decisions. Advances in technology have made it possible to provide managers with decision support systems (DSS) that provide managers with a lot of flexibility in assembling the data they need for decision making.

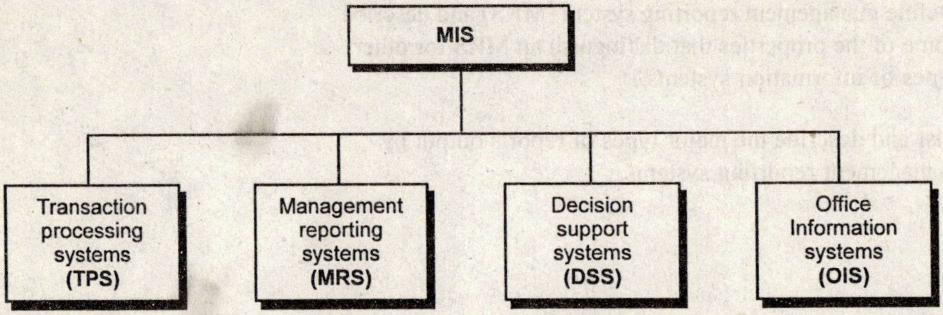

Figure 11.1. *An MIS framework.*

We begin this chapter by reviewing the framework that we have used to classify information systems throughout this text. Keeping this classification system in mind is especially important as you read this chapter and the next three. Then, we will cover some general properties of transaction processing systems. From there, we cover specific transaction processing subsystems—payroll, order entry, inventory, accounts receivable, and several others. Finally, we turn to management reporting systems, discussing their nature and evolution from by-products of transaction processing systems, and providing several examples.

A Management Information Systems Framework

Many terms characterize the types of information systems found in organisations. We frequently hear about "data processing systems," "management information systems," "decision support systems," "executive information systems," "marketing information systems," and "expert systems," to cite just a few. Their meanings are often unclear because these terms are used loosely by people who are not computer professionals and because they are constantly being redefined by changes in technology.

In this section, we will review the framework first presented in Chapter 1 for studying these terms. It is this framework and the nature of the systems represented in it that form the core of our discussion in this part of the textbook.

In Chapter 1, we defined a management information system (MIS) to be any system that provides people with either data or information relating to an organisation's operations. Management information systems support the activities of employees, owners, customer, and other key people in the organisation's environment, either by efficiently processing data to assist with the transaction workload or by quickly and effectively supplying information to authorized people. As described in Chapter 1, computer-based management information systems may be composed of any or all of the following component subsystems.

Role of Transaction Processing Systems

A transaction processing system (TPS) supports the processing of a firm's business transactions. For example, the TPS of a department store can record customer purchases, prepare billings to customers, and order merchandise from suppliers—as well as interrelate these task and others into an overall accounting system. The TPS of a college or university, on the other hand, helps perform such tasks as enrolling students in courses, billing students for tuition, and issuing paychecks to faculty. The transaction processing system associated with a large pension fund may assist stockbrokers in executing buy and sell orders, then help with accounting for those transactions.

Transaction processing systems keep an organisation running smoothly by automating the processing of the voluminous amounts of paperwork that must be handled daily. These systems includes the accurate recording of transactions, as well as the control procedures used in issuing such documents as paychecks, invoices, customer statements, payment reminders, tuition bills, and student schedules. Unlike other MID components, the TPS of an organisation may be far-reaching, extending completely through and out of the organisation, linking together the entire financial system, factory, customers, and suppliers. The movement toward electronic data interchange (EDI) and the establishment of electronic link with suppliers and customers is an example of an extension of a organisation's TPS. EDI and other systems [for example, electronic funds transfer (EFT), image processing, and document management systems] could radically reduce the total amount of physical paperwork that organisations' transaction processing systems have traditionally had to handle.

In this Chapter, we will cover the traditional types of transaction processing systems and subsystems that are found in most businesses. In addition, we will look at transaction processing-related EDI and interorganisational systems (IOS) that span two or more businesses.

Sometimes, the term *data processing system* is used synonymously with the term "transaction processing system" because the primary purpose of these systems is to effectively process the data that arise from transactions. Alternatively, the term "operations" is frequently used to describe the transaction processing component of an MIS.

Role of Management Reporting Systems

A management reporting system (MRS) is an information system that provides predefined types of information to management for relatively structured types of decisions. As opposed to focusing purely on data and the efficient processing of data (which characterized transaction processing systems), management reporting systems focus on information and, occasionally, on effectiveness. Later in this chapter, we will look in depth at management reporting systems and how they provide decision-making information to managers.

Sometimes, the term "management information system" is used synonymously with the term "management reporting system." In fact, to most computer professionals in the late 1960s and early 1970s, management information systems referred specifically to the hardcopy, management-oriented reports that existed beyond transaction-oriented data processing. At that time, the taxonomy of business systems consisted only of TPS and MIS, which were considered two distinct components. Today, some people still regard MIS as being rigidly defined this way; they regard such newer developments as decision support systems (DSS) and office information systems (OIS) as concepts that are distinct from MIS.

As mentioned, the term "management information system" was used widely for many years—and it's not easy to overcome an old habit. However, many researchers today regard management information systems as an evolving, umbrella concept that covers a wide variety of systems—which is evident by the numerous books titled *Management Information Systems* or *Information Systems.* Also, it can be confusing to use MIS as both an umbrella concept and as a differently defined subset of that concept. So, management reporting system (MRS) will be used in this text to represent the MIS subsystem that issues preformatted reports to managers. MIS will be used as the umbrella concept that incorporates TPS, MRS, DSS, OIS, and knowledge-based systems. We hope that this will minimize confusion in this text.

Role of Decision Support Systems

A *decision support system (DSS)* provides tools that enables managers to develop information in the manner that best suits the decisions they are currently trying to make. Unlike the MRS, which delivers specific types of information in a preplanned format, the DSS provides the manager with the computing and communications capabilities to develop his or her own decision models, databases, and report formats. Decision support systems often also focus on such areas as flexibility in meeting a variety of continually changing needs, heavy user/display device interactions, and trial-and-error modeling processes.

Over the years, a variety of decision support systems have evolved. For example, decision support systems targeted to executives are often called executive information systems (EIS) or *executive support systems (ESS)*. Group decision support systems (GDSS)—which support the work activities of work groups—are also quite common. The terms "sales support system" and "marketing information system" pop up occasionally, although it is often unclear whether they are referring to DSS. MRS, TPS OIS, or knowledge-based systems (or all of these!) targeted to selling applications.

Role of Knowledge Based Systems

Chapter 12 will cover decision support systems and their characteristics. Chapter 13 will then discuss the closely related topic of *knowledge-based systems,* which includes expert systems (ES), artificial intelligence (AI), and neural networks. Although these systems probably offer the greatest potential benefits to the DSS area, they could actually benefit any of the application areas under the MIS umbrella. In the future, knowledge-based systems are likely to be infused into virtually every type of organisational information system, including TPS, DSS, EIS, and office systems. Because of this, knowledge-based systems are not shown separately in the MIS framework.

Office Systems (Office Automation System)

Office automation (OA) has traditionally referred to a wide variety of computer-based technologies that make office workers more productive. The diverse set of OA tools that enhance office productivity, efficiency, and effectiveness are often collectively called office information systems (OIS). These will be discussed in Chapter 14.

The taxonomy (classification system) just described does not always provide distinct boundaries that allow a given system to be neatly put into only one category. For example, many office systems can also be classified as decision support systems or DSS tools (such as spreadsheets), which can make office workers more productive and also help managers make better decisions. The blurry line between decision support systems and office systems should be expected because most decision maker work in some type of office environment.

As another example of ambiguity, a database management system that manges transaction data for a firm might also offer some decision support. For instance, if a customer calls up L. L. Bean to order a down jacket and finds that none is currently in stock, but that some will arrive from the supplier in 11 days, that customer is encountering a transaction processing system that may help to keep the customer's business through effective data management and better decision support. This is the case of a traditional transaction processing system that, through advances in technology, has a DSS-like, value-added addition. And—also out of step with tradition—the decision maker (the customer) is outside the organisation.

The main point of these last examples is to show that, although we can distinguish among TPS, MRS, DSS, and office systems to some extent, these once distinct "island of technology" are today blending together in many different ways. Considering how to typologize the overall system is often more of an academic than a practical exercise.

Computer-Based Transaction Processing

Computer-based transaction processing systems are often considered the bread-and-butter MIS application. No matter how nervous upper management in a medium to large organisation is about spending in the information systems area, it knows that it cannot pull the plug on its TPS and survive.

Many of these organisations have had computer-based transaction processing systems since the 1950s. Most of these systems more than paid for themselves and have justified a full-time support staff consisting of computer professionals. Most transaction processing systems have been—and still are—mainframe-oriented. IBM equipment and their compatibles currently claim the lion's share of the transaction processing marketplace and are expected to hold onto this lead throughout the 1990s.

Today, many firms consider transaction processing to be their most important computer application. A surprisingly large number of firms, however, have not carried computer-based information processing far beyond the transaction processing stage.

Because most firms of any size have transaction processing systems in place, this market is not growing as quickly as those for DSS products, knowledge-based systems, and office information systems. In another sense, transaction processing systems are relatively entrenched; many firms have millions of dollars invested in their transaction processing systems and think largely in terms of maintaining or modifying their current systems, rather than replacing them with entirely new systems.

However, the possibility of extending current transaction processing systems across traditional organisational boundaries, to tie in customers and suppliers more closely, has given many transaction processing systems a new slant. Transaction processing systems in many organisations today are used in this way as competitive weapons. Additionally, the move from dumb terminals to intelligent microcomputer-based workstations is expected to alter transaction processing in other ways, such as by distributing certain traditionally mainframe-based centralized transaction processing functions closer to their functional areas.

The Nature of Transaction Processing

For many businesses, a transaction refers to an exchange of goods or services for money. For example, suppose a retailer buy 100 sleeping bags from a wholesaler. From the retailer's end, inventory is increased and a counterbalancing promise to pay the wholesaler is established. When payment is eventually made, the retailer loses cash—but this is counterbalanced by eliminating the payable charge on its records. Organisations such as academic institutions and hospitals have other ways of defining and dealing with transactions. In general, a **transaction** is a recorded business event, often reflecting a routine exchange that affects the financial well-being of an organisation.

As noted previously, a transaction processing system (TPS) supports the processing of an organisation's transactions. This includes accounting for the transactions on its record, as well as providing support activities such as sending out payment reminders (which, although not transactions themselves, are related to transactions). Recently, gaining competitive advantage has become a transaction processing concern in some firms, especially those that are working to tie customers and suppliers together more closely with the organisation's traditional TPS via electronic linkages.

Functions of Transaction Processing

Three functions performed by most transaction processing systems are book-keeping, issuance, and control reporting.

- **Book-keeping.** Book-keeping involves keeping accurate records of a firm's business transactions. Virtually every organisation is involved with day-to-day business transactions between groups such as customers and vendors. For example, banks typically use both human tellers and automatic teller machines to record deposits and withdrawals of accounts holders. The airlines have reservation systems that keep track of all tickets purchased by passengers. Supermarkets and department stores capture customer item purchases with a variety of sophisticated input (for example, point-of-sale) equipment. Colleges and universities record student registrations and fees paid by students. All of these tasks involve keeping accurate records of the firm's business transactions.

In most organisations, bookkeeping involves generally accepted principles of financial accounting. However, financial accounting data are often not all the data that many managers need to help them make decisions. For example, the book value of an asset might not reflect the asset's true worth to the organisation.

- **Issuance.** Issuance refers to the production of such documents as paychecks, invoices, periodic statements (monthly telephone and credit card bills, for example), and payment reminders. The creation of these documents is absolutely necessary to the effective operation of the company; that is, these documents are not discretionary, as are many other types of MIS related documents (such as interoffice memos and informational reports). The documents associated with transaction processing systems are discussed more fully in the section on the transaction processing cycle.
- **Control reporting.** Reports that are produced as a by-product of transaction processing operations, and that also serve operation-control purposes, are called **control reports.** For example, as paychecks are prepared in batches, *payroll edit report* is generally produced to show who was paid what amount. This report can be used to ensure that paycheck amounts are accurate before the paychecks are actually distributed. In transaction processing systems that handle large volumes of business transaction, an **error report** is often used to flag invalid transactions that were rejected by the system and must be reprocessed. In other situations, an exception report can be used to flag unusual transactions, such as a check for an exceptionally large amount. We will look at other types of reports associated with the transaction processing cycle in the next section of the chapter.

Role of Information Technology in Transaction Processing/ Significance of IT in Transaction Processing

The earliest transaction processing systems were manual systems. Clerks would record transactions in a journal or on numbered, multipart forms. These transactions would later be transferred, manually, to a central system of handwritten records or file folders representing individual customers or suppliers. These records would be set up to trigger statements to customer or checks to suppliers. Many small businesses still operate with manual transaction processing systems; however, inexpensive and easy-to-use computer technology is finding its way into more small businesses.

To most businesses, manual systems present numerous problems that are solvable by computer and communications technologies:

- **Error level.** With manual systems, an uncomfortable level of error often exists. Frequently, clerks look up the wrong prices, add prices incorrectly on invoices, or produce garbled journal entries or source documents. Sickness, worry, moodiness, and other inherently human variables can also contribute to high error rates in manual systems.
- **Temporary or permanent loss of data.** Source documents and file folders are easily lost or misplaced. This often results in lost customer payments and delayed purchases or payments.
- **Labour intensity.** Manual systems are labour intensive and, therefore, costly. For instance, data from a single transaction often have to be transcribed several times, and many types of low-volatility data (data that change infrequently, such as product descriptions and customer names or addresses) have to be re-recorded by clerks every time a new transaction takes

place. Additionally, a lot of time is wasted coordinating data from departments; for instance, making phone calls to trace the status of a customer order.

- **Poor level of service.** As can be surmised from the last example, the level of service support in manual systems is often inferior. For instance, customers like to know immediately if goods are in stock, when goods not in stock will be arriving, when they can expect an order to arrive, what their current status is regarding payments, and so on. This level of information support is difficult to achieve with a manual system.
- **Poor response.** Virtually everything takes longer to do with a manual system. For example, when orders are taken, the order-entry department might have to contact the accounts receivable department for a credit check before an order can be validated. Today, many computerized order-entry operations are connected to a centralized database and, when a customer telephones, credit status can be verified immediately. As another example, if a manager wants to find out if a customer has ordered a specific type of product in the last month, the manager might have to search through mounds of documents to find the answer.

As technologies such as computers and communications became available to handle the transaction processing workload, MIS departments responded to it in different ways. Some organisations simply took their manual systems and coded them directly into the computer. Thus, all of the bugs in their manual systems were inherited by their computer systems. Other organisations realized that technology can change the way people work. Thus, they re-thought their transaction processing systems before automating them.

For example, an organisation not taking full advantage of available technology may design its transaction processing system as a file-processing counterpart to handwritten, multipart source documents. In such a system, as each electronic document is originated, it is sent to several files; each file gets a page of the multipart form. As documents are processed by a department, they are sent along to other files. In other words, every paperwork operation resembles its counterpart in the manual system; the only difference is that the documents and the file folders are electronic.

Some of the problems associated with manual systems may still exist in these types of electronic systems. For example, if a copy of a document is corrected in one electronic file folder, the correction will not necessarily be reflected in other copies of the document in other electronic folders—thereby producing inconsistent, data and data integrity problems such as those discussed in Chapter 7. In contrast, an organisation concerned with taking full advantage of information technology is likely to migrate to a database management system. This can eliminate problems such as redundant data and poor data integrity, and may also integrate transaction data in a way that makes the system more useful and more responsive to queries.

Besides enabling transaction processing systems to be more efficient, technology has changed transaction processing in other ways. For example, information technology is one of the main reasons why credit cards proliferate in our society. Also, without computerized transaction processing systems, check processing would still be slow and clumsy. Many firms would not be able to handle anywhere near the number of customers that they do today, or to supply anything close to the level of service, or make available the multitude of products that their customers request.

Today, inexpensive computer and communications devices are setting up two new challenges to transaction processing using the TPS as a competitive weapon and getting better information more quickly to the right people. The next section explores how these and other benefits of high technology are being specifically incorporated into transaction processing systems.

The Transaction Processing Cycle

Transaction processing systems capture and process transaction data. The data that are captured and processed are used to update organisational files and databases. Transaction databases are among the most extensive, richest, and most detailed sets of data created and stored by organisations. This data, or at least parts of this data, frequently serve as inputs for the other types of systems. Reports generated by the MRS typically assemble and summarize data that were initially captured by the TPS. TPS data also often "feed" DSS, EIS, and knowledge-based systems implemented within the organisation.

Figure 11.2 depicts the transaction processing cycle. It consists of five basic parts: data entry, transaction processing, file and database processing, document and report generation, and inquiry processing. Each of these parts is summarized next.

Data Entry (Collecting, Recording, Coding and Editing Transaction Data)

The first step in the transaction processing cycle involves data entry. Data entry concerns collecting, recording, coding, and editing transaction data. In a CBIS, transaction data must be converted to a form that can be entered directly into the computer system for processing.

In traditional systems, data entry typically starts by capturing transaction data on *source documents* such as purchase orders, payroll time sheets, and order invoices. These documents are usually batched and transferred to data-entry specialists. After a manual audit, which is an editing process (often consisting of only a visual inspection of the source documents for omissions and obvious inaccuracies), data from acceptable source documents are converted to machine-readable form. Unacceptable source documents found by this process are often returned to their originators so that they can be corrected. The conversion to machine-readable form often means using a key-to-tape or key-to-disk system—data from the source documents are placed directly onto tape or disk for later processing. Prior to processing, the machine-readable transaction data are further edited, then sorted.

Traditional data-entry systems are giving way to automated data-entry systems in a growing number of organisations. Each of these methods reduces or eliminates many of the activities, people, and media required by traditional data-entry systems. Figure 11.5 provides an example of an automated data-entry system. Electronic data interchange (EDI) systems and document management systems are also changing the ways in which transaction data and source documents are captured, stored, and handled by organisations.

Transaction Processing and File/Database Updating

After data are in machine-readable form, the transactions must be processed. This can be accomplished in two basic ways: (1) batch processing (or batch updating), in which transaction data are accumulated over a period of time and then processed periodically as a batch, and (2) real-time processing, in which each transaction is processed immediately after it occurs. Batch processing is still heavily used by organisations; however, the use of real-time processing is growing and should eventually become the primary means of processing transaction data, especially in medium and large businesses.

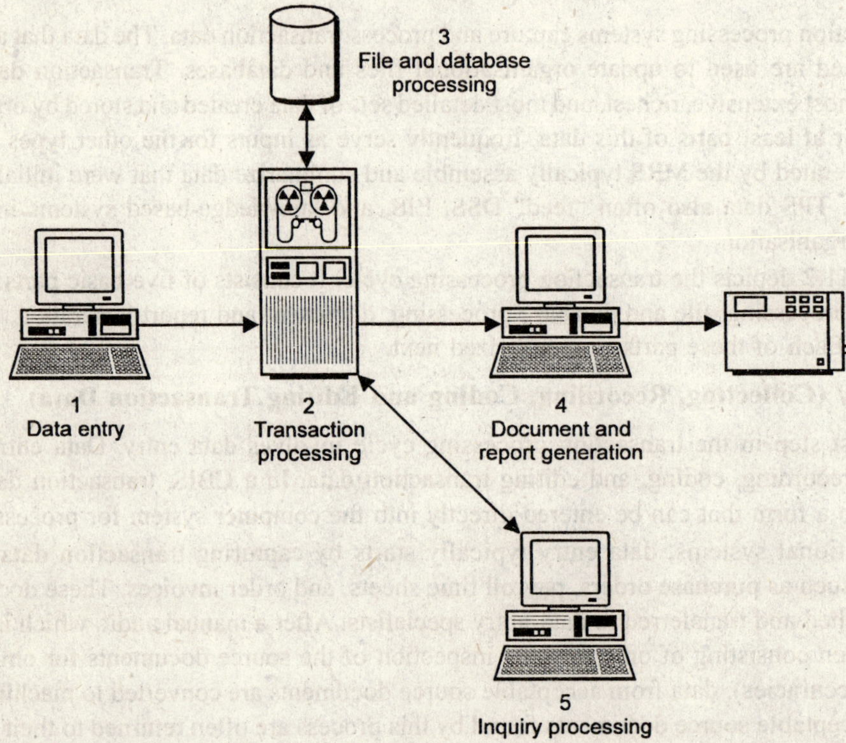

Figure 11.2. *The transaction processing cycle. Most transaction processing systems use a five-step process. The process begins with capture and entry of transaction data, then continues with the actual processing of transaction data and updating of files and/or databases. After these processing and updating tasks conclude, document and report generation and inquiry processing activities can occur.*

Figure 11.6 illustrate how a batch processing system works. The goal of most batch processing programs is to update organisational master files by incorporating data from transaction files. Such updating is done periodically (for example, daily, weekly, or monthly), depending on how current the information needs to be to make business decisions.

Real-time processing, systems process transaction data (plus update files and databases) immediately as it is captured; batches are not accumulated for later processing. On-line terminals or source data automation equipment is used to input data directly into the computer; files and databases are stored on online direct access storage devices (DASD). Records and other data elements contained in these files and databases are updated immediately in real-time transaction processing system. Figure 11.7 provides an example of a real-time transaction processing system.

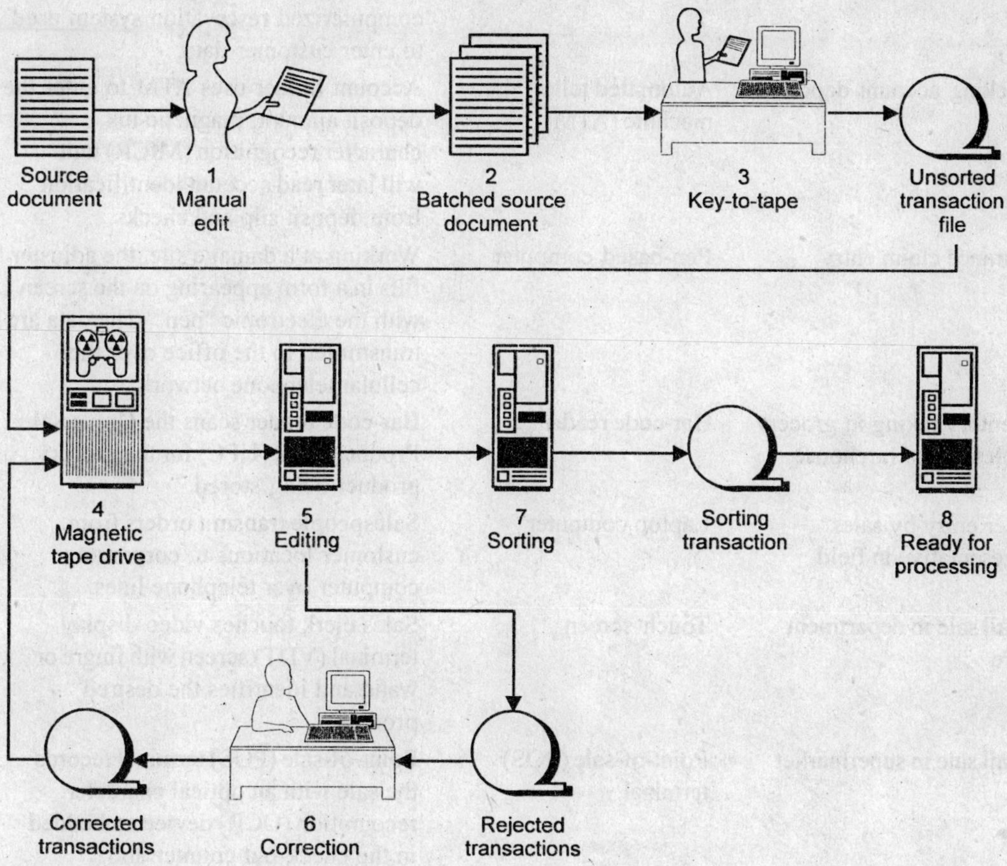

Figure 11.3. A traditional data-entry system. In such systems, prior to processing, source documents containing transaction data are manually edited, batched, and keyed onto tape or disk. Once entered into the computer system, the data are edited again, corrected as necessary and sorted before they are used to update files and databases, generate reports, and so on.

Document and Report Generation

The final stages of the transaction processing cycle typically involve the generation of outputs such as documents and reports. Documents produced by a TPS are called *transaction documents,* which may be categorized as follows:

- **Information documents.** These documents verify, confirm, or prove that transactions have occurred or were attempted. Sales receipts, order confirmations, customer invoices, and customer statements may be generated to document that a transaction took place. A credit rejection notice may serve to communicate that a transaction was attempted, but refused because of a problem in the customer's credit history.

Type of Transaction	Data-Entry Device	Direct Data-Entry Example
Airline reservation	CRT terminal	On-line terminal connected to airline's computerized reservation system used to enter customer data.
Checking account deposit	Automated teller machine (ATM)	Account holder uses ATM to enter the deposit amount; magnetic ink character recognition (MICR) unit will later read account identification from deposit slip and checks.
Insurance claim entry	Pen-based computer	Working at a damage site, the adjuster fills in a form appearing on the screen with the electronic "pen." The data are transmitted to the office over the cellular telephone network.
Inventory taking in grocery wholesaler's warehouse	Bar-code reader	Bar-code reader scans the Universal Product Code (UPC) for the grocery product being stored.
Order entry by sales representative in field	Laptop computer	Salespeople transmit orders from customer locations to corporate computer over telephone lines.
Retail sale in department store	Touch screen	Sales clerk touches video display terminal (VDT) screen with fingre or wand and identifies the desired product.
Retail sale in supermarket	Point-of-sale (POS) terminal	Point-of-sale (POS) terminal records the sale with an optical character recognition (OCR) device embedded in the check-out counter and transmits the data to a computer.
Spoken inventory query	Voice input device	Item is identified by numeric code spoken into microphone.
Unattended gasoline purchase	"Smart-card" reader	Smart-card reader accepts smart card. Funds are transferred automatically from customer's to vendor's account.

Figure 11.4. *Some of the ways in which transaction data can be directly entered into a transaction processing system. Many of these approaches enhance user productivity, customer service, and operational efficiency.*

- **Turnaround documents.** Some invoices and customer statements contain a perforated tear-off portion that should be returned to the sender, along with the customer's payment. When this type of document is generated by the TPS, it is known as a turnaround document. Many turnaround documents used today can be read by magnetic (for example, if MICR is used) or OCR (optical character recognition) scanners after they return to the organisation.

- **Action documents.** Action documents initiate actions or transactions on the part of recipients. A paycheck, for example, authorizes a bank to cash or otherwise process an employee's check. A purchase order similarly authorizes a supplier to send needed items to the organisation that submitted it.

As noted previously in this chapter, a TPS can also provide several types of reports or on-screen displays related to transaction data capturing and processing. These are not specifically tailored to management use, as are the types of reports mentioned in the MRS section of this chapter, but may still be reviewed by managers. The major types of these include:

- **Accounting statements.** These must be generated for legal purposes and legally document the financial performance of a business. These may include general ledger summaries, cash flow statements, balance sheets, and income statements; all of these are directly related to transaction processing activities. The role of most of these will be clarified in the following section on TPS subsystems.
- **Control listings.** Control listings are detailed reports that describe each transaction occurring during a specific time period. These are sometimes called transaction logs. A payroll register, for example, will list every check issued by the payroll system.
- **Edit reports.** Reports that describe errors encountered during processing (or traditional data entry) are often called edit reports. Transactions involving invalid account numbers, incorrect totals, and missing data are usually listed in edit reports.

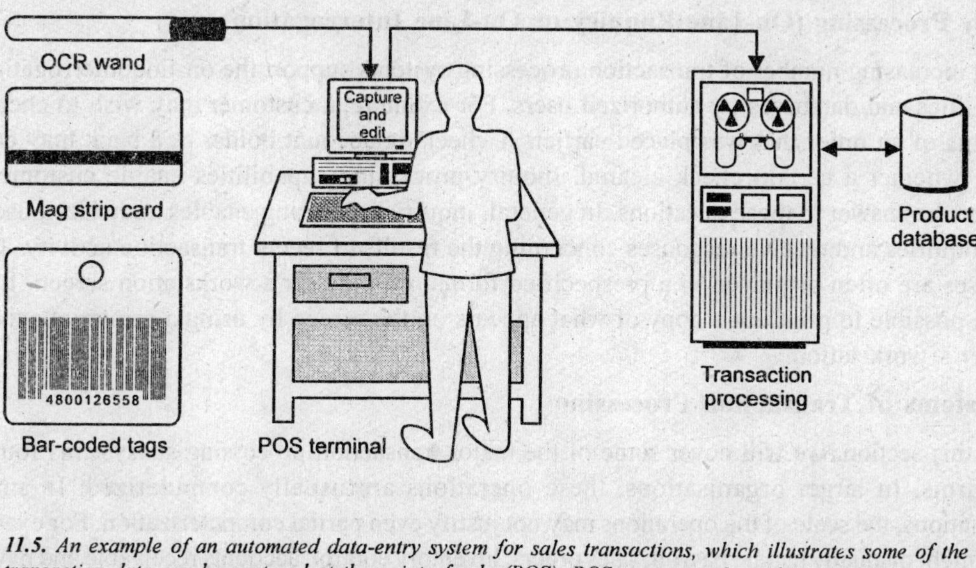

Figure 11.5. An example of an automated data-entry system for sales transactions, which illustrates some of the ways in which transaction data can be captured at the point of sale (POS). POS systems such as this are common in the retail industry.

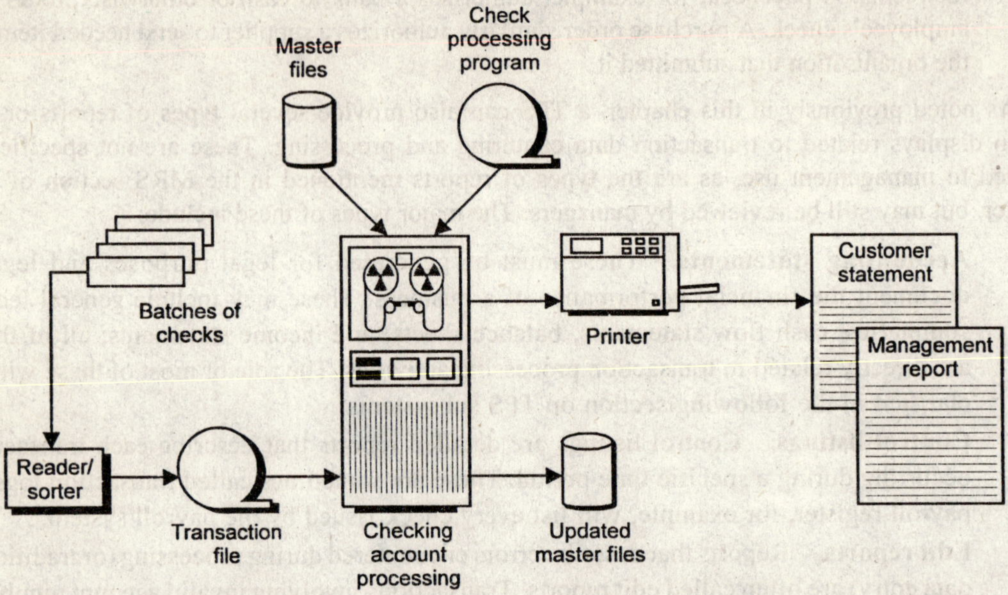

***Figure 11.6.** An example of a batch processing system. In this banking example, batches of checks are accumulated and processed. In most banks, this occurs on a daily basis.*

Inquiry Processing (On-Line Enquiry or On-Line Interrogation)

An increasing number of transaction processing systems support the on-line interrogation of on-line files and databases by authorized users. For example, a customer may wish to check on the status of an order that was placed earlier. A checking account holder at a bank may call to inquire whether a certain check cleared. Inquiry processing capabilities enable customers to discover the answer to these questions. In general, inquiry processing enables authorized users to make inquiries and receive responses concerning the results of recent transaction activity. These responses are often displayed in a prespecified format on the user's workstation screen. It may also be possible to print out a copy of what appears on the screen by using a printer attached to the user's workstation.

Subsystems of Transaction Processing

In this section, we will cover some of the major transaction processing subsystems found in most firms. In larger organisations, these operations are usually computerized. In smaller organisations, the scale of the operations may not justify even partial computerization. For example, clerks might manually handle payroll, sales orders, inventory control, accounts receivable and payable, and general ledger. However, because of the pace and complexity of business today, plus the low cost and relative ease of computing and communications technologies, virtually all but the smallest firms have technology-based transaction processing systems.

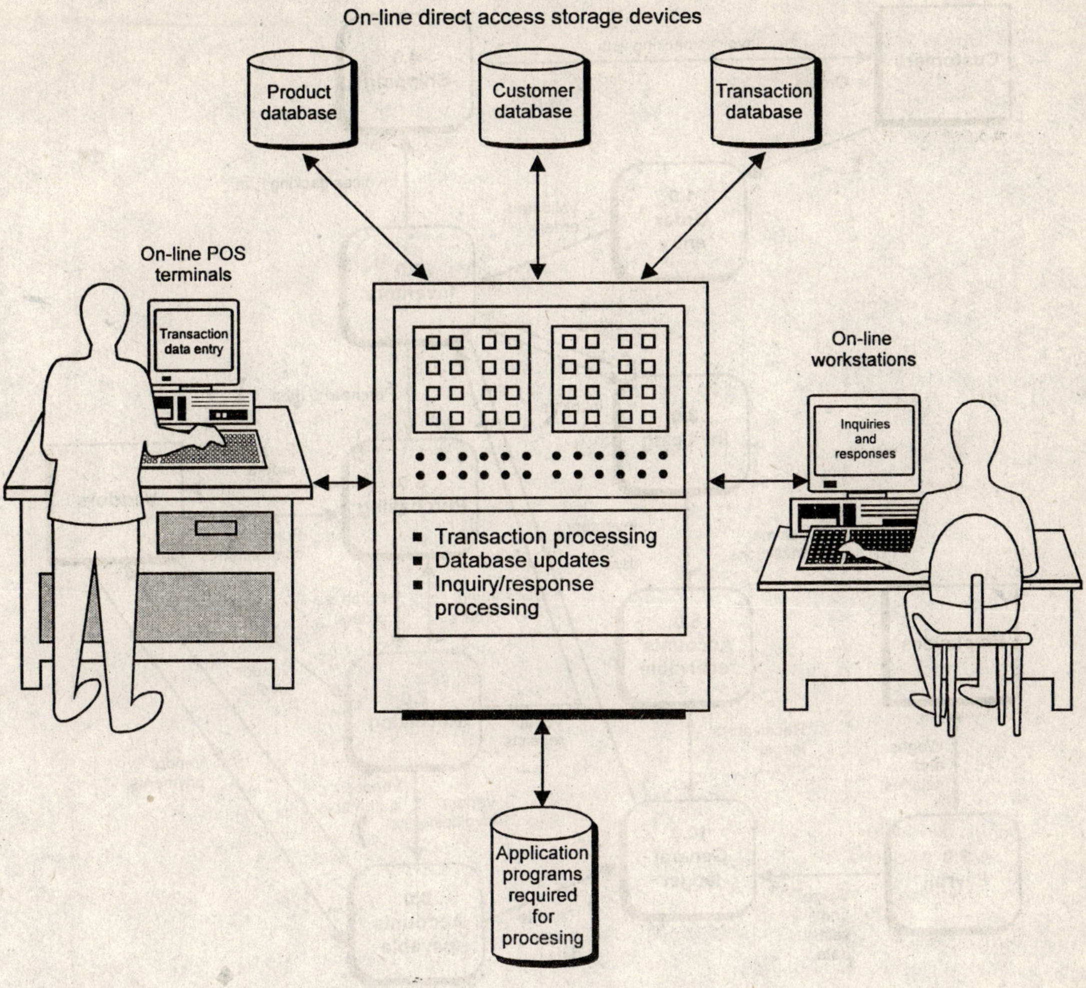

Figure 11.7. *An example of a real-time sales processing. In real-time systems, transaction processing, inquiries, and file/database updates are performed immediately, using on-line devices.*

An example of how the transaction processing subsystems that we will cover in this chapter can be interrelated is shown in the data flow diagram in Figure 11.8. This diagram could provide an illustration of the interrelationships between data processing activities carried out by merchandising firms such as department stores, which sell products manufactured by other companies. It could also depict the transaction processing operations of a wholesale distribution firm. The traditional functions of the subsystems shown in Figure 11.8 are briefly, as follows:

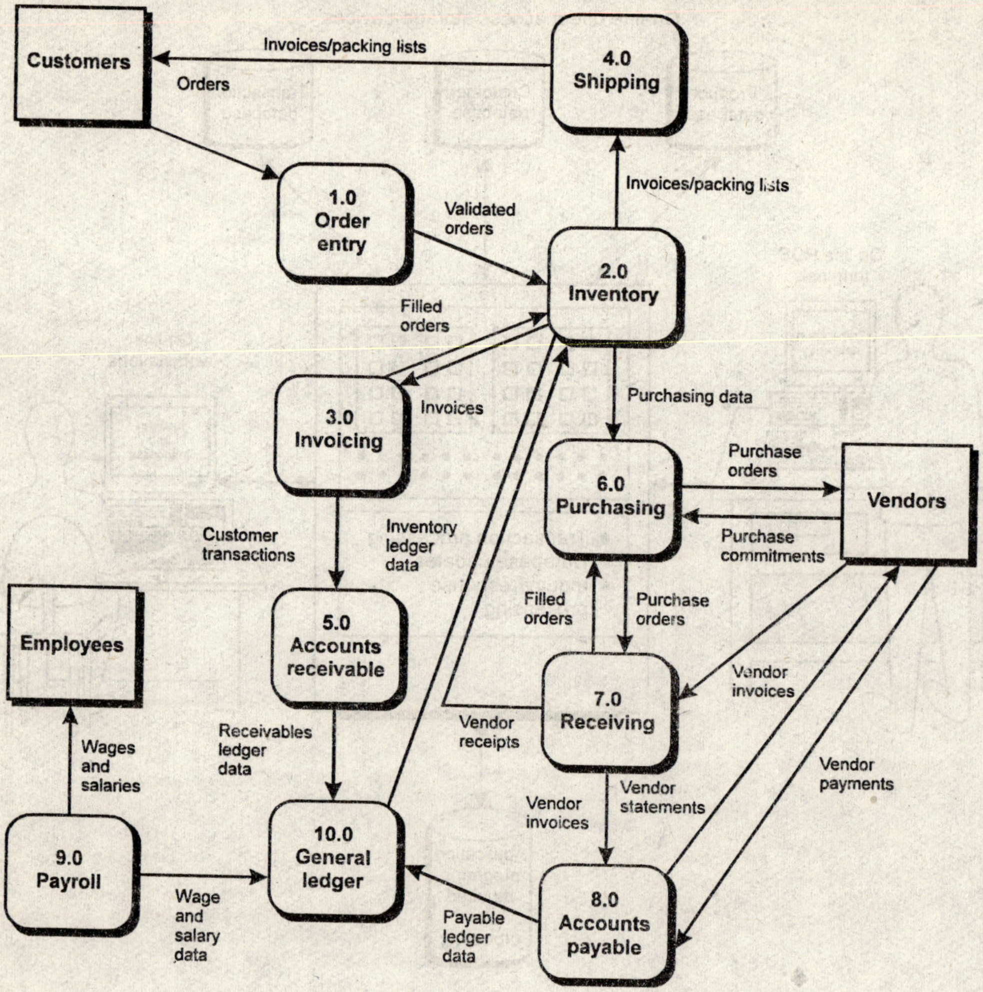

Figure 11.8. An example of how the various subsystems of an organisation's transaction processing system may interrelate.

- **Payroll** Pays employees.
- **Order entry** Records customer purchases.
- **Inventory** Manages the goods available for sale.
- **Invoicing** Produces invoices.
- **Shipping** Gets goods from the firm into the hands of customers.
- **Accounts receivable** Manages customer accounts and sends statements to customers.

- **Purchasing** Coordinates orders with vendors.
- **Receiving** Receives both shipments from vendors and returns from customers.
- **Accounts payable** Manages payments to vendors.
- **General ledger** Ties all of the transaction processing subsystems together.

Each subsystem serves a variety of purposes; we will cover each subsystem more extensively later. Because adequately representing an entire transaction processing system in a single data flow diagram is such a massive undertaking, three simplifying guidelines were followed in preparing Figure 11.8: (1) no data stores are shown, (2) report information normally provided to management for control purposes is omitted, and (3) exception procedures such as stockouts and complaints are omitted. The diagram does, however, effectively show how transaction processing subsystems may interrelate. For example, customer orders typically trigger demands on inventory. A products are sold, invoices are created and the receivables subsystem is notified that money is due. Also, goods have to be scheduled for shipment and, as stocks deplete, orders must be placed with suppliers.

The systems designed to support transaction processing operations are primarily data-oriented. Accurate data must be printed on paychecks, reflected in bills to customers, and used to update and maintain customer, supplier, employee, and asset records. Some of these data can be used for decision-making purposes as well, but supporting internal decision making is not the primary purpose for capturing them. In practice, it is often difficult to delineate where the TPS ends and other MIS subsystems, such as the MRS, begin.

Payroll

The transaction processing subsystems used to produce paychecks for employees are called **payroll processing systems.** These systems also must produce data for tax purposes, such as W-2 forms and reports to federal, state, county, and city tax offices. Additionally, payroll processing systems must keep track of such items as Social Security payments, union dues, and group insurance deductions.

In many organisations, payroll is the first transaction processing subsystem to be computerized because it is relatively straight forward and independent of other system. Although a wide variety of additional requirements have made payroll processing systems more complex than they were in the 1950s, they are still among the simplest of the transaction processing subsystems to implement.

Payroll processing must interface with the general ledger system, which integrates transactions from a variety of other transaction processing subsystems. In addition, there may be a link between payroll and production control systems—for instance, a job-shop system in which the hours put in by employees on jobs are charged against those jobs. Payroll systems, of course, must also often interface with the transaction processing systems of those banks in which direct deposits are made for employees.

Payroll processing is usually a batch operation. Many organisations that pay employees once a month will prepare paychecks at the end or middle of the month. Other organisations prepare paychecks for all employees on a weekly or bi-weekly basis. Many organisations pay some types of workers on a weekly basis, others bi-weekly, and still others only one a month. Hence, the complexity of the payroll subsystem may vary considerably among organisations.

Order Entry

The **order-entry system** is the transaction processing subsystem that processes customer orders. Orders may come from a variety of sources—perhaps by mail, phone, and fax—from customers who are ordering on a demand basis. They can also be generated by "ticklers" within the order-entry system itself; for instance, if customers are scheduled to have goods delivered on a regular, periodic basis. An order-entry subsystem for the mail portion of a mail-order catalog firm is depicted in the data flow diagram of Figure 11.9.

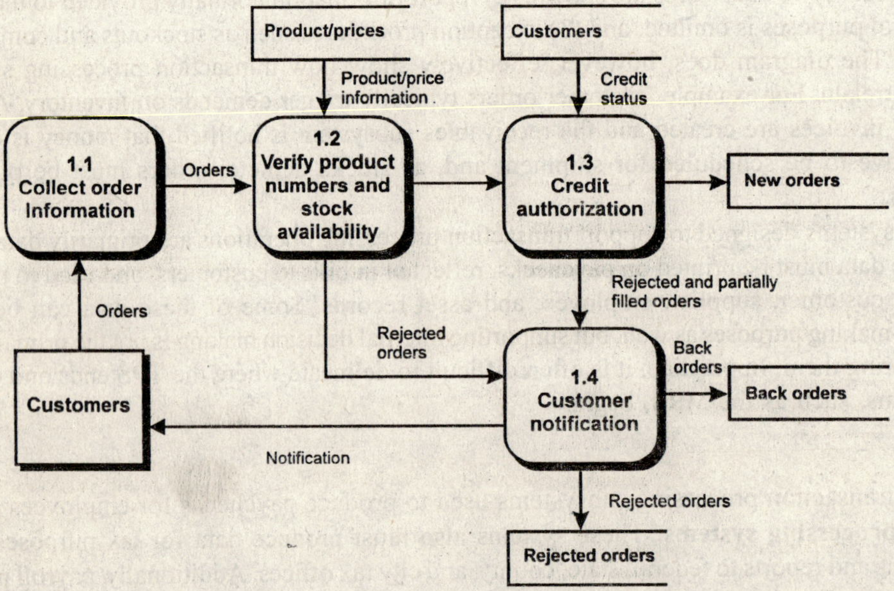

Figure 11.9. An example of a data flow diagram for an order-entry subsystem.

In most instances, as each order is received by mail or by phone, the product numbers and product descriptions in the order are checked for accuracy. Also, stock levels in inventory are checked to determine what portion of the order can be filled immediately. At this point, the order is identified as either one that can be partially or completely filled, or one that cannot be filled at all. Orders that, for one reason or another, cannot be filled are deemed "rejected" and sent to the customer notification operation. In the case of a rejected order, a letter may be sent to the customer that explains the specific nature of the problem (such as a product being out of stock or the presence of conflicting information on the order). In some cases, the customer may be notified of such problems by phone. Orders that can be partially or completely filled are "costed out" with respect to item prices and subtotals then sent on to the credit authorization step. Here, given such factors as the charge amount associated with the order, the method of payment, and the credit status of the customer, the part of the order that can be filled may be approved or disapproved. Approved orders are sent to the warehouse for filling; as noted above, rejected orders and orders that can only be partially filled result in some type of customer notification.

The earliest computer-based order-entry systems did little more than keep track of orders in a systematic way. Communications technologies facilitated distributed order-entry systems—for example, the airline reservations systems that allow worldwide computer-based bookings by thousands of travel agents. Database technology boosted further the power of many order-entry systems, enabling order-entry/sales personnel to interrelate data from various sources to help speed up or to close orders. For instance, personnel who are skilled at searching through databases of product information can rapidly provide customers with option from which to choose, closing a sale while the customer is still on the phone—and still in buying mood.

Today, many firms are tying important customer more closely into their order-entry systems with electronic data interchange (EDI) and interorganisational information systems (IOS), using their order-entry systems as competitive weapons to lock in these customers and lock out competitors. One such example is American Hospital Supply (AHS) Corporation, one of the nation's largest distributors of hospital equipment and supplies. AHS was the first hospital supply company to provide their customers with terminals that hooked into AHS's order-entry system. Using an on-line catalog, customers can place orders electronically with AHS. The system also apprises the customer of the expected delivery date and generates invoicing, shipping, and inventory information for AHS. By making it convenient for customers to place orders and by offering incentives for customers to use their system, AHS makes it difficult for customers to leave them. Also, by realizing that once employees in customer-ordering departments learned how to use AHS's system, they would be more reluctant to learn a competitor's system, AHS had, in effect, locked out most competitors.

Similar competitive stories are told in other industries. American Airlines reservations systems, SABRE, is another example of how an order-entry/transaction processing system can initially give a company a competitive advantage and force competitors to develop comparable systems. In the case of SABRE, that initial advantage has been sustained quite well over time. According to survey report two of every five airline tickets were booked via SABRE. Numerous other examples of the strategic use of order-entry systems were presented in previous chapters.

Another novel way in which organisations are using telecommunications to extend their order-entry systems is by using laptops and pen-based computers to collect and transmit customer orders. By providing these types of computers to travelling, salespeople, customer orders can be collectual in electronic form. These can then be transmitted to the home office in batches—perhaps from the salesperson's hotel room at the end of the day (many hotel rooms now have modern jacks)—or even instantly via a cellular phone system. Expediting customer orders by using such systems often improves customer service and reduces the amount of paperwork that salespeople need to do, thereby giving them more time to contact potential customers and service existing accounts.

Fax systems provide customers with other ways to place orders. Today, the order forms inserted in most mail-order catalogs not only contain instructions about placing phone orders (usually through a no-cost-to-the-customer 800 number), but also provide another 24-hours 800 number for faxing the order form to the retailer. In many of these systems, faxed order forms may never be converted back to a paper documents by the recipient; instead, these are captured by computer fax boards and routed to electronic files containing images of the faxed document, which can then be viewed on a display screen.

Inventory/Stock

The quantity of product that a merchandising firm has available to sell at any given time is called its *inventory.* An **inventory system** monitors the quantity of each product available for sale and helps ensure that proper stock levels are maintained.

Inventory does not necessarily refer exclusively to physical merchandise or to goods available for immediate delivery. In airline passenger reservation systems, for instance, inventory corresponds to the number of seats available on flights; in the registration system at a atypical university or college, inventory corresponds to the openings available in each class. In the auto industry, where electronic information networks let dealers know what has been scheduled for production, inventory is often perceived as representing the total of current and projected vehicles for sale. By using such networks to "sell production," Volvo Cars of North America reduced the amount of time its Swedish imports had to wait at port in Newark, New Jersey, from 20 to 3 days.

In addition to helping managers maintain reasonable inventory levels, inventory systems generate a variety of useful information to management. For instance, management can find out which products are moving fastest or slowest from inventory, the rate of inventory turnover (the number of times that the value of inventory is sold in a period), profitability per square foot of shelf space, facts about any active backorders, the average time it takes to fill backorders, and so on. Figure 11.10 provides a screen showing the types of inventory-status information commonly available in an inventory database. Some companies have this information available in on-line databases for interested and authorized management personnel. For example, a manager using a fourth-generation language (4GL) might issue a command such as

```
DISPLAY PRODUCT-NUMBER FOR SALES < 100 UNITS
```

to query an inventory database about slow-moving items (that is, those selling fewer than 100 units in last week).

Figure 11.11 gives a data flow diagram for the inventory system of our mail-order firm. In this example, new orders are received regularly from the order-entry subsystem of Figure 11.9. These orders, as well as backorders, are filled from available stock. In our example, where stock is not available to completely fill a new order, part of that order is put on backorder. In some companies, however, the entire order may be put on backorder if part of it cannot be filled. A backorder notice is usually sent to the customer as part of the order-entry process.

In most organisations, as orders are filled, an invoice or packing slip is placed inside the box– except perhaps for customers on account. The box is sent to the shipping department with shipping orders, and the transaction data are sent to accounts receivable. When stock is low or insufficient, the purchasing department will be notified (possibly by electronic means) of the items out of stock and the reorder amount. Many companies have specific reorder-point and order-quantity policies; that is; when the stock of item X reaches a level of Y units, immediately reorder Z units. As stock is replenished, this is duly noted in the inventory records.

In the data flow diagram shown in Figure 11.11, we considered the inventory system of a merchandising firm, an organisation that buys finished products and resells them in virtually the same form. The inventory systems of manufacturing firms, which make new products from raw materials, are a bit more complicated.

GROUP: GARDEN PRODUCTS 3/15/93

PRODUCT	PRODUCT DESCRIPTION	BEG QTY	QTY REC	QTY SOLD	ON HAND	ON ORDER	TOTAL AVAILABLE	UNIT PRICE
8410	GLOVES	100	50	40	110	10	120	16.50
8420	SPRINKLER SYSTEM	0	0	0	10	10	20	47.00
8425	PRUNING SAW	15	30	10	35	10	45	24.00
8426	HAND WEEDER	20	10	15	30	10	40	10.00
8442	SPRAY GUN	30	10	30	10	0	10	15.00
8444	WATER COMPUTER	0	0	0	0	50	50	65.00
8445	WATERING CAN	250	40	80	210	10	220	30.00
8451	SPADE	200	100	50	250	0	250	18.00

0 : NEXT SCREEN 1 : PREVIOUS SCREEN 2 : GOTO MENU 3 : EXIT

***Figure 11.10.** A display screen showing inventory data.*

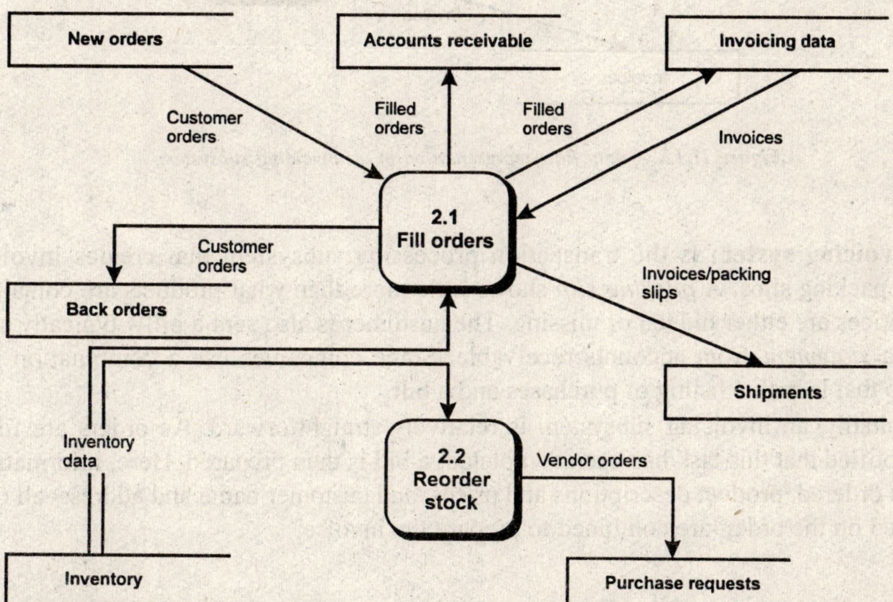

***Figure 11.11.** An example of a data flow diagram for an inventory subsystem.*

A growing trend in both merchandising and manufacturing systems is for firms to tie their ppliers into their inventory systems. This results in shifting inventory handling costs to the supplier, cilitates shopping electronically among suppliers for the lowest prices (if several suppliers are tied), and enables a firm to have greater control over the availability of goods from suppliers. Such interorganisational and EDI systems are buyer-initiated in some instances, and seller-initiated in others. The buyer might initiate a system like this to realize benefits such as those we described. In these instances, carrying higher inventories might be viewed by the seller as a strategy necessary for locking in the buyer and locking out competitors.

Often, the arrival of supplier inventories is timed so that goods arrive barely in time to be used at the retailer or factory destination. Consequently, these close-to-the-bone inventory-carrying systems are known as *just-in-time (JIT)* systems. JIT systems help the receiving organisation reduce inventory-related costs, including overhead expenses, maintenance costs, and taxes. Such systems are used extensively in Japan and contribute to that nation's industrial success. JIT systems are becoming more widely used worldwide; advances in communications and information technology facilitate the spread of such systems.

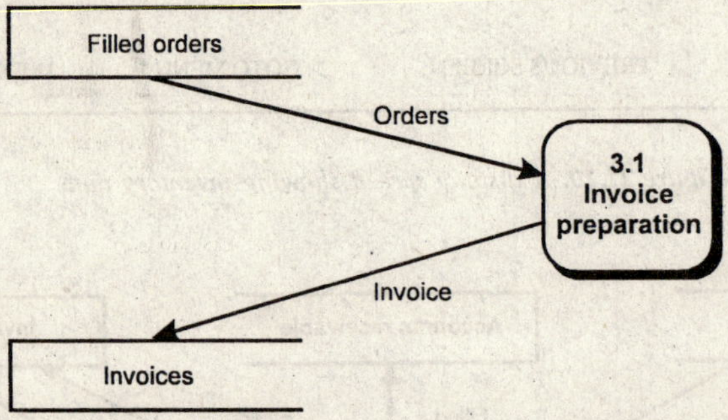

Figure 11.12. *A data flow representation of an invoicing subsystem.*

Invoicing

The **invoicing system** is the transaction processing subsystem that creates invoices and sometimes, packing slips. A *packing slip* shows little more than what products are contained in a shipment; prices are either hidden or missing. The customer is also sent a bill—typically called an *invoice* or a *statement* from accounts receivable. Some companies use a combination invoice/ packing slip that is both a listing of purchases and a bill.

Conceptually, an invoicing subsystem is relatively straightforward. As orders are filled, the system is notified that this task has been completed; a bill is then prepared. Here, information such as the items ordered, product descriptions and prices, and customer name and address–all of which are contained on the order–are combined to prepare the invoice.

Shipping

The **shipping system** is conceptually simple. Sealed, addressed packages of goods are received from inventory, often with shipping instructions. Shipping instructions generally specify a particular shipping method (for example, C.O.D., Federal Express, or UPS), and may provide a warning to shippers (for example, "Fragile" or "Do Not Bend"). When no shipping method or warning is specified, the shipping department will attempt to ship the goods in the most cost-effective, reliable way to the customer. If the goods are valuable in any way, insurance is often another factor in shipping.

Technology has affected the shipping operation in several ways. For instance, computer and communications systems make it much easier to succeed in the overnight package delivery business. Also, technology increased the number of shipping options enormously, especially when the product being shipped is information-intensive. Information technology has also materially affected the tracing of shipped goods—giving the shippers another "value-added service" to differentiate themselves from competitors. For example, one overnight delivery service advertise that, in 30 minutes or less, it can let a sender (or receiver) know the exact location of a package while it is en route. This is possible because the bar code on each package is read every time it is loaded onto the next shipping vehicle.

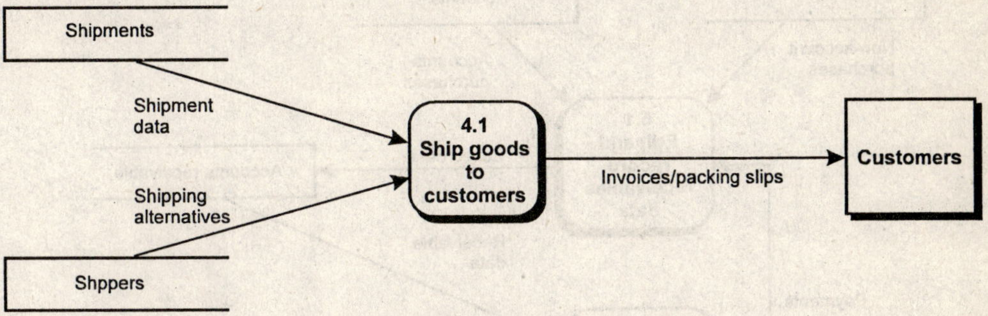

Figure 11.13. A data flow representation of a shipping subsystem.

Accounts Receivable (A/R System or Receivable System)

In many firms, customers pay by credit card or have goods charged to their accounts. The **accounts receivable (A/R) system** (or receivable system) is the transaction processing subsystem that manages customer purchase records, payments, and account balances.

Figure 11.14 shows the accounts receivable subsystem for our mail-order firms. As goods are packaged for shipment in the inventory subsystem, either a packing slip or a combination invoice/packing slip is usually enclosed in the shipping carton. Customers who have established accounts may not be invoiced with each shipment. These customers are typically billed monthly through statements that are similar to those received from credit card or telephone companies. Whatever the method of billing, all customer purchase transactions are sent to the receivables department, where they are edited and made part of the regular receivables files. As payments are received from customers, these too are reflected in the receivables files. Other tasks performed from data in a receivables system include analyzing sales patterns and producing information on current and past sue accounts. While the accounts receivable function may not be set up exactly like this in other organisations, substantial similarities will probably exist.

Because accounts receivable reflects such a large percentage of the revenue coming into a firm, it generally gets a great deal of attention. Computerized accounts receivable systems enable a firm to keep track of outstanding balances, and most firms know that the longer a bill is left unpaid, the smaller the chance that it will ever be collected. Also, the more money tied up in receivables, the less money the firm has to invest in financial markets or new opportunities.

Westinghouse's advanced industrial systems division provides just one of many examples in which technology has helped reduce the receivables burden. Receivables were lowered almost 50 percent over previous levels by having service technicians file job reports electronically. This change in procedure also cut ten days off the manual billing process.

Allied Stores—a big, New York-based, Canadian-owned retailer whose holdings include stores such as Stern's, Jordan Marsh, and Brooks Brothers–is one of many organisations that has streamlined its customer-payment-reminder operations. Before computerization, this task involved a lot of manual paperwork. Now, many reminder situations are handled by phone. When confronting a tardy consumer, the information the caller needs conveniently pops up on a display terminal.

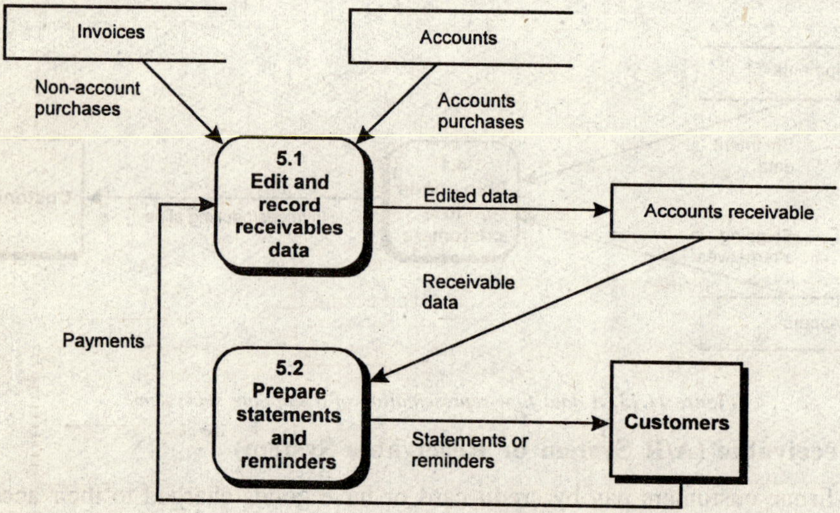

Figure 11.14. A data flow representation of an accounts receivable subsystem.

Purchasing through Central Purchasing Department

Many companies use a central purchasing department to procure the goods they need. The advantages of a centralized purchasing department are cost control, vendor control, and taking advantage of discounts realized by quantity buying. The major disadvantage is inconvenience to the other departments in the organisation for whom the goods are being purchased.

As requests are made to the purchasing department by telephone, interoffice memos, computer, or other means, they are formally logged into a purchase request file that is part of a **purchasing system.** At that point, buyers in the purchasing department begin the vendor-selection process.

In many cases, this decision is relatively routine. Generally, the buyer first contacts a salesperson in the vendor organisation to get a satisfactory price and delivery commitment. Then, the buyers prepares a formal *purchase order.* In many companies, the standard operating procedure is to send one copy of the purchase order to the vendor and a second copy to the receiving department so its personnel can verify the contents of the shipment when it arrives; a third copy is kept on file in the purchasing department as an "open order." As soon as the receiving department accepts the goods, the purchasing department is notified so that it can close out the purchase order.

In many companies, the purchasing operation is heavily computerised. Purchase requests are created electronically and sent by electronic mail (or other data communication) systems to the company's central purchasing department. If a request is approved, the resulting active purchase orders can be electronically prepared and stored in a database so that approval, purchase, shipment, receipt, and payment information is available in central place. This saves time-consuming phone calls and shuffling through paperwork to find the current status of a request. Document management systems and image-processing systems may also help reduce paper shuffling by scanning all important documents and forms into accessible databases.

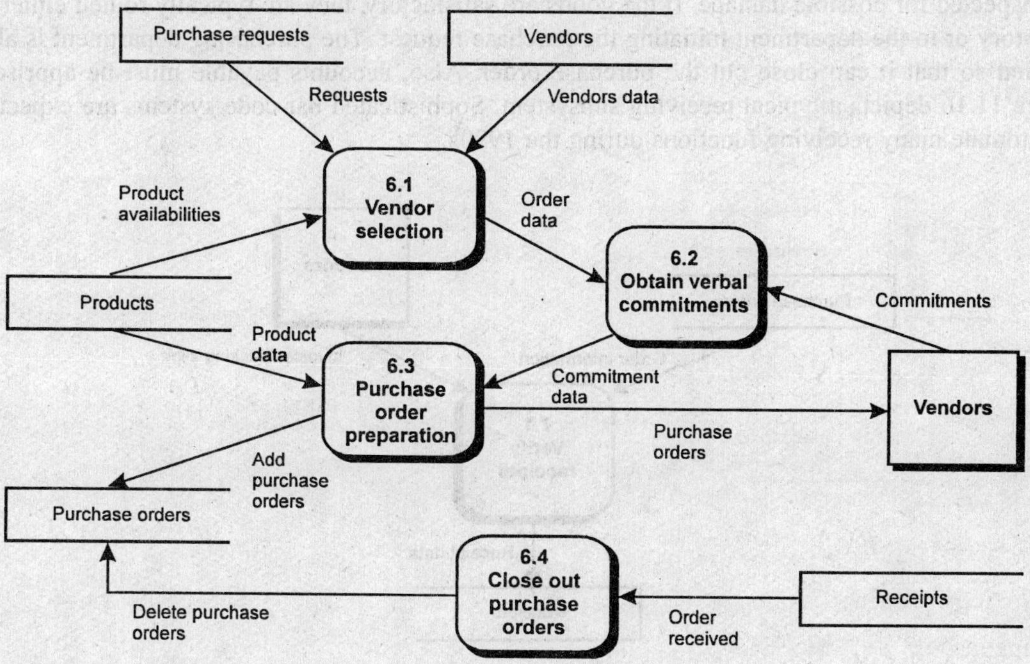

Figure 11.15. A data flow representation of a purchasing subsystem.

In firms that are electronically linked to suppliers, purchasing agents can often search through vendor databases to find the lowest prices. These types of interorganisational systems and/or EDI systems are increasingly common in many industries.

Technology is used in many new and creative ways to create electronic purchase orders. Levi Strauss, for instance, is one of the many apparel manufactures that communicate electronically with retailers, who send them electronic purchase orders. They developed a system named LeviLink, which affixes bar codes on products at factories and traces goods through retail channels. For examples, at Designs, Inc., a Massachusetts-based retailer with over 40 stores, data on sales of specific Levi Strauss products are collected in POS computer/cash registers. These data are sent nightly to Designs' mainframe computer, which sends Levi Strauss an electronic order each weekend. Such electronic purchase orders represent 25 percent of the total orders for Levis. Other electronic purchase order systems are common in the grocery and automotive supply industries.

Receiving

Receiving means is to receive, Check, Accept or Reject goods that Vendors Ship. The function of a **receiving system** in a receiving department is to receive, inspect, and accept or reject goods that vendors ship. As goods are received, the shipping cartons are opened, the contents are checked against the information on the purchase order, the price of the shipment is verified, and the goods are inspected for possible damage. If the goods are satisfactory, they are typically routed either to inventory or to the department initiating the purchase request. The purchasing department is also notified so that it can close out the purchase order. Also, accounts payable must be apprised. Figure 11.16 depicts a typical receiving subsystem. Sophisticated bar-code systems are expected to automate many receiving functions during the 1990s.

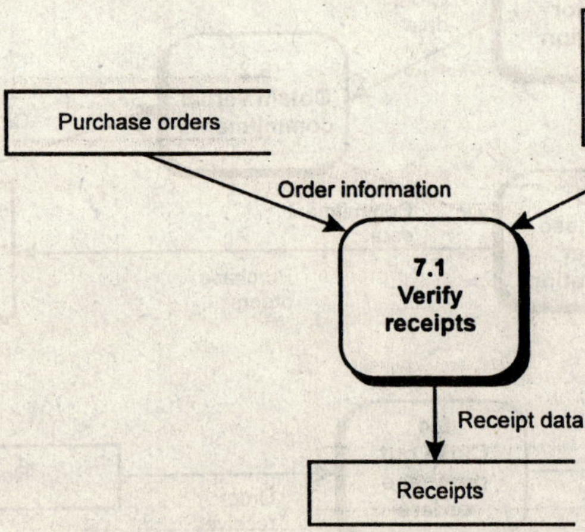

Figure 11.16. A data flow diagram representing a receiving subsystem.

Accounts Payable System or Simply Payable System

Most firms have accounts with their major suppliers (vendors). The **accounts payable (A/P) —or simply "payables"—system** is the transaction processing subsystem that handles payments to suppliers. It keeps track of invoices from suppliers, determines the optimum time to pay invoices, produces checks to pay invoices, and performs cash management activities (thereby ensuring that cash is always available when bills must be paid).

Figure 11.17 shows a data flow representation of the payables system. A payable is a liability that is created as soon as goods (or services) are received from vendors. The invoices and statements are validated against the actual receipt of goods found in the receipt file and, if all of the information is in order, the payable is created on the books. At this point, as many as 30, 60, or 90 days may elapse before the bill is actually paid, depending on the terms of the vendor. As soon as the payment is made and recorded, the payable is closed out.

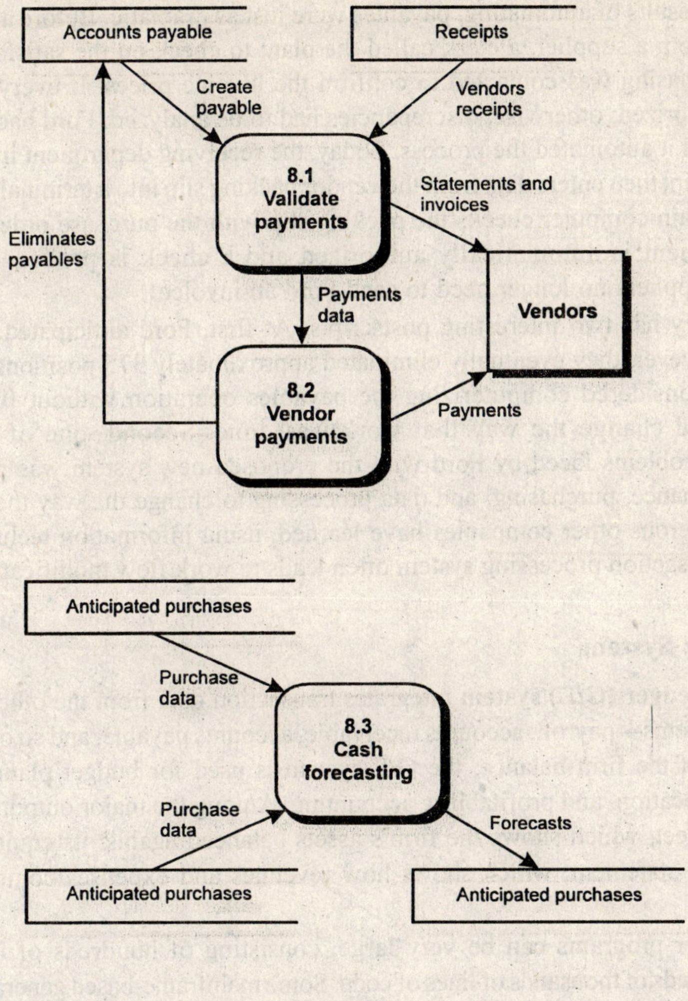

***Figure 11.17.** A data flow diagram representing a payables subsystem.*

Also shown in the data flow diagram is another important part of many payables functions: cash forecasting. This task involves ensuring that enough cash is available to meet vendor obligations as they occur. To prepare the cash forecast, the payables group should be notified of all purchase obligations as soon as these obligations occur (which may be well ahead of the actual receipt of the goods). Any information about anticipated purchases should also be included in the cash forecast. An abundance of cash forecasting software is available commercially to assist with these tasks.

As one example of how technology has changed the payables function, a manufacturer of glass, paint, and chemicals used to pay "dozens, even hundreds" of invoices to some of their suppliers every month. Using a computer systems to automate their payables, the organisation consolidates bills and now writes one check per month to each supplier.

At Ford, the results of automating, payables were just as dramatic. Before automation, when an invoice arrived from a supplier, a clerk called the plant to check on the satisfactory arrival of the parts. Then, purchasing was contacted to confirm the invoice prices. If everything was in order, payment was authorized; otherwise, discrepancies had to be analyzed. Ford had 500 people paying bills this way until it automated the process. Today, the receiving department inspect and approves the goods coming in, then enters data from the vendor packing slip into a terminal tied to a centralized computer. This main computer checks the packing slip with the purchase order and, if everything is in order, payment is automatically authorized and a check is produced. Under ordinary circumstances, suppliers no longer need to send Ford an invoice.

The Ford story has two interesting postscripts. At first, Ford anticipated that only 100 jobs would be cut; however, they eventually eliminated approximately 375 positions. This was because Ford originally considered computerizing the payables operation without first looking at how technology would change the way that work was done. Second, one of the most difficult implementation problems faced by Ford with the proposed new system was getting people from manufacturing, finance, purchasing, and data processing to change the way they performed work. As Ford and numerous other companies have learned, using information technology to automate one part of its transaction processing system often leads to work flow modifications throughout the organisation.

General Ledger System

The **general ledger (G/L) system** integrates transaction data from the other major transaction processing subsystems—payroll, accounts receivable, accounts payable, and so on. Besides ensuring that the records of the firm balance, the G/L system is used for budget planning, responsibility reporting, cost allocation, and profitability accounting. Among the major outputs of the G/L system are the balance sheet, which shows the firm's assets balanced against its equities, and the profit-and-loss (income) statement, which shows how revenues and expenses contribute to the firm's profit or loss.

General ledger programs can be very large, consisting of hundreds of integrated program modules and hundreds of thousands of lines of code. Some mainframe-based general ledger application packages commonly used in industry are IBM's Interactive Financial System, MSA's General Ledger Accounting System, Dun & Bradstreet Software's General Ledger: Millenium, and Cinamon's Control: Financial.

Transaction Processing in Functional Areas or in Practice

In many firms, transaction processing operations similar to those described in this chapter are computerized. On the whole, transaction processing operations are very easily structured and ideal for processing by computer. Also, the benefits of transaction processing to the firm—carrying lower inventories or cutting unnecessary jobs, for example—are relatively easy to quantify and to justify to management.

Many companies have had their transaction processing applications computerized for years. COBOL has traditionally been the language of choice for these applications, and IBM mainframes the usual hardware choice. A lot of these applications were first coded years ago in COBOL, and then modified or rewritten to reflect both new processing environments and changing business conditions. While both COBOL and mainframes are deeply entrenched in the transaction processing world, many observers feel that they will give way to fourth-generation languages (4GL) and microcomputer-based local area network (LAN) eventually. Such changes will evolve slowly.

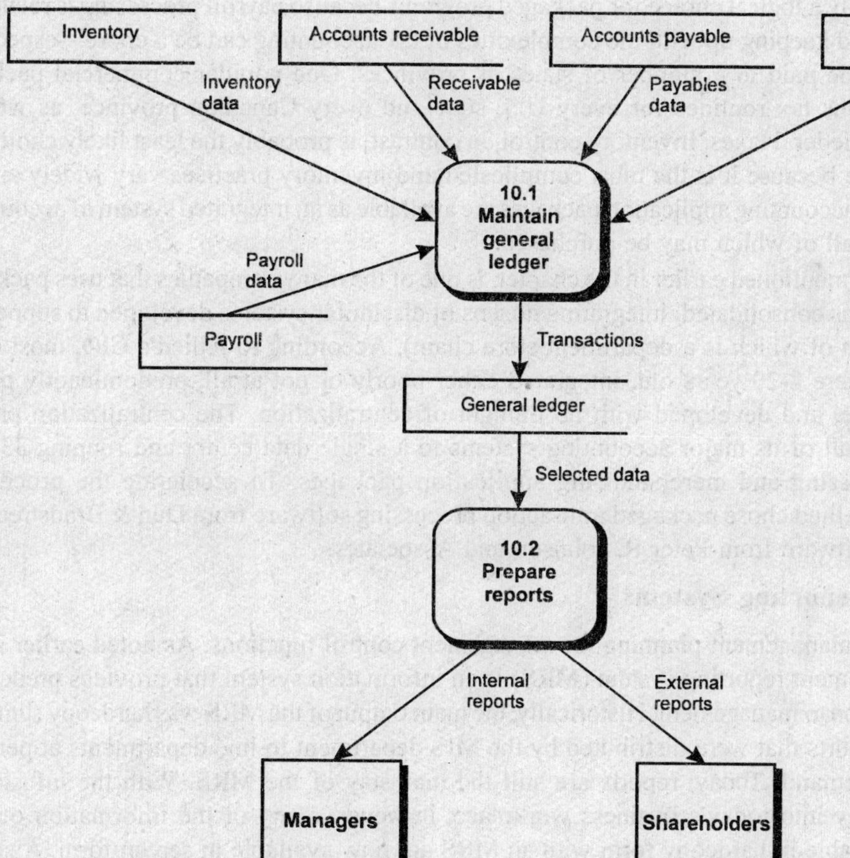

Figure 11.18. A data flow diagram representation of a general ledger system

Regarding the historical evolution of the transaction processing environment, programs had to be modified or overhauled as transaction processing systems moved from tape to disk and later, from file-oriented environments to database environments. For such applications as order entry, programs had to be overhauled as transaction processing systems evolved from card-oriented batch environments into terminal-oriented, real-time environments. Many transaction processing systems were modified over the years to reflect moves from centralized decision-making environments to decentralized ones (and possibly back again the other way), and to accommodate interorganisational links to customer and suppliers. The interorganisational links have caused some companies to look upon their transaction processing systems as potential competitive weapons, and not merely as efficiency-oriented paperwork processors. Fortunately, the accounting practices of most businesses do not change drastically, and this provides some stability to transaction processing.

When a firm is new or is overhauling one of its present transaction processing subsystems, it can either develop the application in-house or buy a prepackaged application package. Payroll processing is usually a logical choice for packaged programs because payroll processing is relatively uncomplicated, and keeping up with the complexities of tax accounting can be a chore—especially when taxes must be paid to a number of states or provinces. One popular commercial package, ALLTAX, maintains tax routines for every U.S. state and every Canadian province, as well as routines for every federal taxes. Inventory control, in contrast, is probably the least likely choice for packaged software because it is the most complicated and inventory practices vary widely among companies. Many accounting application packages are available as an integrated system of accounting functions, any or all of which may be purchased.

Allied Stores, mentioned earlier in the chapter, is one of the many companies that uses packaged software. Allied has consolidated, integrating dozens of dissimilar systems developed to support its six divisions (each of which is a department store chain). According to Allied's CIO, most of its current systems were 8-20 years old, integrated either poorly or not at all, predominantly paper-based, hard to use, and developed with no thought of centralization. The centralization project involved shifting all of its major accounting systems to a single data centre and running 33 new transaction processing and merchandising application packages. To accelerate the process of implementation, Allied chose packaged transaction processing software from Dun & Bradstreet and merchandising software from Peter R. Johnson and Associates.

Management Reporting Systems

It is used for management planning for management control functions. As noted earlier in the chapter, a management reporting system (MRS) is an information system that provides predefined types of information to management. Historically, the main output of the MRS was hardcopy summary and exception reports that were distributed by the MIS department to line departments at periodic intervals or on demand. Today, reports are still the mainstay of the MRS. With the infusion of display technology into today's business workplace, however, many of the information outputs traditionally available in hardcopy form with an MRS are now available in screen form. Also, the range of report types in much greater. For example, the continuously scrolled displays at airports showing arrivals and departures of planes (or those at brokerage houses showing change in stock prices) provide predefined and structured types of information. The form of this information, however, would not traditionally be considered a report.

Management reporting systems are used for both management planning and management control functions. Earlier in the chapter, we covered a few other types of reports, such as edit reports and error reports, that primarily serve operational control functions. Edit and error reports are generally not included under MRS; instead, they are more closely identified with the transaction processing systems they serve. Because MRS reports are associated with managerial decision making and not with the operations functions of a TPS, their value is often hard to quantify.

Origin of Management Reporting Systems

When management reporting systems were first introduced in the late 1950s, they were virtually all by-products of routine transaction processing operations. For example, when bills were batched at the end of a period, a variety of informative hardcopy reports could be produced by the computer—showing how customer purchases were distributed among various products, which sales regions or sales groups accounted for the greatest portion of sales, which customer accounts were overdue, and so on. Some of the types of information produced were new to managers. Other types of information had been available for years with manual systems; the computer merely improved their accuracy and sped up their availability to users. When a particular report request was desired by management, it was formally coded (usually in COBOL) and made available. Many management reporting systems were targeted to the information needs of middle-level managers—in contrast to transaction processing systems, which generally met the needs of lower levels of management.

By the mid-1960s, users and computer professionals felt comfortable with the outputs produced by computers, and many organisations became over-optimistic regarding what these systems could do. At this time, computers beat skilled masters at playing chess, and mathematical techniques were developed to demonstrate how adept computers were at finding optimum solutions to complex operational problems. Many computer professional discussed the immediate viability of "total systems"—systems that integrated every part of the organisation by computer. And some bewildered executives, who knew nothing about computers other than that they were amazing machines, made unwise business decisions. When many of these ambitious efforts failed, MIS was tagged with much of the blame. The failures notwithstanding, many less pretentious management reporting systems did well for companies and are still going strong. The following examples show how management reporting systems are used today in organisations:

- Every Tuesday morning, the CEO of a medium-sized company receives a computer report summarizing product sales of the previous week. The same report is also available to the sales department. The program producing the report was originally written in COBOL in 1975 and has since been modified several times to reflect new decision-making needs.
- The registrar of a university wanted a report that both identified minority students majoring in the social sciences and showed which of those students were receiving financial aid. Six months after a formal request was made for such a program to the MIS department, a computer services programmer produced the report, using a 4GL with strong report-generating capabilities.

In organisations where the MRS is developed by the MIS department, a formal proposal often must be submitted first. The proposal then competes with other MIS projects. If approved; the appropriate resources are scheduled for it. Many firms have a visible backlog of 2–4 years on proposals. This, in turn, has created an even greater invisible backlog—requests that are not submitted because users do not want to wait.

Types of Reports (Scheduled, Exception, Demand)

An MRS can produce either hardcopy report output or display output. As mentioned earlier, hardcopy reports are the most common form of output produced by an MRS.

Reports produced by management reporting systems usually fall into one of three categories: scheduled reports, exception reports, and demand reports.

- **Scheduled reports.** **Scheduled reports** (sometimes called periodic reports) are those that are issued periodically. Two examples of such reports are daily production reports and monthly performance reports. These types of reports can be used either for planning or control purposes.
- **Exception reports.** **Exception reports** are issued when something unusual takes place that requires the attention of management. For instance, an expense overrun would likely trigger the generation of an exception report. Exception reports are used primarily for control purposes.
- **Demand reports.** **Demand report** are generated when someone with authority requests such a report. An example is an executive asking for a financial report on a merger candidate.

Most of the reports produced by an MRS are either scheduled reports or exception reports. With the heavy application backlog that is now typical of many large firms, and with easy-to-use spreadsheet and database software available, many managers are taking the do-it-yourself approach to demand reporting.

How to Structure Report Content

The information contained in the reports generated by the MRS should provide decision makers in the organisation with the information they need. Ideally, the informational content of each MRS report should be relevant, timely, accurate, and verifiable.

Relevance refers to the usefulness of the report contents. In general, the goal of an MRS is to provide report recipients with information that meets their specific decision-making needs. Decision makers are unlikely to use reports containing minimal levels of relevant data. Designing reports that maximize useful information while minimizing irrelevant information usually involves taking the recipient's level in the management hierarchy into account. Managers at lower levels in the organisations typically need more detailed information than top-level managers, who tend to prefer highly summarized, aggregated information. Managers at the top of the hierarchy are also more likely than low-level managers to need information that has an external focus. The report recipient's functional speciality should also be taken into account (for example, accounting personnel should be provided with information that is relevant to accounting decisions, while marketing managers should be provided with marketing-related information). Balancing completeness (providing all the information that the decision maker needs) with conciseness (providing only the information needed) is one of the challenges that report designers face when deciding on the relevance of report contents.

Timeliness refers to the extent to which the information is delivered to decision makers in time for them to use it. Ideally, timely reports should be provided to decision makers when needed—on demand, in some instances. Accurate, relevant reports that reach the user prior to decision making are more likely to be incorporated into the decision-making process—and may lead to more effective decisions. When reports arrive too late, they are virtually useless—even if their contents are relevant to the decisions being made.

Accuracy, in the most basic sense, refers to the degree to which the information contained in the report is free of errors. This also implies that the information in the report is current and reliable.

If the MRS regularly generates reports that contain inaccurate information, decision makers will soon ignore the reports and are likely to brand them (and in some cases, the entire MRS) as unreliable and not useful for decision making. Reports that consistently contain inaccurate data or information will be treated by decision makers as if they are unimportant.

Verifiability refers to what extent a report's accuracy can be substantiated by other business data that the organisation has captured and stored. Reports about transaction processing activities, for example, should be traceable via *audit trails* to the actual transaction on which the reports are based. Reports that are easily verifiable are likely to be trusted by organisational decision makers and therefore used during the decision-making process.

Properties of Management Reporting Systems
Support structured and semistructured decisions, primarily at the middle and lower management levels
Provide fixed types of information, in an established format; the information requirements of users are normally known and stable
Often implemented with voluminous, hardcopy reports, requiring each user to search specifically for key information
Usually require a formal request to be submitted; formal systems development may be required to approve the request.
Often require a formal run schedule
Usually consist of internal operational data, rather than data about the external environment
Usually more concerned with data about the past than data relating to the future
Often oriented to summary and exception reporting

Figure 11.19. *Characteristics properties of management reporting systems. Many management reporting systems specialize in producing periodic reports from operational-level transaction processing data. These reports are used for a wide variety of planning, monitoring, and control activities.*

Importance of MRS Outputs in Management

MRS output can appear in a hardcopy report format or—like the examples of the airline arrival/departure and brokerage house screens presented earlier—in display format. In an MRS, display information is usually made available on either perpetually scrolled screens that are not turned off and are not user-controlled (such as those at airports or in brokerage houses) or on conventional display workstations, where fixed, predefined screens can be summoned by users on demand.

What distinguishes a display-oriented MRS from a DSS is flexibility. The format and types of information on MRS screens are predefined; the format and types of information on DSS screens are not. In a DSS, users are provided with the capabilities to generate their own information, usually in their own way.

No matter what type of output is used, the format should be clear (easy to read and understand), presented in a useful form (for example, narrative, numeric, or graphic), and sequenced in a logical matter (one that follows typical decision-making patterns). Decision making may also be enhanced by using formats that highlight important or exceptional information that should not be overlooked by the decision maker.

Summary/Conclusion

A management information system (MIS) is any system supporting the timely use, management, and processing of data or information by authorized people in the organisation's environment. Management information systems are composed of any or all of four component subsystems: transaction processing systems (TPS), management reporting systems (MRS), decision support systems (DSS), and office information systems (OIS), Expert systems and other knowledge-based systems are being increasingly used in conjunction with each of these subsystems.

A transaction may be defined as a routine business event—an exchange that affects the financial well-being of an organisation. A TPS, then, is a system that supports the processing of an organisation's transactions.

All transaction processing systems perform three functions: bookkeeping, issuance, and control reporting. Bookkeeping involves keeping accurate records of a firm's transaction. Issuance involves the production of business documents, such as paychecks and invoices. Control reports, such as edit reports and error reports, are by-product of a TPS that exist for control purposes.

Manual systems present a number of problems that are often solvable by computer technology. Manual systems are error-prone; they result in data getting easily lost or misplaced. They are labour intensive, their level of service is often low, and they provide poor response to information requests. Computer-based management systems have both overcome the inefficiencies associated with manual transaction processing and have evolved so that transaction processing systems can be used as competitive weapons.

The transaction processing, cycle consists of five major segments: data entry, transaction processing, file/database updating, report/document generation, and inquiry/response processing. Data entry may involve off-line key-to-media input and editing in batch processing systems. Alternatively, on-line input from source data automation terminals—along with immediate processing and file updating—is possible in real-time processing systems. After files and databases are updated, inquiries may be made by authorized users. A number of transaction processing subsystems are found in most firms. The payroll processing system, one of the oldest computerized system in many firms, produces paychecks for employees and data for tax purposes, Payroll processing is usually a batch process.

Order-entry systems process customer orders. Today, many firms use these systems strategically; for instance, by developing interorganisational information systems (IOS) or electronic data interchange (EDI) systems that the customers in more closely and keep competitors out.

An inventory system monitors the quantity of each product available for sale and helps ensure proper stock levels. IOS and EDI systems are also used with inventory systems in order to the suppliers more closely to the firm. Just-in-time systems ensure that inventory supplies arrive just when needed, so that the organisation avoids high inventory costs.

The invoicing system, which is a comparatively simple system, creates invoices and /or packing slips. The shipping system receives goods from inventory and ships them out according to instructions. Technology has increased the number of shipping options.

Accounts receivable (A/R) systems manage customer purchases payments and account balances. Because accounts receivable reflects a large percentage of the revenue coming into a firm, it receives a lot of attention.

The purchasing system assists with the acquisition of goods. Purchasing department personnel often select a vendor, prepare a purchase order, and send the order to the vendor (with copies to the other departments that need them). In many organisations, the purchasing operation is highly computerized so that no physical copies of the purchase order need to be sent; only one copy exists in a central database. The receiving system receives, inspects, and accepts or rejects goods that vendors have shipped.

The accounts payable (A/P) system handles payments to suppliers. It assists with managing vendor's invoices, help determine the optimum time to pay invoices, produces checks, and assists with cash management activities.

The general ledger (G/L) system integrates transaction data from all the other transaction processing subsystems. It is used for budget planning, responsibility reporting, cost allocation, and profitability accounting. It is also used to prepare the firm's balance sheet and profit-and-loss (income) statement.

Management reporting systems (MRS) provide predefined types of information to management, which uses them for management planning and control functions. First introduced in the 1950s, management reporting systems are by-products of transaction processing systems. Today, many management reporting systems are still linked to transaction processing systems, although some have independent sources of data.

The most common type of output produced by an MRS is hardcopy reports—usually scheduled reports, exception reports, and demand reports. Ideally, the information contained in MRS reports is timely, relevant, accurate, and verifiable.

12

Decision Support Systems

- Define decision support system (DSS) and describe some of the properties that distinguish a DSS from other types of information systems
- Differentiate among structured, semistructured, and unstructured decisions
- Identify the types of processing tasks commonly performed by a DSS
- Differentiate among specific decision support systems, DSS generators, and DSS tools
- Name several types of user interfaces commonly employed by decision support systems
- Provide Several examples of DSS applications
- Describe the characteristics of group decision support systems (GDSS) and how they may be implemented
- Describe the types of decisions made by executives and the properties that characterize those decisions
- Define executive information system (EIS) and list the characteristics of executive information systems

During the 1970s, systems designed to help decision makers devise solutions to unstructured and partially structured problem evolved. These systems largely consist of tools that can be customized in a variety of ways to solve computationally or clerically intensive problems. Such systems are particularly useful to higher-level managers whose requirements for information are somewhat unpredictable. They are called decision support systems (DSS).

We look at the types of processing needs for which a DSS is most useful and some of the software and hardware packages specifically designed for decision support. Then, we discuss the characteristics of group decision support systems (GDSS) and the software and hardware configurations associated with them. Finally, we turn to executive information systems (EIS) and explore their potential for improving the quality of strategic-level planning and control.

Introduction to DSS

The term "management information system" was first coined to distinguish the systems that merely process transaction data from systems whose primary purpose is to provide information. The first information-oriented MIS possessed the characteristics of the management reporting systems (MRS) that is, they provided fixed, preformatted information in a standardized way. Typical outputs of this type were computer-produced, hardcopy summary and exception reports that a company's MIS department might circulate periodically to various middle managers.

As developments in interactive display technology, microcomputing, and easy-to-use software systems changed the way in which managers were provided with information—and led to a growing understanding of how technology could support difficult decisions—a new term was coined to distinguish this new system from a report-based MRS. This new term— "decision support system" —resulted from the fact that these systems were more flexible and adaptable to changing decision-making requirements than traditional management reporting systems.

In this text, we define a **decision support system (DSS)** as a system that provides tools to managers to assist them in solving semistructured and unstructured problems in their own, somewhat personalized, way. Often, some type of modeling environment—perhaps a very simple environment such as the one accompanying a spreadsheet package—is involved. A DSS is not intended to make decisions for managers, but rather to provide managers with a set of capabilities that enables them to generate the information they feel is needed to make decisions. In other words, a DSS supports the human decision-making process, rather than providing a means to replace it.

Systems that replace human decision making—rather than support it—are sometimes called *programmed decision systems.* These systems are used to make routine, structured decisions, such as approving loans or credit, reordering inventory, triggering reminder notices, and selecting audit samples. In programmed decision systems, the focus is on doing something more efficiently; in decision support systems, the focus is on helping decision makers become more effective.

Technically, a DSS does not need to involve high technology. For example, to a writer, a selected group of journal and text resources at a local library—and a strategy for using those resources—may serve as part of a decision support system. To a novice accountant in a large accounting firm, the advice offered by a senior tax partner may be part of that novice's decision support system. In this technology-oriented text, however, we will assume that all of the decision support systems discussed are computer-based information systems (CBIS).

DSS Goals and Applications

Few terms have been redefined as many times in technical literature, or defined in so many different ways at any single point in time, as the decision support system. Today, most researchers agree that decision support systems are characterized by at least three properties: (1) they support semistructured or unstructured decision making, (2) they are flexible enough to respond to the changing needs of decision makers, and (3) they are easy to use. Here, we will look at both of these properties and at other properties that—while not mandatory for a DSS—are common to most of them.

Semistructured and Unstructured Decisions

Structured decisions are those that are easily made from a given set of inputs. These types of decisions—such as deciding to issue a reminder notice if a bill is overdue or deciding to sell a stock under a given set of market conditions—can be programmed fairly easily. Unstructured decisions and semistructured decisions, however, are decisions for which information obtained from a computer system is only a portion of the total knowledge needed to make the decision.

The DSS is particularly well adapted to help with semistructured and unstructured decisions; however, it can be designed to support structured decision making as well. A manager, for instance, can browse through data at will (perhaps at a display terminal). When enough information is gleaned from this process to supplement other information (perhaps some of it noncomputer-based), a decision can be reached. In a well-designed DSS, the depth to which the available data can be tapped for useful information often is limited only by the time and patience of the manager.

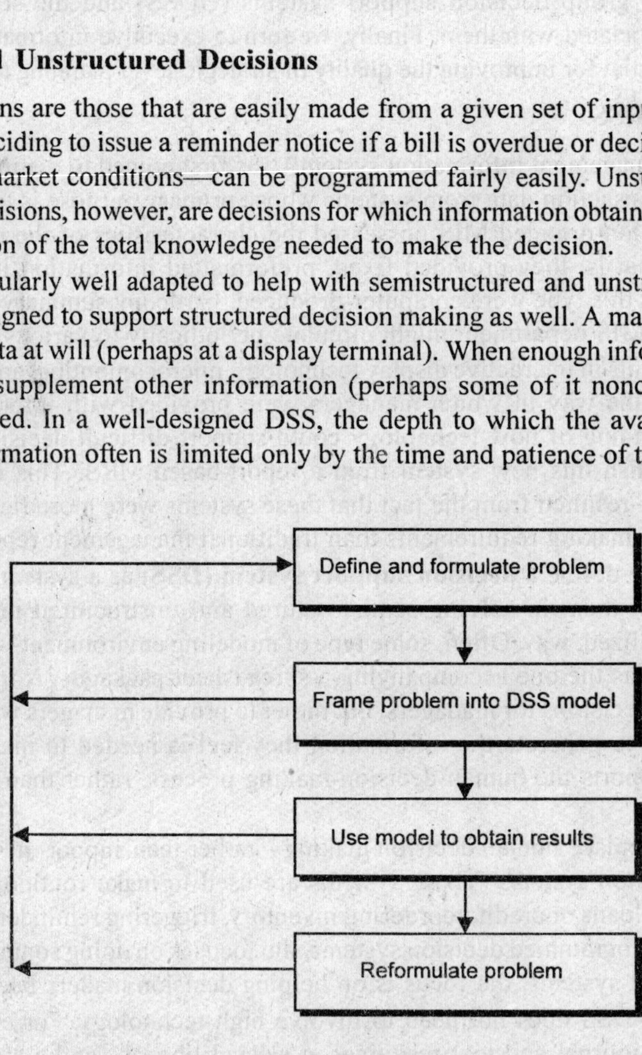

Figure 12.1. Steps in solving a problem with a DSS.

In Figure 12.1, we see how a semistructured problem might be solved by using a DSS. The problem is first defined and formulated. It is then modeled with DSS software. Next, the model is run on the computer to provide results. The modeler, in reviewing these results, might decide to completely reformulate the problem, refine the model, or use the model to obtain other results. For example, a user might define a problem that involves simulating cash flows under a variety of business conditions by using financial modeling software. The DSS model is then run, providing results. Depending on what the results of the model indicate about cash flow, the user might decide to completely remodel the problem, make small modifications to the current model, run the model under a number of new assumptions, or accept the results. For instance, if the model revealed inadequate cash flows to support organisational operations, model modifications should be developed and run. The modification process might continue for several iterations until an acceptable cash flow is identified.

Ability to Adapt to Changing Needs

Semistructured and unstructured decisions often do not conform to a predefined set of decision-making rules. Because of this, their decision support systems need to provide for enough flexibility to enable users to model their own information needs, and should be capable of adapting to changing information needs.

Often, the specification involves a lengthy, customized application program, supporting documentation, and a run schedule. For example, a production manager might make a formal request to the MIS department for a monthly report. The utility of such a report is usually then assessed by a committee and, possibly, scheduled for development. (As noted in previous chapters, many MIS departments are saddled with a 2-to-4 year application backlog and may be unable to fulfil the manager's request immediately.) After the report is designed and a program is written specifically to generate it, the types of information supplied to the manager by that report are "frozen." If information needs change substantially, another formal report request must be submitted to get the program rewritten.

The DSS designer understands that managers usually do not know what information they need in advance and, even if they did, those information needs constantly change. Thus, rather than lock the system into rigid information-producing requirements, capabilities and tools are provided to enables users to meet their own output needs.

Flexibility in a DSS is of paramount importance. Information requests made to a DSS will often be relatively unsystematic and idiosyncratic. For example, a sales manager at a display device might request the price of a specific product. A few seconds later, the manager might change her mind and ask for a listing of the vendors of several other products. The next request, a couple of minutes later, may be ranking of the top salespeople in a particular sales region over the last two months. A report might even be requested at the end of the session, combining data from several of these inquiries.

Since the demands made by the user on the DSS are not fully predetermined, the user might request information in any of a variety of formats. In well-designed decision supports systems, managers can ask spontaneous questions, as these questions occur to them, and receive almost immediate responses. The manager can make many requests without being sure at any point where the search for information will lead next. The manager often needs a variety of tools to satisfy such requests: formulas, functions, sorts, graphs, formal models, and so on. The outputs from a DSS may also be used to prepare customized outputs for examination by other people; for example, a manager preparing presentation graphics for a meeting.

Ease of Learning and Use of Decision Support Systems

Since decision support systems are often built and operated by users rather than by computer professionals, the tools that a company them should be relatively easy to learn and use. Software tools often employ user-oriented interfaces—grids, graphics, nonprocedural fourth-generation languages (4GL), natural English, and easily read documentation—to make it easier for users to conceptualize and perform the decision-making process. As is the case with most computer applications during the 1990s, graphical user interfaces (GUI) are becoming more common in decision support systems. Also, such tools often liberally employ a number of help aids—memory joggers, useful diagnostics, a help feature, and undo commands—because general users typically do not have the skills to interpret cryptic error messages.

Although interactive display devices are not considered a requirement for a DSS, many decision support systems employ them. First, display devices provide users with relatively fast, often real-time, responses, thus enabling the process depicted in Figure 12.1 to be conducted as rapidly as the user wants. Fast electronic responses facilitate maintaining a train of thought as the problem-solving process takes place; real-time responses assure the user that up-to-date (that is, really useful) data are being supplied to the decision-making process. In addition, interactive systems enable the user to base each new request on the system's responses to earlier requests. In non-interactive systems, if a decision must be made within a certain time frame and system turnaround time is slow, managers are often forced to batch together a large number of potentially useful requests; this can involve a lot of extra contingency planning. The point here is that although interactive display devices are not required for a DSS, they do help to make many decision support systems friendly and useful.

Other Properties of DSS

By being focused on solving semistructured and unstructured problems, decision support systems are especially useful to the decision-making needs of higher-level managers. This is not to imply that decision support system cannot benefit managers or non-managers at lower level—in fact, they often do. But decision-making needs at lower levels can be anticipated better than at higher levels, so certain aspects of decision support systems, such as their calculator-type tools and modeling capabilities, may be unnecessary in decision support systems that support lower-level managers.

To increase the quality of the decisions made by managers, most decision support systems incorporate models tailored to the decision-making environment. In some cases, the models are developed by professionals who are skilled in model-building techniques. But more often, the models are user-developed. Because of this, decision support systems require an interface that provides users with the tools to build their own models and an intuitive conceptual framework so that users can assess their own progress. Later in the chapter, we will look at executive information systems (EIS), which rely less on the use of user-constructed models than do traditional decision support systems.

Another general property of many (but not all) decision support systems is that they are harder to cost-justify to management than, for example, transaction processing systems. Often, it is difficult to assess whether a DSS will actually improve the quality of a decision. Even if most people agree that decision making will be improved, it is hard to quantify the benefits directly attributable to the DSS. For example, a manager might claim that use of a spreadsheet package enabled a budget to be prepared more quickly and with a higher level of quality than was previously possible. An observer, on the other hand, might argue that the manager got so carried away with what the spreadsheet software could do that what should have taken five minutes to submit in handwritten form took an hour. These reservations notwithstanding, many DSS tools are so inexpensive and so easy to implement that many managers have installed them anyway—feeling, perhaps, that they really cannot afford to get bogged down in traditional cost justification. Figure 12.2 provides a summary of general properties found in some or all decision support systems.

PROPERTIES OF DECISION SUPPORT SYSTEMS
Decision Support Systems are Typically Characterized by:
Support for semistructured and unstructured decision making
Flexibility in specifying output requirements
Ease of use and ease of development for non-professionals
Fast response
High degree of user control and interaction
In Addition, Many are Characterized by:
Middle or top management focus
Interactive capabilities
Use of models
Difficulty in cost justifying
Evolutionary development
Focus on managerial effectiveness, rather than efficiency

***Figure 12.2.** Properties of decision support systems. What specifically constitutes a DSS is a rapidly evolving issue.*

Components of a DSS (Hardware, Software)

The primary components of a DSS are illustrated in Figure 12.3. As this figure shows, a combination of hardware, software, and data is necessary to provide interactive decision support for managers and users (who are also part of the DSS). The major features of the hardware and software components of a DSS are summarized as follows:

- **Hardware.** In order to provide interactive capabilities, microcomputers may be used on a stand-alone basis or may be connected to larger computer systems (by telecommunication links) that have DSS software, models, and data resources. Interactive display terminals may be used in place of microcomputers when DSS software, models, and data resources all reside on host computers. In stand-alone systems, DSS software, models, and data may be stored on a single microcomputer; communications software may be used to enable decision makers to access external databases such as those provided by the information utilities.
- **Software.** The software packages used to develop and maintain decision support systems are usually called **DSS generators;** these typically contain modules for database, model, and dialogue management.

The *database management* module makes it possible to create, maintain, and query DSS databases. As Figure 12.4 shows, the database management component allows for DSS databases to be created by extracting data from external and internal (both corporate and personal) sources. This module typically has many of the same capabilities for interrogation and maintenance found in the database management systems. A relational database management system is often better suited for such usage than are either hierarchical or network database management systems. The retrieval, data reconfiguration, selection, and projection tasks described in the following section are typically associated with the database management module of the DSS generator.

The *model management* component makes it possible to create, maintain, and apply quantitative, mathematical, and other models that manipulate DSS data. As you can observe in this figure, the model database may consist of a wide variety of models and data manipulation tools. The calculator activities, functions, and analysis tools (for example, statistical optimizing and sensitivity analysis tools) described in the next section may all be aspects of the model management module. Many of the software packages discussed in the "DSS Development" section of this chapter may also be included in the model management component. Note that the exact contents of the model base are built on the needs of individual decision makers.

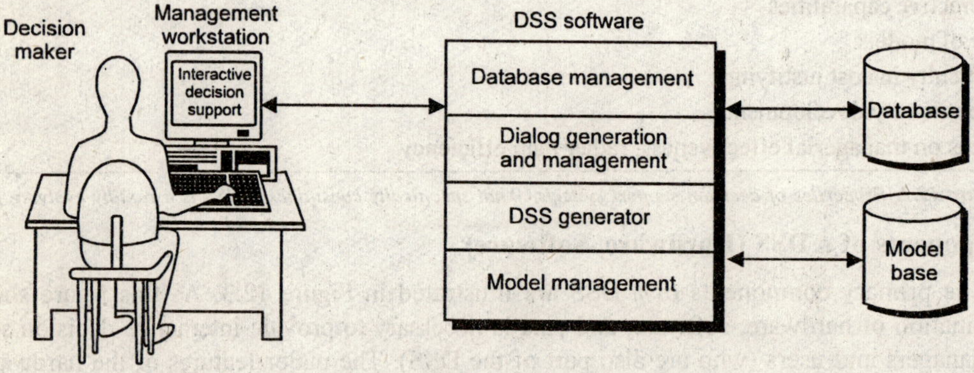

Figure 12.3. *Components of a DSS. Decision support systems consist of hardware, software, data, and decision makers. The main categories of DSS software include the database management software, dialogue generation and management software, DSS generator, and model management software.*

The *dialogue management* module provides the user with the easy-to-operate interfaces (such as screen formats) that supports flexible, interactive input and output. It is illustrated more fully in Figure 12.6. The support interfaces, commands, and templates described in the "DSS Development" section of the chapter are aspects of the dialogue management component.

Putting a DSS to Work

In this section, we will look at some of the tasks commonly performed by decision support systems. Four tasks that we address in this section are information retrieval, data reconfiguration, calculator activities, and analysis.

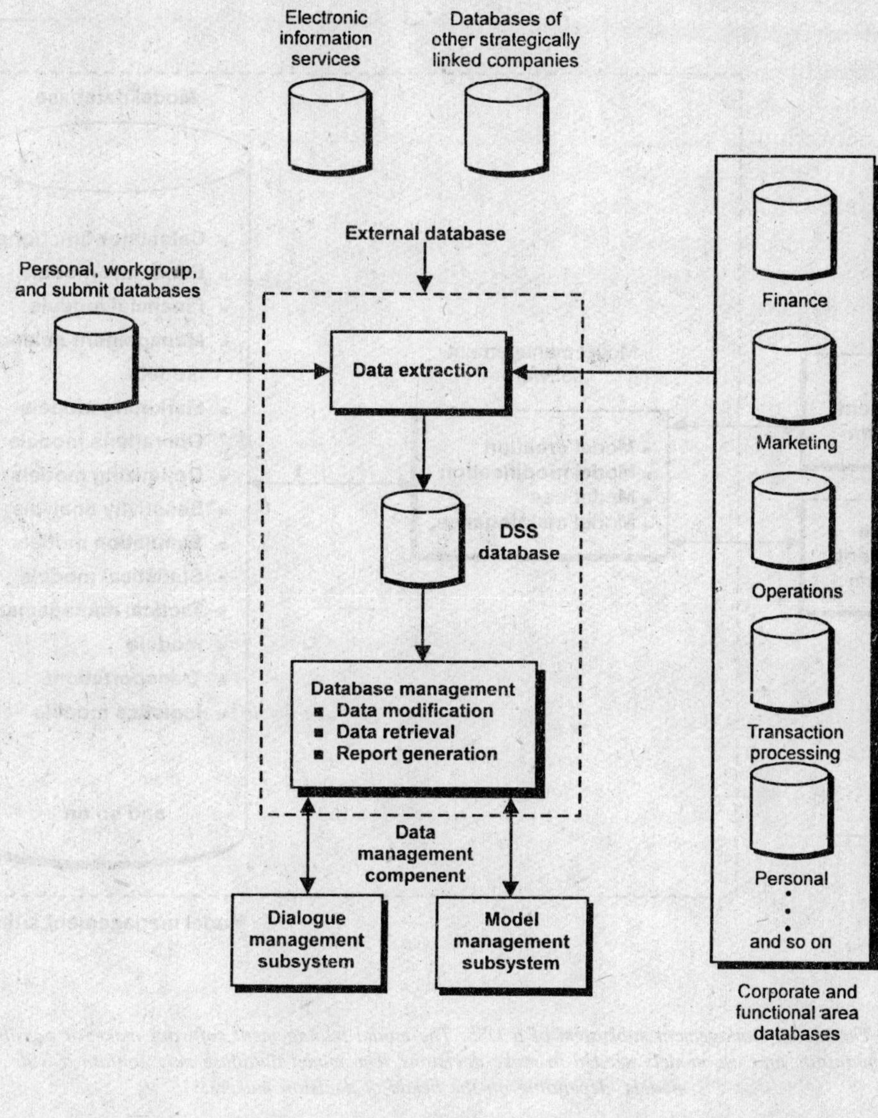

Figure 12.4. *The data management subsystem of a DSS. The data management subsystem allows the user to create DSS databases by extracting data from other databases and, in some systems, databases that are external to the organisation.*

Informational Retrieval

Information retrieval in a DSS environment refers to the act of extracting information from a database, or from data files, for the purpose of making decisions. As described earlier, the retrieval is often carried out at an interactive display station, where each new set of information obtained can be used to direct the search for other types of information.

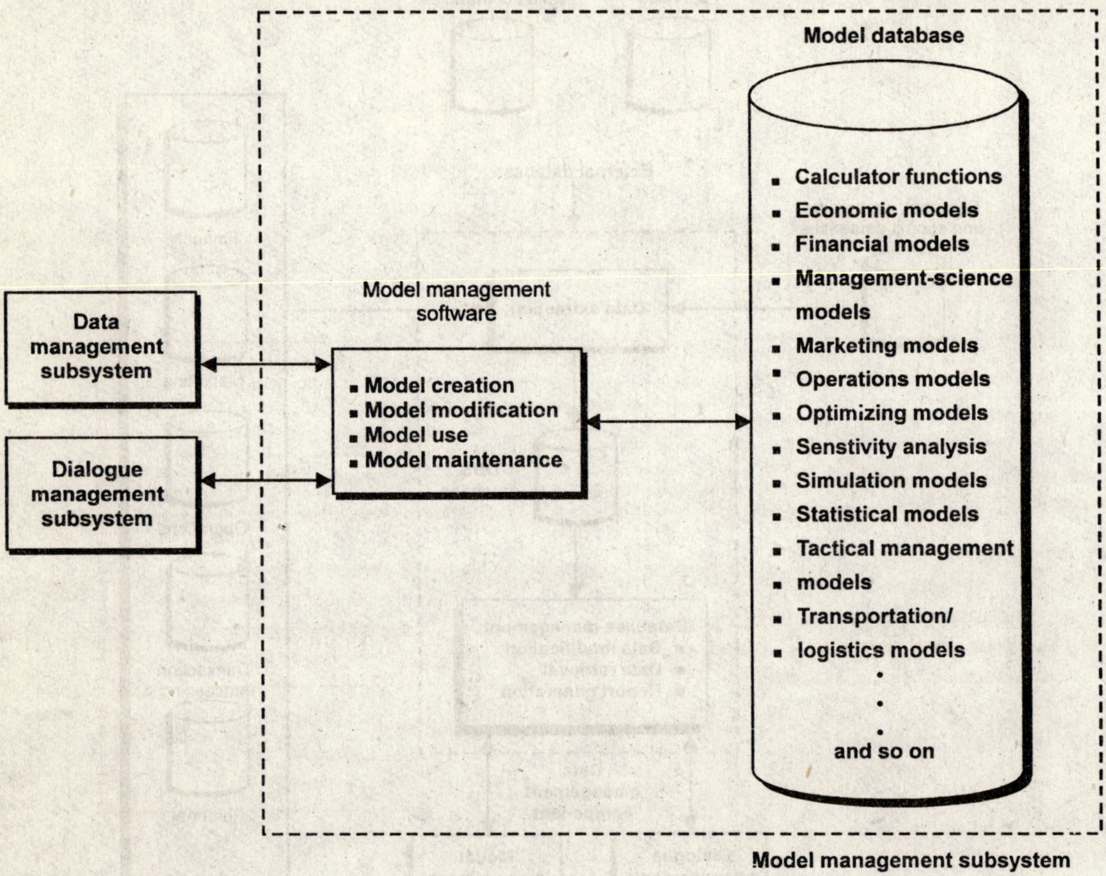

Figure 12.5. The model management subsystem of a DSS. The model management software makes it possible for users to create, maintain, and use models needed to make decisions. The model database may contain a wide variety of models, depending on the needs of decision makers.

The decision maker using the DSS might retrieve small bits of information at the display workstation. If the amount of information needed is extensive, or if the information must be put into permanent form so it can be studied later, the decision maker might ask the DSS to prepare a comprehensive printed report.

Usually, the sequence of retrievals made by the user is unanticipated. For example, the manager might see a few startling pieces of information on the display and, as a result of these, suddenly produce a report that provides more detail about the situation. Or the manager might continue to use the DSS in a display retrieval mode, looking for different types of information on different types of products, in random order.

At upper levels in the management hierarchy, the decision maker often wants access to internal and external databases. Many decision support systems designed for use by higher-level managers make it possible to access the on-line databases provided by information utilities.

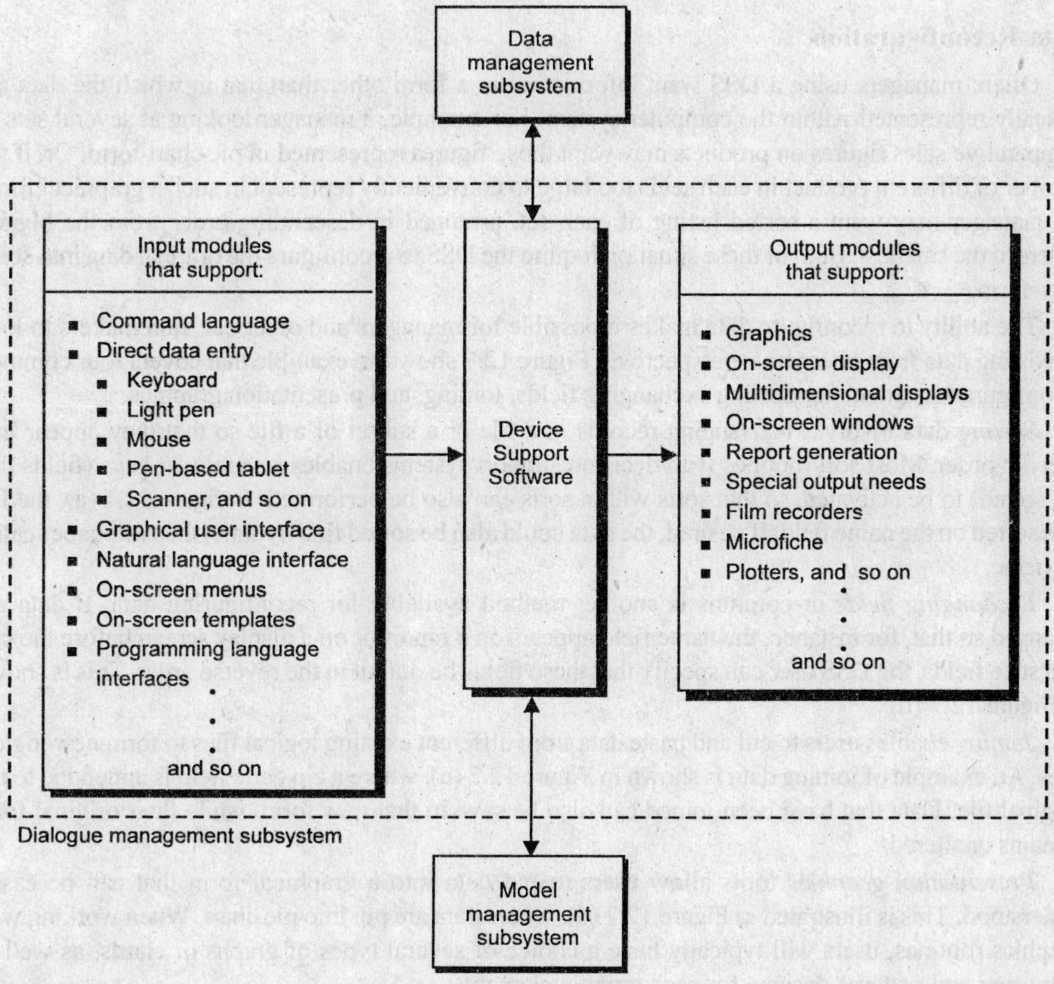

Figure 12.6. *The dialogue management subsystem of a DSS. The dialogue management system provides users with a flexible, interactive interface for input, processing, and output.*

Selection and Projection

Two common types of retrieval are selection and projection. With respect to logical data files, *selection* involves separating out records that have specific characteristics; for example, identifying all males over age 65 in an employee file or database. *Projection*, with respect to logical files, involves obtaining only certain fields of data; for example, extracting all names and phone numbers from an employee file or database. Of course, retrieval often involves a combination of both selection and projection—for example, determining only the names and phone numbers of all male employees over age 65.

Data Reconfiguration

Often, managers using a DSS want information in a form other than that in which the data are logically represented within the computer system. For example, a manager looking at several sets of comparative sales figures on products may want those figures represented in pie chart form. Or, if the number of different product in each set is too large to conveniently represent in such a graphical form, the manager may want a sorted listing of each set, arranged in descending order from the biggest sellers to the smallest. Both of these situation require the DSS to reconfigure the original data into some new form.

The ability to reconfigure data makes it possible for managers and other decision makers to look at existing data from alternative perspectives. Figure 12.7 shows an example that covers four common reconfiguration situations: sorting exchanging fields, joining, and presentation graphics.

Sorting data involves rearranging records in a file or a subset of a file so that they appear in a specific order. Most sort routines with decision support systems enables several sort keys (fields that are sorted) to be activated, so that sorts within sorts can also be performed. In figure 12.7 (a), the file was sorted on the name field. If desired, the data could also be sorted first by state, then (alphabetically) by name.

Exchanging fields or columns is another method available for reconfiguring data. If data are arranged so that, for instance, the name field appears on a report or on a display screen before the city and state fields, the DSS user can specify that these fields be output in the reverse order. This is shown in Figure 12.7 (b).

Joining enables users to cut and paste data from different existing logical files to form new logical files. An example of joining data is shown in Figure 12.7 (c), where a zip code field is appended to the original file. Data that have been joined can also be save in that new form, while their original form remains unaltered.

Presentation graphics tools allow users to put data into a graphical form that can be easily understood. This is illustrated in Figure 12.7 (d), where data are put into pie chart. When working with graphics routines, users will typically have a choice of several types of graphs or charts, as well as colouring and patterns designs for each graphic element.

Calculator Activities

Calculator activities refer to the set of tasks that normally can be done with a calculator. These activities are generally implemented either by having the user write out a complete formula, specifying all the variables involved and how arithmetic operations should be performed on them, or by having the user summon a function resident in the DSS or DSS tool.

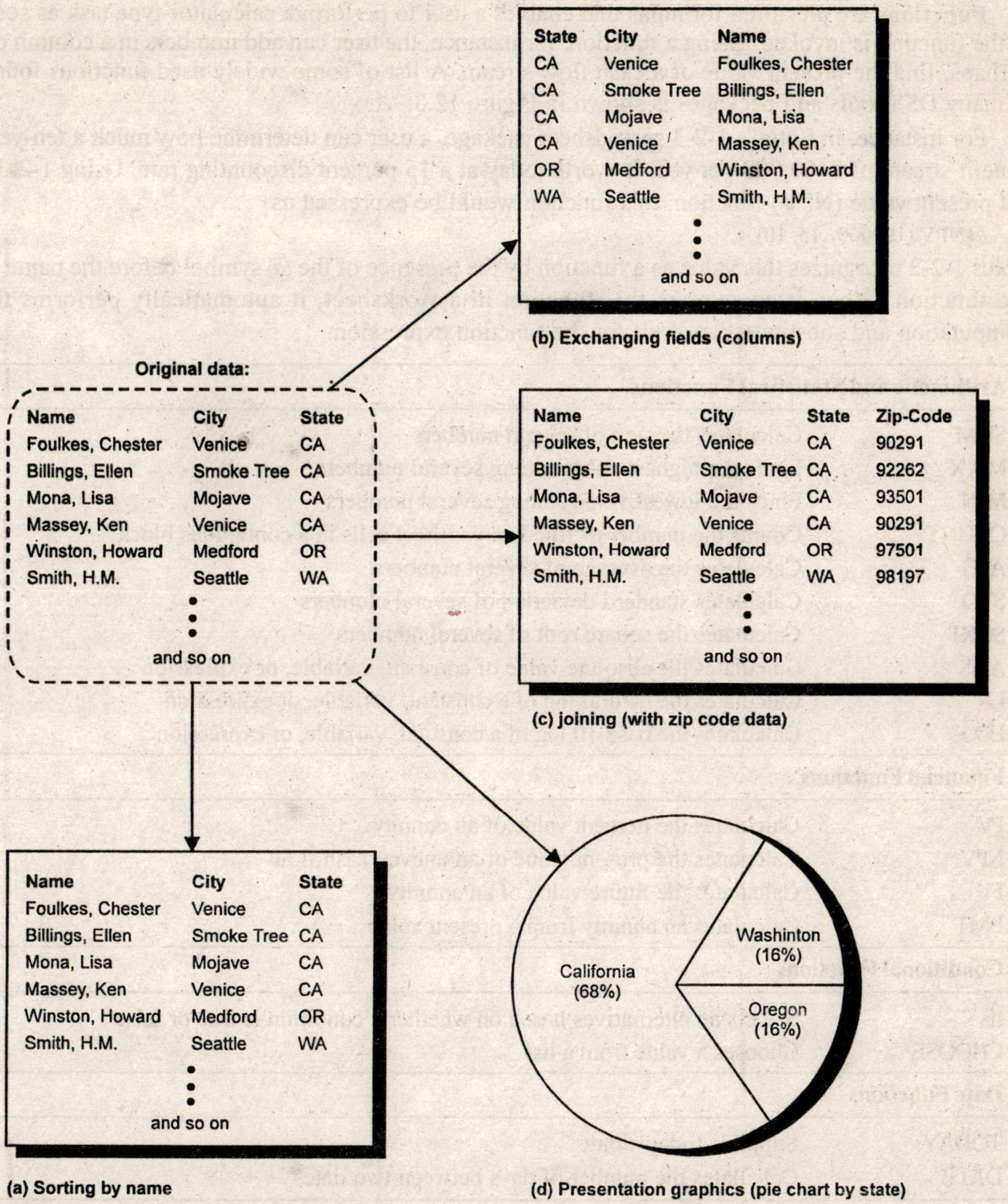

Figure 12.7. Examples of reconfiguring data.

Functions (Prestored Formulas)

Functions are prestored formulas that enables a user to perform a calculator-type task as soon as the function is invoked. Using a function, for instance, the user can add numbers in a column or, perhaps, find the present value of a cash flow stream. A list of some widely used functions found in many DSS tools and packages is shown in Figure 12.8.

For instance, in Lotus's 1-2-3 spreadsheet package, a user can determine how much a ten-year benefit stream of $100,000 per year is worth today at a 15 percent discounting rate. Using 1-2-3's net present value (NPV) function, this function would be expressed as

@NPV (100000, .15, 10)

Lotus 1-2-3 recognizes this value as a function by the presence of the @ symbol before the name of the function. When it encounters this function in a worksheet, it automatically performs the computation and substitute the result for the function expression.

Arithmetic and Statistical Functions	
SUM	Calculates the sum of several numbers
MAX	Finds the highest value among several numbers
MIN	Finds the lowest value among several numbers
COUNT	Counts the number of filled spreadsheet cells in a contiguous block
AVG	Calculates the average of several numbers
STD	Calculates standard deviation of several numbers
SQRT	Calculates the square root of several numbers
ABS	Calculates the absolute value of constant, variable, or expression
LN	Calculates the natural log of a constant, variable, or expression
LOG	Calculates the base-10 log of a constant, variable, or expression
Financial Functions	
PV	Calculates the percent value of an annuity
NPV	Calculates the present value of an uneven cash flow
FV	Calculates the future value of an annuity
PMT	Calculates an annuity from a present value
Conditional Functions	
IF	Selects an alternatives based on whether a condition is true or false
CHOOSE	Chooses a value from a list
Date Functions	
TODAY	Supplies today's date
DATE	Calculates the number of days between two dates

Figure 12.8. *Some commonly used calculator functions.*

Analysis

Analysis refers to using a DSS to review a set of facts and to assist in drawing conclusions based on those facts. Because the decision support environment is semistructured, both the user and machine interact in this process. Four widely used types of DSS analysis tools, or techniques brought by users to the DSS environment, are statistical tools, optimizing tools, what-if analysis, and artificial intelligence routines.

Statistical Tools

Statistical tools enable users to perform a variety of statistical operations on data, as well as to do a number of other data-handling tasks, such as distributing data into categories of the user's choosing. Statistical operations normally include regression analysis (procedures used to discern patterns in or make predictions from a set of data), correlation analysis (tools used to find the strength of association among data), and a variety of statistical inference methodologies (procedures such as analysis of variance, t-test, Chi-square analysis, and confidence limits; they can be used to determine whether a conclusion drawn from data is statistically significant).

Statistical methods are usually descriptive or predictive in nature; that is, they describe patterns among data or forecast events based on present or past happenings. In addition to the standard statistical tools mentioned here, many packages offer a variety of specialized tools, such as factor analysis, discriminant analysis, and cluster analysis (see Figure 12.9). Some of the most widely used statistical tools in business are the variety of regression routines used for forecasting purposes. These are particularly valuable when strategic plans are being formulated.

Operation	Description
Test of hypothesis	Determine whether a hypothesis is statistically significant
Correlation analysis	Determine the strength of association among a number of a variables
Regression analysis	Determines a mathematical relationship that shows how variables may be related
Analysis of variance (ANOVA)	Shows whether differences among groupings of observations are statistically significant
Nonparametric statistics	A collection of inference methods used for small samples or for cases where the underlying probability distribution is unknown
Discriminant analysis	A multivariate, regression-like technique used when the dependent variable (Y variable) is scaled into categories (such as users versus nonusers)
Cluster analysis	A method that classifies observations into groups in such a way that the similarities within groups are minimized and the difference between groups are maximized
Factor analysis	A method that reduces a large number of variables into a smaller number of factors, while retaining most of the information in the process
Forecasting techniques	A collection of methods—including regression analysis, exponential smoothing, the Box-Jenkins techniques, input/output analysis, and econometric techniques—that is used to predict the future from a set of observations

Figure 12.9. *Operations found in many statistical packages. Software packages that are heavily oriented toward forecasting techniques are often called forecasting packages. Many statistical packages also include routines for summarizing, sorting, and classifying data. Some also include graphics generation features.*

Mathematical Optimizing Tools

A number of mathematical optimizing tools were introduced in earlier chapters. Among these techniques are inventory control models, mathematical programming, Monte Carlo simulation, queuing theory, and network modeling. All of these mathematical modeling tools can be used to recommend certain choices to the decision maker, and many of them can generate a rich assortment of descriptive and predictive information as well. One of the most widely used optimizing techniques for business decision makers is the Monte Carlo simulation.

Typically, in decision support environments that feature one or more optimizing tools, the user can choose specific parameters (variables) for the models as well as determine, to a limited extent, how certain relationships are to be specified among those parameters. The specified models and its data are then input to the computer and the results noted. At the point, the user either accepts the information or reformulates the problem and again goes through the process suggested in Figure 12.1.

Flexibility really sets a DSS apart from an MRS with respect to developing such models. With a DSS, the user can dynamically specify variables and values for models, and even build models without strict guidelines. With an MRS, the user is licked into a prespecified model.

What-If Analysis

What-if analysis is a non-probabilistic simulation technique that enables a user to reformulate a problem repeatedly until helpful information is obtained. For example, a manager might use a DSS generator (such as Execucom's IFPS/Plus, Figure 12.10) to build a DSS to maximize the net income for a new product in the coming year. IFPS/Plus is an updated version of IFPS (Interactive Financial Modeling System)—one of the best known and most widely used modeling packages.

```
                      IFPS/PLUS
                 OPTIMIZATION OPTIONS

      MODEL:   FORECAST
               VARIABLE                COLUMNS(S)            VALUE
  OBJECTIVE:   MAXIMIZE NET INCOME          TOTAL
  DECISIONS:   SALES GROWTH RATE             1993
CONSTRAINTS:   DEBT TO TOTAL CAPITAL    1988-1992    =         40%
               CURRENT RATIO            1998-1992    =       4.00X
               END OPTIMIZATION
               ENTER THE CONSTRAINT VALUES YOU WISH TO USE
```

Figure 12.10. Using Execucom's IFPS/Plus for what-if analysis. Each time the user solves the problem shown, the objective, decisions, or constraints can be changed. Here, the user could run the model again, changing the debt-to-capital ratio from 40 percent to some other value.

Often, in the course of using a DSS generator to solve a problem, more than one set of estimates may be needed. What if the debt-to-capital ratio is 10 percent to high? What happens if sales projections are 10 percent too low? What if bank borrowing rates increase by 2 percent? Or what if product development is delayed by a year? DSS generators make it quite easy for users to develop multiple sets of estimates. However, DSS generators are not the only tools that can perform what-if analysis; spreadsheets are also well suited for this.

Refiguring calculations on the basis of all these what-if can take weeks to do by hand, but they are standard in the DSS world. For each what-if query, all the managers need do is change an underlying assumption or the value of a parameter and re-run the model. At the end of the interactive session, several of these runs can be used to make decisions and, perhaps, convince other management members of the appropriateness of the chosen action.

In certain contexts, what-if analysis is called *sensitivity analysis.* The goal of sensitivity analysis is to find out how sensitive a solution suggested by a model is to changes in the model parameters. For example, it might be useful for a bank manager to know how much change should be expected in the profitability of a project if mortgage rates were to change by a quarter of a percent in the next month. Or a chemical producer might want to know that $60,000 per month could be saved in production costs if only the availability of a raw material could be increased by 10 percent.

Artificial Intelligence or Expert System

Artificial intelligence (AI) or expert system routines may dramatically improve the usefulness of the analysis function of a DSS. In the next chapter, we will look in depth at the role played by AI and other knowledge-based systems throughout MIS. Here, we will consider only one example of using AI to enhance a DSS: why analysis, the AI-based explanation feature that goes one step beyond the traditional what-if analysis that is available with most decision support systems.

IFPS/Plus explanation

MODEL: INCOME

GROSS PROFITS WENT DOWN IN YEAR 3 BECAUSE RAW MATERIAL AND DIRECT LABOR INCREASED. THIS RESULT WAS PARTIALLY OFFSET BECAUSE REVENUE INCREASED.

GROSS PROFIT = REVENUE - RAW MATERIAL - DIRECT LABOR - PACKAGING - DISTRIBUTION

	YEAR 2	AMOUNT CHANGE	YEAR 3
GROSS PROFITS	142140	-326	141814
RAW MATERIAL	231840	83170	315010
DIRECT LABOR	154560	49980	204540
REVENUE	621000	132825	753825

WHY DID GROSS PROFITS GO DOWN IN YEAR 3?

"Why" question posed by user

Figure 12.11. *Using Execucom's IFPS/Plus for why analysis. At the bottom of the screen is a natural language query posed by the decision maker in response to the computations at the centre of the screen. At top is the resulting IFPS/Plus explanation.*

Why analysis is a technique in which, after inspecting the results of DSS computations on-screen, the user can ask the DSS to explain why something happened. Figure 12.11 shows the use of why analysis with Execucom's IFPS/Plus modeling package. The AI feature embedded in the package evaluates the significance of key indicators that influence the results of previous computations and responds with its "opinion" as to why the event happened.

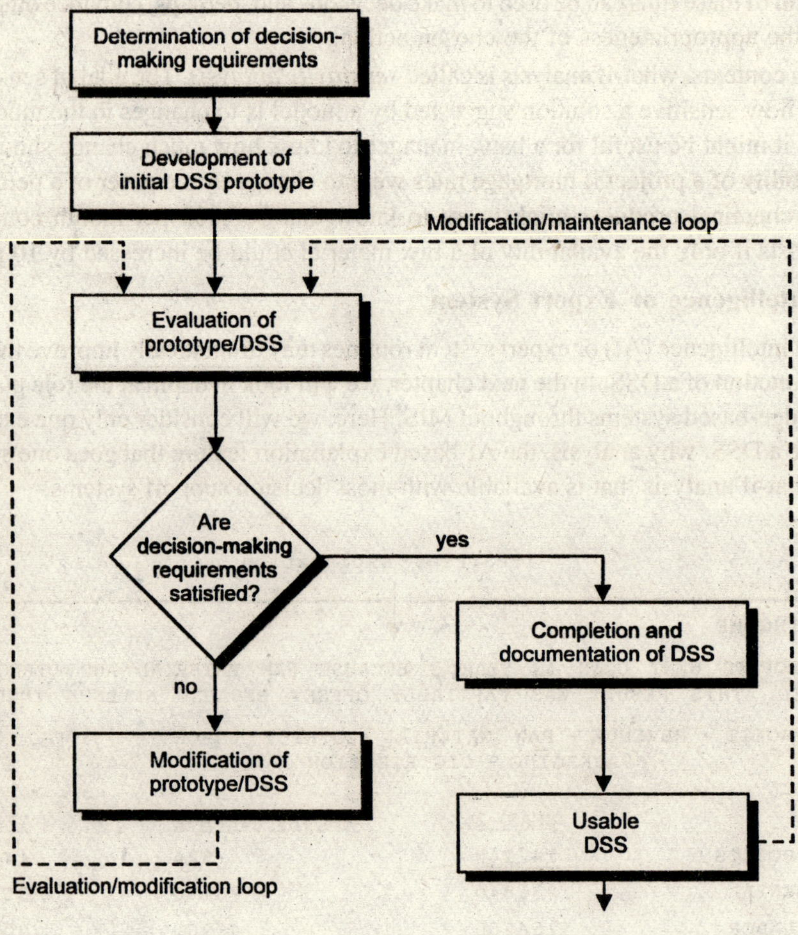

***Figure 12.12.** The DSS development process. In many instances, after decision-making needs are identified and an initial prototype developed, several evaluation/modification iterations may be needed before the DSS is ready for use.*

How to Develop DSS

Decision support systems are usually created in an evolutionary manner. Figure 12.12 illustrates the general nature of the DSS development process. Once user decision-making needs are identified, a preliminary model (prototype) of the DSS is constructed. After the user has some initial experiences with the DSS prototype, it may be refined to provide better results. This process may continue for several iterations. Many decision support systems rely heavily on models and, theoretically, the building of models that have recurring utility is never complete. In this sense, the DSS is never finished; after the initial final product is built, the DSS continues to evolve.

Products of DSS

Hardware and software products used to develop and implement decision support systems abound in the marketplace. Here, we will first consider how these products may be classified. Then, we will look at the variety of software tools that are often used to develop decision support systems and that may also be embedded in them. Finally, we will explore the types of user interfaces that may be found in decision support systems.

Products falling under the DSS umbrella into three categories: specific decision support systems, DSS generators, and DSS tools.

A **specific DSS** allows one or more decision makers to deal with a specific problem or set of related problems. For example, a specific DSS is used by the city of San Jose, California. The DSS enables police officers planning patrol beats to call up maps of their areas and try various allocations of officers to these beats. For each proposed what-if allocation, the DSS provides a measure of effectiveness. A specific DSS might be programmed from scratch by an organisation (and expensive alternative) or developed from a DSS generator.

A DSS generator is a package of related hardware and software (and, often, procedures and data) that allows the user to quickly and easily build a specific DSS. For instance, the police-beat DSS just described was built with a DSS generator called Geodata Analysis and Display System (GADS). GADS has also been used to build other decision support systems having nothing to do with police beats—for example, building a decision support system to assist in the routing of IBM copier repairpeople. The generator software is often an application package that enables the user to customize the generator to a specific application. An example of a DSS generator, IFPS/Plus, was used earlier. Figure 12.13 provides an overview of IFPS/Plus's capabilities.

A **DSS tool** is a hardware, software, procedure, or data element that enables the user to build either a specific DSS or a DSS generator. For instance, such spreadsheet products as Lotus's 1-2-3 and Computer Associates' SuperCalc—both general-purpose "calculators"—can be used as DSS tools. When Lotus 1-2-3 is combined with a microcomputer, a monitor, and a printer, and the operating systems software to build a system that allows a specific sales manager to review the performance of his or her salespeople, the resulting product is a specific DSS. Figure 12.14 lists numerous DSS tools, specific decision support systems, and DSS generators found in business settings.

Tools Required for DSS Development

From our discussion, it should be apparent that many different types of software tools can be used to build decision support systems. While the variety of such software tools is large (and increasing), by far the most common are database management systems, spreadsheets, and modeling packages.

Role of Database Management Systems

Many decision support systems are used in combination with some type of database. This is especially true for decision support systems that are need strong support in the information-retrieval area. Often, the 4GL available with the database management system—the sophisticated software system that controls database-related activities—is used to build the DSS. The 4GL is also likely to be part of the dialogue management system of the resulting DSS.

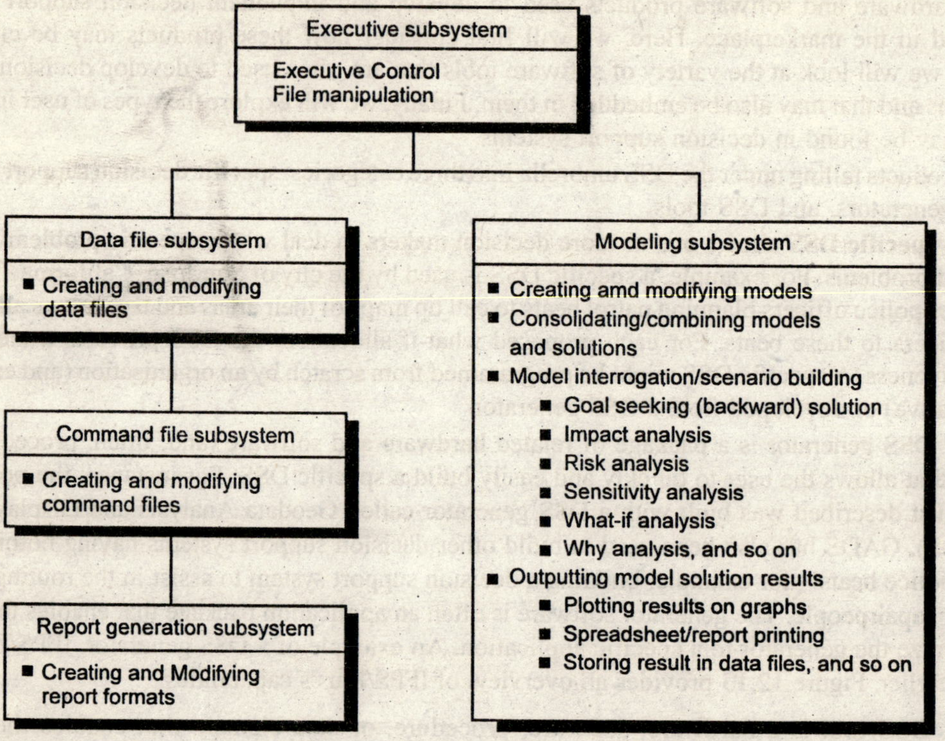

Figure 12.13. *An example of the components of a DSS generator: Execucom's IFPS/Plus. The orientation of IFPS/Plus toward interactive decision support is shown in this depiction of the package's major components.*

Relational database management systems are ideal for situations in which unanticipated types of accesses to a database are expected. This often happens in decision support environments, where information needs are semistructured or unstructured and the DSS is independent from the transaction processing system. Relational database data exist in the form of tables, and those tables can be related in any authorized manner chosen by the user. This design contrasts with hierarchical and network databases, paths where predictable types of accesses are normally encountered and predefined paths are built for those accesses by a data administrator. In the latter types of databases, the user cannot easily relate data in a way that does not correspond to a predefined path.

Although hierarchical and network database models are less suitable in terms of providing the flexibility needed by a DSS, and the transaction processing data typically managed with these models are less suitable for the decision-making needs of upper-level management, both of these traditional types of database models are commonly seen in DSS environments that support middle- and lower-level management. Two examples are a DSS that enables a salesperson to inspect levels of current inventory on a display terminal in order to find substitute products in an out-of-stock situation, and a DSS that allows a credit manager to decide whether to authorize certain customer purchases. In both cases, the DSS must access data managed by the TPS.

SPECIFIC DECISION SUPPORT SYSTEMS

Company	Specific Decision Support Systems
American Airlines	Pricing decision and choosing air routes
First United Bank Corporation	Evaluating investments
Frito-Lay, Inc	Pricing, advertising, and promotion decisions
IBM	Determining routing for repairpeople
National Gypsum	Corporate planning and forecasting
Southern Railway	Dispatching and routing trains
Texas Oil and Gas	Evaluating potential drill sites
LTV Corporation	Finding best sale terms of downtown office
Wells Fargo Bank	Planning postmerger operations
Zale Corporation	Evaluating potential retailing sites

DSS GENERATORS

Product	Vendor
EMPIRE	Applied Data Research, Inc.
EXPRESS	Management Decision System, Inc.
GADS	IBM
Accent R	National Information Systems
MODEL	Lloyd Bush and Associates
SIMPLAN	Simplan Systems Inc.
System W	Comshare, Inc.
IFPS/Plus	Execucom Systems Corporation

DSS TOOLS

- Microcomputer systems
- Database management systems
- Display devices
- General-purpose programming languages
- Optimization tools
- Statistical tools
- Spreadsheet packages
- Graphics generators

Figure 12.14. Examples of specific decision support systems, DSS generators, and DSS tools.

With the movement toward object-oriented programming, object-oriented databases (OODB) will probably become part of the data management component of decision support systems in the near future. Image-based databases are also likely to become facts of some decision support systems. Apple's HyperCard and similar products already enable users to develop graphically oriented databases. HyperCard allows the user to work on a graphical screen as if he or she were working naturally at a desk. Basically, HyperCard operates by allowing users to create a set of computerized index cards—and this set can be huge. These cards can be related to one another in a user-designated manner and accessed by selecting them with a mouse.

Spreadsheets (Sophisticated Electronic Calculators)

Spreadsheets are sophisticated electronic calculators—with special strengths in the areas of calculator activities, data reconfiguration, and what-if analysis. Many of them also have a number of advanced modeling functions (such as regression analysis). In spreadsheet packages, data are usually contained directly in worksheet cells that are arranged in a grid that looks similar to accounting paper.

Product	Vendor
Javelin	Javelin Software
IFPS/Plus	Execucom Systems Corporation
Encorel	Ferox Microsystem Inc.
Infotab	National CSS
Business Modeler	Business Model Systems, Inc.
EMS	Economic Sciences Corporation
Enterprise	Citishare, Inc.
Simplan	Simplan Systems, Inc.
XSIM	Chase Decision Systems
System W	Comshare Inc.
Express	Management Decisions, Inc.

Figure 12.15. Some of the commercially available modelling packages targeted to business applications. As spreadsheet provide an increased number of modelling functions, the distinction between spreadsheets and modelling packages is becoming blurry.

Spreadsheets are useful over an extremely wide number of decision support applications. Despite their popularity, spreadsheets also have several weaknesses, such limited report writing flexibility (in some products, what you see on your display screen is all you can get in print), program-data dependence, and some (especially those found in integrated packages) lack audit trail capabilities to trace edits or updates. For the most part, spreadsheets are used in personal types of applications, where data are manually input and the spreadsheet software becomes a "souped-up electronic calculator" that can do a lot of recalculating and displaying in a short span of time.

Although spreadsheet packages and applications have traditionally been two-dimensional, the trend today is toward multidimensionality. Many managers want to see their organisations in more than two dimensions. For instance, three dimensions would enable a manager to look at accounts for each division by month; five dimensions would allow the manager/ to also view these accounts by product line and by distribution channel. Today, only the full-fledged modelling packages provide superior multidimensional facilities.

Modelling Packages

Modelling packages are specially designed to enable the user to construct complex quantitative algorithms, such as financial simulations or sales forecasting models. Most modelling packages are equipped with several analysis tools, including sophisticated statistical and optimizing techniques.

Many of the most popular modelling packages, such as IFPS/Plus, began on mainframes. Modelling packages enable easy integration of data into several dimensions, the building of very sophisticated types of models, and sophisticated types of analysis. Also, there is a central repository for data, whose form is independent of the model being developed. Some modelling packages also have built-in artificial intelligence capabilities.

A financial model that integrates revenues, costs, and profits of products with time periods, geographic areas, organisational units, product lines, and customer types might help answer such questions as: What will happen to profits if the Western Region's sales of products X to consumer accounts increased by 20 percent? How much would labour costs for product Y, produced by Divisions A and B, have to be lowered to increase by 5 percent the overall return on sales by the enterprise? Why are profits lower in Division A than Division B? Such questions are so difficult to answer by conventional means that they would probably never be asked if modelling packages were not available.

In choosing a modelling package as opposed to a spreadsheet, the user basically trades an easy-to-follow grid for the power of the fully featured model. A variety of modelling packages are listed in Figure 12.15. As Spreadsheets develop more mathematical modelling capabilities, the line that separates spreadsheets from traditional modelling packages is blurring.

User Interfaces (Software/Hardware)

Users must interact with a DSS through some type of hardware/software interface, which is commonly called the **user interface**. The hardware part of the user interface often consists of either a display terminal or a personal computer workstation hooked up to a multiuser computer (for example, a mainframe) or a stand-alone personal computer. A keyboard and a mouse are used for operator input. The software part of the interface typically involves invoking commands, fillings in templates, and/or making physical modifications. Graphical user interfaces (GUI) are becoming more common in decision support systems, just as they are in most other software packages and systems.

Major criteria for designing or choosing the interface are ease of learning and use for the DSS user. Thus, when designing interfaces such as those described here, developers should consider human memory capacity, the likelihood of errors (and the user's having to fix them), the sophistication of the operator, and so on.

Command Interfaces with the Help of 4GL or Mouse

Issuing commands is the traditional way that both users and computers professionals interact with computer systems. Commands should be issued in the easiest possible way. This often means employing either a fourth-generation language (4GL) to allow the user to write out simple commands, or using a pointing mechanism (such as a mouse) so that the user can point to commands or icons on a graphically oriented display-screen menu. In a well-designed DSS, users have the option of issuing commands (the method usually favoured by sophisticated users) or pointing (the method often chosen by beginners).

Of the DSS approaches covered earlier, modelling tools require the heaviest use of written commands; spreadsheets, the heaviest use of pointing mechanisms. Users of a spreadsheet's macro facility (which enables users to write and store keystroke sequences as small programs called macros) will experience both writing certain commands and pointing to certain others—all in the course of working with the spreadsheet. Database environments use both fourth-generation languages and menus extensively to drive applications.

A growing trend in command language-based decision support systems is the use of a natural-language command interface. With such a facility, the user and machine communicate is a user-familiar language such as English. A good command language should enable the user to build a customized "front end" to the DSS (perhaps a sequence of prompts, menus, or self-loading batch files) and to develop his or her own functions or features (for example, a library of special routines).

Pointer mechanisms and graphic-oriented screens also represent a distinct trend in the evolution of decision support systems. They allow DSS users—any of whom are unsophisticated in the use of computer technology and are not proficient at keyboarding—to work quickly, without having to learn a complicated and fastidious language syntax. Many industry observers predict that graphical user interfaces, fueled by powerful 80386-, 80486-, 68030-, and 68040-based microcomputers in the business mainstream, will completely overhaul end-user computing efforts in the coming decade.

Templates

A templates is a prelabelled screen that only needs to be filled in with data. Data are usually typed into specific location on the screen, and each of these locations is controlled by an algorithm that instructs the DSS what to do with the data. An example of a template and its use was provided earlier in the book. Templates are widely used in database, modelling, and spreadsheet environments, and they are appropriate in any other application environment that must make a large amount of data entry as easy as possible for the user or operator.

Structural Modification

Physical structural modification refers to allowing the DSS user to physically structural alter a model represented on the screen. For example, a spreadsheet user who inserts or deletes a row or a column has physically modified the worksheet model. The user of a digitizing tablet can often alter a graphical model represented on a display screen by "painting" modifications with the tablet's stylus.

The newer graphically oriented operating systems—such as Windows, OS/2, and Macintosh System 7—are bringing fresh meaning to physical modification. For example, in these environments, it is quite easy to add a narrative explanation developed in a word-processing package to a spreadsheet (or add a graph generated from a database) in order to create a technical report. As new versions of the DSS tools and software described previously are released, physical modification should become even easier.

Examples of Decision Support System

Now that we have explored some of the characteristics, components, developments, and properties of decision support systems, let's turn to a few examples that show how they are used in a variety of application environments.

A Wall Street DSS

A growing number of brokerage firms and investment banks use decision support systems when making investment decisions concerning the assets they control. The strategies behind these decisions are based both on a trader's sense of the market's direction and on the DSS's ability to identify subtle trends or disturbances in the market prices of securities and options.

A National Forest DSS

The Staff managing a U.S. national forest built a land management database with a commercial DBMS package. The database contained information on characteristics of lands within the forest, broken down by specific land areas. A 4GL that accompanied the DBMS allowed the staff to model the expected behaviour of forest fires under specific combinations of terrain, natural barriers, forest vegetation, and weather.

A fire broke out in the forest one summer and the staff had to decide on a suppression or containment strategy. Using the DSS, the staff simulated various scenarios that showed how the fire would spread. They also determined how each fire-fighting strategy would fare each scenario, and at what cost. All of this took two hours; at the end, an all-out suppression strategy was selected. One fire official estimates that using computer-based decision support systems to simulate the spreading and fighting of forest fires saves about $10 million in fire-fighting efforts in just one year.

A Contract Negotiation DSS

An executive, about to negotiate an important contract with a client, used an ordinary spreadsheet package to model anticipated profits. Before the meeting with the client, the executive also used the spreadsheet package to build a set of mathematical models that would evaluate his financial position if the client were to propose any one of several possible contractual arrangements. When the meeting took place, his preparation enabled the executive to make immediate decisions and push the meeting toward the outcome he wanted. The executive completed a quick deal that gave him a favourable contract.

An Oil Executive's DSS

An executive vice-president at a major oil company spends 30–40 minutes a day at his desktop terminal, looking at internal data, global trends, and competitive pricing. During that time, he accesses a company database for the internal data he needs and two commercial databases for external data. The executive claims that he has more information in less time than ever before.

An Environmental DSS

Traditionally, the Environmental Protection Agency (EPA) deals separately with air pollution, water pollution, and land pollution in a given area. With the aid of high technology, the department can now integrate data from each of these pollution sources. For example, one DSS can answer such questions as: "To what extent will greater emissions restrictions reduce risk to humans?" Or, "What percentage of the pollutants in an area are attributable to such general sources as cars, as opposed to large industrial facilities?" In developing the DSS, the EPA involved local officials in the decision-making process; the result is a system that is usable by some people who never interacted with a computer before.

Group Decision Support Systems

Decision support systems have generally resulted in better support for individual decision making and having often resulted in better decisions. However, many DSS approaches and techniques are not suitable for group decision-making environments. In many organisations, managers spend 80 percent or more of their time in committee meetings and other group decision-making settings. While decision support systems are designed to enhance individual decision making, group decision support systems provide effective support in group decision-making settings.

Sub Components of a GDSS

Group Decision Support Systems (GDSS) consist of the hardware, software, data, and models that are needed to support the decision-making activities of particular groups. A GDSS possesses a number of features that distinguish it from a traditional DSS. Figure 12.16 illustrates how a GDSS is usually configured. The typical configuration consists of many of the elements found in a DSS: a model base, a database, and dialogue management systems. Groupware and the GDSS processor are unique features.

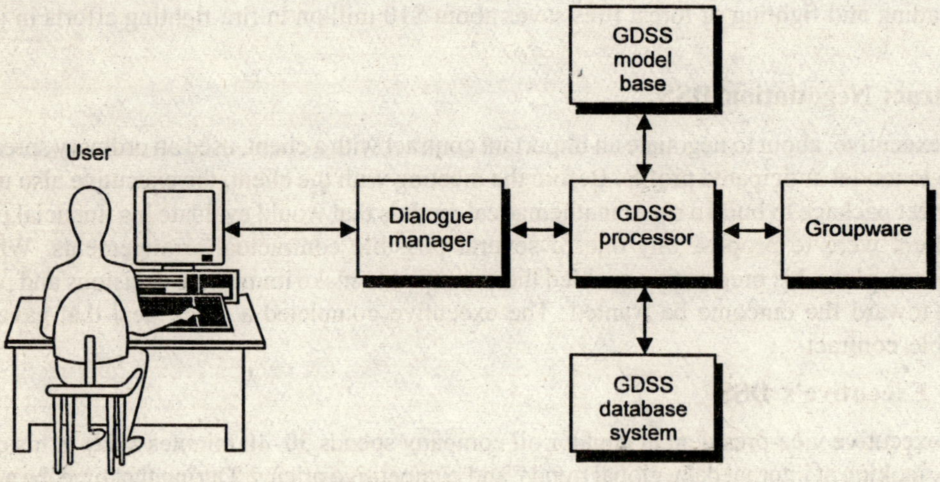

Figure 12.16. The components of a group decision support system (GDSS).

The GDSS *model base* consists of the mathematical, quantitative, and analytic models and tools that the group needs to make its decisions. As with an individual DSS, the models included in the model base will vary as a function of the needs of the decision-making group.

Many group decision support systems allow group members to have simultaneous access to common files and databases so that all members of the group can work on the same task at the same time. The GDSS *database system* makes this possible. Like traditional DSS database systems, the GDSS database system may extract data from personal, corporate, and external databases.

A GDSS may also include groupware—software that helps group members generate alternatives, analyze data, evaluate the choices, and reach decisions. Groupware packages are designed to allow group members—where workstations are connected by a telecommunication network (usually a local network)—to join together on a common project. Packages are available to support cooperative work and collaborative work. Besides group decision making, these packages support other work group activities—for example, electronic mail among group members, joint word processing of a document, and joint what-if analysis of an electronic spreadsheet. GDSS software may include word processing and text manipulation, database and file manipulation, spread or worksheet capabilities, graphics capabilities, decision-making aids (for example, mathematical, management science, and other analytical approaches), and communications facilities.

The *GDSS processor* consists of one or more computer systems that coordinate the processing activities of group members. This may be a dedicated server of one or more microcomputers in a LAN. In some cases, it may be a mainframe or microcomputer, especially when wide area group decision support systems are desired.

The *GDSS dialogue manager* helps group members communicate with each other and to interface with the other GDSS components. In many cases, one or more *group facilitators* or "chauffeurs"—individuals skilled in using GDSS technology—play a special role in coordinating group decision making. Chauffeurs facilitate the flow of information between group members and what appears on the "public screens"—the on-screen displays available to all group members—during a work session. Special software supports the facilitator running the meeting.

GDSS Configurations

Group decision support systems can be configured in numerous ways. The actual configuration used in dependent on the needs of the group, the types of decisions that are supported, the frequency of GDSS use, and the geographic location of group members. Four alternative configurations follows:

- **Decision room.** In the decision room approach, all the GDSS technology is in a single location, usually a single room. This may be feasible when decision makers are brought together to work on common project; for example, when they all work in the same building or geographic area. Groups such as production management teams, market research groups, and financial analysis groups may all benefits from the decision room approach. Several universities and other organisations have developed GDSS decision rooms that serve as models for implementation in other organisations.
- **Local area network.** In the LAN approach, GDSS technology is not concentrated in a single location, but is spread out among several locations within the same building or limited geographic area—usually in the offices of group members.
- **Teleconferencing.** The teleconferencing approach ties together multiple widely dispersed decision rooms. Teleconferencing technology—electronically connects the widely distributed (even globally distributed) decision rooms.
- **Wide area decision network.** The wide area decision network is essentially a WAN version of the local area network GDSS approach. GDSS technology is distributed among

group members (not concentrated in decision rooms) and connected by private or public WAN telecommunication links. The group facilitator and group members may all be at different, geographically dispersed locations. If several group members are found at each of the remote sites, several group facilitators may be involved in the coordination of GDSS work sessions.

Group decision support system may also be classified by the level of support that they provide to group members. *Level-1 group decision support systems* provide technology that enables group members to electronically communicate with one another. All of the configurations just described have Level-1 capabilities. *Level-2 group decision support systems* provide support for group decision-making processes in addition to the communication capabilities provided by Level-1 group decision support systems. Level-2 group decision support systems typically furnish groupware that supports joint modelling and analytical approaches; they also provide the software support needed for determining group preference through voting, ranking, rating, and other means. The Delphi Technique, the Normal Group Technique (NGT), brainstorming, and other group creativity enhancement approaches may also be supported by a Level-2 GDSS. A *Level-3 group decision support system* provides all the capabilities of a Level-2 GDSS and also supplies facilities for formalizing group interaction patterns.

Aim and Objectives of GDSS

Group decision support systems provide many unique features that go beyond those found in traditional decision support systems. When determining whether or not to implement a GDSS, managers should consider whether or not the proposed systems achieve the following goals:

- **Ease of use.** Group decision support systems that are complex or hard to operate are not likely to be used. Groups often have less tolerance than individuals for systems that are difficult to learn. Hence, a GDSS should be easy to master and perceived as usable—and useful—by group members.
- **Provision of both general and specific support.** The GDSS should provide support for both general and specific types of problems. It should support a wide range of group decision-making capabilities, as well as ensuring that specific groups can tailor the GDSS to support the decisions that they need to make. The provision of general and specific support should occur over the long run. It should be possible to expand and modify the model base as the needs of the group and the organisation change over time.
- **Promotion of positive group behaviour.** A number of approaches may be used to promote positive behaviour among group members. Structured group decision-making activities—such as the Nominal Group Technique (NGT), the Delphi Technique, and brainstorming—can enhance group decision-making processes, as well as the group decisions that are reached. GDSS designers are now incorporating many of these features into commercially available GDSS packages; the availability of these options should be considered by potential adopters.
- **Suppression of negative group behaviour.** An effective GDSS will minimize counterproductive behaviour among group members. For example, it will make it difficult for an individual to dominate the decision-making process and thereby inhibit input from

other group members. A well-designed GDSS will also discourage one or more group members from sidetracking the group into non-productive areas. Procedures for effectively planning and managing GDSS meetings are incorporated into many GDSS packages. It is wise for potential to consider group decision support systems that possess these features.

Group decision support systems are becoming more widely used. Studies indicate that both private and public sector organisations are very interested in group decision support systems. They should be commonplace by the year 2000.

Information System of Executives

An executive information system (EIS)—which is sometimes referred to as an executive support system (ESS)—is a DSS that is designed to meet the special needs of top-level managers. Some people use the terms "EIS" and "ESS" interchangeably, but others do not. Any distinction between the two usually is because executive support systems are likely to incorporate additional capabilities such as electronic mail. In this section, we first cover those people in organisations that are considered to be executives and examine the types of decisions they make. Then, we turn to the nature of executive decisions and the types of information that executives need most. Finally, some of the special characteristics of executive information systems—beyond those of other decision support systems—are discussed.

Executives (Manager/Top of the Organisational Hierarchy)

An **executive** can probably best be described as a manager at or near the top of the organisational hierarchy who exerts a strong influence on the course taken by the organisation. The slots in a firm considered to be executive positions vary from company to company. For example, in IRM-oriented firms, the chief information officer (CIO) is usually an executive who participates in key strategic decisions. In other firms, the CIO is a middle manager (who often has a title other than CIO). And sometimes, the person in charge of an organisation's CBIS is basically a data processing director.

Figure 12.17 shows the executive positions found in many corporations. A board of directors sits on top of most corporations. Board members are nominated for their positions by existing board members and by members of the organisation's top corporate management; the final choices are ratified by stockholders. The board members, in turn, select the president. The president, or chief executive officers (CEO), is the person charged with the responsibility of operating the company effectively. In some cases, there are separate president and CEO positions, but most commonly, the president also holds the title of CEO.

The majority stockholders, in effect, own the company. Like the executives who run the company, they can exert a major influence on its mission, scope, and general direction. New vice-presidents in the functional areas are often selected by an *executive group*, which consists of the CEO and existing functional vice-presidents. In some organisations, the executive group acts in an advisory capacity to the president, who ultimately makes all the decisions; in others, the executive group can veto decisions made by the president and make decisions of their own.

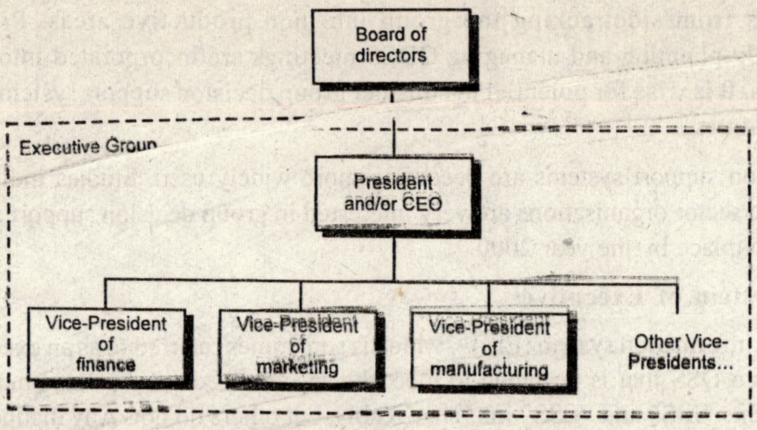

Figure 12.17. *Examples of executive positions in organizations.*

Executive Roles and Decision Making

Most executive decisions fall into one of three classes: strategic planning, tactical planning, and "fire-fighting" activities. Also, executives need a certain degree of control to ensure that these activities are carried out properly.

Strategic Planning (Long Range Planning)

Strategic planning involves determining the general, long-range direction of the organisation, typically, the CEO is ultimately responsible for the development of strategic plans. In firms with a participative style of management, members of the executive group help in formulating a strategic plan. In some cases, they can even veto the plan if, in their judgment, it seems likely to fail, or if it appears to violate the organisation's mission statement. The strategic plan sets the stage for all other major forms of decision making within the company.

Tactical Planning

Whereas strategic planning addresses the general concerns of the firms, tactical planning refers to the how, when, where, and what issues involved with carrying out the strategic plan. Although executives will not normally be concerned with tactical details, they do need to worry about general tactics. For example, the vice-president of finance must address how the firm can best achieve a balance between debt and equity financing. And the marketing vice-president will need to consider which classes of products the company should produce to be successful in the marketplace.

Fire-Fighting

Major problems arise sometimes that must be resolved by someone at an executive level. For example, if a company is involved in a big lawsuit that threatens its financial solvency, an executive must get involved. Other possible fire-fighting activities include damage caused to a major [illegible] facility, the announcement of an important product by a competitor, a strike, and a sharp reversal of the economy. Many of these events will call for key alterations in plans.

General Control

In addition to planning and fire-fighting, executive management also needs to exert some general control over the organisation. For example, if the strategic plan calls for a 20 percent increase in profitability, feedback is needed to ensure that certain actions taken within the organisation are accomplishing that objectives. Thus, executives will also periodically review key performance data to see how they compare against planned amounts.

The Executive Decision-making Environment

Refer back to the executive decision-making environment shown in Figure 12.18. The three main data sources for executive information are as follows:

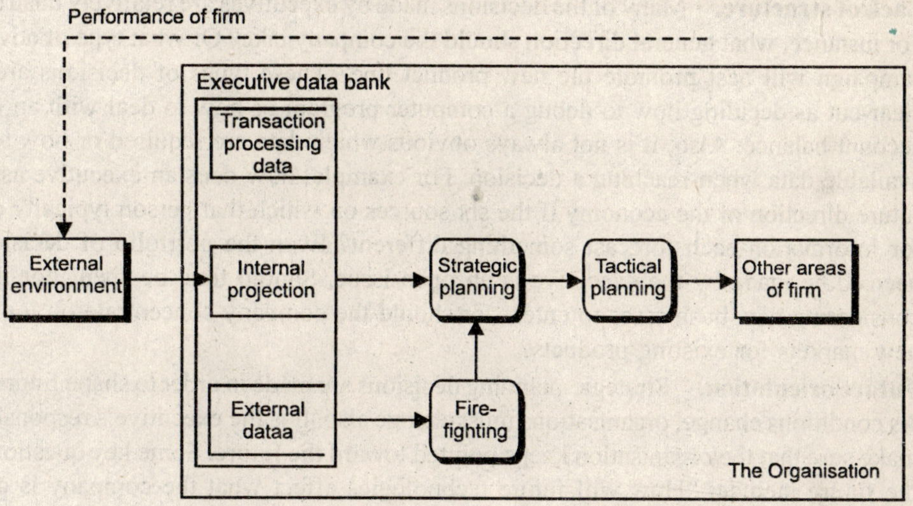

***Figure 12.18.** A data flow representation of the executive decision-planning environment. Corresponding control activities exist for each of the planning functions shown in this figure.*

- **Transaction processing data.** These data, generated from transaction processing systems, usually reflect the past and current performance of the firms. Thus, these data are most useful for normal control purposes and have relatively little value in long-range planning.
- **Internal projections.** These data shows the operating objectives for each functional area, expected revenues, budgets and planned expenses, and the overall financial plan for keeping the company afloat. Some of these projections covers a multiyear period and most useful for assessing the current profile of the company.
- **External data.** Although executives use internal data such as those supplied from transaction processing systems and internal forecasts, most of the data they use in decision making—in fact, the most critical data, and those used as the basis for strategic planning and handling fire-fighting efforts—come from the external environment. In many instances, it is only through environmental scanning and monitoring that strategic opportunities and competitive threats (both immediate and long-term) can be identified.

The types of decisions that executives must make are broad. Often, executives make these decisions based on a vision they have regarding what it will take to make their companies successful. To a large extent, executives rely much more on their own intuition than on the sophisticated analytical skills that are required of specialists. Weston Agor claims that executives "have a sense or vision of what is coming—and how to move their organisations in response to that vision. They are particularly adept at generating new ideas and in providing ingenious solutions to old problems. They also function best in crises or situations of rapid change." The intuitive character of executive decision making is reflected strongly in the types of information found most useful to executives.

Five characteristics of the types of information used in executive decision making are lack of structure, high degree of uncertainty, future orientation, informal sources, and low level of detail. These are discussed next and are summarized in Figure 12.19.

- **Lack of structure.** Many of the decisions made by executives are relatively unstructured. For instance, what general direction should the company take? Or what type of advertising campaign will best promote the new product line? These types of decisions are not as clear-cut as deciding how to debug a computer program or how to deal with an overdue account balance. Also, it is not always obvious which data are required or how to weigh available data when reaching a decision. For example, how does an executive assess the future direction of the economy if the six sources on which that person typically depends for information each forecast something different? Even the portfolio of decisions that need to be made by the executive is an open issue. Should time be spent, for instance, considering new businesses to enter—or should the company concentrate on looking for new markets for existing products?
- **Future orientation.** Strategic-planning decisions are made in order to shape future events. As conditions change, organisations must change also. It is the executive's responsibility to make sure that the organisation keeps pointed toward the future. Some key questions about the future include: "How will future technologies affect what the company is currently doing? What will the competition (or the government) do next? What products will consumers demand five years from now? Where will the economy move next, and how might that affect consumer buying patterns?" As you can see, the answers to all of these questions about the future external environment are vital.
- **Informal sources.** Executives, more than other types of managers, rely heavily on informal sources for key information. For example, lunch with a colleague in another firm might reveal some important competitor strategies. Informal sources such as television might also feature news of momentous concern to the executive—news that he or she would probably never encounter in the company's database or in scheduled computer reports. Besides business meals and the media, some other important informal sources of information are meetings, tours around the company's facilities to chat with employees, brainstorming with a trusted colleague or two, and social events.
- **Low level of detail.** Most important executive decisions are made by observing broad trends. This requires the executive to be more aware of the large overview than the tiny items. Even so, many executives insist that the answers to some questions can only be found by mucking through details.

Properties of Executive Information	
Lack of structure	Informal sources
High degree of uncertainty	Low level of detail
Future orientation	

Figure 12.19. Properties of information used in executive decision making. The strategic nature of executive decisions makes the information needs of executives different from those of ordinary managers.

Role of Executive Information System and its Characteristics

Because executives deal primarily with data about the external environment and data that come from informal sources, they are usually less reliant on direct contact with information technology than other types of manager. When information from their company's computers is needed, many chief executive officers make their subordinates retrieve that information. Because executive information needs are more ambiguous than those of other levels of management, computers have historically been less useful to executives. Many executives have little hands-on experience with computers and don't fully appreciate how information technology can improve their personal productivity and decision-making skills.

Both business conditions and technology have changed dramatically in the last several years, however. Today, executives should turn directly to computers and other information technology for certain types of information in many important situations. According to Stephanie Wilkenson, a study at MIT's Sloan School of Management found that the use of computers by executives is a "steadily growing phenomenon, one that can have major impacts on the nature of executive work and the way organisations functions."

Information technology and application software have become increasingly user-friendly. Operating systems with graphical user interfaces (GUI), such as Windows, have helped stimulate chief executive officer's interest in using computers. In addition, on-line computer services that carry environmental information such as news, industry and economic reports, and worldwide and government data, are used more frequently by executives.

Stephanie Wilkenson writes that one executive, who uses a computer daily to check external trends and internal data, claims, "I have more information than I would have normally received had I called the vice-president... and asked, 'How are we looking today?' "This same executive also relates, "Often, use of the computer leads to a tendency to look at more future-oriented marketing data and less traditional financial data." Claims another executive, "Because I'm a CEO, I have to focus on what's going on outside the company. In terms of my time at the computer, I probably spend two-thirds of it looking at Dow Jones News Service. I get a great deal of information about what's going on in the food industry this way. It is much easier than having my secretary watch newspapers and clip articles." Today, business is often conducted at such a fast pace that even executives find it increasingly difficult to survive without computers.

Computers can also lead to improving executive confidence. In Stephanie Wilkenson's article, one executive mentions, "I don't feel I work faster, just better...It's not really that I'm saving time, because now I'll dig deeper for more information. I'll do extra things to make the quality of my decisions better. When the quality is better, my decisions are more defensible. It makes me more confident." According to Sloan School research, in fact, increased confidence is an advantage of computers mentioned commonly by executives—confidence in the accuracy of the information obtained, in the decisions made on the basis of that information, and in having control of the enterprise. A research associates at Sloan's Center for Information Systems Research (CISR) claims that, "Better control leads to more focus on the future... The executive thinks, 'We're on track; I'll know if we go off track. Now I can think about the future.'"

All of these considerations brings us to some of the properties commonly found in executive support systems. Among these properties are those shown in Figure 12.20 and described in the following subsections.

Common EIS Capabilities	
Strategic-planning support capabilities	Exceptional ease of learning and use
External environment focus	Customization
Broad-based computing ability	

Figure 12.20. Common EIS capabilities. EIS are becoming more common in organisations as an increasing number of executives recognize them as a key to remaining competitive in today's dynamic business environment.

Strategic-Planning Support

Since many executives consider strategic planning to be their top priority, it is essential that designers of executive information systems address this particular need. The designer should be familiar with strategic planning and critical success factor (CSF) models to determine how information technology might enhance the organisation's strategic-planning process. The greatest success in this area has been providing the executive with comprehensive retrieval capabilities so that he or she can quickly pull together the information needed to form a profile of an organisation or organisational unit, a situation, or an important client.

External Environment of Executives

Because events takings place in the environment are so important to executives, information about such events is usually among their most important needs. Thus, many executives information systems include links to commercial databases, such as those of Dow Jones News and Compustat, as well as to specialized databases that provides more specific types of consumer, industry, economic, and worldwide data. An adequate communication gateway is, of course, necessary so that the executive can access these data.

Broad-Based Computing Capabilities

Usually, executives do not have a strong need for modelling tools. Because executive decision making is less structured than that taking place at lower levels of the organisations, their decision environments are more difficult to model. Also, since executives spend most of their time considering broad matters—for instance, pondering direction and dealing with competitors' strategies—they are generally less directly involved with quantitative detail and analysis; which is delegated to staff. Thus, most of their computing needs are relatively simple. Such tasks as information retrieval, spreadsheeting, and graph generation usually top the list of executive computing needs.

Exceptional Ease of Learning and Use

In most organisations, the time of executives is considered more valuable than that of any other worker. Hence, the support systems that cater to executives should reflect this. For instance, since presentation graphic can communicate information much more rapidly than can tabular data, a strong and easy-to-use graphics generator is a helpful tool in many executive information systems. Also, any issues dealing with the user interface become more worthy of close scrutiny; for instance, the ease of use of any command language, the availability of pointing devices and graphical user interfaces, fast response time, customized front-ends, non-cryptic error handling, and so on.

Customization

Because an executive's time is so precious relative to other employees, and the decisions made by executives are so critical to an organisation livelihood, special care must be given to the design of each EIS. Often, this means tailoring the basic model of an EIS to meet the special needs of each executives who wants to use it. For instance, if a million-dollar-a-year executive needs frequent, fast access to an internal financial database—data that might take the average employee ten instructions to access—it is usually worth assigning a programmer to write a special macro that enables the executive to access this data with only one or two keystrokes.

Availability of EIS Products Commercially

Many EIS generators—EIS development packages—are commercially available. Commander EIS (from Comshare, Inc.), Command Center (from Pilot Executive Software), Executive Edge (from Execucom Systems Corporation), and Express EIS (from Information Resources, Inc.) are among the market leaders in the U.S. RESOLVE is another leading product, especially in Europe.

Studies on EIS implementation shows that thousands of companies have implemented executive information systems. Usually, the executive information systems provide executives with access to financial data, marketing and sales information, human resources information, manufacturing data, and competitive/strategic information. Electronic mail, access to external news and databases, word processing, spreadsheet, and automated filing capabilities are also common in business executive information systems. While it is often expensive to develop and maintain an EIS, many organisations feel that enhanced top-level decision making is a benefit that more than balances out any costs associated with the system.

Summary/Conclusion

A decision support system (DSS) provides managers with the tools to assist them in making semistructured and unstructured decisions in their own way. In addition to focusing on semistructured and unstructured decisions, decision support systems facilitate outputs that are not predefined and that are easy to use.

Structured decisions are those that can be made easily from a given set of inputs. Semistructured and unstructured decisions, however, are those for which information obtained from a computer system is, at most, only a portion of the total needed for sound decision making.

DSS outputs are not predefined because managers do not always know in advance the types of information they will need. Besides, even if managers did know these types of information, their information needs constantly change. Thus, flexibility in a DSS is of paramount importance. Decision support systems must also be easy to learn because the users are not computer professionals. Other common properties found in decision support systems are fast response, a high degree of user control and interaction, interactive display technology, and the use of models.

The components of a DSS are the DSS generator, the model management system, the database management system, and the dialogue management system. The DSS generators is the software that is used to develop the DSS and coordinate its processing tasks. The model management system makes it possible to create, maintain, and apply the mathematical and analytical models that are used by the decision maker. The database management system enables users to create, maintain, and interrogate DSS database and to extract data from both internal and external database as necessary. The dialogue manager provides the interface between the user and the other DSS components; typically, the interface is interactive and flexible.

Four common tasks performed by decision support systems are information retrieval, data reconfiguration, calculator activities, and analysis. Information retrieval in a DSS environment usually refers to extracting information from a database or form data files in order to make a decision. Two types of retrieval are selection and projection.

Decision support systems also reconfigure data into forms other than the way they are logically represented in the computer system. They do this by enabling users to sort, exchange fields, join data, and use presentation graphics.

A DSS also enables users to perform calculators activities—a set of tasks that is normally done with a calculator. Such activities are implemented either by having the user writeout a complete formula or by having him or her summon a function resident in the DSS. Functions are presented formulas that perform calculator-type tasks.

A DSS is performing analysis when it allows users to review facts and draw conclusions based on those facts. Four types of DSS analysis tools or techniques are widely used. Statistical tools enables users to perform a variety of statistical operations on data, including regression analysis and correlation analysis. Optimizing tools are mathematical modelling tools that recommend certain choices to a decision maker. What-if analysis is a non-probabilistic technique that enables a user to reformulate a problem repeatedly, with different values for problem parameters, in the process of getting useful information. Artificial intelligence (AI) routines also improve the usefulness of the analysis function. One such routine is why analysis, a technique that enables the user to ask the DSS why something happened.

Under a framework proposed by R. H. Sprague and E. D. Carlson, DSS products are classified as specific decision support systems. DSS generators, or DSS tools. A specific DSS allows decision makers to handle a specific problem or set of related problems. A DSS generator is a package of related hardware and software that allows the user to quickly and easily build a specific DSS. A DSS tools refers to hardware, software, procedure, or data elements that enable decision makers to build either a specific DSS or a DSS generator.

Numerous software tools can be used to build decision support systems, including database managemcnt systems, spreadsheets, and modelling packages. Database management systems are most useful for information retrieval; spreadsheets, for simple types of analysis and reports. Modelling packages enable users to construct complex quantitative algorithms.

Users must interact with a DSS through a hardware/software interface called the user interface. The software part of the interface typically involves issuing commands, filling in templates, and/or making physical model modifications. Commands can be either typed in or pointed to. A template is a prelabelled screen that must be filled in with data.

Group decision support system (GDSS) are decision support systems that support the decision-making activities of work groups. Many of the components of a GDSS resemble similar components in traditional decision support systems. A GDSS is composed of a model base, a GDSS processor, a dialogue manager, a database system, and special software known as groupware. Groupware enables group members to simultaneously work on the same word-processing document, do group what-if analysis on a spreadsheet, and perform other cooperative task such as generating and evaluating alternative solutions to a problem.

Group decision support systems may be configured in several ways. In decision room configurations, all GDSS technology in located in the same room; decision makers come to the room to use the GDSS. GDSS technology is distributed to group member offices or work areas in LAN GDSS configurations. When group member offices are geographically dispersed, a WAN GDSS configuration may be used. Numerous remotely distributed decision rooms can be electronically linked in the videoconferencing configuration.

Group decision support systems should be easy to use and should provide users with both general and specific decision support. A well-designed GDSS also facilitates productive behaviour among group members and helps to suppress counterproductive behaviours.

An executive information system (EIS) is a DSS designed to meet the special needs of executives. Executives are people at or near the top of an organisational hierarchy who exert a strong influence on the course taken by the organisation. These usually include the board of directors, the president or chief executive officers (CEO), and various vice-presidents.

Most executive decisions involve strategic planning, tactical planning, and fire-fighting activities. They also involve exerting some control over the organisation in order to ensure that plans are implemented. Executive information come from three main data sources: transaction processing data, internal projections, and external data.

Executive decisions are generally broad, and based to a large extent on intuition. These characteristics are reflected in the executive decision-making environment, which is itself characterized by a lack of structure, a high degree of uncertainty, a future orientation, use of informal sources, and a low level of detail.

To meet these challenges, executive information systems commonly have the following properties: an external environment focus, a strategic-planning capability, ease of learning and use, and custom tailoring to meet the unique needs of individual executives. A number of EIS software packages are commercially available. Executive information systems should become more prevalent during the 1990s.

13

Knowledge-Based Systems

- Define artificial intelligence
- Discuss the main areas of AI research
- Describe the components of an expert system
- Provide examples of the use of expert systems in business
- Describe the process used to develop expert systems
- Describe some of the limitations of expert systems
- Describe the characteristics of neural networks and how they are used by organisations

The term "artificial intelligence" connotes a futuristic world that is still over the horizon—a world populated by androids and computers such as HAL, the processor in the movie 2001: *A Space Odyssey.* Although many researchers in the field of artificial intelligence do perceive such a world as an attainable reality, most successful efforts in artificial intelligence today are much less ambitious. This led some people to argue that the term "artificial intelligence" may be a poor one, since it connotes a capability that is today impossible to deliver.

In this chapter, we will explore the evolution of the artificial intelligence field and examine in depth the component of artificial intelligence with perhaps the greatest impact on MIS: expert systems. In doing this, we look at why expert systems and other knowledge-based systems are needed, how they work, how they differ from conventional computer-based applications, and what are some of their inherent limitations. We also examine some examples of knowledge-based systems found in practice.

Although knowledge-based systems are most closely associated with decision support functions, they are applicable to virtually any area under the MIS umbrella—including transaction processing systems, management reporting systems, and office systems.

Artificial Intelligence

A computer is a device that, given some instructions, can perform work at extremely fast speeds by drawing upon a large memory. It can also be programmed to draw certain types of conclusions on the basis of the input it receives or the results of computations it performs. A good deal of human mental activity involves these same processes. For this reason, the abilities that can be imparted to computers to enable them to display intelligent, human-like behaviour is commonly referred to as artificial intelligence (AI).

Origin of Artificial Intelligence

The term "artificial intelligence" was coined in the mid-1950s by John McCarthy at a conference at Dartmouth College. One of the features of that conference was a software processor that manipulated symbols instead of numbers (as such language processor as LISP and Prolog do today). Developers claimed that the processor, which proved several mathematical theorems, possessed a certain amount of "artificial intelligence."

As AI evolved, it was put to work solving a number of tasks. For instance, it continued to be used in the field of mathematics to prove theorems and to solve complex problems. In the field of gaming, researchers developed AI programs to play and win at tic-tac-toe, checkers, and chess. At the Massachusetts Institutes to Technology (MIT), one researcher, Joseph Weizenbaum, created a psychiatry "expert" named Eliza, who would listen to the woes of human patients and diagnose their mental ills. Since the types of tasks performed by the programs involved in these applications required human intelligence, most people assumed that such programs possessed artificial intelligence.

This assumption was not always accurate, however. For instance, some of the early chess programs relied more on the brute force of the computer than they did on methods of intelligence. Many of these programs would calculate the effects of thousands of moves and countermoves and make their recommendations based on what appeared to be the best of these. But this is not usually the way that human chess players think. The chess experts instead rely on intuitive rules of thumb—called *heuristic*—to base their moves. One widely used heuristic, for instance, is to control the centre of chess board. As chess programs incorporated these heuristics, they truly embodied artificial intelligence techniques. Better yet, they improved dramatically, rivaling humans at the expert-level class in chess.

The exact definition of artificial intelligence is still hotly debated. Certainly, a lot of systems appear at first glance to fall under the general category of artificial intelligence—such as the early, brute force chess-playing programs that really display very little human-like intelligence. Two cornerstones of intelligent behaviour are the ability to understand natural languages and the ability to reason. It follows, then, that computer systems providing capabilities in these areas, at a performance level that would be regarded as intelligent if observed in humans, should be considered AI-based systems. Thus, in this text we will consider **artificial intelligence (AI)** as a capability in computer systems to provide a level of performance that reflects human-like intelligence. Later, we will look at some technical characteristics that distinguish knowledge-based systems from conventional computer programs.

Applications of Artificial Intelligence

Today, the five main areas of AI research are expert systems, natural languages vision systems, robotics, and neural networks, as Figure 13.1 illustrates.

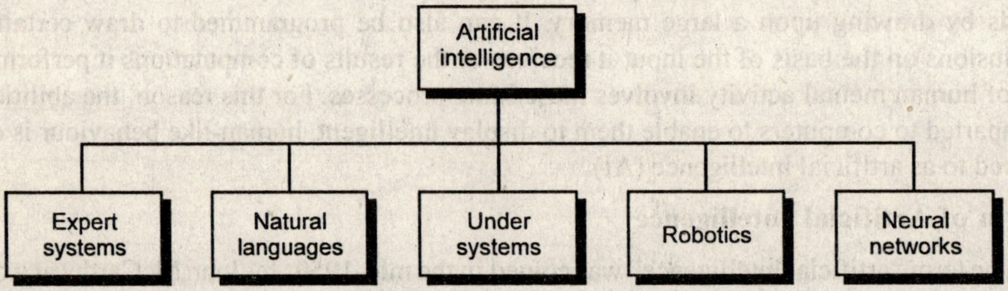

***Figure 13.1.** Areas of artificial intelligence (AI). While AI already influences the activities of some of today's managers, most industry observers feel that its effects will be more profound and widespread in the future.*

Expert Systems

Expert systems are software system that imitate the reasoning processes of human experts and provide decision makers with the type of advice they would normally receive from such human experts. For instance, an expert system in the area of investment portfolio management might ask its user a number of specific questions relating to investments for a particular client. How does the client feel about risk versus growth? How much can be invested? Does the client refuse to invest in any particular companies? Does the client have any preferences regarding specific types of securities? And so on. As each question is posed interactively to the user, and after each user responds, the expert system dynamically formulates the next question to be asked, until a suitable portfolio is recommended. In reaching the decision, the system draws from an enormous database of stocks descriptions and histories, research reports, and economic forecasts. The user involved here may be either a professional investment adviser or the actual client. The investment advisor may be using the expert system to uncover possibilities that he or she would never have imagined when advising the client.

A number of expert system application areas in business are listed in Figure 13.2. We will cover several current and proposed business-related application areas in depth later in the chapter. Most of the success in expert systems has been in rather narrow, specific areas; for instance, diagnostics in the medical field or advice in the tax-planning area. Less success has been achieved in developing highly generalized expert systems that are useful in all application areas.

BUSINESS APPLICATIONS OF EXPERT SYSTEMS	
Accounting and Finance	
Providing tax advice and assistance	Selecting forecasting models
Helping with credit-authorisation decisions	Providing investment advice
Marketing	
Establishing sales quotas	Assisting with marketing timing decisions
Responding to customer inquiries	Determining discount policies
Referring problems to telemarketing centres	
Manufacturing	
Determining whether a process is running correctly	Scheduling job-shop tasks
	Selecting transportation routes
Analysing quality and providing corrective measures	Assisting with product design and facility layouts
Maintaining facilities	
Personnel	
Assessing applicant qualifications	Giving employees assistance at filling out forms
General Business	
Assisting with project proposals	Educating trainees
Recommending acquisition strategies	Evaluating performance

Figure 13.2. *Examples of business application of expert systems. The number and variety of these and other knowledge-base systems increase every year.*

Natural Language System is Based on Natural Languages

The area of **natural-languages systems** involves using the computer to communicate with users in natural languages such as English, Spanish, French, or Chinese. Although it is relatively easy for the computer to provide natural-language output, input is much more difficult. For instance, although the definitions of the words can be stored in a dictionary, the way in which combinations of words—or sentences—convey meaning is rather complex. Also, people often misuse words or use them in strange contexts. And even when humans finish communicating an idea or an intention, it is not always clear what they are trying to say.

Progress in natural-language interfaces has been somewhat slow, but nonetheless fruitful in some areas. The momentum for the development of such systems has increased in recent years. A few software products that allow users to issue natural-language commands are listed in Figure 13.3. As you can see, to date, many of the natural-language application have concerned database queries and report generation.

Natural-Language Systems and Applications

Product	Vendor	Description
Clout	Microrim, Inc.	Natural-language interface for Microrim's System V and R: Base 5000 database systems
Eliza	Artificial Intelligence Research	Natural-language interaction with a "psychotherapist"
EnQuery	Datamate Co.	Natural-language interface for COBOL, report-writing application
EQL (English Query Language)	Information Builders Inc.	Natural-language interface for PC/Focus
Guru	MDBS Inc.	Natural-language interface combined with database management, text processing, spreadsheet, graphics, 4GL, and communications capabilities
HAL	Lotus Development Corporation	Natural-language interface for Lotus 1-2-3
IA (Intelligent Assistant)	Symantec	Natural-language interface for Q&A integrated software package.
K-Chat	MDBS Inc.	Natural-language interface for knowledge Man database system
Natural Language	DEC	Natural-language interface to direct marketing database
NLQ (Natural Language Query)	Battelle	Natural-language interface for Oracle and DB2
PC-IQ	Solutions, Inc.	Natural-language interface that converts natural-language commands to DOS
Prolog-86	Solution Systems	Programming language for creating natural-language interface
Ramis II English	On-Line Software	Natural-language interface for Ramis II application generator
SAS/English	SAS Institute	Natural-language interface for querying and reporting data from SAS data sets and external sources
Savvy	Excalibur Technologies Corp.	Natural-language-based database system
Voice Navigator	Articulate Systems Corporation	Natural-language interface that allows users to attach verbal notes to reports

Figure 13.3. Examples of natural-language systems and applications.

Vision Systems with the Help of Human Eye

Vision systems are computer system performing tasks that could, at one time, only be done through the use of the human eye. They often work through a technique called pattern recognition. For example, vision systems are commonly used today to inspect parts of subassemblies for defects. Such a systems has a number of image patterns of defects stored in a database, and it consults these to determine whether the item beings inspected is defective. This task is not as simple as it seems. Strong , accessing, and comparing a large number of images is difficult. Also, in some systems, if the item being inspected is tilted the wrong way, it has to be reoriented so that it is identifiable by the vision software.

Robotics

Robotics have artificial intelligence it works on artificial intelligence concerned with the design, manufacture, and implementation of robots. Robots are computer-controlled devices that mimic the motor activity of human beings.

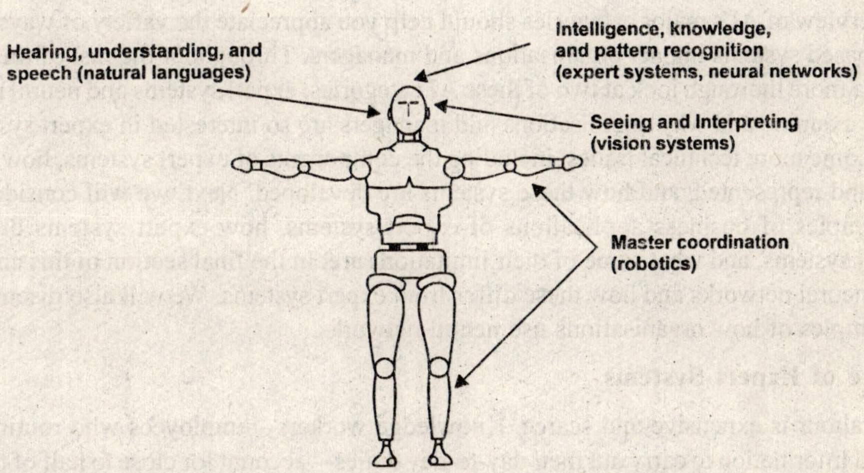

Figure 13.4. The ultimate AI product—an android. Such a product will be the beneficiary of the labours of all five AI areas—expert systems, natural language, vision systems, robotics, and neural networks

Robots have been used in a wide variety of areas, with probably the greatest success in manufacturing. There, they perform jobs that are considered too dangerous, strenuous, monotonous, or expensive for humans to do. And often, robots can perform these jobs faster and better. For instance, IBM claims that the printer for its new line of PS/2 computers is more reliable due to robot manufacturing. Virtually no human hands touch these printers as they evolve from parts, to assembly, to testing, and finally to packaging. Robots are used in a variety of other settings: manufacturing cars, dipping parts into dangerous chemicals, spraying paints, mining coal, and so on. In Japan, they are even used to prepare sushi.

Although it may seem that many of these robots are "dumb," they are often aided by the other AI techniques—expert system, natural languages, and vision systems—to identify objects and states in their environments so they can act accordingly. The ultimate AI product, of course, will be a robot that is virtually indistinguishable from a human being—the android of science fiction fame. That, of course, is still far from realization. Even the androids popularized by the film industry (for example, 3CPO of *Star Wars*) and television (such as Commander Data on "Star Trek: The Next Generation") are roles filled by human actors.

Neural Networks

Perhaps the greatest amount of recent AI development is in the area of neural networks. **Neural networks** are knowledge-based computer systems that emulate the human brain's pattern recognition process. Neural-net systems aren't preprogrammed to provide predicable responses like conventional algorithms, even those found in expert systems; instead, they are designed to "learn" by observation and repetition. Some of the neural nets developed are software programs that work on conventional computers. Several organisations, however, developed hardware-based neural nets that often use parallel processing and interconnected nodes to simulate how the human nervous system works. Examples of business applications of neural networks can be found in the box—as well as in the more detailed discussion of neural networks later in this chapter.

This overview of AI's major categories should help you appreciate the variety of ways in which knowledge-based systems impact organisations and managers. Throughout the rest of this chapter, we will take a more thorough look at two of these AI categories: expert systems and neural networks. We will first examine and why organisations and managers are so interested in expert systems. We then turn to some more technical issues, including the components of expert systems, how expertise is captured and represented, and how these systems are developed. Next, we will consider several specific examples of business applications of expert systems, how expert systems differ from conventional systems, and what some of their limitations are. In the final section of this chapter, we will look at neural networks and how these differ from expert systems. We will also discuss several specific examples of how organisations use neural networks.

Significance of Expert Systems

Expert labour is expensive and scarce. Knowledge workers—employees who routinely work with data and information to carry out their day-to-day duties—account for close to half of business's labour bill. The "star"—the sharpest and most knowledgeable workers—are not easy to find and keep, and companies are often faced with a shortage of talent in key positions. Moreover, no matter how bright or knowledgeable certain people are, they often can handle only a few factors at a time. Both the limitations imposed by human information processing capability and the rushed pace at which business is conducted today put a practical limit on the quality of human decision making.

In order to maintain a competitive edge, companies need to hone the decision-making skills of the personnel they currently have. The following are a number of ways that expert systems might help in this (adapted from John F. Magee):

- You manage a firm that bids on numerous projects; most of them are unique. You have a lot of background data on competitors and their bidding strategies, potential sources of delays, and so forth. Experienced project managers could use these data to arrive at sound bidding strategies; however, you have no experienced managers in your firm. An expert system could capture the lines of thinking of a first-rate project manager, combining competitor data, data about the target project, and data about your firm's tendencies toward risk, pricing, and contracting. Thus, the expert system could provide decision support to inexperienced managers and guide them through the bidding process.

- You are a life insurance agent. Your market has changed in recent years and you now compete with banks, brokerage houses, money-market fund managers, and a host of other new players, in addition to other life insurance agents. Your firm is pushing a variety of new products—universal life insurance and venture capital funds, for instance–with which you are not completely familiar. Also, your client are becoming more inquisitive and sophisticated, and many of the questions you field seem to require a specialist in both tax and financial planning. An expert system could be used to great advantage here to build sophisticated, knowledge-based, tax- and financial-planning support systems to provide agents with a competitive edge when handling inquisitive clients.
- Your firm sells complex, custom-built products that are assembled mostly from standard components. Frequently, orders are changed as a product is being built. Because the products are complex, the changed specifications called in by a customer often do not agree with other specifications that are still in place. These discrepancies can be caught by a sharp engineer, but few engineers are knowledgeable enough about all phases of product assembly to notice subtle irregularities. Also, identifying an error and resolving it take time. An expert system could be used productively here to check new specifications to ensure that they are both internally consistent and fit with other product specification.

Figure 13.5 gives a summary of the benefits that expert systems provide to the organisation. As Figure 13.5 indicates, expert systems help to preserve expertise, make expertise available on demand, and help novices learn how experts tackle complex problems. They can also be used for strategic or competitive advantage.

Benefits of Expert Systems
Preserves knowledge that might be lost through retirement, resignation, or death of an acknowledged company expert
Puts information into an active form so it can be summoned almost as a real-life experts might be summoned
Assists novices in thinking the way experienced professionals do
Is not subject to such human fallings as fatigue, being too busy, or being emotional
Can be effectively used as a strategic tool in the areas of marketing products, cutting costs, and improving products

Figure 13.5. *Benefits of expert systems. The benefits cited above can help organisations lower costs, increase sales, increase productivity, and provide better service. Significant competitive advantage can also result from the appropriate application and use of expert systems.*

Still, expert systems are not always the answer to managerial or organisational problems. They may not be appropriate in all situations. Some of the properties that potential applications should possess to qualify for expert system development are summarised in Figure 13.6. When the conditions specified in Figure 13.6 are satisfied, a proposed expert system has the potential to positively contribute to organisational functioning. If these conditions are not satisfied, managerial caution about expert system development is warranted.

Components of an Expert System/Rule Based Expert System

Technically, knowledge can be represented in several ways in an expert system: through rule-based systems, frame-based systems, predicate-based systems, and other representation schemes. Rule-based systems are, by far, the most common in practice; those are the types of systems that we explore here.

The components of a **rule-based expert system** are shown in Figure 13.7. In the following subsections, we describe the purposes of each of these software and data components, as well as the roles of experts, knowledge engineers, and users in developing and working on these systems.

Expert System Suitability Criteria	
Availability	One or more experts are capable of communicating how they go about solving the problem to which the expert system will be applied.
Complexity	Solution of the problems for which the expert system will be used is a complex task that requires logical inference processing which would not be easily handled by conventional information processing.
Domain	The domain, or subject area, of the problem is relatively small and limited to a relatively well-defined problem area.
Expertise	Solutions to the problem require the efforts of experts. That is, only a few people possess the knowledge, techniques, and intuition needed.
Structure	The solution process must be able to cope with ill-structured, uncertain, missing, and conflicting data, and a dynamic problem-solving situation.

Figure 13.6. Factors to consider when determining if an expert system should be developed in a potential application area.

Knowledge Based System

At the centre of any rule-based expert system is its **knowledge base**, which contains specific facts about the expert area and rules that the expert system will use to make decisions based on those facts. The knowledge base represents the total available data bank for the expert system; it consists primarily of facts and rules. The expert system's inference engine (discussed later) draws from the knowledge base to reach conclusions.

The **rules** in the knowledge base are usually coded in the form

IF X THEN Y

where X is a conditions and Y is an action to be taken if the condition is true. For example, if a company policy states that credits is to be automatically authorized only if a customer's total outstanding balance does not exceed $1,000 and the customer has made no more that two credits purchases already today, the policy can be coded into the following rules:

- Rule 1: Authorise credit if total customer balance after transaction will be less than or equal to $1,000.
- Rule 2: Authorise credit if customer has made not more than two credit purchases already today.

Some of the facts in the knowledge base that are applied to these rules are the names and account numbers of current credit customers, the current outstanding balances and credit limits of each of these customers, proposed purchase amounts, and a list of lost or stolen cards.

One of the biggest frontiers in the knowledge-base area is the use of *multiple domains* of expertise—that is, the use of more than one knowledge base. For instance, the example provided earlier of the insurance agent needing both expert tax and financial advice is a good candidate for an expert system with two knowledge bases. With such a system, a set of rules must be developed to bridge the knowledge bases and resolve any conflicts.

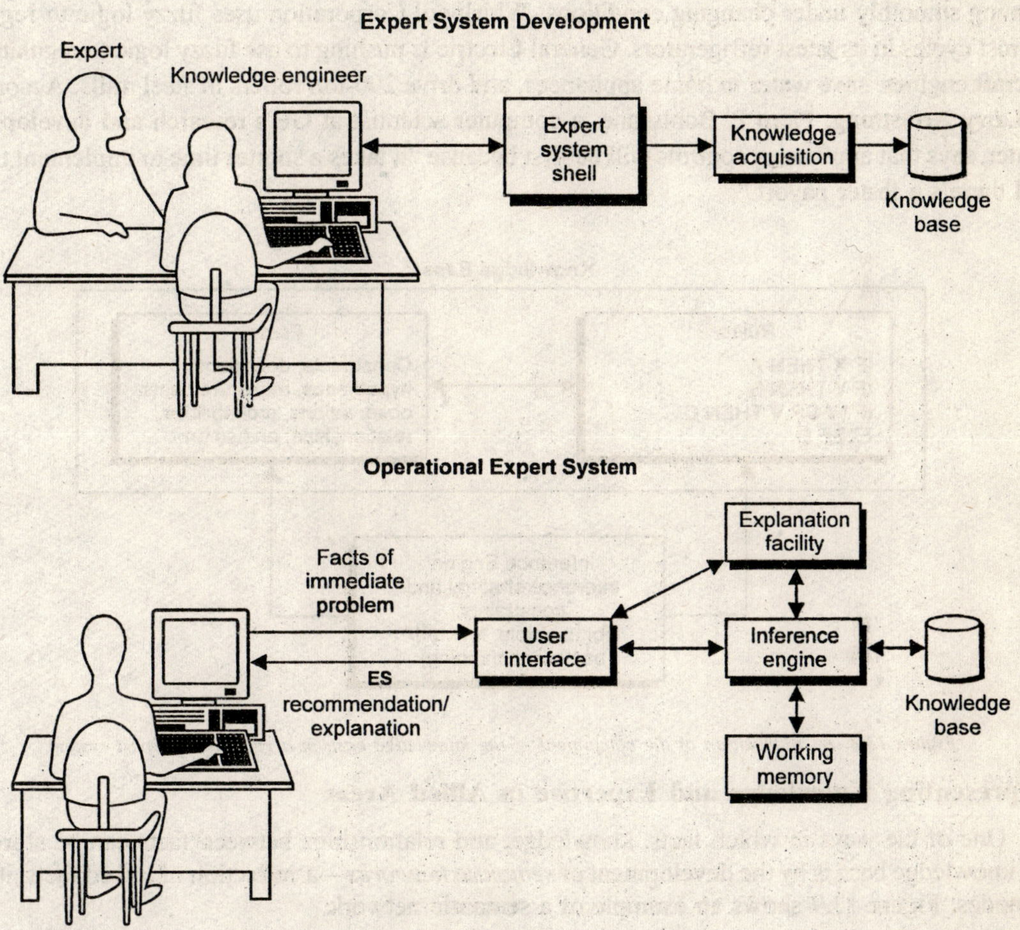

Figure 13.7. The main components of an expert system.

Fuzzy Logic (Binary Logic)

Still another forntier is in the area of *fuzzy logic.* Most expert systems today are only capable of dealing with "binary logic"—yes or no, true or false. If expert systems are to truly incorporate human thinking patterns, they must handle such imprecise terms as "most," "many," or "some."

Fuzzy logic is the brainchild of Lofti A. Zedah, a retired computer science professor from the University of California at Berkeley. Larry Armstrong cities Zedah as saying, "Fuzzy logic accepts the facts that 99.9% of human reasoning is not precise, and it tries to conform to it." Organisations are finding that for some applications, fuzzy logic can provide better and higher quality results than traditional approaches. Fuzzy logic appliances and business applications have been popular among Japanese manufacturers for awhile, but have only recently become popular with U.S. companies. Ford Motor Company, for example, is developing a fuzzy logic system to keep a car's engine running smoothly under changing conditions. Whirlpool Corporation uses fuzzy logic to regulate defrost cycles in its latest refrigerators. General Electric is pushing to use fuzzy logic to regulate jet-aircraft engines, save water in home appliances, and drive 200-ton rollers in steel mills. According to Larry Armstrong, Piero P. Bonissone, a computer scientist at GE's research and development center, says that appliances controls will be first because "it takes a shorter time to implement them, and there's a faster payoff."

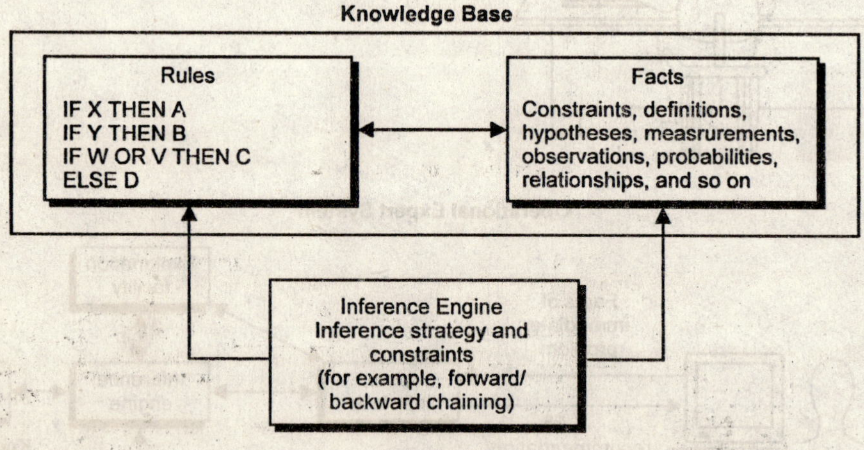

Figure 13.8. An illustration of the component of the knowledge base in a rule-based expert system.

Representing Knowledge and Expertise in Allied Areas

One of the ways in which facts, knowledge, and relationships between facts can be stored in the knowledge base is by the development of *semantic networks*—a collection of linked facts, items, or nodes. Figure 13.9 shows an example of a semantic network.

Frames may also be used to capture and store knowledge in a knowledge base. *Frames* essentially develop relationships among facts about a specific objects or entry. For all practical purposes, a frame is an "object" used in an experts system context—much of the current object-oriented technology is derived from earlier AI experiences with frames.

Frames consist of "slots" in which facts about the entity are entered. Frames that share similar characteristics (for example, where the information in slots is identical for two or more entities) can be related to one another. Frames and relationships between frames are illustrated in Figure 13.10.

Objects are a final, yet-emerging, way of representing knowledge in the knowledge base of an expert system. Previously in the text, we described object-oriented programming (OOP) and object-oriented databases (OODB). Software is now available that enables programmers to develop *object-oriented expert systems*. In these systems, an *object* consists of data values used to describe the attributes of an entity, as well as the operations that can be performed upon the data. The development and use of object-oriented expert systems should expand dramatically during the remainder the 1990s.

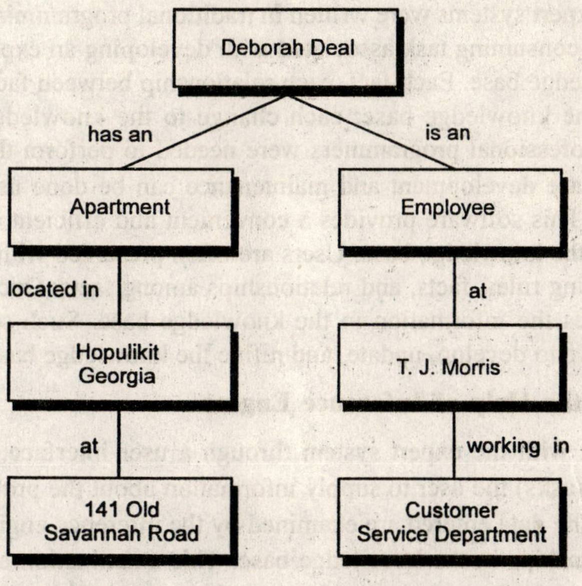

***Figure 13.9.** An example of a semantic network. This example demonstrates the relationship between items in a knowledge base that contains information on the individual Deborah Deal.*

Inference Engine (Forward Chaining and Backward Chaining)

The **inference engine** is the systems of programs that drives the expert system. The role of the inference in the overall expert system was depicted in Figures 13.7 and 13.8. These programs consult the knowledge base as they seek answers. In essence, the inference engine applies the facts and rules in the knowledge base(s) to the data about the problem supplied by users.

Inference engines operate with either a forward-chaining or backward-chaining mechanism: some operate with both. A **forward-chaining** mechanism first examines the knowledge base and the problem at hand; then, it attempts to discover a solution. For instance, a medical expert system may be used to examine a patient's symptoms and provide a diagnosis. Based on the symptomology, the expert system might locate several diseases that the patient may have. With **backward chaining,** on the other hand, the inference engine starts with a hypothesis or goal (such procedures are often called goal-driven inferential processes), which it then checks against the facts and rules in the knowledge base for consistency. So, for instance, the expert system might be given the goal to "find this patient's disease(s) and would work back from there, asking questions as necessary to confirm or refute candidate diagnoses."

Acquisition for Knowledge Subsystem

The **knowledge acquisition subsystem** is the software component of an expert system that enables the **knowledge engineer**, a specialized systems analyst responsible for designing and maintaining the expert system, to build and refine and expert system's knowledge base. The knowledge engineer works with the knowledge acquisition subsystem to model decision logic, derive heuristics, and update the knowledge base.

In the past, when expert systems were written in traditional programming languages, one of the most difficult and time-consuming task associated with developing an expert system was creating and updating the knowledge base. Each fact, each relationship between facts, and each rule has to be programmed into the knowledge base; each change to the knowledge base also had to be programmed. Often, professional programmers were needed to perform these chores.

Now, knowledge base development and maintenance can be done using special, reasonably user-friendly software. This software provides a convenient and efficient means of capturing and storing the contents of the knowledge base. Users are often presented with easy-to-operate menus and templates for entering rules, facts, and relationships among facts. Once these are entered, the software correctly stores the information in the knowledge base. Such software makes it much easier and less expensive to develop, update, and refine the knowledge base.

User Interface with the Help of Inference Engine

User often interact with the expert system through a user interface. In most instances, the expert system prompts (asks) the user to supply information about the problem and the user types in the requested data. The data entered are examined by the inference engine and compared to the facts, rules, and relationships in the knowledge base. This examination and comparison process results in the system continuing to prompt the user for more information until the system has enough data about the current problem so that it can reach a conclusion. Thus the user interface for an expert system is highly interactive.

Another component of the user interface enables users and decision makers to design, create, and update an expert system. This component also is typically interactive and often provides users with menus and templates.

Ideally, the user interface should enables the user (decision maker) to communicate with the expert system in his or her own natural language—English, French, Japanese, or whatever—without needing to learn rigid, programing language syntax. However, as pointed out earlier in the text, **natural-language interfaces** are still in their infancy, but are expected to become more common in expert systems (and other information technology applications) in the years ahead.

Explanation Facility

After users supply information about the current problem-solving situation, the expert system reaches a conclusion and/or makes a recommendation (which can be output to a screen, printer, or storage device) about what should be done. In many instances, users are also interested in knowing the line of reasoning followed by the expert system in drawing conclusions. If this line of reasoning seems faulty to the user, the conclusions reached by the expert system may be considered invalid. The **explanation facility** communicates to a user the logic followed in reaching a decision and, in

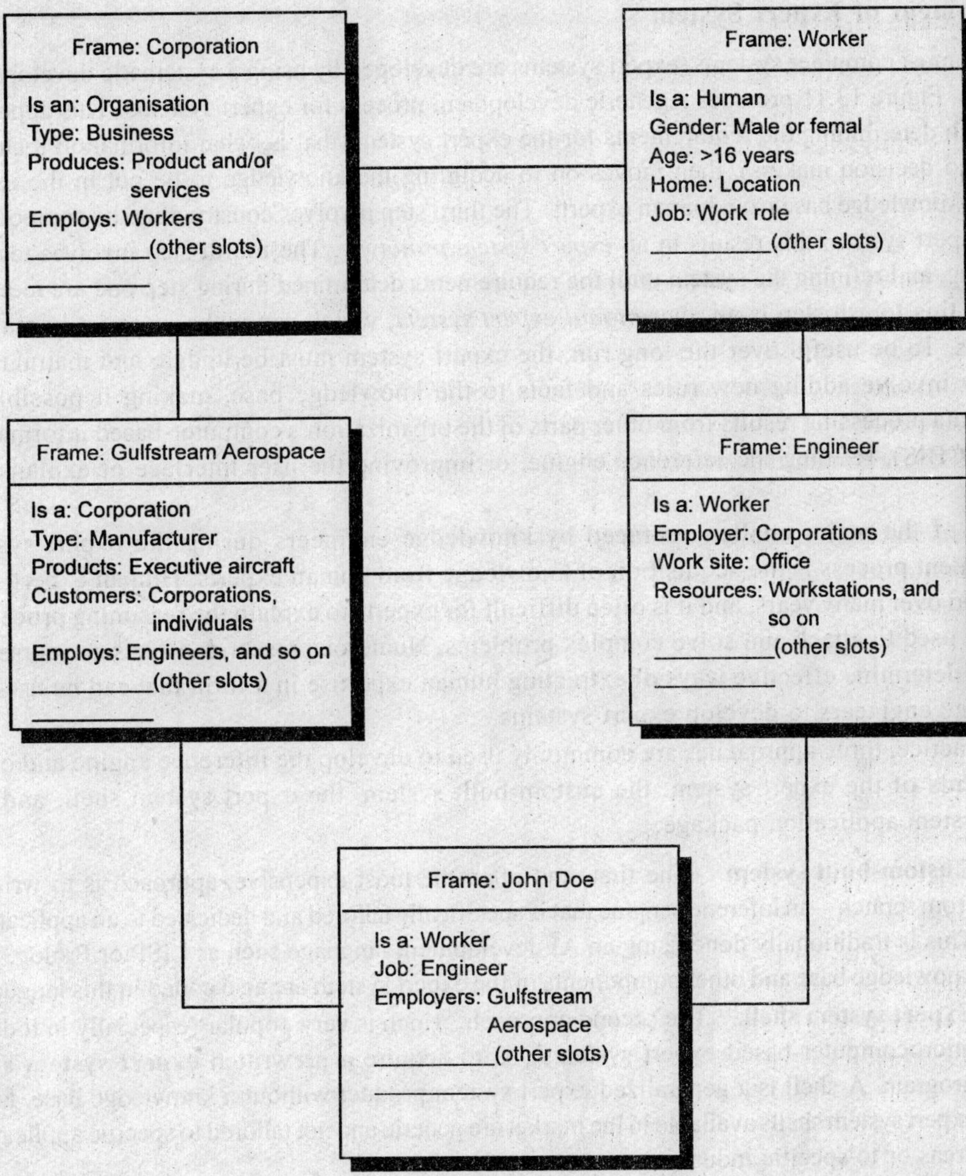

***Figure 13.10.** An example of a frame-based expert system knowledge base. The information in the "slots" in frames is used to interrelate frames.*

some cases, may also attempt to explain the importance of certain information inputs. Also, if the expert system cannot draw a conclusion, it should display what it has uncovered and let human experts use these facts to their advantage.

Development of Expert System

Like most computer systems, expert systems are developed by using a systematic development approach. Figure 13.11 provides a generic development process for expert systems. This approach starts with determining the requirements for the expert system (that is, what information it should provide to decision makers), then moves on to acquiring the knowledge to be put in the expert system's knowledge base from human experts. The third step involves constructing the components of the expert system; this results in an *expert system prototype*. The fourth step involves testing, debugging, and refining the system until the requirements determined during step one are met.The result of this fourth step is an *operational expert system*, which can make or assist in making decisions. To be useful over the long run, the expert system must be update and maintained; this may involve adding new rules and facts to the knowledge base, making it possible to extract data processing results from other parts of the organization's computer-based information system (CBIS), refining the inference engine, or improving the user interface or explanation facility..

One of the major challenges faced by knowledge engineers during the expert system development process is the acquisition of knowledge from human experts. Human expertise is developed over many years, and it is often difficult for experts to explain the reasoning processes that they used to attack and solve complex problems. Numerous research efforts are currently trying to determine effective ways of extracting human expertise in a form that can be used by knowledge engineers to develop expert systems.

In practice, three approaches are commonly used to develop the inference engine and other components of the expert system: the custom-built system, the expert system shell, and the expert system application package.

- **Custom-built system.** The first, and often the most expensive, approach is to write—from scratch—an inference engine that is specifically tailored and dedicated to an application. This is traditionally done using an AI development language such as LISP or Prolog. The knowledge base and other components of the expert system are also coded in this language.
- **Expert system shell.** The second approach, which is very popular (especially in today's microcomputer-based expert systems), is to acquire a prewritten **expert system shell** program. A shell is a generalized expert system product without a knowledge base. Most expert system shells available in the market are generic and not tailored to specific application areas or to specific industries.

  The shell product typically contains a 4GL that will enable the knowledge engineer to develop the knowledge base. Figure 13.12 provides examples of some of the expert system shells on the market today.

  Several factors should be considered when selecting an expert system shell, including the hardware platform (for example, microcomputer, minicomputer, or mainframe) that the system will be developed and utilized on; ease of use; availability of suitable knowledge representation structures (such as frames or objects); availability of appropriate reasoning structures (for example, backward versus forward chaining); the efficiency of the system's "run time" performance (some shell products result in notoriously slow systems); how easy it is to maintain and refine the system; and the compatibility of the product with other components of the organisation's CBIS.

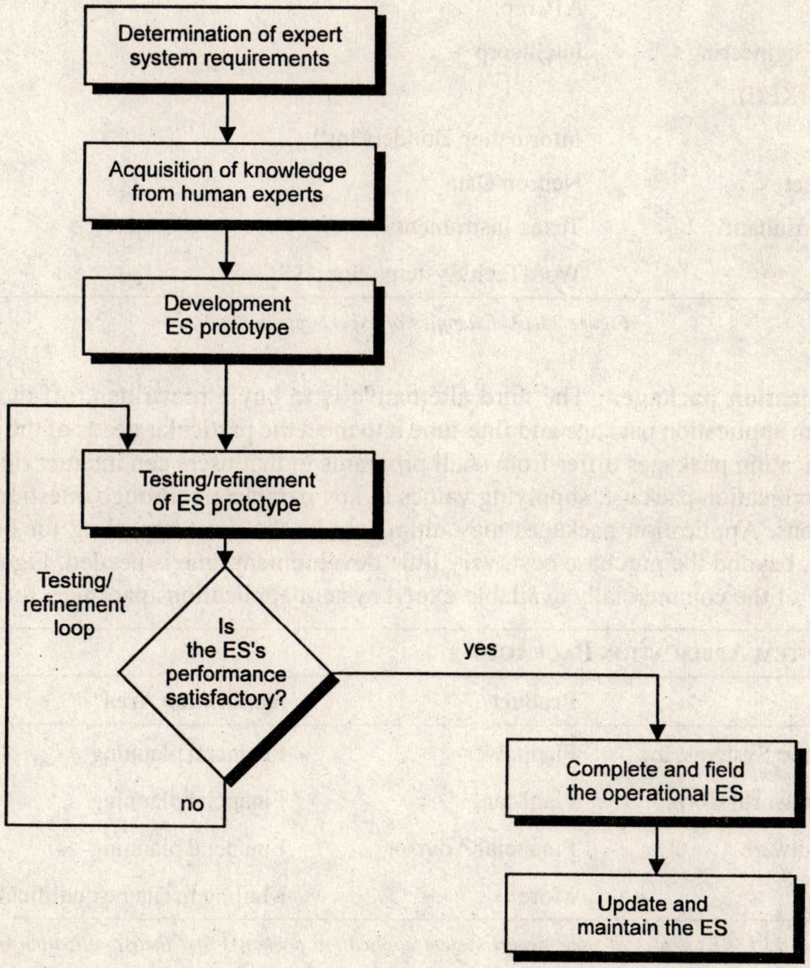

Figure 13.11. *A summary of the steps in the expert system development and maintenance process. After the initial prototype is developed, several testing/refinement iterations may be performed before the operational expert system is put in the field and used.*

Expert System Shells	
Product	**Vendor**
Aion Execution System	Aion Corp.
EXSYS	EXSYS, Inc.
1st-Class Fusion	1st Class Expert Systems
Guru	MDBS, Inc.
KBMS	A1Corp.
Knowledge Engineering Environment (KEE)	Intellicorp
Level 5	Information Builders Int'l.
Nexpert Object	Neuron Data
Personal Consultant	Texas Instruments
VP-Expert	WordTech Systems, Inc.

***Figure 13.12.** Examples of expert system shells.*

- **Application package.** The third alternative is to buy a prewritten, off-the-shelf expert system application package and fine-tune it to meet the particular needs of the organisation. Application packages differ from shell programs in that users can interact right away with the application package, supplying values to key parameters through question-and-answer sessions. Application packages may ultimately be the most appealing for business users since, beyond the purchase cost, very little development time is needed. Figure 13.13 lists some of the commercially available expert system applications packages for business.

Expert System Application Packages		
Vendor	**Product**	**Application Area**
Applied Expert Systems, Inc.	Planpower	Financial planning
Sterling Wentworth Corp.	PlanMan	Financial planning
Palladian Software	Financial Advisor	Financial planning
Persoft, Inc.	More	Mailing list name qualification

***Figure 13.13.** Examples of some expert system application packages and their application areas.*

Once the expert system is developed and implemented, it must be maintained and updated. To properly maintain and update an expert system, users should provide feedback to knowledge engineers on their experiences with the expert system and its explanation facility. If the facility is delivering insufficient or inappropriate conclusion—or if the explanations are based on faulty reasoning processes—the knowledge engineer may have to either modify or add to the rules or facts in the knowledge base—or make changes in the other components of the expert system. Over time, the number of rules in the knowledge base may expand dramatically. For example, the earliest versions of MYCIN—an expert system used to assist in medical diagnosis—contained about 5,000 rules. In its current version, the rule base is over 100,000 rules and the number of illnesses that can be diagnosed also increased (for example, new diseases such as AIDS and lyme disease were added to the knowledge base.)

Implementation of Expert System

The following are some representative examples of the growing use of expert systems in business. These systems are either currently in use or under development. In either case, they will give you a better understanding of both the use and potential of expert systems in business.

Production Schedule

An expert system was designed to analyse a manufacturer's production schedules, optimise the scheduling of resources, and identify opportunities to salvage materials in the rework pile for use in filling customer orders. Traditionally, it cost less for a company to discard unused material than to spend time performing the necessary complex calculations to discover other uses for them. A typical process production factory can have anywhere from 5 to 10 percent of its inventory in a rework pile at any one time. Turning even half of that amount into salable finished goods has a significant impact on the company's bottom line.

Inspection

A parts manufacturer has a vision-aided expert system that compares X-ray images of a machined part with specification drawings. If a defect such as a crack is found, the system directs a carefully aimed laser beam at it to seal the crack and prevent it from spreading. Also, the system creates a report that goes to quality assurance concerning the nature of the defect and the remedy required to correct it.

Assembly

The XCON expert system created and used by Digital Equipment Corporation (DEC) helps to build and assemble computer systems ordered by clients. When a client order is input to the system, it is configured by the system into schedules and diagrams that show the components required by the order and the relationship among those components.

Field Service

A design engineer with Speed Queen uses an expert system to disseminate his expertise to service managers and repair people. They system asks repairpeople a carefully conceived sequence of diagnostic questions, such as: Is the machine turned on? Does the fault lie in the electronic controls or somewhere else? Does the tub fill? This has helped Speed Queen repairpeople to diagnose problems more quickly and to reduce the amount of time it takes to make most types of repairs.

Telephone Repair Through Expert System

NYNEX Corporation, the phone company for much of New York and New England, uses an expert system to assess whether a repair truck really needs to be dispatched when a customer reports a problem. Workers with no expertise in phone repair consult Max (Maintenance Administration Expert), which searches a knowledge base containing thousands of repair records to find one like the caller's problem. NYNEX claims that Max improves customer service and saves an estimated $6 million per year by reducing unnecessary service calls and by decreasing the amount of training needed by the staff that handles customer calls.

Auditing with the Help of Expert System

An expert system helps auditors select auditing procedures with which to verify a firm's accounts receivable. Accounts receivable data such as internal control features and account collectability are input to the program and recommended auditing procedures are output.

Role of Expert System in Tax Accounting

A program called TAXADVISOR assists tax accountants with estate tax planning. The program helps clients arrange financial affairs so that income and death taxes are minimized; while maintaining sound investment decisions and adequate insurance coverage.

Additionally, one public accounting firm feels that its tax experts spend excessive amounts of time working through international tax problems. Coopers & Lybrand developed ExperTAX to assist clients with these and other tax problems.

Financial Planning with the Help of Expert System

A program called **Financial Advisor** incorporates the financial advice of eight faculty members from MIT's Sloan School of Management and ten senior financial officers from major corporations. **Financial Advisor** provides advice on such topics as investment projects, products, and mergers and acquisitions. They system is used in businesses and is available commercially.

Role of Expert System in Investment

A Pennsylvania-based company is currently working on an expert system that combines probability theory, statistical analysis, pattern recognition, and simulation to help investors select stocks and manage portfolio. In tests performed with a prototype of the product, the gain realized was twice that of the Standard and Poor's 500 index.

Personnel with the Help of Expert System

Traveler's Insurance uses an expert system to help employees fill out W-4 tax-withholdings forms. The system alleviates the strain on Traveler's Insurance's personnel department, which was besieged with inquiries from employees having difficulty filling out the forms. The expert system's knowledge base contains both information from the W-4 form and suggestions from the personnel department. The microcomputer-based system asks employees questions about their filing status and produces a complete W-4 form based on their replies.

Knowledge Point developed a product called Personnel Policy Expert, which assists companies in creating complete employees handbooks. It addresses approximately 60 policy issues and helps personnel managers make policy decisions that comply with current labour laws and prevailing personnel practices. The system prompts user for information about the importance of various policies and creates a draft version of the policy statement for inclusion in the handbook.

Importance of Expert System is Sales and Marketing

Traveler's Mortgage Services, a subsidiary of Traveler's Insurance, has a loan prequalification expert system for its sales force. The client provides such facts as monthly payment objectives, data on whether or not it is desirable to minimize closing costs, and qualification data. The expert system output is an approval recommendation and, if the client is approved, a complete mortgage package. According to Janet Mason's article, an assistant vice-president of the firm claims that, "The expert system can work up to six combinations in two seconds, whereas it takes a salesperson 20 to 30 minutes to figure out a single combination."

Credit Authorisation through Expert System

Bad decisions in authorizing credit when merchants phoned for approval cost American Express hundreds of millions of dollars. To curb bad debts, American Express now has an expert system, called Authorizer's Assistant, that helps human authorizers decide whether a potential purchaser should be extended credit. The system gathers important information about a cardholder from 14 databases and compresses it down to two screens, which the human authorizers view to make their final decision as they are on-line with a merchant. In some cases, where the transaction raises absolutely no questions, the system is allowed to make decisions on its own. The case study of expert system of credit authorization is given in the last of the chapter.

Human Services Agency

The U.S. Human Services Agency in Merced County, California, developed an expert system called Magic that decides if applicants should receive welfare benefits. Magic consults a matrix of 6,000 government regulations to determine if an applicant qualifies. While it takes Magic an average of 72 hours to make a decision, it used to take trained clerks as long as three months to make the same decision and to calculate how much and what types of benefits the applicant could receive. Training time for new benefit clerks is dramatically reduced and the delivery of social services to eligible recipients is faster. Magic saves the county over $4 million per year in administrative and training costs.

Significance of Expert System in Medical Prognosis

Medical prognosis concerns what is likely to happen to a patient once they are diagnosed as having a particular disease. Apache III is an expert system that predicts a patient's chances of living or dying. Its knowledge base contains the medical records of thousands of previously diagnosed patients and uses this information, along with the patient's own medical history and changes in the patient's condition, to determine the probability of survival. Studies show that the program can predict more accurately than top-notch doctors. Physicians who use Apache III claim that it helps them to respond the changes in patient conditions more quickly. Hospital administrators like Apache III because it helps the hospital staff control costs by focusing attention on the cases that are most likely to benefit.

Expert Systems Versus Conventional Applications

Many differences exist between the expert system approach and the conventional approach used to develop application software. Four of these differences are covered here:

- In conventional applications, the expert knowledge is buried in code located within the application program. In expert system application, the expert knowledge and heuristics are in a district knowledge base that is located outside the software driving the application (the inference engine).
- Expert systems probe users interactively, in question-and-answer sessions. The answer to an attendant question is used by the expert system to pose the next question. In conventional applications, data are usually supplied all at once—perhaps from a filled-in-template—to the application program for processing.
- In expert system, a large amount of input (the knowledge base) is almost always used to create a small amount of output (such as a medical diagnosis for a specific patient, or the approval or disapproval of credit for a particular customer). Although this is also true today for some conventional applications, most often the reverse is true.

Applications and Limitations of Expert Systems

Although both artificial intelligence and expert systems have great potential, they are sometimes heavily criticized by management as not living up to the fanfare that accompanied them. However, most computer professional are still very positive about these problem-solving approaches. As Clyde Holsapple and Andrew Whinston predict:

> Although artificial intelligence (AI) has scarcely touched today's managers, it will begin to have dramatic and widespread impacts on their activities over the next few years. Looking farther out, to the end of the century, practical fruits form the past 30 years of AI research will be commonplace. The application of artificial intelligence techniques will play a major role in reshaping traditional notions of what organisations are, how they are managed, and how decisions are made. All of this presents a major challenge and an important opportunity to today's managers and organisations. Though the transition will not be without growing pains, it will lead to tremendous increases in the productivity of managers and organizations. Those organisations in the forefront of applying AI methods to aid in management will have distinct competitive advantages over those that lag.

Knowledgeable professionals generally agree with this point of view. Expert systems will indeed eventually infuse themselves deeply into almost all areas of computer processing. They do serve a clear need, and the future technical environment of faster processor chips, parallel processing architectures, and bigger memories that expert systems need to really show their potential power are on their way. AI is not a fad. AI routines will be built into many of today's conventional computer software products, just as microprocessor are already built into hardware products. Within the next decade, look for typical spreadsheet packages, word-processing software, and database management systems to be equipped with artificial intelligence features.

Today, expert system are used mostly to solve narrow problems such as medical diagnosis, aircraft engine analysis, credit approval, tax advice, and oil exploration. These problems involve a small volume of logically complex operations. Also, in each of these problem areas, a relatively universal pattern of logic can be identified (unlike, perhaps, determining the best way to create or to advertise a cereal product). These expert system applications are far removed from mainstream MIS takes such as transaction processing, information retrieval, or budget preparation—many of which involve relatively simple operations. Mainframe-oriented MIS departments have not yet heavily invested in AI, preferring to wait until vendors build a suitable bridge between the artificial intelligence environment and standard, mainframe-based business applications.

Despite the promise of expert systems, they must overcome some tough opposition in order to serve beyond a decision support capacity. As Beau Sheil points out, "Consider the first patient who dies as a result of a bad diagnosis from a robotic doctor. Who will be held responsible?" Furthermore, Sheil cautions:

> It is quite possible that we will never see commercial airlines flown entirely under computer control even if that technology becomes clearly superior—statistically—to human pilots. The reason is that although human pilots crash the occasional plane when trying to land in poor weather, their failures are understandable and thus, though regrettable, can be tolerated. When the mechanical pilot fails, however, even though it might do so much less frequently, it is likely to be by flying a plane into the side of a mountain in broad daylight. And this kind of failure we are unlikely to tolerate, whatever the long-run statistics say.

Neural Networks Works on Artificial Intelligence

Conventional computers, with all of their raw speed, are just not well equipped to handle some types of problems. This is where neural-net computers, or neural nets, can help. These systems, which are built to mimic the way the human brain works, are specially geared to solve pattern-recognition types of problems. For instance, when you recognise a person's face or signature—acts performed so quickly that usually you do not think mush about how this is done—you are really performing pattern recognition. That is, you record and analyse a number of important patterns in an object, comparing them with patterns stored in memory, and then you draw a conclusion (that is, you make an observation).

Neural nets simulate the human pattern-recognition process by arranging processing elements, which often work in parallel, in layers. The connections between layers and between processing elements on the same level form a network. Figure 13.14 illustrate a generic neural network. The lowest layers look at general features of a pattern and pass them up to intermediate layers. For instance, take character recognition. The lower levels might recognise that a character has a few straight lines. The intermediate layers refine the perception of the character, but it is only at the highest layer that the character is recognised—for example, as the letter H.

One of the main reasons why organisations are interested in neural networks is the "learning" capabilities of these systems. The activation of a particular processing element in the neural net depends on which inputs to it were activated and the weights of the inputs activated by other processing units. "Knowledge" is represented by the pattern of connections and weights among the interconnected elements. Storing the pattern of weights and connections provide a baseline against which later inputs can be judged. During "training," the neural net "learns" by adjusting its weights in response to a collection of examples that users provide; each example contains values for both inputs and outputs. Once appropriate weights are determined, they are stored and used to evaluate the activation patterns associated with subsequent inputs. For example, a neural network trained to differentiate between customers who are good and bad credit risk would compare the activation pattern from a new customer's credit data with the pattern associated with known "poor" or "excellent" credit histories. If the new customer's activation pattern is similar to that for poor credit risk customers, then new customer's data could be flagged as a possible credit risk.

Ideally, as neural-net computers mature, they will utilise true parallel processing architectures throughout. Today, many so-called neural-net computers work with software emulation routines or through add-on boards, each of which work together with a conventional serial processor. Over 100 different neurocomputer designs have been implemented.

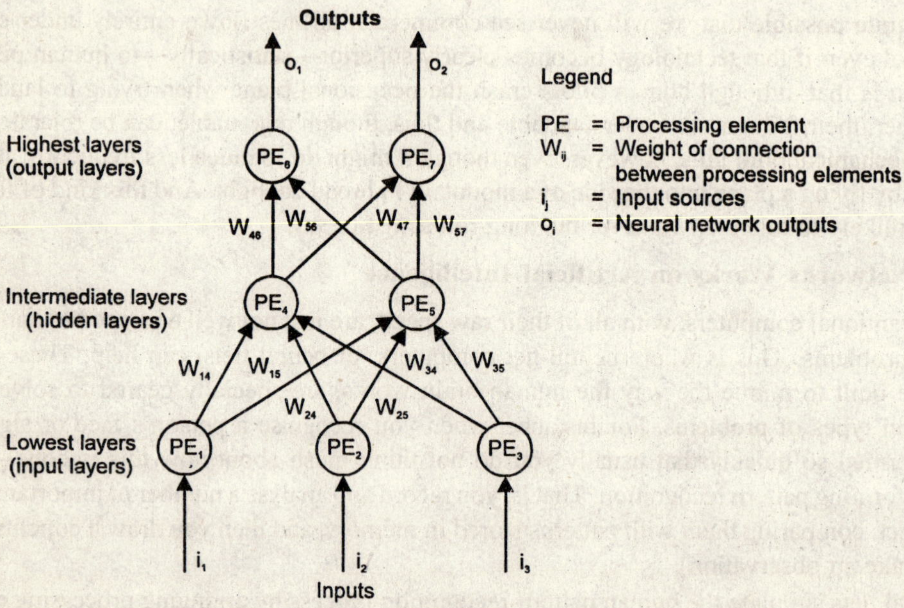

Figure 13.14. The fundamental elements of a neural network.

Neural-net computer have great potential in business, although it will be several more years before a wave of commercially viable product hits the market. Some of the major application areas appear, for the moment, to be handwriting recognition, quality control, and security. Each of these areas depends heavily on some type of pattern recognition: a character, a defect, and a person, respectively.

Several companies are already putting neural networks to use. Ford Motors company implemented a neural network that spots faulty paint jobs. Siemens, a German electrical equipment maker, developed a neural network to check blower motors. Arco and Texaco use neural networks to help pinpoint oil and gas deposits deep beneath the earth's surface. Speigel uses neural networks to determine which individuals in their vast marketing databases are most likely to buy their products. And Shearson Lehman uses neural network to predict the performance of stocks and bonds.

Other neural networks assist quality control in a bottling plant, read handwritten zip codes, and recognise patterns in financial data. Westinghouse is developing a weapon system for the U.S. military that is capable of recognising the image of a tank as ally or enemy—such a system may reduce "friendly fire" losses such as those incurred in 1991's Desert Storm campaign.

Neural network should impact other areas as well, such as looking for trend pattern in sales data, analyzing strategy pattern within companies, looking for duplicate names in mailing lists, and making recommendations on credit or mortgage applications. Anywhere a pattern needs to be analyzed, neural nets should be considered as a solution.

Neural nets are still a fledgling technology, a sparkle in the eye of many technology entrepreneurs. When Edward Rosenfeld, editor of *Intelligence Newsletter*, looked into neural nets in 1984, he counted barely 24 companies doing some work in the field. In 1988, his count reached 175, with at least 125 of these involved in major projects. During the 1990s, neural nets should blossom as a technology and be woven into the MIS fabric of many organisations.

Summary/Conclusion

Artificial intelligence (AI) is the capability of computer systems to perform at a level that would be considered intelligent if observed in humans. Five main areas of AI research exist today: expert systems, natural languages, vision systems, robotics, and neural networks.

Expert systems are software systems that try to provide the type of advice that would normally come form human experts. To date, most successful expert systems have been in rather narrow, specific fields. However, expert systems have been developed for rapidly growing number of fields.

Natural-Language systems are those in which the computer communicates with users in a natural language, such as English or Chinese. The complexity of conveying meaning in a natural language has made progress in this area slow.

Vision systems are systems that perform tasks that could, at one time, only be done through use of the human eye. Image patterns are stored in a database and compared with the item being checked by a machine endowed with "sight."

Robotics is the field of AI concerned with the design, manufacture, and implementation of robots—computer-controlled devices that mimic the motor activity of humans. Robots have had their greatest success in manufacturing, where they perform jobs too dangerous, strenuous, monotonous, or expensive for humans to do.

Neural networks are computer systems that identify objects or patterns in a manner similar to the pattern recognition activities of human brain. These networks are capable of "learning" input and data patterns and subsequently comparing new data and inputs to see how well they fit into learned patterns. Neural networks are implemented by using parallel processing and/or special software.

Expert systems are needed because human expert labour is expensive and scarce. In addition, the quality of human decision making is constrained by the limitations of human information processing and the fast pace of business today.

The most common type of expert system is a rule-based expert system, which consist of numerous components. At the centre of such a system is its knowledge base, which contains all the specific facts about the expert area and the rules the system uses to make decisions based on those facts. The rules in a knowledge base are usually coded in the form:

IF X THEN Y

where X is a condition and Y is an action to be taken if the condition is true. Relationships between facts stored in the knowledge base may be represented as semantic network, frames, or objects.

The inference engine is the system of the computer program that drives the expert system. It applies the rules, facts, and relationships between facts found in the knowledge base to data about the problem input by users. Three approaches are used to develop the inference engine: (1) custom build it; (2) acquire a prewritten, generic expert system shell, or (3) buy a prewritten, commercial application package and fine-tune it to fit the specific needs of the organisation. Inference engines operate with either a forward-chaining mechanism, by which software routines first examine the knowledge base and then attempt to discover a solution—or a backward-chaining mechanism, by which software routines are first given a hypothesis, which they then check against the knowledge base—or by a combination of forward and backward chaining.

The knowledge acquisition subsystem of an expert system is the software component that enables the knowledge engineer to interact with the system. This subsystem makes it possible for the expertise of human experts to be placed in the knowledge base. The knowledge engineer is the MIS professional who design and maintains the expert system.

Users can interact with the expert system through a user interface. Most of these are interactive; users key in responses to questions posed by the expert system. Natural-language interfaces for expert systems are still in their infancy.

The explanation facility communicates to the user the line of reasoning used in reaching a decision. It may also explain the importance of certain inputs, thus attempting to direct the user to a logical conclusion.

Expert systems are used in a variety of business areas, including production, inspection, assembly, auditing, tax accounting, finance, personnel, marketing and sales, field service, investments, and credit authorisation.

Many differences exist between the expert system approach and the traditional approach to developing application software. First, in conventional application, the expert knowledge is buried in code within the application program; conversely, in expert systems, the knowledge is in a distinct knowledge base. Second, in conventional applications, data are usually supplied all at once to the computer system; in expert systems, users are probed interactively and new questions are posed in response to previous answers. Third, in conventional applications, a small amount of input often creates a large amount of output; in expert systems, the reverse is usually true. Finally, in conventional applications, knowledge data are often highly structured and predefined; in expert systems, they are often semistructured.

Although most professionals believe that expert systems will become very important in the future, the use of expert systems is still frequently criticized for not living up to expectations. As experience with expert systems matures, however, and as processor speeds and memories become more capable, expert systems will probably be infused into every important software product that could benefit by some type of expert advice.

Neural networks are also gaining in popularity, especially for pattern recognition tasks. Since these systems can be trained to recognise complex patterns and to compare new inputs against learned patterns, organisations find them useful for many applications, including handwriting recognition, quality control, and spotting patterns in financial information. Hundreds of neural networks have been implemented and many more should be developed in the years ahead.

Case Study

Using an Expert System at American Express

In recent years, one of the best-known business applications of artificial intelligence has been Authorizer's Assistant—a knowledge-based system used by American Express to help credit authorizers make better credit decisions. Expert systems—and a completely revamped credit authorization system—were a logical choice for American Express for numerous reasons. Unlike the credit cards issued by many major banks, the American Express Card has no credit limit. Card holders are also expected to pay their balances in full each month.

Before implementing Authorizer's Assistant, both fraudulent use of charge cards and bad decisions in authorizing credit when merchants called for approval were costing the company hundreds of millions of dollars. Also, the system then in effect was slow and produced inconsistent results. Basically, it required human authorizers to first enter IBM's Transaction Processing facility (TPF) and then use their own judgement to search independently through as many as a dozen IMS databases for specific cardholder information.

In late 1984, American Express executives decided to improve the authorization system. When expert systems were chosen as the route for new systems development, the company contracted with an outside expert system developer to create a preliminary working model of the system—a prototype—to be ready in about a year. The system created by the contractor is an expert system that runs on a microcomputer workstation that has a communications interface. This interface allows the experts system to tap data from the IMS cardholder databases hooked to an IBM mainframe.

When merchants call in for credits approval for a cardholder transaction, the expert system quickly pulls together any relevant database information, evaluates it, and makes either a decision or a recommendation as to whether or not credit should be granted. Usually taken into account are such factors as a cardholder's outstanding balance (the amount of cardholder transactions since the last statement was sent), payment history, buying habits, and the degree of risk involved. Should any warning sighs appear, the system is even capable of asking merchants to obtain further information from the cardholder—such as information that would help to verify the identity of the cardholder.

About a quarter of all transactions processed by Authorizer's Assistant are straightforward enough to require no human intervention. In such cases, the system essentially makes a decision and transmit it to the merchant. The other transactions are referred by the system to human authorizers. Each is accompanied by an identification of the warning sighs, an explanation regarding why the transaction is being referred, a recommendation for credit authorization or denial, and an encapsulation of relevant decision-making data culled from the data bases.

14

Office Information Systems

- Define office information systems (OIS) and office automation (OA)
- Describe the types of workers found in an office
- Describe the evolution that has taken place in office information systems
- Describe the major types of office systems found in organisations
- Identify several benefits derived from implementing office systems in organisations
- Describe some of the challenges and issues associated with implementing office systems in organisation
- Describe the characteristics of integrated office systems

During the past 25 years, computer technology has helped to dramatically increase productivity in the office. The movement toward automation in office tasks in often called office automation (OA). Office automation includes the new hardware and software technologies—word processors, spreadsheet packages, electronic mail, and so on—that make office workers more productive, plus the attendant situations created by OA technologies and the people that use these technologies. These combinations of information technologies that have a dramatic impact on day-to-day office operations are called office information systems (OIS). In this chapter, we explore office information systems and how they evolved.

The chapter begins by discussing the nature of office work and what specifically is covered under office information systems. We explore integrated OIS package, looking at the needs of OIS and where OIS is headed.

Offices and Offices Systems

The basic nature of office work has changed drastically over the past 50 years. At one time, virtually the only role of equipment in the office was to help workers become more efficient. Until the mid-1960s, only the typewriter, phone, copying machine, and electronic adding machines were standard office equipment. Now, as computer technologies have a strong presence in offices, office workers have powerful tools that also make them more effective. For example, word processing and desktop publishing make information much easier to find and modify. Such DSS tools as spreadsheet packages help managers make decisions that are more informed than those they reached when using less powerful calculators.

Here, we will look at the types of workers found in the modern office environment and the types of tasks they perform. Then, we will explore the evolution of computing technologies into office work.

Nature of the Office

Generally, an **office** is a place where staff and line professionals, secretaries, and clerks perform management and administrative tasks. The work performed by office workers is often called white collar work. In recent years, office workers have accounted for about 75 percent of the total business payroll costs in the United States.

Office Employees

Five types of workers can be found in the office: managers, staff professionals, line professionals, secretaries, and clerical personnel. Managers, staff professionals and line professionals are often called **knowledge workers** because their works involves the greatest amount of knowledge of any people in the firm.

- **Managers:** In general, managers spend a lot of time planning, coordinating, and controlling the activities of other people. Some examples are the firm's chief executive officers (CEO), the vice-president of operations, and the head of marketing research.
- **Staff professionals:** Staff professionals support the activities of managers—for example, marketing or operations research analysts. Staff personnel have no direct line responsibility; that is, their role is mostly one of planning, analyzing, and informing management of their findings.

- **Line professionals:** Line professionals include salespeople and purchasing agents. Line professionals typically interact daily with such outside groups as the firm's customer and suppliers.
- **Secretaries:** Secretaries are normally assigned to one or more knowledge workers in an office. They perform such support tasks as typing, filing, answering phones, and keeping appointment calendars.
- **Clerical personnel:** Clerical personnel are normally not assigned to anyone in particular; generally, they support the entire office. Typical types of clerical tasks are filing, typing, and assisting in report preparation.

OA Professionals/OA Experts

In many organisations, a separate support group is responsible for promoting and managing office system technologies. Some firms employ a full-time OA manager with a staff of several people. The OA personnel often perform a variety of representative office tasks on test or demonstration equipment and arrange for product demonstrations within the firm by OIS hardware and software vendors.

Office Work

The management and administrative tasks performed in the office can be divided into five general categories: decision-making, data manipulation, document-handling, communications, and storage activities. All of the offices systems applications that we discuss in the next section of this chapter fall into at least one of these categories.

- **Decision-making:** The main job of the manager is to make decisions. The main job of the staff professional is to assist the manager in this activity. Thus, decision-making is one of the most important tasks performed in the office. Virtually all knowledge workers are involved with key decisions of some type.
- **Data manipulation:** A common office duty is preparing lists and numbers to present at meetings or to discuss with clients over the phone. This type of works involves the manipulation of data—either manually or by computer.
- **Document handling:** A sizable portion of the work done by secretarial personnel, clerical personnel, and line professional is document handling: creating and issuing documents, reviewing and responding to documents, and so on. For example, taking dictation and subsequently typing a letter from it or preparing a written budget bot involve the handling of documents.
- **Communications:** Office workers often spend a lot of time in meetings and on the telephone. Some managers spend almost 50 percent of their time on these communications activities.
- **Storage:** An important office task is keeping accurate records. For example, the shipping office needs to keep records on products leaving the firm and the purchasing office must maintain records of open purchased orders. Also, in most firms, it is important to maintain storage of archival records and to locate those historical records when necessary.

Origin of Office Systems

As mentioned earlier, until the mid-1960s, virtually the only information technologies in the office were typewriters, phones, copying machines, and electric adding machines. Then, in 1964, a seemingly modest typing enhancement—called **word processing**—appeared. Since then, information processing in the office has never been the same.

Among the earliest word processors was the IBM magnetic tape electric typewriter (MT/ST), which stored preprocessed text on a strip of magnetic tape. The tape unit on the MT/ST could be activated by secretary at any time during the regular typing of a letter; it then automatically types a prepared text segment onto a document. Obviously, a lot has changed since 1964. The tape units disappeared long ago, and computer workstations have replaced many standard typewriters.

The introduction of minicomputers and small business computers in the late 1960s and early 1970s also contributed to the alteration of the office's technology. Before then, virtually all computing was highly centralized, performed on mainframes that were located at a single (headquarters) site. Smaller computers made it possible to decentralize computing down to regional sites and individual offices. It was not unusual for large offices, in fact, to own their computers. This trend toward decentralization was called *distributed data processing (DDP)*. What the MT/ST was to the office in the 1960s, DDP was to the office in the 1970s.

Today, because of inexpensive microcomputer systems, quality microcomputer software, electronic mail, local area networking, and gateways to mainframe systems, office technology is changing yet again. The proliferation of computing technologies into office life has been so pervasive, in fact, that computer-illiterate knowledge workers have problems in most of today's offices. Two terms are associated with the computerization of offices in the 1980s and 1990s: office automation (OA) and departmental computing. In this text, office automation is preferred because it is more widely accepted.

Of all the areas currently under the MIS umbrella, the office information systems area is probably the hardest to define because it is composed of many different technologies and overlap considerably with the end-user computing (EUC) and decision support system (DSS) areas. For example, a sales manager using a spreadsheet to model strategies falls under the areas of OIS, DSS, and EUC. If this person is a top-level manager, the spreadsheet may also be part of an executive information system (EIS). If the data are downloaded from a mainframe-based transaction processing system, then the resulting system is also part of a transaction processing system (TPS). Every office worker is a potential end-user, which, to some people, makes OIS a subset of EUC. However, because EUC also covers nonoffice workers, such as those in factories, the topics of end-user computing and development.

The primary purpose of office information systems is to facilitate communication among members of an organisation and between the organisation and its external environment. Ideally, an office information system allows individuals and group members to create, store, and exchange messages through a variety of communications media, including data, documents, images, voice (audio), and video. OA is moving toward the realisation of these ideals. The office of the future will probably have these features and even more. Integrated services digital network (ISDN) should facilitate such communication within and between offices. Advances in electronic data interchange (EDI), image processing, and document management systems should also enable organisations to move toward paperless office operations.

Types of OA Systems

Four major categories of office application are document management systems, message-handling systems, teleconferencing systems, and office support systems. These, and some of the applications that fall under these headings, are summarised in Figure 14.1. Most of the remainder of this chapter will discuss these systems.

Document Management Systems

As Figure 14.1 indicates, document management systems include word processing, desktop publishing applications, and image-processing systems. Intelligent copier systems and other reprographic technologies (systems capable of making multiple copies of a document) are also facets of document management systems. The huge amount of paper documents generated currently makes in this an extremely important OIS area. According to Janet Mann, in the early 1990s, U.S. businesses produced an average of nearly 100 billion original paper documents and 300-400 billion photocopies a year.

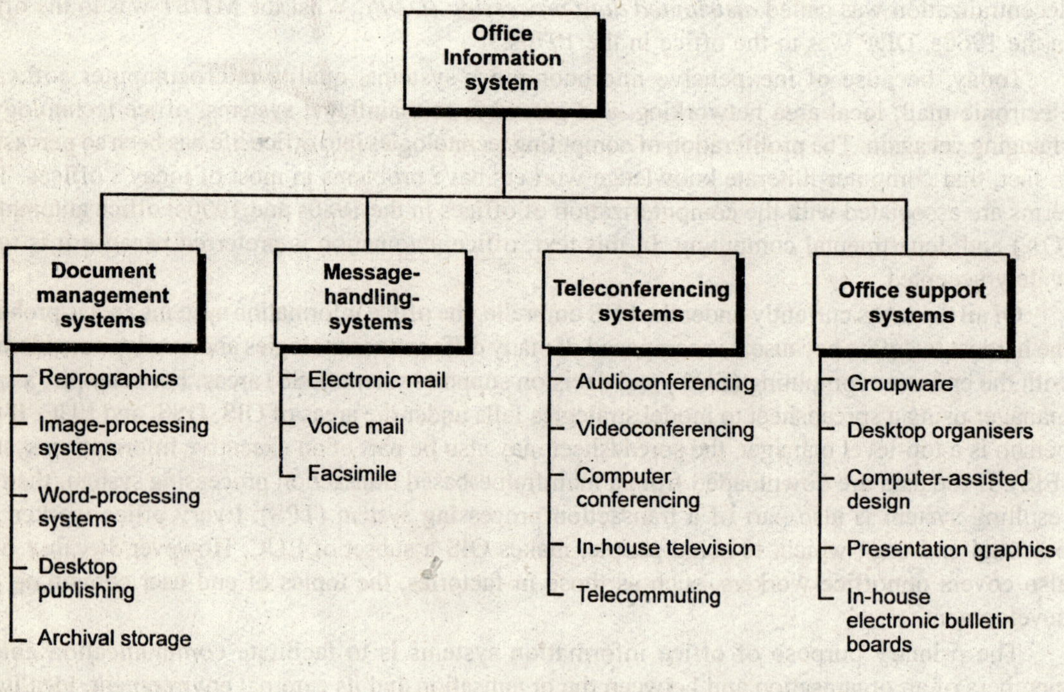

Figure 14.1. The major components of an office information system (OIS).

Word Processing

The most widely used and recognised office-system technology is word processing. Word processing involves hardware and software tools that allow the computer system to become more than a powerful typewriting device. Word processors enables documents to be created and edited electronically, with the assistance of the computer system's processor, memory, and display device.

When the document is finished, it can be stored in secondary storage (typically on disk) or output on the system's printer in a variety of styles. Figure 14.2 lists a number of features commonly found on word processors.

WORD-PROCESSING FEATURES	
Standard Entering and Editing Operations	
Moving the cursor to various places on-screen	Moving and copying blocks of text
Scrolling the document up and down	Searching for text strings
Returning line automatically	Replacing text strings
Inserting and deleting characters and blocks of text	Spelling checker features
	Thesaurus features
Standard Print-Formatting Operations	
Adjusting line spacing	Automatic page numbering, headings, and footings
Indenting blocks of text	Multiple columns per page
Reformatting blocks of text	Selection of tools
Centering text	Selection of fonts
Proportionally spaced characters	Orphan and widow elimination
Advanced Operations	
Mailing list preparation	Cross-referencing
Form-letter boilerplating	Preparing indexes and tables of contents
Math feature	Integrating with spreadsheet programs
Sorting	Desktop publishing features
Redlining and edit tracing	Embedded typesetting codes.

Figure 14.2. Word-processing features. Most word-processing packages perform the same types of operations. Recently, the market leaders have also incorporated several desktop publishing features.

Most of today's word processing uses word-processing software on a general-purpose computer system. These computer systems, of course, can be used for other purposes as well: preparing taxes, extracting records from files, or writing Pascal programs, to name just a few applications. Today, the biggest market for word-processing packages that run on general-purpose computers is in the microcomputing area, where such packages as WordPerfect, Microsoft Word, WordStar, and Ami Pro are among the current leaders. WordPerfect and Microsoft Word alone captured over half of the word-processing market. Many of these packages recently released versions for the Windows operating environment. Newer versions of these packages incorporate numerous graphics and desktop publishing features that were not included in the earlier versions.

As computer networking is now popular, so are "shared" word-processing systems. Shared systems are specifically designed to share the resources of a communication network. Typically, these systems are implemented in one of two ways: (1) as several display terminal workstations that are connected to a host (a midrange or mainframe system) in a star (or hierarchical) configuration, or (2) as a local area network (LAN) consisting of several microcomputer workstations, a file server, a print server, and perhaps other servers as well. In a LAN, the software used may allow workers to concurrently prepare different parts of the same document, sharing their outputs over the network.

Desktop Publishing (DTP)

An office technology that is currently very popular is desktop publishing. **Desktop Publishing (DTP)** involves desktop microcomputer systems that are equipped with special hardware and software features to produce documents that look as through they were done by a professional print shop (see Figure 14.3). DTP users can combine word-processed text with such elements as artwork, photos, and a variety of magazines-style fonts. The overall effect can be stunningly attractive and very effective.

Configuring a Desktop Publishing System

Today, a wide variety of desktop publishing systems is found in the marketplace—at both the low end and the high end. As noted previously, many of the latest versions of the leading word-processing software packages have added desktop publishing features that enable them to be used as low-end desktop publishing systems.

Although a few very low-end packages can run on a regular IBM PS/2 or INM compatible machine—configured with less that IBM of RAM, a dot-matrix printer, and floppy-disk secondary storage—most of them require considerably more power if the user wants to take full advantage of the features they offer, especially the ability to create multicolour layouts and to perform photographic manipulation. Roughly translated, this means that a 32-bit computer, 2-8 megabytes of RAM, a laser printer, and a high-capacity hard disk are needed. Low-end systems typically allow users to combine a variety of graphical fonts onto a page, use prestored art images (called clip art) on pages, and draw line and boxes to highlight text or art. Fonts and clip art software packages can also be purchased separately from third-party vendors to extend the options offered by the original package's vendor.

At high end of the market, numerous additional options are possible. For instance, the user can digitize complex art images such as photos, which are composed of halftones that look good only at high levels of resolution. Also, a much greater variety of options is available with fonts and clip art. For example, both fonts and clip art can be scaled by users to various sizes; these can be created from scratch or edited, as well. Additionally, most high-end packages are designed to interface both laser printers and professional typesetting equipment.

Because graphics require high speeds and large memories, the greater the user's desktop publishing needs become, the more power is required of the desktop publishing system. A relatively unsophisticated desktop publishing application might require a system unit with at least 1MB of RAM and 20MB of hard disk storage; two or four times this amount is often needed for sophisticated applications. Sophisticated applications usually demand a laser printer that works at 300 dpi (dots per inch) resolution or better and can produce colour separations, a full-page or two-page WYSIWYG

(What You See Is What You Get) graphics monitor (that is, one that allows you to see one or two entire 8½ × 11" pages), an image scanner that can both digitize images and recognise text, a digitizing tablet, software to interface with professional typesetting equipment, and several other specialized hardware and software elements.

The complexities of desktop publishing are often ignored or forgotten as users become seduced by the visually enticing images they see in the vendor literature. The extensive hardware and software requirements needed for truly dazzling desktop publishing applications can break some offices' budgets.

***Figure 14.3.** An example of desktop publishing output. Full-featured desktop publishing software packages enable users to create, edit, scale, and combine art, text, and photographic elements on the same page.*

Challenges and Opportunities

To the MIS organisation, beyond the technology of desktop publishing lie many management-oriented challenges and several opportunities. Educating users and establishing standards for use are among these challenges. One of the biggest dangers of implementing desktop systems today is that some users carry DTP to its extreme constantly reworking a document when they could be more effective doing other work. Another problem is the lack of general knowledge about desktop publishing—an application area that just started in the early 1980s.

Regarding opportunities, DTP systems are especially useful to the in-house publishing functions found in many organisations. Because numerous companies have acquired desktop publishing systems, DTP has completely restructured at least one entire industry—the typesetting business.

Desktop publishing also creates an opportunity to differentiate a product. For instance, a factor driving the spread of DTP is a change in people's aesthetic perceptions. A marketing managers in the medical field says, "I can type things up and put it on stationery, and it can be scientifically valid… and people don't look at it." But, claims the manager, when he produces the same document with desktop publishing tools, people will both read it and—because the two-column output looks like something form a scientific journal—give it greater credence.

Some of the leading desktop publishing systems are Aldus Corporation's PageMaker, Xerox Corporation's Ventura Publisher, Quark, Inc.'s Quark Express, Digital Research, Inc.'s, GEM Desktop Publisher, and Laser Friendly, Inc.'s The Office Publisher. Groupware versions of such systems are also used.

Reprographics (Reproducing Multiple Copies)

Reprographics is the process of reproducing multiple copies of a document. Office personnel are usually responsible for making more than one copy of a report, letter, and other documents. When documents are widely distributed either internally or externally, reprographics often includes collating, folding, bindings, and related tasks.

Multiple copies may be made in numerous ways. When only as few copies are needed, it may be cost effective to print out multiple copies using the printer(s) attached to the computer. Most of the time, however, a photocopier is used.

The most sophisticated type of copy equipment currently available is the **intelligent copier system** (or electronic printing system). As Figure 14.4 shows, documents created on microcomputer workstations or display terminals may be electrically transmitted to the intelligent copier. Previously created and stored documents may also be sent directly to the copier so that multiple copies can be made. Additionally, intelligent copiers can transmit documents to other systems. They are often used to merge the stored image of a business form with data supplied by workers at a microcomputer, display terminal, or another computer system—and then they electronically distribute the completed forms; of course, the completed forms can also be printed.

Image-Processing Systems

As mentioned in already, image processing and document management systems are one of the fastest growing types of office systems. **Image-processing systems** (sometimes called electronic image management systems) allow users to electronically capture, store, process, and retrieve images of documents. These documents may include text, numeric data, handwriting, graphics, and photographs; in some cases, these may all be part of the same document. According to Janet Mann, the image-processing segment of the information industry should grow from $1.3 billion in 1990 to $ 8.9 billion in 1995. Most industry experts agree with Mann's assertion that "document imaging technology promises to reduce the problem of paper overload by providing information management with more efficient use of physical storage space and increased productivity." Of course, electronic data interchange (EDI) systems—discussed in earlier chapters—can also reduce an organisation's paper document-handling requirements.

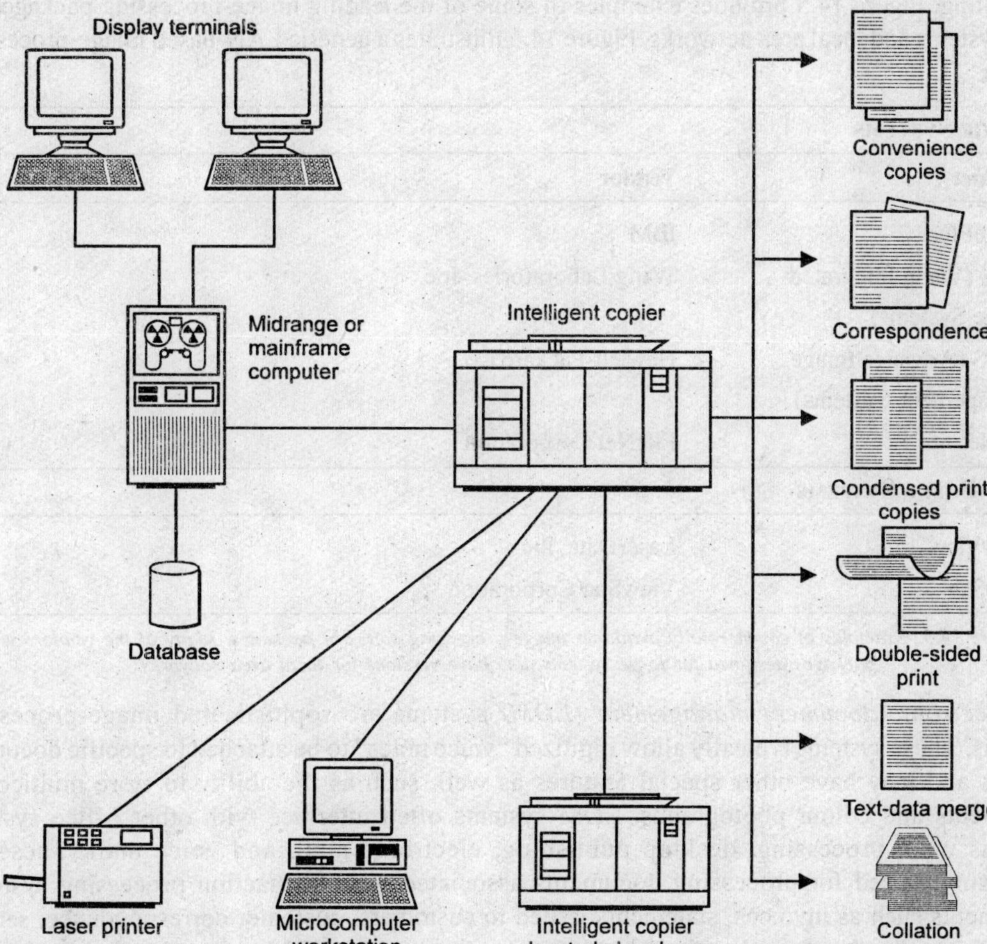

Figure 14.4. *An example of an intelligent copier system. Over time, the capabilities of intelligent copier systems have increased. Most can communicate with other intelligent copiers, computers, and computer networks within the organisation.*

Optical scanning technologies—often called document scanners–are typically used in these systems to input documents. In the past images were often stored on microfilm or microfiche, but microfilm-based systems are rapidly being replaced by optical disk storage technologies. Workstations outfitted with special image-processing circuit broads and software can retrieve document images that were input and stored. Laser printers are rapidly becoming the most commonly used output devices associated with image-processing systems.

As noted in already, image database management systems are becoming more versatile as they are refined. LAN-based image-processing systems are also becoming more common. These often include several servers, each dedicated to a specific function such as database management, scanning, or painting. Figure 14.5 provides examples of some of the leading image-processing packages for large systems and local area networks. Figure 14.6 illustrates a generic LAN-based image-processing system.

Large Systems	
Product	**Vendor**
ImagePlus	IBM
WIIS (Wang Integrated Image Systems)	Wang Laboratories, Inc.
AIMS (Advance Image Management Systems)	Hewlett-Packard Co.
FileNet	FileNet Corporation
LAN-Based Systems	
LaserView	LaserData, Inc.
ViewStar	ViewStar Corporation

Figure 14.5. *Examples of commercially available image-processing software packages. Many of the vendors with packages designed for large systems also have versions for local area networks.*

Electronic document management (EDM) systems are sophisticated image-processing systems. These systems typically allow digitized "voice notes" to be attached to specific document images and may have other special features as well, such as the ability to store multicolour documents and colour photographs. EDM systems often interface with other office systems such as word processing, desktop publishing, electronic mail, and voice mail. These are increasingly used for processing documents associated with transaction processing systems. Documents such as invoices, statements issued to customers, customer correspondence, service requests, application forms, and contracts can be captured by EDM systems and electronically distributes and output whenever needed. Image processing and EDM systems have improved the productivity of office workers, resulting in some significant cost savings. As Jackyln Popuil notes, "Electronic document image-processing systems are becoming more productive, providing faster access at lower costs and enabling managers to make decisions more quickly." Also, these systems have the potential to greatly improve customer service.

Multimedia systems often integrate image processing with text, audio, and video processing technologies. These systems allow users to digitally capture, edit, and combine photograph, video, audio, text, and numeric data in order to develop multimedia presentations, multimedia databases, or interactive video sessions. Interactive video sessions allow users to see and hear prepared materials interactively, either in a prearranged order or randomly. These are often used for training purposes.

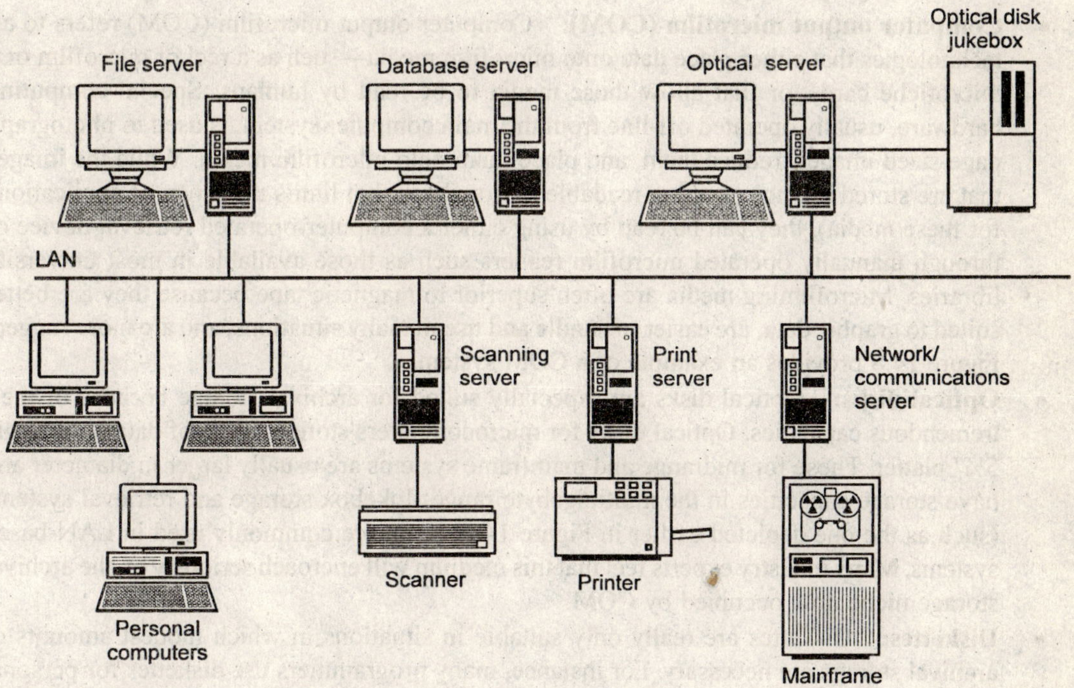

Figure 14.6. A generic LAN-based image-processing system. Most of these systems are found in client/server local area networks with dedicated servers for print, magnetic, and optical storage. Optical storage jukebox systems that hold multiple optical disk are becoming more common.

Archival Storage

As mentioned earlier, one of the key functions in an office is storage. The image-processing and electronic data management systems just discussed are among the hottest technologies for handling business documents. While these are used in an increasing number of organisations, several other traditional storage technologies are still widely used and will exist in some form for many years. For example, numerous organisations, text and numeric data are stored on-line, on fast-access magnetic disk units. In addition, offices usually need archival storage to maintain historical data. To save the expense associated with storage space, handling, and paper costs, archival data was traditionally placed onto various media and stored off-line. Such media are also particularly useful to firms needing to keep large files available that do not have to be updated, or to firms that need to process large amounts of data but find on-line access too expensive.

Four common technologies used to store archival materials are magnetic tape, computer output microfilm (COM), optical disks, and diskettes (see Figure 14.7). These media are also useful for storing backup copies of documents, programs, or data.

- **Magnetic tape:** Magnetic tape is one of the oldest and most common ways of storing data for archival purposes. Tape is inexpensive, compact, and can store rather large text files.
- **Computer output microfilm (COM):** Computer output microfilm (COM) refers to all technologies that either place data onto microfilm media—such as a reel of microfilm or a microfiche card—or that allow those media to be read by humans. Special computing hardware, usually operated off-line from the main computer system, is used to photograph page-sized images, reduce them, and place them onto microfilm media. While the images that are stored are not machine-readable (a drawback that limits the range of applications for these media), they can be read by using either a computer-operated retrieval device or through manually operated microfilm readers such as those available in most university libraries. Microfilming media are often superior to magnetic tape because they are better suited to graphic data, are easier to handle and use in many situations, and are more rugged. Figure 14.8 provides an example of a COM system.
- **Optical disks:** Optical disks are especially suited for archival storage because of their tremendous capacities. Optical disks for microcomputers store 650MB of data on a single 5¼" platter. Those for midrange and mainframe systems are usually larger in diameter and have storage capacities in the multigigabyte range. Jukebox storage and retrieval systems (such as the one depicted earlier in Figure 14.6) are more commonly used in LAN-based systems. Many industry experts feel that this medium will encroach seriously on the archival storage niche now occupied by COM.
- **Diskettes:** Diskettes are really only suitable in situations in which modest amounts of archival storage are necessary. For instance, many programmers use diskettes for personal archival purposes so that backup copies of data or programs can be quickly retrieved. Office personnel can also use diskettes to store electronic copies of important documents. As noted already on storage media and devices, RAID (redundant arrays of inexpensive disks) are now used more widely. RAID may represent a more effective and more secure approach for storing text and data in offices that have increasing archival storage requirements.

Message-Handling Systems

As previously illustrated in Figure 14.1, several important OIS applications can be categorised as message-handling systems. These include facsimile systems, electronic mail, and voice mail systems.

Facsimile (Fax)

Facsimile (fax) systems are commonplace in most organisations today. Fax machines enable hardcopy images of documents, graphics, and photographs to be transmitted from one location to another, either locally or around the world. Both the sending and receiving stations must have faxing equipment for this to happen; however, a relatively stable fax standard now exist that allows virtually any two fax machines to communicate with each other.

Fax machines are basically electronic document delivery systems that combine scanner and modem technology. An optical scanner reduces text or graphic images recorded on paper to electrical impulses that can be transmitted over telephone (or other) networks. Fax machines may be either analog or digital; the digital machines are typically faster. Sending faxed documents normally requires a relatively fast fax modem, about 9600 bps or greater. But even at these speeds, the clarity of some faxed documents may not measure up to the original or even to a photocopy of it. However, the quality of facsimile output is steadily increasing and the latest generation of fax machines utilise laser technology for both higher resolution and higher speed output.

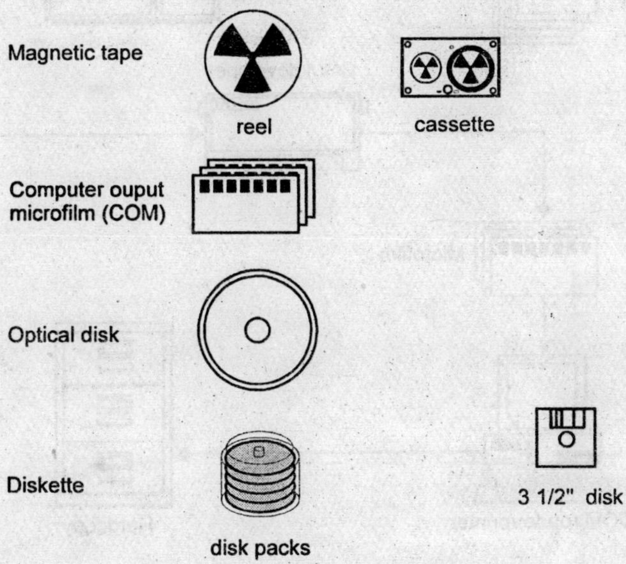

Figure 14.7. *Commonly used archival storage media. The media listed here are useful for both archival purposes and many other applications.*

Today, equipping microcomputer with fax boards, thus empowering them to communicate directly from RAM to a fax unit at another location, is becoming popular. Fax boards and their related software allow users to send documents stored on disk to other facsimile devices and to receive, store, display, and edit fax images transmitted from other fax devices. However, because the output received is a bit-mapped pattern, editing fax images is often difficult. Fax boards typically enable users to print out the documents that are received on dot-matrix or laser printers, which usually results in a better quality of output. However, as noted earlier, many of the new stand-alone fax systems can produce output of comparable quality.

Facsimile technologies often help organisations save money. Usually, the telephone line costs associated with sending a few pages of text are substantially less than sending those same pages by overnight mail. Many sophisticated fax systems can be programmed to send documents at times when phone rates are lowest; for example, between midnight and 6 A.M. Facsimile devices can also be merged with teleconferencing systems to enable participants to share hardcopy materials.

Electronic Mail (E-mail)

Electronic mail (E-mail). Refers to technologies that send messages or documents for one electronic workstation to another. E-mail is the second most commonplace office systems application area (behind word processing).

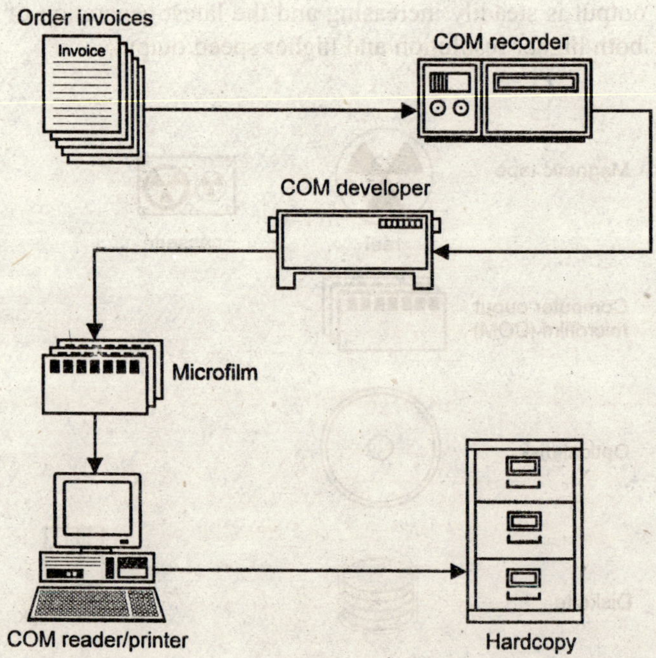

Figure 14.8. *An example of a computer output microfilm (COM) system. COM systems take images and store them on microfilm, which can greatly reduce an organisation's paper management requirements.*

A relatively common form of electronic mail in many organisations is the **electronic mailbox**. This type of system can be implemented in several ways. For instance, employees within a large organisation may have electronic mailboxes that are managed by a mainframe, minicomputer, or local area network. When these employees use a workstation (which may be at their desks), they can call up their personal file—or mailbox—on the E-mail system to see if they have any messages. Or they can send a message to place in someone else's mailbox, as Figure 14.9 illustrates. These types of E-mail systems are typically standard components in integrated office packages, which will be discussed later in the chapter. A second way of implementing a mailbox system is through an outside vendor of such services; CompuServe and GE Information Services are just two of the information utilities that provide E-mail services to subscribers (see Figure 14.10). Here, all the user needs is a microcomputer, a modem, communications software, and an E-mailbox on the vendor's system. E-mailboxes may also be obtained on networks that numerous organisations can access. Bitnet and Internet, for example, provide global E-mail utilities.

```
FRI 15 JAN 1993 8:30 A.M.

You have 3 memos awaiting
You have 8 ticklers
Master menu 1 Calendar
selections: 2 Memo processing
            3 Document processing
            4 Utilities
            5 Exit to system

Enter choice: 2
```

(a) Selecting a choice from the main E-mail menu. Here, the memo processing routine (submenu) is picked.

```
MEMO PROCESSING

Memo processing  1 Create/edit
selections:      2 Read
                 3 File/memo
                   manager
                 4 Search
                 5 Directory
                 6 Exit to
                   master menu

Enter choice: 1
```

(b) Selecting a submenu choice. Here, the user decides to create a new menu or edit an existing one.

```
MEMO CREATION/EDIT ROUTINE

To:          Mark Smith,
Copy to:     T.J. Hall
             Ellen Finkel
Subject:     Meeting of 2/3

The meeting is canceled.

Option desired? (Y/N)  : Y
```

(c) Creating the memo and naming recipients

```
MEMO OPTIONS

Memo Options    1 Edit
selections:     2 Sead
                3 Delete
                4 Store
                5 Print
Enter choice: 2

*** memo sent ***
```

(d) Sending the memo.

Figure 14.9. *Using the electronic mailbox system. Employees in an increasing number of organisations have access to electronic mailboxes that are managed by a mainframe, midrange computer, local area network, or an external information service such as CompuServe. Mailbox systems are often included as standard components in integrated office packages. In the panels illustrated above, user input is highlighted.*

Most types of E-mail can be implemented through non-integrated workstations that can be linked with mainframes through communications software; integrated local interoffice networks and local area networks; or private- or common carrier-based wide area networks. These networking alternatives were covered. Wherever several devices can communicate with each other, the potential for E-mail exists.

A high degree of incompatibility usually exists among competing E-mail systems. Where dissimilar and public E-mail systems interface, some type of gateway is generally necessary to enable them to communicate. The International Standards Organisation (ISO) promotes the X.400 and X.500 standards for E-mail systems. If vendors adhere to these standards, much of the existing incompatibility problems may be resolved. Managers considering adopting a new (or upgrading an existing) E-mail system should probably limit their choices to those that are consistent with the X.400 and X.500 standards.

What the Heck is Groupware?

Groupware is software designed to help members of a committee, project team, or work group coordinate work on common tasks. A wide range of groupware products is available.

- Information-sharing products help work group members exchange data through messaging and database functions. Products such as Notes from Lotus Development Corporation, Topic from Verity, Inc., and Cooperation from NCR Corporation fall into this category.
- Meetingwear or electronic meeting/conferencing products allow two or more users to simultaneously engage in electronic communication via their personal computers. Representative products are Aspects from Group Technologies, Inc., Instant Update from On Technology, Inc., and VisionQuest from Collaborative Technologies Corporation.
- Scheduling products make it easier to arrange meetings or coordinate conferences for a work group. Network Scheduler from Powerscore and Action Plus from Action Plus software are popular.
- Networked office automation software suites such as NewWave Office from Hewlett-Packard and WordPerfect Office from WordPerfect Corporation make it possible for workers to perform various tasks in sync with one another.
- E-mail packages with additional features such as project and task management are also classified as groupware. Higgins from Enable Software, Inc. is one of the best-known products.
- Impressive productivity gains reported by some organisations has fueled interest in groupware; dramatic utilisation increases are expected during the 1990s.

Adapted from LaPlante (1992).

Voice Mail

A **voice mail** system enables a regular voice message, sent over the phone, to be digitally stored at the receiving location. When accessed, the messages is converted back into voice form. These are used by an increasing number of organization and often employ software that runs on the organisation's PBX equipment, rather than on the organisation's host computers.

Voice mail systems require a computer, disk storage, and voice mailboxes that are similar to E-mailboxes. The sending and receiving instrument, however, is the telephone. Like E-mail messages, digitized voice messages can be played back, sent along to one or more other members of the organisation, saved, or deleted. As it is sent along from person to person, a message can usually be voiced-annotated by anyone handling it.

With voice mail, one person calls a voice mailbox rather than a personal phone number. In stand-alone voice systems, the message is simply stored, awaiting pick-up by the person receiving the message; in integrated voice mail/PBX, the message receiver has the option of picking up the phone. People can usually access their voice mailboxes from any telephone (both inside and outside the organisation). The telephone keypad is used to listen to messages in the mailbox, save them, or send them to others. This permits field representatives or travelling executives to maintain contact with the home office and to keep up with their messages. Salespeople can use these systems to enter orders over the telephone from the customer's office. Some universities are using voice mail systems to enable students to register for classes. All of these applications can provide organisations with a competitive edge.

E-MAIL SYSTEMS

Product	Vendor
AT&T Mail	AT&T
Tymnet, OnTyme	British Telecom
InfoPlex	CompuServe
+Mail	Dialcom
Quick-Comm, GEnie	GE Information Services
MCI Mail	MCI
Telemail	Telenet/US Sprint
EasyLink	Western Union

***Figure 14.10.** Examples of publicly available electronic mail systems.*

Teleconferencing Applications

In addition to message-handling applications such as electronic mail and voice mail, an increasing number of organisations provide their employees with other electronic means of communications—especially when they must communicate over long distances. In this section, we will focus on three such systems: teleconferencing, in-house television, and telecommuting.

Types of Teleconferencing

The term **teleconferencing** refers to electronic meetings that involve people who are at physically different sites. Telecommunication technology systems allow meeting participants to interact with one another without travelling to the same location. Three major types of teleconferencing exist: video teleconferencing, computer conferencing, and audio teleconferencing. Wide area group decision support systems (GDSS), such as those described already, often involve some type of teleconferencing.

With video teleconferencing, participants can both see and hear each other. These systems combine voice and television images that allow two or more groups to interact with one another.

Video teleconferencing was first widely demonstrated in 1964 at New York's World Fair when AT&T introduced its picturephone, which dazzled onlookers and gave them a glimpse of what is now fairly common. In the early 1990s, approximately 10-15% of the Fortune 500 companies routinely use video teleconferencing for business meetings. According to Carolyn Brown, in 1990, video teleconferencing was approximately a $60 million market and an application area that should increase at an annual rate of 33.4 percent over the next several years.

Generally, video teleconferencing participants gather in relatively expensive, specially equipped rooms that can handle the complexities of simultaneous video and audio transmission (see Figure 14.11). Anyone who watches the TV program "Nightline," hosted by Ted Koppel, has probably seen an example of video teleconferencing. For instance, resident experts from Miami, New York, and Los Angeles might teleconference to discuss a controversial issue with the host and with each other. During Operation Desert Storm in 1991, all the major television networks—and even the military—widely used teleconferencing to overcome the coordination challenges presented by distance and time zone differences.

In business applications, video teleconferencing can be particularly effective because interaction between people is usually different when they can see each other. A few large hotel chains have invested in video teleconferencing facilities in order to woo their corporate clientele. AT&T, U.S. Sprint, and MCI all have videoconferencing service divisions to assist organisations in the implementation and operation of video teleconferencing systems; many other vendors also provide video conferencing services. Advances in teleconferencing technologies and the advent of ISDN should dramatically increase the use of video teleconferencing.

Computer conferencing involves computer terminals and E-mail or electronic bulletin boards. Conference participants broadcast messages to each other (or post them on a common electronic bulletin board); participants do not have to be present to receive messages. The messages are keyed in and then displayed on computer screens; hence, the "conversations" that take place are electronic. Computer conferencing can be particularly useful in project management and job-shop manufacturing situations. As critical pieces of a project are finished—possibly at numerous geographically dispersed sites—this information is recorded in the public electronic mailboxes of each project manager so that he or she has a real-time update on both costs and progress. The project managers can also communicate with each other through the mailboxes regarding any unusual events or any important matters. Many vendors offer specialized computer conferencing software that coordinates and manages these electronic meetings.

Audio teleconferencing (conference phone calls) enables participants to hear each other only. A speakerphone may be used at one or more locations to allow groups to participate in the meeting. When portions of this book were in preparation, for instance, the publisher arranged an audio teleconference among marketing personnel, the authors, and several specialists in the MIS field. Although the most limited of the teleconferencing procedures discussed here, audio teleconferencing is by far the least expensive. According to Carolyn Brown, about 60 percent of the Fortune 500 companies use audio conferencing every day.

Facsimile devices and other specialized equipment are often used in conjunction with electronic meetings. For example, *electronic blackboards* are now more widely used; these allow participant at one location to write on an "electronic chalkboard" and then transmit the written images to television screens, computer screens, or other electronic blackboards at other locations.

Teleconferencing can save substantial travelling costs and time. Its disadvantages are that it can be expensive and, sometimes, it really cannot be substituted for meeting physically with people—especially in conflict-resolution matters. For instance, the most effective way to show an angry client that the company still cares might be to sacrifice a salesperson's time, have someone physically get onto a plane, and meet with the client at his or her site. A variety of federal, state, and local laws affect the recording of teleconferences. For example, participants must have proven prior knowledge that it is occurring and the room must clearly indicate that a recording is taking place.

In-house Television

One of the newest tools in business, and one that is a beneficial office systems applications, is **in-house television**. With this technology, an organisation invests in a studio, a period of time on a satellite transmitter for broadcasting. Company sites—or even customers—are given satellite dishes so that they can view the broadcast. Scramblers inhibit competitors from gaining access to the transmission.

The list of companies now using in-house television is impressive. Ford, Merrill Lynch, IBM, Eastman Kodak, JC Penney, and Federal Express are among the current users. Many others are considering it. The following list describes the variety of applications for which in-house TV is currently being used:

- Previously, buyers at local JC Penney outlets had to travel to headquarters to select merchandise for their stores. Now, they can use a TV to tune into a JC Penney channel, whose programming resembles a home shopping network that feature JC Penney goods exclusively. The system not only cuts travel costs, but it provides a longer lead time for placing orders and enables buyers to take advantage of any late-breaking consumer trends.
- During the October 1987 stock market crash, Merrill Lynch used in-house TV to broadcast daily briefings from top executives and to field calls from concerned employes. The televised events, which also featured the chairman of the firm, helped to bring some order to the fear and confusion resulting from the chaos.
- Ever want to see yourself on TV? Domino's Pizzas thinks many of its employees do and it is currently using in-house TV as an incentive tool. Any Domino's outlets with great ideas that other outlets should use will get a visit from the company's video team—which stages an on-site show.

In-house TV is relatively new and its creative uses are just beginning. As demonstrated here, it has already shown potential in the areas of competitive advantage, cost cutting, and employee motivation.

Telecommuting

With **telecommuting**, people use communications technology to work at home or in a remote city—and to avoid the usual physical commute to work. Using a remote communications terminal or a microcomputer workstation, for instance, a programmer can do his or her work at home instead of at the office. Or, using the same types of technologies, a Chicago-based lawyer who works alone most of the time might actually live in Sun Valley, Idaho.

Like other system applications, telecommuting has its pros and cons. Advantage include eliminating the time spent travelling and having to deal directly with office politics, which can be very stressful.

Organisations can also bypass the expense of establishing physical office space. And they can often retain a valuable employee that they might otherwise lose. According to Meghan O'Leary, advocates of telecommuting claim that it offers "concrete proof of productivity gains, cost savings, improved morale, and more effective work group communication." However, skeptics argue that there is no substitute for dealing with people face to face, since office politics often determine power structures within the organisation. Also, the organisation loses some control over an employee who telecommutes. In addition, many jobs are not conducive to telecommuting and some employees just do not have the self-discipline required to work productively on their own. Both the positive and negative aspects of telecommuting should be considered carefully by organisations when deciding whether to use this employment option.

Office Support Systems

So far in this chapter, we have discussed some of the major technologies for managing documents, exchanging messages, and holding meetings. In addition to these systems, numerous other application help to coordinates and manage the activities of work groups. These are collectively called office support systems and include groupware and desktop organisers.

Groupware

Groupware consists of software packages designed to support the collaborative efforts of a group of coworkers. Such packages often provide integrated support for many of the typical activities of work groups previously identified, including:

- Word-processing services, including the ability for multiple user to work concurrently on the same document.
- Electronic mail services.
- Voice mail services.
- Computer conferencing services.
- Fax services.
- Access to on-line databases and telecommunication services such as CompuServe.

Groupware packages may also provide group members with other services, such as:

- Project management services.
- Shared "to-do" list and phone number lists.
- Group calendaring and scheduling services.
- Bulletin board services.
- Personal desktop organisers (discussed in the nest section).

Bulletin board services enable users to post information of interest to the other members in the work group. Project management services help ensure that the various activities needed to complete a group project are properly coordinated. Group calendaring and shared to-do lists are similar to the individual calendaring and to-do list modules found in many desktop organisers.

Desktop Organisers

Like electronic mail systems, desktop organisers are generally found at a user's workstation or microcomputer. **Desktop organisers** are software packages that provide users with the electronic equivalent of the organising and coordinating tools found on a typical office desk.

The features in a desktop organisers are often invoked through windows that pop up on the screen when the user presses a certain combination or sequence of keys while working with another application package. For instance, the desktop organisers could be configures such that when the ALT and F4 keys are simultaneously depressed, an electronic calendar may pop up on the screen. If, instead, the ALT and F2 keys are simultaneously depressed, an electronic notepad may appear. After the user works with the summoned feature, another combination of keys returns the user to the exact place in the application program where he or she was. Of course, in the popular operating environments that use graphical user interface (such as Windows, OS/2, and Macintosh Systems 7), a mouse can often point and click on the icon for the desired organisers functions.

Desktop organisers vary regarding the types of features they offer, but many of them offer the following tools, each of which is called a *desk accessory*:

- **Calendar:** Electronic calendars often consist of a series of routines that enable users to make up appointment calendars by the day, week, month, or year. Sophisticated calendar routines on multiuser systems allow users to establish access privileges that enables other authorised users to see their schedules—and, perhaps schedule appointments into certain time slots. *To-do list* generation and modification are coordinated with the calendaring routines in many desktop organisers.
- **Card file:** With a card file feature, the user establishes a type of electronic Rolodex system. For instance, a list of client phone numbers and addresses can be stored. Some packages also provide automatic dialing features so that after a name is selected from this type of file, the modem can dial the number on the record.
- **Notepad:** The notepad feature facilitates the writing of notes as soon as ideas occur to the operator when using an application program. Some packages also allow these notes to be transported back to the resident application program.
- **Clock:** The clock feature enables the operator to keep track of the date and time. In some cases, an alarm feature work in conjunction with the clock, activating an audio unit at the workstation when an important event is about to happen.
- **Calculator:** A calculator facility enables calculations to be done during the course of an application program. Some packages allow these computational result to be imported into the resident application program.

On mainframes and minicomputer systems, desk accessories are often an adjunct feature found in an integrated office system (discussed later in the chapter). On microcomputer systems, desk accessories are usually sold as separate packages (such as Borland International's SideKick—one of the best known and most widely used desktop organiser packages) or they are bundled as an additional feature in a window-based operating environment (such as Windows, OS/2, and Macintosh System 7). Figures 14.11 and 14.12 list many popular groupware and desktop organiser packages for microcomputer.

GROUPWARE	
Product	**Vendor**
BrainStorm	Mustang Software, Inc.
Copy Flow	North Atlantic Publishing System
Document Management Systems	Odesta Corporation
For Comment	Borderbund Software
Lotus Notes	Lotus Development Corporation
Notepad	Notepad Systems International, Inc.
Office Works	Data Access Corporation
Participate	Evertures
Rhapsody	AT&T
Synchrony	Finalsoft Corporation

Figure 14.11. Examples of groupware software packages.

DESKTOP ORGANISERS	
Product	**Vendor**
Action Tracker	Information Research Corporation
Home Base	Brown Bag Software
HQ	TEK Microsystems, Inc.
In Control	Attain Corporation
Integrated Work Station	XYZT Computer Dimension Inc.
Metro	Lotus Development Corporation
MORE	Symantec Corporation
Partner-PC	Time Works Inc.
PC-Desk	Software Studios Inc.
PC-Deskteam	Alternative Decision Software
PolyWindows Desk Plus	PolyTron Corporation
Pop-Up DeskSet Plus	Popular Programs, Inc.
Primetime Personal	Primetime Software, Inc.
SideKick	Borland Corporation
WordPerfect Library	WordPerfect Corporation

Figure 14.12. Examples of desktop organiser software packages.

Other Office Support Applications

As mentioned earlier, a significant overlap often exist between the DSS and office systems areas. Therefore, a number of the DSS tools that were covered in including database management systems, spreadsheets, modelling packages, and graphics generators—are also appropriate for office environments. These technologies can help users to analyse data, retrieve information, and prepare graphs and charts for presentations. Group decisions support systems—(GDSS)—also discussed, are increasingly used in office settings.

Another technology that is frequently used in office environments is computer-aided design (CAD). CAD refers to computer systems that enable designers to work with a display-screen interface and specifications database to design various products. CAD is widely found in engineering environments, but is also used in many office settings; for instance, in an architect's office, where floor plans and building designs can be summoned to the display screen and modified.

Implementing Office Systems

In this section, we will look at some of the ways in which office system applications were successfully implemented in several industries. We will also consider a few of the problems encountered in some unsuccessful OA application, plus several general concerns about OA.

Example of Office Systems Applications

Many success stories are linked to the implementation of office systems. Here are a few of them:

- The U.S. Forest Service (USFS) performed before and after studies of its efforts to automate and electronically link it 900 offices. The post implementation studies reveal that environmental impact statements now take 39 percent less time to prepare and timber contracts take 27 percent less time. As a result of these savings, the USFS trimmed 30 percent off the time it takes to do work and cut its staff by 25 percent.
- At Beneficial Corporation, a large financial services company, a video terminal-based electronic mail system connects 1,200 managers, including the firm's CEO. According to William Bowen, the CEO claims: "I can communicate with or yank figures from any manager, anywhere. We can make a decision now in a quarter to half the time it took before." Eventually, he predicts, the system will change Beneficial's management structure, enabling it to operate with fewer levels of management.
- For several months, an account representative for Metropolitan Life Insurance Company called without results on the pension fund manager of a Chicago firm, attempting to sell him an annuity package that allows client to tailor investments in a portfolio of six different funds. Then one day, the account representative brought in laptop computer and a spreadsheet package. He and the client ran a few what-if analyses. What would happen to the client's total return, for example, if one portfolio were tried instead of another? Thus the account representative answered questions immediately, and a few weeks later, successfully closed the sell.
- In 1986, Hewlett-Packard Company (HP) began a pilot project that equipped 135 of its 1,700 sales representatives with laptop computers to assist them with various time-

consuming tasks. Among these tasks were tracking the status of orders on mainframes and retrieving account histories. Six months after the project began, HO found that the laptops reduced time spent at meetings by 46 percent and decreased travel time to customers by 13 percent. Consequently, time spent with customers increased 27 percent and sales rose 10 percent. Claimed one HP executive, "We changed the way people communicate with their boss and peers." HP is currently equipping all of its sales representatives with laptops and expects benefits to exceed costs by five to ten times in just the first year of implementation.

- At Ace Hardware, outside Chicago, in-house desktop publishing has become the most cost-effective solution to continuing production of Ace's 4,000-page, 45,000-items catalog for its 13 regional warehouses. Each of these catalogs is tailored to specific regions (it is difficult to sell snow shovels in Miami, for instance). With the new system, claims Ace's office systems manager, "One operator in half a day of keyboarding does what dozens of operators and clerk used to do full time." The system saves Ace hundreds of thousands of dollars each year. As an additional benefit, the systems created some new marketing tools that are used for competitive advantage; for instance, a catalog without prices, which dealers can distribute to their commercial and industrial accounts.

Challenges and Issues

As with applications in the DSS area, many offices systems applications are difficult to justify to management by traditional cost-benefit formulas that require reducing benefits to quantifiable terms. A study at Harvard Business School of 40 corporations showed, in fact, that buyers often do not even bother calculating the bottom-line effects of many low-cost end-user systems. Claims James L. McKenney of Harvard, "Most of them did no cost justification at all."

Because little cost justification or analysis made on many office information systems—either before or after purchase—some people wonder if OA really pays off. Although few people question that word processors can produce a finished document from a handwritten draft mush more quickly than a conventional typewriters can, many critics claim that the ease of revision afforded by word processing is often used to overperfect documents. Sometimes, so many draft of a document are churned out by computer-driven printers that the concept of a paperless office seems unattainable. Similarly, electronic mail systems are criticized as a contributing to both a preponderance of trivial messages and an overbroadcasting of messages in general (that is, sending messages to everyone on a list when only a few people really need to see them), thereby using E-mail ineffectively.

Using Information Technology to Tame the Health Care Cost Monster

If a serious illness or injury puts you in the hospital, you will probably feel that no price is too high for the highly skilled doctors and high-tech medical equipment needed to help you recover. However, the medical bills must eventually be paid and businesses, employees, and insurance companies have covered most of them. During the last two decades, annual heath care cost increases have exceeded the inflation rate—in most years by more than a 2 to 1 ratio. Understandably, bringing these rising costs under control is a widespread concern.

Information technology is being used by doctors and hospitals in an increasing number of ways to provide high-quality patient care. However, industry experts feel that billi ons of dollars could be saved each year if hospitals and doctors were also using information technology for the following:

- Electronic management and transmission of patient data—including systems that alert physicians to possible allergic reactions that they might have overlooked.
- Electronic submission and processing of health care claims—including systems that spot irregularities in patient bills.

"DURING THE LAST TWO DECADES, ANNUAL HEALTH CARE COST INCREASES HAVE EXCEEDED THE INFLATION RATE . . ."

- Electronic inventory management systems for hospital supplies.
- The use of videoconferencing for both professional training and remote medical consultations—patients would be able to "visit" specialists on-line from specially equipped offices.

These and many more cost-cutting applications are expected in the years ahead—and this is good news for everyone.

Adapted from Margolis and Booker (1992).

Governmental studies report that, even as corporate spending on computers moves upward (almost 40 percent of U.S. capital spending—almost $100 billion per year—now goes to information systems), white collar productivity has not increased since the early 1970s. An economist in a leading U.S. investment bank underscores these statistics: "There has been virtually no relationship between spending on information systems and productivity."

Unfortunately, the statistics—reflecting many other sources of computer spending in addition to OIS—don't recognise that it may take more effort today, or a redistribution of effort into the office area, just to compete. For instance, increases in government-required paperwork and greater monitoring of the external environment by companies are responsible for many office systems-related expenses. Also, most companies will not send out ordinary letters done on inexpensive office equipment when their competitors use state-of-the-art equipment that produces professional-looking correspondence. The statistics on MIS spending and office productivity also don't recognise the learning curve that exists with new office technologies: it clearly takes time to become proficient with them.

Despite these statistics, companies clearly will not drop word-processing systems and spreadsheet packages and return to electric typewriters and adding machines. As *Business Week* reported, "Haphazard application of office technology... produces poor results. But what pacesetters are finding is that if the right technology is used where it can do the most good... and if the organisation's work structure is adjusted to take advantage of the benefits...gains will result." Adds William Bowen in *Fortune,* "The large payoffs come not from increasing the efficiency with which people perform their old jobs, but from changing the way work is done." The bottom line is that the right technology in the right hands will produce favourable—even astonishingly good—results.

The companies that are most productive with their office systems are usually the ones that relate OIS to clear goals; for example, to make sales representatives productive to the point at which they spend 10 percent more time with customers. Typically they are also the companies that are willing to sufficiently invest in training to ensure that users will make the best use of the office system technologies. As one technology consultant adds, "Winners use their systems in a highly focused way, targeting them at a person or a group and a 'business deliverable' such as closing more sales."

INTEGRATED OFFICE PACKAGES

Product	Vendor
All-in-one	Digital Equipment Corporation
Comprehensive Electronic Office (CEO)	Data General Corporation
Enable OA	The Software Group
Office	Wang Laboratories, Inc.
Office Suite	Lotus Development Corporation
Personal Productivity Center	Hewlett-Packard Company
Professional Office System (PROFS)	IBM
Sperrylink	Unisys

Figure 14.13. Examples of integrated office packages.

The Integrated Office

In the previous sections, we covered several applications areas for computer- and communications-related office technologies. A firm can separately acquire the necessary hardware, software, or services required to implement any of these applications—or it can integrated several of them. Two such integration options are to acquire an integrated office software package and to build a completely integrated office.

Integrated Office Packages

Integrated office packages can be purchased or leased from many software vendors. Typically, an integrated office package features word processing, electronic mail, and several desktop organising routines (such as electronic calendaring). Most of these integrated packages are targeted to large, general-purpose computer systems: mainframes and minis; however, LAN-based integrated packages (such as Enable OA) are also available. The advantages and disadvantages of acquiring an integrated office package are virtually the same as those already discussed, for any other type of integrated software packages.

The Office of the Future

An integrated office packages combines a number of OA-related software functions on a general-purpose computer system; an integrated office (sometimes referred to as the **office of the future**) networks together numerous diverse OIS-related hardware and software activities. An example of an integrated office is provided in Figure 14.14. This might entail integrating any of the following sets of heterogeneous elements:

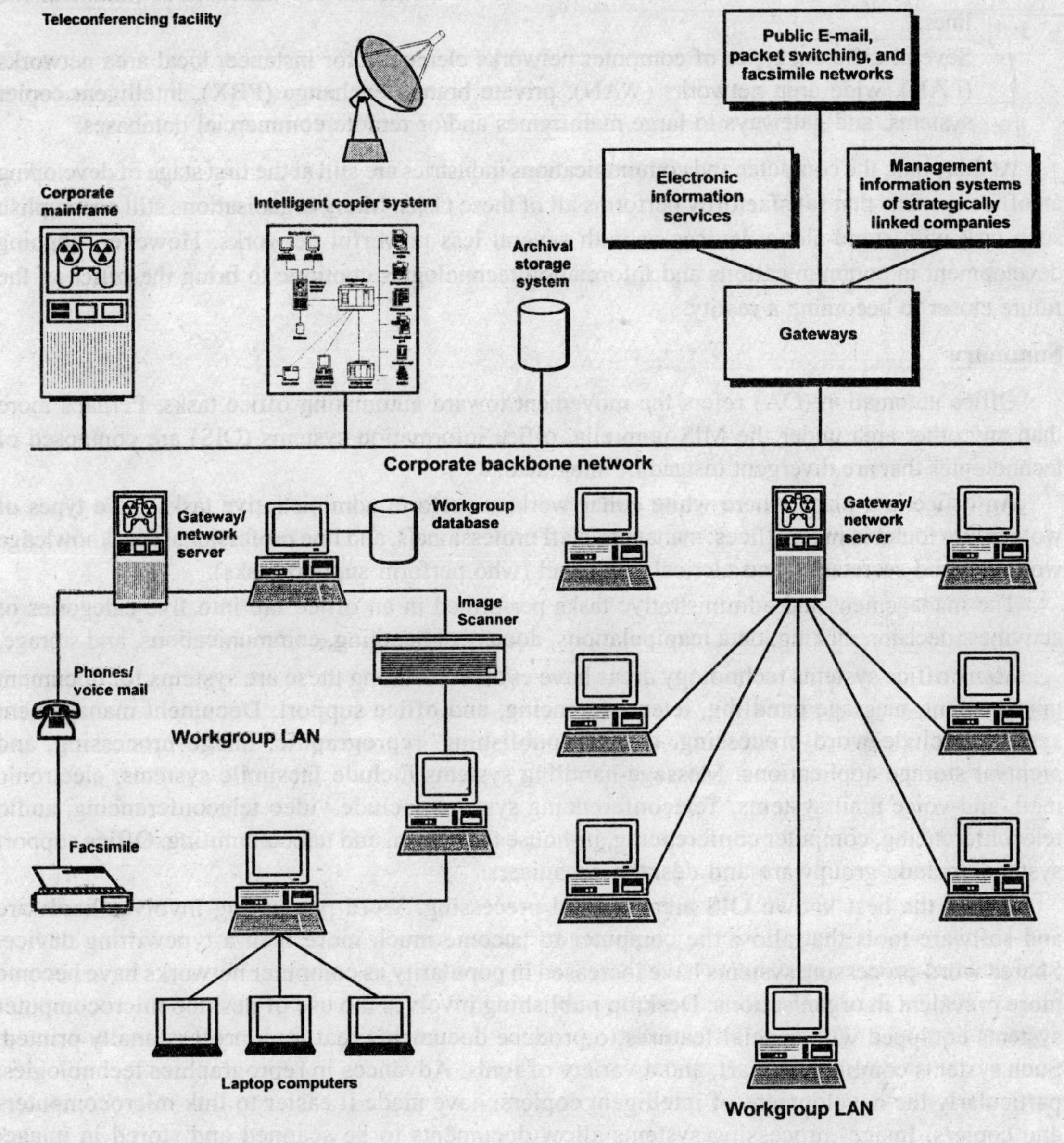

Figure 14.14. An integrated office. The office of the future is designed to integrate numerous separate office functions into a single network.

- The hardware and software products of several vendors.
- Various communications protocols.
- Text, graphics, voice, and video data, some of which will use the same communications lines.
- Several different types of computer networks elements; for instance, local area networks (LAN), wide area networks (WAN), private branch exchange (PBX), intelligent copier systems, and gateways to large mainframes and/or remote commercial databases.

At this point, the computer and communications industries are still at the first stage of developing an office systems that satisfactorily performs all of these tasks. Many organisations still accomplish such task with stand-alone devices or with several less powerful networks. However, ongoing development in communications and information technologies continue to bring the office of the future closer to becoming a reality.

Summary

Office automation (OA) refers the movement toward automating office tasks. Perhaps more than any other area under the MIS umbrella, office information systems (OIS) are composed of technologies that are divergent instead of integrated.

An office is a place where white collar workers perform administrative tasks. Five types of workers are found in most offices: managers, staff professionals, and line professional (the knowledge workers); and secretaries and clerical personnel (who perform support tasks).

The management and administrative tasks performed in an office fall into five categories of activities: decision making, data manipulations, document handling, communications, and storage.

Many office systems technology areas have evolved. Among these are systems for document management, message handling, teleconferencing, and office support. Document management systems include word processing, desktop publishing, reprographic, image processing, and archival storage applications. Message-handling systems include facsimile systems, electronic mail, and voice mail systems. Teleconferencing systems include video teleconferencing, audio teleconferencing, computer conferencing, in-house television, and telecommuting. Office support systems include groupware and desktop organisers.

By far the best known OIS area is word precessing. Word processing involves hardware and software tools that allow the computer to become much more than a typewriting device. Shared word-processing systems have increased in popularity as computer networks have become more prevalent in organisations. Desktop publishing involves the use of desktop microcomputer systems equipped with special features to produce documents that look professionally printed. Such systems combine text, art, and a variety of fonts. Advances in reprographics technologies, particularly the development of intelligent copiers, have made it easier to link microcomputers and copiers. Image- processing systems allow documents to be scanned and stored in image-oriented databases. Most of these systems involve the use of optical storage technologies; LAN-based systems are becoming quite common. Many claims that these are helping organisations make significant strides toward the paperless office. Archival storage refers to off-line storage used for historical and backup materials. Four common technologies for storing archival materials are magnetic tape, computer output microfilm (COM), optical disk, and diskettes.

Facsimile (fax) systems enables hardcopy images to be transmitted between locations. Electronic mail (E-mail) refers to technologies used to send messages or documents from one electronic workstation to another. Electronic mailboxes enables messages to be placed in personal storage areas until they can be accessed by the recipient. Voice mail enables voice messages to be sent via phone lines, digitally stored at the receiving end, and converted back to voice form when accessed.

Another OIS application is teleconferencing: holding meetings among people who are at physically different sites. Three main types of teleconferencing are video, computer, and audio. With in-house television, a relatively new OA area, an organisation invests in a studio, time on a satellite, and a satellite, and satellite transmitter. Restricted broadcast are then prepared by company personnel and shown to employees or authorized outsiders. Telecommuting allows people, through communications technology, to work at home or at remote sites—thus avoiding the physical commute to work. Although this application saves time and money, the organisation loses some control over employees who telecommute.

Groupware packages provide support for work group activities. They provide work groups with a variety of support functions, including the ones summarized earlier. Desktop organisers are software packages that provide users with electronic equivalents of the organising and coordinating tools found on a typical office desk; for example, a calendar, card file, notepad, clock, and calculator.

Office information systems are successfully implemented in many ways. Most problems with implementation stem from a lack of clear goals for office systems. Success, on the other hand, is more likely when the organisation implements new office technologies after a careful strategy is planned.

Individual OA applications can be implemented through integrated office software packages or through a more comprehensive integrated office strategy. The ideal of the later approach is to someday achieve full integration: the office of the future.

Key Terms

- Desktop organiser
- Desktop publishing (DTP)
- Electronic mail (E-mail)
- Electronic mailbox
- Facsimile (fax)
- Image-processing system
- In-house television
- Integrated office package
- Intelligent copier system
- Knowledge worker
- Office
- Office of the future
- Reprographics
- Telecommuting

- Teleconferencing
- Voice mail
- Word processing

Review Questions

1. How are office systems related to end-user computing?
2. What exactly is an office?
3. What distinguishes a knowledge worker from other types of workers?
4. What types of work are performed in offices?
5. What are the characteristics of the major types of office technologies?
6. How have word-processing systems changed over time? What are the characteristics of word-processing packages on the market today?
7. Identify the characteristics of desktop publishing systems.
8. What are the characteristics of reprographic and intelligent copier systems?
9. What are the characteristics and potential advantages of image-processing and document management systems?
10. Identify some media used for archival storage and give an example of a situation in which each type of medium is appropriate.
11. What are the characteristics and potential advantages of facsimile systems?
12. What are the characteristics of electronic mail systems? How are E-mail and voice mail systems different?
13. What is teleconferencing? How do video teleconferencing, audio conferencing, and computer conferencing differ?
14. How do video conferencing, in-house television, and telecommuting differ?
15. What is groupware? What functions may be found in groupware packages?
16. What types of features might be found in a desktop organiser?
17. Describe the office of the future.

Discussion Questions

1. Many people know that various "islands of automation" currently exist within organisations—that is, many different technologies are developing into separate cluster of applications. They also point out that these applications do not communicate with each other. How does OA enter into such a discussion—and, perhaps, even more than other areas under the MIS umbrella (TPS, MRS and DSS)?
2. Does office systems technology seem capable of someday producing the paperless office? Explain why or why not.
3. In what ways, do you feel, will desktop publishing result in both problems and opportunities in the publishing and typesetting industries?
4. Which new technologies do you feel are likely to have the biggest impacts on offices work in the years ahead? Justify your arguments.

CASE STUDY

Global Positioning Systems: Spawning New Commercial Applications

Since 1978, the United States Department of Defense has spent more than $3 billion dollars developing its Navstar Global Positioning System. The systems incorporates a string of 24 satellites orbiting 11,000 miles above the earth. Each of the system's satellites contains four atomic clocks that send out a steady stream of time and location signals. These transmission identify the satellite and is path. Receivers linked to computers in moving vehicles on the ground compare the satellite's signals with their own clocks and use this comparison to calculate the distance between them and the satellite. By locking onto the signals from four satellites, the receiver can determine its location on the earth's surface to within 17.5 yards. By factoring in data from a second stationary receiver on the ground, the location of teh moving vehicle can be calculated within one-half inch.

So what's the big deal? Well, during the Gulf War, soldiers were able to pinpoint their exact positions in an otherwise trackless desert. They did so by taking readings from the satellites, using receivers the size of paperback books. Also, the accuracy of such systems has a wide range of potential business applications that may increase operating efficiency and provide organizations with a competitive edge.

One company that is already taking advantage of the Navstar Global Positioning System is the Minute Man Delivery Service in Gardena, California. It is using the global positioning system (GPS) to dispatch its fleet of 40 trucks more efficiently. In the past, dispatchers had to remember each driver's route and were constantly squawking over two-way radios in order to track their progress. Now, using the GPS, dispatchers are able to instantly pinpoint each truck's location. This makes it easy to alter routes throughout the day—for example, to add last-minute pick-ups—and relative to the old system, trucks can now be dispatched in half the time. This translates into reduced costs, more efficient operations, and improved customer service.

Northwest Airlines is one of several airlines that wants to adapt the GPS for widespread civilian use. By using GPS data, pilots, air traffic controllers, and regional Federal Aviation Administration (FAA) centers can know where every aircraft is at all times. This should make it easier and safer to place planes closer together for landings and takeoffs at crowded airports. Northwest is also working with the FAA to create safer, more efficient flight paths. Both of these applications are likely to reduce jet fuel consumption. Officials at the FAA feel that GPS may make it possible for automated landings and takeoffs in even the densest fog.

Geologists also expect to make good use of the GPS. They should be able to use such systems to monitor subtle changes in the earth's surface—changes that indicate whether an earthquake or volcanic eruption is imminent. Such an application has the potential to save many lives.

Combining GPS signals with other data may open up a number of other interesting applications. For example, the integration of GPS data and digitized land maps could lead to the development of sophisticated, intelligent vehicle-tracking systems. Small computer screens mounted on the dashboard of a car could show drivers how to avoid traffic jam or where the nearest gas station, hospital or automatic teller machine is located. Experts feel that satellite and GPS-oriented intelligent vehicle systems such as that in Orlando, Florida.

More than a dozen companies are profiting from the GPS in another way—by manufacturing and marketing receivers for non-military applications. Sales of such receivers increased tenfold—to more than $600 million—from 1990 to 1993. During this time, Sony released a GPS receiver for hikers. More GPS applications will pop up as the cost of GPS receivers chips drops during the 1990s.

When the Navstar system is fully operational, the Department of Defense intends to continue to artificially degrades the signals from the satellites in order to prevent a potential enemy from using the systems to launch missiles to knock out the satellites. By degrading the signals by a few nanoseconds, the satellite (and ground) locations calculated by receivers may be off by 100 yards. While the Department of Defense expects to provide classified equipment and codes that compensate for signal degradation for commercial applications, these compensating mechanisms will derive up the costs associated with non-military GPS applications.

Section 5

How to Build Management Information System Or Requirements of Information Systems

How to Build Management Information System or Requirements of Information Systems

Correct and complete information requirements are key ingredients in planning organisational information systems, in implementing information systems applications, and in building databases. Despite trends to provide direct support to users major information system applications integrated with databases require careful planning and significant cooperative effort between users and information system professionals. Information requirements determination is a vital part of this cooperative activity. Users are the fundamental source of requirements, but it is difficult for users to define them. Inexperienced analyses often feel that users should tell them what the information requirements are so they can get on with the design and implementation of the system. Experienced analysts know that eliciting correct and complete requirements is one of their most challenging tasks. This section covers a range of topics related to information requirements determination. It should aid both users and analysts to understand better the process of the determination of information requirements and to improve their performance in this task.

The set of chapters thus provides strategies, methods, and concepts to aid users and analysts to define four sets of requirements: the overall plan, application information, requirements, database content, and user interface requirements.

15

Development of Long Range Information Systems

PLANNING FOR INFORMATION SYSTEMS

CONTENT OF THE INFORMATION SYSTEM MASTER PLAN

- Information System Goals, Objectives, and Architecture
- Current Capabilities
- Forecast of Developments Affecting the Plan
- The Specific Plan
- Maintenance of the Master Plan

THE NOLAN STAGE MODEL

- Stages of Information System Growth
- Using the Stage Theory in Planning
- An Evaluation of the Stage Theory

THE THREE-STAGE MODEL OF THE PLANNING PROCESS

STRATEGIC PLANNING STAGE

- Derivation of Information System Strategy from Organisational Plan
- The McFarlan-McKenney Strategic Grid
- Strategy Fit with Organisational Culture
- Strategy Set Transformation

ANALYSIS OF ORGANIZATIONAL INFORMATION REQUIREMENTS

- Define Underlying Organisational Systems
- Develop Subsystem-Manager Matrix
- Define and Evaluate Information Requirements for Organisational Subsystems

RESOURCE ALLOCATION

- Comparative Cost or Benefit
- Portfolio Approach
- Chargeout
- Steering Committee ranking

SUMMARY

The complexity of the information resources environment suggests that planning is vital to success. This chapter surveys the development of an information system plan and outlines the contents of the plan. A stage model of information system growth, which may aid in the development of a plan, is described. There are a variety of methodologies for information system planning; these are classified using a three-stage model. The three stages of strategic planning, organisational information requirements analysis, and resources allocation are then described in more detail.

The type of plan assumed in the chapter is a comprehensive information resources plan which includes all areas of information handling assigned to the chief information executive. The plan will be referred to as an information system plan, master development plan, or information resources plan. The terms are used interchangeably to refer to the comprehensive plan for use of information technology to support organisational strategies, goals, and processes.

Planning for Information Systems

The value of planning is well understood. Companies that plan tend to achieve better results than companies that do not, yet many organisations do not plan or do it poorly.

Planning Shortfalls

"A 1980 Diebold Research Program survey of 150 major corporations...revealed that fully two-thirds (of MIS departments) had a formal planning process with published plans. However, a closer look at these findings shows that 63% of the plans are for three years or less. In other words, only one-fourth of all departments have plans that extend beyond their current backlogs of work.

"A July 1981 sampling of 40 major corporations...revealed how serious the shortfall is in communications planning. Fully 62.5%—25 companies—had either just started planning in the past year or had no plans whatsoever."

An information systems is complex and therefore needs an overall plan to guide its initial development and subsequent change. The plan describes the structure and content of the information system and how it is to be developed. Since all projects cannot be developed and implemented concurrently, priorities must be set. As with other resources in an organisations, information resources are scarce. In a dynamic organisation there are more opportunities for information system applications than can be handled at one time, and therefore an allocation process must be worked out. The master plan, once developed, does not remain constant but must be updated as new developments occur.

A very important fundamental concept of information system planning is that the organisation's strategic plan should be the basis for the MIS strategic plan. Alignment of MIS strategy with organisational strategy is one of the central problems of MIS planning, Methods for achieving this alignment will be discussed later in the chapter.

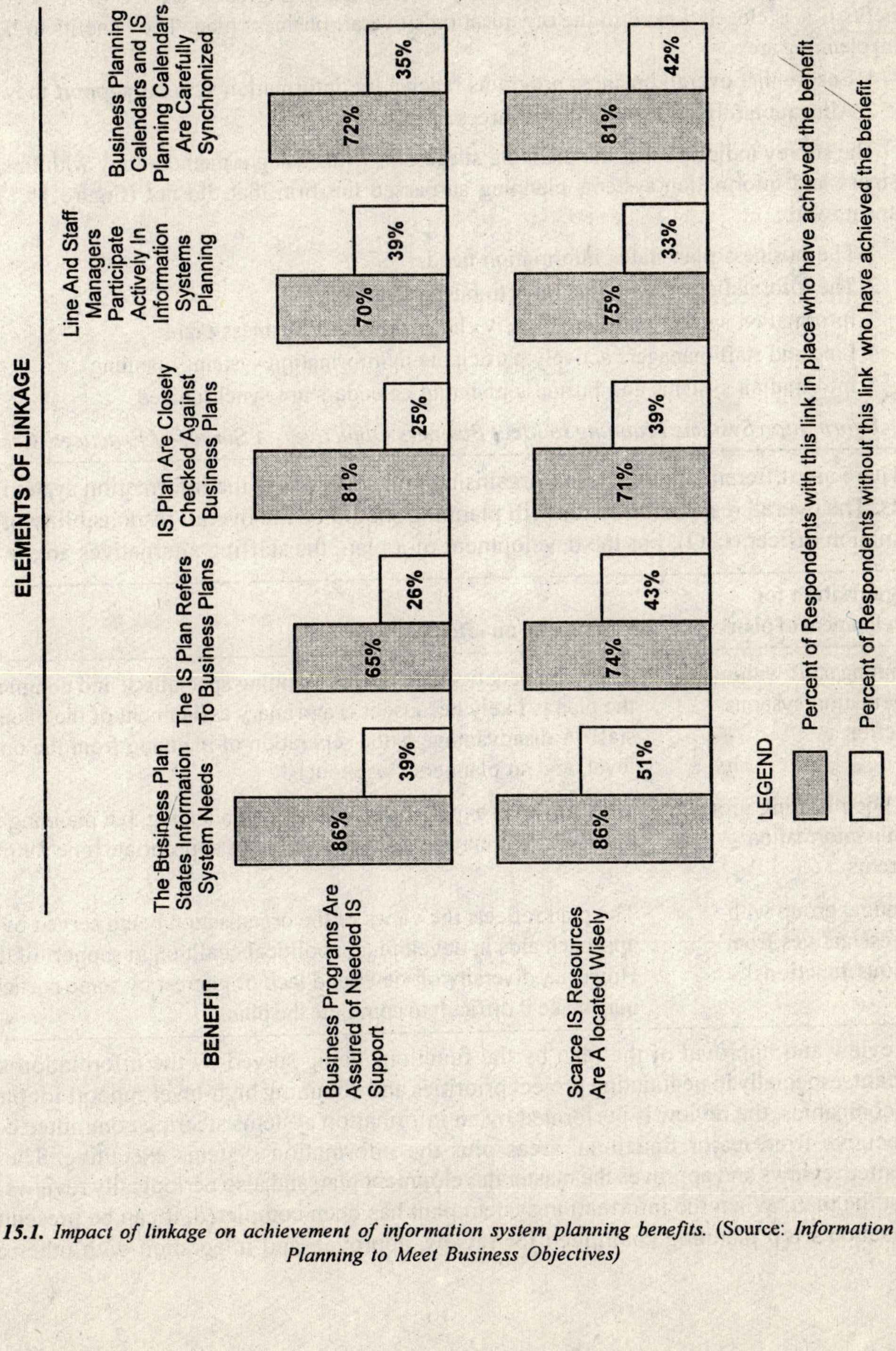

Figure 15.1. *Impact of linkage on achievement of information system planning benefits.* (Source: *Information Systems Planning to Meet Business Objectives*)

Mini Case Study

A survey of 334 corporations by Cresap, McCormick and Paget, Inc., a management consulting firm, provided evidence that information systems planning stands a greater chance of achieving desired benefits if it is closely linked to the organisation's overall business plan. The benefits to be achieved from planning are:

1. Ensure that overall business programs receive the information systems support they need
2. Allocate information systems resources wisely

The survey indicated that the planning success of firms using a methodology with links between business and information systems planning surpassed the firm that did not (Figure 15.1). Linkage elements were:

1. The business plan states information needs
2. The information system plan refer to business plans
3. Information system plans are closely checked against business plans
4. Line and staff managers actively participate in information systems planning
5. Information systems and business planning calendars are synchronized.

Information Systems Planning to Meet Business Objectives: A Survey of Practices, Cresap.

There are different approaches to organising and supervising the information system planning efforts. The overall responsibility for MIS planning should be the overall responsibility of the chief information officer (CIO). For the development of a plan, the staffing alternatives are:

Organisation for development of plan	Comments on effectiveness
Planning staff within information systems function	There are benefits from use of planning specialists, and completion of the plan is likely because it is a primary assignment of the planning staff. A disadvantage is the separation of planning from the operating level, and so planners "lose touch."
Ad hoc planning groups within information systems	Working-level experience is valuable in planning, but planning expertise may be low. It may be difficult to allocate appropriate time for planning.
Planning group with representatives from various functions	The plan reflects the views of the organisation being served by it. This approach aids in developing a political coalition in support of the plan. However, diversity of views and lack of interest by some participants may make it difficult to complete the plan.

Review and approval of the plan by the functions being served by the information system is important, especially in negotiating project priorities and obtaining high-level support for the plan. In some companies, the review is performed by an information systems steering committee composed of executive from major functional areas plus the information systems executive. The steering committee reviews and approves the master development plan and also periodically reviews progress against the plan. When the information system plan has been completed, it can be presented to the organisation's top planning committee for review, approval, and integration with other company plans.

It is desirable to define information systems planning policies and procedures. These establish the information roles of various organisational units, the coordination and integration required by different functions planning for new or revised information resources, and the planning cycle. The allocation of tasks and the assignment of responsibilities to the information systems function should reflect the overall organisational philosophy, culture, and structure. The planning cycle for information systems should conform to the cycle for the organisation plan, so that the information system plan can support and be merged into the overall plan.

Contents of the Information System

The master plan typically has two components—a long-range plan for three to five years (or longer) and a short-range plan for one year. The plan provides a basis for resource allocation and control. The long-range portion provides general guidelines for direction, and the short-range portion provides a basis for specific accountability as to operational and financial performance.

The master development plan establishes a framework for all detailed information system planning. In general, it contains four major sections:

1. Information systems goals, objectives, and architecture
2. Inventory of current capabilities
3. Forecast of developments affecting the plan
4. The specific plan

Although a particular plan may not be organised this way, it should generally cover these topics.

Aim, Objectives and Functions of the Information System

This section of the plan might contain descriptions of the following:

1. Organisational goals, objectives, and strategies
2. External environment (industry, government regulations, customers, and suppliers)
3. Internal organisational constraints such as management philosophy
4. Assumptions about business risks and potential consequences
5. Overall goals, objectives, and strategy for the information system
6. Architecture of the information system

Within the context of overall organisational goals, policy, objectives, strategies, and plans, there should be policy, goals, objectives, strategies, and plans for the information system. The general goals provide guidelines for the direction in which the information system effort should be directed. The objectives are more specific and should be stated so that performance or nonperformance may be measured. For example, a goal might be "to provide information resources on a timely basis to all organisational units." An objective might be "to provide periodic financial reports no later than 36 hours after the end of the period."

The overall architecture or structure of the information system provide a framework for detailed planning. The information architecture defines major categories of information and the major information subsystems or applications.

Current Status

This is a summary of the current status of an information system. It includes such items as the following:

1. Inventory of:
   - **a** Hardware
   - **b** Generalized software (system software, database management system, etc.)
   - **c** Application Systems
   - **d** Personnel
2. Analysis of:
   - **a** Expense
   - **b** Hardware utilisation
   - **c** Software utilisation
   - **d** Personnel utilisation
3. Status of projects in process
4. Assessment of strengths and weaknesses

The purpose of the inventory is to clearly identify the current status of all systems. Applications may be classified by:

1. Major functional systems (such as accounting, marketing, human resources)
2. Organisational strategies (e.g., provides online ordering by customers)
3. Need for maintenance or revision:
   - **a** Applications which are working reasonably well
   - **b** Applications which require revised implementation or improvement
   - **c** Applications which need to be substantially revised or completely replaced by new systems

In the case of personnel, useful classifications might include:

1. Job classification (programmer, operator, etc.)
2. Skill categories (COBOL programming, data communications, etc.)
3. Functional area experience (finance, accounting, manufacturing, etc.)

In each case, the classification should reflect planning concerns. For example, in planning for a shift to facilities for end-user computing, software might be classified with respect to users:

1. Systems software
   - **a** For operations
   - **b** For trained programmers
   - **c** For both programmers and end users
   - **d** For end users
2. Application software
   - **a** Purchased or developed and supported by information systems personnel
   - **b** Purchased or developed by users and supported by information systems personnel
   - **c** Developed and supported only by users.

Forecast of Developments Affecting the Plan

Planning is affected by current and anticipated technology. The impact of such developments as personal computers, local area networks, database management systems, and office automation should be reflected in the long-range plan. It is difficult to estimate technology far into the future, but most developments are announced one or more years before they become generally available. Broad technological changes can be perceived several years before they are implemented. For example, it was known for several years before business-quality personal computers became widely used that this technological development was imminent and that it would have a substantial impact on the design of future systems. Visual display terminals were available for several years before they became widely used. The technological advantages of using visual display were such that it was reasonably obvious they would be an important factor in future systems.

Software availability should also be forecast and the impact on future systems anticipated. For example, in 1965 when IBM announced the System 360, the software trend to COBOL as the dominant business procedural language was under way. Installations that perceived that trend correctly made better decisions than those which chose to ignore COBOL (and other procedure-oriented languages). In 1984, the trend in development software is to fourth generation languages. They are likely to have significant impact on future staffing, provisions for end-user computing, etc.

Methodology changes may also be forecast. Alternative development methodologies should be considered in place of or in addition to traditional life cycle methods. As another example, automated development tools are likely to have an impact and should be examined in the plan.

Environmental developments such as government regulations, tax laws, and competitor actions can also be included insofar as they affect information systems.

The Specific Plan

The plan should cover several years (say three to five) with the upcoming periods (say, the next one or two years) being reasonably specific. The next year should have sufficient detail to contain a budget. The plan should include:

1. Hardware acquisition schedule
2. Purchased software schedule:
   - System software
   - Applications software
3. Application development schedule
4. Software maintenance and conversion schedule
5. Personnel resources required and schedule of hiring and training
6. Financial resources required by object of expenditure (hardware, software, personnel, etc.) and by purpose (operations, maintenance, new development, etc.). Other classifications may also be useful.

Maintenance of the Master Plan/Maintain the Master Plan

As each year passes, the information system plan requires updating. For example, the current status is updated with new equipment and changing personnel figures. Future plans are affected by changes in technology, experience with systems that have been developed, changing needs for new systems, and changes in the organisation. For example, an organisation may have acquired a new division; as a result, the necessity for common information processing, common codes, installation of common systems, etc., may affect the entire plan. A new hardware-software announcement may also affect future plans. Such developments should be assessed, and their impacts should be put into the revision of the plan. Pressures for changes in the plans may come from internal events outside of information systems such as changing financial constraints. The master plan is also updated to reflect the status of systems installed and the progress of new systems.

Events in the external environment may also cause revisions of plans. Examples are government regulations, actions by competitors, etc.

The Nolan Stage Model

Some computer-based information systems are relatively young; others are mature. The Nolan stage model is a framework for information systems planning that matches various features of information systems to stages of growth. It is a contingency theory which states; IF these features exist THEN the information system is in this stage. The basic theme is that an organisation must go through each stage of growth before it can progress to the next one; it thus provides a set of limits to planning if the organisation's current stage of growth can be diagnosed.

Stages in the Growth of Information System

The basic stage model was described by Nolan in 1973-1974 in several articles.[1] These articles identified four stages of information systems growth:

Stage of Growth	Description
Initiation	Early use of computers by small number of users to meet basic organisational needs. Decentralized control and minimal planning.
Expansion (or contagion)	Experimentation with and adoption of computers by many users. Proliferation of applications. Crisis due to rapid rise in costs.
Formalization (or control)	Organisational controls established to contain growth in use and apply cost-effectiveness criteria. Centralization, Controls often prevent attainment of potential benefits.
Maturity (or integration)	Integration of applications. Controls adjusted. Planning well established. Alignment of information system to organisation.

The growth curve of the Nolan Model is the familiar sigmoid or S curve. In a subsequent 1979 *Harvard Business Review* article,[2] Nolan expanded the model to six stages. He also proposed an alternative model in which major changes in technology eliminate the maturity stage. With the introduction of new hardware, software, and system designs, the organisation starts on a new growth curve.

Management responses to growth in computing are reflected in different levels of control or slack with each stage. Control is characterised by management systems and policies which ensure efficiency of computing use. Slack is the lack of controls and the availability of resources to experiment with application features not required to perform basic processing.

Stage	Levels of control or slack
I	Low control. Some slack. Little or no information systems planning.
II	Greater slack in order to encourage use. Lack of planning. Cost rise and costs from lack of integration become visible.
III	High level of controls. Information systems planning is given increased emphasis.
IV	Emphasis on integration. More emphasis on user control of information system costs. Use of databases.
V	Focus on data administration: Some slack to encourage development of systems which contribute to strategic advantage of the organisation.
VI	Application portfolio is complete and matches the organisational objectives.

Nolan makes certain assumptions about the growth dynamics of movement through the stages:

1. Organisational learning permits movement through stages. The limited experimentation of stage I is the basis for the contagion of stage II, and the contagious use allows diffusion of the technology before controls are applied.
2. Stages cannot be skipped because experience in necessary before the organisation is ready for the next stage. If experimentation is not performed, there are no early users to promote contagion. If the organisation goes from initiation to control, diffusion does not occur because controls stifle widespread trial-and-error use.
3. Although there are certain "natural" growth processes involved, the four growth processes can be planned, coordinated, and managed to move through the stages effectively and efficiently. Leadership styles and coalition building shift to meet the needs of each stage. The stages thus represent a sequence for planned and managed change.

Application of Stage Theory in Planning

The stage theory can be used both in diagnosis of current stage of growth and in planning changes to move in a controlled way to the next stage. Not all application subsystems grow at the same rate; accounting may be in stage III with controlled growth, while marketing should be encouraged to look for new applications (needs slack). Diagnosis and planning focus on a set of features associated with each growth process at each stage of growth.

An Evaluation of the Stage Theory

There is ample evidence of significant practitioner acceptance of the stage model:

1. Practitioners generally report it to have high explanatory value, or "face validity."
2. The model has had wide readership. It is one of the "classics" in the field based on frequency of citation.[3]

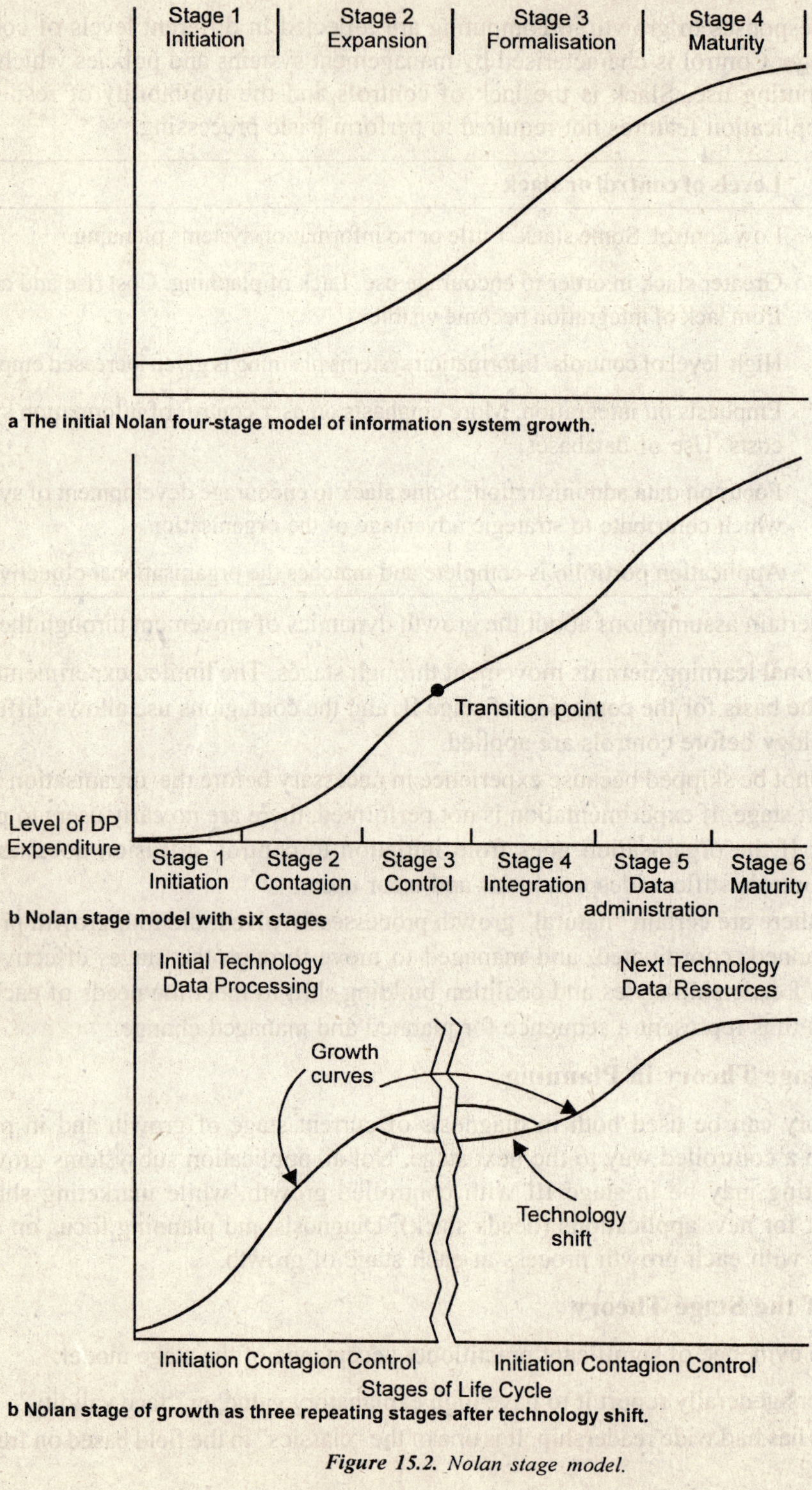

Figure 15.2. Nolan stage model.

3. Over 200 studies of stages of growth in organisations have been performed by the consulting firm of Nolan and Norton, Inc.

The research evidence to date does not support the contingency relationship between stages and features associated with four growth processes at each stage.[4] There may be several explanations for the lack of research evidence:

1. The research designs may not have been adequate.
2. Organisational contingency theories are difficult to "prove" by research because there are so many intervening variables and compensating behaviours.
3. The phenomenon of growth is continuous, yet the stages are discrete. In practice, shifts in stages and their accompanying features occur gradually and at different paces.

King and Kraemer[5] describe the Nolan model as an evolutionist model (a model that characterize change by the direction the change is taking). The model describes the logic of change and the destination that is to be achieved. The strength of an evolutionist model and thus the strength of the Nolan model is its explanation of the logic of development. The weakness of an evolutionist model is lack of specificity; it does not define the mechanisms of change.

On balance, the Nolan stage model is useful conceptual model to understand the general directions of change. At a conceptual level, it aids the planning process by providing a framework for understanding change. The diagnostics measurements and perspective elements of the model should be viewed as general guidelines for information system planning.

Three-Stage Model of the Planning Process

A number of techniques have been proposed for information systems planning. A problem is to evaluate the place of a technique in the flow of activities for developing a long-range information plan and long-range information architecture. The three-stage model of information system planning developed by Bowman, Davis and Wetherbe[6] clarifies the generic planning activities, the order of the activities, and the alternative techniques and methodologies that apply.

Practical guidance for information system planning can be gained from the three-stage model. It can aid in recognising the nature of the planning problems and in selecting the appropriate stage planning. For example, an organisation may view its information system function as not making an adequate contribution to organisational objectives. In seeking to resolve this problem, there may be a proposal to install a chargeout system (located in the resource allocating stage) to make information systems pay their own way. Another organisation may conduct a business systems planning study (a type of organisation information requirements analysis activity) to resolve the same problem of insufficient MIS contribution to organisational objectives. While these activities may result in improved information system services, the planning model suggests that they are probably not the appropriate methodologies in this situation. If the information system function is not responsive to the organisation, the three-stage planning model indicates that a strategic alignment planning effort should precede organisational information requirements and resource allocation.

The three-stage planning model provides insight into the planning process and reduces confusion as to the position of competing planning methodologies. The next three sections will describe the stages in more detail and survey selected methodologies for each planning stage.

Growth Process \ Stage	I	II	III	IV	V	VI
Applications portfolio	Functional cost reduction applications	Proliferation	Upgrade documentation and restructure existing application	Retrofit existing applications using database technology	Organisation integration of applications	Application integration "mirroring" information flows
DP organisation	Specialisation for technological learning	User-oriented programmers	Middle management	Establish computer utility and user account teams	Data administration	Data resource management
DP planning and control	Lax	More lax	Formalized planning and control	Taliored planning and control systems	Shared data and common systems	Data resource strategic planning
User awareness	"Hands off"	Superficailly enthusiatic	Arbitrarily held accountable	Accountability learning	Effectively accountable	Acceptance of joint user and data processing accountability

Figure 15.3. *Matrix of features for growth processes at each stage of growth. (Reprinted by permission of* ***Harvard Business Review.*** *Excerpted from Exhibit 1 from Richards L. Nolan, "Managing the Crises in Data Processing."*

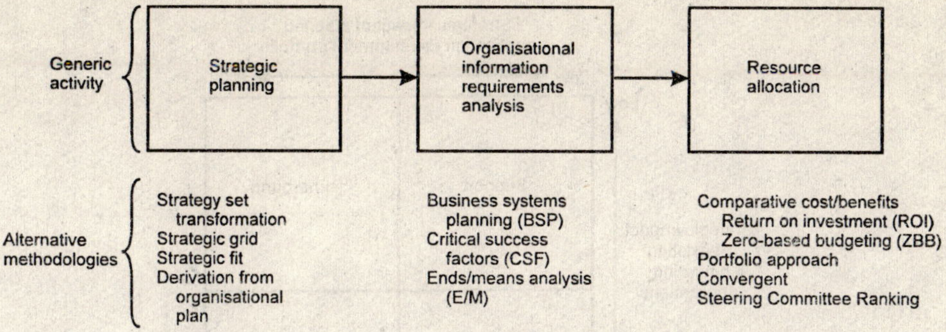

Figure 15.4. *Three stage model of the information system planning process.*

Strategic Planning Stage

The objective of the strategic planning stage of information system planning is to create objectives, goals, and strategies that align with (are derived from) the organisation's objectives, goals and strategies. Four techniques useful in this strategic grid, fit with organisational plan, use of the strategic grid, fit with organisational culture, and strategy set transformation.

Solution of Information System Strategy from Organisational Plan

If the organisation has a plan that reflects organisation goals, objectives, and strategies, information system goal, objectives, and strategy can be derived from it. Each objective, goal, and strategy in the plan is analysed for required information system support. These can then be organised into information system goals, objectives, and strategies. Some examples illustrate the process:

	Organisation plan	**Derivation for information system plan**
Goal	Provide high-quality widgets to the automotive industry	Provide information support for sales of quality widgets
Strategy	Establish quality control program for widgets	Establish quality control database for widgets
Objective	Implement quality circles in Detroit plant by 12/31/XX	1. Implement quality control report suitable for quality circles by 12/31/XX 2. Designs access procedures for quality circle to obtained data from quality control database by 6/15/XX

The McFarlan-McKenney Strategic Grid

One contingency approach to deciding on the information systems planning effort is the McFarlan-McKenney *strategic grid*.[7] The grid defines four types of information systems planning situations depending on the strategic impact of the existing information systems applications portfolio and the strategic impact of the portfolio of applications planned for development (Figure 15.5). The cells define the position of the information systems activity relative to the organisation.

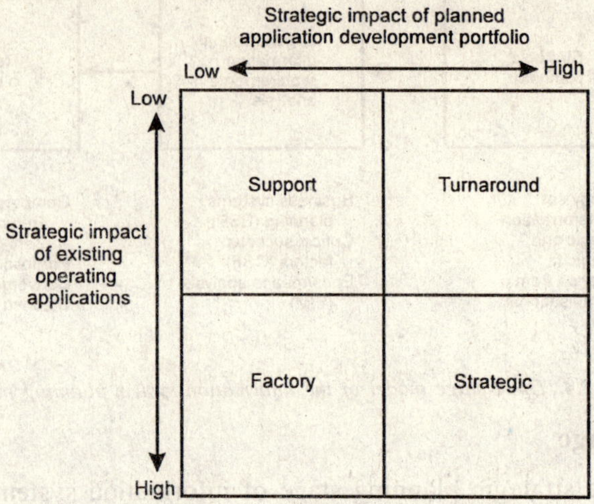

Figure 15.5. *The strategic grid. (Adapted from F. W. McFarlan and J. L. McKenney, Corporate Information Systems Management).*

Strategic. Information system activities are critical to the current competitive strategy and to future strategic directions of the enterprise. Information systems applications are part of new strategic directions.

Factory. Information system applications are vital to the successful functioning of well-defined, well-accepted activities. However, information systems are not part of future strategic operations.

Support. Information system applications are useful in supporting the activities of the organisation. A portfolio weighted to the support cell emphasizes traditional data processing applications. Information system activities are not "vital " to critical operations and are not included as part of future strategic directions.

Turnaround. This is a transition state from "support" to "strategic." The organisation has had support-type applications, but is now planning for applications vitals to strategic success of the organisation.

An analysis of the current and planned portfolio is diagnostic of current status; it can also be used to change directions. The cell can then be used to suggest organisation and management of information systems planning.

The strategic information system grid is a diagnostic tool to understand the role of information systems in an organisation. The position in the grid explains the needed level of top management involvement and the relationship of the information system plan and organisational plan. The disadvantage of the grid is that it explains what is happening rather than what should happen. If an organisation desires to be more strategic in its use of information systems, the grid provides no basis for deciding whether it can be.

Position in grid	Organisation and management of information systems planning
Strategic	Significant general management guidance Integration of corporate planning and information systems planning Need for smooth functioning of information systems activity
Turnaround	Same as strategic
Factory	Less involvement from top management Guidance from corporate plan to maintain information systems alignment Detailed operational and capacity planning by information system function
Support	Little top management involvement Little or no guidance from corporate plan

Strategies Fit for the Organisational Environment

Each organisation has a culture which reinforces values norm, and beliefs about the organisation. Goals, objectives, and strategy for information systems should fit with the culture in order to avoid high resistance and high risk of failure. If the culture is not clear to information systems planners, clues can be obtained from sources such as the following:

1. *Stories.* Particular stories or incidents are repeated in an organisation. An analyst seeking insight into organisational culture should listen to a number of stories. A pattern of meaning will tend to emerge. As an example, a company that emphasises service may repeat incident such as "the time we charted a plane to get an expert here to help a customer get a system running."
2. *Meetings.* The subjects and order of agenda as well as attendees may provide clues as to the items considered important in the organisational as well as which key managers support of block them.
3. *Top management behaviour.* The behaviour of top management generally influences the behaviour of lower levels of management and other organisation members. The way executives spend their time and the questions they ask demonstrate value systems that are likely to be emulated by others in the organisation. Thomas J. Watson of IBM spent significant time on the issue of customer service and wrote frequent memoranda on the subject. His concern was reflected throughout IBM.
4. *Physical layout.* The location of activities and the relative position and size of facilities, offices, etc., provide clues as to importance.
5. *Ritual.* Banquets, parties, orientations, frequently reflect significant organisational values.
6. *Documents.* What is written and to whom, and frequency of correspondence may indicate important beliefs about the ends and means for the organisation.

Strategy Required for Transformation

It is very possible that there is no organisational plan to use in deriving information system goals, objectives, and strategy, and the information system planner must attempt to formulate necessary plans in a void. The strategic grid can be used to estimate the general strategic position of information systems, and organisational culture analysis can help to understand general values and directions, but neither is sufficient to develop information system goals and strategy. A more complete method is strategy set transformation as described by King.[8]

Strategy set transformation is used to produce goals and strategy for the information system by the following steps:

1. Explicate the organisation's strategy set.
   - **a** Delineate the organisation's claimant structure. The clients, claimants, or stakeholders in the organisations are identified. Examples are owners, customers, suppliers and employees.
   - **b** Identify goals for the claimants.
   - **c** Identify organisational goals and strategies for each claimant group.
2. Validate the organisational goals and strategies by asking management to critique the statements. The organisational objectives, strategies, and strategic organisational attributes form the organisational strategy set.
3. Transform the organisational strategy set into the information systems strategy set.
   - **a** Identify one or more information system objectives for each organisational strategy and for each relevant organisational objective and attribute.
   - **b** Identify information system constraints from organisation strategy set and from information system objectives.

As an example of this process, an organisational objectives of improving cash flow may be derived from the profitability goals of shareholders and creditors. An organisational strategy to achieve profitability may be an improvement in credit practices. An information system objective may be to improve speed of billing. Strategic organisational attributes relative to sophistication in use of computers and decision models will be reflected in information system constraints affecting the billing system. These can be expressed in system design strategies such as pilot projects for training, prototyping for development, etc.

Analysis of Organisational Information Requirements

Once goals and strategy have been delineated, the next stage is to obtain organisational information requirements. Information requirements are required at the organisation-wide level for information system planning, identifying applications, and planning an information architecture. More detailed information requirements are required for design of applications. Although the level of specification is different for the organisation and application, many of the methods for obtaining requirements are the same.

The discussion of methods for the determination of information requirements for both organisation and applications. However, to provide insight into the process of obtaining organisational information requirements, an example of an approach used by Wetherbe and Davis[9] that utilizes interviews with key management personnel is described in this section. The method is a synthesis of several existing approaches. In this method, obtaining organisational information requirements consists of several steps:

1. Define underlying organisational subsystems
2. Develop manager by subsystem matrix
3. Define and evaluate information requirements for organisational subsystems

A case study is used to illustrate the method. The company manages leasing of single-family dwellings.

Organisational Subsystems

The first phase of analysis is to define underlying organisational subsystems. The purpose of activity subsystem identification is to subdivide requirements determination by major organisational activity and make the process more manageable. For the home leasing company, the major subsystems are:

Credit
Leasing
Maintenance
Evictions and delinquency
Marketing
Advertising
Accounts receivable and collections
Corporate accounting
Market and product analysis
Client reporting
Appraisal
Insurance
Sales
Personnel administration
Inspections
Audit
Inventory
Legal

These subsystems are obtained by an iterative process of discussing all organisational activities with managers and defining the activities as belonging to broad categories of subsystems. As new activities are considered, they are placed in previously defined categories, or a new category is created.

Develop Subsystem-Manager Matrix in the Organisation

Once the underlying organisational subsystem are defined, the next phase of the organisational information requirements analysis is to relate specific managers to organisational subsystems. The resulting manager-subsystem matrix for the home leasing firm is illustrated in Figure 15.6. Note that the subsystems across the top of the matrix are the same as those identified above.

The matrix is prepared by reviewing the major decision responsibilities of each middle- to top-level manager and associating decision making with specific subsystem. The matrix documents who has major decision-making responsibility for each subsystem. The purpose of this step is to clarify responsibilities and identify those managers to be interviewed relative to each subsystem.

Analysis and Evaluate Information Requirements for Organisational Subsystem

This step obtains the information requirements of each organisational subsystem by group interviews of those managers having major decision-making responsibility for the subsystem. Merely asking managers to define their information requirements is frequently not satisfactory because of the limitations on humans as information processors. It is therefore necessary to provide some structure to aid managers in thinking about information requirements.

Organisational subsystem

Managers	A/R	Credit	Evictions/ delinquent	Inspection	Inventory	Marketing	Advertising	Insurance	Sale	Audit	Appraisal	Personnel/ administration	Legal	Market and product analysis	Corporate accounting	Client reporting
Managers 1	X	X														
Managers 2		X	X													
Managers 3				X		X					X			X		X
Managers 4				X												
⋮																
Managers n										X		X	X		X	

Figure 15.6. Manager by subsystem matrix.

The questions used in eliciting information requirements are derived from three approaches (Business Systems Planning, Critical Success Factors, and Ends-Means Analysis). The questions reflects three ways of thinking about requirements, but each questions also elicits unique requirements. The use of the three types of questions therefore increases the probability of obtaining a complete set of requirements. The three sets of questions are:

- What problems do you have and what information is needed for solving them? What decisions do you make and what information do you need for decision making?
- What factors are critical to the success of your activity and what information do you need to achieve success in them or monitor progress?
- What are the outputs (the ends) from your activities and what information do you need to measure effectiveness in achieving the outputs?
  What resources are used in producing the outputs and what information is needed to measure efficiency in use of the resources?

Interviews typically take two to four hours per subsystem. The maintenance subsystem at the leasing company illustrate the steps of the structured interview.

1. *Statement of purpose.* The first step of the interview is to get the managers to define a statement of purpose for the subsystem under consideration. For example, the purpose of *maintenance* was defined as: Maintain rental property at satisfactory level with minimal cost and process vendor payments.
2. *Subsystem mapping.* The second step of the group interview is to define the relationship of the subsystem to all other subsystems internal to the organisation or entities external to the organisation. It is constructed by drawing the subsystems under consideration in the centre

of a chalkboard or flip chart pad and by drawing around it the subsystems and entities with which it interacts. Next, labelled directional arrows are used to define the types of transactions or information flow that occur. The subsystem mapping makes the managers aware of full-scope of the subsystem under consideration.

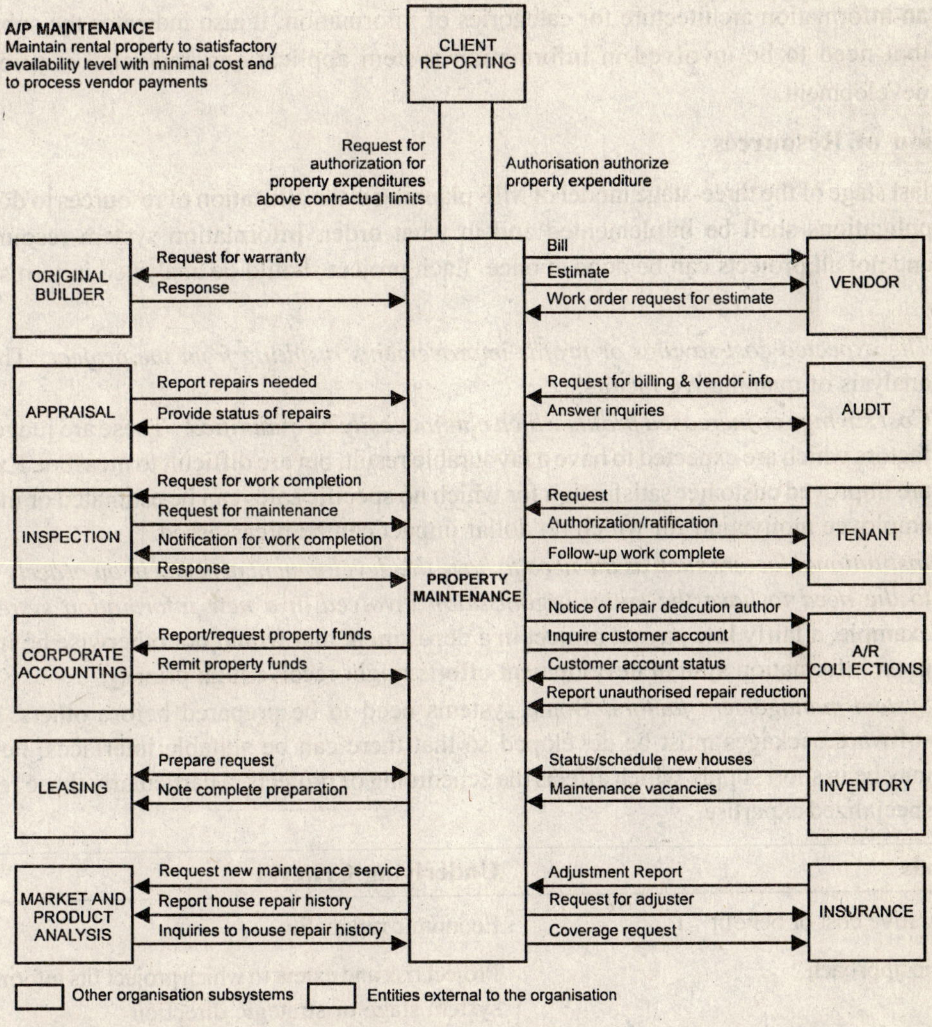

Figure 15.7. Subsystem mapping for maintenance subsystem.

3. *Questions to elicit requirements.* After the subsystem mapping is complete, information requirements are elicited using the three sets of questions.

4. *Define major information categories and classify information requirements.* The grouping of information requirements into broad general categories provide an overall profile of the information needs of the organisation.
5. *Develop information-subsystem matrix.* The information categories are used to create a matrix showing which subsystem uses an information category. Rough measures of importance and current availability are specified (Figure 15.8). The matrix is used to define an information architecture for categories of information. It also indicates the subsystems that need to be involved in information system applications and relative priority for development.

Allocation of Resources

The last stage of the three-stage model of MIS planning is the allocation of resources to determine which applications shall be implemented and in what order. Information system resources are limited, and not all projects can be done at once. Each project should be analys ed in terms of four factors:

1. *The expected cost savings or profits improvements resulting from the project.* This is an analysis of quantitative factors.
2. *Cost savings or increased profits which cannot easily be quantified.* These are judgemental factors which are expected to have a favourable result, but are difficult to measure. Examples are improved customer satisfaction for which no specific sales can be estimated or increased employee motivation for which no dollar impact can be preassessed.
3. *Institutional factors such as the need to have the development proceed in an orderly fashion to the need to have the entire organisation involved in a new information system.* For example, a fairly low payout project in a department that would not otherwise be involved in an information system development efforts might receive high priority.
4. *System management factors.* Some systems need to be prepared before others. Certain software packages must be developed so that there can be suitable interfaces. Personnel may be in short supply which affects the scheduling of projects, a particularly those requiring specialized expertise.

Methods	**Underlying Criteria**
Comparative cost or benefit	Economic rationality
Portfolio approach	Project risk and extent to which project fits information system stage or strategic direction
Chargeout	Value to user (local rationality)
Steering committee ranking	Organisational power, politics, and coalitions

Using the four factors as input, a number of methods have been proposed for allocating scarce development resources with different underlying criteria for decision making. The methods surveyed in this section illustrate some alternatives. The methods may be used singly or in combination.

Comparative Cost or Benefit of the Projects

Projects do not all have the same cost-benefit ratio. Some have a high economic value if successful; others have low payoff. Two methods of rational, economic decision making illustrate the use of economic rationality for allocating resources: return on investment and zero-based budgeting.

Return on investment (ROI) is a classic decision-making approach. In the case of information system projects, each one has quantifiable economic costs and quantifiable economic benefits. Using the streams of costs and benefits, the return of the investment can be calculated. A decision rule based on ROI is to choose projects (among those that are optional) that must have the highest ROI. There are three difficulties with this approach:

1. Many benefits may be difficult to quantify, yet the project is understood to have a high priority.
2. Projects based on ROI alone may not provide a balanced portfolio along other dimensions such as risk.
3. The ROI technique is incremental; it does not cause reconsideration of current applications.

Zero-based budgeting is a procedure to reevaluate all programs, activities, and expenditure in terms of cost or benefits. The steps are:

1. Develop decision packages—documents that describe each activity that can be separately added or dropped. Examples are programs, projects, services, and personnel.
2. Rank packages in order of importance.
3. Allocate available resources to decision packages.

In the case of information systems, zero-based budgeting causes the existing portfolio to be examined along with the proposed portfolio. Each function or area for computer applications starts with a zero base of applications and indicates the priority they assign to applications if they were to add them incrementally. The method appears to be useful for examining the entire allocation of resources; it tends to be very time consuming for regular decision making on projects.

Portfolio Approach for the Projects

The basic idea of the portfolio approach is that projects should be evaluated not only individually but as part of a portfolio of projects that have an overall impact. The portfolio should have an appropriate mixture of risk, support for strategic directions, and applications that fit the stages of growth of the various organisational subsystems.

The portfolio approach has been described by McFarlan[10] with respect to risk; he also applies the approach to project management. Other criteria for building a portfolio are implied by the strategic grid[11] and the stage theory of Nolan.[12]

Portfolio-based risk assessment recognizes that project differ relative to risk of various failure such as schedule failure, cost overrun, performance shortfall, and abandonment. McFarlan identifies three dimensions that contribute to the uncertainty of the success of the project:

1. Project size. Large projects are riskier than small ones.
2. Experience with the technology. Risk is reduced to the extent that the development team

ORGANISATIONAL SUBSYSTEMS

Information categories	Leasing	Maintenance	Accounts/ Receivable	Credit	Evictions/ Delinquent	Inspection	Inventory	Marketing	Advertising	Insurance	Sales	Audit	Appraisal	Personnel/ Administration	Legal	Market and Product Analysis	Corporate Accounting	Client Reporting
Contract	1/3	1/3	1/3	1/2	1/3	1/2	2/3	1/3	2/1	2/3	1/3	1/3	1/3		1/3	1/3	2/3	2/3
Policy/Training	3/3	3/3	3/2	3/3	3/3	3/3		3/3		2/3	2/3	3/3	3/3	2/3	2/2	3/2	3/2	3/2
Customer Financial	2/3		2/3	1/3	2/3		2/3		2/3		1/3	3/2				2/3		
Customer Demographics	2/3		3/2	3/2	3/2		2/3		2/3		2/3					2/3		
Complaint	2/2	2/3	2/2		2/2	3/3	3/3			2/2	3/3	2/3	2/2	3/2	2/2	2/3	2/2	2/2
Leasing/Transactions	2/2		2/3	2/3								1/2			2/2		2/3	2/3
Vendor		2/3	3/2		2/3	3/3	2/3		2/3	2/2	2/3	1/2	1/3		2/3		2/3	
Accounts/Payable		2/2	2/1		2/2				2/3		2/2	1/3	2/3	2/3	1/2		1/3	2/3
Accounts/Receivable		2/1	1/3	1/3	1/3		2/3			1/3	2/3	1/3			1/3		1/3	2/3
Maintenance	2/3	1/3	2/3			1/3	1/3			1/3	2/3	1/3	2/2		1/1	2/2	1/2	2/2
Warranty		2/2				2/2	2/3			1/3	2/2	2/2					1/2	
Inventory	1/3	1/2	1/2		1/3	2/3	3/3	1/3	2/2		2/3				1/1	2/3	1/3	2/2

Key		Availability/value	
Availability		value	
Very =	1	Low =	1
Medium =	2	Medium =	2
Low =	3	High =	3

Figure 15.8. Information categories by organisational subsystems matrix

has experience with the technology being used and the development team and users are knowledgeable in the application area.

3. Project structure. Risk is reduced to the extent the application fits existing structure for performing the task and the organisation demonstrates commitment to the change.

After the risk of each proposed project has been evaluated, the overall riskiness of the portfolio can be assessed. An appropriate balance of risk will depend on factors such as the organisational culture with respect to risk taking, the importance of risk taking to support major shifts in information system strategy, etc.

- A balance between support and strategic applications
- A balance between centralized systems and end-user facilities
- A balance between high risk/high payoff and low risk/low payoff
- A balance between applications for aggressive, mature users and timid, initial users.

Chargeout (Castes of Information Systems)

Chargeout is an accounting mechanism for allocating the costs of information system resources to their users. There are two methods of chargeout. The first is a straightforward allocation of costs to different users in order to give them some idea of how resources are being used. The user has no control over the costs. The primary purpose of this method is to aid in internal control of information system costs. In the second method, users are charged for information services, but they can control costs by reducing services or by choosing alternative methods or suppliers. The latter is consistent with a profit or cost centre concept of local responsibility for costs or profits of the unit. For new system development, the allocation rule is therefore based on whether users are willing to "buy" the application. If the user is willing to pay for development (e.g., a fixed price), the information systems function must allocate necessary personnel resources to accomplish it.

There are significant advantages to the chargeout methods (if it fits the organisation), but it tends to promote local rationality rather than rationality for the entire organisation, and it does not resolve allocation if there are more projects being "brought" than information systems can develop.

Steering Committee Report

In spite of all attempts at rationality and balanced portfolios, significant allocation decisions usually remain to be made. These may be made by a single executive (such as the information system executive); an alternative is a steering committee composed of executives from major functions in the organisation. The important point is that project selection should not fall to lower-level systems planning personnel who have neither appropriate authority nor the broad knowledge of business needs to do it correctly.

An advantage of the steering committee is that it allows for exercise of organisational power and politics. Ideally, it arrives at a plan which is the optimal allocation of resources organisation-wide. It facilitates coalitions and builds support for the allocations and the resulting plan. Disadvantages are the time required for the negotiation of a steering committee and the possibility that "information needy" but less powerful groups will be overlooked.

Summary/Conclusion

The development of an information plan for information system resources is a vital part of good management. There are a variety of approaches to organising for planning; the approach chosen should include appropriate participation and review by the organisation to ensure that the plan meets organisational needs and that it has organisational support. A fundamental principle for the plan is that it should be derived from and conform with the organisation's plan. The contents to the plan demonstrate this conformance and describe how the plan is to be executed.

There are several models that are useful in the planning process and the positioning of an organisations with respect to planning. The Nolan stage model describes the direction of change as organisations adopt information technology and develop organisational mechanisms to benefit from it. The three stage model of MIS planning is a useful framework for describing the stages of planning and the role of methodologies in strategic planning, organisational information requirements analysis, and resource allocation.

Within the information system strategic planning stage, several techniques are available for ensuring strategic alignment with the organisational plan: derivation from the organisational plan, use of the strategic grid, fit with organisational culture, and strategy set formation. Approaches to the information requirements stage will be explained in Chapter 15; this chapter explained an approach to eliciting high level requirements for planning and information architecture through interviews with managers. For the resource allocation stage, four approaches were explained: comparative cost-benefit, portfolio, chargeout, and steering committee ranking.

Notes

1. Cyrus F. Gibson and Richard L. Nolan, "Managing the Four Stages of EDP Growth."
2. Richard L. Nolan, "Managing the Crises in Data Processing."
3. B. Ives and S. Hamilton, "Knowledge Utilization among MIS Researchers."
4. I. Benbasat, A. S. Dexter, D. H. Drury, and R. C. Goldstein: "A Critique of the 'Stage Hypothesis': Theory and Empirical Evidence."
5. John Leslie King and Kenneth L. Kraemer, "Evolution of Organisational Information Systems: An Assessment of Nolan's Stage Model."
6. B. Bowman, G. B. Davis, and J. C. Wetherbe, "Modeling for MIS," *Datamation*, July 1980, pp. 155–162; and B. Bowman, G. B. Davis, and J. C. Wetherbe.
7. F. W. McFarlan and J. L. McKenney, *Corporate Information Systems Management*.
8. W. R. King, "Strategic Planning for Management Information Systems."
9. J. C. Wetherbe and G. B. Davis, "Developing a Long-Range Information Architecture."
10. F. W. McFarlan, "Portfolio Approach to Information Systems," *Harvard Business Review*, September-Oct. 1981, pp. 142–150.
11. McFarlan and McKenney, *Corporate Information Systems Management*.
12. Nolan, "Management the Crises in Data Processing."

16

Procedures for the Determination of Information Requirements

An information system should meet the needs of the organisation it serves, and applications should meet the needs of their users. The requirements for the information system are therefore determined by the strategies, goals, procedures, and behaviour of individuals within the organisation acting individually and collectively. Since this is so, why not ask the participants to describe the requirements for the information system? This chapter will explain why this simple strategy may not be adequate. It will then describe alternative strategies and some criteria for selecting among them.[1]

A Strategic Approach for the Determination of Information Requirements

There are four major reasons it is difficult to obtain a correct and complete set of requirements:

1. The constraints on humans as information processors and problem solvers.
2. The variety and complexity of information requirements.
3. The complex patterns of interaction among users and analysts in defining requirements.
4. Unwillingness of some users to provide requirements (for political or behavioural reasons).

The four reasons for difficulty in arriving at correct and complete requirements for information systems suggest that there should be several general strategies for requirements determination. The selection of a strategy is based on the conditions (contingencies) that apply in a specific case.

An information requirements determination strategy is a general approach to obtaining requirements. The specific procedures are information requirements determination methods. A set of related methods is a methodology (although the terms method and methodology are frequently used interchangeably). Within the broad outlines of a strategy, methods may be used singly or in combination to elicit requirements and to document the results. This is important because methods of documentation frequently contain the implicit assumption that the requirements are known and must only be documented. This chapter will emphasize methods of determination.

Three Levels of Information Requirements

There are three levels at which information requirements need to be established in order to design and implement computer-based information systems:

1. The organisational information requirements to define an overall information system structure and to specify a portfolio of application and databases.
2. The requirements for each database defined by data models and other specifications.
3. The detailed information requirements for an application.

Some methods of requirements determination are more suitable for the less-detailed, broader-scope, organisation-level information requirements, whereas other methods may be more suitable for the more detailed application information requirements. Some methods can be applied to requirements determination at both levels. This chapter will explain specific techniques for information requirements at the level of the organisation and application.

Organisation-Level Information Requirements

Information requirements determination at the organisation or enterprise level is a key element in developing an information system master plan. Often termed enterprise analysis, the process of organisation-level information requirements determination obtains, organises, and documents a complete set of high-level requirements. The requirements are factored into databases and subsystems (a portfolio of applications) that can be scheduled for development. The overall information architecture is defined, and the boundaries and interfaces of the individual applications subsystems are specified.

Database Requirements for Information System

Database requirements arise both from applications and ad hoc queries. The overall architecture for the databases to meet these requirements can be defined as part of organisational information requirements. Major classes of data are defined and associated with organisational processes that require them. There is very little detail in the requirements at this level.

The process of obtaining and organising more detailed database requirements can be divided into defining data requirements as perceived by the user (programs or ad hoc queries) and defining requirements for physical design of the databases. User requirements are referred to as conceptual or logical requirements because the user views of data are separated from the organisation of data in physical storage. User requirements may be derived from existing applications or by data modelling.

The requirements for physical database design are derived from the conceptual requirements, the hardware and software environments, and specifications related to use of the database. Physical database is beyond the scope of this text.

Application-Level Information Requirements

An application is a subsystem of the overall information system structure: it provides information processing for an organisational unit or organisational activity. The process for the determination of information requirements at the application level defines and documents specific information contents plus design and implementation requirements.

There are essentially two types of information system application requirements: social and technical. The social or behavioural requirements, based on job design, specify objectives and assumptions such as the following:

- Work organisation design objectives
- Individual role assumptions
- Responsibility assumptions
- Organisational policies

The technical requirements are based on the information needed for the job or task to be preformed. They specify outputs, stored data, and information processes. A significant part of the technical requirements are associated with the structure and format of data. The formulation of data models is described in the next chapter.

The technical requirements include interface requirements between the user system and the application system. The interface requirements include data presentation format, screen design, user language structure, feedback and assistance provisions, error control, and response time. These interface requirements are explained in Chapter 17.

Constraints on Humans as Specifiers of Information Requirements

Human appear to be so versatile with respect to information use that human constraints or limitations are frequently ignored. Yet "asking" users to define their information requirements will not necessarily yield a complete and correct set of requirements. Are human as information processors, human bias in selection and use of data, and human problem-solving behaviour. The relevance of these limitations to the specification of information requirements will be summarized.

Role of Human in Information Processing

Humans make use of three memories in information processing: external, long-term, and short-term. The limits of short-term memory affect the information requirements obtained whenever the process being used to elicit requirements uses only short-term memory (e.g., an interview in which there is no use of external storage such as notes, reports, or documents). The user beings interviewed cannot hold a large number of items in short-term memory for discussion or analysis purposes and is therefore limited in processing responses. The short-term memorylimitation may also affect the number of requirements that user define as important. In various processing activities using short-term memory, the user may have selectively emphasized a few items of information and recorded these in long-term memory as being the most important. These few requirements may be the only ones recalled when a question is asked.

Short-term memory limitations can be significantly reduced by the use of external memory to store data being processed and by the use of methodologies that systematically elicit and record small numbers of data chunks.

Human Make Biasness and use of Data

There is substantial evidence to show that humans are biased in their selection and use of data.[2] Behaviour resulting in bias. The effects of biases on information requirements determination are summarised below. The net effect on the determination of information requirements is a significant bias toward requirements based on current procedures, currently available information, recent events, and inference from small samples of events. The analyst and user who understand these biases may compensate for them; a significant method of compensation is to provide a structure for eliciting of requirements.

Problem-Solving Behaviour of Humans

The problem space for information requirements determinations is how a particular analyst or user formulated a representation to use in working on information requirements. Methods for the determination of information requirements provide such a structure for the problem space.

The users and analyst involved in the process apply bounded rationality using a somewhat simplified model of the organisation and its information requirements. The completeness and correctness of the requirements obtained are thus limited by the model as well as by the training, prejudice, customs, and attitudes of users and analysts involved in the process. The effect of bounded rationality in analysing information requirements is demonstrated in the behaviour of systems analysts. The low-rated analysts have a poorly developed model and, therefore, a poorly developed search procedure in the problem space.[3] Also, higher-rated analysts consider organisational and policy issues in establishing requirements; low-rated analysts do not.

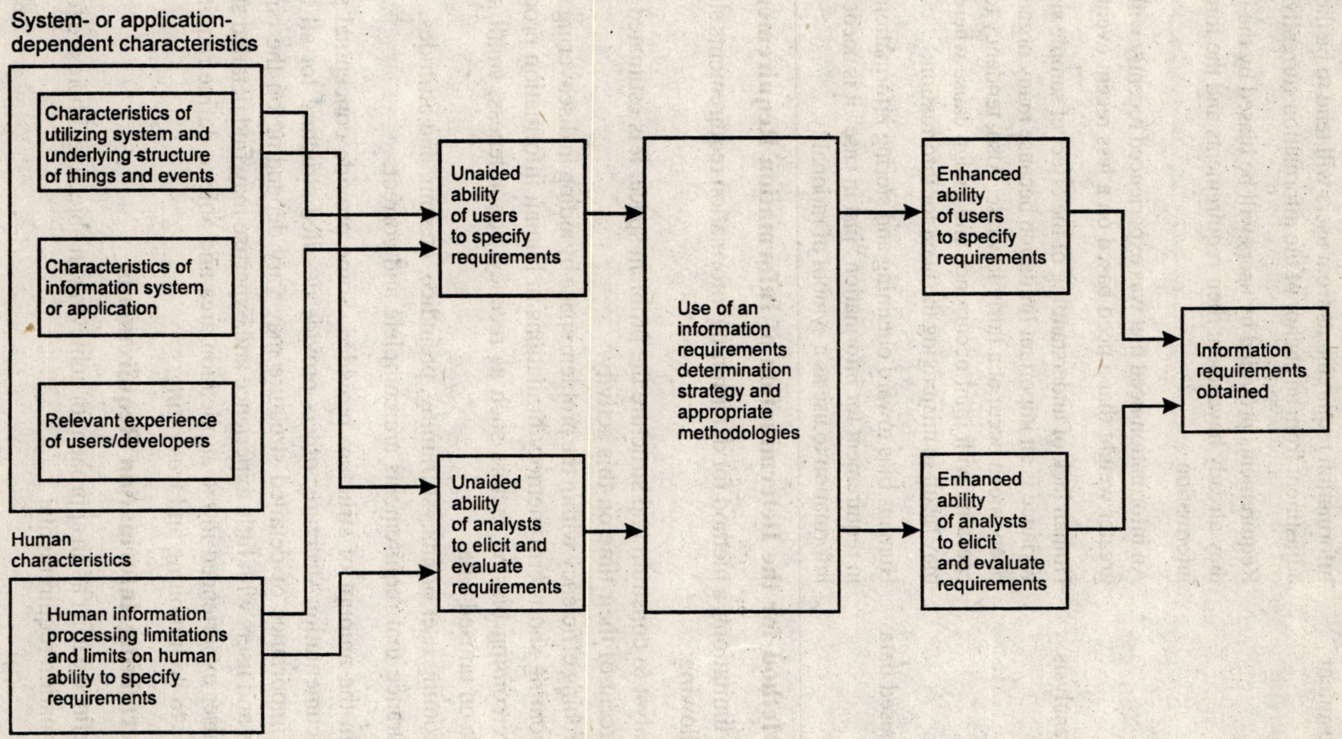

Figure 16.1. Effect of application characteristics, human characteristics, and information determination strategies and methodologies on information requirements obtained.

Human biasing behaviour	Effect on information requirements determination
Anchoring and adjustment	Information requirements from users will tend to be the result of an adjustment from an anchor of the information currently available.
Concreteness	Requirements provided by users will be biased by the information they already have about their requirements and the form of his information.
Recency	An information need that was experienced recently will be given greater weight that a need based on a less recent event.
Intuitive statistical analysis	Human lack of understanding of the effect of sample size of variance is an important limitation because many organisational phenomena occur at a fairly low rate. Also, tendency to identifying causality with joint occurrence and assign cause where none exists may result in misjudging the need for information.
Placing value on unused data	Humans bias toward obtaining and storing information may result in requirement for information "just in case" it is needed or information to use as a symbol of rationality.

Significance of a Method for the Determination of Information Requirements

Based on human limitations, a method for determining information requirements should be able to accomplish the following:

1. Assist an analyst to constrain and structure the problem space. It is estimated that analysts spend 75 percent of their time on this activity.[4]
2. Assist in searching efficiency within the problem space by aiding in discovering requirements and in overcoming short-term memory limitations in human information processing.
3. Assist in overcoming biasing factors such as recency, concreteness, small samples, and placing value on unused data.
4. Aid in overcoming user or analyst training, prejudice, custom, and attitudes.
5. Provide assurance that requirements are complete and correct.

Methods differ in the amount of structure provided. Some provide conceptual structure but little process and documentation structure; others provide detailed structure for all tasks and all documentation. The importance of detailed structure may vary depending on the circumstances. For example, analysts and users with little experience and expertise may find detailed structure very useful; analysts and user experienced in the application area and able to define requirements may find detailed structure to be inhibiting and frustrating.

Strategies for Determining Information Requirements

A strategy was defined earlier as an approach for achieving an objective. There are four strategies for determining information requirements:

1. asking
2. deriving from an existing information system

3. synthesising from characteristics of the utilising system
4. discovering from experimentation with an evolving information system

The set of four strategies is applicable both to determining organisational information requirements and to application requirements. For each strategy, there are a number of methods that are in use or have been proposed. In the discussion of strategies, some methods will be used as illustration; no attempt will be made to provide a comprehensive list.

The Value of a Requirements Study

Perhaps the best way to illustrate the value of an organisation's having an organisational information architecture for MIS is to quote the president of EPIC a year after he personally led the development of their architecture:

I had worked in top management in one of our other subsidiaries and experienced the disappointment that comes from developing systems in the traditional FIFO, piecemeal way with the consequences of redundant, non-integrated and inaccessible information.

When I took over a new subsidiary, I decided there must be a better way. There was. By developing an information architecture before developing systems we have been able to pull all our systems together. Our short-run system decisions are dovetailing into our long-range systems. We know where we are going and getting there.

Beyond that, just the process of going through an organisational information requirements analysis gave me and my management invaluable insight into our business.

Source: J. C. Wetherbe and G. B. Davis, "Developing a Long-Range Information Architecture."

Users Tend to use Mixed Strategies to Identify Requirements

In a research project, information were elicited from executives using two alternative methods:

1. Data analysis (i.e., deriving from data in existing application). Existing reports were examined and data items were dropped or added.
2. Decision analysis (i.e., synthesizing from characteristics of the utilising system). Using a decision flowchart, decision were analysed and informal requirements derived.

The objective was to compare the two approaches. One interesting result was that it was difficult for users to follow a pure strategy; they wanted to use a mixed strategy. Those doing decision analysis kept referring to existing reports and those doing data analysis often analysed the existing data in terms of decisions.

Source: M. C. Munro and G. B. Davis, "Determining Management Information Needs."

Asking

In pure asking strategy, the analyst obtains information requirements from persons in the utilising system solely by asking them what their requirements are. From a conceptual standpoint, the asking strategy assumes that users can structure their problem space and overcome or compensate for biases due to concreteness, recency, small sample size, and unused data. Anchoring by users in formulating responses is assumed to yield satisfactory results. These conditions may hold in very stable systems for which a well-defined structure exists or in systems whose structure is established by law, regulation, or other outside authority. There are a variety of methods for carrying out an asking strategy. Some asking methods are listed below with comments on condition that suggest their use.

Asking method	Description	Condition suggesting use
Closed questions	Each question has a defined set of possible answer from which the respondent selects.	When set of factual responses are known or respondent may not be able to recall all possibilities. Analyst must know all possible responses.
Open questions	No answer provided. Respondent is allowed to formulate response.	When feelings or opinions are important or when respondent has knowledge and ability to formulate responses.
Brainstorming	Group method for eliciting wide variety of suggestion by open flow of ideas.	Used to extend boundaries of problem spaces of participants and elicit nonconventional solutions.
Guided brainstroming	Participants are asked to define ideal solutions and then select the best feasible ideal solution. The IDEALS methods[5] is an example	Used to guide brainstorming to "ideal" solution. Useful where participants have system knowledge, but may be locked into an anchoring and adjustment behaviour.
Group consensus	The participants are asked for their estimates or expectations regarding significant variables. Delphi methods and group norming are examples.	Used to arrive at "best" judgemental estimate of variables that are difficult or impossible to estimate quantitatively.

If a pure asking strategy is followed, one or more of the asking methods are used to elicit requirements, and analysis is limited to consistency checks as requirements are documented. The asking methods can also be used in conjunction with other strategies.

Existence of Information System from the Old Information System

Existing information systems that have an operational history can be used to derive requirements for a proposed information system for the same type of organisation or application. The type of existing information systems that are useful in deriving requirements for future systems are:

1. Existing systems that will be replaced by new system
2. Existing system in another, similar organisation
3. Proprietary system or package
4. Descriptions in textbooks, handbooks, industry studies, etc.

With regard to human problem-solving behaviour, deriving from an existing information system is an explicit use of anchoring and adjustment. Users and analysts explicitly choose an existing systems as an anchor and adjust the requirements from it. Deriving information requirements from an existing information systems has also been termed a data analysis approach[6] since the data inputs and outputs of the existing system are the focus of analysis.

If the information system is performing fairly standard operations and providing fairly standard information for utilizing systems that are stable, the use of an existing systems as an anchor is appropriate. In application systems for some well-defined functions such as payroll, data analysis of an existing systems can be a useful primary method. In the early application of computers to organisational transaction processing and accounting systems, derivation of requirements from the processing performed on the data provided by the existing system was widely used.

Some analysts use data analysis of the existing system as a secondary method for deriving requirements. To avoid being overly influenced by the concreteness of the existing system, they may delay its use until after their primary analysis methods has provided an initial set of requirements.

Synthesis from Characteristics of the Utilising System

Information systems provide information to facilitate the operation of object systems, those that utilise the information. Requirements for information thus stem from the activities of the object system. This suggests that the most logical and complete method for obtaining information requirements is from an analysis of the characteristics of the utilising system. This approach may overcome biases by providing and analytical structure for the problem space of the user or analyst. The object system analysis is therefore appropriate when the utilising system is changing or the proposed information system is different from existing patterns (in its content, form, complexity, etc.), so that anchoring on an existing information system or existing observation of information needs will not yield a complete and correct set of requirements.

Several methods have been proposed for implementing a strategy for determining information requirements from object system analysis. Eight general methods described in this section illustrate the alternatives. Although useful at both organisational level and application level, each method has a primary orientation.

Table 16.1

Characteristics of Methods for Determining Information Requirements

Method	Primary requirements orientation	
	Organisation	Application
1 Normative analysis	X	
2 Strategy set transformation	X	
3 Critical factor analysis	X	
4 Process analysis	X	
5 Ends-means analysis	X	
6 Decision analysis		X
7 Sociotechnical analysis		X
8 Input process-output analysis		X

The description of these methods are very short and provide only an idea of the central focus of each approach. The objectives of this section is not to explain these methods in detail, but to illustrate how the strategy of synthesis from characteristics of a utilising system may be implemented. The common feature of all the methods is that requirements for the information system are obtained from a study of the object or utilising system. The questioning or analysis process in each case begins with the needs, structure, objectives, etc., of the utilising system. When these components are established, they are the basis for deriving the information system requirements.

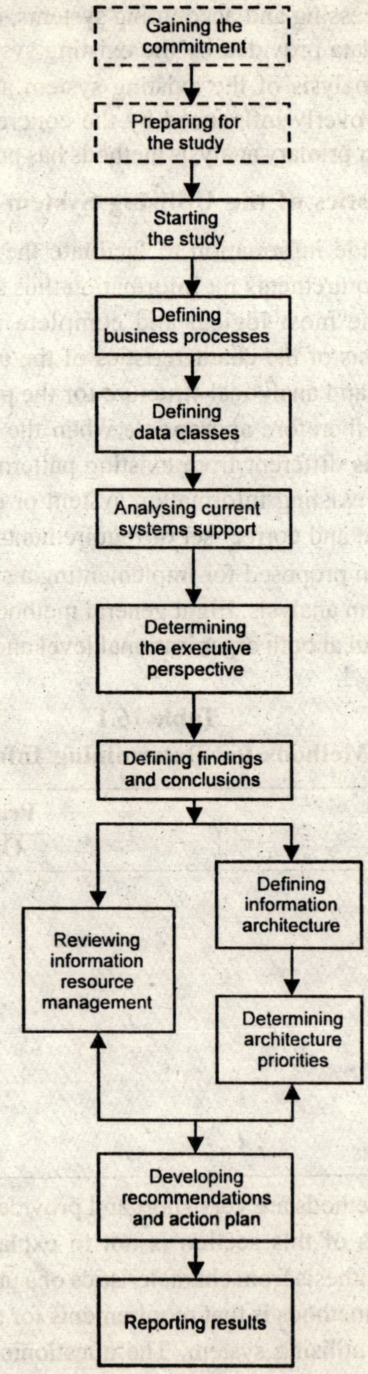

***Figure 16.2.** Steps in defining a proposed information architecture in Business Systems Planning.*

Normative analysis methods are based on the fundamental similarity of classes of object systems. For example, all billing applications perform a set of basic functions that can be prescribed in advance. These fundamental characteristics are the basis for a prescribed or normative set of requirements. Analysis then concentrates on tailoring the normative requirements to meet nonstandard needs of a specific organisation or application.

Strategy set information is a methodology primarily for describing organisation level information requirements[7] from the objectives of the organisation. For example, if an organisational objective is to improve profits and the selected strategy is to change the sale mix to larger proportion of higher gross margin products, the information system requirement derived from this objectives is a gross margin analysis application.

In the *critical factors analysis* approach, information requirements are derived from the critical factors for operating and managing an enterprise. There is therefore a two step process of eliciting the critical factors and then deriving information requirements. An example of critical factors analysis is the Critical Success Factors (CSF) methods.[8] The analyst asks users to define the factors that are critical to success in performing their functions or making decisions. A small number of critical factors usually emerges from this eliciting process. Information requirements can then be derived. It can be used at both the organisation and application level.

Process analysis is another approach to the synthesis of requirements. The idea underlying this approach is that business processes (groups of decisions and activities required to manage the resources of the organisation) are the basis for information systems support. Processes remain relatively constant over time, and the requirements derived from the process will reflect the nontransient needs of the organisation. An example of a process-based methodology is Business Systems Planning (BSP). The method is primarily appropriate for developing an information systems master plan.

BSP is a comprehensive IBM methodology[9] well supported by materials and instruction. Information requirements are derived from the object system in a top-down fashion by starting with business objectives and then defining business processes. Business processes are used as the basis for data collection and analysis. In interviews to clarify processes, executives are also asked to specify key success factors and to identify decisions and problems. Logically related categories of data are identified and related to business processes. This information is used in defining a proposed information architecture. Based on the current systems and proposed information architecture, application priorities are established and migration to databases planned.

Ends-means analysis is a technique for determining requirements based on systems theory.[10] The technique can be used to determine information requirements at the organisational, departmental, or individual manager level.

The technique separates the definition of ends or outputs (goods, services, and information) generated by an organisational process from the means (input and processes) used to accomplish them. The ends or output from one process (whether the process be viewed as an organisational, departmental, or individual process) is the input to some other process. For example, the inventory process provides a part to the production process, the accounting process provides budget information for other organisational processes, and the marketing process products to customer processes.

Managers are first asked to define both ends and means for their unit. They are then asked to describe measurements for effectiveness and efficiency. Effectiveness information requirements are based upon what constitutes effectiveness for outputs and what information or feedback is needed to evaluate effectiveness. Efficiency information requirements are based upon what constitutes in an input and transformation process and upon what information or feedback is needed to evaluate efficiency.

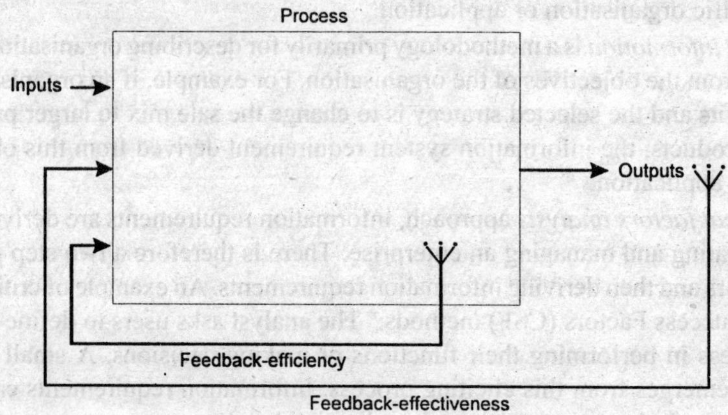

Figure 16.3. *Model of ends-means analysis.*

Ends-means analysis has been used in diverse industrial setting with positive results. Information requirements are determined that are often more far-reaching than requirements generated using other techniques. A problem with many information requirements methods is that they result primarily in efficiency-oriented information. However, manager agree that it is more important to be effective than to be efficient. Ends-means analysis brings out the effectiveness information requirements.

The *decision analysis* method for information requirements determination is performed by the following steps:[11]

1. Identify and prescribe the decision.
2. Define the decision algorithm or decision process. Various documentation methods may be used. Examples are decision flowcharts, decision tables, and decision trees.
3. Define information needed for the decision process.

Decision analysis has been shows to be very useful in clarifying information requirements with users in cases where the decisions process is fairly well defined. For unstructured, poorly understood decision processes, decision analysis does not appear to perform any better than other approaches. Also, decision analysis does not apply to all applications or all information included in applications.[12]

The *sociotechincal analysis* approach[13] consists of two parts: social analysis and technical analysis. The social analysis determines systems requirements relative to the social, human interaction system of the organisation. These requirements include system design features and implementation procedures. The social analysis is performed by studying pattern of social interaction and group behaviour in the current system. Technical analysis is an analysis of variances and control loops that require information.

Requirements for sociotechnical design are usually obtained from participative methods and are oriented to application-level analysis. It is especially appropriate for applications that involve many users, particularly secondary users (such as data preparation personnel), or where the application will significantly change the work environment, social interaction, or job design.

Input-process-output analysis is a system approach. A system is defined in terms of its input, outputs, and transformation processes for receiving inputs and producing outputs. The approach starts in a top-down fashion on an object systems. Subsystems of the object systems are analysed to subdivide them into smaller subsystems, etc., until information processing activities are defined as separate activities with in subsystem. The advantage of analysis based on inputs, processes, and outputs of systems is that it is systematic and comprehensive. By starting at a high level and factoring into subsystems, there is reasonable assurance of completeness. Analysis can be carried to as low a level of detail as desired.

One example of the input-process-output approach is data flow diagrams.[14] When use at a high level of analysis, data flow diagrams are a graphic method for defining inputs, processes, and outputs and for factoring systems into subsystems. The factoring process is top-down and can be carried to the level of program module specification. Other useful methods based on a system approach are SADT (Structured Analysis and Design Techniques)[15] and ISAC (Information Systems work and Analysis of Changes).[16]

Discover with Experiment on Evolving Information System

Traditional procedures for determining information requirements are designed to establish a completes and correct set of requirements before the information system is designed and built. In a significant percentage of cases, user may not be able to formulate information requirements because they have no existing model (either normative or experiential) on which to base requirements. They may find it difficult to deals in abstract requirement or to visualize new systems. User may need to anchor on concrete systems from which they can make adjustments.

Another approach to information requirements determination is, therefore, to capture an initial set of requirements and implement an information systems to provide those requirements. The system is designed for ease of change. As users employ the system, they request additional requirements. After initial requirement establish an anchor, additional requirements are discovered through use of the system. The general approach has been described as prototyping or heuristic development.[17]

Strategy for Finding the Information Requirement

Four strategies have been described for determining information requirements, with each strategy having a number of methods that may be employed. This section will present an approach to the selection of an appropriate primary strategy. The selection procedure is contingent on characteristics of the environment in which the determination of requirement is conducted.

The underlying basis for selecting a strategy is uncertainty with respect to the requirements determination processes. The uncertainty is based on four factors: characteristics of the utilising system, the information system or application, the users, and the analysts.

The approach to selecting an information requirements determination strategy consists of five steps. The steps represent a series of evaluations to establish a basis for selection. The evaluations are not precise, but do provide guidelines for judgment.

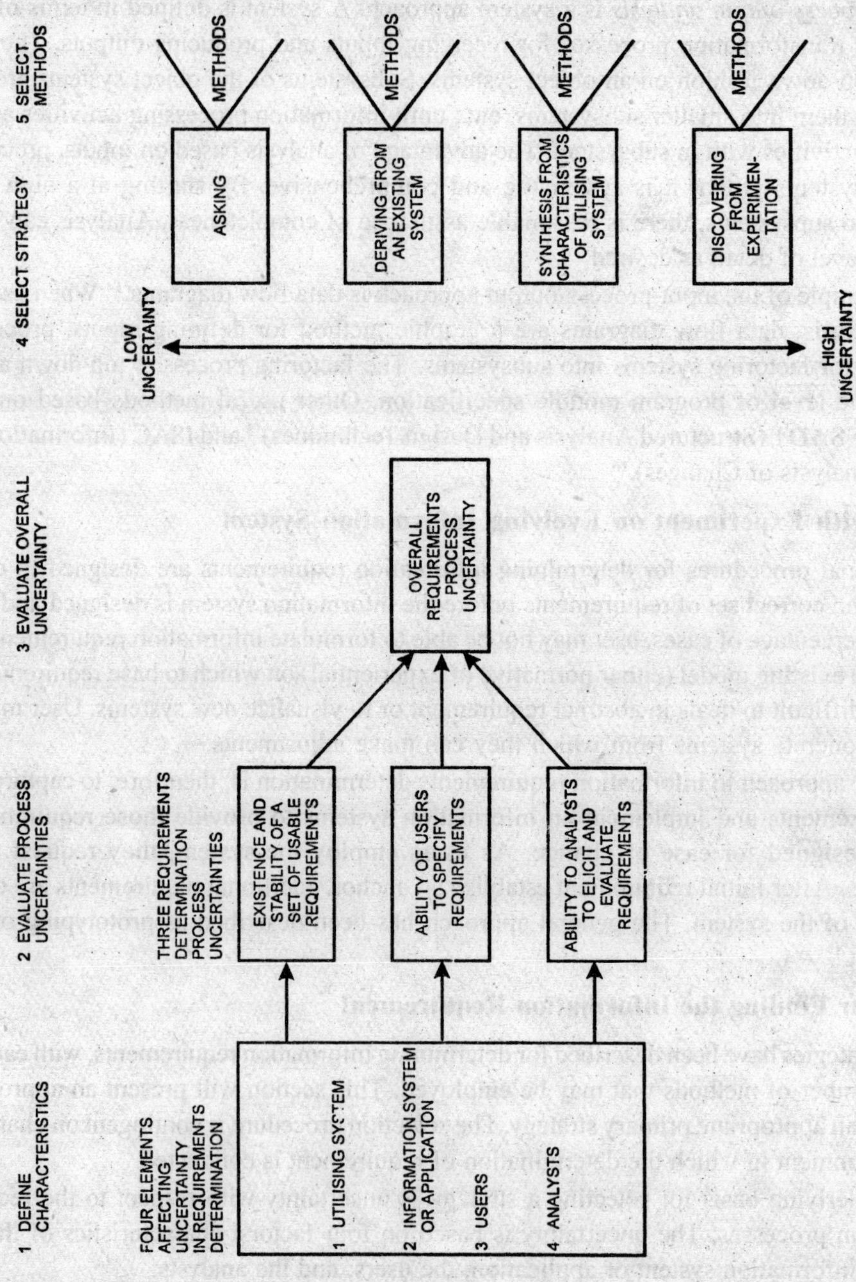

Figure 16.4. Selection of a strategy for the determination of information requirements.

Table 16.2

Steps in Selecting a Strategy and Methods for Determining Information Requirements

1 Identify those characteristics of the four elements in the development process that affect uncertainty in the determination of information requirements:
- Utilising system
- Information system or application
- Users
- Analysts

2 Evaluate the effect of the characteristics of the four elements in the development process on three process uncertainties:
- Existence and availability of a set of usable requirements
- Ability of users to specify requirements
- Ability of analysts to elicit and evaluate requirements

3 Evaluate the combined effect of the process uncertainties on overall requirements uncertainty.

4 Select a primary strategy for requirements determination based on the overall requirements uncertainty.

Uncertainty	*Strategy*
Low	Asking
↑	Deriving from an existing system
↓	Synthesis from characteristics of utilising system
High	Discovering from experimentation

5 Select one or more methods for the set of methods to implement the primary strategy.

Identifying the Characteristics of Elements in the Development Process that Affect Uncertainty

Four elements in the development process affect the level of uncertainty of a strategy for determining information requirements: the utilising systems, the information system or application system, the user, and the analysts. As summarised below, for each of the elements there are characteristics that reduces expected uncertainty as to requirements determination; there are opposing characteristics that increase expected uncertainty.

Evaluating the Effect of the Characteristics of Process Uncertainty

The characteristics of the four elements in the development process affect the uncertainty of determining information requirements by affecting three process uncertainties:

1. Uncertainty with respect to expected and stability of a usable set of requirements.
2. Uncertainty with respect to users' ability to specify requirements.
3. Uncertainty with respect to analyst's ability to elicit requirements and evaluate their correctness and completeness.

The first uncertainty can arise from a number of characteristics of the utilising system. Some examples are

- Lack of a well-understood model of the utilising system. This lack may be reflected in confused objectives, unclear organisation, and poorly defined operating procedures.
- Lack of stability in structure and operation of the utilising system.
- Lack of stability in use of information system. Nonprogrammed activity has a low level of predefined structure, and, therefore, changes in user personnel may create unstable use patterns.

Elements in development process	Characteristics that reduce uncertainty	Characteristics that increase uncertainty
Utilising system	Stable, well-defined systems not in process of change programmed activities or decisions	Unstable, poorly understood system in process of change Nonprogrammed activities or decisions
Information system or application system	Traditional, simple set of requirements Clerical support system	Complex or unusual set of requirements Management support system
Users	One or few users High user system experience	Many users Low user system experience
Analysts	Trained and experienced with similar information system	Little prior training or experience with similar information system

The second process uncertainty about the ability of users to specify requirements is a result not only of human limitations in developing specifications but also of characteristics of the information systems or application. Examples are

- Lack of user conceptual model of the utilising system.
- Lack of structure for activity or decisions being supported.
- Changes in the utilising system.
- Changes in the use of information.
- A complex system.
- A large number of user which will affect level of participation and users' feelings of responsibility in specifying requirements.
- Types of users doing the specifications. Clerical users may be able to specify procedure requirements but not overall content; managers may be better able to specify content than procedures.
- Lack of user experience in the utilising system and lack of experience in type of application being proposed.

The third uncertainty with regard to the ability of the analyst is related to the personal characteristics of the analysts, their general level of training, and prior experience with the same or similar applications. The characteristics of the application that affect users described above also affect the performance of the analyst.

The level of knowledge and experience needed by users and analyst tends to differ for different strategies in the determination of requirements. An asking strategy requires a higher level of user knowledge and experience than an experimental strategy.

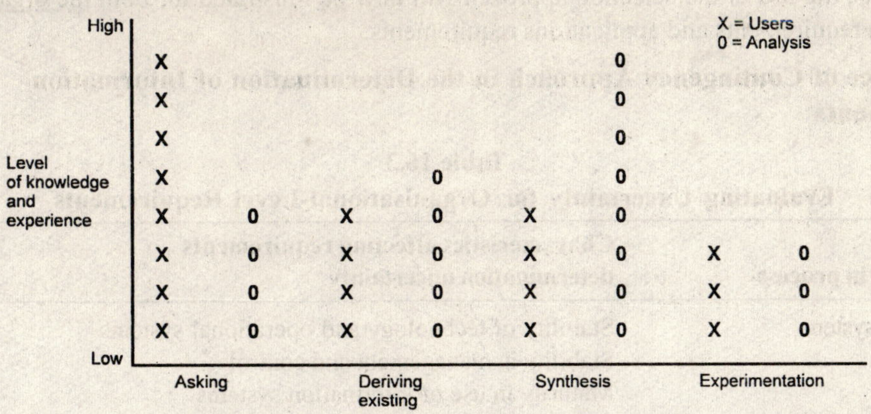

Figure 16.5. *Relative estimated level of knowledge and experience by users and analysts to employ the four requirements determination strategies.*

Evaluating the Combined Effect of the Process Uncertainties on Overall Requirements Uncertainty

The expected overall requirements uncertainty might be estimated directly from the characteristics of the object system, the information system, the users and the analysts. However, it is useful to make this evaluation in two steps:

1. Evaluate the effect of the characteristics of the four elements on the three process uncertainties.
2. Evaluate the three process uncertainties to arrive at an estimated overall level of requirements process uncertainty.

The expected overall level cannot be estimated with certainty, but the insight gained in the three-step evaluation allows a reasonable basis for selection of a strategy.

Selecting a Primary Strategy for Determining Requirements and One or More Methods

The selection of a primary strategy is based on the level of uncertainty in requirements determination. When a strategy has been selected, one or more methods are selected for use. The selection of a primary strategy and associated method(s) does not preclude the use of a secondary strategy and other supplementary methods, but it does assist the analyst in understanding how to deal with the expected level of uncertainty regarding requirements.

Many instalations have adopted a single development methodology to be used for all applications. This has training, supervision, and quality assurance benefits for the organisation. It may, however, mean that some applications are developed with a methodology that is not optimal. In such cases, the strategy selection approach outlined above may aid in encouraging analysts to use alternatives features of the standard methodology or to modify, adjust, or supplement it.

In order to clarify the concept of uncertainty and its effect on determining information requirements, the use of the selection approach will now be illustrated for both the organisational information requirements and applications requirements.

Significance of Contingency Approach in the Determination of Information Requirements

Table 16.3
Evaluating Uncertainty for Organisational-Level Requirements

Elements in process	Characteristics affecting requirements determination uncertainty
Utilising system	Stability of technology and operational systems Stability in management and control Maturity in use of information systems
Information system	Extent to which higher-level management applications are included in scope of systems Complexity and level of integration of information
Users	Level of experience in utilising system Experience in planning information systems
Analysts	Experience in planning information systems

One item of special interest is organisational maturity in the use of a computer-based information system. It is not feasible to implement a complex information system until the organisation has reached a "mature" stage of information processing.

Three examples illustrate the use of the contingency approach for selection of a strategy for determining information requirements for the organisational level.

1. Company A is a small company with a stable technology that has not used computers before. It expects to apply computer processing first to accounting and inventory control. It has an analyst with two years experience. In the list below and in those of the succeeding examples, the second column indicates whether an item increases or reduces uncertainty.

Characteristics of Company	*Effect on Uncertainty*
Stable technology	Reduces
Stable management control	Reduces
Low maturity in computer use	Increases
Clerical level applications	Reduces
Complexity and integration low	Reduces
Experience of analysis	—
Experience of users low	Increases

Based on these characteristics, process uncertainties are classified in the following ways:

- Low uncertainty as to existence and stability of requirements
- Moderate uncertainty as to the ability of users to specify requirements
- Moderate to low uncertainty as to the ability of analysts to elicit and evaluate requirements.

The overall evaluation is moderate to low uncertainty. A requirements strategy might be to derive an initial set of organisational requirements from the existing manual systems.

2. Company B has used computers for traditional accounting but would now like to have management-support applications, decision-support applications, query capabilities, and planning applications. The requirements uncertainty analysis is:

Characteristics of Company	***Effect on Uncertainty***
Stable technology and operational systems	Reduces
Management control changing	Increases
Fairly maturity in use of computers	Reduces
Management-level applications	Increases
Complexity and integration high	Increases
Experience of users low	Increases
Experience of analysts moderate	Increases

An evaluation of these characteristics suggests a moderate to high uncertainty in existence and stability of requirements, a fairly high uncertainty as to the ability of users to specify requirements, and a moderate uncertainty as to the ability of analysts to elicit and evaluate requirements. Overall, there is a moderately high degree of uncertainty in determining requirements, which suggests of synthesising organisational information needs from the characteristics of the utilising system.

3. Company C has a very unstable environment and very poorly developed planning and control information. Management wishes to improve its information systems to provide better information for planning and control.

Characteristics of Company	***Effect on Uncertainty***
Unstable operational processes	Increases
Management control changing	Increases
Low maturity in use of computers	Increases
Complexity and integration high	Increases
Experience of analysts low	Increases
Experience of users low	Increases

An evaluation of the characteristics suggest a high degree of uncertainty for existence and stability of requirements, the ability of users to specify, and the ability of analysts to elicit and evaluate. With this high level of overall uncertainty, the appropriate strategy for determining organisational requirements might be use experimentation with an evolving planning and control system.

Significance of Contingency Approach in Determination of Information Requirements

The characteristics that may be considered in evaluating the uncertainty of requirements processes for an application are summarised in Table 16.4.

Table 16.4
Evaluating Uncertainty for Application-Level Requirements

Elements in process	Characteristics affecting uncertainty in determining requirements
Utilising system	Existence of a model of the system Stability of system Nonprogrammed versus programmed activity stability in information use
Application	High-level versus low-level application Complexity Number of users
Users	Experience with utilising system Experience with application
Analysts	Experience with utilising system Experience with application

The following examples illustrate the use of the contingency theory to select a strategy for determining requirements for an application. In each example, the second column of the list indicates whether an item increases or reduces uncertainty.

1. A balance forward billing and accounts receivable application system for a retail store.

Utilising system has stable, programmed activity	Reduces
Application has stable requirements with fairly small number of users in accounting department	Reduces
User familiarity with system is high	Reduces
Analyst familiarity and experience is reasonably high	Reduces

There is very little uncertainty with respect to the requirements themselves, little uncertainty with respect to the ability of users to provide requirements, and little uncertainty as to the ability of analysts to elicit requirements and evaluate their correctness and completeness. Given this overall low degree of uncertainty, the analyst may use a primary strategy of asking users to define requirements (using open or closed questions). An alternative primary strategy is to derive requirements from an existing billing and accounts receivable system (existing system in this organisation or in another organisation).

2. An integrated online order entry transaction system and management order tracking application to replace a traditional batch system having little management reporting.

Utilising system is stable, mainly programmed activity	Reduces
Application has stable requirements for clerical users and moderately stable requirements for management users. Medium number of users	Reduces
Well defined model of requirements for order entry procedures	Reduces
Less well-defined model of tracking requirements	Increases
Complex system	Increases
User personnel are familiar with order entry requirements	Reduces
Experience of analysts is at least moderate for online systems	Reduces

The overall uncertainty level is moderate, based on the evaluation of three processes:

- Little uncertainty with respect to the order entry functions to be performed and requirements related to these functions. Some uncertainty as to management functions to be supported.
- Little uncertainty as to the ability of users to define transaction entry requirements and medium uncertainty as to ability to define management reporting. Because of online systems, there may also be new social system consideration and human behaviour considerations that users cannot define clearly and completely.
- Moderate uncertainty as to the ability of analysts to elicit requirements and evaluate their correctness and completeness.

Given this overall moderate degree of uncertainty, the analyst may choose to synthesize from the characteristics of the utilising system as the primary strategy for requirements determination. Examples of methods appropriate to this situation are:

- Input-process-output analysis
- Sociotechnical analysis for social and behavioural requirements
- Decision analysis or critical factors analysis for management reporting

3. A management report application for problem identification and problem finding with respect to sales. It includes content of some existing informal, private information systems but does not replace an existing information system application.

Support mixture of programmed and nonprogrammed activities	Increases
Requirements not stable because they are dependent on expertise and decision style of users	Increases
No well-defined model of utilising system and its requirements	Increases
User somewhat unsure of requirements	Increases
Analysts inexperience in specific application because it is unique	Increases

Based on these characteristics, there is uncertainty with respect to processes for determining requirements:

- High uncertainty as to necessary and desirable requirements
- High uncertainty as to the ability of users to specify requirements
- High uncertainty as to the ability of analysts to elicit requirements and assess correctness and completeness

The high level of uncertainty suggests a discovery methodology in which requirements are identified iteratively as the application system evolves.

Summary/Conclusion

The chapter describes factors relevant to the selection of a strategy for determining information requirements. The chapter defines three levels of requirements: organisational information requirements, application-level requirements, and database requirements. The constarints on humans as specifiers of information requirements are explores. Four broad strategies for determining information requirements encompass groups of methods. These strategies are (1) asking, (2) deriving form an existing information system, (3) synthesizing from characteristics of the utilising system, and (4) discovering from experimentation with an evolving information system.

The selection of a strategy is based on uncertainties with respect to processes for determining information requirements. The uncertainty focuses on (1) uncertainty with respect to the existence and stability of a set of requirements, (2) uncertainty with respect to the ability of users to specify requirements, and (3) uncertainty with respect to the ability of analysts to elicit requirements and evaluate their correctness and completeness. These three uncertainties as to the best process for determining information requirements are associated with certain characteristics of the utilising systems, the information system or application, users, and analysts.

The selection of a strategy for determining requirements for both the organisational level and the application level is thus based on an evaluation of the characteristics that determine the three areas of uncertainty. The selection of a primary strategy for determining requirements that satisfies the level of uncertainty points to a set of methods for use. An analysts may choose to use other strategies and methods to supplement the primary determination strategy.

Notes

1. The chapter is based on G. B. Davis, "Strategies for Information Requirements Determination."
2. G. A. Miller, "The Magical Number Seven, Plus or Minus Two: Some Limits on Our Capacity for Processing Information."
3. N. P. Vitalari, "An Investigation of the Problem Solving Behavior of Systems Analysts," unpublished doctoral dissertation. University of Minnesota. Minneapolis, 1981.
4. Vitallari, "An Investigation of the Problem Solving Behavior of Systems Analyst."
5. G. Nadler, *Work Design: A Systems Concepts*, Revised Edition.
6. M. C. Munro and G. B. Davis, "Determining Management Information Needs".
7. W. R. King, "Strategic Planning for Management Information Systems."
8. J. F. Rockart, "Critical Success Factors," *Harvard Business Review*.

9. *Business Systems Planning—Information Systems Planning Guide*, Application manual GE20–0527-3.
10. J. C. Wetherbe and G. B. Davis, "Strategic MIS Planning Through Ends/Means Analysis."
11. R. L. Ackoff, "Management Misinformation Systems,"
12. Munro and Davis, "Determining Management Information Needs."
13. R. P. Bostrom and J. S. Heinen, "MIS Problems and Failures: A Socio-Technical Perspective; Part I: The Causes."
14. The literature on data flow diagrams and structured analysis is fairly extensive. For example, see T. DeMarco, *Structured Analysis and Systems Specification*, Yourdon, New York, 1978; D. T. Ross and K. F. Schoman, Jr.
15. Ross and Schoman, "Structured Analysis for Requirements Definition."
16. M. Lundeberg, G. Goldkuhl, and A. Nilsson, *Information Systems Development: A Systematic Approach*, Prentice-Hall, Englewood Cliffs, NJ, 1981.
17. T. R. Berrisford and J. C. Wetherbe, "Heuristic Development: A Redesign of Systems Design," *MIS Quarterly*, 3:1 March 1979, pp. 11–19.

17

Significance of Database

DATABASES AND DATABASE MANAGEMENT SYSTEMS
- The Database Approach
- Objectives of Databases and Database Management Systems
- The Data Dictionary

DATA MODEL CONCEPTS AND TERMINOLOGY
- Review of Definition
- Relationships
- Constraints
- Schemas and Mappings

NORMALISATION IN DATABASE DESIGN

APPROACHES TO DETERMINATION OF DATA REQUIREMENTS FOR DATABASES
- Development Strategy Based on Overall Architecture
- Evolutionary Development Strategy Based on Existing Files
- Anticipatory Development Strategy

CONCEPTUAL DATA MODELLING
- Chen Entity-Relationship Data Model
- Nijssen's Information Analysis
- Limitations of Conceptual Data Models

SUMMARY/CONCLUSION

One approach to definition of data requirements in an organisations is to specify data only in relation to particular information system applications. There are several difficulties with that approach:

1. Having data "owned" by individual applications may lead to difficulties in data access for other uses, duplicate data, and inconsistencies between data in different files.
2. New applications may be more costly to develop because of the need to build new files, redesign files, or develop interfaces with existing data.
3. Frequently, data needed for analyses and for responding to queries will not be available because no existing application has provided it.
4. Some data may be available for applications, but it may be very difficult and costly to access it for ad hoc query or analysis.

The solution (introduced in earlier chapters) is to establish databases and use a database management system to manage data as a general use resource. However, even with a database, there may be data items that are not available because their use was not anticipated. Much of the data in the database may be derived from the requirements of data processing applications, but many data items that should be in a database are not part of the normal transaction processing or reporting applications.

The subject of this chapter is how to determine the information requirements for organisational databases. The chapter provides conceptual background on databases and reviews the data concepts and terminology. Alternatives for determining current and anticipated database data requirements are reviewed, and two methods for data modelling are explained.

Databases and Database Management Systems

The database is central to a management information system. Although the term "database" is often used to refer to any data available for information processing or retrieval operations, the term implies a particular structuring of the data, both conceptually and in physical storage. This section will provide definitions and background concepts relayed to databases and database management systems.

The Database Approach

A *database* is a mechanized, formally defined, centrally controlled collection of data in an organisation.[1] The data records are physically organised and stores so as to promote shareability, availability, evolvability, and integrity. The database approach is made operational by a *database management system,* or DBMS, a software system which performs the functions of defining, creating, revising and controlling the database. It provides facilities for retrieving data, generating reports, revising data definitions, updating data, and building applications. Many different end users and a variety of application programs can access thee database, and it is desirable to have an organisational function to exercise control over the database. This function is known as *database administration*; the person performing the function is a *database administrator.*

The database management system controls the interaction between the database and application programs prepared by programmers and between the database and nonprogramming or ad hoc users. Accessing or updating items in the database is performed only through the database management system.

There are three classes of users who interact with database management systems. There are languages and instruction procedures appropriate for each of them:

The nonprogramming user. User who is not writing a program to use the database. Usually an analyst or end user with special training. Programs ad hoc queries and reports using a database query language.

The programming user. An application programmer who does the analysis and programming of applications. Uses special database interface instructions to program application access to the database through the database management system. The instructions call the database management system to request data, perform updates, etc. The programming user can also use the database query language for special assignments.

The database administrator (DBA). The DBA uses special instruction and facilities of the databases management systems (*a data definition language* or DDL) to define, create, redefine, and restructure the database and to implement integrity controls.

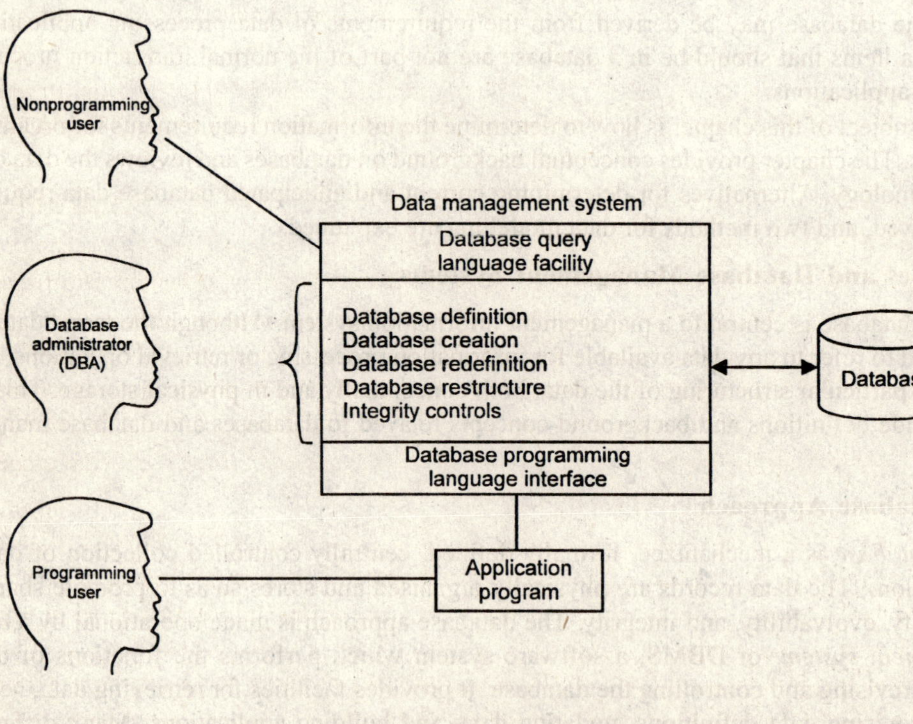

Figure 17.1. *Conceptual model of a database management system. (Adapted from Gordon C. Everest, Database Management: Objectives System Functions and Administration, McGraw-Hill, New York, 1984.)*

Installing a database requires procedures to determine data requirements to be stored in the database and use of software to build the initial database, maintain and recognise the database, provide data to applications programs, and execute ad hoc queries and report request. The database administration function performs or oversees these activities. The focus of this chapter is on the first activity of determining data to be stored.

Aim and Objectives of Database and Database Management Systems

The objectives of the database approach are listed below;[2] they provide a guide to the database requirements process and data modelling.

Database objective	Description
Availability	Data should be available for use by applications (both current and future) and by queries.
Shareability	Data items prepared by one application are available to all applications or queries. No data items are "owned" by an application.
Evolvability	The database can evolve as application usage and query needs evolve.
Data independence	The users of the database establish their view of the data and its structure without regard to the actual physical storage of the data.
Data integrity	The database establishes a uniform high level of accuracy and consistency. Validation rules are applied by the database management system.

Data independence is achieved by separating data from the programs that use it, providing facilities for different user views of the data, and the separation of logical design from physical design. The raw material for the physical design is the logical database design that describes the data as perceived by the users of the database. The shareability objective results in a minimisation of unplanned redundancy. Redundancy occurs when the same data item is stored multiple times. With a database system, it need only be stored once. This reduces inconsistencies and also aids in achieving the objective of data integrity. The data integrity objective is also achieved by having data in the database controlled through the database administration function and data creation, access, and updating controlled by the database management software.

An explanation of the physical design of the database is beyond the scope of this chapter. However, there are many trade-offs to be made in deciding on how to physically structure the data, provide access paths, etc. These trade-offs are between storage utilisation, speed of access, ease of maintenance, and availability of data for a variety of uses. The physical trade-offs may mean that some user requirements are met with fast access times while others are allowed to take significant time to process. The database is not a huge file drawer in which everything is available with equal accessibility. Access paths must be established. By analogy, automobile and truck traffic uses a network of highways, secondary roads, and streets that are predefined. If there is no direct route to a location, a relatively inefficient route may be found using secondary roads and streets. In some cases, no route can be found. In the same way, the physical database design must provide highways for fast data access for the most common needs. Other needs must use less efficient, less direct access paths.

Importance of Data Dictionary

A data dictionary, as the name implies, is a repository of information about data. In some database systems, the stored definitions of data (called schemas) provide all necessary data dictionary information; in others, the data dictionary is supplementary. Although it might be possible in a very small limited database to prepare a manual dictionary, the term refers to a dictionary maintained by special data dictionary software. It contains such information as the following about data:

1. The name of the data item.
2. A description of the data item. The description can be a language description (such as "a unique 9-digit identification code") or a data processing description [such as PIC X(12) for type and number of characters in a field]. The descriptions may also specify allowable values (numeric, range of values, etc.), edit and validation criteria, security, and calculations to determine value, classification, aliases, owner, and number of occurrences.
3. Source of data—various sources of input.
4. Impact analysis—users of the data including screens, reports, programs, and organisational positions that access and use the data item.
5. Key words used for categorising and searching for data item descriptions.

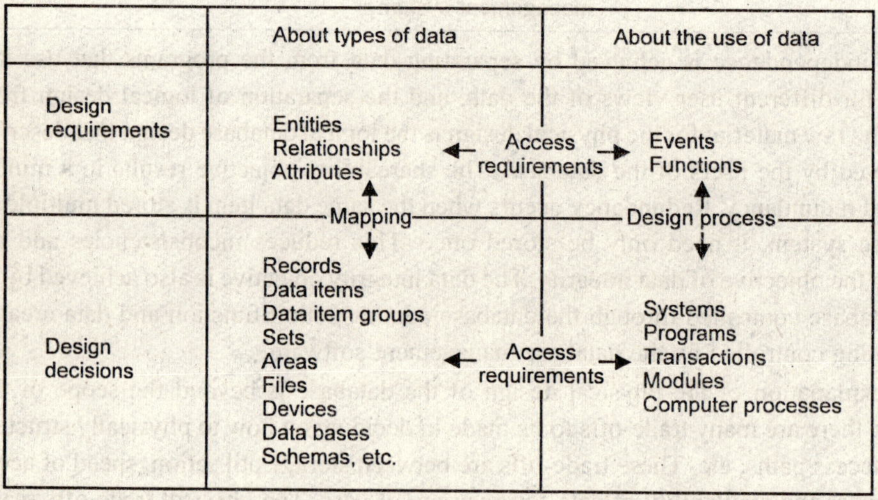

***Figure 17.2.** The Information in a data dictionary, (Source: "The Bristish Computer Society Data Dictionary Systems).*

The information in the data dictionary is about both types of data and uses of data. It relates both to the documentation of design requirements and to design decisions. Entities and attributes document design requirements about types of data; data items and records documents physical design decisions. Events and functions document the end use of data; programs and modules document the physical information processing use of data.

There are three general types of facilities in a data dictionary:

1. **Report facility.** There is detailed reporting on data items and their uses. Cross-reference reports show relationships, and summary reporting provides various summary data.
2. **Control facility.** This defects violations of standards for user authority, documentation, etc.
3. **Excerpt facility.** Specific tasks are performed such as preparation of test data, copying code from existing programs and inserting in programs under development, and copying documentation into source code.

The data dictionary provides lists of data items sequenced alphabetically by classification, keyword, etc. The dictionary provides a consistent official description of data as well as consistent data names for programming and retrieval. For example, the data dictionary can provide a response to specific queries such as all data items describing "product."

The advantages of a data dictionary are not only consistency of data descriptions and naming, but also ease of updating where one data description serves many purposes. For example, if a change is to be made to a product code, some data dictionaries identify every program, input screen, and report in which the data item appears.

Data dictionaries may be used by the database administrator to enforce standards for names and descriptions; those who creates data must follow these standards. Creating a data dictionary requires significant efforts to remove past inconsistencies and ambiguities. The same data items in different applications will have different names, so synonyms must be specified. Also, the same name may have been used in different applications to refer to different data items.

A Difficult Conversation to a Data Dictionary

A medium-large company is considering a data dictionary for documenting existing data and supporting development. The Company uses 3,000 programs that access 2,400 files. However, there has been no consistency of naming, so a file may be referred to by as many as five different names. With an average of three records per file and an average of 10 fields per record, there are a maximum of 12,000 file names, 36,000 record definitions (under the file names), and 360,000 items. There are significantly fewer in actual fact because of the high number of aliases, but there are still a large number.

Data Model Concepts and Terminology

Database design can be divided into three phases:

Phase	Description
Requirements determination	Determination of the data requirements (views) of individual users and applications.
Conceptual (logical) design	Integration of the individual user and application views into an overall conceptual views that resolves view conflicts. There are two parts to this phase: an unconstrained or natural conceptual design and a conceptual design constrained for a particular DBMS.
Physical design	Translating the conceptual design into physical storage structure.

The data modelling procedures described in the chapter refer to requirements determination and development of an overall, natural conceptual model.

Review of Definitions

A data model is a model describing the data in an organisation. It provides a framework for abstracting the essential qualities or characteristics of data. *Data modelling* is the process of abstraction and documentation using a data model.

Data modelling creates hierarchies of abstraction along two dimensions: aggregation and generalisation. Aggregation identifies data item as part of a higher-level, more aggregate descriptor. For example, project number is associated with (part of) a project which is part of an assignment. Generalisation creates categories into which a data item may be classified. For example, employees may be categorised as to age, type of job, type of pay plan, etc. Examples of generalisation of employees by type of job are secretaries, truck drivers, and salespersons.

A data model may be a conceptual model designed to provide user-understandable specifications of data or a physical data model designed to aid in physical database design. The two types of models have also been termed infological (for the human understanding and requirements level) and datalogical (for physical design and implementation).[3] Model can contain some elements of both contain not only conceptual requirements aspects but also physical aspects of data related to implementation.

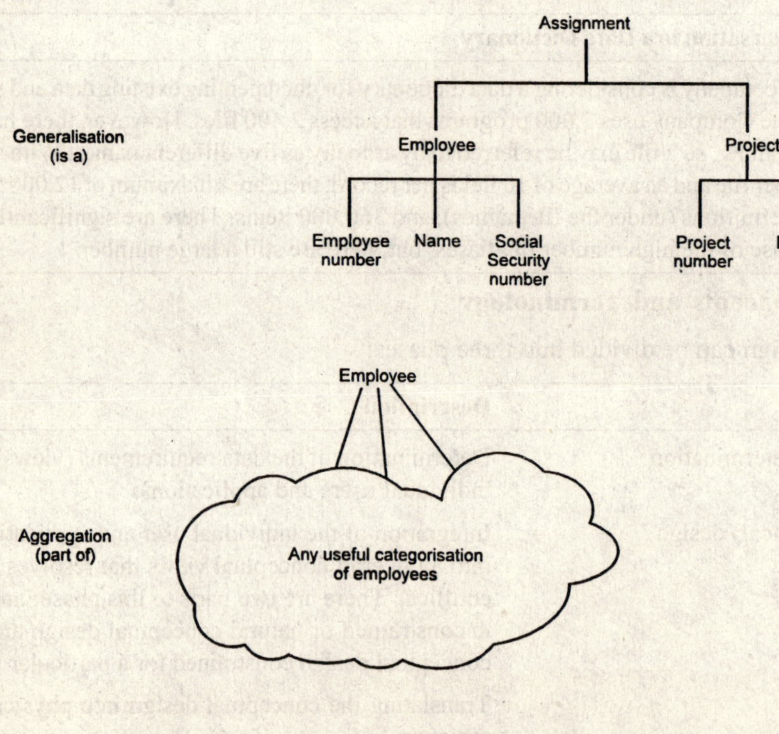

Figure 17.3. Concepts of aggregation and generalisation.

They are summarised below:

Term	Definition
Entity	Any type of "thing" about which information is maintained. A more formal definition is "a category, arbitrarily defined (but agreed to) so that membership within the category can be established (at least at a point in time)."[4]
Attribute	A characteristics of an entity.
Instance	A specific instance of an entity or relationship. Consist of a set of values for attributes of an entity or relationship.
Relationship	Association between entities.
Identifiers	Set of attributes which uniquely identify an instance of an entity or relationship.

An explanation of the relationship among these terms may clarify their meaning. An entity is a category or grouping of things; instances of an entity are members of that category (e.g., EMPLOYEE is an entity and a person who works for the company is an instance of that entity). The description of an entity-instances is a set of values for selected attributes (data items) of the entity-instance (e.g., "John Doe" is the value of the attribute EMPLOYEE-NAME for an instance of the entity EMPLOYEE).

Relationships (One to One, One to Many, Many to Many)

There are three types of relationships among entities. These are recorded during conceptual data modelling and also affect physical database design (Figure 17.4).

Relationship	Explanation
1:1	In a one-to-one relationship, an instance of an entity has a given relationship with only one instance of a second entity. For example, the entity PROFESSOR had the relationship HOLDS for the entity ENDOWED-CHAIR and the ENDOWED-CHAIR entity has the relationship IS HELD BY with the entity PROFESSOR. Since only one professor holds an endowed chair and the endowed chair is held by only one professor, the relationship is 1:1.
1:M	In a one-to-many relationship, an entity has relationships with many instances of another entity. For example, the entity UNIVERSITY has many STUDENTs. but each STUDENT entity instances IS ATTENDING only one UNIVERSITY. Note that if a student can attend many universities, the data model should define a many-to-many relationship.
M:M	In a many-to-many relationship, an entity has relationships with many instances of another entity; and that entity has relationships with multiple entity instances of the first. For example, the entity instances for STUDENT may be REGISTERED IN many different CLASSES, the relationship is many-to-many since each CLASS also has many students.

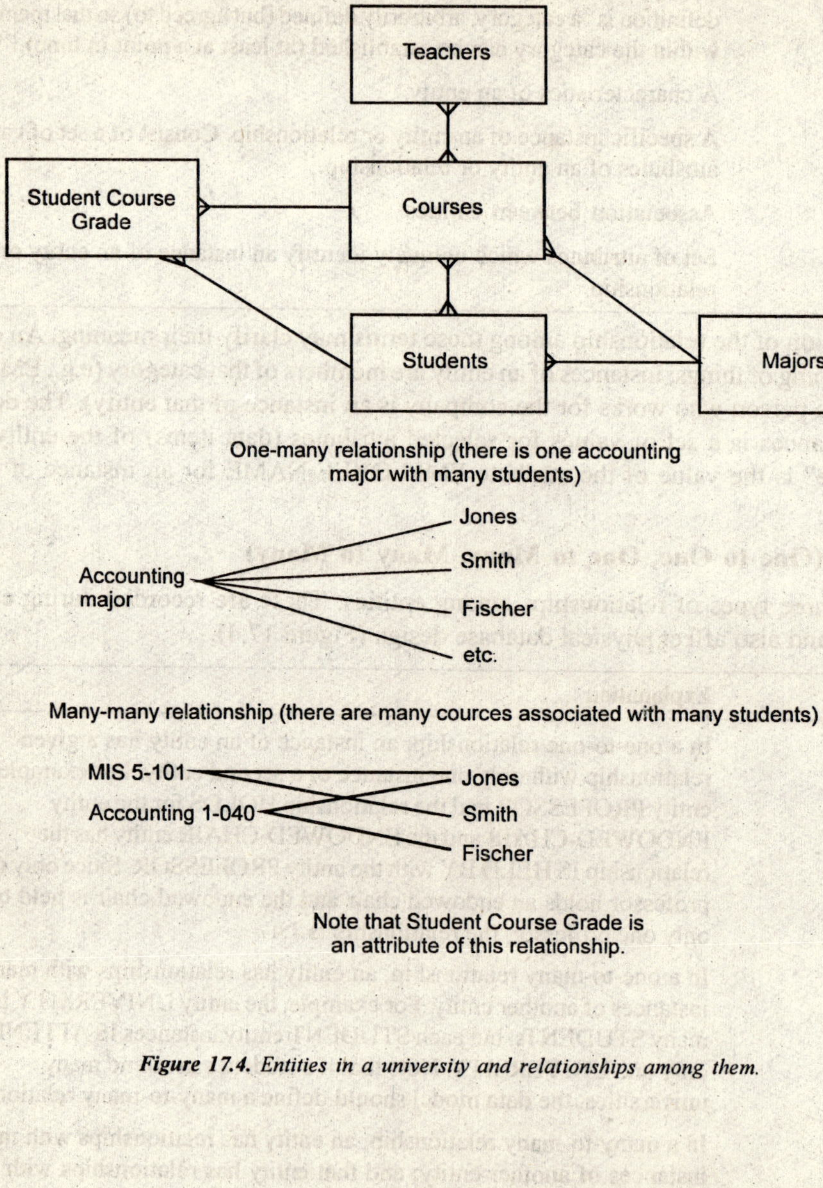

***Figure 17.4.** Entities in a university and relationships among them.*

Constraints (Conditions)

Constraints define conditions that must be met for the data to be complete and correct. Three major types of constraints are on values, dependencies, and referential integrity:

Constraint	Description
Values	The allowable, valid values for attributes may be stated as a list, a range, types of characters, etc. For example, values may be 1, 2, or 3 only, range from 0 to 60, or be numeric only.
Dependencies	The allowable values for attributes may depend on some other value. For example, the allowable values for an employee skill classification are determined by the allowable skills that are part of the employee's department. An employee's eligibility for overtime pay (value for overtime wages) is dependent on his or her employee status code.
Referential integrity	Entities and relationships often have reference conditions that must be met. For example, there may be existence dependencies, in which for one entity to exist, a second entity must also exist. An illustration of this is a sales order; for an order to exist, there must be a customer.

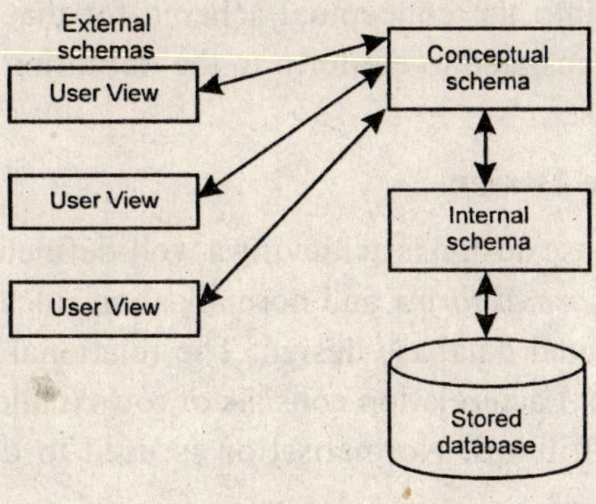

Figure 17.5. A general model of a database system.

Schemas and Mapping (Internal Structure of the Database)

These define categories of data and their properties. The different schemas reflect different views of the database:

- *External schema* or *user schema* is the user's view of a part of the database
- *Conceptual schema* is the overall logical view of the database
- *Internal schema* or *data storage definition* is the way the data is physically organised in storage.

Each user of the database (an application program or a person formulating a query) is concerned with only a small portion of the database. Each user is interested in only a part of the entities in the database, only part of the attributes of those entities, and certain relationships among the entities. The external schema is the user's schema or *user's view* of the data being used.

The conceptual schema (or conceptual model) is the logical view of the entire database. Ideally, the conceptual schema represents as closely as possible the real entities and their relationships. It contains integrity rules and authorization rules, but it does not contain information about how the data items are stored.

The internal schema (or physical data model) describes how the database is organised for physical storage and access. The internal schema includes information or ordering of records, block sizes, storage indexes, use of pointers, and access strategic being used.

A *mapping* is a translation from one schema to another. In order for a user to access data, the user view of the data as reflected in the external schema must be translated into the overall conceptual schema. This is accomplished through *external/conceptual mapping*. In the same way, the *conceptual/internal mapping* translates logical descriptions of data in the conceptual schema to physical locations and access paths in the internal schema.

External schemas that describe overlapping portions of the database in different ways are resolved through the external/conceptual mapping. For example, one application may describe the data item "MAJOR" as having 11 characters while another external schema describes it has having 12 characters. These differences can be handled through the external/conceptual mapping. It first translates each view into the conceptual schema for that field. When the data item is retrieved, its format can be translated to conform to the definition given by the external schema before it is displayed to the user.

Normalisation in Database Design

One of the issues in database design is achieving a well-defined model of data to avoid update anomalies. This is aided by *normal forms* and normalisation rules. The normal forms are easily understood in terms of relational database design. The relational database model describes the database as tables or relations. Each relation consists of rows (called *tuples*) representing entities and columns representing attributes. Normalisation is used to determine how to cluster data items.

There are five normal forms,[6] although fourth and fifth forms are rarely used in practice. They are summarised below and then explained in more detail with an indication of the importance of each. A *key field* in a record is a unique identifier that differentiates the record from any others. The key field may consist of subfields. For example, the key field for a part could consist of two subfields for part number and warehouse number. The other fields in the record are nonkey fields.

The discussion here will focus on second, third, and fourth normal forms. Second and third normal forms deal with single-valued facts, i.e., one-to-one or one-to-many relationships. Fourth normal form is associated with multivalued facts or many-to-many relationships.

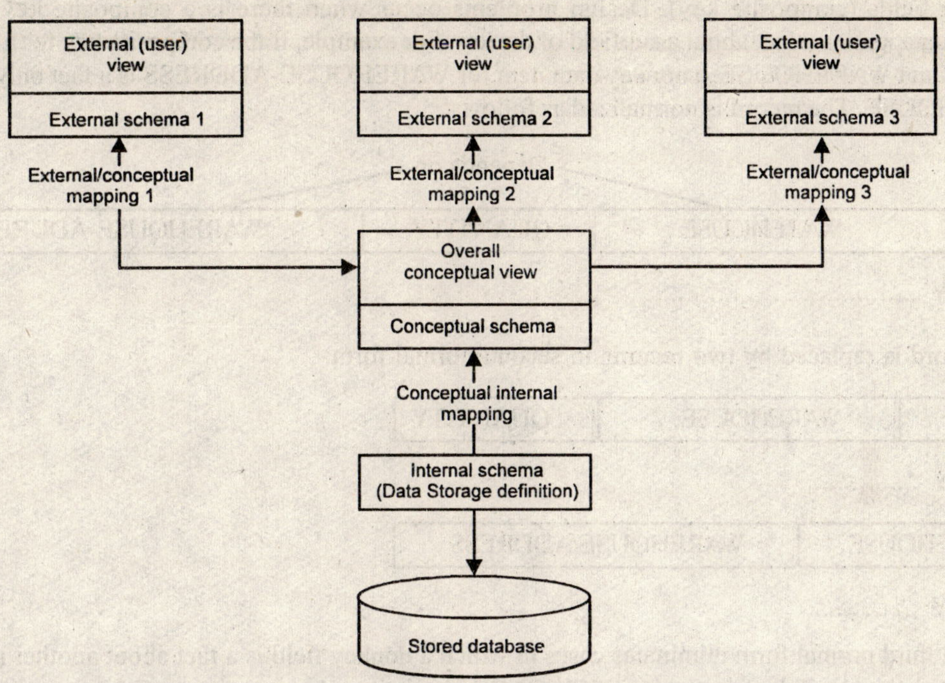

Figure 17.6. Mapping between schemas.

Form	Explanation
First normal form	By definition, all fields in a record in first normal form are atomic or single valued. There are no repeating groups of items.
Second normal form	"Second and third normal forms deal with the relationship between nonkey and key fields. Under second and third normal forms, a *nonkey field* must provide a fact about the key, the whole key, and nothing but the key."[7] In second normal form, no nonkey field is a fact about (depends on) a subset of a key.
Third normal form	No nonkey field is a fact about (depends on) another nonkey field.
Fourth normal form	The key of a record type (that already satisfies third normal form) does not contain two or more independent multivalued facts about an entity.
Fifth normal form	A record in fifth normal form is the same as fourth normal form except in special cases where there is a symmetric constraint.

A record in first normal form can only violate second normal form if the key consists of multiple fields (composite key). Design problems occur when there is a composite key and a nonkey data item is a fact about a subfield of the key. For example, if the composite key for a record is PART and WAREHOUSE, a nonkey data item for WAREHOUSE-ADDRESS is a fact only about WAREHOUSE. The record is normalized as follows:

Depends on

PART WAREHOUSE	QUANTITY	WAREHOUSE-ADDRESS

......KEY ....

The record is replaced by two records in second normal form:

PART	WAREHOUSE	QUANTITY

......KEY ....

WAREHOUSE	WAREHOUSE/ADDRESS

......KEY ....

The third normal form eliminates cases in which a nonkey field is a fact about another nonkey field. For example, if the key field is EMPLOYEE (say, an employee number) and there are nonkey fields for DEPARTMENT and LOCATION of department, the LOCATION is a fact about DEPARTMENT. To place in third normal form, the record definition is replaced by two record types:

Depends on

EMPLOYEE	DEPARTMENT	LOCATION

....KEY ....

The records is replace by two records in third normal form:

EMPLOYEE	DEPARTMENT

....KEY ....

DEPARTMENT	LOCATION

......KEY ....

To look back at the examples for second and third normal forms, the basic problems caused by violation of the forms are the same:

- The item in violation is repeated in every record; therefore, if it changes, every record containing the item must be updated. For example, if the address of the warehouse or the location of a department is changed, every record must be updated. There is significant opportunity for the updating to miss a record and for the records to become inconsistent.
- If there are no records associated with the field violating the normal form, there may be no record in which to store the data. For example, if there are no parts stored in the warehouse, there is no record to keep the warehouse address. Likewise, if a department has no employees, there may be no record in which to store the department location.

Fourth normal form eliminates cases in which the composite key of a record type contains two or more data items that are independent, multivalued facts about an entity. SKILL and LANGUAGE are multivalued (many different skills and many different languages), but there is no logical dependency between a language and a skill. To put into fourth normal form, the data must be represented by two records.

EMPLOYEE	SKILL	LANGUAGE

....KEY...

is replaced by:

EMPLOYEE	SKILL

....KEY..............................

EMPLOYEE	LANGUAGE

....KEY.......................................

Normalisation is a powerful approach to defining the grouping of data items into records. The process of normalisation of records or relations provides both conceptual insight and practical procedures for database design, especially when the database model is relational. Ideally, the database should be in fourth or fifth normal form, but for many situations second or third normal form is acceptable.

Procedures of Determination of Data Requirements for Databases

The development of requirements for a database consists of an overall planning strategy and processes to define an overall architecture, existing requirements, and anticipated requirements. Based on these three processes, there are three alternative requirements development strategies:

- Development strategy based on overall architecture
- Evolutionary development strategy based on existing files
- Anticipatory development design strategy.

Regardless of the strategy chosen for database requirements determination, it should be preceded by an overall planning strategy which defines the basic architecture of the database. The degree of variation between the existing defined database (or files) and the planned overall architecture determines the best strategy for specific requirements development.

The overall architecture for a database is based on two types of requirements:

1. Transaction processing requirements. These are generally defined by existing data processing applications.
2. Management requirements. These include requirements derived from transaction processing as well as new requirements to support management needs not based on transactions or routine reports.

The second type of requirements is the most difficult to obtain. Eliciting these requirements may use a technique such as the one described in chapter 15 or similar techniques for requirements elicitation and architecture design.

The result of such planning is an architecture defining databases, classes of data, attributes, and users and uses for the data.

Development Strategy based on Overall Architecture

The requirements development strategy may be based primarily on an overall architecture for the databases. As individual applications are defined based on the overall architecture, the database requirements of those applications are explicitly defined. All data items do not need to be defined initially, but no data item are added unless there is an identified need either from a new application or form unmet queries.

The data flow diagramming method for application design illustrates an approach to systematic additions to a databases on an overall architecture and a specific application. Data flow diagramming defines application processing and data required to accomplish them. A logical data model is developed that includes all data items identified as being required for the application. The data items are grouped and analysed suing normalisation to ensure a nonredundant model of data. They can be integrated with existing data items using the data dictionary. If data items do not exist, they are added to the database. The data items for the application are analysed as to frequency of access and volume of occurrences, and physical database specifications are prepared.

Evolutionary Development Strategy Based on Existing Files

Some organisations have chosen to not do an overall architecture based on requirements eliciting procedures but to follow an evolutionary strategy. The reasoning is that it is difficult and expensive to develop an overall architecture and that it is better to let the databases evolve through usage. The evolution may occur both from application development and unmet query needs.

1. In the evolution from application development, the existing data files are used as the initial database. As more applications are defined, existing data items are assigned more uses and new data items are added. This approach has special appeal for a database that is expected to show little change in content or pattern of use.
2. In the unmet query evolution, a small initial database is prepared. As it is used, requests for new data items and new data relationships are made. Some items are found to have little or no use. There are additions, deletions, and reorganisation at frequent intervals. The approach is especially useful for small, local databases.

Anticipatory Development Strategy

Rather than only responding to requirements defined by applications or unmet queries, an alternative strategy is to define database requirements in a general way that includes both existing needs and anticipated needs. The approach will be referred to as *conceptual data modelling* to distinguish it form physical data modelling. Other terms are frequently used, such as *semantic data modelling* or *data structure modelling*.

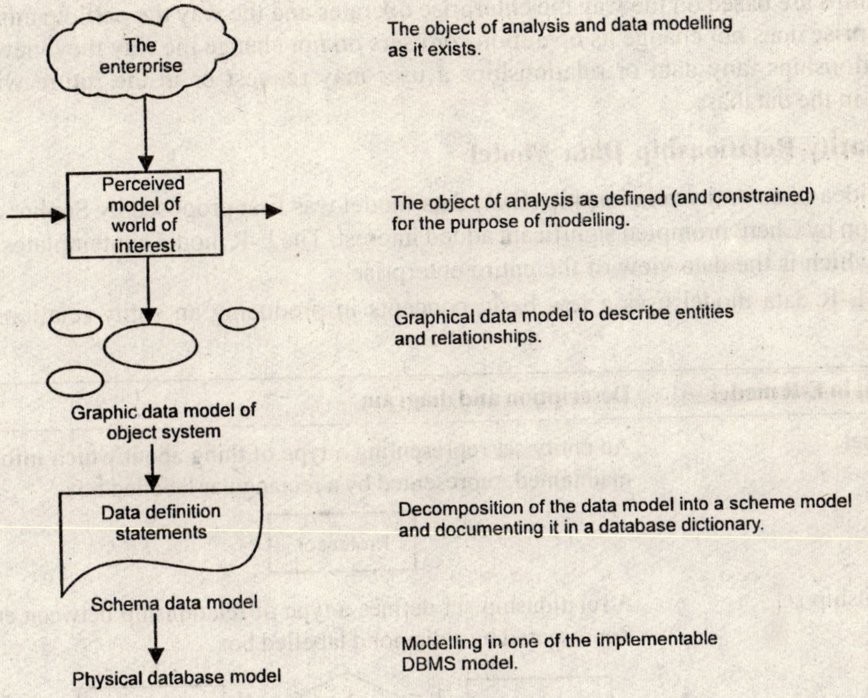

Figure 17.7. *Flow of work from conceptual data modelling to database design.*

The data requirements in the conceptual data modelling strategy are developed from a description of the entities and relationships among entities in the organisation or other object system requiring databases. Two alternative approaches to conceptual data modelling described below illustrate current thinking. There are other alternatives or variations on these approaches, but these will provide a basis for understanding the conceptual and practical issues in defining a complete set of databases requirements including anticipated requirements. The two methods that will be explained illustrate graphic methods and use of a sentences-predicate calculus. The graphic approach is the entity-relationship (E-R) model usually associated with Chen; the sentence-predicate calculus approach is Nijssen's information analysis. Neither will be explained in enough depth for operational use; rather, the objective is to illustrate concepts and ideas of conceptual data modelling and how they are being implemented.

Conceptual Data Modelling (Requirement of Database Model)

The common characteristics of conceptual data modelling methods is the definition of database requirements based on the development of a conceptual model of the organisation (referred to as the "enterprise") and its operations.

Advocates of conceptual data modelling argue that the most stable parts of a data processing systems are data and the data relations. Processing applications and processing functions are more changeable. The fundamental approach to requirements definition should therefore be based on the data. The data structure is theoretically more general than processes because data entities and relationships are based on the way the enterprise operates and the way the participants view data. If the enterprise does not change its operations or users do not change the way they view data entities and relationships, any data or relationships a user may request or in the future will have been included in the database.

Chen Entity-Relationship Data Model

The idea of an entity-relationship (E-R) data model was first proposed by Senko[8] and others. A publication by Chen[9] prompted significant added interest. The E-R model contemplates an enterprise schema which is the data view of the entire enterprise.

The E-R data model uses a few basic concepts in producing an entity relationship diagram (ERD).

Element in E-R model	Description and diagram
Entity set	An entity set representing a type of thing about which information is maintained. represented by a rectangular labelled box. 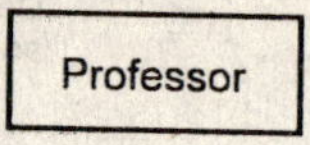
Relationship set	A relationship set defines a type of relationship between entity sets. Represented by a diamond labelled box.  In the above diagram, a PROFESSOR, in an ADVISOR relationship, may relate to many (N) STUDENTS; a STUDENT, in the ADVISOR relationship, has only one advisor PROFESSOR.
Attribute	An attribute associates a set of values (a value set) with an entity set or relationship set and provides an interpretation of the set of values in this context. Represented by a labelled ellipse. 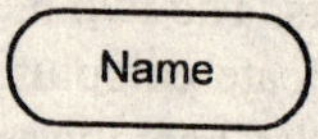

Figure given below uses E-R data model notation to diagram a PROFESSOR who has a NAME (FIRST NAME and LAST NAME) and a SOCIAL SECURITY NUMBER. In other words, the entity PROFESSOR has FIRST NAME as an attribute. There is a set of first name that are the value set for FIRST NAME. There are additional rules and procedures for creating an E-R diagrams and interpreting it. A complete exposition of this modelling approach is beyond the scope of the chapter.

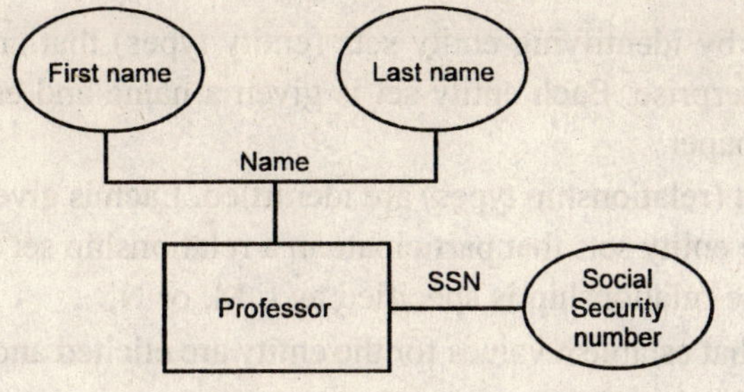

Figure 17.8. *Value set in E-R diagram.*

A Dialogue

Questioner:	"I saw a brochure coming around for a database system called… and I found it strange—in this brochure, they actually suggested you use an entity relationship model to design your database."
Expert:	"I don't see anything strange about being advised to use the entity-relationship model as a design tool and having a relational database as the end result."

An E-R diagram is read by using the names of the entity set plus words that describe the relationships among them. Arcs without labels are read with words such as: of, has, belongs to, and is in. For example, the diagram below could read as "A university has (enrolls) students" and a "students is at (is enrolled at) a university." The university has attributes of university name and university # with university number being an identifier. A student has attributes of students name, student ID #, and social security # with student ID # being part of a unique identifier, the other part being the university name. This simple data model also illustrates the limitations that are incorporate in any data model. The model shows a student with only one university. If a student is attending two or more universities, the data model cannot show it.

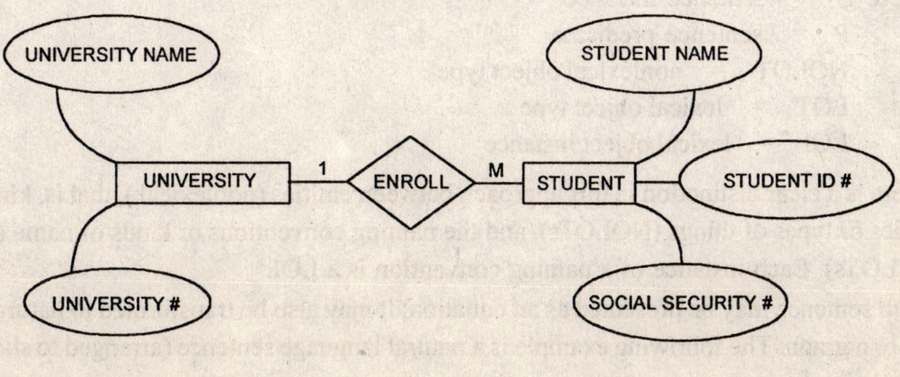

The analyst working with a user (or a user working alone who has received training in data modelling) can use a diagramming technique such as the ERD to develop a user data view of the enterprise and to document that view. For example:

1. The user starts by identifying entity sets (entity types) that are significant for his or her view of the enterprise. Each entity set is given a name and enclosed in a rectangle on a chalkboard or paper.
2. Relationship set (relationship types) are identified. Each is given a name and graphed with a diamond. The entity sets that participate in a relationship set are indicated by connecting with an arc. The relationship is specified as I, M, or N.
3. The attributes that establish values for the entity are elicited and diagrammed with arcs that connect attributes to sets.
4. The process continues until all entity sets, relationship sets, attributes, and values sets have been elicited and diagrammed. The diagram is a tool which allows the analyst and user to discuss the data model and resolve ambiguities.

The drawing of a diagram is only one part of the process of designing a database. However, it can be useful and significant step in preparing the requirements from which to design the physical database.

Analysis of Information by Nijssen[10]

A number of database researchers have suggested other methods for conceptual data modelling. The one chosen for illustration is information analysis by G. M. Nijssen.[11] Other researchers such as William Kent of IBM have proposed similar ideas. Kent describe his approach as "fact-based analysis."[12]

The fundamental data model in the Nijssen approach consists of *deep structure elementary sentences*. These sentences exhibits "deep structure" in the sense that they can be transformed into a variety of other representations (called surface structures). The sentences can be viewed as an extension of a predicate calculus formula. Each sentence takes the form:

S = P (NOLOT, LOT, LOI.....)

where S = sentence instance
P = sentence predicate
NOLOT = nonlexical object type
LOT = lexical object type
LOI = lexical object instance

There is a clear distinction in this approach between entities (nonlexical), that is, kinds, classes, categories or types of things (NOLOTs), and the naming conventions or kinds of name (lexical) for things (LOTs). Each instance of a naming convention is a LOI.

Each sentence may be presented as an equation; it may also be transformed to natural language, a table, or a graph. The following example is a natural language sentence (arranged to show the deep structure):

The EMPLOYEE		(a kind of thing, a NOLOT)
	with EMPLOYEE NUMBER	(a number convention, a LOT)
	37891	(instance of a name, a LOI)
WORKS FOR		(logical predicate, an IDEA)
the DEPARTMENT		(a kind of thing, a NOLOT)
	with DEPARTMENT NUMBER	(a naming convention, a LOT)
	468	(instance of a name, a LOT)

The *role* of every object type in every relationship is defined in the information analysis. In the above sentence, the relationship of EMPLOYEE and DEPARTMENT is explicitly defined as the role "works for."

The example presented in a natural language sentence above is shown below as the table (extended tabular format) with an added set of instances:

EMPLOYEE EMPLOYEE NUMBER WORKS FOR	DEPARTMENT DEPARTMENT NUMBER EMPLOYS	(NOLOTs) (LOTs) (NOLOT ROLEs)
37891	468	Sentence 1
28932	470	Sentence 2

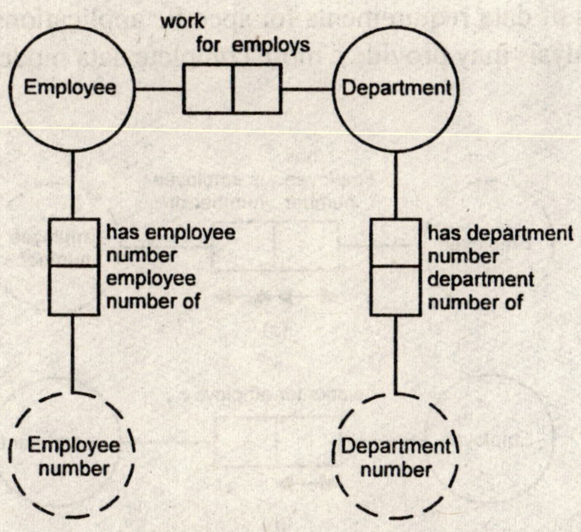

Figure 17.9. *Information analysis conceptual schema in graphic form.*

Figure 17.9 shows the conceptual schema for the same information in graphic form. Since the LOI information is missing, the graph is a general template for all sentences of the same type, in the same way as the table headings above. A NOLOT is graphed as a solid line circle or ellipse; a LOT is diagrammed as a broken line circle or ellipse. The rectangle linking the object type symbols specify role information. Uniqueness is defined for roles by a bar with arrowheads underneath the box. For example, a 1:1 relationship is unique for both roles (thinking in terms of a table with rows, either role defines a unique row in the table), so each has a bar underneath. For a 1:m relationship, the unique role is the "one" role, and a bar underneath it shows this role on the graph. Employee works for only one department. But the department employs many employees. In the case of n:m relationships, a unique row is specified by a combination of both roles, so an underline is placed under both role boxes.

There are additional conventions and rule for both E-R modelling and information analysis, but they are beyond the scope of the chapter. The brief introduction to the two modelling approaches should illustrate the difference between them. In the case of the Chen E-R model, entities, relationships, and attributes are associated and graphed; in the Nijssen information analysis, sentences are formulated and illustrated using natural language, tables, or graphs.

Limitations of Conceptual Data Models

The conceptual data model approach to database requirements has some limitations in arriving at a complete and correct database. Two major limitations are:[13]

1. There are many ways to view an enterprise and many ways to model it. These do not yield exactly the same result. Different analyst and users look at the same thing differently, and they will model it differently.
2. General knowledge is the basis for many data elements. These are not specifically derived from analysis of the enterprise.

For these reasons, a top-down conceptual enterprise approach may be combined with other analyses such as analysis of data requirements for specific applications. The combination of high-level application data analysis may provide a more complete data model.

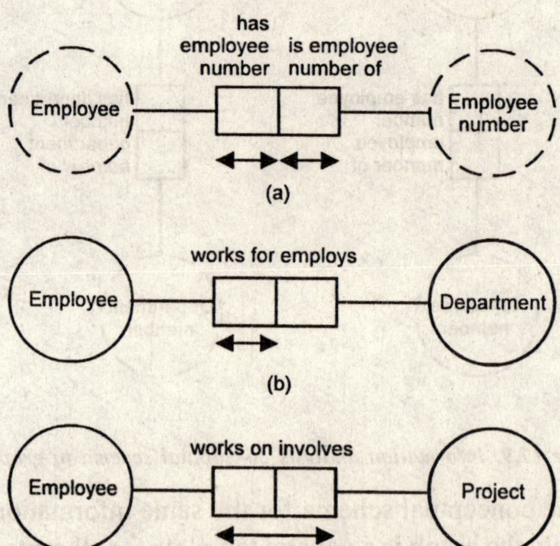

Figure 17.10. Representing cardinality constraints of 1:1, 1:m, and n:m in information algebra graphics.

A Schedule for Data Modelling

A large manufacturing company established a project team of eleven users and eleven data processing personnel to develop a data model for a database for part of its plant. The chronology and volume of activity are instructive.

End of period	*Activity completed*
January	2800 attributes identified.
March	Normalisation
May	Complete data model with 3700 data attributes and 530 data entities representing 40 subject databases and 40 application systems.

Summary/Conclusion

Database is a central concept in the design of organisational information systems. The objectives of a database are availability, shareability, and evolvability of data plus data independence and data integrity. The database concept is made operational by database management system, or DBMS. A supplementary data dictionary is also frequently used.

A data model is a model about the data in an enterprise. It can provide user-understandable specifications of data and physical data specifications. There are three views or schemas in building and using databases: the external schemas is the user's view of the data, the conceptual schema is the overall logical view of the database, and the internal schema or data storage definition is the way the data items are actually stored. Conceptual design of databases is the development and integration of individual user and application views into an overall conceptual view. Physical design is the translation of the conceptual design into physical storage structures.

Normalisation is the process of forming records with key fields and nonkey fields that meet criteria for five normal forms. The normal forms are useful in analysing data, removing unwanted redundancies, and forming logical records prior to physical database design.

Ideally, a database should contain all data items that will be needed by any user of the system, stored in such a way that they can be retrieved. This ideal can rarely be achieved completely; the purpose of information requirements determination for databases is to establish the requirements for data to be stored in a database and the access connections that should be established for retrieval.

A database architecture can be developed by a high-level requirements determination and architecture definition process. Three alternatives strategies may be used subsequent to the planning strategy (or in place of it): development based on overall architecture, evolution from existing data files, or anticipatory development based on conceptual data modelling. Each method has its advantage and disadvantages. The conceptual data modelling approach is described in the chapter because it provides an approach to obtaining requirements that is independent of the function in data processing applications.

Several researchers have contributed to the concepts of conceptual data modelling: the work of Chen and Nijssen are presented in the chapter as examples of graphics-oriented and sentence-predicate calculus-based methods. The elements of the Chen entity-relationship or E-R model are entity set, relationship set, and attributes. With the concept of an enterprise schema, a graphical E-R data model is used to describe entity set relationship, attributes, and value sets. In Nijssen's information analysis, data is defined by sentences having deep structure. The sentences may be presented as natural language statements, tables, or graphs.

Notes

1. Gordon C. Everest, *Database Management: Objectives, System Functions, and Administration.*
2. Everest, *Database Management.*
3. Bo Lundgren, *Theory of Data Bases.*
4. Salvatore T. March, "Techniques for structuring Database Record."
5. T. C. Tsichritizis and A. Klug (eds.), "The ANSI/SPARC DBMS Framework Report of the Study Group on Database Management Systems."
6. This section is based on William Kent, "A Simple Guide to five Normal Forms in Relational Database Theory."
7. William Kent, "A Simple Guide to Five Normal in Relational Database Theory."
8. M. E. Senko, E. B. Altman, M. M. Astrahan, and P. L. Fehder, "Data Structures and Accessing in Data-Base Systems."
9. Peter P. Chen, "The Entity-Relationship Model: Toward a Unified View of Data."
10. This section is based on a working paper by Peter Seddon of the University of Melbourne, Australia.
11. G. M. Nijssen, "Current Issues in Conceptual Schema Concepts," in *Architecture and Models in Data Base Management Systems*, North Holland.
12. W. Kent, "Fact-Based Data Analysis and Design."
13. Based on W. Kent, "Data Model Theory Meets a Practical Application."

18

Requirements of User Interface

Classification of Users

- Developers *versus* Nondevelopers
- Novices *versus* Experts
- Occasional *versus* Frequent Users
- Primary *versus* Secondary Users

Division of Functions Between user and System

Considerations in Design of a user Interface

- Screen Design
- Feedback and Assistance
- Error Control
- Response Time
- Workstation Design

Interactive User Dialog

- Command Languages
- Menus
- Forms
- Icons, Graphs, and Colour
- Natural Language

Alternative Interaction Mechanisms

- Direct Manipulation Systems
- Speech Recognition and Synthesis
- Limitations of Conceptual Data Models

Summary/Conclusion

Computer-based information systems increasingly involve online interaction between the human user and the machine: a critical element of the design of these systems is the user interface. The interface consists of screens, keyboards, devices, languages, and other means by which the human user and the computer system exchange inputs and outputs. Because of the importance of a well-designed user interface in the effective use of a system, a separate chapter is devoted to the topic.

User interface design has received significant attention in recent years. Many "principles" of good user interface design have been developed, much of it focusing on "user friendly" systems and ease of use. Research in this area is frequently characterized as *human factors engineering* or *ergonomics*. Some research related to humans as information processors has been the basis for certain interface design principles; research dealing more specifically with user interface design is reviewed in this chapter.

This chapter provides an overview of important features of user interfaces and develops a contingency approach to the selection of design features. There are many options in user interface design, and the choice of appropriate options depends on factors such as the experience and knowledge of the user and the type of task to be performed. Several guiding principles hold throughout: the system should be flexible, it should be consistent, and it should be perceived as being under the user's control.There principles are discussed in more detail below:

Classification of Users

Classification of users on the basis of their characteristics. This section discusses several different ways of characterizing users. They are not exclusive classifications, in that a user may be characterized in several different ways at the same time.

Developers versus Nondevelopers

An obvious but important distinction in user interface design exists between the developer of the system and the target end user. System developers are those who develop information processing applications and tools for use by other workers, whereas end users are workers who input, manipulate, or retrieve information using the applications and tools. The distinction is particularly important when developers are professional systems analysts who must deal with large, complex systems (for example a large transaction processing system). This causes an emphasis on technical consideration and system control; it often inhibits emphasis on the user interface. In other words, it is often difficult for a system developer both to see the overall technical system and to take a user's view.

To the user, the system is represented primarily by the interface. A complex interface reflects a complex system to the user; a simple interface suggests a simple system to the user. One of the problems illustrated by this distinction is difficulty in communication between system developers and users.

For many types of systems the distinction between developers and nondevelopers is blurred by the introduction of users in the development process. In end-user development, the user and developer can be the same person. Frequently, the developer may be a full-time analyst who is an expert in the user function.

Novices versus Experts

An important distinction directly affecting interface design is the experience level of the user. This experience has two components: the frequency of use of the particular system and the user's general knowledge of computer system concepts. The first component may be referred to as syntactic knowledge and the latter as semantic knowledge.[1]

Ideally, a system should be flexible enough to accommodate both a novice and an expert user. A novice who is unfamiliar with both the system's specific syntax and generalizable (semantic) knowledge about use of computers should be able to get explanations or assistance through the system. On the other hand, an expert who has internalized the system's syntactic structure or has considerable semantic knowledge should be permitted rapid interaction and not be held up by explanations or details that are only required by the novice.

A key design feature of user interfaces is *consistency* in relating to user's general or semantic knowledge. A user faced with a request for a response in a dialog with a computer and an unclear set of choices may borrow from the experience of other computers with similar interfaces to make "an educated guess." "Developers can establish reasonable consistency of interfaces through the development of organisational guidelines and standards for user interface design.[2] For example, all applications needing to save a program or file should use the same command (such as SAVE).

Occasional versus Frequent Users

Another way of categorising of users, related to novices and experts, is occasional versus frequent users. In general, a frequent user will become more expert, particularly in syntactic knowledge; than an occasional one. However, there are other aspects of frequency of use besides the need for training. An occasional user will probably use the system for ad hoc, nonrepetitive processing. A system receiving frequent use is more likely to be used for routine, repetitive activities.

Frequency of use determines directly the amount of training required of the user: the more the expected use of the system, the greater the justification for investment in training time. The amount of training in turn determines the user's skill level after the training period.

After initial training, there is a significant decay in knowledge of system use. Occasional users therefore need to be able to refresh their knowledge of system functions and commands. Commands that use words common to the user and formats that are fairly natural aid in this recall and refreshing of memory.

Primary versus Secondary Users

A final distinction is the type of user or reason for utilising the system. In general, a *primary user* is one who benefits from the system's output, while a *secondary user* is responsible for input into the system and sometimes for output but does not use the output directly in his or her job. The person who utilises the system output also develops it. In some situations, the end user may employ an intermediary. For example, many managers prefer to have the system actually operated by an assistant.

As a contrast to end-user systems that combine primary and secondary user roles, other applications separate the functions. *Data entry* is the team normally used for jobs doing input (and often validation) of large volumes of data. However, data entry of transactions often takes place at the point of origination of the transactions, and those who input data also use the system for inquiry purposes. For instance, a retail sales clerk enters all information about a sale into the computer vi a "point-of-sale" terminal as part of the process of creating a sales receipt. The same system utilised for validation of the customer's credit on a charge account.

Secondary users such as data entry personnel typically perform data input as a major part c their jobs. Therefore, secondary users would be classified as experts rather than novices and a frequent users. As mentioned previously, none of these classes of users is exclusive.

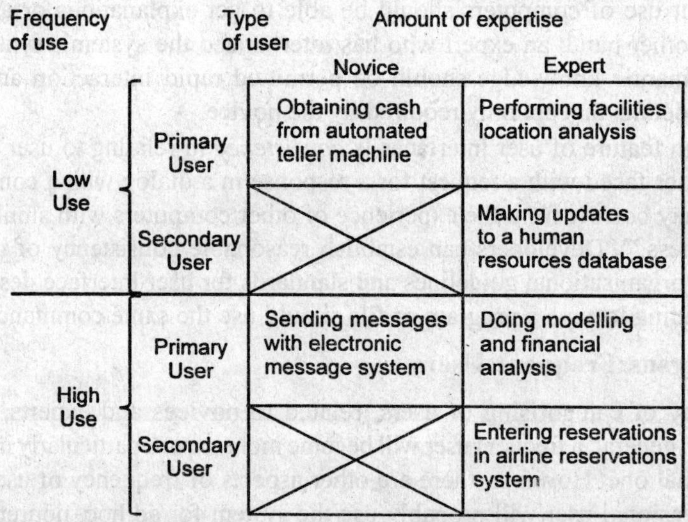

Figure 18.1. Classes of users and examples of system uses.

Division of Functions Between User and System

An important decision which dictates many user interface requirements is the division c functions between the user and the computer system. This issue is related to topics discussed i earlier chapters. Deterministic system and the human as an open, probabilistic system. It wa recommended that a human-machine system should be designed to take maximum advantage c the characteristics of each.

The division of functions between person and machine, regardless of application, has shifte over the last decade from emphasis on machine efficiency to enhancement of human effectivenes The primary reason for this shift has been the declining cost of hardware relative to the cost c human labour. This shift is also reflected in the replacement of many batch processing applicatior by online, interactive systems. The cost of the hardware and software for the user interface ma be a major component of the total cost of application development and operations. However, thes costs are small relative to the typical improvement in the performance of the human system.

The distinction between the negative and positive effects of a computer system on individu quality of work life is related to the division of function between human and machine. A syste which gives the user very little discretion in terms of selection of tasks or pace of work may hav apparent cost advantages, especially if the skills required of the human operator are minimize However, these cost advantages may be lost due to added costs of increased turnover of personn and reduced job commitment. Therefore, whenever possible, a system should be designed so that the user controls the interaction rather than the system. In the long run, a system that is designed well from the user's point of view will result in increased overall performance. The implications of the division of function between person and machine are discussed in more detail in a later section of this chapter. The sociotechnical approach to requirements and to job design is one method to achieve application designs that take advantage of the strengths of both humans and machines to achieve improved quality of work life.

Considerations in Design of a User Interface

In this section, the general components of user interface design are discussed. The next section presents some alternative approaches to interactive user dialog. Underlying the discussion is the premise that selection of an appropriate interface is contingent on the type of user and the type of task to be performed.

The design of user interfaces is the major factor in ease of learning and ease of use. One research study that compared nine text editors showed significant variation in performances of both experts (in terms of error-free time and time spent correcting errors) and novices (in terms of time to learn a core editing task).

Design of Good Screen

A good screen design is clear, uncluttered, and free of irrelevant information. Two useful guidelines for deciding what information should be put on a single screen are the following:[4]

1. Provide only information that is essential to making a decision or performing an action.
2. Provide all related to one task on a single screen. The user should not have to remember data from one screen to the next.

The placement of text and data on a screen affect the user's task of responding. The following are some guidelines for placement based on human information processing limitations plus culture-based habits for processing:

- Place items together that logically belong together (name and address).
- Place items in customary processing order (in the United States: city followed by state followed by postal code.)
- Position most important items (preferably) at left side and arrange in importance from top to bottom.
- Leave sufficient space so that items do not get confused.
- Position items across close enough that the eye does not change rows in moving across. Use guide strips of lines, dots, or dashes if necessary.

The availability of graphics and of colour extend the options available in terms of enhancing clarity of screen design.

Design of data entry tasks for secondary users requires special consideration. The most important issue is whether data items will be keyed from a specially designed source document. If such a document is used, the primary visual focus of the user will be toward the document, and the screen should be designed to reflect the form of the document. Forms-based screens for use with documents are discussed in a later section of the chapter. If data entry does not follow a document, the user's primary focus is toward the screen, and prompts from the system elicit the necessary information. The latter would be the case in any type of telephone request or system where the input values are being captured at the source of the transaction. Examples are point-of-sale retail transactions or banking through an automated teller machine.[5]

Poor Formatting	Better Formatting	Comments
AMOUNT DUE: $ 104.00	AMOUNT DUE: $ 104.00	Don't break a label unless necessary
NAME: KAREN JONES ADDRESS: 310 BLEECKER ST CITY: NEW YORK	NAME: KAREN JONESs ADDRESS: 310 BLEECKER ST CITY: NEW YORK	Use alignment to visually separate labels and responses
IN STOCK: 10 ON BACK ORDER: 20	IN STOCK: 10 ON BACK ORDER: 20	Line up numeric output to support visual comparison
(412) 285-6078	TEL: (412) 285-6078	Use label to avoid misinterpretation
082184	08/21/84	Separate sub-items with symbols

***Figure 18.2.** Examples of good and poor formatting of text and data on screen*

In working with a screen, a user must often look aside at other data or instructions while retaining (and returning to) the original screen. This can be accomplished by *split screens* or *windows*. In the split screen, a portion of the screen, say at the bottom, is used for instructions and reference data. Windows are small areas, overlaid on the screen, in which data or instruction are displayed. Another window may be overlaid on the first, etc. For example, a user may be composing a paper and wish to refer to another text. Using a window, a second text may be read while retaining the original on the screen (obscured in part by the window). When the user is finished, the window may be removed. Or, while reading the window with the second text, the user may desire access to the set of instructions for copying a text. This may be called up in second window (smaller than the first) which is overlaid on the first window.

Feedback and Assistance for MIS

Two types of feedback should be part of a user machine dialog:

1. The system should acknowledge every user request in some way.
2. Additional assistance (such as system status) should be available upon request.

In the first case, the most common form of acknowledgment is the result from the request. However, if the request requires a long time to process, acknowledgment of receipt of the request may be appropriate (see discussion of response times below). For instance, if a user submits a complex query to a large database and the processing time is expected to be fairly long (say 30 seconds), the system may respond, "Your query is being processed there will be a short delay," or "...there will be about a 30 second delay". The user's psychological need for feedback is satisfied by the knowledge that the system has received the query and is not sitting idle.

```
I D A (V.TOPS20.091580)

> ?
YOU CAN HAVE HELP ON ANY OR ALL OF THE FOLLOWING :

  1. GENERAL COMMENTS ABOUT IDA
  2. DATA DEFINITION
  3. DATA EDITING
  4. DATA DISPLAY (PRINT)
  5. DATA DISPLAY (PLOT)
  6. TRANSFORMATIONS
  7. SUMMARY STATISTICS
  8. TABULAR ANALYSIS
  9. REGRESSION ANALYSIS
 10. TIME-SERIES ANALYSIS
 11. PROBABILITY ANALYSIS
 12. MISCELLANEOUS COMMANDS

FOR HOW MANY OF THE ABOVE 13 CATEGORIES DO YOU NEED HELP? 1
* CATEGORY NUMBER(S) :1

WANT ALL OUTPUT FOR "GENERAL COMMENTS" ? NO

1. GENERAL COMMENTS:
WANT INFO ON SIZE OF DATA MATRIX ? YES

A.  MAXIMUM SIZE OF DATA MATRIX IS NORMALLY 500 BY 19.
    COLUMNS OF THE DATA MATRIX ARE REFERRED TO AS VARIABLES
    AND ROWS AS OBSERVATIONS. UNIVARIABLE DATA SHOULD BE
    STORED IN A SINGLE COLUMN. IF YOU HAVE MORE THAN 500
    ROWS IN YOUR MATRIX. YOU MAY REDIMENSION THE SIZE BY
    EXECUTING THE COMMAND "RDIN"

WANT INFO ON PROMPTS ? NO

WANT INFO ON ERROR RECOVERY ? NO

WANT INFO ON ACTIVATING DATA ? NO

WANT INFO ON UPDATING DATA ? NO

END OF GENERAL COMMENTS

> QUIT

STOP
```

Figure 18.3. *Example of user-machine dialog with system prompts.*

Further reassurance meeting the psychological need for feedback is provided by System Status Requests for instance, a user has make a request for a Report and the request has been sent to a "print queue." By typing a simple command such as "information output," the user may see a list of all reports in the print queue and the status in the queue of the report in question.

Another type of feedback provided in user-system dialogs is system prompting. Prompting guides a user step by step through a task. It also may give the range of options available. Prompting is very helpful for novice users, but it may be frustrating to experienced users who have internalized the sequence of steps. Ideally, an experienced user should be able to "turn off" such prompting.

```
@help rdmail
Type in a date and time in TOPS-20 format as follows:

                    MM, DD, YYYY HH:MM
or
                    MMM DD, YYYY
or
                    HH:MM

              The second case will assume time 00:01, and the last
              case will assume today's date. (For example, a valid
              date and time is MAR 16, 1976 15:30)

or            Type an empty line and get all messages since the last
              reading of the message file.

/HELP Print this text
/ALL Types all messages in the file
/PERUSE For perusing messages only
/STOP Will cause RDMAIL to pause after each message typed
/MESSAGE-OF-THE-DAY will use the message of the day file for message
type out
/LIST Will ouput messages to the line printer
```

Figure 17.4. *Example of program documentation accessed online by means of "HELP" command.*

Online assistance is frequently available in the form of optional prompts for help. The help may consist of detailed onlined documentation or a reference to external documentation. A common method of receiving online assistance is the "HELP" function. For instance, a user wishes to run an electronic mail program called "RDMAIL." Rather than searching the computer centre or terminal user library for the system documentation, she types "HELP RDMAIL" on her terminal. The system responds with a brief introduction of the RDMAIL program and the basic commands for using it.

The word HELP may be a poor term, since it connotes distress or emergency. EXPLAIN, INSTRUCT, ASSIST, or a question mark may be used instead. There are several types of help that may be available.[6] These are summarised below:

Type of help	Description
Command assistance	Provides an explanation of how to formulate a specific command. For example, asking for HELP PRINT on one system obtains a brief explanation of the PRINT command and a list of parameters that can be specified with the command.
General help	Provides a list of commands. When a user identifies the command needed, a command assistance HELP may be used. Research indicates that specific command names are remembered more easily than general names. Another method of online assistance is a request for options. In a system where prompts do not appear automatically, a user may type a request for options (such as a question mark) to see a list of alternative responses to a system request. Figure 17.5 shows the uses of requests for system option during a user-system dialog.
Error assistance	Error codes or error notes are frequently insufficient for understanding the error. The HELP facilities may include further explanation of error codes. For example, a user might enter HELP ERROR FORTRAN 31 for an explanation of error 31 in a FORTRAN program execution.
Prompting	When an error is detected, some systems will attempt to prompt the user with information to make a correct entry. For example, if a command is used incorrectly, the response will be an explanation of how to use the command.
Online tutor	A new user (or an infrequent user) may not know how to perform basic operations, so general help and command help are insufficient. The online tutor helps provides a lesson on how to use the system.
Online documentation	The manual is online in addition to or instead of a document manual. The online documentation serves much the same purpose as a command help, but may be in more depth. There is some evidence that written documentation is more effective than online documentation.

Error Control

A basic objective of user interface design is to minimise the errors of the human in the information dialog. A fundamental meaning inherent in "ease of use" and "user friendly systems" is adequate error control.

Regardless of the language structure used, a well-designed user interface should have appropriate error detection mechanisms. The *law of requisite variety* applies to interface design. There should be a system response not only to every correct input but also to every incorrect input.

A well-designed user interface should have four distinct dimension of error control:[7]

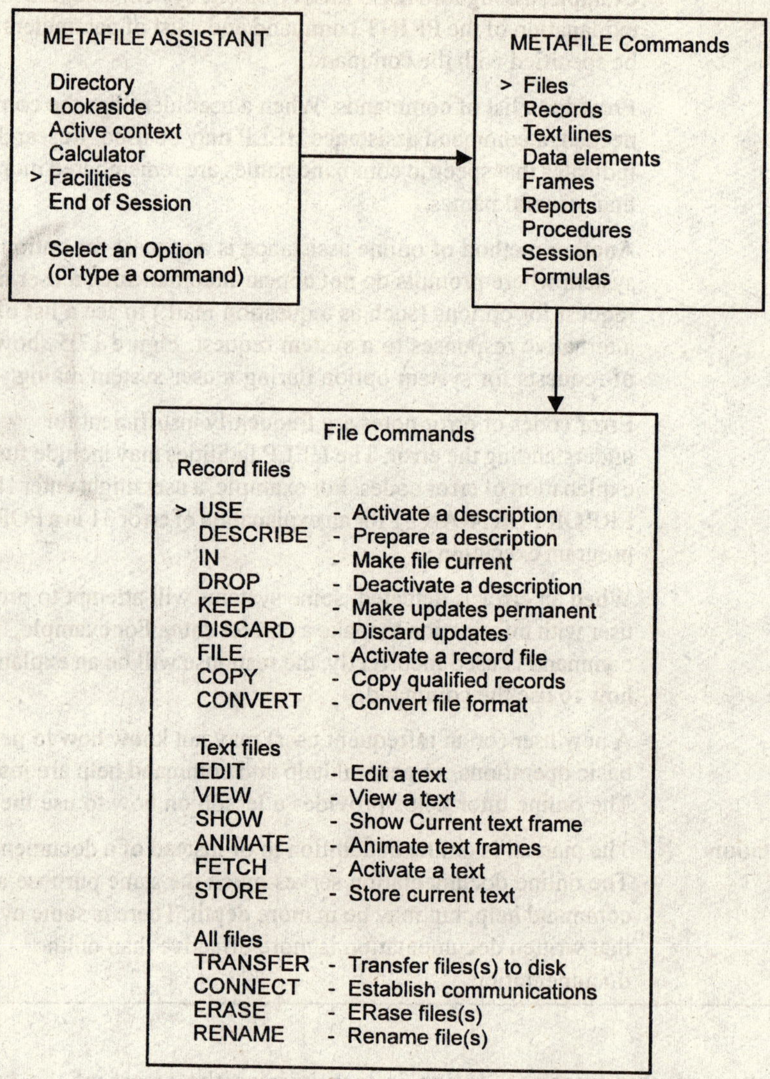

***Figure 18.5.** Example of use of requests for system options in a user-system dialog. First selection of an option gives detailed set and selection of one of these gives a more detailed set of options.*

1. *Error prevention.* As much as possible, the system should provide specific instructions (e.g., prompts, help facilities) so that the user knows exactly what to do and avoids making errors.

2. *Error detection.* When an error is made, the system should identify if clearly and explicitly. However, "polite" error messages are favoured. Common messages such as "FATAL ERROR, RUN ABORTED" and "INVALID COMMAND" are neither polite nor helpful.[8] Notification that an error has been detected should occur immediately. The user should be able to easily identify the error. Finally, no error should cause the system to terminate abnormally; following the law of requisite variety and designing and appropriate control response for every possible input (no matter how incorrect) prevents abnormal program termination from occurring.
3. *Error correction.* Correction should be straightforward and should require rekeying only the portion of the data in error. There is debate over whether systems should attempt correction themselves. For instance, if a system has a total of 50 commands and a user types in a misspelled command, the system can be programmed to estimate through pattern matching which command was meant. In systems where error correction is programmed, the correction is usually posed as a question and the user verifies the correction before it is made.
4. *Error recovery.* Once a command has been accepted, it may still be in error and cause an incorrect action. An important feature of a well-designed system is the ability to "undo" something which has been done. For instance, a user sends an incorrect update to a database. "Undoing" the update is difficult because the old data item was replaced by the new, incorrect data item. However, transactions and before-and-after images of the record being updated are logged by the system, and a procedure should exists to reconstruct the prior state of the database using this data. Having an easy and natural "undo" command can relieve a significant element of stress for novice users who are afraid of doing something wrong that will "wipe out" the system. It is also an important feature of a system used by an expert user who may do things very quickly and need to backtrack as part of the thought process; examples of systems needing this feature are decision support systems and other knowledge work support systems.

Response Time

Response time in an interactive system is the time that elapses between the user keying in a command and the system beginning to display a response. Response times are affected by the system's capacity, the number of other users (if it is a timesharing system), and the complexity of the user's request.

Usually a system design will specify a minimum or average expected response time for a given type of transaction. The response time goal should not necessarily be as fast as possible. It is often more important to have consistent response times for a given level of user expertise for the task to be performed. Some useful guidelines are the following :[9]

1. Frequent, simple commands should take less than a second.
2. For a given command type, response time should be as consistent as possible, even if it takes slightly longer. A maximum response time deviation of no more than 20 percent from the mean has been suggested.
3. Short response times to relatively complex requests may actually increase error rates or inhibit learning.

4. If a response will take a long time (say greater than 10 seconds) a message should be issued within 1 or 2 seconds to give the user feedback. A novice user, in particular, may become frustrated or anxious if the system appears to be idle and waiting for an action.

Another feature of system performances that interacts with response time is display rate. This is the rate at which characters (or graphics) or displayed on the screen. In a terminal connected to a remote computer, display rate is a direct function of the communication speed or baud rate. Display rate is most critical for word processing functions, when an entire screen of text may be redisplayed every time an edit command is issued. With such functions, a display rate of 300 baud (30 characters per second) is extremely slow and can seriously impair performance. At the other extreme 9,600-baud communication speed (or use of a personal computer or intelligent workstation where no data communication is required) permits the entire screen to be redisplayed very quickly and does not impair typing performance. When a person is composing text at a terminal rather than performing bulk typing, slower display rates are generally acceptable. Consistency is also important with display rates in that erratic display rates can be disturbing to users and increase errors.

Design of a Workstation

Much ergonomics research related to computer system use has been concerned with physical aspects such as furniture design, office layout, noise, and lighting. In terms of workstations, guidelines have been developed for size, colour, and positioning of visual display terminal (VDT) screens, measurements of furniture, and keyboard layout.

There have been some concerns that the use of VDTs might adversely affect the health of workers. In a study of 248 office workplace VDT users (and 85 nonuser counterparts) sponsored by the National Institute for Occupational Safety and Health, the results did not support the major concerns. However, certain aspects of working conditions were judged less favourable by VDT users. The chair and workstations configuration affected workers' complains about musculoskeletal disturbances. Workers who use monofocal reading glasses were most affected. Fixed keyboards were also a factor in discomfort. Visual stress was found to be correlated with the illumination levels at both the keyboard and the workplace site.[10]

One example of the evolution of ergonomically designed workstations is the detached keyboard. Many terminals and personal computers in the 1970s had keyboards fixed to the front of the display screen. Most terminals are now designed with detachable, lightweight, adjustable keyboards.

Some major points to consider in choosing appropriate screens and keyboards for particular applications or for general use are highlighted here. References at the end of the chapter provide more detailed guidelines on ergonomic considerations in workstations design.

Considerations in a visual display terminal are the following:[11]

1. The screen should usually be fixed at an angle of 10 to 15 degrees from the vertical, away from the user. Preferably. The tilt should be adjustable, "horizontally as well as vertically.
2. Characters should not flicker or move on the screen.
3. Glare and reflections on the display surface should be minimized.
4. Resolution must provide a sharp image.
5. Character-to-background brightness contrast should be greater than 50 percent. Preferably, the brightness should be adjustable. Screens may offer alternatives of dark on light or light on dark.

Keyboard considerations focus on the physical feel and placement of the keyboards as a whole as well as the placement of individual keys. Keyboard design preferences are often highly individualistic; for this reason an ideal keyboard has as many adjustable features as possible. The following are some examples of ergonomic considerations in the physical design of the keyboard:[12]

1. *Key force*: A range of 15 to 125 grams pressure.
2. *Key spacing:* 18 to 20 millimeters between keys.
3. *Key displacement and activation:* This results in the "feel" of a key when it is pressed.Suggested displacement is 3 to 5 millimeters, with a key activation point requiring an increasing force until contact is made at 65 to 75 percent of downward travel, then a decrease in force so that the point of contact can be felt.
4. *Key shape*: Concave shape, with a matte finish to prevent reflection.
5. *Keyboard slope:* 10 to 15 degrees, preferable adjustable.

Another aspect of keyboard design is a separate numeric keypad. This feature is particularly important if data entry is heavily numeric.

The importance of a well-designed workstation is partially influenced by the amount of time spent on the system. For secondary users, who may spend several hours keying data without breaks, physical features such as lighting and furniture design are especially important.

The layout of the keyboard should fit the convenience of the operator and the task. The keyboard should have all essential keys, and they should be grouped for convenience. Most keyboards have a standard QWERTY keyboard layout because it is the one most skilled typists have learned. Another keyboard layout called the Dvorak, which is based on frequency of character usage, reduces the distance a typical typist's fingers travel by as much as a factor of ten. To date, the Dvorak keyboard has not received widespread acceptance because of the amount of retraining as well as keyboard replacement that would be required. However, its features have now been standardized. Also, microcomputers and word processors can be easily designed to allow the user to specify QWERTY or Dvorak. These developments suggest possible significant future use for the Dvorak layout.

A common feature of most terminal and personal computer keyboards is a set of function keys. Often these are placed separately from the frequently used keys, either to one side or along the top. Functions keys are marked, often in a different colour. They are used to replace keyed commands for frequently used functions. Functions keys are usually assigned by the program in operation, although some systems allow the user to assign function keys to tailor the system. For instance, frequent user of a text editing program may assign certain cursor-positioning functions (end of line, next line, next word, etc.) to function keys.

In summary, workstation design should be carefully considered in light of the type task to be performed. The overall design should emphasise flexibility or easy adjustment to suit individual preferences. The keyboard design, in particular, should emphasise speed, accuracy, comfort, and flexibility.

Interactive User Dialog

Use dialog should be interactive. It can follow different structures. The dialog between user and machine can follow many different structures: command languages, menus, forms, graphics, and natural language. The characteristics of each of these language structures are described in this section. In general, considerations in choosing an appropriate language structure are the expertise of the user, the user's knowledge about the particular problem domains for which the system is used, the physical constraints of the computer and the terminal, and consistency with other dialogs in use.

Command Languages for the Existence of Data

The most common method of user interface dialog is the command language. Most basic computer operating systems utilise a command language to access other applications and perform basic system functions.

A command language generally has a prespecified format for each command. Typically, a command to perform an operation is followed by one or more *arguments* that specify the details for it. For instance, there may be a command rename a file. The user specifies the command RENAME followed by the user-defined current file name and the new file name. Two methods are commonly used:

1. *Keyword.* The user specifies keywords for the arguments:
   RENAME OLD = TEXTFIL2 NEW = TEXTFIL3
2. *Position.* The meaning of the arguments is determined by their position:
   RENAME TEXTFIL2 TEXTFIL3

The advantage of the keyword format is that the user does not have to remember the order of the arguments, whereas in the position format the order is significant and must be memorized. However, the keyword format requires considerably more typing, and the user must remember not only the appropriate arguments but also their associated keywords. The position method tends to be preferred by expert users who know the command formats. Two methods for making position format commands easier for novice users are system prompts and system defaults.

With system prompts, the user types the command, such as RENAME, and then presses a key (such as RETURN or ESC) designated for a prompt. The system then prompts with a keyword indicating the expected argument. For example:

RENAME ? FROMFILE TEXFIL2 ? TOFILE TEXFIL3

In the example above, ***FROMFILE*** and ***TOFILE*** are systems prompts given as a result of the user typing a question mark.

Use of system defaults can increase the efficiency can increase the efficiency of command language. Typically, the command default represents the broadest range for the command and specific arguments are required to narrow the range. For example, a user may wish to list a directory of file names under his account. If the user only specifies "DIR," the system defaults to printing a directory of all files in the account. If he is interested in only those files with the suffix "DOC" or only those created after a certain date, range arguments would follow the command "DIR."

An issue in command language interface design is whether to require the user to enter the full command words or to allow abbreviation. Command abbreviations reduce input time and annoyance associated with system use. In research reported by Benbasat and Wand,[13] truncation was supported as the preferred method for abbreviation. It was found easy to use and implement, it generated few errors, and it led to more abbreviations when commands increased in length or usage.

Command language formats are commonly used in database query languages. Commands have a syntax using natural language words but are restricted to a very specific set of keywords and often a specific ordering.

A Simple SQL query to select and list the name and address of alumni who have a PhD. degree.

```
SELECT    NAME, ADDRESS
FROM      ALUMNI
WHERE     DEGREE = 'Ph.d';
```

An SQL query to select and list the names of alumni who are not donors.

```
SELECT    NAME
FROM      ALUMNI
WHERE     ID NOT IN
          (SELECT ID
          FROM DONORS);
```

An SQL query to list the sum of donations from alumni from Chicago.

```
SELECT    ALUMNI.NAME, SUM(DONORS.AMOUNT)
FROM      ALUMNI, DONORS
WHERE     ALUMNI.CITY = 'CHICAGO' AND
          ALUMNI.ID = DONORS.ID
GROUP BY DONORS.ID ;
```

Figure 18.6. *Examples of database query language (SQL) to access information from a database. Example database contains data on alumni of a university.*

Menus

With the menu format, the user is shown a list of options, usually numbered, and is expected to choose the appropriate option by positioning a cursor or by keying the associated number. A series of menus allows the user to step through a series of hierarchical levels of increasing specificity.

The advantage of a well-designed menu is that it provides a familiar format and a clear set of choices which are well understood by the user. Menus therefore require less training use than command languages. One important feature of a menu structure is the capability of backtracking to a higher (more general level) or of returning to the highest level and starting over. Another useful feature is to refer to similar commands by similar numbers.

One of the major drawbacks to menu selection is its inefficiency for the expert user who wants to go directly to a specific command. An ideal menu interface should have shortcuts. Examples of shortcuts are a menu of menu names so that a user may immediately specify a lower level menu and a feature direct writing of a complex command that bypasses the menu displays.

Forms

In a forms-based interface design, the user "fills in the blanks" on a screen. This type of interface dialog is particularly appropriate for data entry of transactions. As explained earlier, the design of a screen for transaction processing should differ depending on whether the user is working from a transaction document. If a document is used, the screen format should reflect the document layout; if no document is used, the dialog format simulates a form. In both cases, data entry often reflects a "fill in the blanks" Philosophy, with automatic positioning of the cursor to the next field for entry and captions indicating what information goes in each space. Often colour or foreground (bright) and background (dim) character printing differentiates system prompts from user-supplied information on the screen. (See selected references at the end of the chapter for guidelines for caption format, alignment between caption and data entered, spacing, etc.)

The design and programming of screen dialog can be time consuming and difficult if performed using procedural languages such as COBOL. There are software packages that simplify design and programming.

Icons, Graphs, and Colour

Graphical symbols commonly called *icons* may be used in system dialog instead of menus or command languages. A workstation display may show a menu of icons: a desk, an in box, an out box, a file cabinet, a wastebasket. The user moves the cursor to the icon representing the desired function and presses a key to select that icon; either the function is executed or a new set of icons is displayed. Icons and graphics functions may also be used as the basis for creation of complex graphical images that may be displayed on the screen or incorporated in a document. Note icons at left of screen.

Graphics interfaces have had limited use in database query systems via a method known as *spatial data management.*[14] A combination of graphical images, colour, and a joystick manipulation device (explained in the next section) permit the user to traverse through a hierarchical menu by "zooming" in to greater levels of detail.

The ability to combine graphics with colour provides potential for enhancing communication. Colour can be used to highlight a particular aspect of a cluttered display, highlight a change, or separate information categories. Colour is especially valuable in tasks involving identification, searching, and counting.

There can be some problems with using colour. Since it is very noticeable, it can distract a person by highlighting unimportant items or associating different items that are really unrelated. Colour should generally be used carefully, consistently, and sparingly, since irrelevant colours can interfere with the ability to perform tasks. (See Ives in selected references for a summary of graphical user interfaces.)

Natural Language as on Interfaces

The development of natural language interfaces is generally considered part of the domain of artificial intelligence. The goal of for a novice user to communicate with the computer through a natural language such as English. The ultimate objective is for computers to be able to understand natural language in the spoken voice, which would make many of the interface designs already discussed in this chapter unnecessary. In practical terms, natural language interfaces are extremely difficult to implement, although considerable research and development is in progress. An example of a commercial product is Intellect from Artificial Intelligence Corporation.

```
FILE   EMPLOYEE                                        RECORD UPDATE
EMPNO ........................................... 45584
EMPNAME ......................................... PETERSON, N. M.
UNIT ............................................ 2000
JOBCODE ......................................... HEAD
LEVEL ........................................... HEAD
TITLE ........................................... DIVISION MANAGER
SEX ............................................. M
BIRTHDATE ....................................... 280607
PSKILL .......................................... 0110
SSKIL1 .......................................... 6130
SSKILL2 ......................................... 6625
SSKILLS ......................................... 6040
ACTSALARY ....................................... 56000
ARROWS move cursor to change values: RETURN to accept.
```

(a) Screen design not based on a paper form.

```
                                   INDIVIDUAL
INDIVIDUAL NUMBER :________:                             HOUSEHOLD NUMBER :_____:

NAME  LAST :________________:                            FIRST NAME (S) :______________:
   TITLE :______:     SUFFIX :________:            ALTERNATE LAST NAME :______________:

PERSONAL – SEX :_____:            BIRTHDATE :___/___/___:      ROLE IN HOUSEHOLD* :_____:

MARITAL  STATUS* :__:        LAST TRANSITION DATE :___/___/___:

MEMBERSHIP – STATUS* :__:    METHOD* :__:     DATE :_________:
   FORMER CHURCH (DEN LOC CHNAME)* :______________________________________:

RELIGIOUS DATES–  #1 :___/___/___:      #2 :___/___/___:      CHURCH SCHOOL LEVEL :___:

EDUCATION–  ACTIVITI/DIFFERENTIAL* :___:         CURRENT/LAST SCHOOL :______________:
                  LEVEL ATTAINED* :___:          CURRENT/LAST MAJOR :______________:

OCCUPATION– EMPLOYER :________________:          WORK PHONE :___–___ –___X___:
      GENERIC TITLE * :__________________:
                                                 XREF TO SPECIAL NEEDS :____:
OFFICE–  DATE OF LAST CHANGE :___/___/___:       LAST REVIEW BY INDIVIDUAL :__________:
```

(b) Screen design based on a correspoding paper form

Figure 18.7. Examples of forms-based interface designs.

```
1---5---10---15---20---25---30---35---40---45---50---55---60---65---70---75---80
+   +   +   +   +   +   +   +   +   +   +   +   +   +   +   +   +
+   +   +   +   +      EMPLOYEE DATA SCREEN    +   +   +   +   +   +   +
+   +   +   +   +   +   +   +   +   +   +   +   +   +   +   +   +
+---+---+---+---+---+---+---+---+---+---+---+---+---+---+---+---+
+   +   +   +   +   +   +   +   +   +   +   +   +   +   +   +   +
+   +   +   +   +   +   +   +   +   +   +   +   +   +   +   +   +
+  FIRST NAME +    ..............................+   +   +   +   +   +   +   +   +   +
+   +   +   +   +   +   +   +   +   +   +   +   +   +   +   +   +
+--- LAST NAME +---- ............................. +---+---+---+---+---+---+---+---+---+
+   +   +   +   +   +   +   +   +   +   +   +   +   +   +   +   +
+  SOC SEC NUMBER .......................+   +   +   +   +   +   +   +   +   +   +
+   +   +   +   +   +   +   +   +   +   +   +   +   +   +   +   +
+  HIRE DATE  +    .......................+   +   +   +   +   +   +   +   +   +   +
+---+---+---+---+---+---+---+---+---+---+---+---+---+---+---+---+
+   HOURLY RATE    .................   +   +   +   +   +   +   +   +   +   +   +
+   +   +   +   +   +   +   +   +   +   +   +   +   +   +   +   +
+  HOURS +   +   +   +   +   +   +   +   +   +   +   +   +   +   +
+   +   +   +   +   +   +   +   +   +   +   +   +   +   +   +   +
+---+---+---+---+---+---+---+---+---+---+---+---+---+---+---+---+
LINE, COLUMN, CONTENT > 3,25, 'EMPLOYEE DATA SCREEN'
LINE, COLUMN, CONTENT > 8,5, 'FIRST NAME'
LINE, COLUMN, CONTENT > 10,5, 'LAST NAME'
LINE, COLUMN, CONTENT > 12,5, 'SOC SEC NUMBER'
LINE, COLUMN, CONTENT > 14,5, 'HIRE DATE'
LINE, COLUMN, CONTENT > 16,5, 'HOURLY RATE'
LINE, COLUMN, CONTENT > 18,5, 'HOURS'
LINE, COLUMN, CONTENT > 8,20, FIRST-NAME
LINE, COLUMN, CONTENT > 10,20, LAST-NAME,F
LINE, COLUMN, CONTENT > 12,20, SSN, K,F
LINE, COLUMN, CONTENT > 14,20, DATE-OF-HIRE,V,$TODAY
LINE, COLUMN, CONTENT > 16,20, HRLY-RATE,R,2.75,25.00
LINE, COLUMN, CONTENT > 18,20, HOURS,L,20,35,40
LINE, COLUMN, CONTENT > (USER PRESSES RETURN AND THE FORM DEFINITION IS STORED IN THE DICTIONARY)
(DO YOU WISH TO EXECUTE THIS FORM (Y OR N) > Y
```

Figure 18.8. Example of use of a screen generator to create screens for transaction processing.

The primary barrier to development of useful natural language systems is the imprecision of language itself. The objective is to be flexible in stating a query rather than to be forced into the positional or keyword limitations of a command language. However, many ways of phrasing a query (in English for instance) are ambiguous if considered word for word but very understandable to another human. For instance, "Doctor Livingstone, I presume" is understandable in spoken English (in part because of verbal clues such as emphasis and pauses), but in logical analysis, it is incomplete. The words "I presume" require an object to be complete. The analysis that the sentence means "I presume you are Doctor Livingstone" is not impossible, but is very difficult.

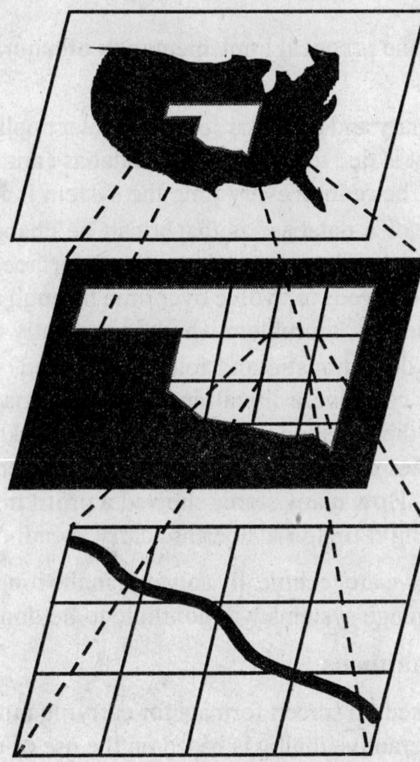

Figure 18.9. *Illustration of progressive "zooming" through a spatial data management system.*

Natural language systems now being developed are "restricted natural language" systems. That is, they are based on a limited domain of inquiry and contain a data dictionary of words and meanings referencing that limited domain. Even within that domain and a given grammar, many phrases which the user would consider "natural" will not be understood. Thus, the language cannot be completely "natural" even within that domain, and the user may become easily frustrated.

Even with the difficulty of a limited domain of specialized knowledge, applications can be developed that "understand" a set of queries greater in scope than command language statements.

The statements below are a dialog using a prototype natural language system. The information desired is exactly the same as that accessed by the command-based query language.

- What are the names and addresses of the alumni who graduated with a Ph.D.?
- Who are the alumni who are not donors?
- List the sum of donations for each alumnus from Chicago.

It should be clear from the example that a restricted natural language is ideal for a novice user with no technical knowledge and no previous training. However, an important drawback of such systems is that they are not efficient for repeated queries or for expert users, since natural language is very verbose and the query requires a great deal more keying than any of the other interfaces discussed in this section.

Several other drawbacks to the practical implementation of natural language systems should be noted:[15]

- The creation of a dictionary and grammar for a particular application is very labour-intensive and the finished product is tied to the particular database and database management system in use. This work must be redone every time the system is installed on a new database.
- One of the advantages of a database is that it can be changed easily. This requires new words to be understood by the natural language interface that were not in its original vocabulary. The interface needs to evolve over time through additions to and changes in its grammar and data dictionary, a problem which is presently difficult.
- A computer system is deterministic and relatively closed, even with a natural language interface. Therefore, it can give a literal answer which may actually be misleading. For instance, an answer to the question. "Which managers make over $15,000 per year" may yield a list of 1,000 names when the more appropriate answer would be "all." Or a response of "none" to the query "How many stores showed a profit on sales of speedboats in region Y?" would be misleading if region Y does not carry speedboats at all.

The problems discussed above are technically solvable in the long run. However, it seems likely that applications of natural language systems will continue to be domain-specific.

Alternate Interaction Mechanisms

The preceding section focused on screen formats for carrying out an interactive dialog with the computer. For the most part, interactive dialog is based on the use of alphanumeric displays and the keyboard. In this section, some alternative interactive mechanisms are considered that do not necessarily emphasise keying skills. The major alternatives are direct manipulation and speech.

Direct Manipulation Systems

The typical user is an expert who uses the system intensively for long periods of time to do many different tasks. Many of the systems developed for this type of support have a common set of interaction principles. Termed *direct manipulation systems,* they are characterized by the following:[16]

- Visibility of the object of interest
- Rapid reversible actions
- Replacement of a command language by direct manipulation of the object of interest.

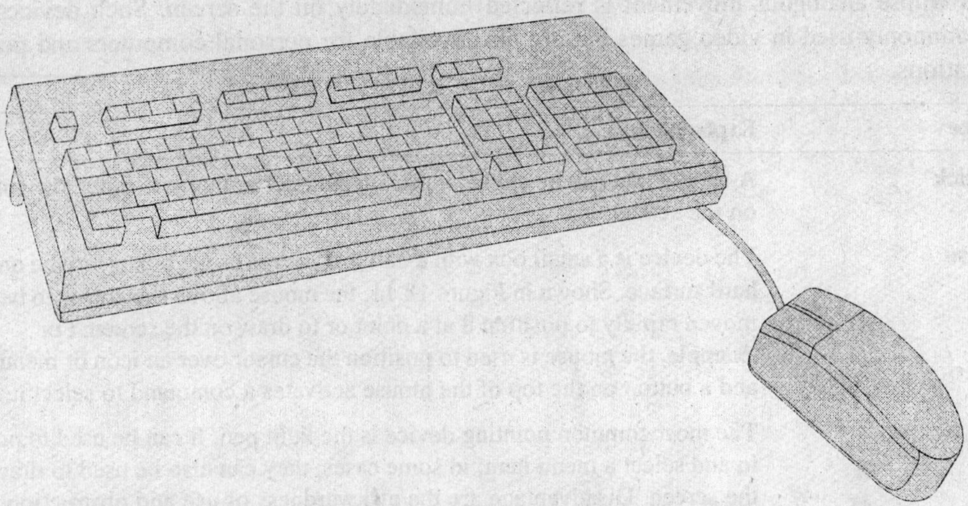

Figure 18.10. A mouse physical manipulation device plus a keyboard.

Many of the examples already described in this chapter. The approach does not necessarily require new technological devices, however, it reflects a philosophy that interaction between the user and the system is performed by a direct interaction of the user with visual presentations or physical manipulation devices.

The system encourages the user to explore its more powerful aspects. Some examples illustrate the philosophy of direct manipulation systems:

1. *Visual display editors.* These editors reflect the notion that "what you see is what you get." Text can be manipulated and viewed on the screen, and the results of an action are displayed immediately. The cursor is moved to the point in the text to be changed; it is manipulated physically by function keys or physical objects, such as a mouse or joystick, that have an intuitive relationship to the movement of the cursor. Commands are easily reversible through the ability to insert or delete characters, words, or lines directly at the point of error.
2. *Electronic spreadsheets.* The electronic spreadsheets simulates visibly traditional accounting spreadsheets. Manipulation of one part of the spreadsheets results in visible changes in the rest, so that the user can readily see results.
3. *Spatial data management.* The notion of using a graphical interface to a database was discussed in the previous section. Actions are easily reversible in that one can zoom back to a higher level of generality and then zoom down to another level of detail on some other object of interest.
4. *Video games.* Video games use colour graphics and even sound to create a rich interface. They are also direct manipulation systems in that commands are directed through physical rotation of knobs or joysticks and results are shown directly on the screen.

Several of the preceding examples incorporated not only keyboard manipulation, but physical devices whose analogous movement is reflected immediately on the screen. Such devices have been commonly used in video games but are also available for personal computers and personal workstations.

Device	Explanation
Joystick	A handle that can be angled vertically and horizontally to move the cursor on the screen.
Mouse	The device is a small box with a ball that moves as the box is moved on a hard surface. Shown in Figure 18.11, the mouse allows the cursor to be moved rapidly to position it at a point or to draw on the screen. For example, the mouse is used to position the cursor over an icon or menu item and a button on the top of the mouse activates a command to select it.
Pointing device	The most common pointing device is the light pen. It can be used to point to and select a menu item; in some cases, they can also be used to draw on the screen. Disadvantage are the awkwardness of use and obstruction of part of the screen when pointing.
Touch-sensitive screen	Touch sensitive screens can be activated by a grid within the screen surface that responds to touch or to a grid of light beams just over the surface of the screen that is broken when a finger or other object comes close to the screen surface.

Speech Recognition and Synthesis

The advantages of voice recognition for data entry are significant; it is fast and accurate, requires minimal training, and frees the user's hands for other operations. Voice recognition systems for limited vocabularies (100 to 400 words) are relatively inexpensive and are very useful for such applications as inventory control inspections. Usually, such systems are speaker-dependent in that the recognition is based on a recording of the speaker's voice patterns.

Dayton's Bridal Registry uses Touch Sensitive Screen

A bride or groom about to be married can register gift preference items at Daylon's departmental store in the Twin Cities of Minneapolis and St. Paul. The list of gifts are not restricted to a few items such as china or crystal. The gift preferences are listed under both bride and groom.

A user of the computer-based registry inputs via a touch sensitive screen. The user touches a designated spot on the screen to indicate bride or groom. The next touch is to indicate the first letter of the last name of the bride or groom. The system displays the persons who have a last name beginning with that letter. The user touches a spot opposite the person being selected. An attached printer provides a list of the gift preference items: when a buyer reports a purchase made, a notation is placed in the list beside the item.

General voice recognition is a much more difficult problem because the normal spoken voice is continuous and often ambiguous. The notion of a "listening typewriter" which can compose a correct written manuscript from speech input is still far from reality, although significant efforts to accomplish it are being made in research laboratories.

Speech synthesis, or the ability of a computer to translate words into speech output, is utilised in telephone information systems. The use of speech output is currently limited to short messages such as telephone numbers, attention-getting devices, and aids to the blind.

Summary/Conclusion

This chapter has explained information system requirements for the user interface. As systems are more commonly used directly by those who benefit from their outputs and who may know very little about their internal aspects, a well-designed interface is critical to the success of a system. Three basic principles that should be incorporated into all interface designs are consistency, flexibility, and user control.

Characteristics of the interface vary according to the degree of expertise of the user and the nature of the task to be performed. The amount of time the user will spend on the system and whether or not he or she benefits from system outputs (primary user) or is responsible primarily for system inputs (secondary user) are also considerations.

The components of the user interface that need to be considered in determining requirements are the language structure, the layout of the screen, the amount of feedback and assistance required, the degree of error control, response time, and ergonomics in workstation design. In terms of interactive dialog design, the most commonly used structures are command languages, menus, and forms images: icons, graphics colour and natural language are also used.

Physical system interface concepts not using the keyboard are direct manipulation and speech. Direct manipulation systems incorporate a manipulation of a visual representation (what you see is what you get) or a manipulation of a physical device. Physical manipulation of objects such as a joystick or mouse are translated into cursor control. Other direct physical manipulation technologies are light pens and touch-sensitive screens. Speech recognition systems are in limited use for specific applications.

Notes

1. B, Shneiderman, *Software Psychology: Human Factors in Computer and Information Systems.*
2. For an example of user interface guidelines developed internally for IBM, see F. H. Otte, "Consistent User Interface," in Y. Vassilou (ed.).
3. T. L. Roberts and T. P. Moran, "The Evaluation of Text Editors: Methodology and Empirical Results,"
4. W. O. Galitz, *Human Factors in Office Automation.*
5. Galitz, *Human Factors in Office Automation.*
6. Raymond C. Houghton, Jr., "Online Help Systems: A Conspectus."
7. Galitz, *Human Factors in Office Automation,*
8. B. Shneidermen, "Direct Manipulation: A Step Beyond Programming Languages."
9. Shneiderman, "Direct Manipulation."
10. S. L. Sauter, M. S. Gottlieb, K. C. Jones, V. N. Dodson, and K. M. Rohrer, "Job and Health Implications of VDT Use: Initial Results of the Wisconsin."

11. C. Raftering and J. Keener, "Providing Terminal Comfort."
12. Galitz, "*Human Factors in Office Automation.*"
13. Izak Benbasat and Yair Wand, "Command Abbreviation Behavior in Human-Computer Interaction."
14. C. F. Herot, "Graphical User Interfaces."
15. S. J. Kaplan and D. Ferris, "Natural Language in the DP World."
16. Shneiderman, "Direct Manipulation."

Select Bibliography

1. "Airborne Information," In "Technology Buyer's Guide," *Fortune*, Winter 1997.
2. ANSI/SPARC Study Group Data Base Management Systems: "Framework Report on Data Base Management Systems," AFIP Press, Montvale, NJ, 1978.
3. Association for Computing Machinery: "The British Computer Society Data Dictionary Systems Working Party Report," *Data Base*, 9:2, Fall 1977, and *SIGMOD Record*, 9:4, December 1977.
4. Atwood, Thomas, "Object Databases Come of Age," *OBJECT Magazine,* July 1996.
5. Babcock, Charled, "OLAP Leads Way to Post-Relational Era," *Computerworld*, November 21, 1997.
6. Bailey, Robert W.: *Human Performance Engineering: A Guide for System Designers*, Prentice-Hall, Englewood Cliffs, NJ, 1982.
7. Barber, Raymond E., and Henry C. Lucas, Jr.: "System Response Time, Operator Productivity, and Job Satisfaction," *Communications of the ACM*, 26:11, November 1983, pp. 972–986.
8. Benbasat, Izak, and Yair Wand: "Command Abbreviation Behavior in Human-Computer Interaction," *Communications of the ACM*, 27:4, May 1984, pp. 376–382.

   Brown, P. J.: "Error Messages: The Neglected Area of the Man/Machine Interface?", *Communications of the ACM*, 26:4, April 1983, pp. 246–249.
9. Benbasat, L., A. S. Dexter, D. H. Drury, and R. C. Goldstein: "A Critique of the 'Stage Hypothesis': Theory and Empirical Evidence," *Communications of the ACM*, 27:5, May 1984, pp. 476-485.
10. Bokin, S.A.: *Data Models: A Sementivc Approach for Database Systems*, M.I.T. Press, Cambridge, MA, 1980.
11. Bowman, B., G. B. Davis and J. C. Wetherbe: "Modeling for MIS," *Datamination*, July 1981, pp. 155–164.
12. Bowman, B., G. B. Davis, and J. C. Wetherbe: "Three Stage Model of MIS Planning," *Information and Management,* 6 February 1983, pp. 11–25.
13. Bowman, V., G. B. Davis, and J. C. Wetherbe: "Modeling for MIS," *Datamination*, July 1980, pp. 166–162.

14. Bruegger, Dave, and Sooun Lee, "Distributed Database Systems: Accessing Data More Efficiently," *Information Systems Management*, Spring 1995.

15. *Business Software Review, Computerworld, PC Magazine, PC Week, Internet World, PC World*, and *Software Digest* are just a few examples of many good magazines for current information on computer software packages for end user, workgroup, and enterprise applications.

16. *Business Systems Planning—Information Systems Planning Guide*, Application Manual, GE20-0527-3, Third Edition, IBM Corporation, July 1981.

17. Cafasso, Rosemary, "Busting Loose," *Computerworld*, April 15, 1996.

18. Card, S., T. Moran, and A. Newell: "Computer Text-Editing: An Information-Processing Analysis of a Routine Cognitive Skill," *Cognitive Psychology*, 12, 1980, pp. 32-74.

19. Card, S., T. Moran, and A. Newell: "The Keystroke-Level Model for User Performance Time with Interactive Systems," *Communications of the ACM*, 23:7, July 1980, pp. 396–410.

20. Card, S., T. Moran, and A. Newell: *Applied Information Processing Psychology: The Human Computer Interface*, Earlbaum, Hillsdale, NJ, 1983.

21. Card, S., T. Moran, and A. Newell: *The Psychology of Human-Computer Interaction*, Earlbaum, Hillsdale, NJ, 1983.

22. Carey, T.: "User Differences in Interface Design," *Computer*, 15:11, November 1982, pp. 14–20.

23. Carlson, Walter M.: "Business Information Analysis and Integration Technique (BIAIT)—The New Horizon," *Data Base*, Spring 1979, pp. 3–9.

24. Carney, Dan, "Congress Fires First Shot in Information Revolution," *Congressional Quarterly Weekly*, February 3, 1996.

25. Carr, Houston, and Charles Snyder, *The Management of Telecommunications*, Burr Ridge, IL: Irwin, 1997.

26. Chan, Hock Chuan; Kee Wei Kwock; and Keng Leng Siau, "User-Database Interface: The Effect of Abstraction Levels on Query Performance," *MIS Quarterly*, December 1993.

27. Chen, Peter P. (ed.): *Entity-Relationship Approach to Systems Analysis and Design*, North-Holland, Amsterdam, 1980.

28. Chen, Peter P.: "The Entity-Relationship Model: Toward a Unified View of Data," *ACM Transactions on Database Systems*, 1:1, March 1979, pp. 9–36.

29. Christ, Richard E.: "Review and Analysis of Color Coding Research for Visual Displays," *Human Factor*, 17:6 December 1975, pp. 542–570.

30. CODASYL Systems Committee, *Feature Analysis of Generalized Data Base Management Systems*, Technical Report, published by several organisations such as the Association for Computing Machinery, New York, May 1971.

31. Codd, E. F.: "A Relational Model of Data for Large Shared Banks," *Communications of the ACM*, 13:6, June 1972, pp. 377–387.

32. Codd, E. F.: "Relational Database: A Practical Formulation for Productivity," *Communications of the ACM*, 25:2, February 1982, pp. 109–117.

33. *Computerworld, PC Week, PC magazine, PC World,* and *PC Today* are just a few examples of many good magazines for current information on computer systems hardware and its use in end user and enterprise applications.
34. *Computing Surveys*, 13:1, May 1981. Entire Issue.
35. Connolly, James, "Buyer's Guide: Win 95 and NT—Taking Root," *Computerworld*, March 11, 1996.
36. Couger, J. Daniel, Mel A. colter, and Robert W. Knapp: *Advanced System Development/ Feasibility Techniques*, Wiley, New York, 1982.
37. Cronin, Mary, *Doing More Business on the Internet,* 2nd ed. New York: Van Nostrand Reinhold, 1996.
38. Cronin, Mary, *Global Advantage on the Internal,* New York: Van Nostrand Reinhold, 1996.
39. Cronin, Mary, *The Internet Strategy Handbook*, Boston: Harvard Business School Press, 1996.
40. Crutice, R. M., and P. E. Jones: "Fundamental of Data Element Definition," *ACM SIGM International Conference on Management of Data*, Ann Arbor, MI, April 29–May 1, 1981, pp. 49–55.
41. Date, C. J.: *An Introduction to Database Systems*, Third Edition, Addision-Wesley, Reading, MA. 1981.
42. Davis, C. G., S. Jajodia, A. Ng, and R. T. Yeh (eds.): *Proceeding of the Third International Conference on the Entitly-Relationship Approach*, Elsevier, New York, 1983.
43. Devoney, Chris, "Look Ms, Know Hands!", *Computerworks*, September 15, 1997.
44. "Digital Imaging," In "Technology Buyer's Guide," *Fortune*, Winter 1998.
45. Doolittle, Sean, "Widening the Pipes," *PC Today*, December 1996.
46. "Dream Machines," In "Technology Buyer's Guide," *Fortune*, Winter 1998.
47. Dreyfus, H., and Associates: *Measures of Man: Human Factors in Design*, Second Edition Whitney Library of Design, New York, 1967.
48. Drury. D. H.: "An Empirical Assessment of the Stages of DP Growth," *MIS Quarterly*, 7:2, June 1983, pp. 59–70.
49. Ehrenreich, S. L.: "Query Languages: Design Recommendations Derived from the Human Factors Literature," *Human Factors*, 23:6, December 1981, pp. 709–725.
50. Ein-Dor, P., and E. Segev: "Strategic Planning for MIS," *Management Science*, 24:15 November 1978.
51. Embly, D., and G. Nagy: "Behavioral Aspects of Text Editors," *Computing Surveys*, 13:1, March 1981, pp. 34–70.
52. Everest, Gordon C.: *Database Management: Objective, System Functions, and Administration,* McGraw-Hill, New York, 1985.
53. Falvin, Matt, *Fundamental Concepts of Information Modeling*, Yourdon, New York, 1981.
54. Friend, David, "Client/Server versus Cooperative Processing: Two Downsizing Topologies Compared," *Information Systems Management*, Summer 1994.

55. Galitz, W. O.: *Human Factors in Office Automation*, Life Office Management Association, Atlanta, GA. 1980.

56. Gibson, Cyrus F., and Richard L. Nolan: "Managing the Four Stages of EDP Growth," *Harvard Business Review*, January–February 1974, pp. 76–88.

57. Gleason, Tim, "The Information Hypeway," *Oregon Quarterly*, Spring 1994.

58. Gordon, L. A. and Danny Miller: "A Contingency Framework for the Design of Accounting Information Systems," *Accounting Organizations and Society*, 1:1, June 1976, pp. 56-69.

59. Gorry, G. A., and M. S. Scott Morton: "A Framework for Management Information Systems," *Sloan Management Review*, 12, Fall 1971, pp. 55–70.

60. Gould, J., J. Conti, and T. Hovanyeez: "Composing letters with a Simulated Listening Typewriter," *Communications of the ACM*, 26:4, April 1983, pp. 295–308.

61. Grover, Varun, and James Teng, "How Effective Is Data Resource Management? Reassessing Strategic Objective, "*Journal of Information Systems Management,* Summer 1991.

62. Gunther, Marc, "The Cable Guys' Big Bet on the Net," *Fortune*, November 25, 1996.

63. Guyon, Janet, "Smart Plastic," *Fortune*, October 13, 1997.

64. "Hardware Technology for Your Job," In "Technology Buyer's Guide," *Fortune*, Winter 1997.

65. Hax, Arnoldo C., and Nicloas S. Majluf: "The Use of the Growth-Share Matrix in Strategic Planning," *Interfaces,* 13:1, February 1983, pp. 46–65.

66. Hax, Arnoldo, and Nicolas S. Majluf: "The Use of the Industry Attractiveness-Business Strength Matrix in Strategic Planning," *Interfaces*, 13:2, April 1983, pp. 53:71.

67. Hedberg, B., and E. Mumford: "The Design of Computer Systems: Man's Vision of Man as an Integral Part of the Systems Design Process," in E. Mumford and H. Sackman (eds.), *Human Choice and Computers,* North-Holland, Amsterdam, 1975, pp. 31–59.

68. Highsmith, J.: "Structural Systems Planning," *MIS Quarterly*, 5:3, September 1981, pp. 35–54.

69. "Home Theatre," In "Technology Buyer's Guide," *Fortune*, Winter 1998.

70. Houghton, Raymond C., Jr.: "Online Help Systems: A Conspectus," *Communications of the ACM,* 27:2, Feburary 1984, pp. 126–133.

71. Hrens, Judith and Chetan Sankar, "Tailoring Database Training for End Users," *MIS Quarterly*, December 1993.

72. *IBM Systems Journal*, 22:2, 1981. Entire Issues.

73. Ives, Blake: "Graphical User Interface for Business Information Systems," *MIS Quarterly* Special Issue, December 1982, pp. 15–48.

74. Jacob, R. J. K.: "Using Formal Specifications in the Design of a Human-Computer Interface," *Communications of the ACM*, 26:4, April 1983, pp. 259–264.

75. Jacobs, April, and Lisa Picatrill, "Microsoft Now Says Thin Is In," *Computerworld*, April 14, 1997.

76. Jacobs, April, "Net Computers End-Run PC Migration Costs," *Computerworld*, February 17, 1997.

77. Jacobsen, Ivar; Maria Ericsson; and Ageneta Jacobsen, *The Object Advantage: Business Process Reengineering with Object Technology,* New York: ACM Press, 1995.

78. Jacobsen, Ivar; Maria Ericsson; and Ageneta Jacobsen, *The Object Advantage: Business Process Reengineering with Object Technology*, New York: ACM Press; 1995.

79. Jenkings, Avery, "Warehouse Woes," *Computerworld*, February 6, 1995.

80. Jenkins, A. M., and R. D. Johnson: "What the Information Analyst Should Know about Body Language," *MIS Quarterly*, 1:3 September 1977, pp. 33–47.

81. Kailash, David, "IBM Boosts Strength of Supercomputer That Beat Kasparov," *PC Today*, November 1997.

82. Kalokota, Ravi, and Andrew Whinston, *Frontiers of Electronic Commerce*, Reading, MA: Addison-Wesley, 1996.

83. Kanter, Jerry: "MIS Long-Range Planning," *Infosystems*, June 1982, pp. 66–70.

84. Kantor, Andrew, and Michael Neubarth, "Off the Charts: The Internet 1996," *Internet World*, December 1996.

85. Kennedy, Ken, and Others, "A Nationwide Parallel Computing Environment," *Communication of the ACM*, November 1997.

86. Kent, W.: "A Simple Guide to Five Forms in Relational Database Theory," *Communications of the ACM*, 26:2, February 1983, pp. 120–125.

87. Kent, W.: "*Data and Reality*, North-Holland, Amsterdam, 1978.

88. Kent, W.: "Data Model Theory Meets a Practical Application," *Conference on Very Large Databases*, Institute of Electrical and Electronics Engineers, 1981.

89. Kerner David V.: "Business Information Characterization Study, "Data Base, Spring 1979, pp. 10-17.

90. King, J. L. and K. L. Kraemer: "Evolution and Organizational Information Systems: An Assessment of Nolan's Stage Model," *Communications of the ACM*, 27:5, may 1984, pp. 466–475.

91. King, W. R., and D. I. Cleland: "The Design of Management Information Systems: An Information Analysis Approach," Management Science, 22:3, November 1974, pp. 286–297.

92. King, W. R.: "Strategic Planning for Management Information Systems," *MIS Quarterly*, 2:1, March 1978, pp. 27–37.

93. King, W. R., "Strategic Planning for Management Information Systems," *MIS Quarterly*, 2:1, March 1978, pp. 27-37.

94. Kirkpatrick, David, "Ten Tech Trends You Can Bet On," *Fortune*, November 10, 1997.

95. Koffler, Richard P.: "The Ergonomic Art," *Datamination*, June 1983, pp. 235–238.

96. Kroenke, David, *Database Processing: Fundamentals, Design, Implementation,* 2nd ed. New York: Macmillan, 1996.

97. Leintz, P. B., and M. Chen: "Long Range Planning for Information Services," *Long Range Planning,* February 1980.

98. London, K.: The People Side of Systems, McGraw-Hill, New York, 1976.

99. Long, Larry: *Design and Strategy for Corporate Information Services: MIS Long-Range Planning*, Prentice-Hall, Englewood Cliffs, NJ, 1982.

100. Lorents, Alden, and James Moragan, *Database Systems: Concepts Management and Applications,* Fort Worth: The Dryden Press, 1998.

101. Lucas, H. C., and J. A. Sutton: "The Stage Hypothesis and S-Curve: Some Contradictory Evidence," *Communications of the ACM*, 20:4, April 1977, pp. 254–259.

102. Lundeberg, Mats Goran Goldkuhl, and Anders Nilsson: "A Systematic Approach to Information Systems Development–I. Introduction," Information Systems, 4, 1979, pp. 1–12.

103. Lundeberg, Mats Goran Goldkuhl, and Anders Nilsson: *Information Systems Development–A Systematic Approach*, Prentice-Hall, Englewood Cliffs, NJ, 1980.

104. Lundgren, Bo: *Theory of Data Bases*, Mason/Charter, New York, 1975.

105. Lynch, Hugh J.: "ADS: A Technique in Systems Documentation," *Data Base*, 1:1 Spring 1969, pp. 6–18.

106. March, S., D. Ridjanovic, and M. Prietula: "On the Effects of Normalization on the Quality of Relational Database Designs, or Being Normal Is Not Enough," *Proceedings Trends and Applications 1984: Making Database Work*, IEEE Computer Society Press, 1984, pp. 257–261.

107. Markus, M. Lynne: *Systems in Organizations: Bugs and Features*, Pitman, Boston, 1984.

108. McCarthy, Williams E.: "An Entity-Relationship View of Accounting Models," *The Accounting Review*, 54:4, October 1979, pp. 667–685.

109. McCracken, Harry, "What's New for '97?" *PC World*, February 1997.

110. McFarlan, F. W., and J. L. McKenney: "The Information Archipelago—Maps and Bridges," *Harvard Business Review*, 60:5, September–October 1982, pp. 109–119.

111. McFarlan, F. W., and J. L. McKenney: *Corporate Information Systems Management: The Issues facing Senior Executives*, Richard D. Irwin, Homewood, IL, 1983.

112. Mcfarlan, F. W., J. L. McKenney, and P. J. Pyburn: "The Information Archipelago—Plotting a Course," *Harvard Business Review*, 61:1, January–February 1983, pp. 145-156.

113. McFarlan, F. W.: "Portfolio Approach to Information Systems," *Harvard Business Review*, September–October 1981, pp. 142–150.

114. McLean: E., and J. Soden: *Strategic Planning for MIS*, Wiley, New York, 1977.

115. Miller, J.C.: "Conceptual Models and Determining Information Requirements," *Proceedings the Spring Joint Computer Conference*, 25, 1964, pp. 609–620.

116. Mumford, E., and M. Weir: *Computer Systems in Work Design: The ETHICS Method*, Halsted (Wiley), New York, 1979.

117. Munro, M.C., and G.B. Davis: "Determining Management Information Needs: A Comparison of Methods," *MIS Quarterly*, 1:2, June 1977, pp. 55–67.

118. Nash, Kim, "Netscape Takes Off the Gloves," *Computerworld*, October 21, 1996.

119. Nijssen, G. M. (ed.): "Current Issues in Conceptual Schema Concepts," in *Architecture and Models in Data Base Management Systems*, North Holland, New York, 1977, pp. 31-65.

120. Nijssen, G. M. (ed.): *Modeling in Data Base Management Systems*, North-Holland, Amsterdam. 1976.

121. Nolan, Richard L.: "Managing Information Systems by Committee," *Harvard Business Review*, July–August 1982.

122. Nolan, Richard L.: "Managing the Computer Resource: A Stage Hypothesis," *Communication of the ACM*, 16:3, March 1973, pp. 399–405.

123. Nolan, Richard L.: "Managing the Crises in Data Processing," *Harvard Business Review*, March–April 1979, pp. 115–126.

124. Norman, Donald A.: "Design Rule Based on Analyses of Human Error," *Communications of the ACM*, 26:4, April 1983, pp. 254–258.

125. O'Mara, Brendan, " Information Superhighway," *Online Access*, Internet Special Issue, April 1994.

126. Pei, Daniel, and Carmine Cutone, "Object-Oriented Analysis and Design: Realism or Impressionism," *Information System Management*, Winter 1995.

127. "Peripherals," In "Technology Buyer's Guide," *Fortune*, Winter 1998.

128. *Psychology Today*, 17:12, December 1983. Entire issue is on "user friendly" machines.

129. Pyburn, Philip J.: "Linking the MIS Plan with Corporate Strategy: An Exploratory Study," *MIS Quarterly*, 7:2, June 1983, pp. 1–14.

130. Quellette, Tim, "Tape Storage Put to New Enterprise Uses," *Computerworld*, November 10, 1997.

131. Roberts, Teresa L., and Thomas P. Moran: "The Evaluation of Text Editors: Methodology and Empirical Results," *Communications of the ACM*, 26:4, April 1983, pp. 265–283.

132. Roche, Edward M., *Telecommunications and Business Strategy*, Fort Worth, TX: Dryden Press, 1994.

133. Rockart, J.F.: "Critical Success Factors," Harvard Business Review, March–April 1979. pp.81–91.

134. Sauter, S. L., M. S. Gottlieb, K. C. Jones, V. N. Dodson, and K. M. Rohrer: "Job and Health Implications of VDT Use: Initial Results of the Wisconsin NIOSH Study," *Communications of the ACM*, 29:4 April 1983.

135. Schlender, Brent, "Sun's Java: The Threat to Microsoft Is Real," *Fortune*, November 11, 1996.

136. Schnaidt, Patricia, *Enterprise-wide Networking*, Carmel, IN: SAM Publishing, 1992.

137. Schneider, Michael L., and C. Thomas (eds.): "The Humanization of Computer Interfaces," *Communications of the ACM*, 26:4, April 1983.

138. Schwartz, M. H.: "MIS Planning," *Datamination*, 16:4, September 1970, pp. 28–31.

139. "Shedding Light on Data Warehousing for More Informed Business Solutions," Special Advertising Supplement, *Computerworld*, February 13, 1995.

140. Sherman, Stratford, "Will the Information Highway Be the Death of Retailing?", *Fortune*, April 18, 1994.

141. Shneiderman, B.: "Direct Manipulation: A Step Beyond Programming Languages," *Computer*, August 1983, pp. 57–69.

142. Shneiderman, B.: *Software Psychology: Human Factors in Computer and Information Systems Winthrop*, Cambridge, MA, 1980.

143. Shneiderman, Ben: *Software Psychology: Human Factors in Computer and Information Systems, Winthrop*, Cambridge, MA, 1980.

144. Simpson, David, "Big Iron Roars," *Datamination*, July 1997.

145. Simpson, David, "New Applications Fuel Servers Sales," *Datamination*, July 1997.

146. Slitz, John, "Object Technology Profiles," Special Advertising Supplement, *Computerworld*, June 13, 1997.

147. Smith, Heather A., and James D. Mckeen, "Object-Oriented Technology: Getting Beyond the Hype," *The Data Base for Advances in Information Systems*, Spring 1995.

148. Smith, J. M., and D. C. P. Smith: "Principles of Database Conceptual Design," *NYU Symposium on Database Design*, New York University, New York, May 18–19, 1978, pp. 35–49.

149. Smith, J. M., and D. C. P. Smith: "Database Abstractions and Aggregations," *Communications of the ACM*, 20:6, June 1977, pp. 405–413.

150. Spiegler, Israel, "Toward a Unified View of Data: Bridging Data Structure and Content," *Information Systems Management*, Spring 1995.

151. Stedman, Craig, "Database Grab Hold of Objects, Multimedia on the Web," *Computerworld*, October 21, 1996.

152. Storey, Veda, and Robert Goldstein, "Knowledge-Based Approaches to Database Design," *MIS Quarterly*, March 1993.

153. "Talk Is Cheaper," In "Technology Buyer's Guide," *Fortune*, Winter 1997.

154. Tarter, Jeffrey: "Ergonomics: A Primer," *Business Computer Systems*, June 1983, pp. 55–72.

155. "Technology Buyer's Guide", *Fortune*, Winter 1998.

156. "The CW Guide to Operating Systems," *Computerworld*, April 24, 1995.

157. The Java Language: A White paper, from java@java.sun.com. Copyright 1996 by Sun Microsystems.

158. The World Wide Web sites of computer manufactures such as Apple Computer, Dell Computer, IBM, Hewlett-Packard, Compaq, and Sun Microsystems are good sources of information on computer hardware developments.

159. The World Wide Web sites of computer manufacturers and software companies like Microsoft, Sun Microsystems, Lotus, IBM, Apple Computer, and Netscape Communications are good sources of information on computer software developments.

160. Tsichritzis, D. C., and F. H. Lochovsky: *Data Models*, Prentice-Hall, Englewood Cliffs, NJ, 1982.

161. Vargo, John, and Ray Hunt, *Telecommunications in Business*, Burr Ridge, IL: Irwin, 1996.

162. Vassiliou, Yannis (ed.): *Human Factors in Interactive Computer Systems*, Ablex Publishing, Norwood, NJ, 1984.

163. Vitalari. N. P. and G. W. Dickson: "Problem Solving for Effective Systems Analysis," *Communications of the ACM*, 26:11, November 1983, pp. 948–956.

164. Von Schilling, Peter, and John Levis, "Distributed Computing Environments: Process and Organization Issues," *Information Systems Management*, Spring 1996.

165. Wetherbe, J. C., and G. B. Davis: "Developing a Long-Range Information Architecture," *Proceedings of the National Computer Conference*, Anaheim, CA, May 1983, AFIPS Press, 52, pp. 261–269.

166. Williams, G.: "The Lisa Computer System," *Byte*, February 1983, pp. 33–50.

167. Williges, R. C., and B. H. Williges: "Modeling the Human Operator in Computer-Based Data Entry," Human Factors, 24:3, 1982, pp. 285–299.

168. Wind, Yoram, and Vijay Mahayan: "Designing Product and Business Portfolios," *Harvard Business Review*, January–February 1981, pp. 155–165.

169. Wong, Harry K. T., and John Mylopoulos: "Two Views of Data Semantics: A Survey of Data Models in Artificial Intelligence and Database Management," *INFOR*, 15:3, October 1979, pp. 344–383.

170. Woodson, Wesley E.: *Human Factors Design Handbook*, McGraw-Hill, New York, 1981.

171. Wrobel, Leo, "Developing Information Highways," *Information Systems Management*, Spring 1996.

172. Wylder, John, "The Network as the Enterprise Database," *Information Systems Management*, Spring 1995.

173. Yadav, Surya B.: "Determining an Organization's Information Requirements: A State of the Art Survey," *Data Base*, 14.3, Spring 1983, pp. 3–20.

174. Yankee Group, "White Paper: Wireless Communications," *Computerworld*, November 14, 1994.

175. Young, J. W. and H. Kent: "Abstract Formulation of Data Processing Problems," *Journal of Industrial Engineering*, November–December 1958. pp. 471–479.

176. Zander, Ed. "Endquotes," *NetReady Adviser*, Winter 1997.

177. Zani, William M.: "Blueprint for MIS," *Harvard Business Review*, November–December 1970, pp. 95–100.

178. Zoglin, Richard, "We're All Connected," *Time*, February 12, 1996.

Index

E

❑❑❑